Leveraging Computer-Mediated Marketing Environments

Gordon Bowen
Regent's University London, UK

Wilson Ozuem
University of Cumbria, UK

A volume in the Advances in Marketing, Customer Relationship Management, and E-Services (AMCRMES) Book Series

IGI Global
DISSEMINATOR OF KNOWLEDGE

Published in the United States of America by
IGI Global
Business Science Reference (an imprint of IGI Global)
701 E. Chocolate Avenue
Hershey PA, USA 17033
Tel: 717-533-8845
Fax: 717-533-8661
E-mail: cust@igi-global.com
Web site: http://www.igi-global.com

Library of Congress Cataloging-in-Publication Data

Names: Bowen, Gordon, 1950- editor. | Ozuem, Wilson, 1974- editor.
Title: Leveraging computer-mediated marketing environments / Gordon Bowen and Wilson Ozuem, editors.
Description: Hershey, PA : Business Science Reference, [2019]
Identifiers: LCCN 2018024608| ISBN 9781522573449 (hardcover) | ISBN 9781522573456 (ebook)
Subjects: LCSH: Internet marketing--Social aspects. | Online social networks. | Social media. | Marketing--Social aspects.
Classification: LCC HF5415.1265 .L4648 2019 | DDC 658.8/72--dc23 LC record available at https://lccn.loc.gov/2018024608

This book is published in the IGI Global book series Advances in Marketing, Customer Relationship Management, and E-Services (AMCRMES) (ISSN: 2327-5502; eISSN: 2327-5529)

British Cataloguing in Publication Data
A Cataloguing in Publication record for this book is available from the British Library.

All work contributed to this book is new, previously-unpublished material. The views expressed in this book are those of the authors, but not necessarily of the publisher.

For electronic access to this publication, please contact: eresources@igi-global.com.

Advances in Marketing, Customer Relationship Management, and E-Services (AMCRMES) Book Series

Eldon Y. Li
National Chengchi University, Taiwan & California Polytechnic State University, USA

ISSN:2327-5502
EISSN:2327-5529

Mission

Business processes, services, and communications are important factors in the management of good customer relationship, which is the foundation of any well organized business. Technology continues to play a vital role in the organization and automation of business processes for marketing, sales, and customer service. These features aid in the attraction of new clients and maintaining existing relationships.

The Advances in Marketing, Customer Relationship Management, and E-Services (AMCRMES) Book Series addresses success factors for customer relationship management, marketing, and electronic services and its performance outcomes. This collection of reference source covers aspects of consumer behavior and marketing business strategies aiming towards researchers, scholars, and practitioners in the fields of marketing management.

Coverage

- Telemarketing
- Customer Relationship Management
- Cases on CRM Implementation
- Cases on Electronic Services
- B2B marketing
- E-Service Innovation
- CRM strategies
- Database marketing
- Relationship marketing
- Web Mining and Marketing

IGI Global is currently accepting manuscripts for publication within this series. To submit a proposal for a volume in this series, please contact our Acquisition Editors at Acquisitions@igi-global.com or visit: http://www.igi-global.com/publish/.

The Advances in Marketing, Customer Relationship Management, and E-Services (AMCRMES) Book Series (ISSN 2327-5502) is published by IGI Global, 701 E. Chocolate Avenue, Hershey, PA 17033-1240, USA, www.igi-global.com. This series is composed of titles available for purchase individually; each title is edited to be contextually exclusive from any other title within the series. For pricing and ordering information please visit http://www.igi-global.com/book-series/advances-marketing-customer-relationship-management/37150. Postmaster: Send all address changes to above address.

Titles in this Series

For a list of additional titles in this series, please visit: www.igi-global.com/book-series

Evaluating the Gaps and Intersections Between Marketing Education and the Marketing Profession
Margarida M. Pinheiro (University of Aveiro, Portugal) Ana Estima (University of Aveiro, Portugal) and Susana Marques (University of Aveiro, Portugal)
Business Science Reference • copyright 2019 • 252pp • H/C (ISBN: 9781522562955) • US $190.00 (our price)

Advanced Methodologies and Technologies in Digital Marketing and Entrepreneurship
Mehdi Khosrow-Pour, D.B.A. (Information Resources Management Association, USA)
Business Science Reference • copyright 2019 • 818pp • H/C (ISBN: 9781522577669) • US $315.00 (our price)

Multifaceted Explorations of Consumer Culture and Its Impact on Individuals and Society
David J. Burns (Kennesaw State University, USA)
Business Science Reference • copyright 2019 • 318pp • H/C (ISBN: 9781522561200) • US $215.00 (our price)

The Role of Language and Symbols in Promotional Strategies and Marketing Schemes
Manuela Epure (Spiru Haret University, Romania) and Lorena Clara Mihăeş (University of Bucharest, Romania)
Business Science Reference • copyright 2019 • 333pp • H/C (ISBN: 9781522557784) • US $205.00 (our price)

Application of Gaming in New Media Marketing
Pratika Mishra (Presidency University Bangalore, India) and Swati Oberoi Dham (New Delhi Institute of Management, India)
Business Science Reference • copyright 2019 • 312pp • H/C (ISBN: 9781522560647) • US $215.00 (our price)

Strategic Perspectives in Destination Marketing
Mark Anthony Camilleri (University of Malta, Malta)
Business Science Reference • copyright 2019 • 411pp • H/C (ISBN: 9781522558354) • US $215.00 (our price)

Corporate Social Responsibility and Strategic Market Positioning for Organizational Success
Carlton Brown (University of Plymouth, UK) and Uzoechi Nwagbara (Sunderland University, UK & Cardiff Metropolitan University, UK)
Business Science Reference • copyright 2019 • 301pp • H/C (ISBN: 9781522554097) • US $195.00 (our price)

Optimizing Millennial Consumer Engagement With Mood Analysis
Sabyasachi Dasgupta (O.P. Jindal Global University, India) and Priya Grover (Symbiosis International (Deemed University), India)
Business Science Reference • copyright 2019 • 351pp • H/C (ISBN: 9781522556909) • US $215.00 (our price)

IGI Global
DISSEMINATOR OF KNOWLEDGE

701 East Chocolate Avenue, Hershey, PA 17033, USA
Tel: 717-533-8845 x100 • Fax: 717-533-8661
E-Mail: cust@igi-global.com • www.igi-global.com

Table of Contents

Section 2
Perspectives and Practice of Computer-Mediated Marketing Environments

Section 3
Opportunities and Challenges in Designing Computer-Mediated Marketing Strategies

Detailed Table of Contents

Social media platforms are the key tools to facilitate online engagement; however, to stimulate a discussion, the content published on the platforms is significant as it must appeal to different consumers. The quality of the content and platform type is key to successful engagement. Maintaining positive relationships with consumers is a vital activity for many brands in social media. Trust, satisfaction, fairness, and mutual dependency are key factors to retaining customers. Moreover, positive brand attitudes and higher purchase intentions were found to be linked to positive evaluations of companies' social media postings. To maintain value, firms use social media platforms that facilitate consumer-to-consumer as well as consumer-to-business engagement. Drawing from social influence theory, this chapter explores how social media marketing content (SMMC) impacts customer retention.

Social media is considered trustworthy by consumers, and this has resulted in a strong consumer focus on social media to acquire information related to products and services. There are various benefits offered by social media, but security is a major concern as viruses and other threats can affect a huge number of users of social media. These platforms are not well governed. Indeed, they are highly decentralized and could easily be accessed, and this presents a high risk of illegal activity. Businesses continue to reap the benefits of incorporating social media into their strategies. There has been a shift in focus from conventional media to online and digital media in the form of social networking sites, wikis, and blogs. This has given rise to viral marketing as a means of effective communication and sharing information. The current chapter aims to explore the relationship between social media and value co-creation.

The active presence of fashion brands online serves as a channel for customers to connect with brands for different intentions. This connection acts as an outlet customers employ in furthering social identity through brand associations. Brand perceptions are accordingly formed among consumers based on the promised functional and symbolic benefits consumption of that brand guarantees. Social media has assumed an integral role in fostering brand-customer relationships that ultimately augment social identity. The following chapter examines the role social media has played on brand perceptions in the fashion apparel and accessories industry from a social identity theory perspective. The chapter focuses on theoretical implications and managerial implications. The concluding section offers some significant roles that social media and social identity may play in keeping up with the design and development of marketing communications programs.

Online behavioral tailoring has become an integral part of online marketing strategies. Contemporary marketers increasingly seek to create an influential environment on social media to empower online users to participate in online brand communities. By interacting in this way, online communities hosted by brands marketers can enhance the nature of the complex interactions that occur amongst those that participate. Such online interactions lead to three different types of social influence compliance, internalization, and identity, which develop the consumers' purchase intentions. This chapter explains how the social influence support the change in beliefs, attitude, and intentions of the online consumers in the user-generated social media networking sites (SNSs). Furthermore, it discusses the functional impact of such online social influence that enables companies to understand the perceptions and needs of online users making sense of how multiple levels of social influence phenomenon on social media impact on consumers purchase intentions.

Information plays an important role in the individual lives of people, and social media as an aspect of online information phenomenon is an exciting topic to explore in terms of its impact on social entrepreneurship. Many theoretical fields have contributed to the development of social entrepreneurship, looking in particular at the financial, political, and psychological impacts. This chapter is unique since it focuses on social enterprises and the impact of evolving technologies on social entrepreneurship. This chapter contributes to the literature on social media usage in social enterprises and offers a better understanding of the issues in the specific context of developing countries.

Section 2
Perspectives and Practice of Computer-Mediated Marketing Environments

Multichannel shopping has changed the way that consumers shop by offering them more choice and convenience. The growing competitive apparel market forces retailers to assess their current marketing strategies and their implementation. It is fundamental that multichannel retailers constantly provide high levels of hedonic shopping value through multichannel shopping in order to stimulate purchase. The purpose of this chapter is to emphasize the importance of hedonic shopping value in the context of multichannel shopping (in store, website, catalogue, mobile, and social media). The benefits of this chapter are evaluation of the strengths and weaknesses of each channel from the perception of the five channels for apparel shopping based on 18 hedonic shoppers in central London by using semi-structured interviews. The result shows that store and website gain the highest in the level of hedonic shopping value for apparel shopping and those are the most likely channels in which hedonic shoppers intend to shop for apparel in the future, while shopping via catalogue shows the lowest score of both hedonic shopping value and purchase intention. This chapter suggests that exploring the hedonic shopping value that consumers derive across five channels can enhance the understanding of hedonic shopping value in the context of the multichannel shopping environment.

Fashion brands have shifted communication to social media as part of evolutionary modern-day marketing approaches to reaching consumers. Brands have adjusted to a vocal customer through back-and-forth interchange on social media platforms that have progressively facilitated for online brand communities. Social media brand communities serve to engage audiences in interactive settings that resonate with individual consumers across different levels. As brand awareness is augmented, brand impressions are conceived, brand-customer relationships are formed, and a sense of community is fostered around a brand, consumers exploit association to such social media brand communities in advancing social identity. The following chapter explores the impact of social media brand communities on Millennials in the fashion industry, while considering the social identity theory. The chapter focuses on theoretical and managerial implications. This chapter considers the influence social media brand communities and social identity may have on a fashion brand.

The success of an online recovery strategy is largely attributed to the provider's response speed. Essentially, engagement in conversation with the customer immediately after he/she complains shortens the pre-recovery phase. Service firms expect complaints from consumers when a service failure occurs. Advances in modern information and communication technologies (ICT) infrastructures have changed the way in which customer-firm interactions take place and the nature of the conduct of services. Computer and internet technologies mean that services can be provided over long distances without the requirement for the physical presence of customers and employees. With the continued rapid development in the field of modern computer-mediated marketing environments (CMME) more and more services will be delivered in technology-mediated environments (TMEs). This chapter provides some insights on failure recovery strategies as competitive tools in computer-mediated marketing environments.

Debates on the importance of user-generated content (UGC) and consumer brand engagement have increasingly gained attention amongst researchers, practitioners, marketing managers, and business leaders. UGC is a concept popularized in the 21st century with the advent and rise of Web 2.0 technology. Web 2.0 has gained recognition due to its novel features that include openness, participation, and the facilitation of the creation and sharing of content. It revolutionized interactions amongst people, and users are now able to share and create personalized content on the internet instead of merely using the content available. The primary objective of this chapter is to evaluate the influence of UGC on consumer brand engagement and discuss its impact on customers and organizational marketing practices.

In omni-channel retailing, the combination of different retail channels along the different customer touchpoints has become the predominant purchasing pattern for customers. The consumers´ purchasing behavior has changed tremendously with the development of e-commerce. The so-called omni-channel customers tend to switch retail channels during their purchasing process. In order to address changing consumer behavior, omni-channel fashion retailing companies still need to learn how to be able to provide an excellent service to these customers. This chapter aims to investigate this phenomenon from the perspective of omni-channel customers.

Understanding the adoption of technologies is crucial for researchers and practitioners, as identifying key factors helps to predict and explain users' attitude towards adopting or rejecting technology. However, as smartphones are well-diffused technologies, there is contention that research efforts shift to understanding their usage comprehensively. As personal technologies that users make meaning of, smartphone usage is assumed to be more comprehensive than that of previous generation mobile phones. This chapter examines how the usage of smartphones is redefining and increasingly adding value to consumer consumption processes.

Digital media literature suggests that social media has eased the process of conceptualizing the customer, inclusive of their perception of fairness in the recovery provision. This is because individuals in social media reveal personal information and engage in online conversation and online communities. However, the inherited risk in social media such as the rapid spread of online negative word-of-mouth and the ease of switching behavior to other online providers no longer permits superficial understanding of customers' perception of failure-recovery experiences. Drawing on extant conceptual theories, the current chapter examines online failure and recovery strategies and argues that effective recovery strategies not only enhance the development of marketing communication programs but act as an effective tool for customer retention.

The ideas of service failure and recovery strategies have been transformed, due to the internet environment, from a consumer-provider perspective to a multifaceted web quality activity. The research on service failure and recovery strategies has been well-developed in terms of the consumer's viewpoint of service as well as the responsibility for recovery conventionally expected to be allotted to the marketer. On the contrary, existing research indicates that there is a limited range of understanding of consumer-website interactivity relating to online service failure and recovery strategies as well as less understanding of the highly diverse characteristics of computer-mediated marketing environments (CMMEs). The perspectives of CMMEs relate to online customer behavior as distinct from conventional behavior. In fact, providers are involved in intense activity in the online environment in terms of market competition, as customers are positioned just a click away from switching providers in the case of service failure.

This chapter demonstrates how to assess the performance of organic and sponsored activities on Facebook using the data available in Facebook Ads Manager, Facebook Page Insights, and Google Analytics. The main aim of the proposed ROI calculation model is to connect common social media marketing objectives with the analytical information available. The main emphasis is put on the technical aspect of ad performance assessment. The authors explain how the Facebook attribution system and post-impression algorithm work, describe the relation between advertising goals and metrics displayed as achieved campaign results, and demonstrate how to derive ROI indexes from different Facebook conversions. The chapter also includes a practical example how to calculate current and future value of ongoing ads.

Together with the internet, social networking sites provide the consumers and the companies with a new marketing channel. In these online platforms, people make groups and come together for specific purposes. This new vivid and productive environment attracts the consumers seeking for product information and the companies trying to be in close contact with the customers. So the traditional WOM (word of mouth) has gained a new momentum and transformed into a new form in this online environment, called e-WOM (electronic word of mouth). Setting out from this recent fact, the chapter aims to give a general review of word of mouth communication starting with the traditional word of mouth and then elaborating e-WOM. It tries to tell about what e-WOM is and how it functions in online environments. As well as the definitions and the explanations of e-WOM, the chapter also aims to give the underlying reasons and the related factors during the process of e-WOM communication, thus putting a general framework for the companies and brands about this new marketing communication.

The concept of nation branding, the origins of the term, and how brand management is applied to obtain the expected results are investigated. Governments are driving nation branding projects, but some, like in the case of the Spanish project Marca España (ME), fail in detailing their objectives. Even when the objectives are weak, it is necessary to evaluate the performance of these projects. This is why some studies and indexes have been created. The indexes distinguish how a country ranks in various areas of study (economic, social, cultural, etc.), and the results are used to measure the efficiency of nation branding. Certain methodologies are used in this study together with various sets of data: from economic indicators and reputation indexes to the digital relevance of Spain.

The impact of identity on brand loyalty has taken precedence as an area of focus in recent marketing research. This has occurred in an era defined by technological revolution, which has created market disruptions, and there are implications for customer-brand relationships. Nonetheless, existing research has failed to acknowledge the impact of socio-psychological attributes and functional utility maximization. Knowledge that illuminates how firms can reposition themselves to sustain brand loyalty when disruptions occur in today's complex and globalized business environment is also required. The chapter presents an empirical investigation into the phenomenon of brand switching behavior among consumers in a specific competitive market, particularly in the smartphone industry. It explores how resistance could be built from an identity theory perspective, as emphasis has historically been placed on the functional utility of products at the expense of social meanings. This chapter provides consideration for market disruptions in the smartphone industry. It confirms that the literature does not capture other non-utilitarian factors such as socio-psychological benefits; hence, there are underlying factors that motivate consumers to continue buying brands they buy.

Preface

Leveraging Computer-Mediated Marketing Environments is an update on how social media has evolved and explore new areas of development such as a tool for value co-creation. These changes have occurred during social media's relatively short-life span. The benefits and challenges of social media can be harnessed and leveraged by the different marketing environments. The book takes a wider perspective of the application of social media so it is not just a marketing tool, but the societal benefits and implications are discussed from a millennial generation viewpoint. Because of the broad coverage of different areas of current and new roles of social media makes this book an important and distinctive reference book for those working in social media marketing and related areas, but also consultancies that specialise in social media or require core understanding on how social media has changed and the increasing potential of its use in a business and societal context. Governmental agencies will have a better understanding of the application of social media and its implication and influence on government policies in future years. Think tanks will also gain value from reviewing this book as it attempts to identify white spaces in marketing and society that could deliver new opportunities for social media in the business environment. Furthermore, academics and market practitioners (not necessarily working in social media) would find the book an invaluable review of the new landscapes in social media. Students would also improve their understanding of social media to give them the necessary depth and detail to galvanise their interest and identify workplace opportunities for social media. The aim of the book is to give its readers a compelling competitive advantage in the field of social media that could be leverage currently and in the future.

The book is structured around three pillars, namely framing and situating computer-mediated marketing environments, perspectives and practice of computer-mediated marketing environments, and opportunities and challenges in designing computer-mediated marketing environments. Thus the chapters will be aligned as follows:

Section 1: Framing and Situating Computer-Mediated Marketing Environments

1. The Dynamics of Social Media Marketing Content and Customer Retention – Michelle Willis
2. Social Media and Value Co-Creation – Kamna Sahni and Kenneth Appiah
3. Social Media and Social Identity in the Millennial Generation – Guida Helal and Wilson Ozuem
4. Exploring the Relationship Between Social Media and Social Influence – Ali Usman and Sebastian Okafor
5. Social Media and Social Entrepreneurship – MD Nazmul Islam and Vivek Chitran

Section 2: Perspectives and Practice of Computer-Mediated Marketing Environments

6. The Differences of Hedonic Shopping Value and Purchase Intention in the Multichannel Shopping Environment for Apparel Shopping – Charanya Nopnukulvised, Laden Aldin, and Gordon Bowen
7. Social Media, Online Brand Communities, and Customer Engagement in the Fashion Industry – Guida Helal
8. Service Failure and Recovery Strategy in Computer-Mediated Marketing Environments – Samuel Ayertey and Kerry Howell
9. User-Generated Content and Consumer Brand Engagement – Mohammed Naeem and Sebastian Okafor
10. The Impacts of Omni-Channel Purchasing Behavior on Service Quality – Elena Patten
11. Smartphones: Resource Dimensions and Uses – IB Sam and Kenneth Appiah
12. Online Service Failure: Understanding the Building Blocks of Effective Recovery Strategy – Yllka Azemi and Wilson Ozuem

Section 3: Opportunities and Challenges in Designing Computer-Mediated Marketing Strategies

13. Competing Through Online Service Failures and Recovery Strategies – Dipen Rai and Dominic Appiah
14. Calculation of Facebook Marketing Effectiveness in Terms of ROI – Tereza Semeradova and Petr Weinlich
15. E-Wom: The New Consumer Megaphone – Underlying Reasons and Related Factors – Esra Guven and Ozlem Isuik
16. The Challenge of Nation Branding in the Digital Age: Case of Spain's Nation Branding Project, Marca Espana – Marca Ciutad, Hamid Jahankhani, and Jim O'Brien
17. Disruptive Technology in the Smartphones Industry: Identity Theory Perspective – Dominic Appiah, Wilson Ozuem, and Kerry Howell

Section 1 is the location of four chapters of which there is a total of thirteen chapters. The first chapter in Section 1 considers social media platforms as a key to customer retention, online engagement and discussion, drawing on social influence theory. Trust, satisfaction, mutual dependency and fairness are key factors in retaining customers. Moreover, positive media posting have a healthy relationship between brand attitudes and higher purchase intentions.

Chapter 2 discuss the nature of social media platform benefits (co-creation) and security issues. Although social media in conjunction with the consumers and firms is a co-creator of economic wealth, the decentralisation of the platform does pose security issues. Social media networking is one strategy that firms reap the benefit, because of its ability to share information and apply viral marketing techniques.

Connecting fashion brands to online consumers is an effective channel to enhance brand intentions is the focus of Chapter 3. The channel connection acts as a further opportunity for brand identity through brand association. Consequently, brand perceptions are also formed and consolidated to generate symbolic and functional benefits. Furthermore, the latter part of the chapter offers suggestions on some of the roles that social media and social identity may play in future-proofing the design and development of marketing communications programmes.

Chapter 4 discusses the technique of tailoring online behaviour. Marketers have wished for a long time to be able to create an influential environment on social media to empower users online to engage in online brand communities. The online interaction lead to three different types of social influence compliance, internalization and identity, these influence purchase intention. Thus the aim of the chapter is to explain how social influence supports the change in beliefs, attitude and the intentions of the online consumers.

The final chapter in Section 1 is Chapter 5. This chapter explores the important role of information in an individual's life, and particularly social media information and its impact on social entrepreneurship. What is unique about the discussion in this chapter is that it focuses on social enterprises and the impact of technologies on social entrepreneurship in the context of developing countries.

Section 2 is structured around five chapters relating to perspectives and practice in computer-mediated marketing environments.

Chapter 6 focuses on the multi-shopping channel environment in the apparel clothing marketing environment. The chapter research aim to assess the hedonic shopping value in several contexts (in store, website, catalogue, mobile and social media). The results from the empirical study suggests the highest level of hedonic shopping value is linked to in store and website channels.

Chapter 7 suggests that brands have adjusted to the vocal customer, by the backward and forward interchange on social media platforms. Brand communities seek to engage customers in an interactive environment at different levels. The special focus of this chapter is the augmentation of brand awareness and how brand impressions are formed in the context of the millennial generation.

Chapter 8 explores the service recovery strategies in the online environment. Essentially, the immediacy of customer conversation and thus engagement once a complaint has been made shortens the pre-recovery phase. Advances in Information, Communication and Technologies infrastructures (ICT) facilitates the immediacy of the conversation and distance is no longer an impediment to engaging in conversation.

Chapter 9 in the group focuses on Use-generated Content (UGC) and consumer brand engagement. UGC has the potential to revolutionise interactions amongst people and reinforce sharing and give them the opportunity to create content and not merely using the available content on the internet.

Chapter 10 discusses omni-channels in the retail environment. The advent of e-commerce has given omni-channel customers the ability to switch retail channels during the purchasing decision making process. To minimise switching retailers will need to provide excellent service.

Chapter 11 develops an understanding of the key factors that help to explain and predict users' attitude to adopting or rejecting technology. The discussion centres around smartphones a deeply-diffused technology and correspondingly the emphasis is on the personal usage of mobile phones and what is the meaning of usage.

Chapter 12 discusses a recurring theme in the digital media literature that social media makes the process of conceptualising customers intentions easier, that is inclusive of their perception of fairness in the online service recovery situation. This is predicated on the behaviour of online consumer, which revealing personal information, engaging in online conversation and belonging to online communities. Thus the chapter aim to explore from the literature online failure and recovery strategies, and further suggest that successful recovery strategies improve customer retention and improve communications.

The final grouping in the book is Section 3, which investigates the opportunities and challenges in designing computer-mediated marketing strategies.

Chapter 13 takes a different perspective on service failure and recovery strategies. Currently, the literature focuses on the consumer's viewpoint. This chapter focuses on consumer-website interactivity relating to online failure and recovery strategies and the characteristics of the computer-mediated marketing environments.

Chapter 14 investigates the performance of organic and sponsored ads on the Facebook platform. The secondary data is evaluated to derive an ROI index for the different ad conversion rates. Moreover, the model uses a practical example to calculate current and future value of ongoing ads.

Chapter 15 gives an account on how WOM is transformed by the online environment. The general discussion on WOM and e-WOM considers the underlying reasons and related factors that make e-WOM an effective communication tool using a general framework.

Chapter 16 discuss nation branding and its context to marketing techniques. Practical use of nation branding includes enhancing country reputation for tourism, gaining FDI momentum, increasing exports and a magnet to attract talent. The chapter uses secondary research including economic, social, cultural and digital indices.

Chapter 17 reflects on brand loyalty as a market disruptor. Knowledge that illuminates how firms can reposition themselves to sustain brand loyalty when disruptions occur in today's complex and globalised business environment is also required. The chapter presents an empirical investigation into the phenomenon of brand switching behaviour among consumers in a specific competitive market, particularly in the Smartphones industry. It explores how resistance could be built from an identity theory perspective, as emphasis has historically been placed on the functional utility of products at the expense of social meanings.

CONCLUSION

This book advances the concepts in computer-mediated marketing and brings practical advice and knowledge that are influential on the online marketing environment and social media platforms. Movement to digital applications is moving at a pace and requires engagement by firms to improve their market position. *Leveraging Computer-Mediated Marketing Environments* attempts to assist and promote the new marketing concepts of the offline and social media environments. Furthermore, to enable firms to develop a holistic perspective of computer-mediated activities and environments.

Section 1

Framing and Situating Computer-Mediated Marketing Environments

Chapter 1
The Dynamics of Social Media Marketing Content and Customer Retention

Michelle Willis
University of Hertfordshire, UK

ABSTRACT

Social media platforms are the key tools to facilitate online engagement; however, to stimulate a discussion, the content published on the platforms is significant as it must appeal to different consumers. The quality of the content and platform type is key to successful engagement. Maintaining positive relationships with consumers is a vital activity for many brands in social media. Trust, satisfaction, fairness, and mutual dependency are key factors to retaining customers. Moreover, positive brand attitudes and higher purchase intentions were found to be linked to positive evaluations of companies' social media postings. To maintain value, firms use social media platforms that facilitate consumer-to-consumer as well as consumer-to-business engagement. Drawing from social influence theory, this chapter explores how social media marketing content (SMMC) impacts customer retention.

INTRODUCTION AND RATIONALE

Maintaining positive relationships with consumers is a vital activity for many brands in social media. Trust, satisfaction, fairness and mutual dependency are key factors to retaining customers (Nguyen & Mutum, 2012; Koufaris & Hampton-Sosa, 2004; Martínez & del Bosque, 2013). Moreover, positive brand attitudes and higher purchase intentions were found to be linked to positive evaluations of companies' social media postings (Beukeboom, Kerkhof, & de Vries, 2015). To maintain value, firms use social media platforms that facilitate consumer-to-consumer as well as consumer-to-business engagement. However, there is no general classification of what counts as engagement (Vivek, Beatty, & Morgan, 2010) due to the many types of social media platforms and usage purposes.

Online engagement does not solely depend on the medium of technology; Shin's (2018) study on virtual reality environments, described as a type of social media platform (Ngai, Moon, Lam, Chin,

DOI: 10.4018/978-1-5225-7344-9.ch001

& Tao, 2015), concluded that technical quality does not directly impact value or experience. For VR, content that encourages active conversation or community gaming is what motivates human-media interaction and facilitates users' online experience. Harrigan, Soutar, Choudhury & Lowe (2015) agree, stating that customer relationship orientation is needed to drive social media technology. Additionally, the interpersonal communication among users, including communication with the brand, can impact how content is perceived by the majority of observers. Lu, Fan, & Zhou (2016) propose that the presence of social media increases the consumers' trust. This means that exposure to socially shared posts by active sharers can increase the likelihood of purchase intentions, because trust can be established if material content is shared by a mass network or by central social networks.

Various scholars have developed taxonomies of social media in specific areas of study (Kaplan & Haenlein, 2010; Kietzmann, Hermkens, McCarthy, & Silvestre, 2011; Tafesse & Wien, 2017; Vilnai-Yavetz & Levina, 2018). Kietzmann *et al.* (2011) developed the Honeycomb social media model, which focuses on addressing seven functional building blocks: identity, conversation, sharing, presence, relationships, reputation and groups. The model provides guidance on how companies can respond to various audience needs with the social media platforms they use. Kietzmann *et al.* (2011) affirm that their framework is useful for analysis of the increasing number of social media platforms and their various capabilities towards specific user communities. However, the model views the various social media platforms subjectively and focuses on the technology value. The model does not consider the possible social influence that induces online users to engage. Therefore it is important to understand social media content from the perspective of consumers and the social influence behind the content that observers acknowledge to impact their decision-making.

Tafesse & Wien (2017) developed a framework that categorises different social media posts for different online activities from the perspective of customer management and message strategy. The model details various categories of post content and their purpose, providing guidance on maintaining online customer interactions. However, the types of post content categorised in the study were based on a single-message strategy. Customers have multiple interests and reasons for using social media, therefore marketers would likely be expected to generate post content with more than one message strategy. An issue in generating content for brands is posting content that encourages consumers to share or interact based on the content that also benefits the firm.

Akpinar & Berger's (2017) study addresses what type of content is effective and valuable. Their study's findings implied that content that evokes emotion impacts consumers' decision to share or interact. However, Akpinar & Berger (2017) implied that whether the content is emotionally or informatively appealing will depend on the purpose of attracting the consumer. This is supported by Pressgrove, McKeever & Jang (2018) who investigated the likelihood of content being shared on Twitter. Pressgrove *et al.* (2018) concluded that while positive emotions can evoke content sharing, if it does not have a practical significance to the observer, the likelihood of content sharing reduces. Yet unlike Akpinar & Berger's (2017) study, Pressgrove *et al.* (2018) do not specify what content is categorised as informative information or an emotional content, or consider the various engagement purposes. Individuals are likely to use social media platforms for various reasons, so responses will vary.

The studies of Vilnai-Yavetz & Levina (2018) and Fu, Wu & Cho (2017) were undertaken from the perspective of the non-financial motives for sharing e-business content. Both found that self-expression, community connection and belonging were key motivations. It is important for firms to understand how they can develop their social media strategies, by understanding how online consumers access content and what influences them to become interactive based on firm-generated content. However, the study does not consider the non-active social media users who form the majority of the online population. Although that population may be irrelevant to viral sharing activity, it can be argued that their decision to remain with an airline can still be majorly influenced by the type of content posted and shared by the company and its followers.

With the majority of online users being observers rather than content contributors, it is important to understand the extent to which they are socially influenced by followers or company-generated content to remain with airline brands. This can be developed from Dholakia, Bagozzi, & Pearo's (2004) decision-making and participation variable on online communities' frameworks. Two of the main variables include an individual's desire and intention to act and commit with others within an online community. If individuals have a strong social influence over other online consumers, the likelihood of brands being positively perceived by a mass number of social networks would be greater than directly posting content to them. This can be the case even if grouped consumers share similar motivations and values or if the content is directed to a particular audience.

Muller & Peres (2018) analysed the key components of social media networks, such as the quality of networks and their key characteristics that define social influence status. The two key messenger groups identified are market mavens and social hubs; these have access to large volumes of marketplace information or online networks and engage in online activities. These two groups impact consumers' perception of marketing messages and encourage them to share the content. This indicates that the type of information these two main groups deliver and their position in the social media community can impact consumers' brand perception. However, it is important to understand whether the observing social media users perceive these two groups significant to influencing their purchasing intentions and decision to remain with brands.

THEORETICAL CONTEXT

Some scholars define social media as an Internet-based application that builds on technological foundations, consisting of a series of words, images and audio hosted by well-known sites such as Facebook, YouTube, Instagram and blogs (Yates & Paquette, 2011; Bertot, Jaeger, & Hansen, D., 2012; Berthon, Pitt, Plangger, & Shapiro, 2012). In contrast, other scholars define social media as platforms of interaction through user-generated content, promoting the encouragement of individuals or communities to socialise, learn, play, engage and exchange information at their convenience (Kietzmann *et al.*, 2011; Bonsón, Torres, Royo, & Flores, 2010; Fischer & Reuber, 2011; Ozuem, 2016). Although there is no single definition of what social media is, it is clear that social media can be used as a method of online communication to redefine how services are delivered to retain customers (Ayertey, Ozuem, & Appiah, 2018). In general, social media has been defined as a technology and community engagement platform. In addition, there have been various studies of social media that have primarily focused on researching the effects of its activity and connection to online behavioural patterns (Kuksov, Shachar, & Wang, 2013; Blazevic, Wiertz, Cotte, de Ruyter, & Keeling, 2014; Bertot, Jaeger, & Grimes, 2010; Stokinger & Ozuem, 2018).

Kuksov *et al.*'s (2013) study focused on the impact online participants have on companies' management of their brands. Kuksov *et al.* state that brand managers are no longer the key stakeholders for presenting a brand, as social media has more effectively enabled consumers to contribute content. Bertot *et al.* (2010) highlight the notion that social media facilitates collaboration, participation and empowerment to enable online users to interact. This, according to Hennig-Thurau, Malthouse, Friege, Gensler, Lobschat, Rangaswamy, & Skiera (2010) is more effective because consumer-generated content spreads more quickly and is more readily available. In addition, Gensler, Völckner, Liu-Thompkins, & Wiertz (2013) argue that consumer-generated brand stories add to a brand's identity. Consequently, when consumers volunteer content or their own networks, they impact not only the image of the brand but also the authenticity of the brand's social identity. However, the availability of technology that enables interaction does not mean that users will respond in the same way even when provided with equal access to do so. Gensler *et al.* (2013) and Bertot *et al.* (2010) do not specifically mention the various motivations online users have to participate in social media or how firms can use social media to encourage online observers to take part in online discussions.

Every online user will deliver different volumes and types of engagement, resulting in brands receiving different response outcomes for their online content. Blazevic *et al.* (2014) studied the extent to which an individual will probably participate in online interaction in contrast to another who will not, even when equal access and motivational settings are available. The study aimed to examine the difference between online and offline interaction behaviours. Blazevic *et al.*'s study (2014) recorded three themes that characterise general online social interaction behavioural patterns:

1. **The Level of Interaction:** The amount of interactive behaviour from different participants, from lurking to contributing content
2. **Social Preferences:** The level of wanting to be a part or a creator of online community interaction or a discussion
3. **Enjoyment in Interaction:** The extent to which an individual enjoys the online interactive exchange with others

These themes suggest that interactivity is a feature not only linked to technology but also to the consumer focused in the online discussion. Wiertz & de Ruyter (2007) support this argument that online interaction does not solely depend on the medium of technology, but on the individuals who make the decision to use those facilities. Blazevic *et al.* (2014) found that there is a clear distinction between online and offline communication, which they determined from the groups involved in online communication. When communicating online, individuals are more likely to interact with strangers, rather than people they are familiar with. Consequently, the participation or disclosure of information online may be different, or limited, in contrast to the disclosure of information in conversations in an offline environment. This means that there is a difference in types of online consumers, the lurkers or observers, and the contributors that post or participate in online activities (Schlosser, 2005).

Various researchers have found that active contributors constitute a small population in contrast with the number of lurkers, who mainly observe content posted by others (Cothrel & Williams, 1999; Kozinets, 1999; Preece, Nonnecke, & Andrews, 2004). Therefore, technology platforms do not guarantee consumer engagement, and each user, even with common interests and goals, will respond differently to content posted online. Yet it is important to note that individuals who are active posters may be more willing to communicate in online situations rather than offline. Consequently, mass online content is still likely to be generated by the small population of contributors, but it will depend on the nature of the interaction in which they are participating.

Brands that publish SMMC on their fan pages are one method of producing popularity among other brands and encouraging online interaction. De Vries, Gensler, & Leeflang (2012) argued that a range of characteristics of brand posts can impact the brand's popularity. The first characteristic discussed is the vividness of the post, emphasising that the features of the content generate a variety of attitudes towards the brand. Various researchers have found that stimulating the vividness of the post can be achieved through different forms of online features, such as pictures and animations (Fortin & Dholakia, 2005; Goldfarb & Tucker, 2011; Goodrich, 2011). Such elements that augment the richness of a post's features can generate different perspectives of the brand from various observers (Coyle & Thorson, 2001). Consequently, the response will vary amongst individuals who develop their own attitudes towards such richness that is published. Therefore interactivity will be different across different post and communication channels, which is another key feature examined in the study. Liu & Shrum (2002) explain that the form of the medium of communication that enables groups to interact with each other is vital when communicating online. In contrast, Blazevic *et al.* (2014) disagree that the technology platform is the most important characteristic of online interaction. Nevertheless, it is the platform that impacts the effectiveness of, and access to, online interaction, therefore there is a connection between online interaction levels and the technology platform that enables such interaction.

Additionally, de Vries *et al.*'s (2012) study of brand-related content specifically focuses on the characteristics of information and entertainment. Muntinga, Moorman, & Smit (2011) point out that individuals consume brand-related content to obtain information concerning the brand and its products or services. This implies that brand posts that contain informative content about the brand are more likely to retain a certain volume of popularity. However, another essential point de Vries *et al.* mention is the content that retains consumers' psychological attachment to the brand. According to Taylor, Lewin & Strutton (2011) advertisements with entertaining characteristics can impact the perception of the brand through the advertisement, which can potentially increase the consumers' psychological connection with the brand (Raney, Arpan, Pashupati, & Brill, 2003). While this is the case, it is important for firms to consider the objectives of enhancing the online interaction or the response they aim to attain in relation to the content they publish.

For example, de Vries *et al.* found that entertainment brand posts can contain unrelated content which thus negatively impacts the brands' objective as to how they are perceived. However, in contrast, Berger & Milkman's (2012) work on what makes online content viral found that content will most likely be shared if it evokes high emotions. The study suggested that consumers share content for the purposes of self-presentation, as positive content may reflect a positive image of the sender. Considering the findings in the studies referred to on the relationship between content and online consumers, it can be argued that the online engagement objectives must match the purpose of the content posted. Although online participants have different levels of need regarding what experience they want from the content and the social media tools, brands using social media must incorporate customisation into their posting activity.

Similarly, Kim & Ko (2012) concluded that the entertainment, interaction and trendiness characteristics are important for application to marketing social media activities for luxury fashion brands. By way of contrast, their study deemed the element of customisation and word-of-mouth (WOM) to be equally important. Moon (2002) proposed that consumers perceive personalisation as having a practical and symbolic value. Bernritter, Verlegh, & Smit (2016) confirmed that brand symbolism is a great benefit for for-profit firms due to the emotional attachment it generates from customers, therefore increasing their likelihood to endorse brands through social media. In this way, personalisation can impact consumers' perspectives of the brand's symbol and values, encouraging the practice of individualism amongst online users (Dunne, Lawlor, & Rowley, 2010). When examining customisation of international marketing,

Markus & Kitayama (1991) assert that understanding cross-cultural differences is vital, as a significant example of customisation in online international marketing (Lim, Leung, Sia, & Lee, 2014; Roth, 1995).

Likewise Hudson, Huang, Roth, & Madden's (2016) research in marketing focused primarily on the cultural dimensions of individualism and collectivism, which can be linked to Hofstede's (1984) cultural dimension study. However, establishing the extent to which a country's culture impacts social media activity is difficult, as individual countries also have sub-groups that can be categorised under different social media activities. These individual studies similarly imply that incorporating customisation into social media posts is significant to retaining online engagement. If firms aim to maintain a continuation of online WOM, it is vital to publish content that matches consumers' interests and connects them with other networks with similar interests. This also contributes to maintaining online consumers' interaction, and it is essential to consider the various activities and reasons that motivate individuals to be active on social media platforms that support brands' social media activity.

TECHNOLOGY PLATFORMS AND TAXOMOMIES

Focusing on the subject of social media, the key significant factor is the technology platforms, including Facebook, Twitter, YouTube and Wikipedia. While these platforms are some of the most globally used, the definition of social media is not limited to the platforms mentioned above (Aichner & Jacob, 2015). As there are various types and formats of social media, there is no methodical way in which social media can be categorised. Thus, it is important to distinguish the different types of social media by the definitions of their intended use. Ngai *et al.* (2015) define six categories of different social media platforms as:

- Media sharing sites
    - Platforms such as YouTube and Instagram that enable users to upload and share audio or visual material online with other people or communities.
- Blogs/microblogs
    - These sites are where individuals can post their own written material online for people to read and comment upon the material or subject. Microblogs are mostly for short and high-frequency posting, whereas blogs are similar to a personal online journal. (e.g. Twitter, Tumblr and Blog sites).
- Social bookmarking sites
    - This is the activity of saving and organising specific web contents through the use of tags in order to share with other online users.
- Virtual/online communities
    - These enable the sharing of specific information and interests through interactive tools.
- Social networking sites
    - These are platforms such as Facebook and LinkedIn that facilitate connecting individuals who may share common interests, or building friendships or promoting acquaintance among individuals. These sites allow individuals to post profiles of themselves and upload pictures and videos.

- Virtual worlds
    - Users can create their own personal identity in computer-generated environments to explore communicating with others and joining in activities.

The definitions of these types of social media indicate that the perceived advantages of social media platforms affect the consumers' motivation to use them. Therefore it is clear that the type and purpose of SMMC will be implemented using the method that best suits the aims and objectives of the material posted in regard to generating consumer interaction and engagement.

Over time the various motivations of consumers using social media have increased from 'lurking' to being active participants. As the motivations of use have increased so have studies to understand the usage behaviour of consumers. So with results not drawing the same conclusions or definitions of social media, there is no generally accepted taxonomy to classify social media as a whole. Yet while there is no generally accepted taxonomy, various researchers have found taxonomies for specific studies of social media, especially in the types of users and their motivations for social media usage. For instance, Kaplan & Haenlein (2010) proposed a taxonomy of social media based on media theories, social presence and media richness, and social processes theories, self-presentation and self-disclosure. Taking into account the type of media and its degree of richness, the study focuses on measuring the media richness of six types of social media and the levels of interaction they enable. To illustrate this, Kaplan & Haenlein (2010) found that blogs score the lowest for media richness due to their basic text-based activity, whereas content communities like YouTube and social networking sites like Facebook scored higher for media richness and social presence due to their combination of text-based communication and sharing of other media content such as pictures and videos. This study helps identify the effectiveness of different social media platforms, but it does not consider the various activities that users can undertake using the social media platforms.

Tafesse & Wien (2017) developed a framework that categorises different social media posts for different online activities and communities. These are:

- **Emotional Brand Posts:** Posts consisting of emotion-laden language, inspiring stories or humour to arouse affective responses
- **Functional Brand Posts:** Posts highlighting the qualities of products or services, or benefits of companies and their performance criteria
- **Educational Brand Posts:** help consumers acquire new knowledge or skills
- **Brand Resonance:** Posts highlighting the main characteristics of a brand's identity and image, including logos, slogans and celebrity associations
- **Experiential Brand Posts:** Highlight the personified qualities of the brand, which can come in the form of visualised product launches, sponsored events or festivals
- **Current Event:** Posts commenting on current themes such as cultural holidays or events to initiate conversations
- **Personal Brand Posts:** Posts tailored around consumer relationships, preferences and experiences
- **Employee Brand Posts:** Posts about a company's employees and their roles within the company and even their personal interests
- **Brand Community:** Posts used to promote or reinforce a brand's online community. This involves tagging and user-generated content to encourage users' participation

- **Customer Relationship:** Customer feedback reviews and testimonies to improve the impact of customer relationship in social media channels and encourage others to submit feedback
- **Cause-Related Brand Posts:** These are created by companies to promote social causes they are supporting and aim to inspire customers to support them
- **Sales Promotion Posts:** The purpose of these posts is to attract consumers toward a buying decision; these include price discounts, coupons and product competitions

The social media post categorisation provides a framework that can be used to inspire new brand post ideas and encourage daily customer interaction on social media, and to improve content strategies. The framework supports determining which category of posts should be published frequently and which ones are more likely to generate consumer engagement. However, the limitation to Tafesse & Wien's (2017) framework is that it does not consider brand posts that incorporate multiple messages into a single post. Therefore measuring the effectiveness of a post category becomes complicated if the post's message cannot be linked to a specified category. Furthermore, the model does not provide an in-depth understanding of how online users are influenced by social factors or networks to engage or share content.

Although it is important to know the various online activities, it is important to understand the various characteristics linked to consumers' psychological or social reasons for interacting through social media or sharing particular content. Vilnai-Yavetz & Levina's (2018) study focuses on addressing four non-financial motives for sharing e-business content: self-enhancement; hedonism; community and belonging; and society and business community. Similarly, Fu *et al.* (2017) examined the social and psychological motivations of content sharing on Facebook. The two broad categories they developed were self-interest (achievement, self-expression, loneliness) and communal incentives (connection, altruism, and group joy). This supports that though consumers may share interest in types of content, there are various consumer behavioural characteristics that social media posts must consider to generate the customers' response to act within the social media community.

In comparison, Kietzmann *et al.* (2011) developed the Honeycomb social media model, which focuses on addressing seven functional building blocks: identity, conversation, sharing, presence, relationships, reputation, and groups. Their study addresses these features of social media and how companies respond to them, providing an understanding of the audience for each social media platform and what their engagement needs are. The Honeycomb framework primarily focuses on the ways in which social media activities vary and impact consumers' online activity. While the framework does not provide specific examples of external social influences that motivate consumers to comply with brands' SMMC or activities, it is a useful framework relating to the strategic development of SMMC.

SOCIAL MEDIA MARKETING AND VIRAL MARKETING

Social media platforms have a high volume of online users encountering many brands and their fan pages. A key marketing method suitable for social media applications is viral marketing, as the community element of social media enables brands to take advantage of the large group of people available to transfer marketing messages to their online networks. Some researchers have therefore combined viral marketing and social media marketing into their study (Kozinets, de Valck, Wojnicki, & Wilner, 2010). Viral marketing is a method that uses consumer-to-consumer communication to spread information about a company's product or service. Viral marketing provides the advantage of rapidly transmitting marketing messages to a mass audience (Kaplan & Haenlein, 2011) without the high investment costs of other traditional advertising (Liu-Thompkins, 2012). Viral marketing has been studied in literature under a variety of subject areas including word-of-mouse and word-of-mouth marketing (Kozinets *et al.*, 2010). Previous research on the determinants of viral marketing success has primarily focused on the features of the content (Shehu, Bijmolt, & Clement, 2016; Pressgrove *et al.*, 2018; Peng, Agarwal, Hosanagar, & Iyengar, 2018) and seeding strategies (Hu, Lin, Qian, & Sun, 2018; Muller & Peres, 2018; Hinz, Schulze, & Takac, 2014).

Features of content often primarily focus on creating effective viral messages that encourage consumers to pass the message to others. Kaplan & Haenlein (2011) developed the Viral Marketing Process Model which identifies three main elements in creating viral marketing, one of which includes the content of the marketing message. Akpinar & Berger's (2017) study investigated the likelihood of content becoming viral based on the viewers' emotional response. Their results from the study indicated that content with more emotional appeal was more likely to be shared than informatively appealed content. Additionally, the study concluded that submitting content that has emotional appeal contributes to boosting brand evaluation and purchase intent. In comparison, Pressgrove *et al.* (2018) found that content evoking positive emotions is more likely to go viral than content evoking negative emotions. However, in contrast their study found that only content with practical value was shared on the basis that it was viewed as having practical value or information relevant enough to share with others. Although Pressgrove *et al.* (2018) was based on a study of the platform Twitter, other sites like Facebook and Instagram that have frequent sharing and posting may have different conclusions as to why content goes viral.

As mentioned earlier, social media users range from being simple observers to active sharers of content. Viral marketing can only occur if consumers are willing to share and promote a brand (de Bruyn & Lilien, 2008). It can be argued that the impact of viral marketing campaigns reaching mass audiences is strongly influenced by key consumer seeds that have a strong social influence in online communities. Samadi, Nagi, Semenov, & Nikolaev (2018) developed the two-level network model which separates the potential seeds or influencers from the regular 'influencees'. The first level contains the influencers that can support a campaign through sharing content consentingly, resulting in the content reaching the 'influencees' who are part of the second stage of the model. However, this study is based on the process of 'paid bloggers' being employed or sponsored to generate or share content, and does not provide assumptions for voluntary activation of potential seeds.

Muller & Peres (2018) analysed components such as the quality of networks and identified key messengers and their characteristics to support the viral message process, as follows:

- **Market Mavens:** As the group who are typically the first to receive the message, these individuals have access to large volumes of marketplace information and engage in online discussions with other consumers to spread information.
- **Social Hubs:** These are individuals with large numbers of online connections who pass marketing messages to a large population of consumers.

Kaplan & Haenlein's (2011) model has limitations to providing an understanding of the 'seeds' impacting the successful spread of viral messages. While the model provides general groups that could impact the process of viral marketing, the model does not specify the social position of seeds that have particular influence over other online consumers. A consumer's social network position within an online community can be defined by his/her relationship with other networks (Kiss & Bichler, 2008; Susarla, Oh,

& Tan, 2012). If the individual is central to the online network it is he/she who impacts other consumers' perception of the marketing messages or encourages other networks to share the content the main seed has shared with them (Muller & Peres, 2018). The development of online communities through social media has extended consumer influence beyond immediate close friends to acquaintances and strangers (Duan, Gu, & Whinston, 2008). Therefore mass networks involved in viral marketing may be a significant factor in influencing individuals to join viral marketing campaigns with heavily populated networks. However, this may be more relevant once a viral campaign has established viral attention, hence the small numbers of fundamental consumers at the start of the process are significant in contrast to targeting a large population at the beginning. Overall, despite research into content and senders and receivers, there is limited understanding on what the main drivers are for successful viral marketing efforts (Ferguson, 2008; Kalyanam, McIntyre, & Masonis, 2007). Yet it can be argued that message content and the influence of key individuals that share it are essential fundamentals to viral marketing.

Social Influence Theory

Social influence is considered essential when studying human behaviour; with regard to social media, it is possible that individuals' online behaviour is impacted by the volume of individuals active online. Social influence occurs when an individual adapts his/her behaviour or beliefs to the behaviour of others in the social system (Leenders, 2002). Scholarly research regarding social and communication networks, opinion leadership, source credibility and uses and consumer indulgence can provide insights into the marketing process and motivations of participants (Phelps, Lewis, Mobilio, Perry, & Raman, 2004). Face-to-face interactions are not essential for social influence, as influence is based on the information about other individuals (Robins, Pattison, & Elliott, 2001). With technology in social media advancing further, the role of social influence may be vital to influencing the usage of the various types of technology platforms (Tsai & Bagozzi, 2014).

Trusov, Bodapati & Bucklin (2010) studied the types of social network users that influence others. They believed that aspects of online social networks like MySpace and Facebook are similar to types of interactions found on consumer product review sites. However, they found that differences in different social network sites were too numerous for them to be treated in the same way. These differences included the volume of people involved and the motives and nature of interactions in online communities. Previous studies had focused more on aggregated group influence than individual influence within groups (Dholakia, Bagozzi, & Pearo, 2004; Godes & Mayzlin, 2004). Trusov *et al.* (2010) found that having a long list of networks does not have a significant influence. Hence it is likely that online users will rely on a small percentage of individuals they are connected to online, supporting the concept that the information or nature of the influencer is key.

Bagozzi & Dholakia's (2002) study adopted a marketing lens to identify two key social influence variables: group norms and social identity. By incorporating the social psychological model of goal-directed behaviour and social identity theory, Bagozzi & Dholakia modelled group participation as a function of individual and social determinants. However, their model has limitations. First, they consider social influence variables to be caused by external forces, and do not consider the background or experience of group norms or social identity. Furthermore the study is limited to virtual communities and does not consider the distinctions among different virtual communities. Dholakia *et al.*'s (2004) study is built on Bagozzi & Dholakia's (2002) framework, but includes the background experience of social influences in the model. Dholakia *et al.*'s model comprises three factors: value perception, social influence variables and decision making, and participation. The value perception consists of five individual value groups:

- **Purposive Value:** Value derived from accomplishment of a pre-determined instrumental purpose (including giving and receiving information).
- **Self-Discovery:** Understanding the notable, unique aspects of one's self through social interactions, supporting individuals to determine their preferences and values.
- **Maintaining Interpersonal Interconnectivity:** The social benefits resulting from online social networks.
- **Social Enhancement:** Value obtained from gaining acceptance and approval from other members, and the image they develop from being a contributor.
- **Entertainment Value:** A result from having fun interacting with others.

Finally there are three main decision-making and participation variables, namely:

- **Desire:** An individual's motivation to favour acting as part of an online community
- **We-Intentions:** An individual's commitment to co-operate actively in agreement with others
- **Participation Behaviour:** Frequency of online behaviour

Dholakia *et al.* (2004) hypothesised that strong group norms indirectly generate consent among members regarding when and how they engage in online interactions. In other words, group norms encourage mutual agreements among members regarding participation details. Research on group negotiation shows that group norms enable co-operative motivation among group members (Weingart, Bennett, & Brett, 1993). Therefore the stronger the group norms, the greater the likelihood of individuals' choice to jointly accommodate their preferences and commitments with others.

Cheung & Lee (2009) investigated important aspects of the social influence processes and their roles in influencing online behaviour. Their model illustrates that intentions to continue using a virtual community are determined by satisfaction, commitment and group norms. These are then affected by online users' needs for purposive value, self-discovery, entertainment value, social enhancement, and maintaining interpersonal inter-connectivity. The model focuses on two behavioural intentions of online members: the intention to continue use and the intention to recommend. Cheung & Lee concluded that satisfaction has the strongest impact on the intention to recommend, as satisfied consumers will engage favourably with firms (Yang & Peterson, 2004). This aspect of satisfaction can be applied to the context of a virtual community. If members are satisfied with their experience, they are more likely to share their positive experiences.

However, Cheung & Lee did not find a connection between satisfaction and commitment. It can be argued that the sense of belonging impacts commitment, which can link with group norms that individuals share with others (Helal & Ozuem, 2018). In this way they generate satisfaction due to the virtual community facilitating individuals' social position in the community. However, this study was only applied to understanding virtual communities. With more social media platforms allowing social interaction it is important to apply an understanding of users' engagement on different platforms. Cheung, Chiu, & Lee's (2011) study hypothesised that individuals with strong social identity generate strong intentions to interact online. Yet it is important to note that individuals' perspectives of online interaction will affect the social influence they accept. So the behavioural outcome of individuals generated will be different even when they are provided with equal access to online platforms. Moreover, it is important to understand the social factors rather than the intended social action (Cheung & Lee, 2009; Dholakia *et al.,* 2004).

According to Prentice-Dunn & Rogers (1985) social influence is strong when individuals belong to groups. Hence it can be argued that when individuals have limited knowledge, the social influence is likely to be high. For example, Cohen & Golden (1972) and Venkatesan (1966) found that social influence is high if product quality detail is unclear. This perspective can be applied to users on social media who may place value on brands based on the volume of online WOM which may reduce individuals' uncertainty. An understanding of human behaviour can be drawn from Kelman's (1958) social influence theory. Kelman states that an individual's attitudes, beliefs and behavioural outcomes are influenced by others through three processes, which are:

- **Compliance**: is assumed to occur when individuals accept influence and adopt the encouraged behaviour to gain rewards or avoid punishment
- **Identification:** Occurs when individuals adopt a behaviour to create or maintain a connection with other individuals or groups
- **Internalisation:** is the adoption of decisions based on finding similarity of one's value systems with other group members

According to Cheung & Lee (2010) earlier models of human behaviour have primarily centred on subjective norms of social influence, which can be linked to the compliance process of Kelman's theory. The limitation of Kelman's model however is that it does not measure the growth of relationships between variables, such as social factors and social identity, or apply them to measuring social interaction. Kelman's research was primarily focused on attitude change, tested scientifically, in contrast to investigating a social community, which limits the understanding of variables influencing social interaction in social media. However, Kelman's theory can contribute to extended studies of different users on social network sites, as many social media may well move through the three different processes. This is supported by Karahanna, Straub, & Chervany (1999) and Taylor & Todd (1995) who compared experienced and inexperienced Internet users, finding that subjective norms are less influential in decisions for usage among experienced users.

CONCLUSION AND MANAGERIAL IMPLICATIONS

Social media has the potential to increase firms' value as a result of maintaining an online interaction with their customers. As well as using social media to connect with peers, many individuals require organisations to adopt a similar level of interaction with their consumers (Hanna, Rohm, & Crittenden, 2011; Ansarin & Ozuem, 2015). Therefore many firms are expected to increase their use of social media as a medium to maintain personal communication with their customers and monitor their online interaction behaviour. According to Trainor (2012), CRM is defined as a customer-facing activities and technology activity combined to create online conversations and develop customer relationships. Wang & Kim (2017) further point out that CRM involves firms managing knowledge about the customers' buying habits in order to personalise product and service offers for individual customers. Research by Xiang, Du, Ma & Fan (2017) has identified social media as significant in motivating users to engage in knowledge-sharing and has recognised that social media incorporates a 'human side' in customer knowledge management (Carlson *et al.*, 2018).

A good relationship between firms and customers is vital for CRM. However, what makes a good relationship in CRM is not always clear. A study by Hajli, Shanmugam, Papagiannidis, Zahay, & Richard (2017) implied that customers' social participation with preferred brands in online communities impacts the relationship quality regarding trust, loyalty and enhancing customer-brand relationships. Kamboj, Sarmah, Gupta, & Dwivedi's (2018) study tested Hajli *et al.*'s (2017) study by assessing the effects of social media participation motivations, including building interpersonal relations, entertainment, brand likeability, information seeking and incentives, and the consequent effect of customer participation on brand trust and brand loyalty. According to Kamboj *et al.* (2018) the findings of the study supported that customer participation in online brand communities leads to brand trust and loyalty and to co-creation of SMMC. The study therefore establishes a link between brand trust and brand loyalty through brands' social media communities.

Kamboj *et al.*'s (2018) findings can be confirmed by Sashi's (2012) model of the process of customer engagement, which confirms that customer engagement focuses on satisfying customers by providing superior value to build trust and commitment in long-term relationships in order to compete with other suppliers. Social media interaction facilitates the process of forming permanent relationships between sellers and buyers. The process of creating a customer engagement cycle has been used in reference to the purchase cycle process which represents customers' stages of purchase decision-making. Sashi (2012) has highlighted the notion that social media enables frequent, faster and richer interactions among groups of people. However, his study does not take different social media platforms into account or examine the advantages and disadvantages of each stage of the engagement cycle regarding social media use. Understanding how social media platforms like Facebook or YouTube combine with CRM to produce affective and calculative commitment is vital. This can be studied with the research into social influence.

According to Üstüner & Godes (2006) social media technology has the potential to support firms in obtaining effective sales through CRM, by enabling them to understand their customers' perspective of the brand. The application of social media to CRM can also support firms in developing strategies for customer solutions and improving the effectiveness of online operations to manage the high demand from customers. Yet while social media is viewed as significant in customer knowledge management, particularly for the personalisation of service and product offers and encouraging consumers' motivation to share knowledge (Moe & Schweidel, 2017; Ozuem and Tan, 2014), it is important to point out that social media alone will not have a direct impact on maintaining online customer relationships. Consequently, the firms' capabilities in facilitating and managing social media platforms and the discussions taking place on them will generate the effectiveness of social media in CRM. Trainor, Andzulis, Rapp, & Agnihotri's (2013) study concluded that social media technology should be used to develop capabilities in online consumer relationships. Therefore social media is vitally significant in maintaining online communication and customer knowledge management, but firms have to organise effective social media activities to generate customer interaction in order to obtain the required information and sustain customers' satisfaction with the brand.

REFERENCES

Aichner, T., & Jacob, F. (2015). Measuring the degree of corporate social media use. *International Journal of Market Research*, *57*(2), 257–276. doi:10.2501/IJMR-2015-018

Akpinar, E., & Berger, J. (2017). Valuable Virality. *JMR, Journal of Marketing Research*, *54*(2), 318–330. doi:10.1509/jmr.13.0350

Ansarin, M., & Ozuem, W. (2015). Social media and online brand communities. In Computer-Mediated Marketing Strategies: Social Media and Online Brand Communities (pp. 1-27). IGI Global.

Ayertey, S., Ozuem, W., & Appiah, D. (2018). Service Failure and Recovery Strategy in Computer-Mediated Marketing Environments. *Global Business and Technology Association Conference.*

Bagozzi, R. P., & Dholakia, U. M. (2002). Intentional social action in virtual communities. *Journal of Interactive Marketing*, *16*(2), 2–21. doi:10.1002/dir.10006

Berger, J., & Milkman, K. L. (2012). What makes online content viral? *JMR, Journal of Marketing Research*, *49*(2), 192–205. doi:10.1509/jmr.10.0353

Bernritter, S. F., Verlegh, P. W., & Smit, E. G. (2016). Why nonprofits are easier to endorse on social media: The roles of warmth and brand symbolism. *Journal of Interactive Marketing*, *33*, 27–42. doi:10.1016/j.intmar.2015.10.002

Berthon, P. R., Pitt, L. F., Plangger, K., & Shapiro, D. (2012). Marketing meets web 2.0, social media, and creative consumers: Implications for international marketing strategy. *Business Horizons*, *55*(3), 261–271. doi:10.1016/j.bushor.2012.01.007

Bertot, J. C., Jaeger, P. T., & Grimes, J. M. (2010). Using ICTs to create a culture of transparency: E-government and social media as openness and anti-corruption tools for societies. *Government Information Quarterly*, *27*(3), 264–271. doi:10.1016/j.giq.2010.03.001

Bertot, J. C., Jaeger, P. T., & Hansen, D. (2012). The impact of polices on government social media usage: Issues, challenges, and recommendations. *Government Information Quarterly*, *29*(1), 30–40. doi:10.1016/j.giq.2011.04.004

Beukeboom, C. J., Kerkhof, P., & de Vries, M. (2015). Does a virtual like cause actual liking? How following a brand's Facebook updates enhances brand evaluations and purchase intention. *Journal of Interactive Marketing*, *32*, 26–36. doi:10.1016/j.intmar.2015.09.003

Blazevic, V., Wiertz, C., Cotte, J., de Ruyter, K., & Keeling, D. I. (2014). GOSIP in cyberspace: Conceptualization and scale development for general online social interaction propensity. *Journal of Interactive Marketing*, *28*(2), 87–100. doi:10.1016/j.intmar.2013.09.003

Bonsón, E., Torres, L., Royo, S., & Flores, F. (2012). Local e-government 2.0: Social media and corporate transparency in municipalities. *Government Information Quarterly*, *29*(2), 123–132. doi:10.1016/j.giq.2011.10.001

Carlson, J., Rahman, M., Voola, R., & De Vries, N. (2018). Customer engagement behaviours in social media: Capturing innovation opportunities. *Journal of Services Marketing*, *32*(1), 83–94. doi:10.1108/JSM-02-2017-0059

Cheung, C. M., Chiu, P. Y., & Lee, M. K. (2011). Online social networks: Why do students use facebook? *Computers in Human Behavior*, *27*(4), 1337–1343. doi:10.1016/j.chb.2010.07.028

Cheung, C. M., & Lee, M. K. (2009). Understanding the sustainability of a virtual community: Model development and empirical test. *Journal of Information Science*, *35*(3), 279–298. doi:10.1177/0165551508099088

Cheung, C. M., & Lee, M. K. (2010). A theoretical model of intentional social action in online social networks. *Decision Support Systems*, *49*(1), 24–30. doi:10.1016/j.dss.2009.12.006

Cohen, J. B., & Golden, E. (1972). Informational Social Influence and Product Evaluation. *The Journal of Applied Psychology*, *56*(1), 54–59. doi:10.1037/h0032139

Cothrel, J. P., & Williams, R. L. (1999). On-Line Communities: Helping Them Form and Grow. *Journal of Knowledge Management*, *3*(1), 54–60. doi:10.1108/13673279910259394

Coyle, J. R., & Thorson, E. (2001). The effects of progressive levels of interactivity and vividness in web marketing sites. *Journal of Advertising*, *30*(3), 65–77. doi:10.1080/00913367.2001.10673646

De Bruyn, A., & Lilien, G. L. (2008). A multi-stage model of word-of-mouth influence through viral marketing. *International Journal of Research in Marketing*, *25*(3), 151–163. doi:10.1016/j.ijresmar.2008.03.004

De Vries, L., Gensler, S., & Leeflang, P. S. (2012). Popularity of brand posts on brand fan pages: An investigation of the effects of social media marketing. *Journal of Interactive Marketing*, *26*(2), 83–91. doi:10.1016/j.intmar.2012.01.003

Dholakia, U. M., Bagozzi, R. P., & Pearo, L. K. (2004). A social influence model of consumer participation in network-and small-group-based virtual communities. *International Journal of Research in Marketing*, *21*(3), 241–263. doi:10.1016/j.ijresmar.2003.12.004

Duan, W., Gu, B., & Whinston, A. B. (2008). The dynamics of online word-of-mouth and product sales—An empirical investigation of the movie industry. *Journal of Retailing*, *84*(2), 233–242. doi:10.1016/j.jretai.2008.04.005

Dunne, Á., Lawlor, M. A., & Rowley, J. (2010). Young people's use of online social networking sites–a uses and gratifications perspective. *Journal of Research in Interactive Marketing*, *4*(1), 46–58. doi:10.1108/17505931011033551

Ferguson, R. (2008). Word of mouth and viral marketing: Taking the temperature of the hottest trends in marketing. *Journal of Consumer Marketing*, *25*(3), 179–182. doi:10.1108/07363760810870671

Fischer, E., & Reuber, A. R. (2011). Social interaction via new social media: (How) can interactions on Twitter affect effectual thinking and behavior? *Journal of Business Venturing*, *26*(1), 1–18. doi:10.1016/j.jbusvent.2010.09.002

Fortin, D. R., & Dholakia, R. R. (2005). Interactivity and vividness effects on social presence and involvement with a web-based advertisement. *Journal of Business Research*, *58*(3), 387–396. doi:10.1016/S0148-2963(03)00106-1

Fu, P. W., Wu, C. C., & Cho, Y. J. (2017). What makes users share content on Facebook? Compatibility among psychological incentive, social capital focus, and content type. *Computers in Human Behavior*, *67*, 23–32. doi:10.1016/j.chb.2016.10.010

Gensler, S., Völckner, F., Liu-Thompkins, Y., & Wiertz, C. (2013). Managing brands in the social media environment. *Journal of Interactive Marketing*, *27*(4), 242–256. doi:10.1016/j.intmar.2013.09.004

Godes, D., & Mayzlin, D. (2004). Using Online Conversations to Study Word-of-Mouth Communication. *Marketing Science*, *23*(4), 545–560. doi:10.1287/mksc.1040.0071

Goldfarb, A., & Tucker, C. (2011). Online display advertising: Targeting and obtrusiveness. *Marketing Science*, *30*(3), 389–404. doi:10.1287/mksc.1100.0583

Goodrich, K. (2011). Anarchy of effects? Exploring attention to online advertising and multiple outcomes. *Psychology and Marketing*, *28*(4), 417–440. doi:10.1002/mar.20371

Hajli, N., Shanmugam, M., Papagiannidis, S., Zahay, D., & Richard, M. O. (2017). Branding co-creation with members of online brand communities. *Journal of Business Research*, *70*, 136–144. doi:10.1016/j.jbusres.2016.08.026

Hanna, R., Rohm, A., & Crittenden, V. L. (2011). We're all connected: The power of the social media ecosystem. *Business Horizons*, *54*(3), 265–273. doi:10.1016/j.bushor.2011.01.007

Harrigan, P., Soutar, G., Choudhury, M. M., & Lowe, M. (2015). Modelling CRM in a Social Media Age. *Australasian Marketing Journal*, *23*(1), 27–37. doi:10.1016/j.ausmj.2014.11.001

Helal, G., & Ozuem, W. (2018). Social Identity Matters: Social Media and Brand Perceptions in the Fashion Apparel and Accessories Industries. In Digital Marketing Strategies for Fashion and Luxury Brands (pp. 326-361). IGI Global.

Hennig-Thurau, T., Malthouse, E. C., Friege, C., Gensler, S., Lobschat, L., Rangaswamy, A., & Skiera, B. (2010). The Impact of New Media on Customer Relationships. *Journal of Service Research*, *13*(3), 311–330. doi:10.1177/1094670510375460

Hinz, O., Schulze, C., & Takac, C. (2014). New product adoption in social networks: Why direction matters. *Journal of Business Research*, *67*(1), 2836–2844. doi:10.1016/j.jbusres.2012.07.005

Hu, H. H., Lin, J., Qian, Y., & Sun, J. (2018). Strategies for new product diffusion: Whom and how to target? *Journal of Business Research*, *83*, 111–119. doi:10.1016/j.jbusres.2017.10.010

Hudson, S., Huang, L., Roth, M. S., & Madden, T. J. (2016). The influence of social media interactions on consumer–brand relationships: A three-country study of brand perceptions and marketing behaviors. *International Journal of Research in Marketing*, *33*(1), 27–41. doi:10.1016/j.ijresmar.2015.06.004

Kalyanam, K., McIntyre, S., & Masonis, J. T. (2007). Adaptive experimentation in interactive marketing: The case of viral marketing at Plaxo. *Journal of Interactive Marketing*, *21*(3), 72–85. doi:10.1002/dir.20086

Kamboj, S., Sarmah, B., Gupta, S., & Dwivedi, Y. (2018). Examining branding co-creation in brand communities on social media: Applying the paradigm of Stimulus-Organism-Response. *International Journal of Information Management*, *39*, 169–185. doi:10.1016/j.ijinfomgt.2017.12.001

Kaplan, A. M., & Haenlein, M. (2010). Users of the world, unite! The challenges and opportunities of Social Media. *Business Horizons*, *53*(1), 59–68. doi:10.1016/j.bushor.2009.09.003

Kaplan, A. M., & Haenlein, M. (2011). Two hearts in three-quarter time: How to waltz the social media/viral marketing dance. *Business Horizons*, *54*(3), 253–263. doi:10.1016/j.bushor.2011.01.006

Karahanna, E., Straub, D. W., & Chervany, N. L. (1999). Information technology adoption across time: A cross-sectional comparison of pre-adoption and post-adoption beliefs. *Management Information Systems Quarterly*, *23*(2), 183–213. doi:10.2307/249751

Kelman, H. C. (1958). Compliance, Identification, and Internalization: Three Processes of Attitude Change. *The Journal of Conflict Resolution*, *2*(1), 51–60. doi:10.1177/002200275800200106

Kietzmann, J. H., Hermkens, K., McCarthy, I. P., & Silvestre, B. S. (2011). Social media? Get serious! Understanding the functional building blocks of social media. *Business Horizons*, *54*(3), 241–251. doi:10.1016/j.bushor.2011.01.005

Kim, A. J., & Ko, E. (2012). Do social media marketing activities enhance customer equity? An empirical study of luxury fashion brand. *Journal of Business Research*, *65*(10), 1480–1486. doi:10.1016/j.jbusres.2011.10.014

Kiss, C., & Bichler, M. (2008). Identification of influencers—measuring influence in customer networks. *Decision Support Systems*, *46*(1), 233–253. doi:10.1016/j.dss.2008.06.007

Koufaris, M., & Hampton-Sosa, W. (2004). The development of initial trust in an online company by new customers. *Information & Management*, *41*(3), 377–397. doi:10.1016/j.im.2003.08.004

Kozinets, R. V. (1999). E-Tribalized Marketing? The Strategic Implications of Virtual Communities of Consumption. *European Management Journal*, *17*(3), 252–264. doi:10.1016/S0263-2373(99)00004-3

Kozinets, R. V., De Valck, K., Wojnicki, A. C., & Wilner, S. J. (2010). Networked narratives: Understanding word-of-mouth marketing in online communities. *Journal of Marketing*, *74*(2), 71–89. doi:10.1509/jmkg.74.2.71

Kuksov, D., Shachar, R., & Wang, K. (2013). Advertising and Consumers' Communications. *Marketing Science*, *32*(2), 294–309. doi:10.1287/mksc.1120.0753

Leenders, R. A. J. (2002). Modeling Social Influence Through Network Autocorrelation: Constructing the Weight Matrix. *Social Networks*, *24*(1), 21–48. doi:10.1016/S0378-8733(01)00049-1

Lim, K. H., Leung, K., Sia, C. L., & Lee, M. K. (2004). Is eCommerce boundary-less? Effects of individualism–collectivism and uncertainty avoidance on Internet shopping. *Journal of International Business Studies*, *35*(6), 545–559. doi:10.1057/palgrave.jibs.8400104

Liu, Y., & Shrum, L. J. (2002). What is interactivity and is it always such a good thing? Implications of definition, person, and situation for the influence of interactivity on advertising effectiveness. *Journal of Advertising*, *31*(4), 53–64. doi:10.1080/00913367.2002.10673685

Liu-Thompkins, Y. (2012). Seeding viral content: The role of message and network factors. *Journal of Advertising Research*, *52*(4), 465–478. doi:10.2501/JAR-52-4-465-478

Lu, B., Fan, W., & Zhou, M. (2016). Social presence, trust, and social commerce purchase intention: An empirical research. *Computers in Human Behavior*, *56*, 225–237. doi:10.1016/j.chb.2015.11.057

Markus, H. R., & Kitayama, S. (1991). Culture and the self: Implications for cognition, emotion, and motivation. *Psychological Review*, *98*(2), 224–253. doi:10.1037/0033-295X.98.2.224

Martínez, P., & del Bosque, I. R. (2013). CSR and customer loyalty: The roles of trust, customer identification with the company and satisfaction. *International Journal of Hospitality Management*, *35*, 89–99. doi:10.1016/j.ijhm.2013.05.009

Moe, W., & Schweidel, D. (2017). Opportunities for innovation in social media analytics. *Journal of Product Innovation Management*, *34*(5), 697–702. doi:10.1111/jpim.12405

Moon, Y. (2002). Personalization and personality: Some effects of customizing message style based on customer personalities. *Journal of Consumer Psychology*, *12*(4), 313–326. doi:10.1207/15327660260382351

Muller, E., & Peres, R. (2018). The effect of social networks structure on innovation performance: A review and directions for research. *International Journal of Research in Marketing*. doi:10.1016/j.ijresmar.2018.05.003

Muntinga, D. G., Moorman, M., & Smit, E. G. (2011). Introducing COBRAs: Exploring motivations for brand-related social media use. *International Journal of Advertising*, *30*(1), 13–46. doi:10.2501/IJA-30-1-013-046

Ngai, E. W., Moon, K. L. K., Lam, S. S., Chin, E. S., & Tao, S. S. (2015). Social media models, technologies, and applications: An academic review and case study. *Industrial Management & Data Systems*, *115*(5), 769–802. doi:10.1108/IMDS-03-2015-0075

Nguyen, B., & Mutum, D. S. (2012). A review of customer relationship management: Successes, advances, pitfalls and futures. *Business Process Management Journal*, *18*(3), 400–419. doi:10.1108/14637151211232614

Ozuem, W. (2016). User-generated content and perceived customer value. In *Competitive Social Media Marketing Strategies* (pp. 50–63). IGI Global. doi:10.4018/978-1-4666-9776-8.ch003

Ozuem, W., & Tan, K. (2014). Reconciling Social Media with Luxury Fashion Brands: An Exploratory Study. In Digital Arts and Entertainment: Concepts, Methodologies, Tools, and Applications (pp. 1546-1574). IGI Global.

Peng, J., Agarwal, A., Hosanagar, K., & Iyengar, R. (2018). Network Overlap and Content Sharing on Social Media Platforms. *JMR, Journal of Marketing Research, 55*(4), 571–585. doi:10.1509/jmr.14.0643

Phelps, J. E., Lewis, R., Mobilio, L., Perry, D., & Raman, N. (2004). Viral Marketing or Electronic Word of-Mouth Advertising: Examining Consumer Responses to Pass Along Email. *Journal of Advertising Research, 44*(4), 333–348. doi:10.1017/S0021849904040371

Preece, J., Nonnecke, B., & Andrews, D. (2004). The Top 5 Reasons for Lurking: Improving Community Experiences for Everyone. *Computers in Human Behavior, 20*(2), 201–223. doi:10.1016/j.chb.2003.10.015

Prentice-Dunn, & Rogers, R.W. (1985). Effects of Public and Private Self Awareness on Deindividuation and Aggression. *Journal of Personality and Social Psychology, 43*, 503–513.

Pressgrove, G., McKeever, B. W., & Jang, S. M. (2018). What is Contagious? Exploring why content goes viral on Twitter: A case study of the ALS Ice Bucket Challenge. *International Journal of Nonprofit and Voluntary Sector Marketing, 23*(1), e1586. doi:10.1002/nvsm.1586

Raney, A. A., Arpan, L. M., Pashupati, K., & Brill, D. A. (2003). At the movies, on the web: An investigation of the effects of entertaining and interactive web content on site and brand evaluations. *Journal of Interactive Marketing, 17*(4), 38–53. doi:10.1002/dir.10064

Robins, G., Pattison, P., & Elliott, P. (2001). Network Models for Social Influence Processes. *Psychometrika, 66*(2), 161–190. doi:10.1007/BF02294834

Roth, M. S. (1995). The effects of culture and socioeconomics on the performance of global brand image strategies. *JMR, Journal of Marketing Research, 32*(2), 163–175. doi:10.2307/3152045

Samadi, M., Nagi, R., Semenov, A., & Nikolaev, A. (2018). Seed activation scheduling for influence maximization in social networks. *Omega: The International Journal of Management Science, 77*, 96–114. doi:10.1016/j.omega.2017.06.002

Sashi, C. M. (2012). Customer engagement, buyer-seller relationships, and social media. *Management Decision, 50*(2), 253–272. doi:10.1108/00251741211203551

Schlosser, A. E. (2005). Posting Vs. Lurking: Communicating in a Multiple Audience Context. *The Journal of Consumer Research, 32*(2), 260–265. doi:10.1086/432235

Shehu, E., Bijmolt, T. H. A., & Clement, M. (2016). Effects of Likeability Dynamics on Consumers' Intention to Share Online Video Advertisements. *Journal of Interactive Marketing, 35*, 27–43. doi:10.1016/j.intmar.2016.01.001

Shin, D. (2018). Empathy and embodied experience in virtual environment: To what extent can virtual reality stimulate empathy and embodied experience? *Computers in Human Behavior, 78*, 64–73. doi:10.1016/j.chb.2017.09.012

Stokinger, E., & Ozuem, W. (2018). The intersection of social media and customer retention in the luxury beauty industry. In Digital Marketing and Consumer Engagement: Concepts, Methodologies, Tools, and Applications (pp. 1305-1328). IGI Global.

Susarla, A., Oh, J. H., & Tan, Y. (2012). Social networks and the diffusion of user-generated content: Evidence from YouTube. *Information Systems Research*, *23*(1), 23–41. doi:10.1287/isre.1100.0339

Tafesse, W., & Wien, A. (2017). A framework for categorizing social media posts. *Cogent Business and Management*, *4*(1), 1284390. doi:10.1080/23311975.2017.1284390

Taylor, D. G., Lewin, J. E., & Strutton, D. (2011). Friends, fans, and followers: do ads work on social networks?: how gender and age shape receptivity. *Journal of Advertising Research*, *51*(1), 258–275. doi:10.2501/JAR-51-1-258-275

Taylor, S., & Todd, P. (1995). Assessing IT usage: The role of prior experience. *Management Information Systems Quarterly*, *19*(4), 561–570. doi:10.2307/249633

Trainor, K. J. (2012). Relating social media technologies to performance: A capabilities-based perspective. *Journal of Personal Selling & Sales Management*, *32*(3), 317–331. doi:10.2753/PSS0885-3134320303

Trainor, K. J., Andzulis, J. M., Rapp, A., & Agnihotri, R. (2013). Social media technology usage and customer relationship performance: A capabilities-based examination of social CRM. *Journal of Business Research*, *67*(6), 1201–1208. doi:10.1016/j.jbusres.2013.05.002

Trusov, M., Bodapati, A. V., & Bucklin, R. E. (2010). Determining influential users in internet social networks. *JMR, Journal of Marketing Research*, *47*(4), 643–658. doi:10.1509/jmkr.47.4.643

Tsai, H-T., & Bagozzi, R.P. (2014). Contribution behavior in virtual communities: cognitive, emotional, and social Influences. *MIS Quarterly*, *38*(1), 143–163.

Üstüner, T., & Godes, D. (2006). Better sales networks. *Harvard Business Review*, *84*(8), 102–112. PMID:16846193

Venkatesan, M. (1966). Experimental Study of Consumer Behavior, Conformity and Independence. *JMR, Journal of Marketing Research*, *3*(4), 384–387. doi:10.2307/3149855

Vilnai-Yavetz, I., & Levina, O. (2018). Motivating social sharing of e-business content: Intrinsic motivation, extrinsic motivation, or crowding-out effect? *Computers in Human Behavior*, *79*, 181–191. doi:10.1016/j.chb.2017.10.034

Vivek, S. D., Beatty, S. E., & Morgan, R. M. (2012). Customer engagement: Exploring customer relationships beyond purchase. *Journal of Marketing Theory and Practice*, *20*(2), 127–145. doi:10.2753/MTP1069-6679200201

Wang, Z., & Kim, H. G. (2017). Can Social Media Marketing Improve Customer Relationship Capabilities and Firm Performance? Dynamic Capability Perspective. *Journal of Interactive Marketing*, *39*, 15–26. doi:10.1016/j.intmar.2017.02.004

Weingart, L. R., Bennett, R. J., & Brett, J. M. (1993). The impact of consideration of issues and motivational orientation on group negotiation process and outcome. *The Journal of Applied Psychology*, *78*(3), 504–517. doi:10.1037/0021-9010.78.3.504

Wiertz, C., & de Ruyter, K. (2007). Beyond the Call of Duty: Why Customers Contribute to Firm-hosted Commercial Online Communities. *Organization Studies*, *28*(3), 347–376. doi:10.1177/0170840607076003

Xiang, Z., Du, Q., Ma, Y., & Fan, W. (2017). A comparative analysis of major online review platforms: Implications for social media analytics in hospitality and tourism. *Tourism Management*, *58*, 51–65. doi:10.1016/j.tourman.2016.10.001

Yang, Z., & Peterson, R. T. (2004). Customer perceived value, satisfaction, and loyalty: The role of switching costs. *Psychology and Marketing*, *21*(10), 799–822. doi:10.1002/mar.20030

Yates, D., & Paquette, S. (2011). Emergency knowledge management and social media technologies: A case study of the 2010 Haitian earthquake. *International Journal of Information Management*, *31*(1), 6–13. doi:10.1016/j.ijinfomgt.2010.10.001

KEY TERMS AND DEFINITIONS

Consumer Engagement: A communication connection between an organisation and consumers through different channels of communication. This can be linked to the customers experience in communicating with organizations regarding its products and services and how effective it is in retaining customer satisfaction.

Influencer Seeding: Influential individuals within a large network that promote brands and their messages on various social media channels to attract the larger target audience to brands. These individuals are highly significant to starting viral marketing campaigns.

Message Strategy: A plan on how to attract target markets to a brand, its services and products and equity through creative and persuasive marketing messages.

Social Influence: The change in behavior, opinions, and emotions of an individual caused as a result of their perception of themselves in relation to the influence, group, or society. Social influence can be seen in socialization, conformity, obedience, compliance, and sales and marketing.

Social Media: Communication channels facilitated through websites and applications linked to social networking, forums, wikis, and microblogging dedicated to community interaction, collaboration, and content sharing.

User-Generated Content: Content such as images, videos, text, and audio that have been created and posted on social media platforms by unpaid contributors or fans of a brand.

Viral Marketing: A marketing technique that encourages online users to share marketing messages to other users or sites, potentially increasing the message's visibility and effect to a larger audience.

Chapter 2
The Dynamics of Social Media and Value Co-Creation

Kamna Sahni
University of the West Scotland, UK

Kenneth Appiah
University of Cumbria, UK

ABSTRACT

Social media is considered trustworthy by consumers, and this has resulted in a strong consumer focus on social media to acquire information related to products and services. There are various benefits offered by social media, but security is a major concern as viruses and other threats can affect a huge number of users of social media. These platforms are not well governed. Indeed, they are highly decentralized and could easily be accessed, and this presents a high risk of illegal activity. Businesses continue to reap the benefits of incorporating social media into their strategies. There has been a shift in focus from conventional media to online and digital media in the form of social networking sites, wikis, and blogs. This has given rise to viral marketing as a means of effective communication and sharing information. The current chapter aims to explore the relationship between social media and value co-creation.

INTRODUCTION

There is increasing understanding in literature that social media is evolving to offer the consumer platforms to connect with others with the help of user-generated content in the form of images, text, videos and audio recordings (Kaplan & Haenlein, 2010; Kietzmann, Hermkens, McCarthy, & Silvestre, 2011). This has encouraged user participation that is not restricted in any form. The social media platforms allow users to participate in a conversation and share views and reviews about products and services. According to Hanna *et al*. (2011), businesses influence consumers and consumers influence brand messages. Social media offers opportunities for customers to contribute to a value co-creation process with companies.

A number of studies have depicted various ways in which businesses can take advantage of and produce worth from user participation on social media platforms (Di Gangi & Wasko, 2009; Bechmann & Lomborg, 2013; Nambisan & Nambisan 2008; Prahalad & Ramaswamy, 2004a). The growing importance

DOI: 10.4018/978-1-5225-7344-9.ch002

of social media has provided benefits such as: (a) building a network, content contribution by customers and updating content; (b) helping to enhance the growth of a company and foster innovation; and (c) trading the information obtained from digital profiles. Therefore, with the help of social media businesses and consumers get involved in different co-creation processes, which include designing and developing products, services and service support ideas (Nambisan & Nambisan, 2008; Prahalad & Ramaswamy, 2004a). Allan (2005) also noted that companies' online views and collaboration have the potential to enhance the characteristics of products by taking on board user-generated content on social media.

The digitalisation aspect of the social media platforms enables consumers to have better knowledge related to the products and services and thus to participate in the value co-creation process and interact more with the brands (Aluri *et al.*, 2015; Chathoth *et al.*, 2014; Lin *et al.*, 2018). Business can enhance the customer experience by employing the benefits of social media. Applying social media as a tool for managing the experience of the customer is vital in a highly competitive market scenario. Businesses have also acknowledged the prospect of utilising social media as a marketing tool within their operations (Fischer & Reuber, 2011; Luo, Zhang, & Lui, 2015; Mangold & Faulds, 2009 ; Ozuem & Yankova, 2015). Previous studies highlighted the adoption of the types of tools mentioned by Siamagka, Christodoulides, Michaelidou, and Valvi (2015). According to Kaplan and Haenlein (2010) and Kietzmann, Hermlens, and Silverstre (2011), social media has developed to provide to consumers with opportunities to become involved in an exchange of ideas through video content, images, text, and audio. According to Gallaugher and Ransbotham (2010), interactions and collaborations between organisations and consumers have become simpler and more common than in the past.

Numerous studies have highlighted the benefits of using social media for value co-creation in various sectors. For example, Cao, Ajjan, and Hong (2013) have applied social media to educational outcomes in college teaching. Xie and Stevenson (2014) applied social media in digital libraries. Kao *et al.* (2016) investigated co-creating value with consumers through social media using a service firm. Islam, Agarwal, and Ikeda (2015) conceptualised the business notion of value co-creation in the framework of libraries. Santos, Alves, and Brambilla (2016) examined value co-creation in retail using social networks. Social media has helped to develop better relationships between businesses and various stakeholders. Social media has gained paramount importance and is greatly used by the masses due to its user-friendly nature and easy access to the Internet.

CONTEXTUALISATION: SOCIAL MEDIA

Social media is a global and useful application that is based on the technological foundations of the World Wide Web. It is a means of social interaction that is facilitated by the Internet. There has been rapid progress in the usage of the Social Media Applications (SMA) in recent years. Social media has made customers more aware about businesses and their products. It has also resulted in stronger connections between buyers and sellers. Social media is grounded on the technologies of Web 2.0 (Hew & Cheung, 2012). Web 2.0 has experienced exponential growth that has resulted in the development of new technologies. Kaplan and Haenlein (2010) and Daugherty, Eastin, and Bright (2008) note that Web 2.0 technologies empower end-users to be able to use different kinds of media content like video, audio, images and comments. Customers can review, create, comment and share content on social media with the help of online networks. Customers thus have uninterrupted access to businesses, brands and marketers (Chau & Xu, 2012).

Social media has affected the life of people over the past decades. The main objective of social media was to connect people socially but subsequently it has broadened from connecting people to connecting industries. Many definitions of social media have been developed based on various studies. Most of them have a similar indication: that social media encompasses platforms that are Internet-centred and encourages an unrestricted stream of user-generated material (Kaplan & Haenlein, 2010; Safko, 2010; Kietzmann, Hermkens, McCarthy, & Silvestre, 2011; Hanna, Rohm, & Crittenden, 2011; Luo, Zhang, & Duan, 2013; Ngai, Tao, & Moon, 2015; Stokinger & Ozuem, 2015).

A social media platform is a channel used for communication, not only amongst people who want to connect with their friends and relatives, but also by businesses who seek to interact with other organisations and users. It is an efficient method for individuals to communicate, interact and connect within their networks. At the same time, social media is used by many businesses to advertise products and services and to interact with customers and prospective customers. Social media compromises two-way communication and offers opportunities for the individuals and businesses to take advantage of the network of people and valuable digital space for the exchange of electronic word-of-mouth (e-WOM) (Kaplan and Haenlein 2011). Social media differs from traditional communication methods in facilitating two-way communication. Examples of one-way, traditional methods of communication include newsletters, magazines, television, billboards, and radio (Hasan, 2011; Mangold & Faulds, 2009). Social media is better than traditional methods of communication as it enables two-way communication and is technologically more hi-tech. There has been a shift in focus from conventional media to online and digital media in the form of social networking sites, wikis and blogs. This has given rise to viral marketing as a means of effective communication and sharing information (Hutton & Fosdick, 2011). Businesses influence consumers and consumers influence brand messages (Hanna *et al.*, 2011). Social media presents a strong opportunity for customers to exchange views with hundreds and even thousands of customers worldwide. Businesses are not the only source of brand communication. Social media helps businesses to formulate strategies and reduce R&D costs. Using social media organisations can collect information, develop databases and improve service delivery (Barnes, 2010). They can also extend their geographical presence as social media has worldwide reach (Wright *et al.*, 2010). Social media is preferred by many organisations and customers over traditional forms of media to explore information (Mangold & Faulds, 2009).

Social media has many advantages so many businesses harness these to interact with their customers. Taylor (2009) argues that social media is a highly effective global application. It is a powerful personalised tool which individuals can use to create and circulate matter by participating in discussions. Taylor (2012) asserts that from a promotion and marketing perspective, the biggest opportunity associated with any digital medium is interactivity. Social media is no different from another digital medium when it comes to interactivity. It affects not only our daily lives but also the business activities we are familiar with. There has been a steady increase in the number of businesses adopting social media to market their goods and services. It is also utilised by firms to expand upon their conventional marketing activities. In the marketing strategies literature, social media is simply approached as a new method, but its purposes are far from new. Social media are used by businesses to grow sales and to improve reputation (Sapena & Paniagua 2014). Organisations can take advantage of and create value from consumer involvement in social media. Bechmann and Lomborg (2013) suggest that value can be created in the form of networks which facilitate the ability to update and contribute content. Social media also enhances organisational development and innovation of new products and services. It supports the trading of information and data across numerous digital profiles.

Social media is considered trustworthy by consumers and this has resulted in a strong consumer focus on social media to acquire information related to products and services (Foux, 2006). There are various benefits offered by social media, but security is a major concern (Parameswaran & Whinston, 2007). Viruses and other threats can potentially affect a huge number of users of social media. These authors argue that such platforms are not well governed. Indeed, they are highly decentralised and could easily be accessed and this presents a high risk of illegal activity. Businesses continue to reap the benefits of incorporating social media into their business strategies. The main features of social media are conversation, participation, community formation, information openness and connectedness (Chan-Olmsted *et al.*, 2013).

Ward and Ostrom (2006) draw attention to some of the disadvantages of social media for businesses. They suggest that social media helps organisations to access valuable knowledge about their customers including their personal information, interests and preferences. However, when customers are not happy with particular goods or services they will use social media to complain and this can affect their loyalty towards brands. Such views can, in turn, influence others that are exposed to them. It is very difficult to control the creation of User Generated Content (UGC) in various forms such as comments, views and reviews on social media. Social media is not a closed system and marketers must be aware of the associated risks. Marketers are concerned about this, as only a single unfavourable input to an official website, blog or forum online can have lasting effects on the reputation of businesses (Ryan & Jones, 2009).

There are two different perspectives relating to the applicability of social media. Some scholars who have discussed the benefits of using social media have noted that organisations are willing to adopt social media to enhance their business. In contrast, others are reluctant to adopt social media due to its open nature, which means that anyone can share a negative experience quite easily. These two contrasting perspectives have resulted in a growing body of research associated with social media. Some has assessed the impact of social media on businesses and consumers. Consumers have gained power because social media has enabled them to raise negative opinions related to products and services. This power helps to reduce physical and psychological costs to consumers (Ayertey, Ozuem, & Appiah 2018). Social media, as a term, describes a dynamic and evolving set of technologies (Kane *et al.*, 2013). It has been described as a 'moving target' (Sinha *et al.*, 2013; Hogan & Quan-Haase, 2010).

Safko (2010, p. 4) describes social media in general terms, noting that it is composed of two words, i.e. 'social' and 'media'. Social satisfies the 'instinctual needs we humans have to connect with other humans' and the 'need to be around and included in groups of similar like-minded people with whom we can feel at home and comfortable sharing our thoughts, ideas, and experiences'. Media, in this context, refers to 'media we use with which we make connections with other humans'. Such media are 'technologies we use to make those connections'.

Social Media From Technological Perspective

Evolving digital technology has enabled consumers to dynamically regulate how and when they interact with businesses to structure personalised product experiences and co-create value with businesses and other customers (Gummesson & Mele, 2010). Various scholars have defined social media from a technological perspective (Kaplan & Haenlein, 2010; Coursaris, 2013; Mangold & Faulds, 2009; Rodriguez *et al.*, 2012). Social media is the study of digital traces of online user activities with a strong focus on the organisational usage of technological platforms. Social media has also been discussed in terms of both the material and virtual worlds, and is considered to represent several technological artefacts from the material and virtual dimensions. It supports different actors in diverse communication activities to create UGC to enhance and sustain social relationships, and to allow other computer-facilitated interactions and collaborations (Coursaris, 2013, p. 703).

In addition, social media has been defined by Kaplan and Haenlein (2010) as an example of Web 2.0. The authors suggest that social media is 'a group of Internet-based applications that build on the ideological and technological foundations of Web 2.0 and that allow the creation and exchange of user-generated content'.

O'Reilly (2005) suggests that 'Web 2.0 refers to developments in online technology that enable interactive capabilities in an environment characterised by user control, freedom, and dialogue'. In the same vein, Paris, Lee, and Seery (2010) define social media as 'a second generation of web development and design features, social media websites facilitate communication, information sharing, and collaboration among people'. It can therefore be concluded that social media websites enable two-way communications, the sharing of the information and relationship building amongst people, all facilitated by second generation web technology and its attendant design characteristics.

According to Kaplan and Haenlein (2010), Web 2.0 content is altered continuously by all actors by means of sharing and collaboration. Web 2.0 is based on technologies that facilitate the creation of highly interactive platforms that help people and groups of people to share, review, co-create and amend content that is generated by users. The term 'social media' has wide implications and includes all websites based on the technological foundations of Web 2.0 that empower operators to produce UGC that can be shared. Such content is created and replicated on the social media networks by users of Web 2 technology. The content that is created can be shared amongst other members of social media websites which are linked to users. Other members may have different opinions and can reply in alternative ways to the content created by the original users since the process is entirely interactive in nature.

Kaplan and Haenlein (2010) discuss the use of social media within businesses. They identify various ways in which social media can be used by businesses to communicate internally and externally. Businesses can use social media to share information internally amongst staff members, and externally in the form of consumer-to-consumer communication. They can also communicate using social media with other external stakeholders of the organisation and they can communicate beyond organisational boundaries based on a consumer-to-organisation format. This kind of communication presents an implementation challenge for many organisations due to their conventional hierarchies and centralised control structures. The authors suggest that social media is an online communications tool that encourages users to share views and exchange information. The sharing and exchange of views results in the creation and exchange of UGC. This definition covers various types of social media. Amongst the different kinds of social media, Social Networking Sites (SNS) are the most popular formats, and the most resonant example is Facebook. Other kinds of social media include formats that allow users to upload and share various types of media such as photos, text messages, and audio and video files. These include Flickr, YouTube, and podcasts. Finally, there are some innovative types of social media that comprise virtual worlds, widgets, and crowdsourcing.

Social Media and Symmetrical Communication

The success of social media depends on the capability of the various applications available to enable two-way symmetrical communication between corporations and communities across the Internet. Gurnig (2009) and Phillips (2009) note that two-way communication is regarded as a critical success factor by organisations that seek to create and sustain strong relationships with the public. Phillips (2009) discussed the concept of two-way symmetrical communication and indicated that novel media tools differ with respect to their capability to facilitate communication in two directions. For instance, the interactional levels of Facebook and Twitter can be regarded as very symmetric since they permit extraordinary levels of interactions. In contrast, content-sharing sites including Wikipedia entries and blogs enable one-way asymmetrical communications. These tools have low levels of feedback facilitating two-way systems of communication with the public. This has resulted in a better understanding of the individual features of each social media application and has simultaneously helped to inform best practice in terms of communicating with the public using social media.

According to Rodriguez *et al.* (2012), social media has been considered as a linkage that can facilitate:

- The creation of content
- Online reviews
- Online dialogue
- Real-time feedback
- The creation and maintenance of relationships and group building.

In addition, social media influences the user's network and wider society based on the cumulative number of social networking sites (Curran & Lennon, 2011). Social media possesses all the features of Internet-based platforms and its core characteristic comprises innumerable directions of communication. Interactions are more extreme, richer and larger in magnitude than traditional forms of media. The numbers of spectators are higher, and the scale and reach are greater (Sawhney *et al.*, 2005). Social media is therefore more effective than traditional methods of communication due to the kinds of two-way communication that it enables. Social media helps businesses to create and maintain strong relationships with their stakeholders. Social media also provides a platform for consumers to express their views about businesses and their products and services, whether these are positive or negative. This helps businesses to maintain a public presence. Social media is an efficient method that can be used to communicate and interact. Social media brand communities provide substantial occasions for firms to provide resources, typically in the form of posts, e.g. the posts generated by the firms (Kumar *et al.*, 2016). Posts also permit social group members to create their own resources in the form of user-generated content posted on the sites (Schamari & Schaefers, 2015)

Social networking sites offer a simpler mode to encounter information and to share information with other users. This results in decentralised user level content (Abrahams *et al.*, 2012). There are several kinds of social networking sites that enable different kinds of social interactions. Interactions can occur in the form of social viral activities and community engagement (Kapoor & Dwivedi, 2015; Li & Shiu, 2012). Social media depends on users to co-create content (Kim *et al.*, 2010). Social media comprises content produced by consumers and which is known as UGC. Such UGC is publicly available, immediately distributable, and creative in nature. UGC is not generated through professional content creation practices (Habibi *et al.*, 2014). Social media that is based on Web 2.0 is extremely popular and has intensified online social networks in the e-commerce field. Web 2.0 has been defined as a range of technologies that permit operators to produce content, communicate, and share content across social networks with other users, communities, and virtual worlds. Less effort is required compared to analogue forms of media. These tools and technologies highlight the power of operators to choose, filter, circulate and amend information (Tredinnick, 2006) in addition to partaking in the creation of content in social media.

The spectrum of online media is very broad and has empowered consumers in electronic markets. They can now opine about products and services on social media based on UGC. Offering an opinion can take the form of numeric scores which are structured and/or unstructured. An example of the latter might be written comments (Cheung & Thadani, 2012). The data generated based on both approaches helps traders and shoppers by empowering them to reach more informed conclusions (Lukyanenko *et al.*, 2014a). In contrast, it was claimed by Lukyanenko and Parsons (2015) that both kinds of UGC produced by casual content providers can lead to unclear, unrelated and even inconsistent messages when they refer to the same product or service.

A vast amount of structured and unstructured UGC is produced at a very fast pace as public users create a great deal of content. The Organisation for Economic Co-operation and Development (OECD) has defined UGC as information that: 'is published on a Web site that is publicly accessible or available to a select group of people … demonstrates some degree of creativity (and) is not created for commercial purposes' (Kaplan & Haenlein, 2010, p. 61). Structured UGC on web pages shares a number of qualities and comprises fixed scales including overall structured ratings or detailed ratings based on scales including Likert scales (Dellarocas, 2010). Unstructured UGC refers to product reviews, blogs, discussion forums, free-formatted texts, and rich media data; or even sensory data (Leskovec, 2011; Lukyanenko & Parsons, 2015). The most common form of unstructured data includes written comments associated with brands, products, services and traders. It appears that communication between businesses and customers results in the generation of UGC. Such content can be structured or unstructured, but the format of content is equally important and can empower organisations and consumers to make more efficient decisions.

Social media is used by firms in three ways. The first approach sees social media used as a traditional marketing method, and the businesses' key objective is to create an economic Return on Investment (RoI). A second approach is the traditional-experimental approach. Based on this, the economic features are also linked with social interactions (social-RoI). The third approach is the experimental approach which sees firms incorporate a human voice into social media platforms. The main aim is to influence the thoughts of consumers, businesses and brands (Dijkmans, Kerkhif, Buyukcan-Tetic, & Beukeboom 2015). Firms are aware of the consequences of adopting social media and are equally aware of its impacts on consumers and the power that social media provides to customers to involve them in the development of digital business (Kaplan & Haenlein, 2010). In contrast, Fournier and Avery (2011) note that firms are the 'uninvited gate crashers' of social media. They debate the main purpose of social media and suggest it can link individuals rather than impose businesses and brands on social media audiences.

Social media is an important factor that inspires the behaviour of consumers in the form of opinions, usage, awareness, intentions, evaluations, information sharing and purchasing habits (Chang, 2008). Social media permits interconnectivity between users and between content and communication technologies (Dann & Dann, 2011; Stokinger & Ozuem, 2014). Social media can be adopted by businesses to enhance their conventional marketing activities. This can help businesses to increase their sales, improve their reputation and enhance their brand image. In contrast, a dearth of knowledge and skills essential for the successful implementation and management of social media could negatively affect the benefits derived from social media.

WEB-ENABLED MARKETING ECOSYSTEM

Social media has been examined from a marketing perspective by various scholars including Weinberg (2009), Solomon & Tuten (2015) and Gordhamer (2009). Social media marketing is a novel marketing strategy. Businesses embrace social media to enhance their reach to customers using virtual networks.

'Social media marketing is the utilisation of social media technologies, channels, and software to create, communicate, deliver, and exchange offerings that have value for an organisation's stakeholders' (Solomon & Tuten 2015, p. 73.1).

Social media marketing has been defined by Weinberg (2009, p.3) as 'the process that empowers individuals to promote their websites, products, or services through online social channels and tap into a much larger community that may not have been available via traditional channels'. It can be concluded that social media marketing is a process that helps businesses to utilise the web to create awareness about products and information that would be more difficult to spread via traditional marketing methods. Organisations also use social media applications as platforms to inform prospective clients about the current state of the organisation. This includes communicating strategies and the possible introduction or promotion of novel models or merchandise to provide up-to-date news about the business. Social media marketing has been debated from the perspective of relationship marketing by Gordhamer (2009). The author suggests that firms should move away from 'trying to sell' towards an ethos of 'making connections' with customers. This suggests that organisations should focus on constructing relationships with current and potential customers. This is crucial to encourage repeat purchasing and greater brand loyalty amongst customers. He also suggests that currently, customers are busy but they are more powerful than ever before. Therefore, organisations must be easily accessible through social media communications channels like Facebook, Twitter, blogs and forums. They must always be accessible so that customers can reach them easily. Jan and Khan (2014) further suggest that social media is a modern tool used by businesses to build extremely strong public relationships with customers across virtual networks.

Social media (SM) is continuously growing and performing a progressively important function in marketing. It enhances the communications of organisations in their dealings with other businesses, societies and people (Kietzmann, Hermkens, McCarthy, & Silvestre, 2011). Social media is harnessed as additional marketing channels by businesses and marketers who value the fact that such platforms can be used to correspond or interact with consumers and prospective consumers (Gummerus, Liljander, Weman, & Pihlstrom, 2011). Many scholars have noted an upsurge in the number of firms adopting social media to conduct marketing activity and augment traditional marketing efforts (Dahnit, Oztamur, & Karahedilar, 2014). As stated by Barnes (2010), social media offers huge benefits and opportunities. Thus, it is very important for businesses to implement social media successfully as part of a well-organised marketing strategy. It is essential for businesses to fully utilise the opportunities offered by social media platforms.

The web-enabled marketing ecosystem has huge power. It has upgraded and intensified the way in which buyers communicate among themselves and with companies. Consumers are using this as a channel to harmonise their everyday activities, which is not possible in the case of traditional communication methods. The computer-mediated marketing environment has improved relationships between friends, consumers and organisations. This has resulted in better attachment among individuals and businesses (Ozuem, Howell, & Lancaster, 2008). Businesses can no longer depend on the one-way communication of traditional marketing, which has become outdated. Due to this, two-way communication has gained more authority as it does not diminish the power of the consumers but takes them as an integral part of the communication process (Andersen, 2001; Ozuem, Howell, & Lancaster, 2008).

The roles of marketers have reduced due to the dominance of consumers. All kinds of information are easily available to consumers thanks to the user-friendliness and reach of the Internet. Accordingly, businesses using traditional organisational communication frameworks may be viewed as having features that are non-transparent (Ozuem & Tan, 2014).

The benefits of social media, its easy accessibility and significance for efficient marketing communications have received great consideration (Bolton *et al.*, 2013; Hamid, Akhir, & Cheng, 2013; Hanna, Rohm, & Crittenden, 2011; Hoffman & Fodor, 2010; Mangold & Faulds, 2009; Ozuem & Stokinger, 2015, Ozuem, Howell & Lancaster 2008).

It has been argued that social media not only helps individuals to promote their websites, products or services but enables them to develop two-way communication by providing opportunities for stakeholders to co-create value. The current paper defines social media as ***the process that empowers individuals to promote their websites, apps, products, or services through online social channels and tap into a much larger community that may not have been available via traditional channels, which results in opportunities for the users of these social media sites to co-create value for them and other users.***

SOCIAL MEDIA AND VALUE CO-CREATION

The importance of customer engagement in marketing activity has been highlighted in the work of Hollebreek (2011) and Brodie *et al.* (2011). This concept has been examined in virtual contexts by Brodie *et al.* (2013), Hollebreek *et al.* (2014), Kao *et al.* (2016), and Tregua *et al.* (2015). Customer engagement has been defined as ‘a psychological state which occurs by virtue of interactive, co-creative customer experiences with a focal object (e.g. a brand) within a dynamic, iterative process of service relationships that co-create value’ (Brodie *et al.*, 2011, p. 258). It can be inferred that customer engagement with organisations can guide the process of value co-creation with the help of experiences and ‘engagement objects’ as they are called by Brodie *et al.* (2013, p. 109). The satisfaction levels of consumers and their loyalty are affected by customer engagement since customers are allowed to customise the subject matter of their experience (Pine & Gilmore, 1999)

Interactions among the members with posts generate both value-in-use and value-in-context for society as a whole and also serve as the basis for further resources for participants’ interactions, creating continuing opportunities for value creation and value co-creation (Sorensen *et al.*, 2016). There is a difference between the terms value creation and value co-creation. Value creation is the creation of value-in-use by customers when they use products or services. Value co-creation is based on interactions between businesses and customers (partners). Such interactions can be understood to represent the convergence between organisations and customer spheres of influence (Gronroos & Voima, 2013). Value co-creation not only encompasses an association with customers, but also includes collaborating with associates to model new services and improve customer value (Jaakkola *et al.*, 2012). Value co-creation has been defined as ‘the joint collaborative, concurrent, peer-like process of producing new value, both materially and symbolically’ (Galvagno & Dalli, 2014, p. 644).

Scholars are interested in how resourcefully businesses can inspire and determine ways to successfully inspire and enable consumers to co-create value on social media platforms. The significance of the process is extensively recognised in the literature on service-dominant logic and co-creation (Maglio *et al.*, 2009; Payne *et al.*, 2009). The process of co-creation takes place due to a combination of activities between traders and producers that ensures the supply of ‘unique’ value to customers. The same experience of added value will not give same level of satisfaction to two different customers since all interactions are unique (Cova, Dalli, & Zwick, 2011). Consumers can be regarded as partial workforces as they are moderately accountable for the result of the co-created service (Xie, Bagozzi, & Troye, 2008; Bowers, Martin, & Luker, 1990). Based on this concept, producers and consumers are much more integrated than they are based on conventional views, and consumers adopt the role of prosumers who 'undertake value creating activities that result in the production of products they eventually consume and that become their consumption experiences' (Xie *et al.*, 2008, p. 110). In Service Dominant Logic (SDL), the customer is always the co-creator of value. Vargo and Lusch (2004) identify two-way interactions in SD logic as the main concept of value co-creation between the service provider and the customer (Prahalad & Ramaswamy, 2000, 2004b). Vargo and Lusch (2006, p. 181) emphasised that the value-creation process takes place not when the output is manufactured, but when a product or service is consumed or used by a customer. Resources cannot create value on their own. Rather, the customer is the co-creator of value in SD logic. Potential value is realised from resources when resources are used in context and are combined with other resources (Vargo & Lusch *et al.*, 2008). SD logic perceives all actors, especially customers and businesses, as accomplishing an identical phenomenon, i.e. integrating resources to enhance their own situation or wellbeing (Vargo & Lusch, 2011).

SD logic is based on the principle that all providers are service providers; i.e. all marketing exchanges are service-dominant, and hence, service is the central basis of exchange (Vargo & Lusch, 2004, 2008). Therefore, SD logic contradicts the function of the traditional goods-dominant logic of the role of exclusive value creator. Companies and consumers are value co-creators in SD logic (Vargo & Lusch, 2008). Gronroos and Gummerus (2014) support this concept and suggest that the consumer is the sole value creator whereas companies occupy the normal position of the value facilitator. The exceptions to this are situations where interactions exist. They also note that firms can only co-create value when they interact with customers (Grönroos & Gummerus, 2014). These interactions are not occasional. Businesses and consumers usually participate in service-by-service interactions to attain new resources which are integrated with pre-existent resources. Value creation must not be considered as something that takes place through the manufacturing process. Instead, it is directed by the customers in their respective consumption circumstances (Vargo & Lusch, 2004, 2008a; Gronroos, 2008a, b; Strandvik *et al.*, 2012). Customers are perceived to be active operant resources rather than passive targets of marketing actions that finally control and create value in numerous value-creating processes. They can restructure their functions from consumer, to contributor, to creator (Tapscott & Williams, 2006). There is therefore a shift of focus from value creation toward value co-creation. It appears that consumers can actively take part by contributing their resources towards the creation of modified products and services. They can employ their resources for the creation of tailor-made products and services according to their needs. Consumers can be regarded as partial workforces as they are moderately accountable for the result of the co-created service (Xie, Bagozzi, & Troye, 2008; Bowers, Martin, & Luker, 1990). Based on this concept, producers and consumers are much more integrated than they are based on conventional views, and consumers adopt the role of prosumers who 'undertake value creating activities that result in the production of products they eventually consume and that become their consumption experiences' (Xie *et al.*, 2008, p. 110).

The advantage of involving customers at this level with the help of the co-creation model gives the customer a feeling of pride as an outcome of a co-created accomplishment (Moreau and Herd, 2010; Roberts *et al.*, 2013). A variety of research has explored the ways in which value is co-created by trader and purchaser. For example, the fundamentals of service science applying the value co-creation concept were explained by Maglio and Spohrer (2008). Perks *et al.* (2012) examined the value co-creation process in motor insurance through the lens of radical service innovation. Dong, Evans, and Zou (2008) explored service failure in relation to value co-creation. Vargo *et al.* (2008) and Payne, Storbacka, and Frow (2008) created models to realise value co-creation in service systems, and managing value co-creation. In the case of tourism, involving customers helps increase loyalty, faith and brand evaluations (So, King, & Sparks, 2014). Xiang *et al.* (2015) concluded that the growing popularity of the Internet for trip choices is understandable since the Internet offers greater quality information and a richer experience than ever before. Kaplan and Haelein (2010) and Mangold and Faulds (2009) note how remarkably social media has altered the tools and strategies applied by businesses to interconnect and create loyal customers in B2C settings. Research has also explored social media uses by manufacturing organisations for product development or modifications to existing product support (Nambisan & Nambisan, 2008; Prahalad and Ramaswamy, 2004a). The ways in which products and services are created are very different (Sampson & Froehle, 2006) and the methods used for the marketing of products and services also vary (Song, Di Benedetto, & Song, 2010). More studies should be conducted to explore the drivers of co-creation activities that relate to the actions of firms and processes (Van Doorn *et al.*, 2010).

In the product development process, social media can be utilised very efficiently. Extra and significant information can be gained about the products on the social media platform. The use of social media is not only restricted to the promotion of the products. It can be very efficiently incorporated in the process of product development. The cost of collecting huge amounts of information is very low in comparison with the traditional methods of data collection such as surveys and focus group discussions. The quality of information collected on social media is better and the time needed to collect the information is also reduced. It ultimately results in better products for the community (Rathore *et al.*, 2016).

MANAGERIAL IMPLICATIONS AND CONCLUSION

The current paper proposes a number of managerial implications. Businesses must keep in mind that social media tools have made the marketspace very transparent and increased the awareness of consumers in terms of different organisations, products, prices and features of various products and services. The awareness developed due to the Internet, social media, technological advancements and other computed-mediated marketing channels have resulted in making customers and prospective customers very active in creating their experiences by contributing their skills, experiences and knowledge gained through various channels, and they are no longer passive. This has resulted in value co-creation by customers in the process of buying the products and services that meet their individual needs.

The social media ecosystem has resulted in openness and transparency that have increased consumers' knowledge and options. Social media is assisting the development of new products and helping to provide better ideas to businesses for development of new product designs and modification of their products. Social media marketing must be used in conjunction with traditional media to ensure that organisations are not missing out any segment of their target customers and that they are reaping the benefits of the symmetrical communication. Businesses must have a team of members who are well qualified to look after the social media marketing so that none of the queries go unnoticed or unanswered. This team should have good knowledge of social media, its usability and applications. Visually based rather than text-based social media communications should be utilised by businesses as images are more appealing than long text messages that viewers could find boring.

In today's scenario, businesses must focus on the core value of providing excellent customer service. All the activities of the business must be customer-centred and the customers must be the focus of the business. Social media can help business to provide exposure but great customer services are the only key for retaining customers. The business must understand the needs and requirements of its customers and encourage them toward value co-creation. A social media platform helps in reducing research and development costs for the business. The products that are developed after taking suggestions from customers have less chance of product failure and are easily accepted by the customers in the market once the products are launched.

REFERENCES

Abrahams, A. S., Jiao, J., Wang, G. A., & Fan, W. (2012). Vehicle defect discovery from social media. *Decision Support Systems*, *54*(1), 87–97. doi:10.1016/j.dss.2012.04.005

Allan, B. (2005). Social enterprise: Through the eye of consumer. *Social Enterprise Journal*, *1*, 57–77. doi:10.1108/17508610580000707

Aluri, A., Slevitch, L., & Larzelere, R. (2015). The effectiveness of embedded social media on hotel websites and the importance of social interactions and return on engagement'. *International Journal of Contemporary Hospitality Management*, *27*(4), 670–689. doi:10.1108/IJCHM-09-2013-0415

Anderson, P. H. (2001). Relationship development and marketing communication: An integrative model. *Journal of Business and Industrial Marketing*, *16*(3), 167–183. doi:10.1108/08858620110389786

Ayertey, S., Ozuem, W., & Appiah, D. (2018). Service failure and recovery strategy in computer- mediated environments. *Global Business and Technology Association Conference*, Bangkok, Thailand.

Barnes, N. G. (2010). Tweeting and blogging to the top. *Marketing Research*, *22*(1), 8–13.

Bechmann, A., & Lomborg, S. (2013). Mapping actor roles in social media: Different perspectives on value creation in theories of user participation. *Sage (Atlanta, Ga.)*, 767–679. doi:10.1177/1461444812462853

Bolton, R. N., Parasuraman, A., Hoefnagels, A., Migchels, N., Kabadayi, S., Gruber, T., ... Solnet, D. (2013). Understanding Generation Y and their use of social media: A review and research agenda. *Journal of Service Management*, *24*(3), 245–267. doi:10.1108/09564231311326987

Bowers, M. R., Martin, C. L., & Luker, A. (1990). Trading places: Employees as customers, customers as employees. *Journal of Services Marketing*, *4*(2), 55–69. doi:10.1108/EUM0000000002512

Brake, D. K., & Safko, L. (2009). So exactly what is the social media? In *The social media bible: Tactics, tools and strategies for business success* (p. 6). John Wiley & Sons.

Brodie, J. R., Ilic, A., Juric, B., & Hollebeek, L. (2013). Consumer engagement in a virtual brand community: An exploratory research. *Journal of Business Research*, *66*(1), 105–114. doi:10.1016/j.jbusres.2011.07.029

Brodie, J. R., Juric, B., & Ilic, A. (2011). Consumer engagement: Conceptual domain, Fundamental propositions and implications for research. *Journal of Service Research, 14*(3), 252–271. doi:10.1177/1094670511411703

Cao, Y., Ajjan, H., & Hong, P. (2013). Using Social Media Applications for Educational Outcomes in College Teaching: A Structural Equation Analysis. *British Journal of Educational Technology, 44*(4), 581–593. doi:10.1111/bjet.12066

Chan-Olmsted, S. M., Cho, M., & Lee, S. (2013). User Perceptions of Social Media: A comparative study of perceived characteristics and user Profiles by social media. *Journal of Communication and Media Technologies, 3*(4).

Chang, C. C. (2008). Factors influencing visual comfort appreciation of the product form of digital cameras. *International Journal of Industrial Ergonomics, 38*(11), 1007–1016. doi:10.1016/j.ergon.2008.04.002

Chathoth, P. K., Ungson, G. R., Harrington, R. J., & Chan, E. S. W. (2014). Barriers affecting organisational adoption of higher order customer engagement in tourism service interactions. *Tourism Management, 42*(3), 181–193. doi:10.1016/j.tourman.2013.12.002

Chau, M., & Xu, J. (2012). Business intelligence in Blogs: Understanding consumer interactions and communities. *Management Information Systems Quarterly, 36*(4), 1189–1216. doi:10.2307/41703504

Cheung, C. M. K., & Thadani, D. R. (2010). The state of electronic word-of-mouth research: A literature analysis. In *Proceedings of Pacific Asia Conference on Information Systems.* Taipei, Taiwan: AIS Electronic Library (AISeL).

Cheung, C. M. K., & Thadani, D. R. (2012). The impact of electronic word-of-mouth communication: A literature analysis and integrative model. *Decision Support System, 54*(1), 461-470. doi:org/. doi:10.1010/j.dss.2012.06.008

Coursaris, O. W.V., & Constantinos, K. (2013). Organizational Social Media: A Comprehensive Framework and Research Agenda. In *46 Hawaii International Conference on system Sciences*. Michigan State University.

Cova, B., & Dalli, D. (2009). Working consumers: The next step in marketing theory? *Marketing Theory, 9*(3), 315–339. doi:10.1177/1470593109338144

Curran, J., & Lennon, R. (2011). Participating in the conversation: Exploring adoption of online social media. *Academy of Marketing Studies Journal, 15*(1), 21–38.

Dann, S., & Dann, S. (2011). *E-marketing: theory and application*. Basingstoke, UK: Palgrave Macmillan. doi:10.1007/978-0-230-36473-8

Daugherty, T., Eastin, M., & Bright, L. (2008). Exploring Consumer Motivations for Creating User-Generated Content. *Journal of Interactive Advertising, 8*(2), 16–25. doi:10.1080/15252019.2008.10722139

Dellarocas, C. (2010). Online reputation systems: How to design one that does what you need. *Sloan Management Review, 51*(3), 33–38.

Di Gangi, M., & Wasko, M. (2009). The Co-Creation of Value: Exploring User Engagement in User-Generated Content Websites. *Pre-ICIS 8th Annual JAIS Theory Development Workshop.*

Di Gangi, P. M., & Wasko, M. (2009). Open innovation through online communities. In Knowledge management and organizational learning. Springer. doi:10.1007/978-1-4419-0011-1_13

Dijkmans, C., Kerkhif, P., Buyukcan-Tetic, A., & Beukeboom, C. J. (2015). Online Conversation and Corporate Reputation: A Two-Wave Longitudinal Study on the Effects of Exposure to the Social Media Activities of a Highly Interactive Company. *Journal of Computer-Mediated Communication*, *20*(6), 632–648. doi:10.1111/jcc4.12132

Dong, B., Evans, K. R., & Zou, S. (2008). The effects of customer participation in co-created service recovery. *Journal of the Academy of Marketing Science*, *36*(1), 123–137. doi:10.100711747-007-0059-8

Fischer, E., & Reuber, A. (2011). Social interaction via new social media: (How) can interactions on Twitter affect effectual thinking and behavior? *Journal of Business Venturing*, *26*(1), 1–18. doi:10.1016/j.jbusvent.2010.09.002

Fournier, S., & Avery, J. (2011). The uninvited brand. *Business Horizons*, *54*(3), 193–207. doi:10.1016/j.bushor.2011.01.001

Foux, G. (2006). Consumer generated media: Get your consumers involved. *Brand Strategy*, *202*, 38–39.

Gallaugher, J., & Ransbotham, S. (2010). Social Media and Customer Dialog Management at Starbucks. *MIS Quarterly Executive*, *9*(4).

Galvagno, M., & Dalli, D. (2014). Theory of value co-creation: A systematic literature review. *Managing Service Quality*, *20*(4), 643–683. doi:10.1108/MSQ-09-2013-0187

Gordhamer, S. (2009). *4 ways Social media is changing Business.* Retrieved from http://Mashable.com /2009/09/22/Social-Media-Business

Gronroos, C., & Gummerus, J. (2014). The service revolution and its marketing implications: Service logic versus service–dominant logic. *Managing Service Quality*, *24*(3), 206–229. doi:10.1108/MSQ-03-2014-0042

Gronroos, C., & Voima, P. (2013). Critical service logic: Making sense of value creation and co-creation. *Journal of the Academy of Marketing Science*, *41*(2), 133–150. doi:10.100711747-012-0308-3

Grunig, J. E. (2009). Paradigms of global public relations in an age of digitalisation. *Prism*, *6*(2).

Gummerus, J., Liljander, V., Weman, E., & Pihlstrom, M. (2012). *Consumer motivations to join a Facebook brand community. In Marketing Fields Forever 2012.* Emeralds.

Gummerus, J., Liljander, V., Weman, E., & Pihlström M. H. (2011). *Consumer motivations to join a facebook brand community.* Marketing Fields Forever: Academy of Marketing Conference, Liverpool, UK.

Gummesson, E., Lusch, R. F., & Vargo, S. L. (2010). Transitioning from service management to service-dominant logic: Observations and recommendations. *International Journal of Quality and Service Sciences*, *2*(1), 8–22. doi:10.1108/17566691011026577

Gummesson, E., & Mele, C. (2010). Marketing as value co-creation through network interaction and resource integration. *Journal of Business Market Management*, *4*(4), 181–198. doi:10.100712087-010-0044-2

Habibi, M. R., Laroche, M., & Richard, M.-O. (2014). Brand communities based in social media: How unique are they? Evidence from two exemplary brand communities. *International Journal of Information Management*, *34*(2), 123–132. doi:10.1016/j.ijinfomgt.2013.11.010

Hamid, N. R, & Akhir, R. M., & Cheng, A. Y. (2013). Social media: An emerging dimension of marketing communication. *Journal of Management and Marketing Research*, *12*, 4–11.

Hanna, R., Rohm, A., & Crittenden, V. L. (2011). We're all connected: The power of the social media ecosystem. *Business Horizons*, *54*(3), 265–273. doi:10.1016/j.bushor.2011.01.007

Hew, K. F., & Cheung, W. S. (2012). *Use of Web 2.0 technologies in K-12 and higher education: The search for evidence- based practice. In Education Research Review 9*. Singapore: National Institute of Education, Nanyang Technological University.

Hoffman, D. L., & Fodor, M. (2010). Can You Measure the ROI of Your Social Media Marketing? *Sloan Management Review*, *52*, 1.

Hollebeek, L. D. (2011). Demystifying customer brand engagement: Exploring the loyalty nexus. *Journal of Marketing Management*, *27*(7-8), 785–807. doi:10.1080/0267257X.2010.500132

Hollebeek, L. D., Glynn, M., & Brodie, R. J. (2014). Consumer Brand Engagement in Social Media: Conceptualization, Scale Development and Validation. *Journal of Interactive Marketing*, *28*(2), 149–165. doi:10.1016/j.intmar.2013.12.002

Horgan, B., & Quan Haase, A. (2010). Persistence and Change in Social Media. *Bulletin of Science, Technology & Society*, *30*(5), 309–315. doi:10.1177/0270467610380012

Hutton, G., & Fosdick, M. (2011). The globalisation of SM, consumer relationships with brand evolve in the digital age. *Journal of Advertising Research*, *3*(4), 564–570. doi:10.2501/JAR-51-4-564-570

Islam, A., Agarwal, N. K., & Ikeda, M. (2015). Conceptualizing value co-creation for service innovation in academic libraries. *Business Information Review*, *32*(1), 45–52. doi:10.1177/0266382115573155

Jaakkola, E., Helkkula, A., & Stenroos, L. A. (2012). Service experience co-creation: Conceptualization, implications, and future research directions. *Journal of Service Management*, *26*(2), 182–205. doi:10.1108/JOSM-12-2014-0323

Jan, A., & Khan, M. F. (2014). Social Media Is Nothing but a Public Relation Tool. *International Journal of Business and Management*, *2*(12), 272–277.

Kane, G. C., Alavi, M., Labianca, G., & Borgatti, S. P. (2014). What's different about social networks? A framework and research agenda. *Management Information Systems Quarterly*, *38*(1), 274–304. doi:10.25300/MISQ/2014/38.1.13

Kao, T. Y., Yang, M. H., Wu, J.-T. B., & Cheng, Y.-Y. (2016). Co-creating value with consumers through social media. *Journal of Services Marketing*, *30*(2), 141–151. doi:10.1108/JSM-03-2014-0112

Kaplan, A. M., & Haenlein, M. (2010). Users of the world, unite! The challenges and opportunities of social media. *Business Horizons, 53*(1), 59–68. doi:10.1016/j.bushor.2009.09.003

Kaplan, A. M., & Haenlein, M. (2011). Two hearts in three-quarter time: How to waltz the social media/viral marketing dance. *Business Horizons, 54*(3), 253–263. doi:10.1016/j.bushor.2011.01.006

Kapoor, K. K., & Dwivedi, Y. K. (2015). Metamorphosis of Indian electoral campaigns: Modi's social media experiment. *International Journal of Indian Culture &Business Management, 11*(4), 496–516. doi:10.1504/IJICBM.2015.072430

Kietzmann, J. H., Hermkens, K., McCarthy, I. P., & Silvestre, B. S. (2011). Social media? Get serious! Understanding the functional building blocks of social media. *Business Horizons, 54*(3), 241–251. doi:10.1016/j.bushor.2011.01.005

Kim, W., Jeong, O. R., & Lee, S. W. (2010). On social web sites. *Information Systems, 35*(2), 215–236. doi:10.1016/j.is.2009.08.003

Kumar, A., Bezawada, R., Rishika, R., Janakiraman, R., & Kannan, P. K. (2016). From social to sale: The effects of firm-generated content in social media on consumer behaviour. *Journal of Marketing, 80*(1), 7–25. doi:10.1509/jm.14.0249

Leskovec, J. (2011). *Social media analytics: tracking, modelling and predicting the flow of information through networks.* Tutorial in ACM SIGKDD Conference, San Diego, CA.

Li, Y. M., & Shiu, Y. (2012). A diffusion mechanism for social advertising over microblogs. *Decision Support Systems, 54*(1), 9–22. doi:10.1016/j.dss.2012.02.012

Lin, S., Yang, S., Ma, M., & Huang, J. (2018). Value co-creation on social media: Examining the relationship between brand engagement and display advertising effectiveness for Chinese hotels. *International Journal of Contemporary Hospitality Management, 30*(4), 2153–2174. doi:10.1108/IJCHM-08-2016-0484

Lukyanenko, R., & Parsons, J. (2015). Information quality research challenge: Adapting information quality principles to user-generated content. *ACM Journal of Data and Information Quality, 6*(1), 1–3. doi:10.1145/2723166

Lukyanenko, R., Parsons, J., & Wiersma, Y. F. (2014a). The IQ of the crowd: Understanding and improving information quality in structured user-generated content. *Information Systems Research, 25*(4), 669–689. doi:10.1287/isre.2014.0537

Luo, N., Zhang, M., & Lui, W. (2015). The effects of value co-creation practices on building harmonious brand community and achieving brand loyalty on social media. *Computer in Human Behaviour*, 492-500.

Luo, X., Zhang, J., & Duan, W. (2013). Social Media and Firm Equity Value. *Information Systems Research, 24*(1), 146–163. doi:10.1287/isre.1120.0462

Maglio, P. P., & Spohrer, J. (2008). Fundamentals of service science. *Journal of the Academy of Marketing Science, 36*(1), 18–20. doi:10.100711747-007-0058-9

Mangold, W. G., & Faulds, D. J. (2009). Social media: The new hybrid element of the promotion mix. *Business Horizons, 52*(4), 357–365. doi:10.1016/j.bushor.2009.03.002

Moreau, C. P., & Herd, K. B. (2010). To each his own? How comparisons with others influence consumers' evaluations of their self-designed products. *The Journal of Consumer Research, 36*(5), 806–819. doi:10.1086/644612

Nagi, T. (2015). Social media research: Theories, constructs, and conceptual frameworks. *International Journal of Information Management, 35*(1), 33–44. doi:10.1016/j.ijinfomgt.2014.09.004

Nambisan, S., & Baron, R. A. (2009). Virtual customer environments: Testing a model of voluntary participation in value co-creation activities. *Journal of Product Innovation Management, 26*(4), 388–406. doi:10.1111/j.1540-5885.2009.00667.x

Nambisan, S., & Nambisan, P. (2008). How to Profit from a Better Virtual Customer Environment? *MIT Sloan Management Review, 49*(3), 53–61.

Ozuem, W., Howell, K. E., & Lancaster, G. (2008). Communicating in the new interactive marketspace. *European Journal of Marketing, 42*(9/10), 1059–1083. doi:10.1108/03090560810891145

Ozuem, W., & Stokinger, E. (2015). Social media and customer retention: Implications for the Luxury Beauty Industry. In K. Wolfe (Ed.), *Computer-Mediated Marketing Strategies*. Hershey, PA: IGI Global.

Ozuem, W., & Tan, K. (2014). Reconciling Social Media with Luxury Fashion Brands: An Exploratory Study. In Handbook of Research on Management of Cultural Products: E-Relationship Marketing and Accessibility Perspectives. IGI Global.

Ozuem, W., & Yankova, I. (2015). Social Media and customer experience. In K. Wolfe (Ed.), *Computer-Mediated Marketing Strategies*. Hershey, PA: Business Science Reference.

Parameswaran, M., & Whinston, A. B. (2007). social Computing: An Overview. *Communications of the Association for Information Systems, 19*, 762–780.

Paris, C. M., Lee, W., & Seery, P. (2010). The role of social media in promoting special events: Acceptance of Facebook events. *Information and Communication Technologies in Tourism, 14*, 531–541.

Payne, A., Storbacka, K., & Frow, P. (2008). Managing the co-creation of value. *Journal of the Academy of Marketing Science, 36*(1), 83–96. doi:10.100711747-007-0070-0

Perks, H., Gruber, T., & Edvardsson, B. (2012). Co-creation in Radical Service Innovation: A Systematic Analysis of Microlevel Processes. *Journal of Product Innovation Management, 29*(6), 935–951. doi:10.1111/j.1540-5885.2012.00971.x

Phillips, D., & Young, P. (2009). *Online Public Relations: A practical guide to developing an online strategy in the world of social media* (2nd ed.). London: Kogan Page Limited.

Prahalad, C. K., & Ramaswamy, V. (2004a). *The future of competition: Co-creating unique value with customers*. Boston, MA: Harvard Business School Press.

Rathore, A., Ilavarasan, V., & Dwivedi, Y. K. (2016). Social media content and product co-creation: An emerging paradigm. *Journal of Enterprise Information Management, 29*(1), 7–18. doi:10.1108/JEIM-06-2015-0047

Robert, G., Astrid, S., & Bart, N. (2013). Social Media Affecting Tour Operators' Customer Loyalty. *Journal of Travel & Tourism Marketing*, *30*, 1–2, 41–57. doi:10.1080/10548408.2013.750993

Rodriguez, M., Peterson, R. M., & Krishanan, V. (2012). Social media's influence on business-to business sales performance. *Journal of Personal Selling & Sales Management*, *32*(3), 365–378. doi:10.2753/PSS0885-3134320306

Ryan, D., & Jones, C. (2009). *Understanding Digital Marketing: Marketing Strategies forEEngaging the Digital Generation*. Glasgow, UK: Marketing Industry Network.

Safko, L. (2010). John Wiley & Sons. In *The social media bible: tactics, tools, and strategies for business success* (2nd ed.; pp. 4–25). Hoboken, NJ: John Wiley & sons.

Sampson, S. E., & Froehle, C. M. (2006). Foundations and implications of a proposed Unified Services Theory. *Production and Operations Management*, *15*(2), 329–343. doi:10.1111/j.1937-5956.2006.tb00248.x

Santos, A. T., Alves, L., & Brambilla, F. R. (2016). *Value co-creation in Retail through the use of social networks*. Retrieved from https://online.unisc.br/seer/index.php/cepe/index

Sapena, J., & Paniagua, J. (2014). Business performance and social media: Love or hate? *Business Horizons*, *57*(6), 719–728. doi:10.1016/j.bushor.2014.07.005

Sawhney, M., Verona, G., & Prandelli, E. (2005). Collaborating to create: The internet as a platform for customer engagement in product innovation. *Journal of Interactive Marketing*, *19*(4), 4–17. doi:10.1002/dir.20046

Schamari, J., & Schaefers, T. (2015). Leaving the home turf: How brands can use web care on consumer generated platforms to increase positive consumer engagement. *Journal of Interactive Marketing*, *30*(5), 20–33. doi:10.1016/j.intmar.2014.12.001

Siamagka, N., Christodoulides, G., Michaelidou, N., & Valvi, A. (2015). Determinants of social media adoption by B2B organisations. *Industrial Marketing Management*, *51*, 89–99. doi:10.1016/j.indmarman.2015.05.005

Sinan, A., Dellarocas, C., & Godes, D. (2013). Introduction to the Special Issue—Social Media and Business Transformation: A Framework for Research. *Information Systems Research*, *24*(1), 3–13. doi:10.1287/isre.1120.0470

So, K. F., King, C., & Sparks, B. (2014). Customer engagement with tourism Brands: Scale development and validation. *Journal of Hospitality & Tourism Research (Washington, D.C.)*, *38*(3), 304–329. doi:10.1177/1096348012451456

Solomon, M. R., & Tuten, T. L. (2015). The Fifth P of Marketing. In *Social media marketing* (p. 1). Thousand Oaks, CA: Sage.

Song, Z. L., Di Benedetto, A. C., & Song, M. (2010). Competitive advantages in the first product of new ventures. *IEEE Transactions on Engineering Management*, *57*(1), 88–115. doi:10.1109/TEM.2009.2013836

Sorensen, A., Andrews, L., & Drennam, J. (2016). *Using social media posts as resources for engaging in value co-creation. The case for social media- based cause brand communities*. doi:10.1108/JSTP-04-2016-0080

Stockinger, E., & Ozuem, W. (2014). Social Media and Customer Retention: Implications for the Luxury Beauty Industry. In *Computer-Mediated Marketing Strategies: Social Media and Online Brand Communities*. Business Science Reference.

Stockinger, E., & Ozuem, W. (2015). Social media and customer retention: implications for the luxury beauty industry. In G. Bowen & W. Ozuem (Eds.), *Marketing strategies: Social media and online brand communities*. Hershey, PA: IGI Global. doi:10.4018/978-1-4666-6595-8.ch009

Stokinger, E., & Ozuem, W. (2015). Social media and customer retention: Implications for the Luxury Beauty Industry. In K. Wolfe (Ed.), *Computer-Mediated Marketing Strategies* (pp. 200–205). Hershey, PA: IGI Global. doi:10.4018/978-1-4666-6595-8.ch009

Strandvik, T., Holmlund, M., & Edvardsson, B. (2012). Customer needing: A challenge for the seller offering. *Journal of Business and Industrial Marketing*, *27*(2), 132–141. doi:10.1108/08858621211196994

Tapscott, D., & Williams, A. (2006). *Wikinomics: How Mass Communication Changes Everything*. New York: Penguin Group.

Taylor, C. R. (2009). The six principles of digital advertising. *International Journal of Advertising*, *28*(3), 411–418. doi:10.2501/S0265048709200679

Tredinnick, L. (2006). Web 2.0 and business. *Business Information Review*, *23*(4), 228–234. doi:10.1177/0266382106072239

Tregua, M., D'Auria, A., & Bifulco, F. (2015). Comparing research streams on smart city and sustainable city. *China-USA Business Review*, *14*(4), 203–215.

Van Doorn, J., Lemon, K. N., Mittal, V., Nass, S., Pick, D., Pirner, P., & Verhoef, P. C. (2010). Customer engagement behavior: Theoretical foundations and research directions. *Journal of Service Research*, *13*(3), 253–266. doi:10.1177/1094670510375599

Vargo, S. L., & Lusch, R. F. (2006). Service Dominant Logic: Reactions, reflections and refinements. *Marketing Theory*, *6*(3), 281–288. doi:10.1177/1470593106066781

Vargo, S. L., & Lusch, R. F. (2008a). Service Dominant Logic: Continuing the Evolution'. *Journal of the Academy of Marketing Science*, *36*(1), 1–10. doi:10.100711747-007-0069-6

Vargo, S. L., & Lusch, R. F. (2011). It's all B2B . . . and beyond: Toward a systems perspective of the market. *Industrial Marketing Management*, *40*(2), 181–187. doi:10.1016/j.indmarman.2010.06.026

Vargo, S. L., & Lusch, R. L. (2004b, May). The Four Services Marketing Myths: Remnants from a Manufacturing Model. *Journal of Service Research*, 324–335. doi:10.1177/1094670503262946

Wang, P., Hongxiu, L., & Suomi. (2016). Value co-creation in Business via social media: A technology Affordance approach. *PACIS Proceedings*, 355.

Ward, J. C., & Ostrom, A. L. (2006). Complaining to the masses: The role of protest framing in customer-created complaint web sites. *The Journal of Consumer Research*, *33*(2), 220–230. doi:10.1086/506303

Weinberg, T. (2009). The New Community Rules: Marketing on the Social Web. O'Reilly.

Wright, E., Khanfar, N. M., Harrington, C., & Kizer, L. E. (2010). The lasting effects of social media trends on advertising. *Journal of Business & Economics Research*, *8*(11), 73–80. doi:10.19030/jber.v8i11.50

Xiang, Z., Gretzel, U., & Fesenmaier, D. (2009). Semantic Representation of Tourism on the Internet. *Journal of Travel Research*, *47*(4), 440–453. doi:10.1177/0047287508326650

Xie, Ch., Bagozzi, R., & Troye, S. (2008). Trying to prosume: Toward a theory of consumers as co-creators of value. *Journal of the Academy of Marketing Science*, *36*(1), 109–122. doi:10.100711747-007-0060-2

Xie, I., & Stevenson, J. (2014). Social media application in digital libraries. *Online Information Review*, *38*(4), 502–523. doi:10.1108/OIR-11-2013-0261

Yang, S., Lin, S., Carlson, J. R. A. N. D., & Ross, W. T. Jr. (2016). Brand engagement on social media on social media: Will firms' social media efforts influence search engine advertising effectiveness? *Journal of Marketing Management*, *32*(5&6), 47–63.

KEY TERMS AND DEFINITIONS

Customer Engagement: Involving customers in sharing, spreading and discussing their knowledge and experiences on the social media platform with the business and other users, thus allowing them to co-create value as co-designers, co-marketers, co-distributors, and co-producers of products/services and magnifying the role of consumers as co-creators of value.

Electronic Word-of-Mouth (E-WOM): The communication via the internet of the views, opinions, or experiences of current, potential, and prior customers related to products, services, or businesses, which could take the form of constructive or adverse statements.

Service-Dominant Logic (SDL): One of the main theories that describe value co-creation between firms and customers. It considers customers as the operant resources which have capabilities of combining their skills, experiences and knowledge in the co-creation process for the advantage of another actor or the self. The main cause of the empowerment of customers is the advanced internet-based technologies that have forced businesses to be more customer-centric.

Social Media: An online platform based on internet technology that facilitates multi-directional communication among users which not only provides space to the participants to connect with their friends and family on a regular basis by sharing their posts, locations and pictures or videos to stay more connected, but also helps them to promote their views and opinions about apps, products or services and their experiences, furthering value co-creation.

Social Media Marketing: Marketing techniques adopted by businesses that are based on the ecosystem of social media to communicate information, knowledge, values, and morals related to the service or product in order to attract customers to interact with the business and help to establish and manage cordial relationships with customers.

Symmetrical Communication: Two-way communication that assists in the development of trust, reliability, transparency, openness, interchange of views and opinions that generate feedback and discussion motivating participants to maintain trusting relationships.

User-Generated Content: The content that is created during the process of sharing the views, opinions and information by consumers on the social media platform. It is very difficult to be controlled in the form of views, comments and discussion from posts, blogs, videos, reviews or any other kind of media that is widely accessible to other consumers.

Value Co-Creation: The creation of value due to the direct interactions between businesses and customers. It is joint actions by a customer and a service provider. It also includes collaborating with associates to model new services and improve customer value. The value is co-created during the resource integration process in which businesses integrate their various resources such as market, individual and public resources and customers integrate individual resources and social network resources.

Chapter 3
Social Media and Social Identity in the Millennial Generation

Guida Helal
American University of Beirut, Lebanon

Wilson Ozuem
University of Cumbria, UK

ABSTRACT

The active presence of fashion brands online serves as a channel for customers to connect with brands for different intentions. This connection acts as an outlet customers employ in furthering social identity through brand associations. Brand perceptions are accordingly formed among consumers based on the promised functional and symbolic benefits consumption of that brand guarantees. Social media has assumed an integral role in fostering brand-customer relationships that ultimately augment social identity. The following chapter examines the role social media has played on brand perceptions in the fashion apparel and accessories industry from a social identity theory perspective. The chapter focuses on theoretical implications and managerial implications. The concluding section offers some significant roles that social media and social identity may play in keeping up with the design and development of marketing communications programs.

INTRODUCTION

Marketing logics and developments have comparably and effectively progressed over the years to parallel the whirlwind innovations that primarily define the fashion industry. The dynamic nature of marketing means fashion companies are relentlessly on guard for the next groundbreaking development (Jayachandran, Gimeno & Varadarajan, 1999; Lusch, 2007; Vargo & Lusch, 2004; Webster, 1992). One case of a sought after phenomenon that has dramatically revolutionised today's society, is the technological Millennial approach to communication. Traditional marketing has gradually lost bearing, as the rigid likes of one-way communication is superseded by active two-way interchange (Houman Andersen, 2001; Ozuem, Howell, & Lancaster, 2008). The shift in communication has consequently encouraged worldwide organisations to assume the likes of Internet technologies along with their varied manifestations, such as social media,

DOI: 10.4018/978-1-5225-7344-9.ch003

as an outlet allowing brands to produce content for followers (Evans, 2012; Hoffman & Novak, 1996; Zarrella, 2009). An abundance of literature has consequently surfaced examining the evolution social media has enthused in routine life (Fischer & Reuber, 2011; Hanna, Rohm & Crittenden, 2011; Hoffman & Fodor, 2016; Huy & Shipilov, 2012; Kaplan & Haenlein, 2010; Kietzmann, Hermkens, McCarthy, & Silvestre, 2011; Michaelidou, Siamagka, & Christodoulides, 2011). Further studies have explored the application of social media within a brand's marketing strategy (Luo, Zhang, & Duan, 2013; Naylor, Lamberton & West, 2012; Simmons, 2008; Tuten & Solomon, 2014).

Kim and Ko (2012) addressed the promising relationship between social media marketing and resultant customer equity among luxury fashion brands. The study aimed to demonstrate †he success luxury fashion brands gain from employing social media marketing activities including entertainment, interaction, or word of mouth. Based on the findings, the study concluded that the use of social media is directly correlated with subsequent enhanced purchase intentions and customer equity within the luxury fashion industry. However, the study paid limited attention to a demographic age that is familiar with social media and able to produce pertinent feedback that enhances the accuracy of research results. An analysis conducted by a statistic portal, Statista, on the worldwide daily usage of social media found that the highest degree of daily social media usage in 2016 was held by global users aged 25 to 34 years old (Statista, 2016). A more recent study revealed the highest time consumption of visual activities on social networking sites such as Facebook and Instagram to be among ages 16-34 years, while preceding generations demonstrated fewer percentages of average time spent participating in such activities (Statista, 2017). The Millennial generation outruns other age groups as the leading social media user. Albeit the current extensive literature investigating social media, few studies have examined the use of social media in the fashion industry, particularly on the Millennial generation.

Social media is a development of the World Wide Web that began gaining ground between the late 1990's and early 2000's, establishing worldwide prominence by the late 2000's (Dewing, 2010). Yet before delving into the profound significance social media has exerted globally, the course of events leading up to its inception are considered

The initiation of the World Wide Web began in the early 1990's upon Tim Berners-Lee linking hypertext technology to the Internet. This allowed for one common worldwide foundation to be formed, whereby networked communication was born (Van Dijck, 2013). The consequent evolution of Web 2.0 brought about social media. Web 2.0 is described as consisting of two features that help define it, and these are *microcontent* and *social media. Microcontent* comprises of pieces of content that express a primary idea. Such pieces cover much less information than websites and may take the form of blog posts, comments, or small images. These are designed for easy upload, reuse, and stimulating participation. The second feature of Web 2.0, *social media* or *social software*, consists of platforms organized around the framework of connecting people to one another. The *microcontent* produced by multiple users creates a page of shared interests different users can access to bond with one another (Alexander & Levine, 2008). In time, the growth of Web 2.0 prompted the birth of two-way communication platforms and the flow of user-generated content, which is today identified as social media (Arora, 2014; Fuchs, 2014; Gillies & Cailliau, 2000; O'Reilly, 2005).

A study conducted by Statista further affirms the significance social media has gained across the fashion industry (Statista, 2016). This study emphasizes the sheer 'clout' that virtual channels have when it comes to the fashion domain through the integration of social media throughout London Fashion Week. The show is a highly anticipated bi-annual fashion trading weeklong event, and in 2014, it generated over half a million mentions on social media. The majority of these mentions emerged over

Instagram. Reports show that user access to fashion brands online is set to reach over one billion users by the year 2020 (Statista, 2016). Additional analyses identified social media as the most commonly used source by Millennials for updates on high-end fashion (Statista, 2017). These figures demonstrate the on-going unification social media has brought about within the fashion world, as more brands race towards social networking sites to attain followers. Online channels offer fashion brands further leeway for original content contribution that facilitates for an intimate connection with Millennials. The social platform cultivates brand-customer relationships, as brands strive to publicly evoke customer loyalty, and customers, in turn, are receptive to demonstrate brand association and acquire the promised relationship equity such brands are perceived to offer (Lemon, Rust, & Zeithaml, 2001; Kim & Ko, 2012; Vogel, Evanschitzky, & Ramaseshan, 2008).

Drawing on social identity, this study investigates the application of social media in advancing online brand communities and relationship equity that consumers chase in enforcing social identity. Social identity theory holds that individuals seek to allocate themselves or others according to social categories (Tajfel & Turner, 1985). Individuals trail the groups that guarantee positive recognition and ultimately enhance the self through association (Ashforth & Mael, 1989; Hogg & Terry, 2000). Numerous studies have explored the tendency of customers to identify with particular brands in forming a desired social identity (Arnett, German, & Hunt, 2003; Bhattacharya & Sen, 2003; Lam, Ahearne, Hu, & Schillewaert, 2010). Consumption can be a significant attribute within an individual's journey to build an identity for his/her own self, as well as for others (Elliot & Wattanasuwan, 1998; Kleine, Kleine, & Kernan, 1993). The consumption of popular culture has been recognized as a paramount contributor to the attainment of social status or social placement for individuals. Fashion, a major segment of present pop culture, has manifested into a prominent facilitator of social enhancement (Barron, 2012). Fashion brands are pursued by consumers with the intention of embracing individuality that, in fact, complies with a universal standard of social classification. People seek to individually speak, behave, or dress in a manner that is perceptible and significant, but that simultaneously resides within putative group norms. A consumer is placed amid two forces, the individual/psychological influence of personal opinions and preferences, and the public/social weight of uniform beliefs and attitudes (Burke, 2006; Carlson, Suter, & Brown, 2008; Nowak, Szamrej and Latané, 1990).

Customers are enticed by a brand's online presence as a means of furthering social identity through brand association, and ultimately this can shape brand perceptions among customers through promised functional and symbolic benefits. Social media embodies the leading channel for casual interactions that develop brand-customer relationships and enrich social identity. Consumer touch points have accordingly been reinvented to accommodate for more than physical exchanges. Rather, brand-customer interaction has ensued beyond the point of sale and into a virtual realm of open interchange (Edelman, 2010; Fromm & Garton, 2013) that has become second nature to the Millennial generation. This study supplements present available research on social media in numerous ways. There exists abundant literature examining the implementation of social media means as marketing tools, however current literature does not account for Millennial presence in investigating the influence social media exerts on brand perceptions in the fashion industry. In exploring the impact social media holds as a marketing instrument, consequent outcomes from this study develop literature concerning the impact of social media on the Millennial age, and this cohort's dependence on social identity in further connecting with brands. This research provides a footing for fashion brands to develop in future research, which might look at how social media accounts can be appropriately handled in targeting consumers. The findings in this study uncovers the imprint social media has provoked on Millennial brand perceptions in the fashion industry.

BACKGROUND

The fashion industry comprises of various sectors from apparel and accessories, perfumes and cosmetics to watches and jewellery. This vast industry has been globally valued at 3 trillion US dollars (approx. 2.4 trillion pounds) with a compound annual growth rate of 2 percent. Positive market figures are anticipated to resume with industry growth projected across major regions such as China, Europe, USA and India, to name a few (Statista, 2016). Sales growth in the fashion industry have noticeably materialised across regions such as Asia Pacific and Europe, with anticipated global fashion industry growth to reach 4.5 percent in 2018 (Statista, 2017). As the fashion world engages a wide scope of sectors, this study focuses on the use of social media among the Millennial generation exclusively within the apparel and accessories sector.

In a study conducted by Deloitte on the global fashion and luxury market in 2016, the apparel and accessories sector demonstrated more than 80% of revenues recorded in the industry for years 2014 and 2015. Consequently, the expected market trends for 2016 demonstrated a 59% increase in the apparel and accessories sector worldwide (Deloitte, 2016). These figures can be expected to materialize among top billionaire players such as Zara (Inditex), LVMH, and H&M, among others (Statista, 2016). Multinational fast-fashion retailer Zara (Inditex) revealed a 10% climb within nine months of fiscal 2017 as the group persisted with its' effective tactic of globally locating flagship stores around peak shopping strips. Inditex complemented its highly visible brick-and-mortar stores with an integrated online-offline model offering same-day delivery and next-day delivery in certain markets (Inditex, 2017). Major competitor, H&M, was ranked one of the world's largest retail companies in 2016 with a 4 percent sales growth in the financial year of 2017. The company acknowledges the prominence of complementing the industry shift moving into 2018, through digital and offline integration of customer interaction and purchase points (H&M, 2017). Parent luxury fashion company LVMH (Moët Hennessy Louis Vuitton) has likewise asserted its place in the fashion industry boasting a revenue growth of 13% in 2017 compared to the previous year. LVMH's *Fashion and Leather Goods* sector exhibited optimistic figures across all luxury brands citing Louis Vuitton's innovative operation as a strong contributor to performance (LVMH, 2018). In an exhaustive forecast titled *The State of Fashion 2018,* conducted by Mckinsey & Company and The Business of Fashion, the report demonstrates an evolving shift in consumer behaviour as online platforms gain primary grounds as points of consumer exposure to brands. Revenue growth is subsequently projected to witness 2-3x increase online in 2018 versus 2015 as consumers push to personalise experiences through online channels and global mobile payment transactions surge (BOF & McKinsey & Co., 2018).

Social media has empowered the fashion industry with the free-flow of content shared between brands and consumers worldwide. Brands are able to penetrate international markets through the likes of Facebook, Instagram and fashion blogs that document the latest runways, campaigns and trends to an active audience. Brand followers likewise share their own content among brands and consumers. This two-way interchange and freedom in exchanging content has allowed brands and customers to connect, customers to express affiliation to brands, and online fashion communities to develop. Such a platform of communication enables vast brand exposure and awareness among worldwide social media users. H&M was recorded to have an average of over 10 million Instagram engagements consisting of likes, retweets and comments across over a one month period, signifying the scope of market saturation a single social media platform is capable of achieving (Statista, 2016).Luxury brands Chanel, Louis Vuitton and Christian Dior were placed in the top most influential luxury brands on social media worldwide as of October 2016 (Statista, 2016). The implementation of social media as a promotional technique has served as a gateway to market prominence as brands are given the opportunity to reach global customers on an intimate level. Consumers are drawn to online platforms to connect with brands in a more unique experience that may contribute to a brand's exclusivity and authenticity.

As affirmed by Van Dijck (2013), upon the initial development of social media, "participatory culture was the buzzword that connoted the Web's potential to nurture connections, build communities, and advance democracy." (Van Dijck, 2013, p.4). Such universal engagement has propelled the immense growth of social media into worldwide cultures. A study by Statista (2018) reveals the enormity social media holds as a defining phenomenon of the present time through a global infiltration of approximately 2 billion active social media users. Instagram, a photo-based application and social networking site, solely yielded a 21% global reach merely one year after its launch in 2013; and reached a record in 2018 of over 800 million monthly active users (Statista, 2018). Social media has infiltrated a generation of devoted users comprising of the Millennial age, as more than 85% of 18-29 years olds use online social platforms (Smith & Anderson, 2018). Fashion leaders Zara and H&M have prevailed among the Millennial age group (Forbes, 2012); a technological age that has grown to embody social media as a key communication portal. By utilizing social media as a major delivery approach, such brands are able to considerably impress their weight within the Millennial market.

MILLENNIAL GENERATION

The Millennial Generation is defined as a demographic cohort born between the early 1980s and the early 2000s. This generation differs remarkably from previous groups, as the Millennial perception of communication is that it is conveniently available and instant, therefore obstacles such as time or geography do not impinge upon the presence of technology (Strauss & Howe, 1991; Lingelbach, Patino, & Pitta, 2012; Rainer & Rainer, 2011). Global boundaries are diminishing as the use of the Internet empowers the Millennial age as a consumer group defined by homogeneous behaviour (Moore, 2012). Millennials worldwide are able to relate through identical behaviour and consumption patterns due to the network of mass media. The innate existence of the Internet has altered their way of interaction and characterised them as *digital natives* (Hershatter & Epstein, 2010; Prensky, 2001). The Millennial generation is the first cohort to entirely absorb social media as the leading source of communication within an era that values public and conspicuous behaviour (Bennett, Matson & Kervin, 2008; Bakewell & Mitchell, 2003; Paulin, Ferguson, Jost & Fallu, 2014). Twenge (2006) and Twenge, Campbell and Freeman (2012) interestingly describe the generation as both "Generation We", concerned with public and environmental obligations, and "Generation Me", stemming from the significance placed on materialistic behaviour and preserving image. Social media offers the platform to express activities, consumption and lifestyles that accentuate the "*me*" quality Millennials seek to achieve.

This cohort has wholly integrated social media into daily activities including the use of such interactive portals to connect to brands (Moore, 2012; Nowak, Thach & Olsen, 2006). Marketers recognise the reliance Millennials place on social media to connect with peers and brands in acquiring relevant information from such networks (Eastman, Iyer & Thomas, 2012; Eastman & Liu, 2012; Hewlett, Sherbin & Sumberg, 2009). The notion of remaining connected to real-time occurrences is an underlying motivation for Millennials to seek social media, and brands to consequently use interactive technologies to directly reach Millennials (Engel, Bell, Meier & Rumpel, 2011; Fiore, Kim & Lee, 2005; Valentine & Powers, 2013). Recurring brand-customer contact bears the potential to evolve into emotional interaction through trust, loyalty and commitment that advances brand equity (Nowak, Thach & Olsen), symbolically influencing Millennial perceptions of brands. The relevance of social media is only expected to grow with continuing consumer dependence on the network to which it caters, and newfound proficiency amongst brands in delivering a unified message worldwide is also set to evolve (Stephen & Galak, 2010; Mangold & Faulds, 2009; Prensky, 2001). Such characteristics justify the worth of social media as a phenomenon that merits exploration.

CONTEXT AND FOUNDATION

Social media has shrewdly manoeuvred its way into people's lives over the past decade. While it may have commenced with the prime intention of socially linking people together, it later developed and was described using broader definitions spanning from connecting individuals to connecting industries. The extensive exploration of this communication portal through numerous studies has generated multiple definitions, all of which tend to highlight a parallel overview: social media comprises of Internet-centred platforms that enable and promote a free flow of user-generated information (Kaplan & Haenlein, 2010; Safko, 2012; Kietzmann, Hermkens, McCarthy, & Silvestre, 2011; Hanna, Rohm, & Crittenden, 2011; Luo, Zhang, & Duan, 2013; Ngai, Tao, & Moon, 2015; Stokinger, & Ozuem, 2015).

Kaplan and Haenlein (2010) define social media as a "group of Internet-based applications that build on the ideological and technological foundations of Web 2.0, and allow the creation and exchange of user generated content." (Kaplan & Haenlein, 2010, p.61). This, much celebrated, definition has prevailed in acknowledging the key role of social media in facilitating the movement of content across a shared floor. Safko (2012) outlines a comparable explanation whilst emphasizing the efficiency social media facilitates in allowing human interactions and relationships to develop. Social media has cultivated an environment driven by an open exchange between networks of users. Ngai, Tao and Moon (2015) recognize the capacity of social media networks to form relationships, but they also discuss the potential of networks to influence career prospects. Building on this progression of explanations, social media can be defined as an evolving phenomenon that continues to mature across society.

Mayfield (2008) describes five characteristics of social media which are 1) *participation* that stimulates sharing 2) *openness,* which eliminates barriers and enables free-flow of information 3) *conversation* generated from the public stream of content shared 4) *community* that develops from open interactions, and 5) *connectedness*, which describes the network created between users. Kietzmann et al. (2011) have likewise categorized social media into seven similar functional blocks and these are 1) *identity,* that considers the degree to which a user is willing to reveal his/her identity 2) *conversation*, which considers the level of communication between users 3) *sharing,* which is the degree of content circulating between users 4) *presence,* which refers to the access given to display available users 5) *relationships* reflect the extent of users relating to one another 6) *reputation* considers the degree to which users can identify their stance within settings, and finally 7) *groups* refers to the ability to form or belong to a community. The functional blocks social media are built on create its flexibility in producing an open environment that consolidates worldwide users and progresses relationships.

Before proceeding to the next section, it is imperative to address the connotation of social media with regards to social networking sites. While social media and social networking sites are frequently used interchangeably, the two terms hold separate meanings. Social media generally concerns collective construction and the circulation of media on a large scale, which can include countless applications and services such as social networking sites, wikis, or podcasts, to name a few (Collin, Rahilly, Richardson, & Third, 2011; Dewing, 2010; Weinberg & Pehlivan, 2011). Social networking sites are web-based services, which are a part of social media and which are crafted for sharing media between networks of users (Collin, Rahilly, Richardson, & Third, 2011). Boyd and Ellison (2008) define social network sites as, "web-based services that allow individuals to 1) construct a public or semi-public profile within a bounded system 2) articulate a list of other users with whom they share a connection, and 3) view and traverse their list of connections and those made by others within the system." (Boyd & Ellison, 2008, p.211). Social networking sites comprise of websites such as Facebook, Instagram or Twitter that characteristically require users to primarily register on the website and create a network, after which content can be shared with networks of connections. The virtually interactive platforms that social media create have induced a shift in the web towards a more people-driven community, whereby regular users influence the content produced (Berthon, Pitt, Planger, & Shapiro, 2012; O'Reilly & Battelle, 2009; Smith, 2009). Account holders now have the liberty of broadcasting (receiving) any message on a global scale with the click of a button. This self-expression encourages a dynamic and democratic setting through which users feel more inclined to engage and share their own opinions (Susarla, Oh, & Tan, 2012). This study focuses on exploring how social media has influenced Millennial brand perceptions through different marketing methods.

Social Media as a Marketing Tool

Social media has progressively emerged on marketing agendas as an influential promotional tool within business operations (Fischer & Reuber, 2011; Luo, Zhang & Duan, 2013; Mangold & Faulds, 2009). This communication portal has compelled organizations to combine different marketing strategies, such as outbound marketing (dispensing promotional messages) with inbound marketing (receiving consumer messages through social media), to achieve an optimized balance of promotion (Smith & Zook, 2011). The viral chatter and ample exposure social media incites, cues brands to capitalize on potential networks as part of founding strong brand-customer relationships within brand communities, while amassing critical customer feedback (Chiu, Hsu, & Wang, 2006; Enders, Hungenberg, Denker, & Mauch, 2008). Brands benefit from eliciting social ties with customers that evoke an exchange of resources, such as trust between users, and facilitate a shared vision for companies that extend beyond overpowered geographic distances and broken organization-customer barriers (Ngai, Tao, & Moon, 2015; Heinonen, 2011; Tsai & Ghoshal, 1998).

Certain axioms are applied in designing attractive platforms for consumers when implementing social media within organizational marketing strategies. These axioms allow companies to reflect on each nation's local economic, political, and cultural stance in communicating with users on social media, while also maintaining consistency of content produced at a global level (Berthon, Pitt, Planger, & Shapiro, 2012; Hinz, Skiera, Barrot, & Becker, 2011). Brands form a universal norm of social network activities that produce memorable content worldwide customers pertain to. Corresponding touch-points are employed to connect with customers throughout the day and ultimately ensure incessant brand awareness (Ashley & Tuten, 2015; Tsimonis & Dimitriadis, 2014).

Viral Marketing and E-WOM

Stealth marketing has permeated industries via engagement of practises, such as viral marketing, that tactfully and subtly promote brands (Kaikati & Kaikati, 2004; Martin & Smith, 2008; Roy & Chattopadhyay, 2010; Ozuem, Borrelli & Lancaster, 2017). Viral marketing is defined as, "the process of getting customers to pass along a company's marketing message to friends, family, and colleagues." (Laudon & Traver, 2015, p.381). The unreserved, free flow quality supporting social media instigates web circulation. One form of viral marketing that has predominantly flourished offline, as an eminent promotional technique is word-of-mouth (Katz & Lazarsfeld, 1955). Word-of-mouth (WOM) has been defined as the exchange of information on a particular subject among consumers (Arndt, 1967; Kaplan & Haenlein, 2011; Stern, 1994).

Buttle (1998) describes WOM according to five characteristics; *valence, focus, timing, solicitation* and *intervention. Valence* considers the positive or negative force WOM may impress on receivers with regards to a brand. According to a study by File et al. (1994), WOM can be appropriately managed to produce a desired effect among customers. The second characteristic Buttle (1998) addresses is the *focus,* which the brand adopts in influencing customers through the management of WOM. *Timing* refers to the use of WOM as a pre-purchase or post-purchase evaluation amongst consumers. *Solicitation* discusses the potential of customers to accept WOM and this may be influenced by the *intervention* of spokespeople, or celebrities hired by the brand. In most cases, WOM is assumed to occur naturally among customers who share brand experiences, and this consequently creates trails of chatter that diffuse across multiple receivers (Anderson, 1998; Bone, 1995; Herr, Kardes, & Kim, 1991; v. Wangenheim & Bayon, 2004). However, brands have managed to exert their own influence over handling WOM, particularly through virtual outlets (Biyalogorsky, Gerstner, & Libai, 2001; Godes & Mayzlin, 2009; Mayzlin, 2006).

A movement of shoppers probing for broader brand reviews and scrutiny has summoned for the progression of traditional WOM to online channels as electronic Word-Of-Mouth (eWOM), consequently unveiling copious volumes of user inputs (Cheung & Thadani, 2012; Chu & Kim, 2011; Trusov, Bucklin, & Pauwels, 2009). Being mindful that while virtual interchange cannot suffice as the sole vehicle to contact in place of conventional offline communication, it bears the competence to act as an adjunct to evolving consumer behaviour (Kozinets, 1999).

Chevalier and Mayzlin (2006) undertook a study to evaluate customer dependence on eWOM. This study compared sales of the same products from different websites. The results demonstrated a discrepancy between the businesses in terms of sales of the same products generated, as the website with more positive feedback submitted on those products generated more sales. Positive eWOM exhibits the capability of shaping customer purchase decisions. However, Schlosser (2005) demonstrates that negative reviews also significantly influence buyer behaviour by discouraging potential customers whilst swaying current customers that have a positive stance towards the brand. You, Vadakkepatt & Joshi (2015) draw on varied factors that may affect the reception of eWOM. The study underlines the potency of eWOM to be dependent on the motivation of the sender. EWOM is accordingly categorised into *organic*, material that an eWOM sender innately chooses to share, or *incentivised eWOM,* material that is induced by the promise of company incentives (You, Vadakkepatt & Joshi, 2015). The latter may not be perceived as genuine or trustworthy.

Electronic word of mouth enables an accumulation of customer feedback that evidently adds to the image of a brand, and shapes a customer's screening process (Baker, Donthu & Kumar, 2016; Chakravarti & Janiszewski, 2003; Dellarocas, 2006; Dhar & Chang, 2009; Trusov, Bucklin, & Pauwels, 2009).

Consumers have gradually come to refer to and rely on eWOM to make purchase decisions. Typically, the consumer decision process involves different stages, beginning with *need recognition, information search, evaluation of alternatives, purchase,* and *post-purchase evaluation* (Solomon, 2012; Liang & Huang, 1998). De Valck, van Bruggen, & Wierenga (2009) conducted a study to explore the influence of virtual communities on the consumer decision processes. The findings reveal that substantial virtual interactions weighed on a number of the phases involved within the decision process; largely the first three stages and the final stage of the process through the retrieval, supply, and discussion of information. This study accentuates the development in decision-making as the profusion of information online contributes to customers' retrieval of choices for needs recognition, information search, alternative evaluation, and encourages supply of experiences in the post purchase stages.

Brand Communities and E-WOM

The accessibility of sharing content online has expedited eWOM's wide reception among Millennials and empowered the upswing of online communities and brand-customer relationships (Gruen, Osmonbekov, & Czaplewski, 2006; Taken Smith, 2012; Veloutsou and McAlonan, 2012). Social media interactions have developed into a trialogue of communication between brands and customers, and among customers as online communities are formed through back and forth user exchanges (Hung & Li, 2007; Mangold & Faulds, 2009; Miller, Fabian, & Lin, 2008). This trialogue is further matured as companies cultivate brand communities to enrich brand-customer relationships and offer customers a platform to bond with one another, eliciting a sense of belonging (Robards & Bennett, 2011; Veloustou & Moutinho, 2009). A tribe of followers is consequently founded based on shared behaviours or preferences around a particular brand (Cova & Cova, 2001).

Muniz and O'Guinn (2001) define brand community as, "a specialized, non-geographically bound community, based on a structured set of social relationships among admirers of a brand." (Muniz & O'Guinn, 2001, p.412). Consumers are gathered under one umbrella of brand devotees irrespective of geographic distances.

According to (Schau, Muniz, & Arnould, 2009), brand community can be categorized into four value-creating activities,

1. Social networking, which centres on building and maintaining relationships within the brand community.
2. Impression management, that involves managing a positive brand image both within and past the brand community.
3. Community engagement, which ensures continuous interaction among members and brand.
4. Brand use, whereby the brand regularly shares guidance for greater utilization of the product.

The population of brand communities on social media has granted companies a leverage of brand impressions that can be crafted and communicated across global networks. A triad of interchange between brand-customer and customer-customer has advanced to produce an unrestricted environment for continuous engagement, relationship growth and, in the long run, customer loyalty (Fischer, Bristor, & Gainer, 1996; Luo, Zhang, & Duan, 2013; Muniz & O'Guinn, 2001; Sheth & Parvatiyar, 1995). Amid the instant communication of social media, brand-customer interaction is escalated as more frequent engagement propels satisfaction, trust and commitment among followers (Jang, Olfman, Ko, Koh, &

Kim 2008; Kim, Choi, Qualls, & Han, 2008; Wirtz et al., 2013). Consistent brand-customer interchange further impels brands to reinforce the brand image among consumers, and evidently create an attractive environment that drives purchase intentions (Adjei, Noble, & Noble, 2009; Lipsman, Mudd, Rich, & Bruich, 2012).

Brand-customer interactions via social media are openly displayed for the entire brand community to see. Brands are even more so compelled to heed and preserve positive customer experiences and customer engagement (Dessart, Veloutsou, & Thomas, 2015; Gu and Ye, 2014; Ozuem, Howell & Lancaster, 2016a). According to Gummerus et al. (2012), a study was conducted on customer engagement with a company Facebook profile. The findings of the study showed that members of online brand communities were predominantly drawn to connect with a brand to seek help or express approval. Brands benefit from creating inviting environments that encourage customers to reach out when given the chance.

Fournier and Lee (2009) identify the development of brand societies as competitive business strategies engineered to produce pools of admirers that sustain stronger brands. This band of followers takes on the role of a buffer, whereby every individual openly demonstrates support for his/her community. An interactive community facilitates the strength of brand impressions beyond the place of purchase into a society of individuals that, in turn, act as ambassadors in further extending the brand name (Dobele et al., 2007; McAlexander, Schouten, & Koenig, 2002). Online brand community members are exposed to large-scale global networks that embody diverse demographics, thus enlisting worldwide users under a common union of social integration. Relationships are formed across worldwide customers that have diverse backgrounds, but share a similar devotion, or following towards a particular brand, and who institute a strong community solely based on that devotion (Brown, Broderick, & Lee, 2007; Jones, 1998). A study on the correlation between the presence of online brand communities and consequent customer purchase frequency demonstrated a parallel link of the variables (Wu, Huang, Zhao & Hua, 2015). Wu, Huang, Zhao & Hua (2015) revealed positive outcomes for brands involved in online communities regardless of the degree of online participation by customers.

Reference Groups

The degree of influence customer interactions are capable of exerting on receivers depends on the credibility and expertise of the sender (Gilly, Graham, Wolfinbarger, & Yale, 1998; Sweeney, Soutar, & Mazzarol, 2008). Messages produced by opinion leaders, or reference groups hold higher appeal and exert greater influence on consumer brand judgments (Flynn, Goldsmith, & Eastman, 1996; Senecal & Nantel, 2004). A reference group is defined as, “that group in which the actor aspires to gain or maintain acceptance: hence, a group whose claims are paramount in situations requiring choice.” (Shibutani, 1955, p.563). Shibutani (1955) portrays the modern world as consisting of mass societies that have been segregated into communities of social groups run by different communication systems, ultimately identified as reference groups. Such social groups have today been utilized in the marketing realm as a means of influencing consumers by assigning more than just a functional use for products. Such products are instead assigned a symbolic significance (Ekinci et al., 2011; Englis & Solomon, 1995; Escalas & Bettman, 2005; Levy, 1959). Hogg et al. (2009) comparably highlight the significance the social environment imposes on consumption through consumers’ symbolic interaction with brands that they perceive and interpret to be embraced or rejected within different social groups. The symbolic value a brand is believed to deliver, weighs heavily on consumption behaviour.

Reference groups may be normative in the sense that family members, friends and peers influence one another through direct interactions. They may be comparative when, for example, public figures set benchmarks that individuals aspire to (Carmeli & Schaubroeck, 2007; Childers & Rao, 1992; Kelley, 1952; Li & Su, 2007). Marketers have long used the exploitation of the demographic, psychographic and cultural characteristics of public figures as a tactic of reference groups (McCracken, 1989; Escalas & Bettman, 2003; Amaldoss & Jain, 2008; Choi & Rifon, 2012; Seno & Lukas, 2007; Ozuem & Tan, 2014). The aspirations of consumers to achieve the perfect self and to belong within a specific social group further drive their idolization of celebrity figures (Amos, Holmes, & Strutton, 2008; Atkin & Block, 1983; Choi & Rifon, 2012). Association with such figures brings them one step closer to achieving their lifestyle objectives. A study conducted on the impact of celebrities using social media to endorse a brand found that the greater the following a celebrity had, the bigger the resulting product exposure and buying intention towards that brand (Jin & Phua, 2014). Social media users are drawn to, and follow brands that reflect the people those users strive to be and emulate through overt consumption of brands. Customers become more committed to virtual communities that not only assist in product research, but more importantly they become attached to communities that enhance their social needs (Dholakia, Bagozzi, & Pearo, 2004; Pentina, Prybutok, & Zhang, 2008).

Within the presence of brand communities, the consumption of brands surpasses their functional use. Brand acquisition becomes symbolic as social gratification is experienced and emotional fulfilment is achieved from the brand (Cova, 1997). Self identification, group identification and involvement in a brand community add to the emotional attachment customers foster for brands. The more emotional feelings are elicited, the greater the prospect that customers will maintain a relationship with the brand (Hwang & Kandampully, 2012). Social media further intensifies customer immersion as the brand assumes a customer-centric approach to generating value within a community built on the principal notion of active engagement with customers (Huy & Shipilov, 2012; Sashi, 2012).

SOCIAL IDENTITY THEORY AND SOCIAL MEDIA

Social media has granted individuals a large platform in relaying identities (Bagozzi & Dholakia, 2002; Bargh & McKenna, 2004; Dholakia, Bagozzi, & Pearo, 2004; Hogg & Reid, 2006; Pentina, Prybutok, & Zhang, 2008; Hennig-Thurau, Gwinner, Walsh & Gremler, 2004; Kane, Alavi, Labianca, & Borgatti, 2014; Schivinski & Dabrowski, 2016; Veletsianos, 2013). By route of social media and subsequent online brand communities, current and aspirational customers are emboldened in voicing affiliation with a brand and consequently augmenting self-presentation. Consumers seek to rely on brands, among the public network of social networking sites, to enhance the self. Customer engagement is consequently heightened and relationships are formed within brand communities as such interchanges promise customers the symbolic benefit of social placement (Algesheimer, Dholakia, & Herrmann, 2005; Ma & Agarwal, 2007; Ren et al., 2012; Zhu & Chen, 2015). Individuals are more compelled to express affiliation with a brand that empowers them to climb the ladder of social enhancement.

Social identification of the self is comprised of two identities, personal and social. Personal identity refers to an identification of personal characteristics; whereas social identity considers a collective identification of the group that the individual belongs to (Luhtanen & Crocker, 1992; Nowak, Szamrej,

& Latané, 1990; Onorato & Turner, 2004). Individuals seek to enhance both identities by embracing behaviour that accentuates their individuality; however, individualism that is socially commended. Customers pursue brands that convey personal attributes, while maintaining societal compliance over a public scale. Drawing on Onorato and Turner's (2004) study to investigate the weight individuals place on either identity, their findings revealed that greater importance is placed on social identity, since personal identity has more of a context-driven, variable nature. Individuals altered their behaviours according to societal standards, especially within circumstances involving high salience. Conspicuous situations influenced individuals to assert behaviour that complied with the salient identity.

Social media is a prime example of a public setting that may exert such social influence. The consolidated global network of users, under a common platform of user-generated content, encourages individuals to express any personal opinion or preference. However, personal identity is shared under the premise that it parallels the salient identity held by the public (Clement & Krueger, 2002; Haslem, Oakes, Reynolds, & Turner, 1999; Hogg & Turner, 1987; Kietzmann, Hermkens, McCarthy, & Silvestre, 2011). Individuals adopt social media as a platform to enforce social inclusion by expressing identical behaviour among the desired social group.

Turner, Oakes, Haslem, & McGarty (1994) describe social identity theory as, "self-categories that define the individual in terms of his or her shared similarities with members of certain social categories in contrast to other social categories." (Turner, Oakes, Haslem, & McGarty, 1994, p.454). Social categories are used as a means of social classification or identification. Individuals form definitions of themselves based on the characteristics of the groups they follow (Hogg & Abrams, 1988; Hogg, Terry, & White, 1995). The self-definition formed by an individual arises from the social categories he/she pursues. Individuals identify themselves with groups of similar social categories that grant them a sense of social consensus from being affiliated with that group (Jenkins, 2008; Tajfel & Turner, 1985; Trepte, 2008). Such social consensus ensures a sense of belonging, and reinforces self-identity. Individuals chase social identification within groups to establish prominent inclusion that is socially recognized (Ashforth & Mael, 1989; Hogg & Terry, 2000). Social identification foments value among individuals as affiliation with the desired group stimulates public perception, and inflates an individual's identity.

Bearden and Etzel (1982) demonstrated a connection between social influence and subsequent consumption behaviour in a study that explored influences between public-private consumption and luxury-necessity dimensions. The findings revealed a significant influence of social reference on the public consumption of luxury products. Motivation for consuming certain products may be elicited through functional values; however noneconomic values are also drawn from investing in the purchases of a particular brand (Arnett, German, & Hunt, 2003; Kleine, Kleine, & Kernan, 1993; Laverie, Kleine III, & Kleine, 2002). Brands are built on foundations of an image and personality that is communicated to the public through brand equity (Aaker, 1996; Keller, 2012). The image of a brand is associated with the brand community it has manifested, and with particular consumers that fit into particular social collectives. Customers seeking to identify with certain groups or consequent statuses may resort to brands and brand communities to advance personal image based on brand equity (Argo, Dahl, & Manchanda, 2005; Gurau, 2012; O'Cass & McEwen, 2004; Bearden & Etzel, 1982). For instance, individuals may adopt pronounced fashion or luxury brands in depicting a level of wealth and establishing identification with a certain socio-economic status.

The desire to establish social consensus among a particular social group drives individuals to exploit brand association across a public platform, like social media. Online brand communities retain a vital presence for consumer assertion of affiliation. Interestingly, brand-customer connections are strengthened as consumers publicly identify with brands in pursuit of building a self-identity based on what that brand represents (Bhattacharya & Sen, 2003; Escalas & Bettman, 2005). Customers form distinct relations with brands through their personal pursuit of gaining the desired social identity.

SOCIAL MEDIA PLATFORMS

Social media constitutes of various Internet-based services enabling audiences to partake in user-generated online interactions; such services range from blogs, wikis, and social networking sites, among others (Campbell, Pitt, Parent & Berthon, 2011, Dewing, 2010; Weinberg & Pehlivan, 2011). Social networking sites especially gained prominence amid recent generations, particularly empowering consumers' open exchange within a formerly restricted market (Bernoff & Li, 2008; Bolton et al., 2013; Dutta, 2010; Hansen, Dunne, & Shneiderman, 2010). The likes of Facebook, Twitter, Instagram, Snapchat as well as blogs have assumed a platform role that has permitted the free-flow of user-generated information among consumers, but also the interchange between companies and customers. While Facebook and Twitter have amassed pronounced success, this study will focus on the surge visual social networking sites such as Instagram, Snapchat and lifestyle blogs have gained in the fashion industry.

Instagram

Social networking sites have created and accelerated dynamic communication settings in which users interchange globally within seconds. This has compelled marketers to adapt accordingly via the utilization of such platforms to promote corresponding brands. One noteworthy social networking site, Instagram, has ensured its mark in generating significant influence, and it has caught the attention of marketers worldwide (Holmes, 2015; Miles, 2014; Kerpen, 2015; Richards, 2015; Macarthy, 2013). Instagram began in 2012 as an easy, direct photo-sharing application, later expanded into a website, allowing universal users to connect through pictures. Almost overnight, Facebook had acquired the application, and Instagram boasted the adoption of over six million users within a six-month period (Holmes, 2015; Miles, 2014). Its simple purpose and layout demonstrated vast success as the mere sharing of photos birthed a fascination for communicating with appealing visuals that ultimately spoke louder than words.

As the name indicates, Instagram revolves around the notion of capturing an 'instant', and sharing it. Unlike Facebook or Twitter, the central theme employs visuals rather than words, aside from the caption or *hashtag*[1], which is part of the post. In addition, through the use of a *hashtag*, the image is shared beyond a constricted line-up of followers (Miles, 2014). The publicity one shared post is capable of accumulating within moments not only underlines the clout the social networking site carries, but also highlights the speed of communication the world has embraced. Marketers have thus assumed their place in such platforms to remain relevant among customers (Kerpen, 2015; Richards, 2015; Macarthy, 2013). Considering the immediacy of Instagram, brands from consequent dynamic industries have found their presence within this progressive portal an effective match in relaying fleeting messages. A study on the influence marketers may expect through Instagram demonstrated the significance a brand successfully exerts on consumers upon employing an active Instagram account with many followers (Veriman, Cauberghe & Hudders, 2017).

Snapchat

One prominent fast-growing social network is Snapchat. Similar to Instagram, Snapchat primarily employs the use of visuals. Founded in 2011, the social networking site was built on the notion of communication via ephemeral photos and videos that last between a timeframe of a few seconds to 24 hours after being posted, to engage its' users in real-time interaction (Snap Inc., 2018). As of the fourth quarter of 2017, Snapchat was reported to have over 185 million active users worldwide on a daily basis, predominantly between the millennial ages of 18 and 24 years old (Statista, 2018). While the social media company is relatively novel to marketers in most industries, the fashion and lifestyle industry holds a leading presence on Snapchat as of late 2017 (Statista, 2018). In a study on the impact of brand presence via Snapchat on college students, Sashittal, DeMar & Jassawalla (2016) produced a figure highlighting the relationship between a brand's use of Snapchat and subsequent brand perception among college students. The results demonstrated greater familiarity linked with brands on Snapchat that ultimately led to intimate brand-customer relationships and emotional association. The higher the brand was placed on an intimacy axis (proportional to its' presence on Snapchat), the more superior that brand's social status was perceived to be (Sashittal, DeMar & Jassawalla, 2016). Another exploratory analysis of brand use of Snapchat demonstrated immense potential for marketers to reach millennials through the spontaneous nature of storytelling and posts on Snapchat (Gomen, Alvarado, Bernabe & Melendez, 2017). As Snapchat is in the midst of being deciphered by marketers, this study indicates significant prospective brand resonance among users if Snapchat is coherently utilised within a brand's marketing communication practice.

An industry that has especially revelled in the use of Instagram and on a successive path in Snapchat is the fashion industry. The nature of immediate and relatively momentary crazes that swarm social networking sites before receding behind the next craze is proportional to the unceasing evolvement the fashion industry is known for. Fashion brand marketers are able to apply this instant marketing tool as a means of promoting ever-changing fashion trends while receiving immediate feedback (Gomen, Alvarado, Bernabe & Melendez, 2017; Kim & Ko, 2012; Sashittal, DeMar & Jassawalla, 2016; Wolny & Mueller, 2013). A brand profits from painting the exact image it wishes to depict on a more intimate level with customers. Instagram and Snapchat serve as channels for brands to interact with, amid key prevailing moments in pop culture to remain relevant among the consuming masses.

Blogs

Apart from operating their own social networking sites and using reference groups, brands have taken the approach of liaising with bloggers to further influence customers (Colliander & Dahlen, 2011). Weblogs or blogs began as dated virtual writing tools for personal use before expanding into globally influential social networking sites run by bloggers of various demographic and geographic backgrounds. Blogs are outlets for any potential bloggers to document life activities, share opinions and feelings and also create relationships with readers in a community (Hsu & Lin, 2008; Kumar, Novak, & Tomkins, 2004; Nardi, Schiano, Gumbrecht, & Swartz, 2004; McKenna & Pole, 2008; Singh, Veron-Jackson, & Cullinane, 2008). This further shapes social identity as readers shadow such blogs as part of an attempt to obtain belonging within a group or community (Dholakia, Bagozzi, & Pearo, 2004; Farrell & Drezner, 2008).

The blog environment of free flowing information within a friendly setting has uniquely captured the attention of marketers to further promote brands as the open nature of blogs, similar to other social media platforms, has minimized the power a brand has over its own reputation (Simmons, 2008). Devoted followers are indirectly fed brand promotions via third parties they occasionally refer to for general advice.

The additional buzz of a brand generated through supplementary websites such as bloggers boosts visibility and allows for further perceptions of brands through eWOM (Weinberg, 2009; Huang, Shen, Lin, & Chang, 2007). Evidently, as users more frequently visit blogs for reference, bloggers gain prominence among users (Colliander & Dahlen, 2011; Rettberg, 2008). Para-social interaction involves the fantasy of having a relationship with a media personality (Horton & Wohl, 1956). While the theory of para-social interaction initially originated from media personalities seen on television or heard on the radio, the following para-social relationship a viewer establishes on television can be paralleled to the relationship a computer-mediated user forms with a brand spokesperson or blogger on social media. Repeated encounters drive customers to develop a strong bond of trust and association with media figures (Ballantine & Martin, 2005; Hoerner, 1999). According to Escalas & Bettman (2017) in a study on consumers' use of celebrities to find belonging, consumers expressed belonging by affiliating to particular brands endorsed by celebrities they established a one-sided (para-social) relationship with. Another study administered on the degree of influence an online personality inflicts on readers indicated that eWOM is received with more credibility and effectiveness when delivered by a particular brand or website representative (Thorson & Rodgers, 2006). Bloggers develop into instrumental reference groups as the pin-up example of trending actions. As consumers develop social identification in which people identify themselves with social groups, consumer behaviour is assessed by brands and reference groups that allow for ideal placement of personal social identity according to model group norms (Langner, Hennigs, & Wiedmann, 2013; Liu & Hu, 2012; Van Knippenberg et al., 2004).

SOCIAL MEDIA ADDED VALUE ON BRANDS

Brand salience is considerably elevated through social media, as one mention of a brand is expected to travel across a global network of receivers. Brand communities accordingly flourish to accommodate wider customer engagement and commitment that progressively fosters into brand loyalty (Chaudhuri & Holbrook, 2001; Chauhun & Pillai, 2013). Companies advancing into a customer-centric environment of users stimulating substantial content require an adjustment of brand promotion that accentuates brand-customer interchange. Considering the paramount importance of brand and customer interactions on social media, managing customers has become an increasingly crucial asset, which is managed comparably to other company assets (Blattberg, Getz, & Thomas, 2001; Da Silva & Alwi, 2008; Hollebeek, Glynn, & Brodie, 2014; Malthouse et al., 2013; Sashi, 2012). The widespread interchange facilitated through social media develops brand perceptions and brand equity that is communicated to all customers alike across prevalent platforms (Keller, 2009; Naylor, Lamberton, & West, 2012). Worldwide users receive the same brand messages that ensure identical brand presentation across all audiences.

Brand equity represents the incremental value that a brand name adds to the product (Feldwick, 1996; Park & Srinivasan, 1994; Rangaswamy, Burke, & Oliva, 1993). Keller (1993) further elaborates on this explanation in noting that "a brand is said to have positive (negative) customer-based brand equity if consumers react more (less) favourably to the product, price, promotion, or distribution of the brand than they do to the same marketing mix element when it is attributed to a fictitiously named or unnamed version of the product or service." (Keller, 1993, p.8). A brand has succeeded in establishing strong brand equity once it exerts a profound impact on a customer that a similar marketing mix approach under a different brand name did not have.

Keller (2001) describes four building blocks that make up customer-based brand equity. These blocks are achieved in sequence and begin with *brand identity*, established through creating *brand salience. Brand salience* is described as the brand awareness customers have, and the degree to which they are able to identify a brand. The second block is *brand meaning,* which involves the perspective image customers have towards a brand or brand image. *Brand meaning* includes *brand performance;* the functional aspect of the product belonging to the brand, and *brand imagery* focuses on more of a symbolic approach to how the customer is fulfilled mentally, emotionally or socially. This may include aspects that consider the demographic and psychographic characteristics of a typical customer, the channel through which the brand is sold, the history and personality of the brand and the overall the manner in which the brand is portrayed to customers.

The third block is *brand responses* that refer to *judgments,* in terms of quality or advantage a brand holds, and *feelings,* in terms of the favourability felt from consuming or being associated with the brand. The fourth and final block is *brand relationships*, which considers *brand resonance* and the degree of commitment, loyalty, or engagement a customer may build with a brand (Keller, 2001). The relationship a customer establishes with a brand involves a series of steps from the point at which a customer primarily becomes aware of a brand to when he/she benefits from it functionally or symbolically, and creates a perception of it. It also extends to the moment at which the customer forms feelings towards a brand, and interacts with it well enough to form a connection.

Aaker (1996) identified a similar method to determine brand equity called The Brand Equity Ten. This proposes four classifications to denote how the customer perceives a brand, and a fifth classification, which measures market behaviour. The first category is labelled *loyalty* and comprises of how much a customer is willing to pay for a brand and consequently how fulfilling the experience of consuming the brand was for the customer. The second category, *perceived quality/leadership*, involves what the customer believes will be achieved in terms of functionality and, more importantly, recognition from investing in the brand. The third set is called *association/differentiation*, which involves key factors that distinguish the brand from other brands within the same industry. The next set considers *value,* and this is mainly centred on notions of what the brand physically offers in return for the price paid. This category also considers *brand personality* and how the customer deems the brand by defining the typical customer. Finally, this measure comprises of *organizational association* that focuses on the credibility and reliability of the company. Lastly the *awareness* set reflects on the extent to which a brand is recognized, remembered and truly considered in the market (Aaker, 1996). This brand equity measurement attempts to pinpoint how a customer primarily assesses a brand, according to different categories, before proceeding to consumption.

After the initial awareness stage of a brand, a perception of the potential advantages of using that brand is drawn from the brand image, before an acquisition is made following customer recognition and evaluations of producing brand equity (Aaker, 1991; Biel, 1993; Kirmani & Zeithaml, 2013; Bong Na, Marshall, & Keller, 1999; Ozuem, Howell & Lancaster, 2016b). Lemon et al. (2001) consider customer equity to be at the heart of any effective business strategy that ensures long-term success. Customer equity is driven by value, brand and relationship equity. Value equity comprises of the price, quality, and convenience of consuming a brand. It also refers generally to how a customer evaluates a brand depending on the perception of what is forgone in exchange for the value of the brand. Brand equity is believed to entice, serve as a reminder of the brand, as well as construct customer attitudes towards the brand. Finally, relationship equity ascertains the emotional bond and the prospect that a customer returns to the brand. Relationship equity may be strengthened by how the brand has promised to enhance social identity through consumption (Lemon et al., 2001). The foundation of brand equity is considered through the potential social media exhibits in generating brand awareness. Moreover, whether by conceptualizing the brand through an ideal customer or considering the possible personality that brand personifies (Hoeffler & Keller, 2002; Brakus et al., 2009; Valette-Florence et al., 2011), the brand image that is drawn from a customer's outlook is the chief reflection that embodies brand perceptions in this study.

Social media retains a reach that extends beyond brand communities to touch on prospective customers. The potential of online platforms drives companies to follow suit in the adoption of social media as a vital portal to communicating brand messages (Tiago & Verissimo, 2014). The widespread chatter social media is capable of steering induces awareness and enriches brand knowledge among potential customers (Barwise & Meehan, 2010; Hoffman & Fodor, 2010; Weinberg & Pehlivan, 2011). Wider brand recognition through exposure triggers reassurance among customers as the presumed risk of interacting with, and purchasing from the brand is reduced (Huang, Schrank, & Dubinsky, 2004). Brand awareness assumes the role of a foundation and paves the way to the development of brand equity. Thus, a brand lacking in awareness is subsequently bereft of equity, as it holds no value among consumers (Hakela, Svensson, & Vincze, 2012; Kumar & Mirchandani, 2012). Exposing a brand through multiple platforms, amid the interactive global interchange of social media, manifests brand awareness that underpins the development of a brand's equity. Once a brand has attained initial attention, the ensuing step comprises of delivering an identifiable brand image that an audience can grasp, relate to, and retain for later use. Park et al. (1986) identified three stages in managing a brand image commencing with the *introduction stage,* during which a brand establishes its image and positioning in the market. This allows it to distinctly communicate itself to customers. The second stage, the *elaboration stage,* centres on developing and augmenting the brand image to create value that is superior to, and provides an edge over competitors. Finally, the *fortification stage,* aims to build a consistent image fit to sheltering all subsequent products produced under the following solitary image of a brand. Companies may have succeeded in accentuating brand images through offline outlets; however the advent of presence and communication through social media has pushed brands to evolve brand promotion in accordance with online channels.

Aaker and Joachimsthaler, (2000) describe brand identity as "a set of brand associations that the brand strategist aspires to create or maintain. These associations imply a promise to customers from the organization members." (Aaker & Joachimsthaler, 2000, p.45). Brand identity represents the core that remains consistent to the company and customers throughout a brand's evolvement into new domains such as social media; and hence it acts as the connection between brand and customer (Aaker, 2004; Ghodeswar, 2008). However, the core that forms brand identity consists of exclusive brand associations. The brand image entails a series of associations of a brand carried in the memory of a customer. Brand association begins with brand awareness as certain brand nodes are initially realized and, with repeated exposure, more information is assembled around the brand (Keller, 1993). Based on the following accumulation, customers construct a meaning around the brand.

Social media allows a brand to translucently communicate its own identity through direct communication while offering transparency to its followers via communal interaction, and subsequent customer profiles. It is in the marketers' hands to generate and maintain brand associations that leave a positive impression and distinguish the consequent brand from competitors (Aaker & Keller, 1990; Pitta &

Katsanis, 1995; Andzulis, Panagopoulos, & Rapp, 2012; Bolton et al., 2013; Huang & Sarigollu, 2012; Kaplan & Haenlein, 2011; Vermeulen & Seegers, 2008). Another study has shown that such virtual presence exposes brands to a greater chance of expression and richer brand associations, impacting brand evaluations and purchase intentions (Naylor, Lamberton, & West, 2012). Brand-mapping techniques have been constructed to assist companies in identifying the associations customers hold of the brand (John et al., 2006). Brands may apply such techniques in generally evaluating where it is positioned in customers' minds.

As social media depicts the brand on a larger scale, brands must remain mindful that exposure and engagement stretches beyond committed customers to a wider audience (Kozinets et al., 2010; Singh & Sonnenburg, 2012) thus appropriate brand presentation and association is exceedingly crucial to users that are less familiar with the brand. Organizations have succeeded in leveraging social media as a means of accentuating brand associations, and evidently brand perceptions, through the publicity of spokespeople and celebrity endorsers (Cornwell, Roy, & Steinard, 2001; Cornwell, Weeks, & Roy, 2005). The use of influential reference groups creates brand associations that are retained in customers' minds and are evidently associated with the attainment of social consensus. The greater prominence brand associations are able to exert, the greater chance a brand can expect to have in achieving strong brand equity and a competitive edge (Cheng-Hsui Chen, 2001). Another association of brand image that influences perceptions is brand personality. Brand personality has been defined as, "the set of human characteristics associated with a brand." (Aaker, 1997, p.347). As part of digesting a brand, consumers tend to anthropomorphize brands in an attempt to further relate to the label on a humanly level and to better envision and grasp an identity. This also helps them to evaluate the brand in terms of a status enhancer and social group admission (Maehle, Otner, & Supphellen, 2011; Plummer, 2000; Wee, 2004). As a brand establishes an image with human traits constituting a personality, and as it depicts this through boundless platforms via social media, a global consumer perception is drawn (Parker, 2009) that brands are significantly able to manipulate through the widespread communication of social media. Consumer preference further grows as the brand becomes easily identifiable and distinguished and as the symbolic values the brand personality imbues allows customers to extract it from a market of competitors (Biel, 1993; Freling & Forbes, 2005). The subsequent surge of preference in a particular brand emanates loyalty and induces emotion towards that brand. Brands are continually in pursuit of expanding interactions with consumers, beyond the point of purchase, into grounds of connection and emotional brand-customer bonding (Malar et al., 2011; Whan Park et al., 2010; Gobe, 2010). Fashion brands have assumed increasingly active roles on Instagram through posts that communicate the latest trends, campaigns and collaborations that feed into the ultimate fantasy of the brand. This approach has enticed customers as communication transpires past the product into a deeper and more authentic feature of the people, time and effort devoted to creating the outcome of the brand customers see. Brands have thus produced a more intimate nature in reaching and relating to customers. Emotional branding, as such, takes on an angle of richer interchange that inspires and manifests into a relationship with customers (Thompson, Rindfleisch, & Arsel, 2006; Roberts, 2006). The overall emotion-stimulating brand experience further evokes contentment and loyalty (Brakus, Schmitt, & Zarantonello, 2009; Sung & Kim, 2010). According to a study performed on potential influencers of brand equity, the method in which a brand communicates itself coupled with consumer interference, through their own input and promotion, enhances brand equity (Valette-Florence et al., 2011). Social media is thus applied as a complement to a brand's strategy in building a presence and image among viewers.

MANAGERIAL IMPLICATIONS AND RECOMMENDATIONS

The outcome of this paper is that it offers an insight into a relatively unexplored area of how social media influences brand perceptions in the fashion industry, particularly among Millennials (Colliander & Dahlen, 2011; Gensler et al., 2013; Kim & Ko, 2012; Moore, 2012; Singh & Sonnenburg, 2012; Taken Smith, 2012). The results suggest there is much for the fashion industry to be optimistic about in reaching customers through social media by identifying a relationship between social media and social identity in influencing brand perceptions. Millennials (today's main users of social media) express social identity through brand affiliation on social media, depending on that brand's social status.

Brands benefit from the use of social networking sites such as Instagram or Snapchat as dynamic platforms to maintain relevance in real-time events. The consistent brand presence allows for powerful resonance as the brand asserts its' existence in consumers' social world. Brands supplement awareness and image through marketing efforts produced on social media (Godey et al., 2016). Instagram, for example, can be used to entice customers, develop relationships and to draw them to the website or, more conventionally, to stores. Lifestyle bloggers, for instance, use Snapchat and Instagram stories to document authentic day-to-day associations to fashion brands through fashion weeks, promotional events, or product endorsements that assist both brand and blogger in preserving social status among audiences. The fashion industry would benefit from employing social networking sites in promoting never-ending new collections, seasons, runways, and campaigns that define the fashion businesses. Finally, the findings from this study can be used to initiate future research based on a larger sample.

The conception of social media induced a shift in brand-customer dynamic causing consumers to possess more power (Hanna, Rohm, & Crittenden, 2011; Kaplan & Haenlein, 2010; Ngai, Tao and Moon, 2015; Ozuem, Howell & Lancaster, 2008). Brands have transferred communication to the virtual realm in being active pursuers of customers. This study presents a richer understanding of how social media has developed in the fashion industry. Industries are moving at a quicker pace and the fashion sector has become the frontrunner in generating a rapid turnover of ever-changing trends to feed the relentless demand of consumerism. The findings of this research demonstrate the significance of social media as a marketing tool in remaining relevant within the modern world, as traditional methods can no longer sustain such power. This study contributes to the existing literature on marketing to the technologically savvy generation of Millennials (Kilian, Hennigs and Langner, 2012; Moore, 2012; Taken Smith, 2011). This age has grown with the presence of technology and resorts to social media for regular interaction. Brands may find social media beneficial for communicating with such customers in real-time. However, Millennials use offline channels as well, and view social media as a complement to traditional brand outlets. Companies should be mindful of creating an online presence that is in keeping with a brand identity. Brands should reconsider handling social media as a separate entity. Rather, social media should be integrated as a key aspect of a marketing strategy. The content produced through social networking sites represents the brand DNA aligned to fit the entire personality of the brand. This study highlights the importance of integrating online channels into business operations when employing social media as a marketing tool among Millennial ages.

This research contributes to the literature on the application of social identity theory within virtual platforms (Bagozzi & Dholakia, 2002; Ozuem, Thomas & Lancaster, 2016; Dholakia, Bagozzi, & Pearo, 2004; Hogg & Reid, 2006; Pentina, Prybutok, & Zhang, 2008). This study acknowledges the motivations behind the use of social media by consumers for social benefits. Social media extends beyond providing a common portal between brands and customers. Rather it acts as a platform for the two to further relationships. Continuous interaction manifests into a society of casual triad interchange that facilitates belonging, and establishes the symbolic benefits of brand association. This study demonstrates that individuals enjoy the pursuit of specific brands to express their sense of belonging to a social group or status. Connecting with a brand becomes a vital facet to satisfy the personal needs of inclusion within a society, but additionally, to flaunt that association to others. Social media provides the public podium of expressing affiliation and fulfilling social identity through brand communities. Brands can profit from offering customers such non-economic values.

REFERENCES

Aaker, D. (1991). *Managing Brand Equity: Capitalizing on the Value of a Brand Name*. New York: Free Press.

Aaker, D. (1996). Measuring Brand Equity Across Products and Markets. *California Management Review*, *38*(3), 102–120. doi:10.2307/41165845

Aaker, D. (2004). Leveraging the Corporate Brand. *California Management Review*, *46*(3), 6–18. doi:10.1177/000812560404600301

Aaker, D., & Joachimsthaler, E. (2000). *Brand leadership*. New York: Free Press.

Aaker, D., & Keller, K. (1990). Consumer Evaluations of Brand Extensions. *Journal of Marketing*, *54*(1), 27–41. doi:10.2307/1252171

Aaker, J. (1997). Dimensions of Brand Personality. *JMR, Journal of Marketing Research*, *34*(3), 347. doi:10.2307/3151897

Adjei, M., Noble, S., & Noble, C. (2009). The influence of C2C communications in online brand communities on customer purchase behavior. *Journal of the Academy of Marketing Science*, *38*(5), 634–653. doi:10.100711747-009-0178-5

Alexander, B., & Levine, A. (2008). *Web 2.0 Storytelling Emergence of a New Game*. EDUCAUSE Review.

Algesheimer, R., Dholakia, U., & Herrmann, A. (2005). The Social Influence of Brand Community: Evidence from European Car Clubs. *Journal of Marketing*, *69*(3), 19–34. doi:10.1509/jmkg.69.3.19.66363

Amaldoss, W., & Jain, S. (2008). Research Note —Trading Up: A Strategic Analysis of Reference Group Effects. *Marketing Science*, *27*(5), 932–942. doi:10.1287/mksc.1070.0350

Anderson, E. (1998). Customer Satisfaction and Word of Mouth. *Journal of Service Research*, *1*(1), 5–17. doi:10.1177/109467059800100102

Andzulis, J., Panagopoulos, N., & Rapp, A. (2012). A Review of Social Media and Implications for the Sales Process. *Journal of Personal Selling & Sales Management*, *32*(3), 305–316. doi:10.2753/PSS0885-3134320302

Argo, J., Dahl, D., & Manchanda, R. (2005). The Influence of a Mere Social Presence in a Retail Context. *The Journal of Consumer Research*, *32*(2), 207–212. doi:10.1086/432230

Arndt, J. (1967). Role of Product-Related Conversations in the Diffusion of a New Product. *JMR, Journal of Marketing Research, 4*(3), 291–297. doi:10.1177/002224376700400308

Arnett, D., German, S., & Hunt, S. (2003). The Identity Salience Model of Relationship Marketing Success: The Case of Nonprofit Marketing. *Journal of Marketing, 67*(2), 89–105. doi:10.1509/jmkg.67.2.89.18614

Arora, P. (2014). *The Leisure Commons*. New York: Routledge.

Ashforth, B., & Mael, F. (1989). Social Identity Theory and the Organization. *Academy of Management Review, 14*(1), 20–39. doi:10.5465/amr.1989.4278999

Ashley, C., & Tuten, T. (2015). Creative Strategies in Social Media Marketing: An Exploratory Study of Branded Social Content and Consumer Engagement. *Psychology and Marketing, 32*(1), 15–27. doi:10.1002/mar.20761

Atkin, C., & Block, M. (1983). Effectiveness of Celebrity Endorsers. *Journal of Advertising Research, 23*(1), 57–61.

Bagozzi, R., & Dholakia, U. (2002). Intentional social action in virtual communities. *Journal of Interactive Marketing, 16*(2), 2–21. doi:10.1002/dir.10006

Baker, A., Donthu, N., & Kumar, V. (2016). Investigating How Word-of-Mouth Conversations About Brands Influence Purchase and Retransmission Intentions. *JMR, Journal of Marketing Research, 53*(2), 225–239. doi:10.1509/jmr.14.0099

Bakewell, C., & Mitchell, V. (2003). Generation Y female consumer decision-making styles. *International Journal of Retail & Distribution Management, 31*(2), 95–106. doi:10.1108/09590550310461994

Ballantine, P., & Martin, B. (2005). Forming Parasocial Relationships in Online Communities. *Advances in Consumer Research. Association for Consumer Research (U. S.), 32*, 197–201.

Bargh, J., & McKenna, K. (2004). The Internet and Social Life. *Annual Review of Psychology, 55*(1), 573–590. doi:10.1146/annurev.psych.55.090902.141922 PMID:14744227

Barron, L. (2012). *Social theory in popular culture*. Basingstoke, UK: Palgrave Macmillan.

Barwise, P., & Meehan, S. (2010, December). The One Thing You Must Get Right When Building a Brand. *Harvard Business Review*.

Bearden, W., & Etzel, M. (1982). Reference Group Influence on Product and Brand Purchase Decisions. *The Journal of Consumer Research, 9*(2), 183–194. doi:10.1086/208911

Bennett, S., Maton, K., & Kervin, L. (2008). The 'digital natives' debate: A critical review of the evidence. *British Journal of Educational Technology, 39*(5), 775–786. doi:10.1111/j.1467-8535.2007.00793.x

Bernoff, J., & Li, C. (2008). Harnessing the power of the oh-so-social web. *Sloan Management Review, 49*(3), 36–42.

Berthon, P., Pitt, L., Plangger, K., & Shapiro, D. (2012). Marketing meets Web 2.0, social media, and creative consumers: Implications for international marketing strategy. *Business Horizons, 55*(3), 261–271. doi:10.1016/j.bushor.2012.01.007

Bhattacharya, C., & Sen, S. (2003). Consumer-Company Identification: A Framework for Understanding Consumers' Relationships with Companies. *Journal of Marketing*, *67*(2), 76–88. doi:10.1509/jmkg.67.2.76.18609

Biel, A. (1993). Converting image into equity in the book. In D. Aaker & A. Biel (Eds.), *Brand equity and advertising: Advertising's role in building strong brands* (1st ed.; pp. 67–82). New York: Psychology Press.

Biyalogorsky, E., Gerstner, E., & Libai, B. (2001). Customer Referral Management: Optimal Reward Programs. *Marketing Science*, *20*(1), 82–95. doi:10.1287/mksc.20.1.82.10195

Blattberg, R., Getz, G., & Thomas, J. (2001). *Customer Equity: Building and Managing Relationships as Valuable Assets*. Boston: Harvard Business School Press.

BOF & McKinsey&Co. (2018). *The State of Fashion 2018*. Retrieved from https://cdn.businessoffashion.com/reports/The_State_of_Fashion_2018_v2.pdf

Bolton, R., Parasuraman, A., Hoefnagels, A., Migchels, N., Kabadayi, S., Gruber, T., ... Solnet, D. (2013). Understanding Generation Y and their use of social media: A review and research agenda. *Journal of Service Management*, *24*(3), 245–267. doi:10.1108/09564231311326987

Bone, P. (1995). Word-of-mouth effects on short-term and long-term product judgments. *Journal of Business Research*, *32*(3), 213–223. doi:10.1016/0148-2963(94)00047-I

Bong Na, W., Marshall, R., & Lane Keller, K. (1999). Measuring brand power: Validating a model for optimizing brand equity. *Journal of Product and Brand Management*, *8*(3), 170–184. doi:10.1108/10610429910272439

Boyd, D., & Ellison, N. (2008). Social network sites: Definition, history, and scholarship. *Journal of Computer-Mediated Communication*, *13*(1), 211.

Brakus, J., Schmitt, B., & Zarantonello, L. (2009). Brand Experience: What Is It? How Is It Measured? Does It Affect Loyalty? *Journal of Marketing*, *73*(3), 52–68. doi:10.1509/jmkg.73.3.52

Brown, J., Broderick, A., & Lee, N. (2007). Word of mouth communication within online communities: Conceptualizing the online social network. *Journal of Interactive Marketing*, *21*(3), 2–20. doi:10.1002/dir.20082

Burke, P. (2006). *Contemporary social psychological theories*. Stanford, CA: Stanford Social Sciences.

Buttle, F. (1998). Word of mouth: Understanding and managing referral marketing. *Journal of Strategic Marketing*, *6*(3), 241–254. doi:10.1080/096525498346658

Campbell, C., Pitt, L., Parent, M., & Berthon, P. (2011). Understanding Consumer Conversations Around Ads in a Web 2.0 World. *Journal of Advertising*, *40*(1), 87–102. doi:10.2753/JOA0091-3367400106

Carlson, B., Suter, T., & Brown, T. (2008). Social versus psychological brand community: The role of psychological sense of brand community. *Journal of Business Research*, *61*(4), 284–291. doi:10.1016/j.jbusres.2007.06.022

Carmeli, A., & Schaubroeck, J. (2007). The influence of leaders' and other referents' normative expectations on individual involvement in creative work. *The Leadership Quarterly*, *18*(1), 35–48. doi:10.1016/j.leaqua.2006.11.001

Chakravarti, A., & Janiszewski, C. (2003). The Influence of Macro-Level Motives on Consideration Set Composition in Novel Purchase Situations. *The Journal of Consumer Research*, *30*(2), 244–258. doi:10.1086/376803

Chaudhuri, A., & Holbrook, M. (2001). The Chain of Effects from Brand Trust and Brand Affect to Brand Performance: The Role of Brand Loyalty. *Journal of Marketing*, *65*(2), 81–93. doi:10.1509/jmkg.65.2.81.18255

Chauhan, K., & Pillai, A. (2013). Role of content strategy in social media brand communities: A case of higher education institutes in India. *Journal of Product and Brand Management*, *22*(1), 40–51. doi:10.1108/10610421311298687

Cheng-Hsui Chen, A. (2001). Using free association to examine the relationship between the characteristics of brand associations and brand equity. *Journal of Product and Brand Management*, *10*(7), 439–451. doi:10.1108/10610420110410559

Cheung, C., & Thadani, D. (2012). The impact of electronic word-of-mouth communication: A literature analysis and integrative model. *Decision Support Systems*, *54*(1), 461–470. doi:10.1016/j.dss.2012.06.008

Chevalier, J., & Mayzlin, D. (2006). The Effect of Word of Mouth on Sales: Online Book Reviews. *JMR, Journal of Marketing Research*, *43*(3), 345–354. doi:10.1509/jmkr.43.3.345

Childers, T., & Rao, A. (1992). The Influence of Familial and Peer-Based Reference Groups on Consumer Decisions. *The Journal of Consumer Research*, *19*(2), 198–211. doi:10.1086/209296

Chiu, C., Hsu, M., & Wang, E. (2006). Understanding knowledge sharing in virtual communities: An integration of social capital and social cognitive theories. *Decision Support Systems*, *42*(3), 1872–1888. doi:10.1016/j.dss.2006.04.001

Choi, S., & Rifon, N. (2012). It Is a Match: The Impact of Congruence between Celebrity Image and Consumer Ideal Self on Endorsement Effectiveness. *Psychology and Marketing*, *29*(9), 639–650. doi:10.1002/mar.20550

Chu, S., & Kim, Y. (2011). Determinants of consumer engagement in electronic word-of-mouth (eWOM) in social networking sites. *International Journal of Advertising*, *30*(1), 47–75. doi:10.2501/IJA-30-1-047-075

Clement, R., & Krueger, J. (2002). Social Categorization Moderates Social Projection. *Journal of Experimental Social Psychology*, *38*(3), 219–231. doi:10.1006/jesp.2001.1503

Colliander, J., & Dahlén, M. (2011). Following the Fashionable Friend: The Power of Social Media. *Journal of Advertising Research*, *51*(1), 313–320. doi:10.2501/JAR-51-1-313-320

Collin, P., Rahilly, K., Richardson, I., & Third, A. (2011). *The Benefits of Social Networking Services. Research Report*. Melbourne: Cooperative Research Centre for Young People.

Cornwell, T., Roy, D., & Steinard, E. II. (2001). Exploring Managers' Perceptions of the Impact of Sponsorship on Brand Equity. *Journal of Advertising*, *30*(2), 41–51. doi:10.1080/00913367.2001.10673636

Cornwell, T., Weeks, C., & Roy, D. (2005). Sponsorship-linked Marketing: Opening the Black Box. *Journal of Advertising*, *34*(2), 21–42. doi:10.1080/00913367.2005.10639194

Cova, B. (1997). Community and consumption. *European Journal of Marketing*, *31*(3/4), 297–316. doi:10.1108/03090569710162380

Cova, B., & Cova, V. (2001). Tribal aspects of postmodern consumption research: The case of French in-line roller skaters. *Journal of Consumer Behaviour*, *1*(1), 67–76. doi:10.1002/cb.54

Da Silva, R., & Alwi, S. (2008). Online brand attributes and online corporate brand images. *European Journal of Marketing*, *42*(9/10), 1039–1058. doi:10.1108/03090560810891136

de Valck, K., van Bruggen, G., & Wierenga, B. (2009). Virtual communities: A marketing perspective. *Decision Support Systems*, *47*(3), 185–203. doi:10.1016/j.dss.2009.02.008

De Veirman, M., Cauberghe, V., & Hudders, L. (2017). Marketing through Instagram influencers: The impact of number of followers and product divergence on brand attitude. *International Journal of Advertising*, *36*(5), 798–828. doi:10.1080/02650487.2017.1348035

Dellarocas, C. (2006). Strategic Manipulation of Internet Opinion Forums: Implications for Consumers and Firms. *Management Science*, *52*(10), 1577–1593. doi:10.1287/mnsc.1060.0567

Deloitte. (2016). *Global Fashion & Luxury Market. Private Equity and Investors Survey 2016*. Author.

Dessart, L., Veloutsou, C., & Thomas, A. (2015). Consumer engagement in online brand communities: A social media perspective. *Journal of Product and Brand Management*, *24*(1), 28–42. doi:10.1108/JPBM-06-2014-0635

Dewing, M. (2010). *Social Media: An Introduction*. Ottawa: Library of Parliament.

Dhar, V., & Chang, E. (2009). Does Chatter Matter? The Impact of User-Generated Content on Music Sales. *Journal of Interactive Marketing*, *23*(4), 300–307. doi:10.1016/j.intmar.2009.07.004

Dholakia, U., Bagozzi, R., & Pearo, L. (2004). A social influence model of consumer participation in network- and small-group-based virtual communities. *International Journal of Research in Marketing*, *21*(3), 241–263. doi:10.1016/j.ijresmar.2003.12.004

Dobele, A., Lindgreen, A., Beverland, M., Vanhamme, J., & van Wijk, R. (2007). Why pass on viral messages? Because they connect emotionally. *Business Horizons*, *50*(4), 291–304. doi:10.1016/j.bushor.2007.01.004

Duggan, M., Ellison, N., Lampe, C., Lenhart, A., & Madden, M. (2015). Demographics of Key Social Networking Platforms. *PewResearch Center*. Retrieved from http://www.pewinternet.org/2015/01/09/demographics-of-key-social-networking-platforms-2/

Dutta, S. (2010, November). What's Your Personal Social Media Strategy? *Harvard Business Review*, 1–5. PMID:21049685

Eastman, J., Iyer, R., & Thomas, S. (2013). The Impact of Status Consumption on Shopping Style: An Exploratory Look at the Millennial Generation. *The Marketing Management Journal*, *23*(1), 57–73.

Eastman, J., & Liu, J. (2012). The impact of generational cohorts on status consumption: An exploratory look at generational cohort and demographics on status consumption. *Journal of Consumer Marketing*, *29*(2), 93–102. doi:10.1108/07363761211206348

Economic Times. (2016). *Zara Key Statistics: A detailed report on how Zara is using social media.* Retrieved from http://retail.economictimes.indiatimes.com/social-analytics/Fashion/Zara/494

Edelman, D. (2010). Branding in the digital age: You're spending your money in all the wrong places. *Harvard Business Review*, (88), 62–69.

Ekinci, Y., Sirakaya-Turk, E., & Preciado, S. (2011). Symbolic consumption of tourism destination brands. *Journal of Business Research*, *66*(6), 711–718. doi:10.1016/j.jbusres.2011.09.008

Elliott, R., & Wattanasuwan, K. (1998). Brands as Symbolic Resources for the Construction of Identity. *International Journal of Advertising*, *17*(2), 131–144. doi:10.1080/02650487.1998.11104712

Enders, A., Hungenberg, H., Denker, H., & Mauch, S. (2008). The long tail of social networking. *European Management Journal*, *26*(3), 199–211. doi:10.1016/j.emj.2008.02.002

Engel, C., Bell, R., Meier, R., & Rumpel, J. (2011). Young consumers in the new marketing ecosystem: An analysis of their usage of interactive technologies. *Academy of Marketing Studies Journal*, *15*(2), 23–44.

Englis, B., & Solomon, M. (1995). To Be and Not to Be: Lifestyle Imagery, Reference Groups, and The Clustering of America. *Journal of Advertising*, *24*(1), 13–28. doi:10.1080/00913367.1995.10673465

Escalas, J., & Bettman, J. (2003). You Are What They Eat: The Influence of Reference Groups on Consumers' Connections to Brands. *Journal of Consumer Psychology*, *13*(3), 339–348. doi:10.1207/S15327663JCP1303_14

Escalas, J., & Bettman, J. (2005). Self-Construal, Reference Groups, and Brand Meaning. *The Journal of Consumer Research*, *32*(3), 378–389. doi:10.1086/497549

Escalas, J., & Bettman, J. (2017). Connecting With Celebrities: How Consumers Appropriate Celebrity Meanings for a Sense of Belonging. *Journal of Advertising*, *46*(2), 297–308. doi:10.1080/00913367.2016.1274925

Evans, D. (2012). *Social Media Marketing: An Hour a Day* (2nd ed.). Indianapolis: John Wiley & Sons Publishing, Inc.

Farrell, H., & Drezner, D. (2008). The power and politics of blogs. *Public Choice*, *134*(1-2), 15–30. doi:10.100711127-007-9198-1

Feldwick, P. (1996). Do we really need 'Brand Equity'? *Journal of Brand Management*, *4*(1), 9–28. doi:10.1057/bm.1996.23

Fiore, A., Kim, J., & Lee, H. (2005). Effect of image interactivity technology on consumer responses toward the online retailer. *Journal of Interactive Marketing*, *19*(3), 38–53. doi:10.1002/dir.20042

Fischer, E., Bristor, J., & Gainer, B. (1996). Creating or escaping community? An exploratory study of Internet consumers' behaviors. *Advances in Consumer Research. Association for Consumer Research (U. S.)*, *23*, 178–182.

Fischer, E., & Reuber, A. (2011). Social interaction via new social media: (How) can interactions on Twitter affect effectual thinking and behavior? *Journal of Business Venturing*, *26*(1), 1–18. doi:10.1016/j.jbusvent.2010.09.002

Flynn, L., Goldsmith, R., & Eastman, J. (1996). Opinion Leaders and Opinion Seekers: Two New Measurement Scales. *Journal of the Academy of Marketing Science*, *24*(2), 137–147. doi:10.1177/0092070396242004

Forbes. (2012). *The Future Of Fashion Retailing -- The H&M Approach (Part 3 of 3)*. Retrieved from http://www.forbes.com/sites/gregpetro/2012/11/05/the-future-of-fashion-retailing-the-hm-approach-part-3-of-3/#49f3d33d6dbf

Forbes. (2015). *H&M Has Largest Audience On Social Media, Latest Data From Sprinklr Shows*. Retrieved from http://www.forbes.com/sites/fionabriggs/2015/12/22/hm-has-largest-audience-on-social-media-latest-data-from-sprinklr-shows/#4ce692054ac0

Forbes. (2016). *The World's Most Valuable Brands*. Retrieved from http://www.forbes.com/powerful-brands/list/#tab:rank_header:oneYearValueChange_industry:Retail

Fournier, S., & Lee, L. (2009, April). Getting Brand Communities Right. *Harvard Business Review*, 2–8.

Freling, T., & Forbes, L. (2005). An empirical analysis of the brand personality effect. *Journal of Product and Brand Management*, *14*(7), 404–413. doi:10.1108/10610420510633350

Fromm, J., & Garton, C. (2013). *Marketing to Millennials*. Barkley, Inc.

Fuchs, C. (2014). *Social Media: A Critical Introduction*. London: Sage Publications, Ltd.

Gensler, S., Völckner, F., Liu-Thompkins, Y., & Wiertz, C. (2013). Managing Brands in the Social Media Environment. *Journal of Interactive Marketing*, *27*(4), 242–256. doi:10.1016/j.intmar.2013.09.004

Ghodeswar, B. (2008). Building brand identity in competitive markets: A conceptual model. *Journal of Product and Brand Management*, *17*(1), 4–12. doi:10.1108/10610420810856468

Gillies, J., & Cailliau, R. (2000). *How the Web was born*. Oxford, UK: Oxford University Press.

Gilly, M., Graham, J., Wolfinbarger, M., & Yale, L. (1998). A Dyadic Study of Interpersonal Information Search. *Journal of the Academy of Marketing Science*, *26*(2), 83–100. doi:10.1177/0092070398262001

Gobé, M. (2010). *Emotional Branding* (2nd ed.). New York: Allworth Press.

Godes, D., & Mayzlin, D. (2009). Firm-Created Word-of-Mouth Communication: Evidence from a Field Test. *Marketing Science*, *28*(4), 721–739. doi:10.1287/mksc.1080.0444

Godey, B., Manthiou, A., Pederzoli, D., Rokka, J., Aiello, G., Donvito, R., & Singh, R. (2016). Social media marketing efforts of luxury brands: Influence on brand equity and consumer behavior. *Journal of Business Research*, *69*(12), 5833–5841. doi:10.1016/j.jbusres.2016.04.181

Gomez, L., Alvarado, Y., Bernabe, K., & Melendez, L. (2017). Snapchat As An Influential Tool For Marketing Communication: An Exploratory Analysis Of Brands Usage. In *2017 Academy of Marketing Science Annual Conference*. Coronado, CA: 2017 Academy of Marketing Science Annual Conference.

Gruen, T., Osmonbekov, T., & Czaplewski, A. (2006). eWOM: The impact of customer-to-customer online know-how exchange on customer value and loyalty. *Journal of Business Research*, *59*(4), 449–456. doi:10.1016/j.jbusres.2005.10.004

Gu, B., & Ye, Q. (2014). First Step in Social Media: Measuring the Influence of Online Management Responses on Customer Satisfaction. *Production and Operations Management*, *23*(4), 570–582. doi:10.1111/poms.12043

Gummerus, J., Liljander, V., Weman, E., & Pihlström, M. (2012). Customer engagement in a Facebook brand community. *Management Research Review*, *35*(9), 857–877. doi:10.1108/01409171211256578

Gurău, C. (2012). A life-stage analysis of consumer loyalty profile: Comparing Generation X and Millennial consumers. *Journal of Consumer Marketing*, *29*(2), 103–113. doi:10.1108/07363761211206357

Hakala, U., Svensson, J., & Vincze, Z. (2012). Consumer-based brand equity and top-of-mind awareness: A cross-country analysis. *Journal of Product and Brand Management*, *21*(6), 439–451. doi:10.1108/10610421211264928

Hanna, R., Rohm, A., & Crittenden, V. (2011). We're all connected: The power of the social media ecosystem. *Business Horizons*, *54*(3), 265–273. doi:10.1016/j.bushor.2011.01.007

Hansen, D., Dunne, C., & Shneiderman, B. (2010). *Analyzing Social Media Networks with NodeXL*. HCIL University of Maryland.

Haslam, S., Oakes, P., Reynolds, K., & Turner, J. (1999). Social Identity Salience and the Emergence of Stereotype Consensus. *Personality and Social Psychology Bulletin*, *25*(7), 809–818. doi:10.1177/0146167299025007004

Heinonen, K. (2011). Consumer activity in social media: Managerial approaches to consumers' social media behavior. *Journal of Consumer Behaviour*, *10*(6), 356–364. doi:10.1002/cb.376

Hennig-Thurau, T., Gwinner, K., Walsh, G., & Gremler, D. (2004). Electronic word-of-mouth via consumer-opinion platforms: What motivates consumers to articulate themselves on the Internet? *Journal of Interactive Marketing*, *18*(1), 38–52. doi:10.1002/dir.10073

Herr, P., Kardes, F., & Kim, J. (1991). Effects of Word-of-Mouth and Product-Attribute Information on Persuasion: An Accessibility-Diagnosticity Perspective. *The Journal of Consumer Research*, *17*(4), 454–462. doi:10.1086/208570

Hershatter, A., & Epstein, M. (2010). Millennials and the World of Work: An Organization and Management Perspective. *Journal of Business and Psychology*, *25*(2), 211–223. doi:10.100710869-010-9160-y

Hewlet, S., Sherbin, L., & Sumberg, K. (2009, July). How Gen Y & Boomers Will Reshape Your Agenda. *Harvard Business Review*.

Hinz, O., Skiera, B., Barrot, C., & Becker, J. (2011). Seeding Strategies for Viral Marketing: An Empirical Comparison. *Journal of Marketing*, *75*(6), 55–71. doi:10.1509/jm.10.0088

H&M. (2017). *The H&M Group's sales development for the full-year 2017 including the fourth quarter 2017*. Retrieved from https://about.hm.com/en/media/news/financial-reports/2017/12/2765961.html

Hoeffler, S., & Keller, K. (2002). Building Brand Equity Through Corporate Societal Marketing. *Journal of Public Policy & Marketing*, *21*(1), 78–89. doi:10.1509/jppm.21.1.78.17600

Hoerner, J. (1999). Scaling The Web: A Parasocial Interaction Scale for World Wide Web Sites. In D. Schumann & E. Thorson (Eds.), *Advertising and the World Wide Web* (1st ed.; pp. 135–147). Mahwah, NJ: Lawrence Erlbaum Associates.

Hoffman, D., & Fodor, M. (2016). Can you measure the ROI of your social media marketing? *Sloan Management Review*, *52*(1), 41–49.

Hoffman, D., & Novak, T. (1996). Marketing in Hypermedia Computer-Mediated Environments: Conceptual Foundations. *Journal of Marketing*, *60*(3), 50–68. doi:10.2307/1251841

Hogg, M., & Abrams, D. (1988). *Social identifications*. London: Routledge.

Hogg, M., Banister, E., & Stephenson, C. (2009). Mapping symbolic (anti-) consumption. *Journal of Business Research*, *62*(2), 148–159. doi:10.1016/j.jbusres.2008.01.022

Hogg, M., & Reid, S. (2006). Social Identity, Self-Categorization, and the Communication of Group Norms. *Communication Theory*, *16*(1), 7–30. doi:10.1111/j.1468-2885.2006.00003.x

Hogg, M., & Terry, D. (2000). Social Identity and Self-Categorization Processes in Organizational Contexts. *Academy of Management Review*, *25*(1), 121–140. doi:10.5465/amr.2000.2791606

Hogg, M., Terry, D., & White, K. (1995). A Tale of Two Theories: A Critical Comparison of Identity Theory with Social Identity Theory. *Social Psychology Quarterly*, *58*(4), 255–269. doi:10.2307/2787127

Hogg, M., & Turner, J. (1987). Intergroup behaviour, self-stereotyping and the salience of social categories. *British Journal of Social Psychology*, *26*(4), 325–340. doi:10.1111/j.2044-8309.1987.tb00795.x

Hollebeek, L., Glynn, M., & Brodie, R. (2014). Consumer Brand Engagement in Social Media: Conceptualization, Scale Development and Validation. *Journal of Interactive Marketing*, *28*(2), 149–165. doi:10.1016/j.intmar.2013.12.002

Holmes, J. (2015). *Instagram black book*. Lexington, KY: Academic Press.

Horton, D., & Wohl, R. (1956). Mass Communication and Parasocial Interaction: Observations on Intimacy at a Distance. *Psychiatry*, *19*(3), 215–229. doi:10.1080/00332747.1956.11023049 PMID:13359569

Houman Andersen, P. (2001). Relationship development and marketing communication: An integrative model. *Journal of Business and Industrial Marketing*, *16*(3), 167–183. doi:10.1108/08858620110389786

Hsu, C., & Lin, J. (2008). Acceptance of blog usage: The roles of technology acceptance, social influence and knowledge sharing motivation. *Information & Management*, *45*(1), 65–74. doi:10.1016/j.im.2007.11.001

Huang, C., Shen, Y., Lin, H., & Chang, S. (2007). Bloggers' Motivations and Behaviors: A Model. *Journal of Advertising Research*, *47*(4), 472–484. doi:10.2501/S0021849907070493

Huang, R., & Sarigöllü, E. (2012). How brand awareness relates to market outcome, brand equity, and the marketing mix. *Journal of Business Research*, *65*(1), 92–99. doi:10.1016/j.jbusres.2011.02.003

Huang, W., Schrank, H., & Dubinsky, A. (2004). Effect of brand name on consumers' risk perceptions of online shopping. *Journal of Consumer Behaviour*, *4*(1), 40–50. doi:10.1002/cb.156

Hung, K., & Li, S. (2007). The Influence of eWOM on Virtual Consumer Communities: Social Capital, Consumer Learning, and Behavioral Outcomes. *Journal of Advertising Research*, *47*(4), 485–495. doi:10.2501/S002184990707050X

Huy, Q., & Shipilov, A. (2012). The key to social media success within organisations. *Sloan Management Review*, *54*(1), 73–81.

Hwang, J., & Kandampully, J. (2012). The role of emotional aspects in younger consumer-brand relationships. *Journal of Product and Brand Management*, *21*(2), 98–108. doi:10.1108/10610421211215517

Inditex. (2017). *Inditex's net sales climb 10% to €17. 96 billion in the first nine months of fiscal 2017.* Retrieved from https://www.inditex.com/article?articleId=541893&title=Inditex's+net+sales+climb+10%25+to+€17.96+billion

Jang, H., Olfman, L., Ko, I., Koh, J., & Kim, K. (2008). The Influence of On-Line Brand Community Characteristics on Community Commitment and Brand Loyalty. *International Journal of Electronic Commerce*, *12*(3), 57–80. doi:10.2753/JEC1086-4415120304

Jayachandran, S., Gimeno, J., & Varadarajan, P. (1999). The Theory of Multimarket Competition: A Synthesis and Implications for Marketing Strategy. *Journal of Marketing*, *63*(3), 49–66. doi:10.2307/1251775

Jenkins, R. (2008). *Social identity (Key Ideas)* (3rd ed.). London: Routledge.

Jin, S., & Phua, J. (2014). Following Celebrities' Tweets About Brands: The Impact of Twitter-Based Electronic Word-of-Mouth on Consumers' Source Credibility Perception, Buying Intention, and Social Identification With Celebrities. *Journal of Advertising*, *43*(2), 181–195. doi:10.1080/00913367.2013.827606

John, D., Loken, B., Kim, K., & Monga, A. (2006). Brand Concept Maps: A Methodology for Identifying Brand Association Networks. *JMR, Journal of Marketing Research*, *43*(4), 549–563. doi:10.1509/jmkr.43.4.549

Jones, S. (1998). Information, Internet and community: Notes toward an understanding of community in the information age. In S. Jones (Ed.), *Cybersocierty 2.0: Revisiting computer-mediated communication and community* (2nd ed.; pp. 1–34). London: Sage Publications. doi:10.4135/9781452243689.n1

Kaikati, A., & Kaikati, J. (2004). Stealth Marketing: How to Reach Consumers Surreptitiously. *California Management Review*, *46*(4), 6–22. doi:10.2307/41166272

Kane, G., Alavi, M., Labianca, G., & Borgatti, S. (2014). What's Different About Social Media Networks? A Framework and Research Agenda. *Management Information Systems Quarterly*, *38*(1), 274–304. doi:10.25300/MISQ/2014/38.1.13

Kaplan, A., & Haenlein, M. (2010). Users of the world, unite! The challenges and opportunities of Social Media. *Business Horizons*, *53*(1), 59–68. doi:10.1016/j.bushor.2009.09.003

Kaplan, A., & Haenlein, M. (2011). Two hearts in three-quarter time: How to waltz the social media/viral marketing dance. *Business Horizons*, *54*(3), 253–263. doi:10.1016/j.bushor.2011.01.006

Katz, E., & Lazarsfeld, P. (1955). *Personal influence*. Glencoe, IL: Free Press.

Keller, K. (1993). Conceptualizing, Measuring, and Managing Customer-Based Brand Equity. *Journal of Marketing*, *57*(1), 8. doi:10.1177/002224299305700101

Keller, K. (2001). *Building a Customer-Based Brand Equity: A Blueprint for Creating Strong Brands*. Marketing Science Institute.

Keller, K. (2009). Building strong brands in a modern marketing communications environment. *Journal of Marketing Communications*, *15*(2-3), 139–155. doi:10.1080/13527260902757530

Keller, K. (2012). *Strategic brand management* (4th ed.). Upper Saddle River, N.J.: Prentice Hall.

Kelley, H. (1952). Two functions of reference groups. In G. Swanson, T. Newcomb, & E. Hartley (Eds.), *Society for the psychological study of social issues, readings in social psychology* (1st ed.; pp. 410–414). New York: Holt.

Kietzmann, J., Hermkens, K., McCarthy, I., & Silvestre, B. (2011). Social media? Get serious! Understanding the functional building blocks of social media. *Business Horizons*, *54*(3), 241–251. doi:10.1016/j.bushor.2011.01.005

Kilian, T., Hennigs, N., & Langner, S. (2012). Do Millennials read books or blogs? Introducing a media usage typology of the Internet generation. *Journal of Consumer Marketing*, *29*(2), 114–124. doi:10.1108/07363761211206366

Kim, A., & Ko, E. (2012). Do social media marketing activities enhance customer equity? An empirical study of luxury fashion brand. *Journal of Business Research*, *65*(10), 1480–1486. doi:10.1016/j.jbusres.2011.10.014

Kim, J., Choi, J., Qualls, W., & Han, K. (2008). It takes a marketplace community to raise brand commitment: The role of online communities. *Journal of Marketing Management*, *24*(3-4), 409–431. doi:10.1362/026725708X306167

Kirmani, A., & Zeithaml, V. (1993). Advertising, perceived quality, and brand image. In D. Aaker & A. Biel (Eds.), *Brand Equity & Advertising: Advertising's Role in Building Strong Brands* (1st ed.; pp. 143–162). Hilldale, NJ: Lawrence Erlbaum Associates.

Kleine, R. III, Kleine, S., & Kernan, J. (1993). Mundane Consumption and the Self: A Social-Identity Perspective. *Journal of Consumer Psychology*, *2*(3), 209–235. doi:10.1016/S1057-7408(08)80015-0

Kozinets, R. (1999). E-tribalized marketing?: The strategic implications of virtual communities of consumption. *European Management Journal*, *17*(3), 252–264. doi:10.1016/S0263-2373(99)00004-3

Kozinets, R., de Valck, K., Wojnicki, A., & Wilner, S. (2010). Networked Narratives: Understanding Word-of-Mouth Marketing in Online Communities. *Journal of Marketing*, *74*(2), 71–89. doi:10.1509/jmkg.74.2.71

Kumar, R., Novak, J., Raghavan, P., & Tomkins, A. (2004). Structure and evolution of blogspace. *Communications of the ACM*, *47*(12), 35–39. doi:10.1145/1035134.1035162

Kumar, V., & Mirchandani, R. (2012). Increasing the ROI of social media marketing. *Sloan Management Review*, *54*(1), 55–61.

Lam, S., Ahearne, M., Hu, Y., & Schillewaert, N. (2010). Resistance to Brand Switching When a Radically New Brand Is Introduced: A Social Identity Theory Perspective. *Journal of Marketing*, *74*(6), 128–146. doi:10.1509/jmkg.74.6.128

Langner, S., Hennigs, N., & Wiedmann, K. (2013). Social persuasion: Targeting social identities through social influencers. *Journal of Consumer Marketing*, *30*(1), 31–49. doi:10.1108/07363761311290821

Laudon, K., & Traver, C. (2015). *E-commerce*. Boston: Addison Wesley.

Laverie, D., Kleine, R. III, & Kleine, S. (2002). Reexamination and Extension of Kleine, Kleine, and Kernan's Social Identity Model of Mundane Consumption: The Mediating Role of the Appraisal Process. *The Journal of Consumer Research*, *28*(4), 659–669. doi:10.1086/338208

Lemon, K., Rust, R., & Zeithaml, V. (2001). What drives customer equity. *Marketing Management*, *10*(1), 20–25.

Levy, S. (1959). Symbols for Sale. *Harvard Business Review*, (37), 117–124.

Li, J., & Su, C. (2007). How face influences consumption. *International Journal of Market Research*, *49*(2), 237–246. doi:10.1177/147078530704900207

Liang, T., & Huang, J. (1998). An empirical study on consumer acceptance of products in electronic markets: A transaction cost model. *Decision Support Systems*, *24*(1), 29–43. doi:10.1016/S0167-9236(98)00061-X

Lingelbach, D., Patino, A., & Pitta, D. (2012). The emergence of marketing in Millennial new ventures. *Journal of Consumer Marketing*, *29*(2), 136–145. doi:10.1108/07363761211206384

Lipsman, A., Mudd, G., Rich, M., & Bruich, S. (2012). The Power of "Like": How Brands Reach (and Influence) Fans through Social-Media Marketing. *Journal of Advertising Research*, *52*(1), 40–52. doi:10.2501/JAR-52-1-040-052

Liu, X., & Hu, J. (2012). Adolescent Evaluations of Brand Extensions: The Influence of Reference Group. *Psychology and Marketing*, *29*(2), 98–106. doi:10.1002/mar.20507

Luhtanen, R., & Crocker, J. (1992). A Collective Self-Esteem Scale: Self-Evaluation of One's Social Identity. *Personality and Social Psychology Bulletin*, *18*(3), 302–318. doi:10.1177/0146167292183006

Luo, X., Zhang, J., & Duan, W. (2013). Social Media and Firm Equity Value. *Information Systems Research, 24*(1), 146–163. doi:10.1287/isre.1120.0462

Lusch, R. (2007). Marketing's Evolving Identity: Defining Our Future. *Journal of Public Policy & Marketing, 26*(2), 261–268. doi:10.1509/jppm.26.2.261

LVMH. (2016). *Interim Financial Report Six-Month Period Ended June 30, 2016*. Retrieved from https://r.lvmh-static.com/uploads/2016/06/lvmh-2016-first-half-financial-report.pdf

LVMH. (2018). *LVMH 2017 record results*. Retrieved from https://r.lvmh-static.com/uploads/2018/01/lvmhannualresults2017va.pdf

Ma, M., & Agarwal, R. (2007). Through a Glass Darkly: Information Technology Design, Identity Verification, and Knowledge Contribution in Online Communities. *Information Systems Research, 18*(1), 42–67. doi:10.1287/isre.1070.0113

Macarthy, A. (2013). *500 Social Media Marketing Tips: Essential Advice, Hints and Strategy for Business*. Charlotte, NC: CreateSpace Independent Publishing Platform.

Maehle, N., Otnes, C., & Supphellen, M. (2011). Consumers' perceptions of the dimensions of brand personality. *Journal of Consumer Behaviour, 10*(5), 290–303. doi:10.1002/cb.355

Malär, L., Krohmer, H., Hoyer, W., & Nyffenegger, B. (2011). Emotional Brand Attachment and Brand Personality: The Relative Importance of the Actual and the Ideal Self. *Journal of Marketing, 75*(4), 35–52. doi:10.1509/jmkg.75.4.35

Malthouse, E., Haenlein, M., Skiera, B., Wege, E., & Zhang, M. (2013). Managing Customer Relationships in the Social Media Era: Introducing the Social CRM House. *Journal of Interactive Marketing, 27*(4), 270–280. doi:10.1016/j.intmar.2013.09.008

Mangold, W., & Faulds, D. (2009). Social media: The new hybrid element of the promotion mix. *Business Horizons, 52*(4), 357–365. doi:10.1016/j.bushor.2009.03.002

Martin, K., & Smith, N. (2008). Commercializing Social Interaction: The Ethics of Stealth Marketing. *Journal of Public Policy & Marketing, 27*(1), 45–56. doi:10.1509/jppm.27.1.45

Mayzlin, D. (2006). Promotional Chat on the Internet. *Marketing Science, 25*(2), 155–163. doi:10.1287/mksc.1050.0137

McAlexander, J., Schouten, J., & Koenig, H. (2002). Building Brand Community. *Journal of Marketing, 66*(1), 38–54. doi:10.1509/jmkg.66.1.38.18451

McCracken, G. (1989). Who is the Celebrity Endorser? Cultural Foundations of the Endorsement Process. *The Journal of Consumer Research, 16*(3), 310–321. doi:10.1086/209217

McKenna, L., & Pole, A. (2008). What do bloggers do: An average day on an average political blog. *Public Choice, 134*(1-2), 97–108. doi:10.100711127-007-9203-8

Michaelidou, N., Siamagka, N., & Christodoulides, G. (2011). Usage, barriers and measurement of social media marketing: An exploratory investigation of small and medium B2B brands. *Industrial Marketing Management, 40*(7), 1153–1159. doi:10.1016/j.indmarman.2011.09.009

Miles, J. (2014). *Instagram power.* McGraw Hill.

Miller, K., Fabian, F., & Lin, S. (2009). Strategies for online communities. *Strategic Management Journal*, *30*(3), 305–322. doi:10.1002mj.735

Moore, M. (2012). Interactive media usage among millennial consumers. *Journal of Consumer Marketing*, *29*(6), 436–444. doi:10.1108/07363761211259241

Muniz, A. Jr, & O'Guinn, T. (2001). Brand Community. *The Journal of Consumer Research*, *27*(4), 412–432. doi:10.1086/319618

Muniz, A. Jr, & O'Guinn, T. (2016). Brand Community. *The Journal of Consumer Research*, *27*(4), 412–432. doi:10.1086/319618

Nardi, B., Schiano, D., Gumbrecht, M., & Swartz, L. (2004). Why we blog. *Communications of the ACM*, *47*(12), 41–46. doi:10.1145/1035134.1035163

Naylor, R., Lamberton, C., & West, P. (2012). Beyond the "Like" Button: The Impact of Mere Virtual Presence on Brand Evaluations and Purchase Intentions in Social Media Settings. *Journal of Marketing*, *76*(6), 105–120. doi:10.1509/jm.11.0105

Ngai, E., Tao, S., & Moon, K. (2015). Social media research: Theories, constructs, and conceptual frameworks. *International Journal of Information Management*, *35*(1), 33–44. doi:10.1016/j.ijinfomgt.2014.09.004

Nowak, A., Szamrej, J., & Latané, B. (1990). From private attitude to public opinion: A dynamic theory of social impact. *Psychological Review*, *97*(3), 362–376. doi:10.1037/0033-295X.97.3.362

Nowak, L., Thach, L., & Olsen, J. (2006). Wowing the millennials: Creating brand equity in the wine industry. *Journal of Product and Brand Management*, *15*(5), 316–323. doi:10.1108/10610420610685712

O'Cass, A., & McEwen, H. (2004). Exploring consumer status and conspicuous consumption. *Journal of Consumer Behaviour*, *4*(1), 25–39. doi:10.1002/cb.155

O'Reilly, T. (2005). *Web 2.0: Compact Definition?* Retrieved from http://radar.oreilly.com/2005/10/web-20-compact-definition.html

O'Reilly, T., & Battelle, J. (2009). *Web Squared: Web 2.0 Five Years On.* O'Reilly Media, Inc.

Onorato, R., & Turner, J. (2004). Fluidity in the self-concept: The shift from personal to social identity. *European Journal of Social Psychology*, *34*(3), 257–278. doi:10.1002/ejsp.195

Ozuem, W., Borrelli, M., & Lancaster, G. (2017). Leveraging the co-evolution of offline and online video games: An empirical study. *Journal of Strategic Marketing*, *24*(1), 75–97. doi:10.1080/0965254X.2015.1076883

Ozuem, W., Howell, K., & Lancaster, G. (2008). Communicating in the new interactive marketspace. *European Journal of Marketing*, *42*(9/10), 1059–1083. doi:10.1108/03090560810891145

Ozuem, W., Howell, K., & Lancaster, G. (2016a). An exploration of consumers' response to online service recovery initiatives. *International Journal of Market Research*, *59*(1), 97–115.

Ozuem, W., Howell, K., & Lancaster, G. (2016b). Understanding technologically induced customer services in the Nigerian banking sector: The Internet as a post-modern phenomenon. *International Journal of Information Technology and Management*, *15*(3), 272–290. doi:10.1504/IJITM.2016.077349

Ozuem, W., & Tan, K. (2014). Reconciling Social Media with Luxury Fashion Brands: An exploratory study. In L. Aiello (Ed.), *Management of Cultural Products: E-Relationship Marketing and Accessibility Perspective*. Hershey, PA: IGI Publications.

Ozuem, W., Thomas, T., & Lancaster, G. (2016). The Influence of customer loyalty on small island economies: An empirical and exploratory study. *Journal of Strategic Marketing*, *24*(6), 447–469. doi:10.1080/0965254X.2015.1011205

Park, C., Jaworski, B., & Maclnnis, D. (1986). Strategic Brand Concept-Image Management. *Journal of Marketing*, *50*(4), 135–145. doi:10.1177/002224298605000401

Park, C., & Srinivasan, V. (1994). A Survey-Based Method for Measuring and Understanding Brand Equity and Its Extendibility. *JMR, Journal ofMarketing Research*, *31*(2), 271–278. doi:10.2307/3152199

Parker, B. (2009). A comparison of brand personality and brand user-imagery congruence. *Journal of Consumer Marketing*, *26*(3), 175–184. doi:10.1108/07363760910954118

Paulin, M. J., Ferguson, R., Jost, N., & Fallu, J. (2014). Motivating millennials to engage in charitable causes through social media. *Journal of Service Management*, *25*(3), 334–348. doi:10.1108/JOSM-05-2013-0122

Pentina, I., Prybutok, V., & Zhang, X. (2008). The role of virtual communities as shopping reference groups. *Journal of Electronic Commerce Research*, *9*(2), 114–136.

PewResearch. (2014). *Social Media Use by Age Group Over Time*. Retrieved 29 September, from http://www.pewinternet.org/data-trend/social-media/social-media-use-by-age-group/

Pitta, D., & Katsanis, L. (1995). Understanding brand equity for successful brand extension. *Journal of Consumer Marketing*, *12*(4), 51–64. doi:10.1108/07363769510095306

Plummer, J. (2000). How Personality Makes a Difference. *Journal ofAdvertising Research*, *40*(6), 79–83. doi:10.2501/JAR-40-6-79-83

Prensky, M. (2001). Digital Natives, Digital Immigrants Part 1. *On the Horizon*, *9*(5), 1–6. doi:10.1108/10748120110424816

Rainer, T., & Rainer, J. (2011). *The Millennials: Connecting to America's Largest Generation*. Nashville, TN: B & H Pub. Group.

Rangaswamy, A., Burke, R., & Oliva, T. (1993). Brand equity and the extendibility of brand names. *International Journal of Research in Marketing*, *10*(1), 61–75. doi:10.1016/0167-8116(93)90034-V

Ren, Y., Harper, M., Drenner, S., Terveen, L., Kiesler, S., Riedl, J., & Kraut, R. (2012). Building member attachment in online communities: Applying theories of group identity and interpersonal bonds. *Management Information Systems Quarterly*, *36*(3), 841–864. doi:10.2307/41703483

Rettberg, J. (2008). *Blogging: Digital Media and Society Series*. Cambridge, UK: Polity.

Richards, M. (2015). *Social Media: Dominating Strategies for Social Media Marketing*. CreateSpace Independent Publishing Platform.

Riedinger, D. (2015). *Likeable Social Media, Revised and Expanded* (2nd ed.). McGraw-Hill.

Robards, B., & Bennett, A. (2011). MyTribe: Post-subcultural Manifestations of Belonging on Social Network Sites. *Sociology*, *45*(2), 303–317. doi:10.1177/0038038510394025

Roberts, K. (2006). *Lovemarks: The future beyond brands* (2nd ed.). New York: PowerHouse Books.

Roy, A., & Chattopadhyay, S. (2010). Stealth marketing as a strategy. *Business Horizons*, *53*(1), 69–79. doi:10.1016/j.bushor.2009.09.004

Safko, L. (2012). *The social media bible: Tactics, tools, and strategies for business success*. Hoboken, NJ: John Wiley & Sons.

Sashi, C. (2012). Customer engagement, buyer-seller relationships, and social media. *Management Decision*, *50*(2), 253–272. doi:10.1108/00251741211203551

Sashittal, H., DeMar, M., & Jassawalla, A. (2016). Building acquaintance brands via Snapchat for the college student market. *Business Horizons*, *59*(2), 193–204. doi:10.1016/j.bushor.2015.11.004

Schau, H., Muñiz, A. Jr, & Arnould, E. (2009). How Brand Community Practices Create Value. *Journal of Marketing*, *73*(5), 30–51. doi:10.1509/jmkg.73.5.30

Schivinski, B., & Dabrowski, D. (2016). The effect of social media communication on consumer perceptions of brands. *Journal of Marketing Communications*, *22*(2), 189–214. doi:10.1080/13527266.2013.871323

Schlosser, A. (2005). Posting versus Lurking: Communicating in a Multiple Audience Context. *The Journal of Consumer Research*, *32*(2), 260–265. doi:10.1086/432235

Senecal, S., & Nantel, J. (2004). The influence of online product recommendations on consumers' online choices. *Journal of Retailing*, *80*(2), 159–169. doi:10.1016/j.jretai.2004.04.001

Seno, D., & Lukas, B. (2007). Exploring the relationship between celebrity endorser effects and advertising effectiveness. *European Journal of Marketing*, *41*(1/2), 121–134. doi:10.1108/03090560710718148

Sheth, J., & Parvatlyar, A. (1995). Relationship Marketing in Consumer Markets: Antecedents and Consequences. *Journal of the Academy of Marketing Science*, *23*(4), 255–271. doi:10.1177/009207039502300405

Shibutani, T. (1955). Reference Groups as Perspectives. *American Journal of Sociology*, *60*(6), 562–569. doi:10.1086/221630

Simmons, G. (2008). Marketing to postmodern consumers: Introducing the internet chameleon. *European Journal of Marketing*, *42*(3/4), 299–310. doi:10.1108/03090560810852940

Singh, S., & Sonnenburg, S. (2012). Brand Performances in Social Media. *Journal of Interactive Marketing*, *26*(4), 189–197. doi:10.1016/j.intmar.2012.04.001

Singh, T., Veron-Jackson, L., & Cullinane, J. (2008). Blogging: A new play in your marketing game plan. *Business Horizons*, *51*(4), 281–292. doi:10.1016/j.bushor.2008.02.002

Smith, A., & Anderson, M. (2018). *Social Media Use in 2018*. PewResearch Center. Retrieved from http://assets.pewresearch.org/wp-content/uploads/sites/14/2018/03/01105133/PI_2018.03.01_Social-Media_FINAL.pdf

Smith, K. (2011). Digital marketing strategies that Millennials find appealing, motivating, or just annoying. *Journal of Strategic Marketing*, *19*(6), 489–499. doi:10.1080/0965254X.2011.581383

Smith, P., & Zook, Z. (2011). *Marketing Communications* (5th ed.). London: Kogan Page.

Smith, T. (2009). The social media revolution. *International Journal of Market Research*, *51*(4), 559–561. doi:10.2501/S1470785309200773

Snap Inc. (2018). Retrieved from https://www.snap.com/en-US/

Solomon, M. (2012). *Consumer behavior* (10th ed.). Pearson Education Limited.

Statista. (2016a). London Fashion Week: Social Buzz 2014. Social Media & User-Generated Content. *Statista - The Statistic Portal*. Retrieved 18 January 2016, from http://www.statista.com/statistics/315224/social-media-mentions-london-fashion-week/

Statista. (2016b). *Leading luxury brands ranked by number of Instagram followers as of October 2016 (in millions)*. Retrieved 29 September 2016, from https://www.statista.com/statistics/483753/leading-luxury-brands-instagram-followers/

Statista. (2016c). *Daily time spent on social networking by internet users worldwide as of 2nd quarter 2016, by age group (in minutes)*. Retrieved 5 March 2018, from https://www.statista.com/statistics/613456/daily-social-media-usage-worldwide-age/

Statista. (2016d). *Global apparel market size projections from 2012 to 2025, by region (in billion U.S. dollars)*. Retrieved 29 September 2016, from https://www.statista.com/statistics/279757/apparel-market-size-projections-by-region/

Statista. (2016e). *Brand value of the leading 10 apparel brands worldwide in 2016 (in million U.S. dollars)*. Retrieved 29 September 2016, from https://www.statista.com/statistics/267931/brand-value-of-the-leading-10-apparel-brands-worldwide/

Statista. (2016f). *Sales of the H&M Group from 2008 to 2015, by country (in million U.S. dollars)*. Retrieved 29 September 2016, from https://www.statista.com/statistics/252187/sales-of-the-hundm-group-by-country/

Statista. (2016g). *Leading luxury brands ranked by number of Instagram followers as of October 2016 (in millions)*. Retrieved 29 September 2016, from https://www.statista.com/statistics/483753/leading-luxury-brands-instagram-followers/

Statista. (2016h). *Leading high street fashion labels ranked by Instagram user engagement as of May 2016*. Retrieved 6 March 2018, from https://www.statista.com/statistics/677609/high-street-fashion-labels-instagram-engagement/

Statista. (2017a). *Daily time spent on social media by social video viewers worldwide as of 2nd quarter 2017, by age group*. Retrieved 5 March 2018, from https://www.statista.com/statistics/267138/social-media-usage-per-day-global-social-video-users-age/

Statista. (2017b). *Sources used by Millennials to hear about the latest high-end fashion or luxury item trends worldwide in 2017*. Retrieved 5 March 2018, from https://www.statista.com/statistics/441758/sources-for-hearing-about-new-luxury-brands-worldwide/

Statista. (2017c). *Worldwide forecasted sales growth in the fashion industry in 2018, by region*. Retrieved 6 March 2018, from https://www.statista.com/statistics/802943/fashion-industry-sales-growth-worldwide-by-region/

Statista. (2018a). *Most famous social network sites worldwide as of January 2018, ranked by number of active users (in millions)*. Retrieved 6 March 2018, from https://www.statista.com/statistics/272014/global-social-networks-ranked-by-number-of-users/

Statista. (2018b). *Number of daily active Snapchat users from 1st quarter 2017 to 4th quarter 2017 (in millions)*. Retrieved 27 March 2018, from https://www.statista.com/statistics/545967/snapchat-app-dau/

Stephen, A., & Galak, J. (2010). The Complementary Roles of Traditional and Social Media in Driving Marketing Performance. *INSEAD Working Papers Collections*, *2010*(97).

Stern, B. (1994). A Revised Communication Model for Advertising: Multiple Dimensions of the Source, the Message, and the Recipient. *Journal of Advertising*, *23*(2), 5–15. doi:10.1080/00913367.1994.10673438

Stokinger, E., & Ozuem, W. (2015). Social media and customer retention in the luxury fashion sector. In G. Bowen & W. Ozuem (Eds.), *Computer-mediated marketing strategies: social media and online brand communities*. Hershey, PA: IGI. doi:10.4018/978-1-4666-6595-8.ch009

Strauss, W., & Howe, N. (1991). *Generations: The History of America's Future*. New York: Morrow.

Sung, Y., & Kim, J. (2010). Effects of brand personality on brand trust and brand affect. *Psychology and Marketing*, *27*(7), 639–661. doi:10.1002/mar.20349

Susarla, A., Oh, J., & Tan, Y. (2012). Social Networks and the Diffusion of User-Generated Content: Evidence from YouTube. *Information Systems Research*, *23*(1), 23–41. doi:10.1287/isre.1100.0339

Sweeney, J., Soutar, G., & Mazzarol, T. (2008). Factors influencing word of mouth effectiveness: Receiver perspectives. *European Journal of Marketing*, *42*(3/4), 344–364. doi:10.1108/03090560810852977

Tajfel, H., & Turner, J. (1985). The Social Identity Theory of Intergroup Behaviour. In S. Worchel & W. Austen (Eds.), *Psychology of intergroup relations* (2nd ed.; pp. 7–24). Chicago: Nelson-Hall.

Taken Smith, K. (2012). Longitudinal study of digital marketing strategies targeting Millennials. *Journal of Consumer Marketing*, *29*(2), 86–92. doi:10.1108/07363761211206339

Thompson, C., Rindfleisch, A., & Arsel, Z. (2006). Emotional Branding and the Strategic Value of the Doppelgänger Brand Image. *Journal of Marketing*, *70*(1), 50–64. doi:10.1509/jmkg.2006.70.1.50

Thorson, K., & Rodgers, S. (2006). Relationships Between Blogs as EWOM and Interactivity, Perceived Interactivity, and Parasocial Interaction. *Journal of Interactive Advertising*, *6*(2), 5–44. doi:10.1080/15252019.2006.10722117

Tiago, M., & Veríssimo, J. (2014). Digital marketing and social media: Why bother? *Business Horizons*, *57*(6), 703–708. doi:10.1016/j.bushor.2014.07.002

Trepte, S. (2008). Social Identity Theory. In J. Bryant & P. Vorderer (Eds.), *Psychology of Entertainment* (2nd ed.; pp. 255–271). New York: Routledge.

Trusov, M., Bucklin, R., & Pauwels, K. (2009). Effects of Word-of-Mouth Versus Traditional Marketing: Findings from an Internet Social Networking Site. *Journal of Marketing*, *73*(5), 90–102. doi:10.1509/jmkg.73.5.90

Tsai, W., & Ghoshal, S. (1998). Social capital and value creation: The role of intrafirm networks. *Academy of Management Journal*, *41*(4), 464–476.

Tsimonis, G., & Dimitriadis, S. (2014). Brand strategies in social media. *Marketing Intelligence & Planning*, *32*(3), 328–344. doi:10.1108/MIP-04-2013-0056

Turner, J., Oakes, P., Haslam, S., & McGarty, C. (1994). Self and Collective: Cognition and Social Context. *Personality and Social Psychology Bulletin*, *20*(5), 454–463. doi:10.1177/0146167294205002

Tuten, T., & Solomon, M. (2014). *Social Media Marketing* (2nd ed.). Boston: Pearson.

Twenge, J. (2006). *Generation Me: Why today's young Americans are more confident, assertive, entitled--and more miserable than ever before*. New York: Free Press.

Twenge, J., Campbell, W., & Freeman, E. (2012). Generational differences in young adults' life goals, concern for others, and civic orientation, 1966–2009. *Journal of Personality and Social Psychology*, *102*(5), 1045–1062. doi:10.1037/a0027408 PMID:22390226

Valentine, D., & Powers, T. (2013). Generation Y values and lifestyle segments. *Journal of Consumer Marketing*, *30*(7), 597–606. doi:10.1108/JCM-07-2013-0650

Valette-Florence, P., Guizani, H., & Merunka, D. (2011). The impact of brand personality and sales promotions on brand equity. *Journal of Business Research*, *64*(1), 24–28. doi:10.1016/j.jbusres.2009.09.015

Van Dijck, J. (2013). *The culture of connectivity*. Oxford, UK: Oxford University Press. doi:10.1093/acprof:oso/9780199970773.001.0001

van Knippenberg, D., van Knippenberg, B., De Cremer, D., & Hogg, M. (2004). Leadership, self, and identity: A review and research agenda. *The Leadership Quarterly*, *15*(6), 825–856. doi:10.1016/j.leaqua.2004.09.002

Vargo, S., & Lusch, R. (2004). Evolving to a New Dominant Logic for Marketing. *Journal of Marketing*, *68*(1), 1–17. doi:10.1509/jmkg.68.1.1.24036

Veletsianos, G. (2013). Open practices and identity: Evidence from researchers and educators' social media participation. *British Journal of Educational Technology*, *44*(4), 639–651. doi:10.1111/bjet.12052

Veloutsou, C., & Moutinho, L. (2009). Brand relationships through brand reputation and brand tribalism. *Journal of Business Research*, *62*(3), 314–322. doi:10.1016/j.jbusres.2008.05.010

Vermeulen, I., & Seegers, D. (2009). Tried and tested: The impact of online hotel reviews on consumer consideration. *Tourism Management*, *30*(1), 123–127. doi:10.1016/j.tourman.2008.04.008

Vogel, V., Evanschitzky, H., & Ramaseshan, B. (2008). Customer Equity Drivers and Future Sales. *Journal of Marketing*, *72*(6), 98–108. doi:10.1509/jmkg.72.6.98

v. Wangenheim, F., & Bayón, T. (2004). The effect of word of mouth on services switching. *European Journal of Marketing*, *38*(9/10), 1173–1185. doi:10.1108/03090560410548924

Webster, F. (1992). The Changing Role of Marketing in the Corporation. *Journal of Marketing*, *56*(4), 1–17. doi:10.2307/1251983

Wee, T. (2004). Extending human personality to brands: The stability factor. *Journal of Brand Management*, *11*(4), 317–330. doi:10.1057/palgrave.bm.2540176

Weinberg, B., & Pehlivan, E. (2011). Social spending: Managing the social media mix. *Business Horizons*, *54*(3), 275–282. doi:10.1016/j.bushor.2011.01.008

Weinberg, T. (2009). *The New Community Rules: Marketing on the Social Web*. Sebastopol, CA: O'Reilly Media, Inc.

Whan Park, C., MacInnis, D., Priester, J., Eisingerich, A., & Iacobucci, D. (2010). Brand Attachment and Brand Attitude Strength: Conceptual and Empirical Differentiation of Two Critical Brand Equity Drivers. *Journal of Marketing*, *74*(6), 1–17. doi:10.1509/jmkg.74.6.1

Wirtz, J., den Ambtman, A., Bloemer, J., Horváth, C., Ramaseshan, B., van de Klundert, J., ... Kandampully, J. (2013). Managing brands and customer engagement in online brand communities. *Journal of Service Management*, *24*(3), 223–224. doi:10.1108/09564231311326978

Wolny, J., & Mueller, C. (2013). Analysis of fashion consumers' motives to engage in electronic word-of-mouth communication through social media platforms. *Journal of Marketing Management*, *29*(5-6), 562–583. doi:10.1080/0267257X.2013.778324

WSJ. (2016). *H&M Hennes & Mauritz AB Series B*. Retrieved from http://quotes.wsj.com/SE/XSTO/HMB/financials

Wu, J., Huang, L., Zhao, J., & Hua, Z. (2015). The deeper, the better? Effect of online brand community activity on customer purchase frequency. *Information & Management*, *52*(7), 813–823. doi:10.1016/j.im.2015.06.001

You, Y., Vadakkepatt, G., & Joshi, A. (2015). A Meta-Analysis of Electronic Word-of-Mouth Elasticity. *Journal of Marketing*, *79*(2), 1–39. doi:10.1509/jm.14.0169

Zarrella, D. (2009). *The Social Media Marketing Book*. Sebastopol, CA: O'Reilly Media, Inc.

Zhu, Y., & Chen, H. (2015). Social media and human need satisfaction: Implications for social media marketing. *Business Horizons*, *58*(3), 335–345. doi:10.1016/j.bushor.2015.01.006

KEY TERMS AND DEFINITIONS

Brand Associations: Brand associations are the main factors that differentiate one brand from another.

Brand Equity: Brand equity is the value of a brand based on the consumer's perception of that brand in his/her mind.

Brand Perceptions: Brand perceptions are consumers' perceptions of the potential advantages, disadvantages or overall image portrayed from consuming a certain brand.

E-WOM: E-WOM involves the online exchange of information about a product among customers.

Fashion Industry: The fashion industry comprises a global enterprise that involves the production, retail, and consumption of clothing.

Millennial Generation: The millennial generation is a demographic cohort born between the early 1980s and the early 2000s and raised in a technological age where communication has become globally boundless.

Social Identity Theory: Social identity theory considers how individuals may classify themselves or others according to certain social categories.

Social Media: Social media comprises internet-centered platforms that enable and promote a free flow of user-generated information.

ENDNOTE

1 A *hashtag* acts as a form of categorization so that any user searching a topic will be exposed to a considerable volume of images (Miles, 2014).

Chapter 4
Exploring the Relationship Between Social Media and Social Influence

Ali Usman
University of the West of Scotland, UK

Sebastian Okafor
University of Cumbria, UK

ABSTRACT

Online behavioral tailoring has become an integral part of online marketing strategies. Contemporary marketers increasingly seek to create an influential environment on social media to empower online users to participate in online brand communities. By interacting in this way, online communities hosted by brands marketers can enhance the nature of the complex interactions that occur amongst those that participate. Such online interactions lead to three different types of social influence compliance, internalization, and identity, which develop the consumers' purchase intentions. This chapter explains how the social influence support the change in beliefs, attitude, and intentions of the online consumers in the user-generated social media networking sites (SNSs). Furthermore, it discusses the functional impact of such online social influence that enables companies to understand the perceptions and needs of online users making sense of how multiple levels of social influence phenomenon on social media impact on consumers purchase intentions.

INTRODUCTION

The transition from traditional modes of marketing to a consumer-centric marketing approach in B2C environments has had an explicit impact on the psychological behaviours of consumers. Such developments have captured the attention of marketers and academic researchers (Michaelidou et al., 2011). The shift to an integrated marketing communication paradigm from traditional media to internet based multi-channel marketing has revolutionised the concept of integrated marketing communication (Huang & Benyoucef, 2013). Furthermore, the continuous development of online media from computer mediated

DOI: 10.4018/978-1-5225-7344-9.ch004

marketing applications to more sophisticated Web 2.0-based social media has dramatically transformed the purchase behaviours of online users by enhancing the speed of communications between businesses and consumers and reducing the costs associated with doing so (Tsai & Men, 2013). The development of social media has become one of the prime tools of online marketing, and this has captured the attention of stakeholders due to its significant impact on promotional communications between businesses and consumers, as well as amongst consumers (Ansarin & Ozuem, 2014). However, the empirical efforts for online consumers behavioural modelling on social media could result in its greater acceptability, making it a real-time online marketing tool for transforming online users into potential customers through change of behaviour via valuable information exchange. The extent to which social media and the development of behavioural modelling based on networked online social interactions can determine changes to purchase intentions and decision making behaviour lacks empirical understanding (Zhu & Chen, 2015). The aim of this chapter is to explain recent changes in the beliefs, opinions, attitudes and intentions of individuals as a result of complex heterogenic online social interactions among online users. Such interactions take place to expedite exchange information. They are valued for facilitating collaborative learning and circulating vital information about products and services (Lim & Heide, 2015). Further, this chapter also reveals how group-based online social interactions develop multiple levels of social influence to create behavioural uniformity among members of online social groups based on social influence.

The development of appropriate marketing and communication strategy on the basis of impartial changes to integrated marketing communication helps businesses to establish a direct connection with end-consumers at relatively low cost, and in an efficient timely manner. Such exchanges can socially influence the purchase behaviour of online users (Bhatli & Mehri, 2015). Businesses can exert significant influence by taking advantage of interactions between online members who join communities to satisfy a need to belong. This is achieved when they associate themselves with certain brand communities to feel socially connected and recognised after interacting with similar, like-minded online users (Bamberg et al., 2007; Zhang et al., 2015). Such an enhanced sense of belonging increases the desire of online users to become part of an online brand community. It also significantly increases the level of trust that exists between online users in financial services and enhances interactions and information sharing between group members who engage with financial services brands. Such online users feel more valued and recognised when associating with certain brands, and this is a direct result of engagement which significantly influences purchase intentions (Zhou, 2011).

Social media is facilitated by Web 2.0 technologies and is based on user-generated content. This is also known as user-generated media since it enables active participation amongst online users allowing them to communicate with, and respond to, promotional content that they interact with on social media (Nelson-Field et al. 2012). User-generated content has changed the layout of social media which helps in shaping the behaviour of customers by making social media a prevalent information source which, as a result, creates positive Electronic Word of Mouth (EWOM) (Ozuem et al. 2015). User-generated media has transformed communication tools and strategies in such a way as to control information and the speed of information that is exchanged. Such control rests with consumers rather than with marketing experts (Gallaugher & Ransbotham, 2010). This phenomenon not only supports two-way communication between consumers and businesses, but also transforms online users into active participants rather than passive recipients of promotional communications based on traditional models of media. For example, on a Social Networking Site (SNS) an online user can actively express his or her views at an individual level or in a group setting. They can circulate messages and evaluate information on the basis of informational exchanges and knowledge sharing. The use of social networking sites for business has greatly enhanced the adaptability of social media as a vital source of promoting products and services and has transformed the behaviour of consumers through education. In this way, online social media users gain more information and knowledge through socialisation.

THEORETICAL CONTEXT

Most previous researchers have approached social media as a vital tool for online marketing communications due to its clear significance within marketing discussions (Holsapple et al., 2018; Yankova & Ozuem, 2014; Brengarth & Mujic, 2016). However, a widely recognised empirically-based definition of social media is still lacking in academic literature. The term social media is defined as the collection of internet-based applications purposely built for the exchange and creation of digital content within the technological foundations of Web 2.0 (Kaplan & Haenlein, 2010). Such technologies are built with the intention of helping companies engage in two-way communications with customers, such as listening to customers and responding appropriately.

Furthermore, Safko & Brake (2009,p.6) defined social media in their research as:

Activities, practices and behaviour among communities of people who gather online to share information knowledge, and opinions using conversational media. Conversational media are Web-based applications that make it possible to create and easily transmit content in the form of words, pictures, videos, and audios.

Constantinides & Fountain (2008) interpret the term social media as a synonym for Web 2.0, suggesting both terms can be used interchangeably. Cox et al. (2008), suggest the term social media means "user-generated content websites" that explain and promote digital content produced by users in the form of podcasts and blogs. Endress (2014) defines social media as social software that enables online users to undertake social networking, including photo sharing, blogging and instant messaging. Social media facilitates instant communication, providing an easy interface for the sharing of digital information to help online users to achieve quick access by removing the barriers to, and inherent time constraints of, traditional media (Azemi & Ozuem, 2014). Social media is a hub and can be simply described as a starting point for acquiring intelligence on the buying behaviour of consumers using social media marketing strategies (Stokinger & Ozuem, 2014). A variety of explanations and definitions have been propounded by various scholars but a universally accepted definition of social media is unavailable in the academic world. The issue of how these scholars have contributed to social media marketing and explained the phenomenon of social media and its implications for social media marketing has been investigated by a number of key authors in the field of digital marketing (Helal & Ozuem, 2017; Hlebec et al., 2015; Carr et al., 2016).

Developments in technology have enabled individuals to interact online and exchange communications through computer mediated online social media. Online social media of the type developed across Web 2.0-based technologies offers online users the ability to communicate and instantly exchange information through multiple forms of social media social networks, social bookmarking and blogs (Holsapple et al., 2018). Online social media has facilitated joint learning through collaboration and social networking which has enabled millions of online individuals to enhance their communication within their social circles. Such users have also been able to communicate promotional and marketing messages to entire populations of online consumers on a consumer-to-consumer communication exchange basis (Muñiz & Schau, 2007). Compared with traditional media and the integrated marketing communication paradigm, new computer-mediated online social media have empowered consumers to communicate, not just amongst themselves, but with companies as well (Dolan & Goodman, 2017). This type of online social communication and the speedy exchange between members of the online platforms it supports strengthens participation by connecting populations of online members. This significantly impacts on their behaviour and mindset (Sinha et al., 2012).

Online social media enables the creation, alteration and modification of user-generated content that is publicly available to online consumers and end-users (Jiang et al. 2009; Herget & Mader, 2009; Litvin et al. 2008). The development of internet-based information technologies and communications platforms facilitated by Web 2.0-based technologies has enabled, not just the publication of user-generated content on social media, but it has also dramatically improved the aesthetics of websites (Brengarth & Mujic, 2016). Depending on the usage and influence of the associated technologies, Web 2.0 offers a unique technological set-up to enhance the use of online applications developed with and based on these technologies. For example, enhancing social networking amongst individuals, collaborative learning and the rapid exchange of information facilitates a form of two-way communication which not only enables online users to receive user-generated content-based messages, but also enables such users to respond to and interact with the sender at the same time (Hearn et al., 2009). This further enables online consumers to potentially engage in communication, information sharing and empowerment in anticipation of some kind of economic exchange between the companies involved and consumers in the form of consumer purchase intentions (Sinha et al., 2012; Zhu et al., 2016). Li & Bernoff (2008) explained that the significance and outcome of online social media from a business perspective differs considerably from the traditional communication paradigm where marketers have been able to control promotional content. This high degree of contrast has implications for businesses in multiple dimensions. First, it allows marketers to communicate promotional content to a wide audience on social media quicker than ever before. Secondly it has supported the efficiency of an integrated marketing communications strategy through cost reduction based on inexpensive, direct engagement and communication with clients on the basis of two-way communication. This is achieved with greater efficiency and a sharper focus greater than any other integrated marketing communication tool (VanMeter et al., 2015; Felix et al., 2017).

Within the context of social media, marketing is understood to be planned and based on an online, inbound consumer-centric strategy that uses social media networking sites as tools to facilitate online interactions and the consumption of user-generated content in the form of blogs, micro-blogs, product ratings, product reviews, group discussions and social book-marking. This creates a two-way communication process between marketers and online consumers (Dang et al. 2014; Bojārs et al. 2008). Social media marketing has been widely used in the context of integrated marketing communications through social networking. Such marketing is considered to be discrete and different from its long-standing existence in the field of sociology (Qi et al., 2018). The term 'social network' is a subset of online communities, platforms, or group pages where users interact and share their ideas and choices with others (Jansen et al., 2009). It is important to note that the terms 'social media' and 'social networking sites' cannot be used interchangeably, as the former is a broader term compared with the latter, which is a component of 'social networking sites'.

Chan & Guillet (2011, p. 347) define Social Media Marketing (SMM) as

A set of Internet-based applications that enable interaction, communication, collaboration of user-generated content and hence, sharing of information such as ideas, thoughts, content, and relationships.

Understanding social media marketing as a platform for the promotion and communication of products and services on social networking sites through user-generated content using Web 2.0 provides a fundamental basis upon which to establish two-way conversation and communications between companies and customers (Kaplan & Haenlein, 2010). User-generated content is the material generated by online members of social media websites, comprising information in the form of blogs, product reviews, videos, micro blogs and informational content, based on experiences of products. Examples include Facebook and YouTube. Cox et al. (2008), note that online users interact with online social media in three ways i.e.: i) by consuming social media, ii) by participating in social media and iii) by producing social media content. Consuming social media involves a range of activities such as using social media to read information and view interactive content without participating in it. Participation concerns user-to-user and user-to-content interactions in which users share their personal experiences about content use. They share content socially and evaluate content on the basis of its value proposition to the public (Jia et al., 2018). Finally, producing user-generated content entails the creation, modification and publication of content generated by a user on social media, such as pictures, videos or podcasts. Such user-generated content on social media sites has drawn the attention of many customers and it plays a significant role in modifying perceptions of, and awareness about, products and services (Füller, 2006).

Malthouse et al. (2013), state that since social media is all about users sharing user-generated content for information and knowledge-sharing purposes, the creation of such content on social media could limit a company's control over its promotional and advertising messages which are accessible to the general public. Such user-generated content and information exchange activities cannot be isolated and limited to a certain group of people on social media, as it is viewed in multiple contexts on social media (Lee, 2018). Thus, whenever a company designs a promotional campaign to target certain users with specific needs, this phenomenon necessarily signifies that the campaign will hit users on social media who are not specifically targeted (Arrigo, 2014). In real-time practice it is almost impossible for organisations to limit the audience of a marketing promotional campaign based on specific needs and requirements (Hajli, 2015). In almost every case, whenever a company launches a promotional campaign directed at a certain group of specific users on social media with defined needs, such promotions must make provision for the high probability of users sharing such advertising information with fellow online social media users regardless of whether they share their specific needs and/or requirements with others. This phenomenon has created a positive impact on viral marketing as part of social media marketing strategies because a considerable audience can be reached with promotional advertisements, encouraging information-sharing amongst social media members (Miller & Lammas, 2010)

Social media explicitly emphasises user-generated communication between consumers and consumers and companies. The importance of web-based technologies, such as Web 2.0, functions is based on the principle of user-generated content and the instant creation and sharing of content amongst communities and groups (Harrysson et al. 2012). The transition of marketing strategies from a company-centric matrix has influenced the target audiences of marketing strategies with the elaboration of the mechanism of online value creation (Lee, 2018). The phenomenon of two-way communications between users, and users and marketers as a function of user-generated content has increased the scope of marketing online due to its extensive influence and ability to target wide audiences within a short time span (Hajli, 2015). Broadly, users participate in value creation by creating innovative activities on the social medium. The vital aspect of users' innovation in terms of online content by adding value to it stems from online engagement with content, where users actively participate in value addition to the online content of promotional campaigns (Weinberg & Pehlivan, 2011). Such a process of adding value can include value creation in the context of a company's promotional campaign achieved when consumers share their personal experiences (Ozuem & Tan, 2014). In so doing they demonstrate loyalty to a certain brand by helping other online users with product evaluation, generating new ideas or sharing information on specific problems (Scott, 2012). Such a process of content modification by users on behalf of the company on social media helps the company to reach increasing numbers of potential customers online. To achieve this they harness contributions made by online users and incorporate value into their promotional campaigns, subsequently changing the online behaviour of consumers (Qualman, 2009). Technological developments in social media fit with the current marketing landscape and challenge the usefulness of traditional media as an influencing agent that can shape consumer behaviour.

Marketers use this phenomenon as a cushion for their online marketing strategies by purposely engaging online users in promotional content, and by further empowering them to share information and knowledge with fellow-users in order to achieve a maximum population of online users exposed to promotional content (Hajili, 2015). However, the limitations related to social media marketing can impose restrictions on the use of social media for marketing purposes. Predominantly, there are two major perspectives that clearly indicate the limitations of social media. The first factor defines the limitations of the social medium on a platform in terms of information exchange and knowledge-sharing, which completely overlook self-expression amongst users. The second factor indicates a limitation of social media as an online social interaction platform where information exchange, knowledge-sharing and online interactions with content are exchanged in a marketing environment inextricably connected to consumption-related activities (Iankova et al. 2018). On social media, social influence stems from social interactions which triggers the development of new attitudes and intentions due to significant changes to consumer behaviour and makes social media an intensely valuable medium for marketing in the current business environment (Qualman, 2009). With particular reference to the emergence of social media websites, user-generated content has undergone a tremendous development whereby online members not only consume but create content and share it on social media. This kind of creation of digital content on social media, and the concurrent consumption of user-generated content has created the phenomenon of "prosumers"; a term used to describe the members of online media who create and at the same time consume digital content (Laestadius & Wahl, 2017). Fuchs (2010) describes the mechanism of prosumers as a process that merges the creation and consumption of user-generated content simultaneously on social media. Such prosumers are both the creators and consumers of content on social media.

Online users interact with social media in multiple ways. For example, the way users participate in the content creation process as active consumers, and the way they act as passive consumers consuming such online content is significant. So too is the process of users acting as facilitators in sharing content and information with fellow-users online. The interactive motive of online users on social media is categorised into two major groups based on the nature of the interaction. The first view holds that online social interactions are based on rational motivation, for example knowledge-sharing and/or advocacy. Similarly, the second view approaches online user interactions as an emotional motivation. An example might be developing social networking by interacting with more social media members and expressing personal views, thereby gaining confidence and identity (Li et al., 2017). Further, the integration of online user interactions combined with complex internet tools and technologies creates electronic word-of-mouth (Balaji et al., 2016). However, this phenomenon is limited in the sense that, when confronted with such an output on certain occasions due to extensive overloading of information, online users face difficulty in choosing the promotional campaign they would like to participate in. In the majority of cases, consumers are drawn to those companies that are most familiar to them.

Contemporary academic research has mainly focused on consumer responses to social media marketing, although significant research has yet to be undertaken regarding the optimisation of social media, which would significantly explain how firms attain greater numbers of customers with rapid customer responses using social networking websites as a trade platform (Chong et al., 2018). Hoffman & Novak (1997) first used the term 'digital medium' as a platform for online marketing to sell goods and services. They used the term "hyper-mediated computer environments" to explain the behavioural targeting of consumers by firms as the root cause of the origin of digital media. They suggested that marketing trends are shifting, with more emphasis on the digital-based marketing of products and services. They affirmed that the traditional communication paradigm, fundamentally based on the traditional promotional mix strategies of integrated marketing communications strategies, must be replaced with a new communication paradigm which explicitly relies on computer-mediated environments and platforms. These must include all forms of social media and potential tools for creating an IMC strategy in online B2C marketing settings (Ozuem et al., 2016). For example, in a computer-mediated environment and in terms of a technological setup, web pages hold key information and are composed of banners and other forms of advertising through which marketers reach customers by tailoring their behaviour when a customer clicks on their details and passes on their information (Chang & Wang, 2008).

Most importantly, this phenomenon speaks to the specific manner of change that impacts on digital searches and online search decision aids in computer-mediated environments (Wu & Chang, 2005). Hoffman *et al.*, (2013) indicate that the development of such computer-mediated environments, with the explicit development of social media, is an evolution of the type of electronic commerce that highlights the impact of social media and social networking on online marketing. This creates a new dimension of online social media marketing called 'social commerce'. Such social commerce is a notable platform for providing online shopping information with the help of social media and social networking sites by engaging the maximum possible number of customers with social network ties, enabling them at the same time to develop a social identity by sharing, recommending, and discovering online financial services information (Vemuri, 2010; Sciglipaglia & Ely, 2006). Such an adaptive process based on technologies elicits the true capabilities of firms in computer mediated environments and creates value for customers in the retail banking industry (Walsh et al. 2004).

Hau & Kim (2011) explained that the concept of social media marketing became operational in the middle of the last decade, when the growing use of these social networking sites made them an important platform for online trade (Sashi, 2012). This created a change for consumers and led them to rely more on online shopping using social media and social networking sites. The most popular of this social networking and social media sites are Facebook, Twitter or Instagram, YouTube & LinkedIn. Chan & Ngai (2011), argue that the motivation of users and their interactions with online promotional messages depends on their perceptions of online advertising and the participation of consumers in online communities. This takes place through discussion and the sharing of advertised information with peers on social networks. This also includes the self-disclosure of behaviour and attitudes in online social communities amongst the participants of a social group (Ouirdi et al. 2015; Chen & Li, 2017). Such self-disclosure and intentional involvement in social media, and engagement with communication, can influence buying decisions (Lin & Utz, 2017). This self-disclosure by consumers on social media takes place in various forms of online media where users create content and share it. The nature of how this takes place depends on their level of engagement and interactivity. This creates a form of social capital based on personal or mutual interactions on social media. It creates common knowledge in relation to consumer-to-consumer information sharing and it encourages discussions and personal experiences through interactions and the sharing of promotional messages. This helps marketers to communicate with online clients using a B2C approach (Iankova et al., 2018). Chang & Zhu (2011) found that individual, personal interactions on any social medium define the personality influences and so-called self- presentation of users. In this way, users share their thoughts, feelings and ideas and are motivated to help develop a relationship and, crucially, an identity, in social circles on social media. Kaplan & Haenlein (2010) classified such individual self-presentation and disclosure which triggers a level of engagement with online users on social media as a form of social media based on individual social presence which is shaped by various levels of self-disclosure and self-presentation.

DEVELOPMENT OF SOCIAL MEDIA

To comprehensively understand the concept of social media, it is first essential to understand the background of its development and the wider implications of Web 2.0, since the concepts of social media and Web 2.0 are closely related and are often used in the same context (Berthon et al. 2012). The term Web 2.0, which is used to describe a subset of the internet, comprises websites on the internet which operate on the principle of user-generated content. These sites facilitate users on the internet and help them to actively participate in altering and editing web content for ease of use (Kang, 2016). Web 2.0 is the composition of images, graphics and texts on the internet based on user-generated content (Ho & Chang, 2010). Jansen *et al.* (2009) argue that Web 2.0 has revolutionised the world on the internet, based on the active participation of users. These users create digital content online rather than act as passive recipients of such content, as was the case in the era of Web 1.0 (Constantinides & Fountain, 2008). They further stated that the development of Web 2.0 has had a considerable impact on the world of the internet. For example, the internet has undergone certain modifications which have led to the development of new internet-based applications and new categorisations of internet-based applications. The most valuable transformation that the internet has undergone with the development of Web 2.0 is the facilitation of user-generated content which has led to the development of social media and other interactive communicational platforms as contributions to the electronic economy (Cox et al., 2008). Further, Web 2.0 categorises internet-based applications as: user-generated content applications which run on Web 2.0 platforms such as social media; digital content communities; online forums; blogs and micro blogs.

Webs 1.0 was based on the arrangement that online users were passive recipients of web content and were unable to alter or create content due to its limited functionality (Newman et al., 2016). The term "Web 2.0" came into focus in 2004 when online network developers integrated Web 2.0 platforms with user-generated content (Newman et al., 2016; Cox et al., 2008). Such user-generated content relaunched the World Wide Web as a platform harnessed by end-users to alter and modify online content and share it on the internet. This sat in stark contrast to first-generation Web 1.0, where users had limited access as passive viewers of content on a website (Rodriguez-Ardura et al., 2010). Further, Web 2.0 evolved as an open foundation platform, supporting the sustainable development of innovative technological applications through the generic features of royalty-free technologies (De Valck et al., 2009). This enabled the establishment of unlimited web-based links to web pages and unrestricted, instant access to those webpages. McQuail (2005), stated that, for the majority of prominent search engines which run on Web 2.0, the smallest unit is a webpage. This is particularly the case with social media, also referred to as Web 2.0 by the majority of users. The smallest entity of social media is considered to be content bits, altered or created by active online social media users in real time. These are commonly known as "user-generated content units". This explains why Web 2.0 and social media differ, as each webpage has several content entries created or altered by users or companies and is greater than the smallest entity on a social medium (Newman et al., 2016).

The development of Web 2.0 is also linked with the evolution of the development of the internet serving as a medium to help share and alter user-generated content online. Jansen et al., (2009), affirmed that the purpose of the development of the internet with subsequent Web 2.0 development is primarily concerned with enabling online feasibility for the general public to more actively engage with the internet to communicate and interact, to form a new era of development towards online democracy (Rainie & Wellman, 2012). As a step further from the development of the internet, the development of Web 2.0 means it is friendlier and easier to use where user-generated content is concerned. This has empowered users and revolutionised the process for marketers and companies to interact and share information with each other (Newman, 2018). Furthermore this second-generation web service has also led to the exchange of digital content in many ways, for example between one-to-many, many-to-many consumers on digital platforms.

Focussing on the basics of the multi-dimensional functionality of Web 2.0, marketers consider it a prime medium for the development of internet-based applications developed using digital content creation. Web 2.0 has become a mass medium, since it encompasses a much wider role than traditional Web 1.0, as it has modernised the structure of online communications, giving a clearer focus regarding the transfer of promotional messages. It has enabled the polarisation of social and digital content-based interactions (Murugesan, 2007). The modernisation of such a mass medium in the form of Web 2.0 has out-performed traditional marketing and communications methods, thanks to instant two-way communication and the ability to reach a far wider audience with quick customer responses (Fuchs et al., 2010). Additionally, it has enabled a power shift on the internet from sender to receiver with more emphasis on information acquisition leading to the transition of the landscape of the marketing mix and orientation of marketing strategies from push to pull (Faci et al., 2017). This seismic change in the paradigm of marketing communications has enabled the communication and interaction processes among online users to enhance the credibility and vitality of online promotions. This is enabled through confident user exchange of information initiated by organisations in an expeditious and convenient way (Newman, 2018). Changes to the behaviour of online stakeholders are an explicit function of Web 2.0 and its interactive features which have made online applications more user-friendly. Consumer interaction-based applications such as social media have empowered consumers to interact as individuals or in communities to seek information and gain wide acceptance in social media circles to create content (Brengarth & Mujkic, 2016; Walther et al., 2012)

Web 2.0 has made social interactions easier through the technologically innovative development of online social communities connecting online users all over the globe. Such users have formed a sophisticated platform of human interaction in a virtual online environment (Al-ghamdi & Al-ghamdi, 2015). Predominantly, Web 2.0 has proven to be the key medium for the development of online communications, linking users around the world and supporting interaction-based applications development such as social media networking sites. An explicit feature of Web 2.0 is its user-friendly interface which has enabled online users to participate in, and control, online interactions, social information sharing, and the promotion of products and services (Dang et al. 2014). With such a user-friendly interface, the development of online communities where consumers become members sharing a common interest and similar characteristics of membership has also been made possible. Such online communities represent evolution in this sense, enabling content consumption by online users who achieve satisfaction by reading and sharing valuable content which enables them to shape their buying behaviour. This in turn has had a subsequent impact on their online purchase decision(s) (Berthon et al. 2012), who noted that, with the development of social networking sites running explicitly on user-generated content, the internalisation of content information shared on social media can be used for both commercial and non-commercial purposes. Within this scenario, consumers use digital content which has originated, not from a commercial source, but from a reference group on a social networking site, in the form of product reviews, experiential product reflections and online user recommendations on Web 2.0 (Michopoulou & Moisa, 2018). The advancement and development of technology such as the development of online search engines, sophisticated mobile communication devices, online social networks and websites for peer-to-peer communications and online group discussions has helped marketers to extend their capacity to form a detailed understanding of online communities, social trends and user preferences regarding buying branded products and services advertised online (Habibi et al., 2014). This has led to the development of social networking sites on the web that has made it easier for online users to develop a greater understanding about how to make a rational choice when it comes to electronically available products and services. Such developments lead to consumer engagement which has a subsequent impact on purchase intentions based on the creation of a sense of loyalty and affiliation between consumers and the brand (Hollebeek et al. 2014). However, the question that remains salient in the literature is whether social media has a direct influence on consumer engagement and interactions. It is not yet known how useful social media is when it comes to boosting the sales revenue of companies by transforming the psychological behavior of online users, or if it has a long-term influence over post-purchase related behavior (Muntinga et al., 2011).

Social Media and Social Influence

Arguably social networking sites such as Facebook, twitter and Instagram transform consumer perceptions and preferences through online social interactions. These include group discussions, information exchange among members. Such group based online interaction together with gratification features of social media such as interactivity and entertainment result in development of social influence through significant change in members' knowledge, attitude and intentions as a result of informational content exchange and increase in value perception (Bagozzi & Lee, 2002). The term social influence is explained as a product of individual group-based online social interactions which are determined by individual attitudes towards perspective social behaviour and value systems (Dholakia et al., 2004). Changes to the behaviour and intentions of individuals are an explicit outcome of the acceptance of social influence in online network-based communities. Hutter et al. (2013) note that such online social interactions and group-based mutual social actions on social media develop social influence which significantly impacts on decision making amongst online members. Furthermore, the consumers' engagement with promotional content together with individual or group level social exchange explicitly add aesthetic value towards developing a rational mindset for making a buying decision (Kozinets et al., 2010).

Previous research has established the connection between social media and the purchase intentions of consumers but there exists a knowledge gap in terms of how social media influences the psychology of consumers and how it motivates consumers to make purchases (Erkan & Evans, 2016; Zhu et al., 2016; Wang et al., 2012; Hutter et al., 2013). In particular, the role of social influence in transforming consumer behaviour and decision-making in terms of social media has yet to be conceptualised on an empirical basis, leaving an extensive knowledge gap. There is scope, therefore, to develop a conceptual framework in relation to social influence and consumer purchase intentions in academic literature. (Dholakia et al., 2004) argued that social influence provides a more subjective understanding of the direct connection between social media and consumer purchase intentions. Social influence is related to the attitude and behaviour of online consumers.

The consumer social influence model includes three fundamental components which are value perceptions, social identity and group norms. These share some similarity with the initial framework of social influence (Kelman, 1958) which includes compliance, internalisation and identity. Kelman (1958), explained that social influence develops at various levels in society; and each level has a unique outcome associated with it. Social influence develops based on mutual agreement to adopt the common attitude and behaviours of the group. An individual either conforms to the new behaviour by accepting it to gain acceptance, or finds a match between his/her personal value system, norms, attitude and behaviour with the group's norms, values and attitudes (Zhou, 2011). In addition, identity-based influence determines self-defined relationships and the acceptance of group behaviour by individuals. In this way an individual can become recognised and accepted by other members in the online media (Shen et al., 2011).

Dholakia et al., (2004) used the social influence theory (Kelman 1958) to determine to measure the participative behaviour of individuals in network based online social communities. The social influence model introduced by Dholakia et al. (2004) contains three components which are: consumer value perceptions; social influence predictors; and decision-making variables. Consumer value perceptions or antecedents of the model include the five-factor framework in relation to the use and gratification paradigm framework which incorporate purposive and self-discovery values as well as the maintenance of interpersonal connectivity, social enhancement and entertainment values (Shen et al., 2011). Consumer value perceptions act as antecedents to the main predictors, group norms and social identities in terms of determining changes in attitude and intention in the form of group based social actions known as we-intentions (Zhou, 2011). The antecedents and social influence framework (group norms and social identity) impact on the mediator variable of desire, which leads to the we-intentions that create changes in participative behaviour (Cheung, 2011). There are two component parts belonging to the social influence group norms of mutual agreement and mutual accommodation, and the three components of social identity and online social communities which are affective identity, evaluative identity and cognitive identity.

However, Dholakia et al.'s (2004) social influence model, the compliance factor (subjective norms) which develops normative social influence has not been included since it is less useful in determining 'we-intentions' in online communities. Furthermore, the value perceptions of consumers are psychological triggers of engagement with online groups on the social media. Such value perception serves as an antecedent and reveals potential clues as to the change in group members' beliefs, intentions and norms. (Dellarocas et al., 2007). Tsai & Bagozzi (2014), argued that individuals accept influence either by becoming active members of online groups by sharing their opinions, ideas and thoughts in group based online interactions or by acting as passive members who receive information and knowledge and accept social influence.

CONCLUSION AND MANAGERIAL IMPLICATIONS

The explicit role of social media in transforming the psychological behaviours of online users and in helping them to make purchase decisions adds economic value to the marketing communications that take place between consumers and companies (Hutter et al., 2013). In addition to the socialisation perspective, social media also helps marketers to promote brands, thereby helping companies to create online brand identity and brand communities (Hajli & Sims, 2015). As a platform of exchange of user-generated content, companies endorse the features and use of brand related products and services with an embedded message of brand value to improve the lifestyle of customers or to meet more specific needs. This is also true of the retail financial services industry where social media has played a prominent role in disseminating information-sharing about the value of financial services. Such data is shared amongst online members on social media (Liang & Chen, 2009).

Developments on social media networking sites gained popularity when the practices of different forms of user-generated content became available on different websites created by end-users. However, in order to qualify as a social networking website, some basic features and regulations must be recognised in order to meet the criteria and requirements. For example, the website must contain online users' profiles, personal content and information in order to enable users to develop a unique identity on a social network and to be able to participate in online communities and establish a connection with other online users. This enables users to post online in online communities and seek out information by reading online blogs and expert testimonials on social media (Alarcón et al., 2018). According to the OECD (2007) for a user-graphic interface to be considered as an online social exchange platform it should fulfil certain requirements. First of all, the content needs to be available online as published content available to a group of online users to access and alter. Secondly, it needs to demonstrate innovation in containing vital information for online users. These characteristics perfectly support the development of social media, which is explained by many researchers as the internet-based applications developed on Web 2.0, helping online users to exchange user-generated content (Dang et al., 2014; Faci et al., 2017). The most recognised forms of user-generated content exchange include micro blogs, weblogs, podcasts, social blogs, ratings and bookmarks, especially on Facebook, which supports group discussions amongst members.

Kietzmann et al., (2011) explained that such interactions reveal the human behavioural matrix on online social platforms. For example, online social networking and group discussions on a Web 2.0-based application increase human exposure to the desired content and information related to consumption, initiating the transition process from ordinary user to potential online consumer (Fu et al., 2018). Such a behavioural matrix supported by online interactions and active membership has dominated Web 2.0 with extensive online traffic enlarging the overall function of user-generated content applications in online behavioural change (Ozuem et al., 2015). Online user traffic on Web 2.0-based applications is based on the act of participation by online users and the heterogeneous nature of interaction. For example, on social networking sites, online users create digital content and interact simultaneously to share information and knowledge. They actively participate in group discussions or become members of a group associated with specific content related to information concerning a product or services, such as product reviews, personal experiences, or post-purchase behaviour. Cheema (2017) argues that, today the exchange of user-generated content on Web 2.0 has enabled the development of many potential social networking websites that provide extensive benefits to online users, such as Facebook, Wikipedia, or LinkedIn.

Such a social influence has unique implications for change in individuals' mindsets on online social medium. Similarly, modification in Dholakia et al.'s (2004) social influence model could enhance the vitality and credibility of its use in determining the purchase intentions in the financial services industry. From a managerial perspective, the framework of the consumers' social influence model has potential significance in explaining the behavioural and attitudinal change of consumers interacting through social media networking sites such as Facebook. Indeed, the research model of this study also functions as an integrated marketing communication process, especially while promoting financial services online (Friedkin & Johnsen, 2011; Mason et al., 2007). Such a cumulative social influence supported by social identity, group association and the value perceptions of consumers will enhance consumer trust in information about financial services in online, group-based social interaction.

REFERENCES

Alarcón, C. N., Sepúlveda, A. N., Valenzuela-Fernández, L., & Gil-Lafuent, J. (2018). Systematic mapping on social media and its relation to business. *European Research on Management and Business Economics*, *24*(2), 104–113. doi:10.1016/j.iedeen.2018.01.002

Ansarin, M., & Ozuem, W. (2014). Social media and online brand communities. In Computer-Mediated Marketing Strategies: Social Media and Online Brand Communities. IGI Global.

Arrigo, E. (2014). Social media opportunities for market-driven firms. In Integrating social media into business practice, applications, management, and models. IGI Global.

Azemi, Y., & Ozuem, W. (2014). Social media and SMEs in transition countries. In Computer-mediated marketing strategies: social media and online brand communities. IGI Global.

Bagozzi, R. P., & Lee, K.-H. (2002). Multiple Routes for Social Influence: The Role of Compliance, Internalization, and Social Identity. *Social Psychology Quarterly*, *65*(3), 226–247. doi:10.2307/3090121

Balaji, M. S., Khong, K. W., & Chong, A. Y. L. (2016). Determinants of negative word-of-mouth communication using social networking sites. *Information & Management*, *53*(4), 528–540. doi:10.1016/j.im.2015.12.002

Bamberg, S., & Hunecke, M., & Blöhbaum. (2007). Social context, morality and the use of public transportation: Results from two field studies. *Journal of Environmental Psychology*, *27*, 190–203. doi:10.1016/j.jenvp.2007.04.001

Berthon, P. R., Pitt, L., & Campbell, C. (2008). Ad lib: When customers create the ad. *California Management Review*, *50*(4), 6–31. doi:10.2307/41166454

Berthon, P. R., Pitt, L. F., Plangger, K., & Shapiro, D. (2012). Marketing meets Web 2.0, social media, and creative consumers: *Implications for international marketing strategy. Business Horizons*, *55*(3), 261–271. doi:10.1016/j.bushor.2012.01.007

Bhatli, D., & Mejri, C. A. (2015). The Influence of Social Media on Consumption Practices. In *Ideas in Marketing: Finding the New and Polishing the Old. Developments in Marketing Science: Proceedings of the Academy of Marketing Science*. Springer. 10.1007/978-3-319-10951-0_289

Bojārs, U., Breslin, J. G., Finn, A., & Decker, S. (2008). Using the Semantic Web for linking and reusing data across Web 2.0 communities. *Journal of Web Semantics*, *6*(1), 21–28. doi:10.1016/j.websem.2007.11.010

Brengarth, L. B., & Mujkic, E. (2016). Web 2.0: How social media applications leverage non-profit responses during a wildfire crisis. *Computers in Human Behavior*, *54*, 589–596. doi:10.1016/j.chb.2015.07.010

Carr, C. T., Wohn, Y. D., & Hayes, R. A. (2016). As social support: Relational closeness, automaticity, and interpreting social support from paralinguistic digital affordances in social media. *Computers in Human Behavior*, *62*, 385–393. doi:10.1016/j.chb.2016.03.087

Chan, N. L., & Guillet, B. D. (2011). Investigation of Social Media Marketing: How Does the Hotel Industry in Hong Kong Perform in Marketing on Social Media Websites? *Journal of Travel & Tourism Marketing*, *28*(4), 345–368. doi:10.1080/10548408.2011.571571

Chan, Y. Y. Y., & Ngai, E. W. T. (2011). Conceptualising electronic word of mouth activity: An input-process-output perspective. *Marketing Intelligence & Planning*, *29*(5), 488–516. doi:10.1108/02634501111153692

Chang, H. H., & Wang, I. C. (2008). An investigation of user communication behaviour in computer mediated environments. *Computers in Human Behavior*, *24*(5), 2336–2356. doi:10.1016/j.chb.2008.01.001

Chang, Y. P., & Zhu, D. H. (2011). Understanding social networking sites adoption in China: A comparison of pre-adoption and post-adoption. *Computers in Human Behavior*, *27*(5), 1840–1848. doi:10.1016/j.chb.2011.04.006

Cheung, C. M. K., Chiu, P.-Y., & Lee, M. K. O. (2011). Online Social Networks: Why Do Students Use Facebook? *Computers in Human Behavior*, *27*(4), 1337–1343. doi:10.1016/j.chb.2010.07.028

Chong, A. Y. L., Lacka, E., Boying, L., & Chan, H. K. (2018). The role of social media in enhancing guanxi and perceived effectiveness of E-commerce institutional mechanisms in online marketplace. *Information & Management*, *55*(5), 621–632. doi:10.1016/j.im.2018.01.003

Constantinides, E., & Fountain, S. (2008). Web 2.0: Conceptual foundations and marketing issues. *Journal of Direct. Data and Digital Marketing Practice*, *9*(3), 231–244. doi:10.1057/palgrave.dddmp.4350098

Cox, C., Burgess, S., Sellitto, C., & Buultjens, J. (2008). *Consumer-Generated Web-based Tourism Marketing*. Queensland, Australia: Sustainable Tourism Cooperative Research Centre.

Dang, Y., Zhang, Y., Hu, P. J.-H., Brown, S. A., Ku, Y., Wang, J.-H., & Chen, H. (2014). An integrated framework for analysing multilingual content in Web 2.0 social media. *Decision Support Systems*, *61*, 126–135. doi:10.1016/j.dss.2014.02.004

De Valck, K., Van Bruggen, G., & Wierenga, B. (2009). Virtual communities: A marketing perspective. *Decision Support Systems*, *47*(3), 185–203. doi:10.1016/j.dss.2009.02.008

Dellarocas, C., Zhang, X., & Awad, N. (2007). Exploring the value of online product reviews in forecasting sales: The case of motion pictures. *Journal of Interactive Marketing*, *21*(4), 23–45. doi:10.1002/dir.20087

Dholakia, U. M., Bagozzi, R. P., & Pearo, L. K. (2004). A social influence model of consumer participation in network- and small-group-based virtual communities. *International Journal of Research in Marketing*, *21*(3), 241–263. doi:10.1016/j.ijresmar.2003.12.004

Dolan, R., & Goodman, S. (2017). Succeeding on social media Exploring communication strategies for wine marketing. *Journal of Hospitality and Tourism Management*, *33*, 23–30. doi:10.1016/j.jhtm.2017.09.001

Endress, T. (2014). Digital Governance and Social Media Engagement. In Computer-mediated marketing strategies: social media and online brand communities. IGI Global.

Erkan, I., & Evans, C. (2016). The influence of eWOM in social media on consumers' purchase intentions: An extended approach to information adoption. *Computers in Human Behavior*, *61*, 47–55. doi:10.1016/j.chb.2016.03.003

Faci, N., Maamar, Z., Buregio, V., Uglijanin, E., & Benslimane, D. (2017). Web 2.0. Applications in the workplace: How to ensure their proper use? *Computers in Industry*, *88*, 1–11. doi:10.1016/j.compind.2017.03.003

Felix, R., Rauschnabel, P. A., Gallaugher, J., & Ransbotham, J. (2010). Social media and customer dialog management at Starbucks. *MIS Quarterly Executive*, *9*(4), 197–212.

Habibi, M. R., Laroche, M., & Richard, M.-O. (2014). The roles of brand community and community engagement in building brand trust on social media. *Computers in Human Behavior*, *37*, 152–161. doi:10.1016/j.chb.2014.04.016

Hajli, N. (2015). Social commerce constructs and consumer's intention to buy. *International Journal of Information Management*, *35*(2), 183–191. doi:10.1016/j.ijinfomgt.2014.12.005

Hajli, N., & Sims, J. (2015). Social commerce: The transfer of power from seller to buyers. *Technological Forecasting and Social Change*, *94*, 350–358. doi:10.1016/j.techfore.2015.01.012

Harrysson, M., Metayer, E., & Sarrazin, H. (2012). How 'social intelligence' can guide decisions. *The McKinsey Quarterly*, 1–9.

Hau, Y. S., & Kim, Y. G. (2011). Why Would Online Gamers Share Their Innovation-Conducive Knowledge in the Online Game User Community? Integrating Individual Motivations and Social Capital Perspectives. *Computers in Human Behavior*, *27*(2), 956–970. doi:10.1016/j.chb.2010.11.022

Hearn, G., Foth, M., & Gray, H. (2009). Applications and implementations of new media in corporate communications: An action research approach. *Corporate Communications*, *14*(1), 49–61. doi:10.1108/13563280910931072

Helal, G., & Ozuem, W. (2017). Social Identity Matters: Social Media and Brand Perceptions in the Fashion Apparel and Accessories Industries. In W. Ozuem & Y. Azemi (Eds.), *Digital Marketing Strategies for Fashion and Luxury Brands* (pp. 326–361). Hershey, PA: IGI Global.

Herget, J., & Mader, I. (2009). Social software in external corporate communications – a conceptional approach towards measuring, assessment and optimization of Web 2.0 activity [Social Software in der externen Unternehmenskommunikation – ein Gestaltungsansatz zur Messung, Bewertung und Optimierung von Web 2.0-aktivita¨ten]. *Information-Wissenschaft und Praxis*, *60*(4), 233–240.

Hlebec, V., Manfreda, K. L., & Vehovar, V. (2015). The social support networks of internet users. *New Media & Society*, *8*(1), 9–32. doi:10.1177/1461444806058166

Ho, H. Y., & Chang, C. P. H. (2010). Influence of message trust in online word-of-mouth on consumer behaviour - By the example of food blog. In *International conference on electronics and information engineering*. Los Alamitos, CA: IEEE.

Hoffman, D.L., & Novak, T. (2013). *Online Experience in Social Media: Two Paths to Feeling Close and Connected*. Academic Press.

Hollebeek, L. D., Glynn, M. S., & Brodie, R. J. (2014). Consumer brand engagement in social media: Conceptualization, scale, development and validation. *Journal of Interactive Marketing*, *28*(2), 149–165. doi:10.1016/j.intmar.2013.12.002

Holsapple, C. W., Hsiao, S.-H., & Pakath, R. (2018). Business social media analytics: Characterization and conceptual framework. *Decision Support Systems*, *110*, 32–45. doi:10.1016/j.dss.2018.03.004

Huang, Z., & Benyoucef, M. (2013). From e-commerce to social commerce: A close look at design features. *Electronic Commerce Research and Applications*, *12*(4), 246–259. doi:10.1016/j.elerap.2012.12.003

Hutter, K., Hautz, J., Dennhardt, S., & Fuller, J. (2013). The impact of user interactions in social media on brand awareness and purchase intention: The case of MINI on Facebook. *Journal of Product and Brand Management*, *22*(5/6), 342–351. doi:10.1108/JPBM-05-2013-0299

Jansen, B. J., Zhang, M., Sobel, K., & Chowdury, A. (2009). Twitter power: Tweets as electronic word of mouth. *Journal of the American Society for Information Science and Technology*, *60*(11), 2169–2188. doi:10.1002/asi.21149

Jia, A. L., Shen, S., Li, D., & Chen, S. (2018). Predicting the implicit and the explicit video popularity in a User-generated Content site with enhanced social features. *Computer Networks*, *140*, 112–125. doi:10.1016/j.comnet.2018.05.004

Jiang, Z., Chan, J., Tan, B. C. Y., & Chua, W. S. (2009). Effects of interactivity on website involvement and purchase intention. *Journal of the Association for Information Systems*, *11*(1), 34–59. doi:10.17705/1jais.00218

Kang, I. (2016). Web 2.0 UGC, and citizen journalism: Revisiting South Korea's Oh my News model in the age of social media. *Telematics and Informatics*, *33*(2), 546–556. doi:10.1016/j.tele.2015.07.007

Kaplan, A. M., & Haenlein, M. (2010). Users of the world, unite! The challenges and opportunities of Social Media. *Business Horizons*, *53*(1), 59–68. doi:10.1016/j.bushor.2009.09.003

Kaplan, A. M., & Haenlein, M. (2011). The early bird catches the news: Nine things you should know about micro-blogging. *Business Horizons*, *54*(2), 105–113. doi:10.1016/j.bushor.2010.09.004

Kelman, H. C. (1958). Compliance, identification, and internalization: Three processes of attitude change. *The Journal of Conflict Resolution*, *2*(1), 51–60. doi:10.1177/002200275800200106

Kietzmann, J. H., Hermkens, K., McCarthy, I. P., & Silvestre, B. S. (2011). Social Media? Get Serious! Understanding the Functional Building Blocks of Social Media. *Business Horizons*, *54*(1), 241–251. doi:10.1016/j.bushor.2011.01.005

Kozinets, R., de Valck, K., Wojnicki, A., & Wilner, S. (2010). Networked narratives: Understanding word-of-mouth marketing in online communities. *Journal of Marketing*, *74*(2), 71–89. doi:10.1509/jmkg.74.2.71

Laestadius, L. I., & Wahl, M. M. (2017). Mobilizing social media users to become advertisers: Corporate hashtag campaigns as a public health concern. *Digital Health*, *3*, 1–12. doi:10.1177/2055207617710802 PMID:29942600

Li, C., & Bernoff, J. (2008). *Groundswell: Winning in a world transformed by social technologies*. Boston: Harvard Business Press.

Li, H., Zhang, Z., Meng, F., & Janakiraman, R. (2017). Is peer evaluation of consumer online reviews socially embedded? – An examination combining reviewer's social network and social identity. *International Journal of Hospitality Management*, *67*, 143–153. doi:10.1016/j.ijhm.2017.08.003

Liang, C., & Chen, H. (2009). How to lengthen, deepen and broaden customer-firm relationships with online financial services. *Journal of Financial Services Marketing*, *14*(3), 218–231. doi:10.1057/fsm.2009.20

Lim, Y.-S., & Heide, B. V. D. (2015). Evaluating the Wisdom of Strangers: The Perceived Credibility of Online Consumer Reviews on Yelp. *Journal of Computer-Mediated Communication*, *20*(1), 67–82. doi:10.1111/jcc4.12093

Litvin, S. W., Goldsmith, R. E., & Pan, B. (2008). Electronic Word-of-Mouth in Hospitality and Tourism Management. *Tourism Management*, *29*(3), 458–468. doi:10.1016/j.tourman.2007.05.011

Malthouse, E. C., Haenlein, M., Skiera, B., Wege, E., & Zhang, M. (2013). Managing Customer Relationships in the Social Media Era: Introducing the Social CRM House. *Journal of Interactive Marketing*, *27*(4), 270–280. doi:10.1016/j.intmar.2013.09.008

Mason, W. A., Conrey, F. R., & Smith, E. R. (2007). Situating Social Influence Processes: Dynamic, Multidirectional Flows of Influence within Social Networks. *Personality and Social Psychology Review*, *11*(3), 279–300. doi:10.1177/1088868307301032 PMID:18453465

McQuail, D. (2005). *McQuail's Mass Communication Theory* (5th ed.). London Sage publishers.

Michaelidou, N., Siamagka, N. T., & Christodoulides, G. (2011). Usage, barriers and measurement of social media marketing: An exploratory investigation of small and medium B2B brands. *Industrial Marketing Management*, *40*(7), 1153–1159. doi:10.1016/j.indmarman.2011.09.009

Michopoulou, E., & Moisa, D. G. (2018). (in press). Hotel social media metrics: The ROI dilemma. *International Journal of Hospitality Management.*

Miller, R., & Lammas, N. (2010). Social media and its implications for viral marketing *Asia Pacific. The Public Relations Journal*, *11*(1), 1–9.

Muntinga, D. G., Moorman, M., & Smit, E. G. (2011). Introducing COBRA: Exploring motivations for brand-related social media use. *International Journal of Advertising*, *30*(1), 13–46. doi:10.2501/IJA-30-1-013-046

Muñiz, A. M. Jr, & Schau, H. J. (2007a). Vigilante marketing and consumer-created communications. *Journal of Advertising*, *36*(3), 35–50. doi:10.2753/JOA0091-3367360303

Murugesan, S. (2007). Understanding Web 2.0. *IT Professional*, *9*(4), 34–41. doi:10.1109/MITP.2007.78

Nelson-Field, K., Riebe, E., & Sharp, B. (2012). What's not to "like?": Can a Facebook fan base give a brand the advertising reach it needs? *Journal of Advertising Research*, 1–8.

Newman, M. C. (2018). Evidence in Social Networks. In M. Newman (Ed.), *The Nature and Use of Eco toxicological Evidence Natural Science* (pp. 219–243). Statistics, Psychology, and Sociology.

Newman, R., Chang, V., Walters, R. J., & Wills, G. B. (2016). Web 2.0—the past and the future. *International Journal of Information Management*, *36*(4), 591–598. doi:10.1016/j.ijinfomgt.2016.03.010

OECD. (2007). *Participative Web: user-created content - OECD*. Available online: http://www.oecd-ilibrary.org/science-and-technology/participative-web-and-user-created-content_9789264037472-en

Ouirdi, M. E., Segers, J., Ouirdi, A. E., & Pais, I. (2015). *Predictors of job seekers self-disclosure on social media*. Computers in Human Behaviour.

Ozuem, W., & Tan, K. (2014). Reconciling Social Media with Luxury Fashion Brands: An Exploratory Study. In L. Aiello (Ed.), *Handbook of Research on Management of Cultural Products: E-Relationship Marketing and Accessibility Perspectives* (pp. 257–285). IGI Global. doi:10.4018/978-1-4666-5007-7.ch013

Ozuem, W., Pinho, C. A., & Azemi, Y. (2016). User-Generated Content and Perceived Customer Value. In W. Ozuem & G. Bowen (Eds.), *Competitive Social Media Marketing Strategies* (pp. 50–63). IGI Global. doi:10.4018/978-1-4666-9776-8.ch003

Ozuem, W., Kerry, H., & Geoff, L. (2008). Communicating in the new interactive marketspace. *European Journal of Marketing*, *42*(9/10), 1059–1083. doi:10.1108/03090560810891145

Ozuem, W., O'Keeffe, A., & Lancaster, G. (2015). Leadership Marketing: An exploratory study. *Journal of Strategic Marketing*. doi:10.1080/0965254X.2014.1001867

Ozuem, W., Borrelli, M., & Lancaster, G. (2015). Leveraging the co-evolution of offline and online video games: An empirical study. *Journal of Strategic Marketing*. doi:10.1080/0965254X.2015.1076883

Qi, J., Monod, E., Fang, B., & Deng, S. (2018). Theories of Social media Philosophical Foundations. *Engineering*, *4*(1), 94–102. doi:10.1016/j.eng.2018.02.009

Qualman, E. (2009). *Socialnomics: How social media transforms the way we live and do business*. Hoboken, NJ: John Wiley & Sons.

Rainie, L., & Wellman, B. (2012). *Networked: the new social operating system*. MIT Press.

Rodriguez-Ardura, I., Martinez-Lopez, F. J., & Luna, P. (2010). Going with the consumer towards the social web environment: A review of extant knowledge. *International Journal of Electronic Marketing and Retailing*, *3*(4), 415–440. doi:10.1504/IJEMR.2010.036885

Safko, L., Brake, D., & David, K. (2009). *The Social Media Bible: Tactics, Tools, and Strategies for Business Success*. Wiley.

Sashi, C. M. (2012). Customer engagement, buyer-seller relationships, and social media. *Management Decision*, *50*(2), 253–272. doi:10.1108/00251741211203551

Sciglipaglia, D., & Ely, D. (2006). Customer account relationships and e-retail banking usage. *Journal of Financial Services Marketing*, *10*(4), 109–122. doi:10.1057/palgrave.fsm.4760026

Scott, J. (2012). *Social network analysis*. Thousand Oaks, CA: Sage.

Shen, A. X. L., Cheung, C. M. K., Lee, M. K. O., & Chen, H. (2011). How Social Influence Affects We-Intention to Use Instant Messaging: The Moderating Effect of Usage Experience. *Information Systems Frontiers*, *13*(2), 157–169. doi:10.100710796-009-9193-9

Sinha, K. S., Subramanian, S., & Bhattacharya, K. C. (2012). The contemporary framework on social media analytics as an emerging tool for behaviour informatics, HR analytics and business process. *Journal of Contemporary Management Issues*, *17*(2), 65–84.

Stokinger, E., & Ozuem, W. (2014). Social media and customer retention: Implication for luxury beauty industry. In Computer-mediated marketing strategies: social media and online brand communities. IGI Global.

Tsai, H.-T., & Bagozzi, R. P. (2014). Contribution Behaviour in Virtual Communities: Cognitive, Emotional, and Social Influences. *Management Information Systems Quarterly*, *38*(1), 143–163. doi:10.25300/MISQ/2014/38.1.07

Tsai, W. S., & Men, L. R. (2013). Motivations and Antecedents of Consumer Engagement with Brand Pages on Social Networking Sites. *Journal of Interactive Advertising*, *13*(2), 2. doi:10.1080/15252019.2013.826549

Vanmeter, R. A., Grisaffe, D. B., & Chonko, L. B. (2015). Of "Likes" and "Pins": The Effects of Consumers' Attachment to Social Media. *Journal of Interactive Marketing*, 70–78.

Vemuri, A. (2010). Getting social: Bridging the gap between banking and social media. *Global Finance*, *24*(5), 20–21.

Walsh, S., Gilmore, A., & Carson, D. (2004). Managing and implementing simultaneous transaction and relationship marketing. *International Journal of Bank Marketing*, *22*(7), 468–483. doi:10.1108/02652320410567908

Walther, J. B., Liang, Y. J., Ganster, T., Wohn, D. Y., & Emington, J. (2012). Online reviews, helpfulness ratings, and consumer attitudes: An extension of congruity theory to multiple sources in Web 2.0. *Journal of Computer-Mediated Communication*, *18*(1), 97–112. doi:10.1111/j.1083-6101.2012.01595.x

Wang, X., Yu, C., & Wei, Y. (2012). Social Media Peer Communication and Impacts on Purchase Intentions: A Consumer Socialization Framework. *Journal of Interactive Marketing*, *26*(4), 198–208. doi:10.1016/j.intmar.2011.11.004

Weinberg, B. D., & Pehlivan, E. (2011). Social Spending: Managing the Social Media Mix. *Business Horizons*, *54*(1), 275–282. doi:10.1016/j.bushor.2011.01.008

Wu, J. J., & Chang, Y. S. (2005). Towards understanding members' interactivity, trust, and flow in online travel community. *Industrial Management & Data Systems*, *105*(7), 937–954. doi:10.1108/02635570510616120

Yankova, I., & Ozuem, W. (2014). Social Media and its Implications for Marketing Communications. In Computer-mediated marketing strategies: social media and online brand communities. IGI Global.

Zhang, L., Tam, V. C., Wan, W. W., Wu, P., & Luk, C. L. (2015). An exploratory study on school children's intent attributions for parental structuring behaviours. *Psychological Reports*, *116*(1), 249–273. doi:10.2466/21.PR0.116k17w3 PMID:25668329

Zhou, T. (2011). Understanding online community user participation: A social influence perspective. *Internet Research*, *21*(1), 67–81. doi:10.1108/10662241111104884

Zhu, Y. Q., & Chen, H. G. (2015). Social media and human need satisfaction: Implications for social media marketing. *Business Horizons*, *58*, 335–345.

Zhu, Z., Wang, J., Wang, X., & Wan, X. (2016). Exploring factors of user's peer-influence behaviour in social media on purchase intention: Evidence from QQ. *Computers in Human Behavior*, *63*, 980–987. doi:10.1016/j.chb.2016.05.037

KEY TERMS AND DEFINITIONS

B2C: The business environment where firms directly communicate and promote their products and services to the consumers through adopting multiple media and using integrated marketing communication strategies.

Purchase Intention: The willingness of a customer to buy a product or service in a certain condition.

Social Influence: The phenomenon which explains the change in the individuals' beliefs, attitudes, and intentions occurs at different levels because of social interaction between an individual and another individual or a group of individuals.

Social Interaction: The communication or contact of an individual with another individual or a group of individuals in the society for purpose of information exchange, entertainment, or to maintain essential social connection.

Social Media: Web 2.0-based application that runs on the principles of user-generated content, facilitating the online users to create, share, modify, and alter the digital content enabling the two-way communication on internet.

User-Generated Content: UGC represents all the ways by which users create and exchange digital content and use social media on the technological basis of Web 2.0.

Web 2.0: Web 2.0 is a platform in which software and digital content are not only produced and published by individual companies and people but are also produced and developed by different participants in a continuous and collaborative manner.

Chapter 5
Social Media and Social Entrepreneurship

Md Nazmul Islam
University of West of Scotland, UK

Vivek Chitran
University of Cumbria, UK

ABSTRACT

Information plays an important role in the individual lives of people, and social media as an aspect of online information phenomenon is an exciting topic to explore in terms of its impact on social entrepreneurship. Many theoretical fields have contributed to the development of social entrepreneurship, looking in particular at the financial, political, and psychological impacts. This chapter is unique since it focuses on social enterprises and the impact of evolving technologies on social entrepreneurship. This chapter contributes to the literature on social media usage in social enterprises and offers a better understanding of the issues in the specific context of developing countries.

BACKGROUND AND INTRODUCTION

Previous work has established a lengthy list of internal and external aspects that affect the acceptance of IT by SMEs (Ahmad et al., 2014; Brunswicker and Vanhaverbeke, 2013; Ongori and Migiro, 2010; Venkatraman and Fahd, 2016). Research also holds that internal factors are more influential than external factors in terms of the acceptance of IT in business (Fernández-Olmos and Ramírez-Alesón, 2017). The characteristics of leaders, entrepreneurs and administrative experts including creativeness, age and experience/knowledge of IT are particularly salient in terms of the impact that they have (Fernández-Olmos and Ramírez-Alesón, 2017; Fosso Wamba & Carter, 2014).

Other issues such as virtual benefits (Mehrtens, Cragg, & Mills, 2001; Pillania, 2007), ease of practice (Lane, Wafa and Hassan, 2014; Yang et al., 2014) the size of the business (Bogataj Habjan and Pucihar, 2017) and its structural readiness (Son and Han, 2011; Alshawi and Goulding, 2008) also have an impact on the adoption of IT in businesses. On the other hand, Government support, as well as rules and procedures and the nature of the business and national setting (Gunasekaran and Ngai, 2009), are the key external factors that influence IT adoption.

DOI: 10.4018/978-1-5225-7344-9.ch005

Recently, the role of SM has captured the imagination of business researchers and academics. Organizations recognize the tactical value of social media and are making advances in terms of how it can be used strategically. On the other hand, they are taken as an influential means for concluding the worldwide digital gaps (Ali, 2011; Ozuem, Prasad and Lancaster, 2016). Social media can also exert a powerful influence over social conduct, social relations and socio-politics (Stepanova, 2011). Moreover, the dissemination of SM within organizations produces both prospects and challenges (Deng, Joshi, & Li, 2015).

THEORETICAL CONTEXT: SOCIAL MEDIA AND SOCIAL ENTREPRENEURSHIP

Social connection is considered a fundamental component in terms of the psychology of communities (Laroche et al., 2012). The evolution of technology from telegraph, radio and telephone to the computer and other modern devices has made it easier and faster for people to maintain interactions with each other. In an era of rapid technological development and ubiquitous digital technologies, the use of social media is possibly the most notable contribution in the field of networked society (Vodanovich et al., 2010; Harris, Rae & Misner, 2012). Recent studies demonstrate that around the globe there are now over one billion people that use social media for different purposes (Karikari et al., 2017; Anderson et al., 2016). This has revolutionised the process of obtaining information and this has in turn created increased online brand assurance amongst customers (Hammedi et al., 2015; Pagani and Malacarne, 2017; Brodie et al., 2013; Chang et al., 2015; Kim, 2016; Kumar et al., 2016).

Social media is comparatively a recent phenomenon facilitated by increasing global access to the internet. This has given rise to the concept of the so-called "Networked Society" (Castells 2003). The origins of social media interacting can be traced to the advent of Bulletin Board Systems (BBS) in 1978, where users could log in to share software and information as well as to send messages and post to public communication panels. At the same time, because of the increasing interest and availability of home computers, social media became increasingly familiar to users (Kaplan and Haenlein, 2010). More importantly, this BBS is considered as a predecessor of the World Wide Web.

In 1979, Tom Truscott and Jim Ellis, from Duke University came up with the idea of "Usenet", which was a worldwide conversation or communications system that allowed users to post public messages over the internet (Kaplan and Haenlein, 2010). This platform was mainly used for posting articles or news. The idea came into being in a major way in 1980. The difference between BBS and Usenet was the dependency of Usenet on a server to create a news feed and to forward messages and information to different servers. BBS was based on central administration or a server.

In 1991 the discovery of the World Wide Web (WWW) provided new energy to connect the nerd culture with an increasing counterculture. After successfully change the dot. Communism to dot. Commercialism, Web 1.0 had been changed into the new form of two-way communication with the launch of Amazon and eBay in the early 2000s. Consequently, web 2.0 has grown to facilitate a more democratic style of interaction among users (Kaplan and Haenlein, 2010). Indeed, Web 2.0 is predominantly an exchange process for gaining access to resources and co-creating value (Finch et al., 2012).

In 1997 Bruce and Susan Abelson initiated ''Open Diary,'' which was a premature social networking site that combined all online diary writers into one segment (Kaplan and Haenlein, 2010). At the same time Six Degree, which is considered the first distinguishable social media site was also formed in 1997 (Grizane and Jurgelane, 2017; Boyd and Ellison, 2007). This site added features which allowed users to create individual profiles and make friends with other users. SixDegrees.com permitted users to make personal profiles, invite Friends and browse the profiles of other users. Six Degrees endorsed itself as a means to allow individuals to send messages to others. Although this social networking site managed to attract millions of individuals, it closed in 2000 as a consequence of unsustainable business operations.Blogging sites were formulated in 1999 and added a new arm to the establishment of social media. Blogging remains popular among social media users. Blogging was first called "weblogging" in 1997 later transformed into "Blogging". The format because very popular (Kaplan and Haenlein, 2010).

In 2000 with the evolution of social networking sites like Myspace, LinkedIn and Facebook, and the increasing access to high-speed Internet services, social media usage grew ever more popular. The appearance of several sites changed how people in general, and entrepreneurs, in particular, shared common interests. For example, applications like Photobucket and Flickr delivered give photo sharing services to users. At this point social networking because a key consumer trend and sites such as Facebook and Twitter became, for some, an essential part of daily life. Around 2003 social media began to focus on conventional organisations and mass audiences. MySpace, which acquired around $580 million when it first appeared, is considered to be the first example of an SNS which managed to attract mainstream media attention.

Although several explanations exist regarding social media, there remains no objectively recognised definition, in terms of both functional and theoretical contexts (Treem & Leonardi, 2012; Omosigho and Abeysinghe, 2012; Kaplan & Haenlein, 2010; Xiang & Gretzel, 2010). Currently, existing definitions have either emphasized the specific structures of social media that have since become out-dated (Grizane and Jurgelane, 2017; Boyd & Ellison, 2007; Kaplan & Haenlein, 2010) or have focussed on the energetic aspects of social media usage (Scott & Orlikowski, 2014). As a consequence of the incessant and rapid advancement of Social media, it is difficult to define it using a single perspective (Kane et al., 2014).

This chapter focuses on both the substantial features of social media and the dynamic interpretations of social media. The concept of social media can be defined using different perspectives, and each explanation tends to have been instigated by the insight brought to bear from each corresponding study (Kaplan and Haenlein, 2010). In terms of behavioural observation, social media has been defined as a set of actions, performances, and behaviours of groups of people who gather to share information, knowledge, and views using familiar online media (Safko, 2012; Zafarani & Liu, 2014). In other words, social media is more about the thoughts that people produce and share rather than their perceptions (Lincoln, 2010). Three main characteristics of social media from a behavioural perspective are constructive, shared aptitude and conversation enabler (Lincoln, 2010; Ahlqvist et al. 2008). Constructive social media users add value to the sites or apps they use in social interactions. Social media diverts private individuals to become the pioneers of particular sources of information by sharing thoughts, perceptions and knowledge online. Social media platforms have continued to prosper and to shape society (Richey, 2016).

On the other hand, shared aptitude in the context of social media means working collectively and efficiently without any geographical restrictions. Social media is a collaborative tool which is easily adaptable and flexible in nature (Wang, Yu and Wei, 2012; Georgescu & Popescul, 2015; Ozuem, Prasad and Lancaster, 2016). Social media represents the evolution of a process of content distribution through social communications. The idea of enabling conversation is one of the key features of social media. The term 'enabler' refers to the use of social media practices and actions to achieve a course or function. Kadam, & Ayarekar (2014) suggested that the interactive nature of social media sites breaks down class and other barriers. Wikipedia, which has the ultimate aim to produce encyclopaedic content employs shared perceptions and contributions from a number of Web users. Wikipedia is an example of using social media as an enabler.

From a media viewpoint, Social media is an upgraded version of mass media and niche media. Social media has three explicit features. First, social media is collaborative. Thus, several authors have described social media as a mode of receiving and publishing messages to extensive audiences who can empower an exchange of dyadic and networked collaboration (Järvinen, Tollinen, Karjaluoto, & Jayawardhena, 2012; Lacka & Chong, 2016). Russo, Watkins, Kelly, and Chan (2008) defined social media as a collaborative platform that supports online communications and networking. Secondly, the content generated in social media is mainly produced by users rather than professionals. Finally, social media stresses the centrality of content and community rather than information.

From a conceptual perspective, social media is a platform on which people interact and it is constructed based on three key principles of content, communities and Web 2.0. This new way of communication enables users to generate, share, exchange and observe content in simulated groups and networks (Stockdale, Ahmed and Scheepers, 2012; Ahlqvist, Bäck, Halonen and Heinonen, 2008). Thus, social media is not viewed equally amongst business practitioners or academics and the concepts of Web 2.0 and User Generated Content are complex (Kaplan and Haenlein, 2010; Laroche et al., 2012). According to Boyd and Ellison, (2007) the socially interactive nature of social media encompasses content, communities and Web 2.0 technologies and delivers services through web-based and mobile applications.

For hundreds of years, the construction and propagation of content have been evolving, and the possibilities for typical users to interconnect and influence mass audiences have only recently been realised with the arrival of Web 2.0 technologies. According to Kaplan and Haenlein, (2010) Web 2.0 was first evaluated in 2004 as a means of generating and publishing content and applications by software inventors and users in a collaborative manner. The author's introduced Web 2.0 as a platform for the revolution of social media, and a symbol of a new conceptual and technological foundation. From his point of view, Web 2.0 signifies an ideological and scientific revolution with elementary functionalities in terms of where the World Wide Web (WWW) can be accessed by operators and end-users. Therefore Web 2.0 is considered as a key platform to produce and establish software and content in a collaborative manner instead of at the individual level (Kaplan and Haenlein, 2010).

Web 2.0 tends to refer to the broad phenomenon of social media. However, in this study, the term is used to review the technical aspects of social media. Web 2.0 incorporates a diverse range of applications

Figure 1. Social media under a conceptual perspective

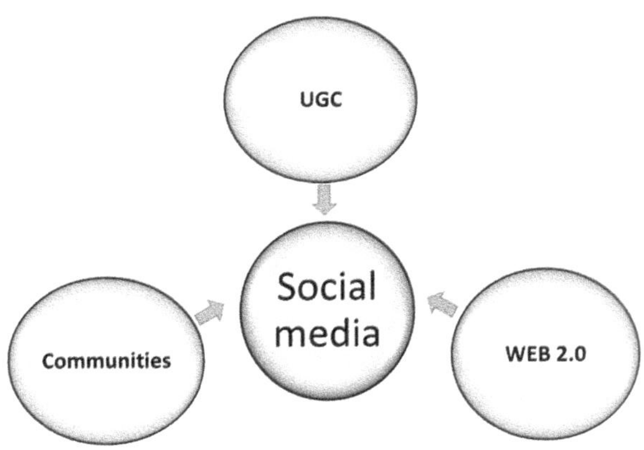

including wikis, blogs, podcasts, social networking sites, debate forums, conference spaces, direct messaging, group journals and address records, cybernetic offices, joint whiteboards presentation systems and many more. Web 2.0 provides the possibility of an enhanced interactive setting that enables a high grade of interaction, support, alliance and assembly amongst users (Barnes et al., 2012). The features of Web 2.0 offer the opportunity to overcome the restrictions of distance for all businesses, whether large, medium or small (Barnes et al., 2012). In addition, Web 2.0 delivers the combined collaborative and participatory approaches to relationship building using tactics such as consumer relationship management. It depends on enterprise applications which are intricate and expensive (Barnes et al., 2012). Thus, industries all around the world are beginning to extensively embrace Web 2.0 in order to forge closer links with stakeholders in more effective ways (Barnes et al., 2012). However, Constantinides and Fountain (2008) suggest that the particular nature of Web 2.0 has not been fully understood and, more importantly, there is no universal definition of the term. Therefore, from a practical viewpoint, the term Web 2.0 is not universally understood (Barnes et al., 2012).

On the other hand, Ahlqvist et al. 2008 consider User Generated Content (UGC) to be something that users can engender and share on the web. However, Kaplan and Haenlein (2010) view UGC as the overall procedure through which individuals make use of social media. The term UGC is useful to distinguish between the various types of media content like audio, video, images, information, labels, assessments, playlists and so on that are publicly available.

User Generated Content (UGC) can be described as the collaborative outputs of all the opportunities that people take advantage of in social media settings (Ozuem, Almeida, and Azemi, 2016; Kaplan and Haenlein, 2010). UGC comprises several forms of media content which are openly accessible and formed by end-users; from text to video and audio resources (Kaplan and Haenlein, 2010). Tang, Fang, and Wang (2014) define UGC simply as media content used to exchange information and views with users. Others have also suggested that UGC is content that is made available on the web which is codified by users without having professional knowledge and practice. Such users, however, have a certain amount of creative ability (Shao, 2009; Christodoulides, Jevons, & Bonhomme, 2012; Organization for Economic Cooperation and Development, 2007).

UGC has the ability to appear in many forms and formats. Letters in newspapers can be regarded as the oldest examples of UGC whereby users had the ability to modify written content in newspapers (Fill, 2009). Currently, Most UGC takes the form of online media which ranges from podcasts, online forums, 'comments', pictures and videos, blogging and reviews (Simon, 2016).

Therefore, UGC is any form of content from digital images, videos, audio files, statements, tweets and blog discussions to forum posts, and everything in between which has been generated by amateur contributors or users. This form of content sharing is considered the consequence of users that endorse brands, rather than content created by the brand itself.

Social Media from a communication perspective refers to the revolution that occurred following the dawn of the information age which expanded human intellect and enhanced social practices and the sharing of intelligence. From this point of view, social media lets users create, discover, share, appraise, and collaboratively create information which is easily accessible online to mass audiences. This suggests that social media has changed the way we communicate from one-to-many (monologue) to many-to-many (dialogue).

Remarkably, even though experts have sought to define social media, limited attention has been given to exploring how organisations define and understand social media (Treem & Leonardi, 2012). The internet plays an integral role in the development of all types of businesses by giving them chances to diverse forms of social media tools like Facebook, Twitter and Instagram. These are used by millions of people on an hourly basis. On the other hand, through peer communications, social media exert a significant influence over consumer purchasing behaviours (Wang et al., 2012; Lueg et al. 2006; Okazaki 2009). At the same time, social media which can be used as powerful marketing tools can support enterprises to create new and dynamic business prospects (Jagongo and Kinyua, 2013). According to Hennig-Thurau et al., (2004) social media has changed the nature of communication between manufacturers and marketers and their targeted clients. Social media is now instrumental in the strategies of several industries (Laroche et al., 2012).

Conversely, social networking provides access to the resources businesses require that are normally very difficult for them to reach (Jagongo and Kinyua, 2013). Social media resources can increase contact between customers and suppliers. It can promote innovation and drive organisations to engage in strategic partnerships (Della Corte, Iavazzi and D'Andrea, 2015). In addition, social media is a platform for businesses to inspire and enhance the sense of intimacy and meaningful relationships they maintain with their customers (Felix et al., 2017; Mersey, Malthouse, & Calder, 2010; Swani, Brown, & Milne, 2014). It also creates more potential to link up with corporate allies internationally (Drummond, McGrath and O'Toole, 2017; Michaelidou, Siamagka, & Christodoulides, 2011). Kim and Ko (2012) and Ozuem, Howell and Lancaster, (2008) see social media as a two-way direct communications medium whereby marketers and consumers both contribute to a new way of trading, servicing and generating corporate models and standards. This would suggest that social interactions via social media are useful for communicating with likeminded individuals and for establishing networks with the public. Hogan & Quan-Haase, (2010) labelled social media as a "moving target" while Sorenson, (2013) contended that social media belongs to a period of rapid development that, at its peak, will overtake anyone's aptitude to make sense of it.

By reviewing different opinions about social media, it can be determined that social media is a platform which allows users to publish and observe a diverse form of information. It can thus be implemented as a strategy for marketing, which involves continuous updating. Enterprises continue to enjoy a variety of advantages from social media. Such a platform of communication has very wide reach. It is low cost to use and offers effective and efficient communications potential (Kaplan and Haenlein, 2010; Kim and Ko, 2012). Businesses can draw attention to different types of users in different parts of the world and they can link with current loyal, and potential customers (Wang et al., 2016; Schultz et al., 2012; Della Corte et al., 2015). This can be carried out effectively and in a more affordable way than with traditional media (Wang et al., 2012). Social media swap physical immediacy for a virtual interface (Barnes et al., 2012). Interaction is vibrant for business actors who can assemble resources quickly to build links (Finch et al., 2012).

Currently, corporate social networking platforms create the opportunity to involve the consumer to generate value in online experiences with offline outcomes. Moreover, whether carried out to fulfil needs or to enjoy interactions in social media platforms, individuals like the idea of contributing, creating and participating online (Laroche et al., 2012). Thus, consumer socialization means that this new and alternative way of communications has changed consumer behaviour permanently. (Lueg et al. 2006; Okazaki 2009).

The intense level of competency of social media compared to traditional ways of communicating through networks has encouraged established leaders to use online content such as Twitter, Facebook, Skype, LinkedIn and so on to build a more sustainable and dynamic environment for their businesses (Kaplan & Haenlein, 2010). The arrival of social media has created powerful options for relational and logistic communication (Lovejoy and Saxton, 2012). Therefore, it can be argued that social media provides an opportunity for all types of businesses to widen their scope and grow their operations to even greater levels of capacity.

Previous studies have claimed that non-profit making enterprises are unable to practice or adopt websites and that social media is underrealized as a tactical, collaborative stakeholder engagement tool (Kent, Taylor, &White, 2003; Saxton, Guo, & Brown, 2007; Chang et al., 2015; Kim, 2016). This perception was perhaps formulated due to a lack of opportunity to create more communications sites with comment options and argument panels. The arrival of social media sites like Facebook and Twitter make those observations invalid since they are free to use and have built-in interactive features (Lovejoy and Saxton, 2012). Therefore, any business, whether large or small, profit or non-profit can generate an online site and start to build a network and grow business activity.

Regardless of the prevalence and rising concentration on social media, an empirical enquiry is only in its embryonic stage. Research has demonstrated the importance and impact of social media usage for consumer marketing (Quinton & Wilson, 2016; Siamagka, Christodoulides, Michaelidou, & Valvi, 2015; Swani et al., 2014) as well as the implications and practices of social media in firms (Treem & Leonardi, 2012; Koch, Leidner and Gonzalez, 2013; Leonardi, 2014). Other research has focussed on branding in large organisations (Ali, Jiménez-Zarco, & Bicho, 2015; Hudson et al., 2015; Kilgour, Sasser, & Larke, 2015; Colleoni, 2013; Arora & Predmore, 2013; Dahnil, Marzuki, Langgat, & Fabeil, 2014). Yet very little has been written about the impact on or usage of social media in SMEs (Dahnil et al., 2014; Wang et al., 2016; Öztamur & Karakadilar, 2014) especially in social entrepreneurial firms.

Social Media as a Strategic Weapon

Although the literature exposes the various theoretical benefits of social media, most of these are operational in nature rather than strategic (Barnes et al., 2012). The adoption of ICTs has been considered a strategic weapon to reach an extensive market and compete with big enterprises for some time (Safari et al., 2015; Ongori and Migiro, 2010). Social media can be used as a tool to develop a dynamic strategy in business (Williams & Williams, 2008). Social networking sites have become central aspects of network resources for administrations. They add strategic value to business performance (Zhou, Wu, & Luo, 2007). Since they offer businesses the potential to interact with distant audiences, social media also create the opportunity to determine new prospects in business strategies. Social media, which offer a widespread source of information, have transformed the strategies of many companies (Mangold & Faulds, 2009). Once introduced as a part of business strategy, social media can play a significant role in managing customer relationships, enhancing communication and facilitating the sharing of knowledge amongst all stakeholders.

Social media help businesses to understand what the public think about their brands, and help them better understand competitors. This helps to inform future strategies. At the same time, social media can help firms to better engage with existing customers (Della Corte et al., 2015). They can influence customers to make repeat purchases. Social media offers an adaptive and sustainable business strategy to entrepreneurs by helping them to join forces and share a diverse range of knowledge with their networks (Drummond et al., 2017). However, Jagongo & Kinyua, (2013) suggest that policymakers in the world of social media should offer constructive online surfing tariffs and e-business strategies in order to inspire entrepreneurs to engage with technological advantages which could add a new dimension to any business format.

Social Entrepreneurship

Any discussion related to "social entrepreneurship" must begin with the term "entrepreneurship" (Martin and Osberg, 2007). Entrepreneurship is a leading component of economic growth and expansion (Anokhin et al. 2008; Rani 2013; Kedmenec et al. 2015). Alongside economic progression, entrepreneurship influences and transforms social conditions (Harding, 2007). Gurol & Atsan, (2006) claim that entrepreneurship is an engine to create new job opportunities, as well as social modifications. On the other hand, it is recognised as a potential breeding ground for technological advancements as well as product and market revolution (Mueller and Thomas, 2000). Entrepreneurship is the process of starting up a business and then contributing to the development of a strong economic position (Harding, 2007). Entrepreneurship is a process which seeks opportunities without concern for the currently controlled resources (Stevenson and Jarillo, 1990). Miller (1983), categorises entrepreneurial behaviour as "innovation, proactiveness and risk-taking". On the other hand, Shane (2003) states that revolution, evaluation and exploitation are all key aspects of entrepreneurship.

Dess et al. (1999) argue that there are two different ways of setting up corporate entrepreneurship. One is to develop an entirely new way to trade, and the other is to alter the present circumstances and curricula via strategic revitalization. Messeghem, (2003) agrees and suggests that launching a business is just a technique which is associated with nursing entrepreneurial behaviour. Such behaviour involves generating or adding to new activity as part of entrepreneurial actions (Stevenson and Jarillo, 1990; Messeghem, 2003). In this sense, the entrepreneur can come up with a new product or service in existing markets to dominate market share and to increase value for the enterprise (Certo and Miller, 2008).

Messeghem, (2003) also suggests that the dynamic detection of new opportunities is part of entrepreneurship and is a tactical dimension of the firm. According to Alvord et al. (2004), entrepreneurship is the process of forming a viable business organization. Thus, it can be said that entrepreneurship is the creation of value through innovation. However, entrepreneurial research has both academic and practical importance which invite further research (Abdulwahab and Al-Damen, 2015).

Social entrepreneurship is the arena in which entrepreneurs modify their actions to be directly knotted with the pivotal goal of bringing social value (Abu-Saifan, 2012). Last few decade, social entrepreneurship has become a progressively important global cultural phenomenon (Dacin et al. 2011; Thompson et al. 2000) because of the failure of government and other responsible authority to lessen toughest and most intractable social challenges such as poverty, social expulsion, and the diverse nature of environment (Harding, 2007).

According to Alvarez and Barney, (2007) the idea of developing new value is vital for the field of entrepreneurship and spreading this sense to the land of social entrepreneurship has directed to an evolving research stream of concentration to scholars (Mair & Martı, 2006; Austin et al., 2012; Certo and Miller, 2008; Trivedi and Stokols, 2011; Peredo and Chrisman, 2006; Dacin et al. 2011; Schendel and Hitt, 2007).

Social entrepreneurship is a multidimensional concept concerning the entrepreneurially virtuous activities to eradicate social problems or attain the social objectives (Mort et al., 2003; Thompson, 2002). Even though social entrepreneurship is comparatively new, the practice of this phenomenon is considerably older and has been undertaken with government support by private foundations for many years. Social entrepreneurship is a creative activity that can support needy and relegated groups and take an approach to explain social difficulties in inventive ways (Noruzi, Westover, & Rahimi, 2010;

Unkwu, Jude and Obiajulu, Egbunike and Ozuem, 2016). Social entrepreneurship has been the subject of a great deal of academic attention in recent decades.

Awareness of social entrepreneurship within the academic world and amongst government only developed in the 1990s. This took place alongside the evolution of new media in the 2000s. In 2004, social co-operatives were launched in the UK to help social businesses to harness their returns and resources for social purposes. As the borders between government, not-for-profit, and commercial sectors have become increasingly blurred, and as further ground-breaking and profitable ways of addressing social problems have emerged, there has been a greater focus on how ideas like social entrepreneurship can address critical social problems (Dees & Anderson, 2003).

Even though the focus on social-oriented business has increased over the years (Dacin et al. 2011; Thompson et al. 2000), it is clear that the concept of social entrepreneurship remains indistinct (Haugh, 2005; Robinson and Lo, 2005; Certo and Miller, 2008; Dacin et al. 2011). Scholars like Smith, Bell and Watts, (2014) have suggested that more comprehensive research to look at how advanced social projects are determined is essential in order to comprehend the phenomena more clearly. In addition, since much research has emphasized the charitable nature of social enterprises, their commercial role has never fully come into focus (Dees, 1998).

In this study the process of resource mobilization in terms of developing market strategy considered as a leading research gap. During the growth phase, every organisation requires doing their marketing broadly which involve extensive resource acquisition. The selection of this gap was determined by many aspects. Regardless of the dominant theoretical evidence on the role of marketing in the development of commercial businesses, it is a surprising fact that there is a lack of academic research on marketing in the context of social enterprise (Agafonow, 2014; Shaw & Carter, 2007). On the other hand, to obtain the required funding, influence customers perception, spread business activity and distinguishable business model, social enterprises need to promote themselves (Agafonow, 2014).

Compared to developed countries, in developing countries like Bangladesh, Social enterprises operate in a condition of resource constrained. Regularly they are competing with several other organizations for resources together with the shortage of capital and expert employees. Lack of adequate funding is considered as a primary obstacle for the growth of social enterprises in developing countries especially in the Asian region (Kim and Lim, 2017).

Social media can deliver an excellent return for entrepreneurs and can help them to capitalise on social investments. Currently, almost all types of businesses are engaging in social networking communications (Bughin, 2008). The cooperative actions of entrepreneurial organisations and their partners through two-way communication on social media platforms has proven productive (Lacka & Chong, 2016; Singaraju et al., 2016). The co-creation of new products, facilities, concepts and systems has been accelerated with the evolution of social media (Drummond et al., 2017).

MANAGERIAL IMPLICATIONS

Social media has modified the way businesses deal with customers (Nadeem, 2012). Blogs, social networking sites, content communities, virtual worlds and collaborative projects collectively represent groups of individuals that generate and distribute content internally and outside of specialised practices. It is now one of the core elements of communicating with consumers (Ozuem, Patel, Howell, and Lancaster, G., 2017). Businesses are starting to form expressive and constant affairs that comprise regular connections with their clients. This new description of customer engagement permits firms to establish reliable relations that spread and exist a long time.

Research increasingly reveals numerous motives for the uptake of social media usage amongst companies (Scott & Orlikowski, 2014; Uyar and Boyar, 2015; Leonardi,2014). In several cases, researchers have focussed on the practice of internal social media stands (Scott & Orlikowski, 2014; Lee, 2016; Huang, Baptista & Galliers, 2013) by prominent companies communicating with international networks (Karjaluoto and Ulkuniemi, 2015). In this sense, social media offers many interactional benefits and outcomes that were previously difficult, and often impossible to attain. Social media facilitates an innovative way to share knowledge (Koch, Leidner and Gonzalez, 2013) and a new means to reach geographically isolated users (Scott & Orlikowski, 2014). Kaplan and Haenlin (2010) have underscored the significance of social media platforms and proposed some approaches to adopting social media in business. There is scope to explore social media more strictly in terms of its uses in social enterprise.

Indeed, most academic literature examines commercial enterprises rather than social enterprises when it comes to social media. A consequence of this is that researchers have perhaps overlooked an essential context (Lewis, 2015; Koch Gonzalez & Leidner, 2012; Vandenbosch and Eggermont, 2016; Kaplan and Haenlein, 2010) and have tended to depend on the inaccurate hypothesis that social entrepreneurs understand and thus unable to take full advantage from social media (Ho, 2016). Besides, such assumptions do overlook the fast-paced nature of technology and variation in the types of users and business settings that are implicated.

REFERENCES

Abdulwahab, M., & Al-Damen, D. (2015). The Impact of Entrepreneurs' Characteristics on Small Business Success at Medical Instruments Supplies Organizations in Jordan. *International Journal of Business and Social Science*, *6*(8), 164–175.

Abu-Saifan, S. (2012, February). Social Entrepreneurship: Definition and Boundaries. *Technology Innovation Management Review*, 22-27.

Agafonow, A. (2014). Value Creation, Value Capture, and Value Devolution. *Administration & Society*, *47*(8), 1038–1060. doi:10.1177/0095399714555756

Ahlqvist, T., Back, A., Halonen, M., & Heinonen, S. (2008). *Social media roadmaps: exploring the futures triggered by social media*. VTT. Retrieved from http://www.vtt.fi/inf/pdf/tiedotteet/2008/t2454.pdf

Ahmad, S., Abu Bakar, A., Faziharudean, T., & Mohamad Zaki, K. (2014). An Empirical Study of Factors Affecting E-Commerce Adoption among Small- and Medium-Sized Enterprises in a Developing Country: Evidence from Malaysia. *Information Technology for Development*, *21*(4), 555–572. doi:10.1080/02681102.2014.899961

Ainin, S., Parveen, F., Moghavvemi, S., Noor, I. J., & Nor Liyana, M. S. (2015). Factors influencing the use of social media by SMEs and its performance outcomes. *Industr Mngmnt & Data Systems*, *115*(3), 570–588. doi:10.1108/IMDS-07-2014-0205

Alalwan, A., Rana, N., Dwivedi, Y., & Algharabat, R. (2017). Social media in marketing: A review and analysis of the existing literature. *Telematics and Informatics*, *34*(7), 1177–1190. doi:10.1016/j.tele.2017.05.008

Ali, A. H. (2011). Power of Social Media in Developing Nations: New Tools for Closing the Global Digital Divide and Beyond, The. *Harv. Hum. Rts. J.*, *24*, 185.

Ali, I., Jiménez-Zarco, A. I., & Bicho, M. (2015). Using Social Media for CSR communication and engaging stakeholders. *Developments in Corporate Governance and Responsibility*, *7*, 165–185. doi:10.1108/S2043-052320150000007010

Alshawi, M., & Goulding, J. (2008). Organisational e-readiness: Embracing IT for sustainable competitive advantage. *Construction Innovation*, *8*(1), ci.2008.33308aaa.001. doi:10.1108/ci.2008.33308aaa.001

Alvarez, S., Barney, J., & Anderson, P. (2013). Forming and Exploiting Opportunities: The Implications of Discovery and Creation Processes for Entrepreneurial and Organizational Research. *Organization Science*, *24*(1), 301–317. doi:10.1287/orsc.1110.0727

Alvord, S. H., Brown, L. D., & Letts, C. W. (2004). Social entrepreneurship and societal transformation: An exploratory study. *The Journal of Applied Behavioral Science*, *40*(3), 260–282. doi:10.1177/0021886304266847

Anderson, S., Hamilton, K., & Tonner, A. (2016). Social labour: Exploring work in consumption. *Marketing Theory*, *16*(3), 383–400. doi:10.1177/1470593116640598

Anokhin, S., Grichnik, D., & Hisrich, R. D. (2008). The journey from novice to serial entrepreneurship in China and Germany: Are the drivers the same. *Managing Global Transitions*, *6*(2), 117–142.

Arora, P., & Predmore, C. E. (2013). Social media as a strategic tool: Going beyond the obvious. *Advanced Series in Management*, *11*, 115–127. doi:10.1108/S1877-6361(2013)0000011010

Austin, J., Stevenson, H., & Wei-Skillern, J. (2006). Social and commercial entrepreneurship: Same, different, or both? *Entrepreneurship Theory and Practice*, *30*(1), 1–22. doi:10.1111/j.1540-6520.2006.00107.x

Barnes, D., Clear, F., Dyerson, R., Harindranath, G., Harris, L., & Rae, A. (2012). Web 2.0 and micro-businesses: An exploratory investigation. *Journal of Small Business and Enterprise Development*, *19*(4), 687–711. doi:10.1108/14626001211277479

Bogataj Habjan, K., & Pucihar, A. (2017). Cloud Computing Adoption Business Model Factors: Does Enterprise Size Matter? *The Engineering Economist*, *28*(3).

boyd, d., & Ellison, N. (2007). Social Network Sites: Definition, History, and Scholarship. *Journal of Computer-Mediated Communication*, *13*(1), 210-230.

Brodie, R. J., Ilic, A., Juric, B., & Hollebeek, L. (2013). Consumer engagement in a virtual brand community: An exploratory analysis. *Journal of Business Research*, *66*(1), 105–114. doi:10.1016/j.jbusres.2011.07.029

Brunswicker, S., & Vanhaverbeke, W. (2013). *Open Innovation in Small and Medium-Sized Enterprises (SMEs): External Knowledge Sourcing Strategies and Internal Organizational Facilitators.* SSRN Electronic Journal.

Bughin, J. (2008). The rise of enterprise 2.0. *Journal of Direct Data and Digital Marketing Practice*, *9*(3), 251–259. doi:10.1057/palgrave.dddmp.4350100

Castells, M. (2011). A network theory of power. *International Journal of Communication*, *5*, 773–787.

Certo, S., & Miller, T. (2008). Social entrepreneurship: Key issues and concepts. *Business Horizons*, *51*(4), 267–271. doi:10.1016/j.bushor.2008.02.009

Chang, C.-C., Hung, S.-W., Cheng, M.-J., & Wu, C.-Y. (2015). Exploring the intention to continue using social networking sites: The case of Facebook. *Technological Forecasting and Social Change*, *95*, 48–56. doi:10.1016/j.techfore.2014.03.012

Christodoulides, G., Jevons, C., & Bonhomme, J. (2012). Memo to marketers: Quantitative evidence for change. How user-generated content really affects brands. *Journal of Advertising Research*, *52*(1), 53–64. doi:10.2501/JAR-52-1-053-064

Colleoni, E. (2013). CSR communication strategies for organizational legitimacy in social media. *Corporate Communications*, *18*(2), 228–248. doi:10.1108/13563281311319508

Constantinides, E., & Fountain, S. (2008). Web 2.0: Conceptual foundations and marketing issues. *Journal of Direct. Data and Digital Marketing Practice*, *9*(3), 231–244. doi:10.1057/palgrave.dddmp.4350098

Dacin, M., Dacin, P., & Tracey, P. (2011). Social Entrepreneurship: A Critique and Future Directions. *Organization Science*, *22*(5), 1203–1213. doi:10.1287/orsc.1100.0620

Dahnil, M. I., Marzuki, K. M., Langgat, J., & Fabeil, N. F. (2014). Factors Influencing SMEs Adoption of Social Media Marketing. *Procedia: Social and Behavioral Sciences*, *148*, 119–126. doi:10.1016/j.sbspro.2014.07.025

Dees, J. G. (1998). *The meaning of social entrepreneurship.* Comments and suggestions contributed from the Social Entrepreneurship Funders Working Group.

Dees, J. G., & Anderson, B. B. (2003). For-Profit Social Ventures. *International Journal of Entrepreneurship Education*, *2*, 1–26.

Della Corte, V., Iavazzi, A., & D'Andrea, C. (2015). Customer involvement through social media: The cases of some telecommunication firms. *Journal of Open Innovation: Technology, Market, and Complexity*, *1*(1), 10. doi:10.118640852-015-0011-y

Deng, X., Joshi, K., & Li, Y. (2015). Introduction to the Social Media and Enterprise Minitrack: Job and Work Design Issues. In *System Sciences (HICSS), 2015 48th Hawaii International Conference on* (pp. 1818–1818). IEEE.

Dess, G. D., Lumpkin, G. T., & McGee, J. E. (1999). Linking Corporate Entrepreneurship to Strategy, Structure, and Process: Suggested Research Directions. *Entrepreneurship Theory and Practice*, *23*(3), 85–102. doi:10.1177/104225879902300306

Drummond, C., McGrath, H., & O'Toole, T. (2017). The impact of social media on resource mobilisation in entrepreneurial firms. *Industrial Marketing Management.*

Drummond, C., McGrath, H., & O'Toole, T. (2017). The impact of social media on resource mobilisation in entrepreneurial firms. *Industrial Marketing Management.*

Durkin, M., McGowan, P., & McKeown, N. (2013). Exploring social media adoption in small to medium-sized enterprises in Ireland. *Journal of Small Business and Enterprise Development*, *20*(4), 716–734. doi:10.1108/JSBED-08-2012-0094

Felix, R., Rauschnabel, P. A., & Hinsch, C. (2017). Elements of strategic social media marketing: A holistic framework. *Journal of Business Research*, *70*, 118–126. doi:10.1016/j.jbusres.2016.05.001

Fernández-Olmos, M., & Ramírez-Alesón, M. (2017). How internal and external factors influence the dynamics of SME technology collaboration networks over time. *Technovation*, *64-65*, 16–27. doi:10.1016/j.technovation.2017.06.002

Fill, C. (2009). *Marketing communications: Interactivity, communities and content* (5th ed.). Harlow, UK: Prentice Hall/Financial Times

Finch, J., Wagner, B., & Hynes, N. (2012). Resources prospectively: How actors mobilize resources in business settings. *Journal of Business Research*, *65*(2), 164–174. doi:10.1016/j.jbusres.2011.05.017

Fosso Wamba, S., & Carter, L. (2014). Social Media Tools Adoption and Use by SMEs: An Empirical Study. *Journal of End User and Organizational Computing*, *26*(1), 1–16. doi:10.4018/joeuc.2014040101

Georgescu, M., & Popescul, D. (2015). Social media–the new paradigm of collaboration and communication for business environment. *Procedia Economics and Finance*, *20*, 277–282. doi:10.1016/S2212-5671(15)00075-1

Grizane, T., & Jurgelane, I. (2017). Social Media Impact on Business Evaluation. *Procedia Computer Science*, *104*, 190–196. doi:10.1016/j.procs.2017.01.103

Gunasekaran, A., McGaughey, R., Ngai, E., & Rai, B. (2009). E-Procurement Adoption in the Southcoast SMEs. *International Journal of Production Economics*, *122*(1), 161–175. doi:10.1016/j.ijpe.2009.05.013

Gurol, Y., & Atsan, N. (2006). Entrepreneurial characteristics amongst university students. *Education + Training*, *48*(1), 25–38. doi:10.1108/00400910610645716

Hammedi, W., Kandampully, J., Zhang, T. T., & Bouquiaux, L. (2015). Online customer engagement: Creating social environments through brand community constellations. *Journal of Service Management*, *26*(5), 777–806. doi:10.1108/JOSM-11-2014-0295

Harding, R. (2007). Understanding social entrepreneurship. *Industry and Higher Education*, *21*(1), 73–86. doi:10.5367/000000007780222723

Harris, L., & Rae, A. (2009). Social networks: The future of marketing for small business. *The Journal of Business Strategy*, *30*(5), 24–31. doi:10.1108/02756660910987581

Haugh, H. (2005). A research agenda for social entrepreneurship. *Social Enterprise Journal*, *1*(1), 1–12. doi:10.1108/17508610580000703

Hennig-Thurau, T., Gwinner, K. P., Walsh, G., & Gremler, D. D. (2004). Electronic Word-of-Mouth Via Consumer Opinion Platforms: What Motivates Consumers to Articulate Themselves on the Internet? *Journal of Interactive Marketing*, *18*(1), 38–52. doi:10.1002/dir.10073

Ho, T. (2016). Private Entrepreneurs in China: Social Entrepreneurs or Social Menaces? *Chinese Public Administration Review*, *3*(1/2), 14. doi:10.22140/cpar.v3i1/2.52

Hogan, B., & Quan-Haase, A. (2010). Persistence and Change in Social Media. *Bulletin of Science, Technology & Society*, *30*(5), 309–315. doi:10.1177/0270467610380012

Huang, J., Baptista, J., & Galliers, R. (2013). Reconceptualizing rhetorical practices in organizations: The impact of social media on internal communications. *Information & Management*, *50*(2-3), 112–124. doi:10.1016/j.im.2012.11.003

Hudson, S., Roth, M. S., Madden, T. J., & Hudson, R. (2015). The effects of social media on emotions, brand relationship quality, and word of mouth: An empirical study of music festival attendees. *Tourism Management*, *47*, 68–76. doi:10.1016/j.tourman.2014.09.001

Jagongo, A., & Kinyua, C. (2013). The Social Media and Entrepreneurship Growth (A New Business Communication Paradigm among SMEs in Nairobi). *International Journal of Humanities and Social Science*, *3*(10), 213–227.

Järvinen, J., Tollinen, A., Karjaluoto, H., & Jayawardhena, C. (2012). Digital and social media marketing usage in B2B industrial section. *Marketing Management Journal, 22*(2).

Kadam, A., & Ayarekar, S. (2014). Impact of Social Media on Entrepreneurship and Entrepreneurial Performance: Special Reference to Small and Medium Scale Enterprises. *SIES Journal of Management, 10*(1).

Kane, G., Alavi, M., Labianca, G., & Borgatti, S. (2014). What's Different About Social Media Networks? A Framework and Research Agenda. *Management Information Systems Quarterly*, *38*(1), 274–304. doi:10.25300/MISQ/2014/38.1.13

Kaplan, A. M., & Haenlein, M. (2010). Users of the world, unite! The challenges and opportunities of Social Media. *Business Horizons*, *53*(1), 59–68. doi:10.1016/j.bushor.2009.09.003

Karikari, S., Osei-Frimpong, K., & Owusu-Frimpong, N. (2017). Evaluating individual level antecedents and consequences of social media use in Ghana. *Technological Forecasting and Social Change*, *123*, 68–79. doi:10.1016/j.techfore.2017.06.023

Karjaluoto, H., & Ulkuniemi, P. (2015). Digital communications in industrial marketing. *Journal of Business and Industrial Marketing*, *30*(6). doi:10.1108/JBIM-04-2013-0092

Kedmenec, I., Rebernik, M., & Perić, J. (2015). The Impact of Individual Characteristics on Intentions to Pursue Social Entrepreneurship. *Ekonomski Pregled*, *66*(2), 119–137.

Kent, M. L., Taylor, M., & White, W. J. (2003). The relationship between Web site design and organizational responsiveness to stakeholders. *Public Relations Review*, *29*(1), 63–77. doi:10.1016/S0363-8111(02)00194-7

Kilgour, M., Sasser, S. L., & Larke, R. (2015). The social media transformation process: Curating content into strategy. *Corporate Communications*, *20*(3), 326–343. doi:10.1108/CCIJ-07-2014-0046

Kim, A., & Ko, E. (2012). Do social media marketing activities enhance customer equity? An empirical study of luxury fashion brand. *Journal of Business Research*, *65*(10), 1480–1486. doi:10.1016/j.jbusres.2011.10.014

Kim, D. (2016). Value ecosystem models for social media services. *Technological Forecasting and Social Change*, *107*, 13–27. doi:10.1016/j.techfore.2016.03.010

Kim, D., & Lim, U. (2017). Social Enterprise as a Catalyst for Sustainable Local and Regional Development. *Sustainability*, *9*(8), 1427. doi:10.3390u9081427

Kim, H. D., Lee, I., & Lee, C. K. (2013). Building Web 2.0 enterprises: A study of small and medium enterprises in the United States. *International Small Business Journal*, *31*(2), 156–174. doi:10.1177/0266242611409785

Koch, H., Leidner, D., & Gonzalez, E. (2013). Digitally enabling social networks: Resolving IT-culture conflict. *Information Systems Journal*, *23*(6), 501–523. doi:10.1111/isj.12020

Kumar, A., Bezawada, R., Rishika, R., Janakiraman, R., & Kannan, P. (2016). From social to sale: The effects of firm-generated content in social media on customer behavior. *Journal of Marketing*, *80*(1), 7–25. doi:10.1509/jm.14.0249

Lacka, E., & Chong, A. (2016). Usability perspective on social media sites' adoption in the B2B context. *Industrial Marketing Management*, *54*, 80–91. doi:10.1016/j.indmarman.2016.01.001

Lane, P., Wafa, S., & Hassan, R. (2014). Perceived Usefulness and Perceived Ease of Use of E-Commerce Adoption among Entrepreneurs in Sabah. *Kuwait Chapter of Arabian Journal of Business and Management Review*, *3*(9), 94–103. doi:10.12816/0018333

Laroche, M., Habibi, M. R., Richard, M. O., & Sankaranarayanan, R. (2012). The effects of social media based brand communities on brand community markers, value creation practices, brand trust and brand loyalty. *Computers in Human Behavior*, *28*(5), 1755–1767. doi:10.1016/j.chb.2012.04.016

Lee, J., & Hong, I. B. (2016). Predicting positive user responses to social media advertising: The roles of emotional appeal, informativeness, and creativity. *International Journal of Information Management*, *36*(3), 360–373. doi:10.1016/j.ijinfomgt.2016.01.001

Leonardi. (2014). Social media, knowledge sharing, and innovation. *Information Systems Research*, *25*(4), 796–816. doi:10.1287/isre.2014.0536

Lewis, S. (2015). Reciprocity as a Key Concept for Social Media and Society. *Social Media + Society*, *1*(1).

Lincoln, S. (2010). *Mastering Web 2.0*. London: Kogan Page.

Lovejoy, K., & Saxton, G. (2012). Information, Community, and Action: How Nonprofit Organizations Use Social Media*. *Journal of Computer-Mediated Communication*, *17*(3), 337–353. doi:10.1111/j.1083-6101.2012.01576.x

Lueg, J. E., Ponder, N., Beatty, S. E., & Capella, M. L. (2006). Teenagers' Use of Alternative Shopping Channels: A Consumer Socialization Perspective. *Journal of Retailing*, *82*(2), 137–153. doi:10.1016/j.jretai.2005.08.002

Mair, J., & Marti, I. (2006). Social entrepreneurship research: A source of explanation, prediction, and delight. *Journal of World Business*, *41*(1), 36–44. doi:10.1016/j.jwb.2005.09.002

Mangold, W. G., & Faulds, D. J. (2009). Social media: The new hybrid element of the promotion mix. *Business Horizons*, *52*(4), 357–365. doi:10.1016/j.bushor.2009.03.002

Martin, R. L., & Osberg, S. (2007). Social Entrepreneurship: The Case for Definition. Stanford Social Innovation Review, 29–39.

Mehrtens, J., Cragg, P. B., & Mills, A. M. (2001). A model of Internet Adoption by SMEs. *Information & Management*, *38*(3), 165–176. doi:10.1016/S0378-7206(01)00086-6

Mersey, R. D., Malthouse, E. C., & Calder, B. J. (2010). Engagement with Online Media. *Journal of Media Business Studies*, *7*(2), 39–56. doi:10.1080/16522354.2010.11073506

Messeghem, K. (2003). Strategic entrepreneurship and managerial activities in SMEs. *Estados Unidos, 21*(2), 197–212.

Michaelidou, N., Siamagka, N. T., & Christodoulides, G. (2011). Usage, barriers and measurement of social media marketing: An exploratory investigation of small and medium B2B brands. *Industrial Marketing Management*, *40*(7), 1153–1159. doi:10.1016/j.indmarman.2011.09.009

Miller, D. (1983). The Correlates of Entrepreneurship in Three Types of Firms. *Management Science*, *29*(7), 770–791. doi:10.1287/mnsc.29.7.770

Mort, G. S., Weerawardena, J., & Carnegie, K. (2003). Social entrepreneurship: Towards conceptualisation. *International Journal of Nonprofit and Voluntary Sector Marketing*, *8*(1), 76–89. doi:10.1002/nvsm.202

Mueller, S. L., & Thomas, A. S. (2000). Culture and entrepreneurial potential: A nine-country study of locus of control and innovativeness. *Journal of Business Venturing*, *16*(1), 51–75. doi:10.1016/S0883-9026(99)00039-7

Nadeem, M. (2012). Returning Customer: Was That A Planned Purchase? *Skyline Business Journal*, *7*(1), 11–17.

Noruzi, M. R., Westover, J. H., & Rahimi, G. R. (2010). An Exploration of Social Entrepreneurship in the Entrepreneurship Era. *Asian Social Science*, *6*(6), 3–10. doi:10.5539/ass.v6n6p3

Okazaki, S. (2009). The Tactical Use of Mobile Marketing: How Adolescents' Social Networking Can Best Shape Brand Extensions. *Journal of Advertising Research*, *49*(1), 12–26. doi:10.2501/S0021849909090102

Omosigho, O., & Abeysinghe, G. (2012). Evaluating readiness of organizations to adopt social media for competitive advantage. *Information Society (i-Society), 2012 International Conference on*, 16-21.

Ongori, H., & Migiro, S. (2010). Information and communication technologies adoption in SMEs: Literature review. *Journal of Chinese Entrepreneurship*, *2*(1), 93–104. doi:10.1108/17561391011019041

Organization for Economic Cooperation and Development. (2007, April 12). *Participative web: User-created content*. Retrieved from http://www.oecd.org/sti/38393115.pdf

Öztamur, D., & Karakadilar, I. S. (2014). Exploring the role of social media for SMEs: As a new marketing strategy tool for the firm performance perspective. *Procedia: Social and Behavioral Sciences*, *150*, 511–520. doi:10.1016/j.sbspro.2014.09.067

Ozuem, W., Almeida Pinho, C., & Azemi, Y. (2016). User-Generated Content and Perceived Customer Value. In *Competitive Social Media Marketing Strategies. Mission* (pp. 50–63). Hershey, PA: IGI Global. doi:10.4018/978-1-4666-9776-8.ch003

Ozuem, W., Howell, K., & Lancaster, G. (2008). Communicating in the new interactive marketspace. *European Journal of Marketing*, *42*(9/10), 1059–1083. doi:10.1108/03090560810891145

Ozuem, W., Patel, A., Howell, K., & Lancaster, G. (2017). An exploration of consumers' response to online service recovery initiatives. *International Journal of Market Research*, *59*(1), 97–119.

Ozuem, W., Prasad, J., & Lancaster, G. (2016). Exploiting online social gambling for marketing communications. *Journal of Strategic Marketing*, *26*(3), 258–282. doi:10.1080/0965254X.2016.1211728

Pagani, M., & Malacarne, G. (2017). Experiential engagement and active vs. passive behaviour in mobile location-based social networks: The moderating role of privacy. *Journal of Interactive Marketing*, *37*, 133–148. doi:10.1016/j.intmar.2016.10.001

Peredo, A. M., & McLean, M. (2006). Social entrepreneurship: A critical review of the concept. *Journal of World Business*, *41*(1), 56–65. doi:10.1016/j.jwb.2005.10.007

Pillania, R. (2007). Organisational issues for knowledge management in SMEs. *International Journal of Business and Systems Research*, *1*(3), 367. doi:10.1504/IJBSR.2007.015835

Quinton, S., & Wilson, D. (2016). Tensions and ties in social media networks: Towards a model of understanding business relationship development and business performance enhancement through the use of LinkedIn. *Industrial Marketing Management*, *54*, 15–24. doi:10.1016/j.indmarman.2015.12.001

Rani, S. H. (2013). Antecedents and Consequences of Entrepreneurial Quality among Graduate Entrepreneurs. *Asian Journal of Business and Management Sciences*, *2*(9), 44–55.

Richey, M. (2016). *Exploring social media use in small firms: a cultural toolkit perspective* (PhD thesis). Loughborough University.

Robinson, J. A., & Lo, J. (2005). *Bibliography of Academic Papers on Social Entrepreneurship*. New York: New York University.

Russo, A., Watkins, J., Kelly, L., & Chan, S. (2008). Participatory communication with social media. *Curator (New York, N.Y.)*, *51*(1), 21–31. doi:10.1111/j.2151-6952.2008.tb00292.x

Safari, F., Safari, N., Hasanzadeh, A., & Ghatari, A. (2015). Factors affecting the adoption of cloud computing in small and medium enterprises. *International Journal of Business Information Systems*, *20*(1), 116. doi:10.1504/IJBIS.2015.070894

Safko, L. (2012). *The social media bible* (3rd ed.). Hoboken, NJ: John Wiley & Sons.

Saxton, G. D., Guo, C., & Brown, W. (2007). New dimensions of nonprofit responsiveness: The application and promise of Internet-based technologies. *Public Performance & Management Review*, *31*(2), 144–173. doi:10.2753/PMR1530-9576310201

Schendel, D., & Hitt, M. A. (2007). Introduction to volume 1. *Strategic Entrepreneurship Journal*, *1*(1–2), 1–6. doi:10.1002ej.16

Schultz, R. J., Schwepker, C. H., & Good, D. J. (2012). An exploratory study of social media in business-to-business selling: Salesperson characteristics, activities and performance. *Marketing Management Journal*, *22*(2), 76–89.

Scott, S., & Orlikowski, W. (2014). Entanglements in Practice: Performing Anonymity Through Social Media. *Management Information Systems Quarterly*, *38*(3), 873–893. doi:10.25300/MISQ/2014/38.3.11

Shane, S. (2003). *A general theory of entrepreneurship: The individual-opportunity nexus*. Cheltenham, UK: Edward Elgar Publishing Limited.

Shao, G. (2009). Understanding the appeal of user-generated media: A uses and gratification perspective. *Internet Research*, *19*(1), 7–25. doi:10.1108/10662240910927795

Shaw, E., & Carter, S. (2007). Social entrepreneurship: Theoretical antecedents and empirical analysis of entrepreneurial processes and outcomes. *Journal of Small Business and Enterprise Development*, *14*(3), 418–434. doi:10.1108/14626000710773529

Siamagka, N. T., Christodoulides, G., Michaelidou, N., & Valvi, A. (2015). Determinants of social media adoption by B2B organizations. *Industrial Marketing Management*, *51*, 89–99. doi:10.1016/j.indmarman.2015.05.005

Simon, J.P. (2016). User generated content – users, community of users and firms: Toward new sources of co-innovation? *Info*, *18*(6), 4–25.

Singaraju, S. P., Nguyen, Q. A., Niininen, O., & Sullivan-Mort, G. (2016). Social media and value co-creation in multi-stakeholder systems: A resource integration approach. *Industrial Marketing Management*, *54*, 44–55. doi:10.1016/j.indmarman.2015.12.009

Smith, R., Bell, R., & Watts, H. (2014). Personality trait differences between traditional and social entrepreneurs. *Social Enterprise Journal*, *10*(3), 200–221. doi:10.1108/SEJ-08-2013-0033

Son, M., & Han, K. (2011). Beyond the technology adoption: Technology readiness effects on post-adoption behavior. *Journal of Business Research*, *64*(11), 1178–1182. doi:10.1016/j.jbusres.2011.06.019

Sorenson, O. (2013). Status and reputation: Synonyms or separate concepts? *Strategic Organization*, *12*(1), 62–69. doi:10.1177/1476127013513219

Stepanova, E. (2011). The role of information communication technologies in the "arab spring.". *Ponars Eurasia*, *15*, 1–6.

Stevenson, H. H., & Jarillo, J. C. (1990). A Paradigm of Entrepreneurship: Entrepreneurial Management. *Strategic Management Journal*, *11*, 17–27.

Stockdale, R., & Standing, C. (2004). Benefits and barriers of electronic marketplace participation: An SME perspective null. *Journal of Enterprise Information Management*, *17*(4), 301–311. doi:10.1108/17410390410548715

Swani, K., Brown, B. P., & Milne, G. R. (2014). Should tweets differ for B2B and B2C? An analysis of fortune 500 companies' Twitter communications. *Industrial Marketing Management*, *43*(5), 873–881. doi:10.1016/j.indmarman.2014.04.012

Tang, T., Fang, E., & Wang, F. (2014). Is neutral really neutral? The effects of neutral user generated content on product sales. *Journal of Marketing*, *78*(4), 41–58. doi:10.1509/jm.13.0301

Thompson, J., Alvy, G., & Lees, A. (2000). Social entrepreneurship - A new look at the people and the potential. *Management Decision*, *38*(5), 328–338. doi:10.1108/00251740010340517

Treem, J. W., & Leonardi, P. M. (2012). Social Media Use in Organizations: Exploring the Affordances of Visibility, Editability, Persistence, and Association. *Communication Yearbook*, *3*(6), 143–189.

Trivedi, C., & Stokols, D. (2011). Social Enterprises and Corporate Enterprises: Fundamental Differences and Defining Features. *The Journal of Entrepreneurship*, *20*(1), 1–32. doi:10.1177/097135571002000101

Unkwu, Obiajulu, & Ozuem. (2016) Understanding Social Entrepreneurship: An Exploration of Theory and Practice. *World Journal of Social Sciences, 6*(3), 86-99.

Uyar, A., & Boyar, E. (2015). An Investigation Into Social Media Usage of Publicly Traded Companies. *Journal of Corporate Accounting & Finance*, *27*(1), 71–78. doi:10.1002/jcaf.22113

Vandenbosch, L., & Eggermont, S. (2016). The Interrelated Roles of Mass Media and Social Media in Adolescents' Development of an Objectified Self-Concept. *Communication Research*, *43*(8), 1116–1140. doi:10.1177/0093650215600488

Venkatraman, S., & Fahd, K. (2016). Challenges and Success Factors of ERP Systems in Australian SMEs. *Systems*, *4*(2), 20. doi:10.3390ystems4020020

Vodanovich, S., Sundaram, D., & Myers, M. (2010). Digital Natives and Ubiquitous Information Systems. *Information Systems Research*, *21*(4), 711–723. doi:10.1287/isre.1100.0324

Wamba, S. F., & Carter, L. (2014). Social Media Tools Adoption and Use by SMES: An Empirical Study *Journal of Organizational and End User Computing*, *26*(2), 1–17. doi:10.4018/joeuc.2014040101

Wang, X., Yu, Y., & Wei, Y. (2012). Social media peer communication and impacts on purchase intentions: A consumer socialization framework. *Journal of Interactive Marketing*, *26*(4), 198–208. doi:10.1016/j.intmar.2011.11.004

Williams, T., & Williams, R. (2008). Adopting social media: Are we leaders, managers or followers? *Communication World*, *25*(4), 34–37.

Xiang, Z., & Gretzel, U. (2010). Role of social media in online travel information search. *Tourism Management*, *31*(2), 179–188. doi:10.1016/j.tourman.2009.02.016

Yang, H., Lee, J., Park, C., & Lee, K. (2014). The Adoption of Mobile Self-Service Technologies: Effects of Availability in Alternative Media and Trust on the Relative Importance of Perceived Usefulness and Ease of Use. *International Journal of Smart Home*, *8*(4), 165–178. doi:10.14257/ijsh.2014.8.4.15

Zafarani, R., & Liu, H. (2014). Behavior Analysis in Social Media. *IEEE Intelligent Systems*, *29*(4), 1–4.

Zhou, L. X., Wu, W. P., & Luo, X. M. (2007). Internationalization and the performance of born-global SMEs: The mediating role of social networks. *Journal of International Business Studies*, *38*(4), 673–690. doi:10.1057/palgrave.jibs.8400282

KEY TERMS AND DEFINITIONS

Online Communities: A group of people who have shared interest and communicate through interactive platforms such as discussion boards, websites, e-mail, and chat.

Social Entrepreneurship: Social entrepreneurship mainly focuses on identifying various intractable social difficulties with the innovative concept to eliminate those problems as well as to elevate economic value and the condition of the society.

Social Marketing: Social marketing is the Combination of the concepts of commercial marketing and the social sciences. This is one of the cost-effective and most sustainable idea to influence an individual's behavior.

Social Media: Social media is a platform which allows to publish and observe the diverse form of information and thus it can be implemented as a strategy for marketing and communication, which involves continuous updating.

Social Networking Sites: Social networking sites give the opportunity to create and share a personal profile in the form of text, photo, video and audio in order to connect with other users.

User-Generated Content: User-generated content can be described by way of any form of content, it can refer to digital images, videos, audio files, statements, tweets, blog discussion form posts, and everything in between which has been generated and placed by amateur contributors or users.

Web 2.0: Web 2.0 consider as a platform to produce and established software and content in a collaborative manner instead of the individual company.

Section 2

Perspectives and Practice of Computer-Mediated Marketing Environments

Chapter 6
The Differences of Hedonic Shopping Value and Purchase Intention in the Multichannel Shopping Environment for Apparel Shopping

Charanya Nopnukulvised
Cardiff Metropolitan University, UK

Laden Husamaldin
University of West London, UK

Gordon Bowen
Regent's University London, UK

ABSTRACT

Multichannel shopping has changed the way that consumers shop by offering them more choice and convenience. The growing competitive apparel market forces retailers to assess their current marketing strategies and their implementation. It is fundamental that multichannel retailers constantly provide high levels of hedonic shopping value through multichannel shopping in order to stimulate purchase. The purpose of this chapter is to emphasize the importance of hedonic shopping value in the context of multichannel shopping (in store, website, catalogue, mobile, and social media). The benefits of this chapter are evaluation of the strengths and weaknesses of each channel from the perception of the five channels for apparel shopping based on 18 hedonic shoppers in central London by using semi-structured interviews. The result shows that store and website gain the highest in the level of hedonic shopping value for apparel shopping and those are the most likely channels in which hedonic shoppers intend to shop for apparel in the future, while shopping via catalogue shows the lowest score of both hedonic shopping value and purchase intention. This chapter suggests that exploring the hedonic shopping value that consumers derive across five channels can enhance the understanding of hedonic shopping value in the context of the multichannel shopping environment.

DOI: 10.4018/978-1-5225-7344-9.ch006

INTRODUCTION

The Internet has recently caused a shift towards the multichannel retail strategy. Multichannel shopping has currently become a purchasing pattern in which consumers use multiple channels such as retail stores, websites, television, catalogues and mobile to purchase products or service (Goldsmith and Flynn, 2005; Hsiao et al., 2012; van Dijk et al., 2005; Schoenbachler and Gordon, 2002). Multichannel strategy is more than the different channels to reach consumers but rather how the consumers use and interact across channels (Schoenbachler and Gordon, 2002). Hence, the consumer journey become more complex (Wolny and Charoensuksai, 2014). As channels differ in their constraints and advantages, consumers also perceive the shopping experience differently across channels (Chatterjee, 2010; Levin et al., 2003; Pinto, 2013). Consumers may undoubtedly perceive different levels of hedonic shopping value and purchase intention across channels. This chapter will cover five different channels: store, website, catalogue, mobile and social media. The understanding of hedonic shopping value and purchase intention that consumers derive from each channel is essential for the implementation of a multichannel retail strategy.

HEDONIC SHOPPING VALUE

Babin et al. (1994) defined shopping value as the outcome of a shopping experience. They proposed two fundamental dimensions of shopping values, which are the hedonic and utilitarian benefits of a shopping trip. Shopping is normally characterised by both values but with different weight depending on the shoppers, products, shopping condition and their interaction (Chung, 2015). Moreover, consumers can perceive both hedonic and utilitarian shopping value at the same time in one shopping experience (Babin et al., 1994). Consumers perceive utilitarian value from purchasing what they need while simultaneously perceiving hedonic shopping value from the enjoyment of the shopping experience itself.

Babin et al. (1994) defined hedonic shopping value as the potential entertainment and emotional worth of the shopping experience. Overby and Lee (2006) describe hedonic shopping value as an overall assessment of experiential benefits such as pleasure and entertainment. Hedonic shopping value is more subjective and personal than utilitarian shopping value (Babin et al., 1994). Hedonic shopping value is derived from exploration and entertainment (Davis, 2013). Consumers regularly seek pleasure rather than task completion from a shopping experience. Increased arousal, fun, fantasy fulfilment, entertainment, freedom and escapism all indicate a hedonically valuable shopping experience (Babin et al., 1994). Moreover, shopping activity can provide hedonic shopping value with or without purchase (Chang, 2001; Irani and Hanzaee, 2011).

On the contrary, utilitarian shopping value reflects a shopping trip as task-specific, rational and goal-fulfilling (Batra and Ahtola, 1991). Overby and Lee (2006) defined utilitarian shopping value as an overall assessment of functional benefits and economic value. Utilitarian shopping value is seen as work or missions to be accomplished (Holbrook and Hirschman, 1982). Utilitarian shopping value is derived from cost-effectiveness and convenience (Davis, 2013). The hedonic shopping value aims to measure whether consumers enjoyed apparel shopping, hence for the purpose of this chapter, hedonic shopping value therefore refers to the degree to which consumers derived hedonic value from shopping activity in a particular channel (store, website, catalogue, mobile and social media).

Hedonic Shoppers

Hedonic shoppers and utilitarian shoppers understand differently when it comes to a perceived shopping value (Kazakeviciute and Banyte, 2012). Hedonic shoppers are people who are deeply involved in the satisfaction of shopping (Kirgiz, 2014). Hedonic shoppers may shop for various reasons apart from economic reasons, such as a desire for new trends, socialisation, reducing tension and shopping for others (Arnold and Reynolds, 2003). Hedonic shoppers spend a longer time than average on a shopping trip since they find that the time spent on shopping is pleasant and rewarding (Bellenger and Korgaonkar, 1980). Hedonic shoppers can be seen as impulsive buyers since they are more likely to be engaged with unplanned purchases (Scarpi, 2006).

While hedonic shoppers are motivated towards shopping and looking for fun, amusement, fantasy and sensory stimulation, utilitarian shoppers consider shopping to be a necessary task involved with rational buying motives (Babin et al., 1994; Batra and Ahtola, 1991). Utilitarian shoppers look for convenience in a shopping experience that makes their lives easier (Kim, 2002). Unlike hedonic shoppers, utilitarian shoppers are generally information seekers who search for information through various channels about products that will help them to decide which products to buy (Timothy, 2005). However, they do not necessarily end up with an actual purchase (Kazakeviciute and Banyte, 2012). Still, hedonic shoppers can also be seen as information seekers when they are browsing even though they may or may not have products in their mind (Nurmikko, 2011). Yet they purchase on impulse.

Hedonic shoppers are more likely to be women than men because women generally prefer to go shopping more than men (Tifferet and Herstein, 2012). Men are found to be utilitarian type consumers because they would rather look for apparel to fulfil a practical use (Babin et al., 1994). They see shopping as a task that they want to accomplish within the least possible time and with the least effort (Cardoso and Pinto, 2010). Compared to women, men are not likely to relate with emotional need in order to drive their purchase (Parker, 2011). In contrast, women view shopping as more than just a purchase, and they look at the overall shopping experience (Tifferet and Herstein, 2012). Women usually spend more time shopping, and look for more information and more options than men (Cardoso and Pinto, 2010).

Purchase Intention

Purchase intention refers to the likelihood that consumers are willing to purchase certain products or services again after they have evaluated that the products or services are worth buying (Hosein, 2012; Madahi and Sukati, 2012; Whitlark et al., 1993). Purchase intention reflects the subjective value of individuals' plans, goals or expectations of what they will do in the future (Armstrong, 2001; Chih and Lin, 2010). Consumers with an intention to purchase certain products will have a higher actual purchase rate (Armstrong, 2001). Therefore, purchase intention can be used to predict consumer purchase behaviour (Chih and Lin, 2010). However, it does not always result in an actual purchase (Kotler et al., 2013). Purchase intention in this chapter refers to the degree of possibility of purchasing apparel through a particular channel (store, website, catalogue, mobile and social media) in the future (Whitlark et al., 1993).

Multichannel Shopping

Multichannel shopping is becoming the standard for retailers rather than complementary technology due to the boom of online purchases (Mintel, 2011). Apart from traditional retailing formats such as store, website, television and catalogue, consumers can shop from mobile phones and even via social media. Multichannel retailing offers many benefits not only to retailers but also to consumers. For retailers, the new online channel can be used to support the entire purchase, and at the same time it can be considered a complementary service for a company (Karimi, 2013). The multichannel retail strategy increases the opportunity to drive traffic and sales across channels (Berman and Thelen, 2004). The greater the number of channels, the more consumers can be reached, and the more effectively consumer needs can be catered for (Berman and Thelen, 2004). Therefore, multichannel shopping helps consumers to step closer to make a purchase (Mintel, 2011). On the other hand, the benefits of multichannel shopping help consumers to increase trust and reduce risks that come from online purchasing (Görsch, 2002). For example, consumers can see the products in-store before purchasing online, or they can return items in-store that they purchase online (Görsch, 2002). Furthermore, multichannel shopping increases levels of convenience and degrees of control now that they can choose different channels for their shopping activities (Görsch, 2002). Multichannel shopping extends choice of sources of product information, product choices and different ways to obtain the products (Schoenbachler and Gordon, 2002). However, not all consumers take advantage of this wider channel choice, as some channels are still not available and some consumers still prefer to shop in traditional stores. Although buying in-store is still the most popular channel, the Internet is involved in many in-store purchases since some consumers browse online before buying their apparel in stores (Balasubramanian et al., 2005; Mintel, 2013; Sarkar, 2011). Thus, the distinction between shopping in-store and online has become increasingly blurred (Mintel, 2013).

Channel Proliferation

There are various factors affecting consumers' channel choice such as consumers' objectives, consumers' characteristics, product characteristics, channel characteristics and organisational factors (Balasubramanian et al., 2005; Black et al., 2002; Chiang et al., 2006; Gupta et al., 2004; Schoenbachler and Gordon, 2002). Consumers' channel choice is complex and dynamic (van Dijk et al., 2005). The preference of their channel choice depends on which channel suits them best and how they can achieve a maximum outcome for the minimum cost (van Dijk et al., 2005).

However, it can be concluded that consumers choose to purchase in a certain channel due to three major factors: convenience, product availability and price (Katawetawaraks and Wang, 2011). Consumers choose to shop where it is convenient for them (Hsiao et al., 2012). When shopping from online channels, consumers can shop anywhere at any time without being concerned as to whether the stores are closed (Katawetawaraks and Wang, 2011). Hence, it can be seen that consumers use online shopping to save time and effort (Hsiao et al., 2012). In terms of product availability, consumers may not find specific sizes of products in-store (Mintel, 2011). Therefore, they search for real-time stock availability online and place an order from an online channel instead (Mintel, 2011). In addition, consumers may use multichannel shopping to seek special offers (PwC, 2011). They use the benefits of multichannel shopping to compare prices before making a decision about which channel to buy from (PwC, 2011). They think they would make better decisions by comparing prices between offline and online channels (Verhoef et al., 2007).

Nevertheless, perceived risks are still a major barrier in online purchase (Katawetawaraks and Wang, 2011; Schröder and Zaharia, 2008). Perceived risks in online commerce are related to the uncertainties consumers feel when they believe that the Internet is unsafe or that there will be negative consequences when they engage with online purchasing (Glover and Benbasat, 2011). Therefore, perceived risks are linked to consumers' trust in online purchase and these risks cause some consumers to be reluctant to purchase from the Internet (Glover and Benbasat, 2011). Those issues include *product risks* from inability to see and try a product on before making a purchase decision (Goldsmith and Flynn, 2005; Yu, 2009), *convenience risks* that may arise from technology such as technical difficulties or the complexity of websites including delayed delivery (Chiu et al., 2014; Rosa, 2012; Sarkar, 2011) and *financial risks* that may occur from insecurity of credit card usage such as the risks of personal information being exposed or money lost during an online transaction (Rosa, 2012; Sarkar, 2011).

THE HEDONIC BENEFITS DERIVED FROM EACH CHANNEL

Shopping channels differ in their constraints and advantages, such as whether a channel is used primarily for purchase or for information, whether it is physical or virtual, the degree of accessibility, the type of communication that a channel permits, the nature of its interface, its level of convenience, how easily the consumer is able to switch from one channel to another, the degree of flexibility and the ability to record the history of consumers' behaviour (Dholakia et al., 2010). Hence, some channels are more appropriate for certain situations (Gefen and Straub, 2003).

In Store

Shopping in stores still remains the most popular channel in multichannel strategies (Balasubramanian et al., 2005; Mintel, 2011; Sarkar, 2011) due to the fact that consumers prefer to have the experience of visiting stores, seeing what new items there are and trying products on as well as substitute products before making a purchase (Falk, 2014). Moreover, they can collect the products immediately after they make a purchase without having to wait for a delivery (Berman and Thelen, 2004; Chatterjee, 2010; Falk, 2014). Kim (2002) explains that consumers may go shopping in-store just to get out of their home, to relieve boredom and stress. Arnold and Reynolds (2003) also state that consumers enjoy shopping in traditional stores because of their need to socialise. Shopping as a social activity can be done only in stores, whereas through other channels it cannot (Berman and Thelen, 2004). Arnold and Reynolds (2003) further pointed out that traditional stores allow consumers to experience pleasure from shopping with friends and family members and bonding with others during shopping trips. Thus, store employees could enhance consumer experience through personal interaction (Cottet et al., 2006; Olsen and Skallerud, 2011). Cox et al. (2005) imply that shoppers enjoy being pampered by store employees due to their personal service. On the other hand, some consumers prefer to have less personal contact with others and will go online instead (Balasubramanian et al., 2005). According to Nicholson et al. (2002) and Cox et al. (2005), shopping in stores can be seen as a leisure activity. They stated that consumers are excited and motivated by the store atmosphere such as lighting, background music and overall store layout. Therefore, creating a pleasant environment for shopping in-store can motivate consumers to stay longer and return to the store more often (Kim, 2002). However, the disadvantages of shopping in stores can be seen as overcrowding and queuing to pay and travel costs (Katawetawaraks and Wang, 2011; Nicholson et al., 2002). Moreover, product information is limited since consumers have to rely on packaging, labels and store employees' knowledge (Noble et al., 2005).

Website

Consumers can now have 24/7 access to the global market and to markets without retail stores (Berman and Thelen, 2004). Making a purchase at home and waiting for the products to be delivered to the doorstep are the key that stimulates consumers to shop online (Ramayah and Ignatius, 2005). Moreover, shopping from websites enables consumers to avoid service personnel or social contact when mood is low (Nicholson et al., 2002). Websites provide consumers with a wide range of information and are easy to access (Noble et al., 2005). Hence, websites are commonly used to search about product features and to compare offers and prices across online retailers (Berman and Thelen, 2004; Chatterjee, 2010; van Dijk et al., 2005). In addition, the application of technology on websites can now provide interactive features such as image enlargement, mix-and-match facilities, three-dimensional virtual models and virtual fitting rooms that allow consumers to have actual experience with the products (Lee et al., 2010). The technological advances can create positive website shopping experiences and decrease perceived risks from website shopping (Blázquez, 2014; Cai and Xu, 2011). However, the disadvantages of websites include the inability to see the products before purchasing, poor quality illustrations of products, delayed delivery, products not meeting with expectations (size, fabric, colour), unclear product description, lack of human contact and transaction-related risks (Kim, 2002; Mintel, 2014; Nicholson et al., 2002).

Catalogue

The benefit of printed catalogues is their portability (Berman and Thelen, 2004). Catalogue shopping is convenient since consumers can shop anywhere at any time of the day (Goldsmith and Flynn, 2005). They are easy to read and can be picked up repeatedly (Nicholson et al., 2002). Consumers see catalogues as relaxing reading in their leisure time (Nicholson et al., 2002). Catalogues are often seen as lookbooks to get ideas about product information (Rud and Wong, 2011). Catalogue shopping can be a resource to inspire consumers or to interest them in products they would not have had in mind beforehand (Rud and Wong, 2011). Moreover, Fiore (2002) explains that shopping via catalogues provides sensory and affective pleasure through colourful pictures, and that catalogues are able to stimulate consumers to imagine themselves using the products. However, there is some evidence that shows the decline of shopping via catalogues in traditional post-based mail order since consumers often channel-shift from catalogue to online channel (Goldsmith and Flynn, 2005). Nevertheless, printed catalogues can be used to stimulate consumers to purchase though online or in-store shopping (Mintel, 2011). However, the amount of information provided in catalogues is restricted (Noble et al., 2005). Catalogues make less information available to consumers compared to the Internet (Noble et al., 2005). Therefore, consumers might find that the information provided in catalogues does not meet their needs (Noble et al., 2005).

Mobile

Mobile is the channel closest to consumers since the mobile phone is a portable device which is easy to carry around. Consumers are able to use mobiles instantly and more frequently compared to personal computers (Lu and Su, 2009). The unique characteristic of shopping via mobile is that consumers can access online anywhere and at any time while they are on the move or even in severe time constraints (Lu and Su, 2009; Yang and Kim, 2012). The ability to search for information while shopping is the main reason that mobile shopping is different from shopping from websites (Yang and Kim, 2012).

Consumers use their smartphones or tablets to find information such as product details, opening times, store locations and latest offers, whether they are in-store or not (Falk, 2014). Moreover, mobile devices, especially tablet computers offering good screen size, are easy to hold and browse, have a touchscreen interface and click-to-order features that can enhance consumer experience (Mintel, 2011). Consumers can enjoy the fun through the features in mobile applications and the easy-purchase experience (Chen et al., 2009). Bruner and Kumar (2005) agreed that the enjoyment from mobile shopping comes from the ease of use and the sense of control. However, the limitations of mobile commerce are still found to be a small screen and limited data processing capacity and network connection (Yang and Kim, 2012; Lu and Su, 2009).

Social Media

Social commerce merges e-commerce with social media (Anderson et al., 2011). Social media is a place where consumers can stay tuned to their favourite brands (Ramlugun, 2014). Marketers and retailers use social media to reach their consumers (Ramlugun, 2014). Social media allows consumers to browse and place orders easily at any time and at a reduced cost (Cha, 2009). This is because social media provides consumers with a wide variety of products, which makes their information search and product selection easier (Paquette, 2013). Consumers perceive arousal from the trend of discovering new fashions, products and brands through their followers in social media (Mikalef et al., 2013). Furthermore, Ramlugun (2014) points out that product browsing via social media creates a sense of adventure. This is because social media platforms effortlessly provide non-stop updates of the latest products in contrast to traditional stores.

Consumers are able to exchange and share messages in real time, such as posting, sharing pictures and comments and peer support with their networks (Pozza, 2014; Ramlugun, 2014). Since social media allows consumers to communicate directly with retailers, they can ask for information about products and report problems with products and services via social media (Paquette, 2013). In addition, retailers use social media to support in-store activities, which in turn boosts traffic and sales. Furthermore, consumers tend to share information with their friends after browsing (Paquette, 2013; Mikalef et al., 2013; Shankar et al., 2011). Hence, word-of-mouth or, in this case, positive feedback from a peer about a product is a strong motivator for future purchasing. Conversely, however, negative comments and feedback including product reviews from social media will subsequently affect consumers' decision-making (Pfeffer et al., 2014). Social media has become an essential tool for retailers to build relationships with consumers (Pozza, 2014). The wide range of consumers utilising social media means that most target markets can be reached (Cha, 2009). Retailers use social media to enhance their brand image, for targeting advertising and creating social interaction and social networking with other social network members so as to reach potential buyers (Kang et al., 2014; Saravanakumar and SuganthaLakshmi, 2012). In addition, retailers employ social media to promote their brands and share promotions. Hence, the influence of social media motivates shoppers to buy products (Mintel, 2014).

METHODOLOGY

The sample is based on 18 participants achieved through data saturation. Semi-structured interviews using snowball sampling were employed to show the outcomes. Due to the scope of this chapter, all samples had to be hedonic shoppers who are very satisfied with apparel shopping, currently reside in central London and have purchased apparel through more than one channel (store, website, catalogue, mobile and social media) within the past 12 months. The preliminary questions are designed to eliminate unqualified participants in order to ensure the representativeness of the sample and the validity of this research. The researcher asks a few questions about their shopping behaviour in order to make sure that they are *Hedonic shoppers*. If they have positive feelings towards apparel shopping that correspond to the research of Babin et al. (1994) such as that they feel that shopping for apparel is truly a joy, apparel shopping is a very good time out, the time spent on apparel shopping is enjoyable, or they feel that apparel shopping like an escape, the researcher will catagorise them as *Hedonic shoppers*. The semi-structured interviews were audio-recorded and transcribed using thematic analysis via *NVivo*.

RESULTS AND DISCUSSION

The result focuses on how consumers perceive different levels of hedonic shopping value across the five channels of store, website, catalogue, mobile and social media. The result from the semi-structured interviews shows that website is the most enjoyable channel for apparel shopping, followed by store, mobile, social media and catalogue respectively. This outcome is inconsistent with Balasubramanian et al. (2005), Mintel (2013), Sarkar (2011) and Wolny and Charoensuksai (2014) which state that shopping in-store is the most popular channel for shopping for apparel in multichannel strategies. Nevertheless, there is no significant difference between website and store. Accordingly, it can be concluded that store and website equally gain a significant level of hedonic shopping value.

The findings from the semi-structured interviews show that the major reason that hedonic shoppers enjoy shopping from a website is that they find it easy to use. Respondent No. 7 explains that:

It is easier to access, some websites have styles that you can link together, for example Topshop and H&M. They allow you style them up and if you like that style you can buy the whole outfit, so it is easier for me.

Furthermore, hedonic shoppers enjoy shopping for apparel from websites because it is convenient for them. The result is consistent with the research of Kim (2002) who points out that the key benefit of searching and purchasing from a website is that it is convenient and easy. Respondent No. 2 gives a reason for enjoying shopping via a website:

Website because it fits my work and lifestyle. Websites are convenient for me.

Hedonic shoppers also fond of website shopping because of product variety. This outcome shows the similarity with the research of Berman and Thelen (2004) that consumers can access the global market and some of the products on a website might not available in-store. Respondent No. 17 states in relation to shopping via website that:

It has more variety, you can see a model wearing it and sometimes they have a catwalk. Online, it is better.

For store, the ability to try the clothes on (2 out of 6) is still the major reason that hedonic shoppers like shopping in-store. Respondent No. 18 states the reason that:

I love to go in-store more than others, I can try the clothes on and see the clothes before I purchase. Sometimes, when you order online, it depends on the company, it might be difficult to return it if it does not fit right.

Additionally, hedonic shoppers enjoy shopping for apparel in-store because they can physically see the products. This reason is coherent with the research of Mintel (2011) that consumers prefer to go to stores because of the ability to see the products and try them on before purchasing. Respondent No. 13 explains that:

It is because it's convenient and you get availability of different sizes. And you can accessorise the items as well whereas online, you cannot tell how it will physically look and what accessories you can match with it. In-store, you can do it.

Another reason that hedonic shoppers enjoy shopping in-store is immediate possession. This finding is supported by Berman and Thelen (2004) and Chatterjee (2010) and Falk (2014) who point out that shopping in-store allows consumers to purchase and collect the products immediately without having to wait for a delivery. Respondent No. 3 states:

In-store because I can be there with the product, also I can take it home straightaway.

Shopping in-store was also found to be a relaxing activity. Arnold and Reynolds (2003) state that consumers are excited and motivated through store atmospheres. Respondent No. 4 states in relation to this point that:

When you shop in-store. I find that you don't mind about the time. You are just browsing.

Furthermore, hedonic shoppers enjoy being spoiled by store employees through the service. This finding is consistent with the research of Cox et al. (2005) who emphasise that consumers are pleased to be served through store service and they enjoy it when store employees spend time helping them. Respondent No. 8 give a reason that:

You get the whole experience, you get the customer service. You can feel the clothing and you can try your clothes on. You get a 360 degree retail experience. It is just nice.

For mobile, the main reason is that they enjoy shopping via mobile because it is convenient when they are on the go. This finding is supported by Yang and Kim (2012). The unique benefit of mobile is that it is portable and can be carried around (Lu and Su, 2009). Hence, the ability to shop anywhere and at any time when they are on the go offers hedonic shoppers an omnipresent shopping experience (Yang and Kim, 2012). Respondent No. 16 states:

Because it is convenient wherever I am. You can access it anywhere at any time.

However, social media and catalogue are found to be the least enjoyable for apparel shopping. The key reason most of the respondents do not choose catalogue, social media and mobile is that they do not use them for apparel shopping. Only one respondent from 18 rates catalogue as the most enjoyable channel for shopping for apparel. The same situation happens in social media. The main reason that hedonic shoppers enjoy shopping via catalogue is for ideas. Catalogue shopping for *Hedonic shoppers* seems to be as a lookbook for dress-up ideas and inspiration (Rud and Wong, 2011). Respondent No. 12 states that:

It gives ideas about what goes with what, new trends and it is convenient for me.

For social media, the reason given is that it is easy to access and convenient to use. This finding is linked to the research of Cha (2009) and Paquette (2013) that social media is easy to use in searching for information. Respondent No. 15 states in relation to social media shopping that:

It is easy and convenient. I can access anytime. When you see someone's clothes, you can search for it like on Pinterest.

The findings show that hedonic shoppers are concerned about making online payment. They do not feel secure when it comes to online payment. It is seen that this perceived risk is the major barrier in online purchase, which is supported by the research of Katawetawaraks and Wang (2011) and Schröder and Zaharia (2008) who point out that many consumers are aware of transaction-related risks when they shop online. Respondent No. 4 states in relation to shopping via mobile that:

I don't like shopping via mobile. Mobile is not a secure thing for a payment.

For purchase intention, all channels differed significantly in order of probability: store, website, mobile, social media, and catalogue. The result shows that catalogue shopping is the least popular channel among hedonic shoppers to shop for apparel. The main reasons that hedonic shoppers intend to purchase in-store in the future are that they can try apparel on and physically see the products. Again, this is is related to the market research of Mintel (2011) which points out that the ability to see the items and try them on before make a purchase are the unique benefits from shopping in the store channel. Respondent No. 3 states the reason:

In stores because you'll get pleasure from touching the products and trying them on.

Furthermore, hedonic shoppers choose to purchase in-store in the future because they can get products immediately. This is also related to the research of Berman and Thelen (2004) and Chatterjee (2010) and Falk (2014), who mention that there is no need to wait for delivery when shopping in-store since consumers can take products with them immediately after purchase. Respondent No. 13 explains:

In-store because it is convenient, you can get the products immediately whereas online you have to send it back and change the size if it's not right and in-store you can try it on as well.

Another reason that hedonic shoppers intend to shop in store in the future is that it is an enjoyable activity when they have the time for it. This is linked to the research of Kim (2002) pointing out that consumers may go to shop in-store just to get out of their home, to relieve boredom and stress and enjoy crowds. Respondent No. 7 explains that:

It would be in-store if I have time. It is easier. When I go to buy jeans, I end up buying tops and jackets as well. It is more enjoyable in that way.

On the other hand, hedonic shoppers switch to websites because it is time-saving for them and easy to access. Respondent No. 5 in the semi-structured interviews states that:

I will carry on with websites because it saves me a lot of time and is easier.

They also intend to purchase via website in the future because it is convenient. These two main reasons can be linked to the research of Kim (2002) who emphasises that the key benefits of shopping via website are convenience and ease of use. Respondent No. 10 gives a reason for purchasing via website in the future that:

I prefer to purchase online because I don't have to leave my house. I can do it at my convenience at home.

Hedonic shoppers also find that websites provide more variety of products and they therefore intend to shop through websites in the future. This outcome is related to the research of Berman and Thelen (2004) pointing out that shopping via website has more variety of products since consumers can access the global market. Respondent No. 15 gave the reason:

Website because it has more variety than in-store.

Furthermore, hedonic shoppers are willing to shop via websites to avoid people. This is supported by Nicholson et al. (2002) who found that shopping via website can enable avoidance of social contact. Respondent No. 8 gave a reason for purchasing via website in the future that:

I will continue buying from websites. I think it's a bit too busy in-store especially at this time of the year. Christmas and January, it is going to be absolutely horrible for shopping. I will stay away from the stores as much as possible.

The only reason that hedonic shoppers choose to purchase apparel via mobile in the future is because it is handy and quick. This is related to the research of Yang and Kim (2012) pointing out that the ability to search for information when they are on the move is the reason why mobile shopping is different from shopping from websites. Respondent No. 14 states in relation to this point that:

It's handy and quick to use.

In contrast, the main reason that *Hedonic shoppers* will purchase via social media in the future is its exclusiveness. Respondent No. 1 states that:

Social media is probably the way forwards because you might not find it in- store or it might be exclusively online only.

Furthermore, they intend to purchase via social media in the future because of product variety. This is supported by Paquette (2013) who points out that social media sites provide consumers with a wide variety of products. Respondent No. 15 give a reason that:

It has more variety.

Lastly, some *Hedonic shoppers* may choose to purchase via catalogue in the future because it is easy. Respondent No. 12 give the reason:

Catalogue because it is easier.

Some of them also intend to purchase via social media in the future because it is convenient. Respondent No. 4 states a reason for purchasing via social media that:

It is more convenient for me.

It can be seen from the repetitive answers that the main reasons that they like certain channels are almost the same as why they choose to purchase in those channels in the future. The findings show that consumers do perceive different enjoyment (which is a sub-dimension of hedonic shopping value) and purchase intention when they shop across channels. Hence, the findings can be beneficial to marketers to evaluate the strengths and weaknesses of each channels from the perception of hedonic shoppers.

CONCLUSION

The challenge for the multichannel strategy is to understand clearly how consumers use or evaluate different channels to purchase from. Hence, understanding the perception of each channel among hedonic shoppers across five channels is important for any apparel business. The strengths and weaknesses of each channel are the key to maintain or minimise in order to increase sales in certain channels.

Multichannel retailers need to constantly monitor their services. Adding hedonic features to every channel is essential in order to motivate hedonic shoppers to purchase. This research finds that store and website are the most enjoyable channels to shop in for apparel. Furthermore, those are the most likely channels in which hedonic shoppers intend to shop for apparel in the future. Hence, marketers should focus closely on these two channels. Maintaining an enjoyable shopping experience in those channels is crucial in order to gain more sales. At the same time, the negative perceptions of each channel have to be reduced.

REFERENCES

Anderson, M., Sims, J., Price, J., & Brusa, J. (2011). Turning 'like' to 'buy' social media emerges. *Strategy &*, 1–12.

Armstrong, J. S. (2001). *Principles of forecasting: A handbook for researchers and practitioners illustrated* (J. S. Armstrong, Ed.). New York: Springer Science & Business Media. doi:10.1007/978-0-306-47630-3

Arnold, M. J., & Reynolds, K. E. (2003). Hedonic shopping motivations. *Journal of Retailing*, *79*(2), 77–95. doi:10.1016/S0022-4359(03)00007-1

Babin, B. J., Darden, W. R., & Griffin, M. (1994). Work and/or fun: Measuring hedonic and utilitarian shopping value. *The Journal of Consumer Research*, *20*(4), 644–657. doi:10.1086/209376

Balasubramanian, S., Raghunathan, R., & Mahajan, V. (2005). Consumers in a multichannel environment: Product utility, process utility, and channel choice. *Journal of Interactive Marketing*, *19*(2), 12–30. doi:10.1002/dir.20032

Batra, R., & Ahtola, O. T. (1991). Measuring the hedonic and utilitarian sources of consumer attitudes. *Marketing Letters*, *2*(2), 159–170. doi:10.1007/BF00436035

Bellenger, D. N., & Korgaonkar, P. K. (1980). Profiling the recreational shopper. *Journal of Retailing*, *56*(3), 77–91. Available at http://connection.ebscohost.com/c/articles/4667116/profiling-recreational-shopper

Berman, B., & Thelen, S. (2004). A guide to developing and managing a well-integrated multi-channel retail strategy. *International Journal of Retail & Distribution Management*, *32*(3), 147–156. doi:10.1108/09590550410524939

Black, N. J., Lockett, A., Ennew, C., Winklhofer, H., & McKechnie, S. (2002). Modelling consumer choice of distribution channels: An illustration from financial services. *International Journal of Bank Marketing*, *20*(4), 161–173. doi:10.1108/02652320210432945

Blázquez, M. (2014). Fashion shopping in multichannel retail: The role of technology in enhancing the customer experience. *International Journal of Electronic Commerce*, *18*(4), 97–116. doi:10.2753/JEC1086-4415180404

Bruner, G. C. II, & Kumar, A. (2005). Explaining consumer acceptance of handheld internet devices. *Journal of Business Research*, *58*(5), 553–558. doi:10.1016/j.jbusres.2003.08.002

Cai, S., & Xu, Y. (2011). Designing not just for pleasure: Effects of web site aesthetics on consumer shopping value. *International Journal of Electronic Commerce*, *15*(4), 159–188. doi:10.2753/JEC1086-4415150405

Cardoso, P., & Pinto, S. (2010). Hedonic and utilitarian shopping motivations among Portuguese young adult consumers. *International Journal of Retail & Distribution Management*, *38*(1), 538–558. doi:10.1108/09590551011052124

Cha, J. (2009). Shopping on social networking web sites: Attitudes toward real versus virtual items. *Journal of Interactive Advertising*, *10*(1), 77–93. doi:10.1080/15252019.2009.10722164

Chang, E. (2001). *The mediating role of hedonic shopping value in apparel shopping satisfaction*. Oregon State University.

Chatterjee, P. (2010). Multiple-channel and cross-channel shopping behavior: Role of consumer shopping orientations. *Marketing Intelligence & Planning*, *28*(1), 9–24. doi:10.1108/02634501011014589

Chen, X., Li, M., & Fang, Q. (2009). Factors influencing consumption experience of mobile device: A study from experiential view. *Proceedings of the International Conference on Electronic Business (ICEB)*, 701–710.

Chiang, W. K., Zhang, D., & Zhou, L. (2006). Predicting and explaining patronage behavior toward web and traditional stores using neural networks: A comparative analysis with logistic regression. *Decision Support Systems*, *41*(2), 514–531. doi:10.1016/j.dss.2004.08.016

Chih, W., & Lin, Y. 2010. The study of the effects and consequences of perceived website attitude. *Proceedings of the 12th International Conference on Electronic Commerce*, 18–20.

Chiu, C.-M., Wang, E. T. G., Fang, Y.-H., & Huang, H.-Y. (2014). Understanding customers' repeat purchase intentions in B2C e-commerce: The roles of utilitarian value, hedonic value and perceived risk. *Information Systems Journal*, *24*(1), 85–114. doi:10.1111/j.1365-2575.2012.00407.x

Chung, Y.-S. (2015). Hedonic and utilitarian shopping values in airport shopping behavior. *Journal of Air Transport Management*, *49*, 28–34. doi:10.1016/j.jairtraman.2015.07.003

Cottet, P., Lichtlé, M. C., & Plichon, V. (2006). The role of value in services: A study in a retail environment. *Journal of Consumer Marketing*, *23*(4), 219–227. doi:10.1108/07363760610674347

Cox, A.D., Cox, D., & Anderson, R.D. (2005). Reassessing the pleasures of store shopping. *Journal of Business Research, 58*(3), 250–259.

Davis, L. (2013). Exploring Chinese consumers' shopping value across retail outlets. *International Journal of China Marketing*, *14*(1), 51–64.

Dholakia, U. M., Kahn, B. E., Reeves, R., Rindfleisch, A., Stewart, D., & Taylor, E. (2010). Consumer behavior in a multichannel, multimedia retailing environment. *Journal of Interactive Marketing*, *24*(2), 86–95. doi:10.1016/j.intmar.2010.02.005

Falk, J. (2014). *Physical mobile interaction in omni-channel retailing: Using the customers' smartphone to interact with smart objects in a store*. Linköping University.

Fiore, A. M. (2002). Effects of experiential pleasure from a catalogue environment on approach responses toward fashion apparel. *Journal of Fashion Marketing and Management: An International Journal*, *6*(2), 122–133. doi:10.1108/13612020210429467

Gefen, D., & Straub, D. (2003). Managing user trust in B2C e-services. *e-Service Journal*, *2*(2), 7–24. doi:10.2979/esj.2003.2.2.7

Glover, S., & Benbasat, I. (2011). A comprehensive model of perceived risk of e-commerce transactions. *International Journal of Electronic Commerce*, *15*(2), 47–78. doi:10.2753/JEC1086-4415150202

Goldsmith, R. E., & Flynn, L. R. (2005). Bricks, clicks, and pix: Apparel buyers' use of stores, internet, and catalogs compared. *International Journal of Retail & Distribution Management*, *33*(4), 271–283. doi:10.1108/09590550510593202

Görsch, D. (2002). Multi-channel integration and its implications for retail web sites. *Ecis*, 748–758. Available at: http://aisel.aisnet.org/ecis2002/11

Gupta, A., Su, B. C., & Walter, Z. (2004). Risk profile and consumer shopping behavior in electronic and traditional channels. *Decision Support Systems*, *38*(3), 347–367. doi:10.1016/j.dss.2003.08.002

Holbrook, M. B., & Gardner, M. P. (2000). Illustrating a dynamic model of the mood-updating process in consumer behavior. *Psychology and Marketing*, *17*(3), 165–194. doi:10.1002/(SICI)1520-6793(200003)17:3<165::AID-MAR1>3.0.CO;2-5

Hosein, N. Z. (2012). Measuring the purchase intention of visitors to the auto show. *Journal of Management and Marketing Research*, *9*, 1–18.

Hsiao, C.-C., Yen, H. J. R., & Li, E. Y. (2012). Exploring consumer value of multi-channel shopping: A perspective of means-end theory. *Internet Research*, *22*(3), 318–339. doi:10.1108/10662241211235671

Irani, N., & Hanzaee, K. H. (2011). The mediating role of hedonic value in apparel shopping satisfaction. *World Applied Sciences Journal*, *12*(3), 1715–1729.

Kang, J.-Y. M., Johnson, K. K. P., & Wu, J. (2014). Consumer style inventory and intent to social shop online for apparel using social networking sites. *Journal of Fashion Marketing and Management*, *18*(3), 301–320. doi:10.1108/JFMM-09-2012-0057

Karimi, S. (2013). *A purchase decision-making process model of online consumers and its influential factor a cross sector analysis*. University of Manchester.

Katawetawaraks, C., & Wang, C. L. (2011). Online shopper behavior: Influences of online shopping decision. *Asian Journal of Business Research*, *1*(2), 66–74. doi:10.14707/ajbr.110012

Kazakeviciute, A., & Banyte, J. (2012). The relationship of consumers' perceived hedonic value and behavior. *Inzinerine Ekonomika-Engineering Economic*, *23*(5), 532–540.

Kim, Y.-K. (2002). Consumer value: An application to mall and internet shopping. *International Journal of Retail & Distribution Management*, *30*(12), 595–602. doi:10.1108/09590550210453075

Kirgiz, A. (2014). Hedonism, A consumer disease of the modern age: Gender and hedonic shopping in Turkey. *Global Media Journal*, *4*(8), 200–213.

Kotler, P., Armstrong, G., Harris, L., & Piercy, N. F. (2013). *Principles of marketing* (European edition). Pearson Education Limited.

Lee, H.-H., Kim, J., & Fiore, A. M. (2010). Affective and cognitive online shopping experience: Effects of image interactivity technology and experimenting with appearance. *Clothing & Textiles Research Journal*, *28*(2), 140–154. doi:10.1177/0887302X09341586

Levin, A. M., Levin, I. P., & Heath, C. E. (2003). Product category dependent consumer preferences for online and offline shopping features and their influence on multi-channel retail alliances. *Journal of Electronic Commerce Research*, *4*(3), 85–93. Available at http://www.csulb.edu/web/journals/jecr/issues/20033/paper1.pdf

Lu, H.-P., & Su, P. Y.-J. (2009). Factors affecting purchase intention on mobile shopping web sites. *Internet Research*, *19*(4), 442–458. doi:10.1108/10662240910981399

Madahi, A., & Sukati, I. (2012). The effect of external factors on purchase intention amongst young generation in Malaysia. *International Business Research*, *5*(8), 153–159. doi:10.5539/ibr.v5n8p153

Mikalef, P., Giannakos, M., & Pateli, A. (2013). Shopping and word-of-mouth intentions on social media. *Journal of Theoretical and Applied Electronic Commerce Research*, *8*(1), 17–34. doi:10.4067/S0718-18762013000100003

Mintel. (2011). *Multi-channel retailing*. Author.

Mintel. (2013). *Clothing retailing*. Author.

Mintel. (2014a). *E-commerce*. Author.

Mintel. (2014b). *Fashion online*. Author.

Nicholson, M., Clarke, I., & Blakemore, M. (2002). 'One brand, three ways to shop': Situational variables and multichannel consumer behaviour. *International Review of Retail, Distribution and Consumer Research*, *12*(2), 131–148. doi:10.1080/09593960210127691

Noble, S. M., Griffith, D., & Weinberger, M. G. (2005). Consumer derived utilitarian value and channel utilization in a multi-channel retail context. *Journal of Business Research*, *58*(12), 1643–1651. doi:10.1016/j.jbusres.2004.10.005

Nurmikko, S. (2011). *Implications of hedonic and utilitarian information search and social media browsing on purchase value*. Aalto University.

Olsen, S. O., & Skallerud, K. (2011). Retail attributes' differential effects on utilitarian versus hedonic shopping value. *Journal of Consumer Marketing*, *28*(7), 532–539. doi:10.1108/07363761111181527

Overby, J. W., & Lee, E. J. (2006). The effects of utilitarian and hedonic online shopping value on consumer preference and intentions. *Journal of Business Research*, *59*(10-11), 1160–1166. doi:10.1016/j.jbusres.2006.03.008

Paquette, H. 2013. *Social Media as a Marketing Tool: A Literature Review*. Academic Press.

Parker, M. (2011). *Gender differences between hedonic and utilitarian purchase behaviors concerning out-of-stock apparel*. Ashland University.

Pfeffer, J., Zorbach, T., & Carley, K. M. (2015, March). 2014. Understanding online firestorms: Negative word-of-mouth dynamics in social media networks. *Journal of Marketing Communications*, *20*(1-2), 117–128. doi:10.1080/13527266.2013.797778

Pinto, N. 2013. Understanding the barriers to online shopping among Indian consumers. *International Journal of Research in Humanities, Arts and Literature, 1*(3), 35–44. Available at: http://oaji.net/articles/488-1393060393.pdf

Pozza, I. D. (2014). Multichannel management gets 'social'. *European Journal of Marketing*, *48*(7/8), 1274–1295. doi:10.1108/EJM-10-2012-0598

PwC. (2011). *Pick 'n' Mix: Meeting the demands of the new multi-channel shopper*. Author.

Ramayah, T., & Ignatius, J. (2005). Impact of perceived usefulness, perceived ease of use and perceived enjoyment on intention to shop online. *ICFAI Journal of Systems Management, 3*(3), 1–16. Available at: http://ramayah.com/journalarticlespdf/impactpeu.pdf

Ramlugun, V. G. (2014). The Scope of social media browsing and online shopping for mauritian e-retailers: A study based on utilitarian and hedonic values. *Review of Integrative Business and Economics Research*, *3*(2), 219–241.

Rosa, M. I. (2012). *Omni-channel retailing: Is its 'order online pick-up in store' service viable in the Portuguese grocery industry?* Universidade Católica Portuguesa.

Rud, M., & Wong, S. K. B. (2011). *Turning a new page: Co-creation in practice through the study of C-G lookbook*. Lund University.

Saravanakumar, M., & Sugantha Lakshmi, T. (2012). Social media marketing. *Life Science Journal*, *9*(4), 2012.

Sarkar, A. (2011). Impact of utilitarian and hedonic shopping values on individual's perceived benefits and risks in online shopping. *International Management Review*, *7*(1), 58–65. Available at http://uxscientist.com/public/docs/uxsci_50.pdf

Scarpi, D. (2006). Fashion stores between fun and usefulness. *Journal of Fashion Marketing and Management*, *10*(1), 7–24. doi:10.1108/13612020610651097

Schoenbachler, D. D., & Gordon, G. L. (2002). Multi-channel shopping: Understanding what drives channel choice. *Journal of Consumer Marketing*, *19*(1), 42–53. doi:10.1108/07363760210414943

Schröder, H., & Zaharia, S. (2008). Linking multi-channel customer behavior with shopping motives: An empirical investigation of a German retailer. *Journal of Retailing and Consumer Services*, *15*(6), 452–468. doi:10.1016/j.jretconser.2008.01.001

Shankar, V., Inman, J. J., Mantrala, M., Kelley, E., & Rizley, R. (2011). Innovations in shopper marketing: Current insights and future research issues. *Journal of Retailing*, *87*(Suppl. 1), S29–S42. doi:10.1016/j.jretai.2011.04.007

Tifferet, S., & Herstein, R. (2012). Gender differences in brand commitment, impulse buying, and hedonic consumption. *Journal of Product and Brand Management*, *21*(3), 176–182. doi:10.1108/10610421211228793

Timothy, D. J. (2005). *Shopping tourism, retailing and leisure*. Channel View Publications. doi:10.21832/9781873150610

van Dijk, G., Laing, A., & Minocha, S. (2005). Consumer behaviour in multi-channel retail environments: Consumer movement between online and offline channels. *5th American Marketing Association/ Academy of Marketing Joint Biennial Conference 'Marketing: Building Business, Shaping Society'*.

Verhoef, P. C., Neslin, S., & Vroomen, B. (2007). Multichannel customer management: Understanding the research-shopper phenomenon. *International Journal of Research in Marketing*, *24*(2), 129–148. doi:10.1016/j.ijresmar.2006.11.002

Whitlark, D. B., Geurts, M. D., & Swenson, M. J. (1993). New product forecasting with a purchase intention survey. *The Journal of Business Forecasting Methods & Systems*, *12*(3), 18. Available at https://www.questia.com/library/journal/1P3-574939/new-product-forecasting-with-a-purchase-intention

Wolny, J., & Charoensuksai, N. (2014). Mapping customer journeys in multichannel decision-making. *Journal of Direct, Data and Digital Marketing Practice, 15*(4), 317–326. Available at: http://www.palgrave-journals.com/doifinder/10.1057/dddmp.2014.24

Yang, K., & Kim, H.-Y. (2012). Mobile shopping motivation: An application of multiple discriminant analysis. *International Journal of Retail & Distribution Management*, *I*(10), 778–789. doi:10.1108/09590551211263182

Chapter 7
Social Media, Online Brand Communities, and Customer Engagement in the Fashion Industry

Guida Helal
American University of Beirut, Lebanon

ABSTRACT

Fashion brands have shifted communication to social media as part of evolutionary modern-day marketing approaches to reaching consumers. Brands have adjusted to a vocal customer through back-and-forth interchange on social media platforms that have progressively facilitated for online brand communities. Social media brand communities serve to engage audiences in interactive settings that resonate with individual consumers across different levels. As brand awareness is augmented, brand impressions are conceived, brand-customer relationships are formed, and a sense of community is fostered around a brand, consumers exploit association to such social media brand communities in advancing social identity. The following chapter explores the impact of social media brand communities on Millennials in the fashion industry, while considering the social identity theory. The chapter focuses on theoretical and managerial implications. This chapter considers the influence social media brand communities and social identity may have on a fashion brand.

INTRODUCTION

Marketing advancements have continued to mature as contextual disciplines dependent on factors such as the economy, society, technology, globalisation, or emerging markets, among other elements (Sheth, 2011; Sheth & Sisodia, 1999; Zinkhan & Hirschheim, 1992). These external realities allow for ever-evolving marketing logics that industries venture to embrace (Jayachandran, Gimeno, & Varadarajan, 1999; Vargo & Lusch, 2004). The Internet is a paramount example of a revolutionary influence that has radically transformed interaction in today's society. The modernised Millennial take on communication

DOI: 10.4018/978-1-5225-7344-9.ch007

marks the extensive assumption of Internet manifestations, such as social media, that have facilitated dynamic interchange. Social media platforms have notably crept into marketing operations as lead tools in reaching, sharing and interacting with customers (Hudson, Huang, Roth, & Madden, 2016; Chappuis, Gaffey & Parvizi, 2011), as traditional marketing regresses from providing the active two-way interchange social media encapsulate (Houman Andersen, 2001; Ozuem, Howell, & Lancaster, 2008). Brands have accordingly adjusted to online communication channels in the chase to ensure timely prominence among consumers within an inviting setting (Evans, 2012; Hoffman & Novak, 1996). Over the years, the fashion industry among others has invested in social media presence in hopes of reaping the benefits direct, two-way interchange promises to provide through online brand-customer interactions (Kim & Ko, 2012; Phan; Thomas & Hein, 2011; Helal & Ozuem, 2017). Expansive literature has been produced on the development of social media in routine interactions and its potential leverage on consumer intentions (Fischer & Reuber, 2011; Hoffman & Fodor, 2016; Huy & Shipilov, 2012; Kaplan & Haenlein, 2010; Kietzmann, Hermkens, McCarthy, & Silvestre, 2011; Qualman, 2013). Additional studies have examined the principles of applying social media within a brand's marketing strategy (Habibi, Laroche & Richard, 2014; Naylor, Lamberton, & West, 2012; Simmons, 2008).

Kim and Ko (2012) examine the success of luxury fashion brands utilising social media activities, including interaction or word-of-mouth, in securing encouraging customer intentions. The findings reveal a parallel relationship between the two factors as greater application of social media activities resulted in positive purchase intentions and overall customer equity in consumption of luxury fashion brands (Kim & Ko, 2012). Nevertheless, the study was performed on a broad age pool that gave limited attention to the leading social media demographic age to yield relevant responses that produce precise results. Habibi, Laroche, and Richard (2014) address the evolution of brand communities to online platforms by exploring the building blocks of a social media brand community in impacting brand trust. The results revealed a generally positive link between social media brand community interaction and consequent brand trust. However, the study was performed on a broader age group on a wide range of brand communities from various industries. This paid limited attention to an age pool that has most integrated social media into different branches of daily life. It also posits limitations since a general sample of brand communities and industries was used, which may result in lenient definitions of what constitutes a brand community and being a part of it, thus producing general results. An annual demographic analysis by PewResearch Center demonstrated that the highest percentage of social media usage was exhibited by ages 18 to 29 years between years 2006 to 2018 (Smith & Anderson, 2018). Among the current vast literature examining the evolution and implementation of social media, few have investigated the influential use of social media brand communities on Millennials in the fashion industry.

The discipline of marketing has been on an evolutionary path from a tangible focus on commodities to an emphasis on an intangible approach of service marketing (Vargo & Lusch, 2004; Lusch, 2007; Vargo, Lusch, & Morgan, 2015; Hunt & Madhavaram, 2015). Marketing practices have progressed to a logic that places power on creating value and relationships with customers (Grönroos & Voima, 2013; Prahalad & Ramaswamy, 2000). Lusch (2007) dissects the development of marketing practices into three stages over the past 100-year period. The first stage begins with "to market", which involves the idea of the supplier and buyer once being separate and marketers working to bring products into the market to bridge that gap. The expansion of the industry sector advanced marketing focuses to "market to", involving generating demand from customers. Finally, the third stage, "market with", transforms the customer from a mere receiver of promotion and persuasion to a contributor of value through brand-customer interaction (Lusch, 2007). Brands have recognised the significance of creating consequential interactions with consumers (Ramaswamy, 2008). As interaction is the core of co-creating value, brands are pressed to visit the process of value creation in more depth to accommodate a more active customer (Prahalad & Ramaswamy, 2004).

Prahalad and Ramaswamy (2004) suggest the DART model as the central building blocks for co-creating value. The first block, *dialogue*, includes receiving and sharing information and conversation with customers. *Access*, the second block, considers the degree to which both brand and customer can access information. Third, *risk assessment*, involves the potential risk or harm consumers may be exposed to from consumption of a product. Consumers are informed of full risks and hold responsibility for consumption. Finally, *transparency* reflects on the adaptation of firms from vague to the present-day transparent sharing of product detail with consumers. The four building blocks merge to create an environment that reinforces engagement between brand and customer. By sharing information, awareness and responsibility, participation is created between brand and customer as well as customers among one another, forming a community (Hatch & Schultz, 2010; Muniz & O'Guinn, 2001; Pongsakornrungslip & Schroeder, 2011). Brand communities are important in building unique social structures between affiliates of the community (Muniz & O'Guinn, 2001). Brand communities have been transposed to online communities that allow members to venture into novel, prevalent channels (Romero & Molina, 2011), and foster brand-customer relationships from ongoing social interactions (Manville, 2004). Brand presence on social media outlets has brought about social media brand communities with devotees across varied geographic points (Habibi, Laroche, & Richard, 2014; Pitta & Fowler, 2005). Greater reliance is allotted to social media sites for worldwide information acquisition than traditional media channels (Mangold & Faulds, 2009; Schivinski & Dabrowski, 2016).

Social media was developed from the World Wide Web as an Internet-based service that granted users a platform to exchange user-generated content (Dewing, 2010). The World Wide Web came about in 1991 as a result of Tim Berners-Lee connecting hypertext technology to the Internet and establishing networked communication (Van Dijck, 2013). This later evolved to Web 2.0 as an interactive channel for networked bodies (O'Reilly & Battelle, 2009; Paroutis & Al Saleh, 2009; Solomon & Schrum, 2007). Tim O'Reilly (2005) described Web 2.0 as having a core with "a set of principles and practices that tie together a veritable solar system of sites that demonstrate some or all of those principles, at a varying distance from that core" (O'Reilly, 2005). Web 2.0 introduced collaborative platforms that created community spaces for users to participate, share and connect with other networks of users (Van Dijck, 2013). The progression of Web 2.0 triggered a hike in user-generated communication platforms, which is today recognised as social media (Arora, 2014; Fuchs, 2014; Gillies & Cailliau, 2000; O'Reilly, 2005).

A study conducted on the number of worldwide social network users from the years 2010 to 2021 demonstrates a significant rise in active users every year, with almost 1 billion users in 2010 to a projected 3 billion active users by 2021 (Statista, 2017). An analysis performed on various sources utilised by Millennials worldwide to acquire updates on fashion trends revealed social media to be the first go-to informant of the latest styles (Statista, 2017). Social media continue to be notably integrated in the fashion world, with Milan Fashion Week in 2016 displaying Instagram traffic of over 60 per cent of users following personal contacts or bloggers to keep informed of the latest happenings (Statista, 2016). The following analyses expose the level of influence social media practices have gained in communicating trends in the fashion industry. Online platforms grant fashion brands the prospect of exercising novel, real-time content across a wider scope of recipients. Millennials innately embrace social media as an outlet for information, entertainment, and social interaction (Kilian, Hennigs, & Langner, 2012; Williams, Crittenden, Keo, & McCarty, 2012; Whiting & Williams, 2013). These social platforms cultivate social contact into relationships among users, allowing for brands to evoke customer loyalty, develop intimate relationships, and create a promised relationship equity that both customer and brand can benefit from (Lemon, Rust, & Zeithaml, 2001; Kim & Ko, 2012; Vogel, Evanschitzky, & Ramaseshan, 2008).

From a social identity perspective, this chapter examines the use of social media brand communities and relationship equity that appeal to customers in invoking social identity. Social identity theory sees that an individual seeks to assign him/herself or others to social groups that carry a symbolic value (Tajfel, 1972). An individual pursues social groups that promise positive recognition and contribute to self-quality through association (Ashforth & Mael, 1989; Hogg & Terry, 2000). There are a number of studies examining consumers' motives to associate with particular brands in developing desired social identities (Arnett, German, & Hunt, 2003; Bhattacharya & Sen, 2003; Lam, Ahearne, Hu, & Schillewaert, 2010). Product and brand consumption may act as imperative contributors in an individual's quest to form his/her own identity, as well as decipher others' (Elliot & Wattanasuwan, 1998; Kleine, Kleine, & Kernan, 1993). Popular culture consumption is perceived to be an enabler of social status for individuals. Fashion is a pivotal example of influential pop culture that aids in inflating social placement (Barron, 2012). Social placement is advanced by way of flaunting discernible fashion labels that exemplify an individuality/lifestyle comparable to a desired social group conceived on the premise of that lifestyle. Fashion brands serve as a means that consumers capitalise on in their chase to exert a 'distinctive' identity among a social circle of similar social identities. Individuals enforce inclusion by mirroring an identity imposed by a social collective and instilled by its respective followers, indicating the dependence of self-identity on identities in a sought community (Ashmore, Deaux, & McLaughlin-Volpe, 2004; Heere et al., 2011).

Online brand presence ventures beyond a purpose of mere visibility to become a symbolic motive that consumers interact with in furthering social identity through brand association. Social media brand communities evolve as integral grounds for perceived functional and symbolic benefits brands can offer customers. Brands have gained a reach of customers that goes beyond physical touch-points limited by brick-and-mortar stores. Brand-customer interaction has extended past the point of sale into ongoing engagement over a virtual communicative world (Edelman, 2010; Fromm & Garton, 2013) that the Millennial generation has grown with. There is vast literature exploring the application of social media marketing practices; however, the available research does not acknowledge Millennial interaction in social media brand communities in the fashion industry. This research aims to develop literature regarding the impact social media brand communities have exerted as marketing instruments on Millennials, and this cohort's reliance on social identity in interacting with brands. This study offers a basis for fashion brands to further develop in potentially consolidating online brand communities on social media in suitably pursuing consumers.

BACKGROUND

The apparel market, which may comprise clothing, footwear and accessories, is globally valued at an estimated 2.4 trillion US dollars, with a projected progressing growth in coming years (McKinsey, 2016). The McKinsey Global Fashion Index anticipates an industry sales growth in 2018 to potentially reach 4.5 per cent, with major growth originating from Asia-Pacific and Latin American regions (BOF & McKinsey & Co., 2018). According to an extensive study, The State of Fashion 2018, performed by the UK-based Business of Fashion and renowned McKinsey & Company, the fashion industry is expected to experience internal and external transformative shifts. Consumers' digital adoption tips the power of control into the consumers' domain, as shoppers become key players in sharing product information among one another. Moreover, an active consumer demands an omni-channel journey commencing with online platforms such as information search points on social media to brand websites, in-store click-and-collect and comparable services that facilitate the move between offline and online channels (BOF & McKinsey & Co., 2018). Brands are consequently encouraged to re-invent user-experiences through digitisation. Digitising communication via social media produces direct, personalised relationships between brands and customers as networking sites grant leeway for immediate interaction. As the fashion world delves into new-age communication, this study explores the use and impact of social media brand communities among the Millennial generation in the apparel sector.

The worldwide penetration of social networks sits at approximately 71 per cent in 2018, with an estimated growth to over 73 per cent by 2021 (Statista, 2017). This indicates the degree of global online infiltration in daily interaction. Social network penetration may vary from one region to another. Statistics from January 2018 reveal a 70 per cent social media penetration in North America, followed by 66 per cent in Europe and nearing percentages from Asia-Pacific (Statista, 2018). Social network region penetration demonstrates the worldwide saturation of online channels in offering communicative platforms for users of broad geographic locations to partake in. Brands can ensure universal presence through the reach of social media outlets. Fashion brands such as H&M, Zara, Louis Vuitton and Chanel, among others, have scored high social visibility percentages over social networking sites (Statista, 2016). Strong virtual visibility can be attributed to a social media platform like Instagram, which boasts a 98-percentage penetration rate by fashion brands (Statista, 2016). Top fashion players are taking advantage of conspicuous social networking sites in maintaining awareness and presence among consumers. Fashion brands similarly demonstrated one of the highest penetration rates on Snapchat, with visual posts ranging from images to live video shares (Statista, 2017).

Social media has transported the fashion industry into a digitised realm of free-flow content exchanged between brands and consumers worldwide. Brand-customer relationships cultivate over a common floor of interchange, intensifying brand communities and enriching consumers' inclination to affiliate with a brand. The model of consumer-driven content becomes a key contributor to brand perceptions (Berthon, Pitt & Campbell, 2008; Christodoulides, Jevons, & Bonhomme, 2012). Consumers openly share opinions, reviews, devotion, and association to a brand among one another. This use of virtual platforms evokes brand impressions that resonate with customers, demonstrating encouraging links between a brand's social media activity and corresponding brand recognition (Hutter, Hautz, Dennhardt & Fuller, 2013). Customers pursue association with a brand's community as part of an agenda to build their own social identity based on what that brand is perceived to denote (Bhattacharya & Sen, 2003; Escalas & Bettman, 2005). Lemon, Rust, and Zeithaml (2001) emphasise customer equity as a pivotal footing to any marketing strategy in a study that investigates three drivers of customer equity: brand, value or relationship equity. Value and brand equity involve a consumer's assessment of a brand based on what is given up for brand purchase and overall perception of the brand, respectively. Relationship equity alludes to a brand-customer connection that exceeds objectivity; rather, it implicates a deeper relation that bonds customers to brands. Meaningful attachments can be created by incentives that offer aspirational value of brand consumption (Lemon, Rust, & Zeithaml, 2001). Hosting social media brand communities can build emotional ties between members and motivate consumers to seek brand affiliation for the perceived value of social enhancement.

Social media is conceived on the foundation of free-flowing content from any participating user, invoking universal engagement across global cultures (Van Dijck, 2013). According to Evans (2012), "Social media is the democratisation of information, transforming people from content readers to content publishers. It is the shift from a broadcast mechanism to a many-to-many model, rooted in conversations between authors, people, and peers" (Evans, 2012, p. 32). A sense of equality is instilled among parties as any one user can contribute or receive material. By route of social media, conversations have reformed to embody a casual, back-and-forth standard for interacting.

The Millennial age has extensively integrated social media into daily communication across a range of platforms. Social networks such as Facebook, Twitter and Instagram are used to share the latest on ample subjects including politics, economy, and society. Numerous studies have shown the Millennial generation of ages 18 to 29 years to be the highest age group utilising social media platforms for regular use (Deloitte, 2017; Smith & Anderson, 2018; Statista, 2016). The Millennial generation is the demographic cohort following Generation X. This cohort does not have precise beginning and end dates but some researchers believe Millennials' birth years fall between the early 1980s and the early 2000s (Ng, Schweitxer, & Lyons, 2010; Rainer & Rainer, 2011). However, Howe and Strauss (2000) define the generation as individuals born between 1982 and 2004. Millennials move between different convenient and immediate communication avenues (Rainer & Rainer, 2011). This cohort esteems virtual socialisation and community environments (Bolton et al., 2013). The absorption of Internet communication technologies blurs geographic boundaries, allowing worldwide Millennials to merge through homogeneous behaviour (Moore, 2012). As collective, global platforms expose Millennials to harmonised experiences that shape values and attitudes, marketers gain the intelligence to target Millennial groups based on those values (Schewe & Meredith, 2004).

CONTEXT AND FOUNDATION

Social media has continued to assert influence as an imperative instrument in daily life for over a decade. Its initiation offered a foundation for user-generated content originally used by individuals before maturing into a virtual phenomenon adopted by individuals, corporations and industries alike (Hennig-Thurau et al., 2010; Kaplan & Haenlein, 2012). Expansive literature has been dedicated to the explanation and thorough examination of social media (Hanna, Rohm, & Crittenden, 2011; Kaplan & Haenlein, 2012; Kietzmann, Hermkens, McCarthy, & Silvestre, 2011; Mangold & Faulds, 2009; Murugesan, 2007; Whiting & Williams, 2013; Williams, Crittenden, Keo, & McCarty, 2012). Kaplan and Haenlein (2010) famously defined social media as a "group of Internet-based applications that build on the ideological and technological foundations of Web 2.0, and allow the creation and exchange of user generated content" (Kaplan & Haenlein, 2010, p. 61). Social media offers a networked culture fuelled by easy information reach and accessibility (Van Dijck & Poell, 2013). Content is produced and circulated by online users to inform one another of various issues, including product and service reviews (Blackshaw & Nazzaro, 2006). This has produced an age of technologically skilled Millennial consumers, liberated by the free-flow distribution of online platforms (Kozinets, 1999; Williams, Crittenden, Keo, & McCarty, 2012). Online users are empowered to contribute and engage in social interactions (Fischer & Reuber, 2011; Susarla, Oh, & Tan, 2012) that can coalesce into collective influences capable of weighing on other individual users, consumers, and organisations (Parameswaran & Whinston, 2007).

In a study deliberating the rationale of using social media based on extensive research on existing uses and gratifications literature, Whiting and Williams (2013) identified seven themes including social interaction, information seeking, passing time, entertainment, relaxation, communicatory utility, and convenience utility. These themes produce a framework for social media use that is highly dependent on social connectivity to self-educate and associate with others. Simple back-and-forth dialogue on niche topics induces connections between users that potentially prosper into communities (Hansen, Schneirderman, & Smith, 2011). As individuals are motivated to voice opinions, consumers gain cumulative force among brands allowing for 'bottom-up marketing' (Karpinski, 2005). Marketers strive to reach consumers through collaborative engagements. Social media platforms share communities that marketers employ to engross audiences and exert influence on consumers (Hanna, Rohm, & Crittenden, 2011). Brands and customers are presented the opportunity to connect and form relationships and attachments through online communities on social media. Before proceeding to the exploration of online communities, it is important to define what brand communities entail.

The notion of brand communities has gained immense grounds among researchers, marketers and organisations over the years (Muniz & O'Guinn, 2001; Cova & Pace, 2006; Stokburger-Sauer, 2010; McAlexander, Koenig, & Schouten, 2006; Schau, Muniz, & Arnould, 2009). Marketers have progressed beyond an individualistic approach to a communal outlook of consumption (Cova, 1997). A 'tribal' effect has been identified through social dynamics that display individuals being influenced by groupings they identify with (Cova & Cova, 2002; Gainer & Fischer, 1994). One-on-one relationships between brand and customer have regressed in effectively securing outcomes (Berry, 1995; Iacobucci, 1994) as the recognition of social influence has provoked marketing interest in brand communities (Cova & Cova, 2002; Dholakia, Bagozzi, & Pearo, 2004; McAlexander, Koenig, & Schouten, 2006; Schouten & McAlexander, 1995). Muniz and O'Guinn (2001) define brand community as a non-geographically bound group of social relationships among consumers of a brand, who share common admiration and interest toward the brand. Communities have three core indicators, the first being consciousness of kind, which is the feeling that links community members to one another while separating them from non-members of the community (Bagozzi & Dholakia, 2006; Gusfield, 1978; Muniz & O'Guinn, 2001). Weber (1978) recognises shared consciousness as a sense of belonging. The second marker is shared rituals and traditions that evolve over the brand's history and allow for a symbolic community culture (Muniz & O'Guinn, 2001). The third indicator of community is the responsibility members develop towards other members, the community, and the brand (Muniz & O'Guinn, 2001). These core components form the foundation of a community by which brands and members connect, grow and form relationships.

McAlexander, Schouten, and Koenig (2002) conceptualised a customer-centric model of brand community stressing the gravity of customer experience in sustaining brand communities. The model holds the customer at the centre of the equation with member and brand integration resulting in positive relationships and ensuing aftermaths. McAlexander, Schouten, and Koenig (2006) further dissect the model by examining four component relationships within a brand community. *Customer-product relationship* considers the tangible product that is exchanged between brand and customer, or in the case of an intangible exchange, the quality and experience acquired. Positive outcomes from this exchange result in stronger consumer-perceived identity from being connected with a brand. *Consumer-brand relationship* emphasises the emotional and symbolic connections customers establish with a brand. *Customer-institution relationship* reflects on the relationship developed between the customer and the company to which the brand belongs that ultimately contributes to loyalty. Finally, the *customer-customer relationship* examines the tribal influence word-of-mouth yields among customers. The collective leverage of customers sways other community members' purchase intentions, experiences, and behaviour (McAlexander, Schouten, & Koenig, 2006). The thorough breakdown of integrated relationships within brand communities accentuates the intricate dynamics a brand community surmises and strives to harmonise to succeed.

Consumers are presented greater networking opportunities with similar individuals through the vast reach of social media (Mangold & Faulds, 2009). Kozinets (1999) addressed the tribalising of society through virtual networked communications he refers to as 'e-tribalizing'. Online communities act as supplements marketers can employ to understand consumer behaviour (Kozinets, 1999; Kozinets, 2002) in the manner that social media exposes organisations to insightful information on consumers. While the Internet has always been a host to collective interactive settings as online forums, social media platforms such as social networking sites have displayed more life-like interactions since users are encouraged to use their own identity and connect with their offline networks (Ross et al., 2009). Marketers gain a deeper perspective on consumers, as interpersonal relationships and behaviours are made public through networked platforms like Facebook or Instagram.

Habibi, Laroche, and Richard (2014) underscore five elements that differentiate social media based brand communities from other brand communities. The first aspect is the *social context* and detailed information social media platforms offer on community members. The second dimension that makes social media a unique host of brand communities is the flexible *structure* communities are able to offer. Thirdly, the immense *scale* social media brand communities are capable of obtaining is affirmed by the reach that social media platforms retain. The fourth crucial element to brand communities that is profoundly accentuated in social media's articulate characteristic is *storytelling*. Social media offers platforms for appealing posts through visuals and texts that spur interaction among community members. The final feature is *affiliated brand communities* that may come about from interactive members further interlinking through related smaller sects within a brand community (Habibi, Laroche, & Richard, 2014). The nature of social media produces brand communities with charismatic environments that customers can relate to in self-expression and ultimately brand identification. Online social networks are an essential contributor to valuable brand communities, offering human connections and memorable experiences (Fournier & Lee, 2009). Marketers can expect to offer customers an experience beyond the purchase of a product by exercising brand communities among worldwide networks on social media.

ADDED VALUE THROUGH SOCIAL MEDIA BRAND COMMUNITIES

Brands recognise the advantages of engaging in the two-way communication social media entails as a potential for leveraging brand-customer interactions (Hudson, Huang, Roth, & Madden, 2016; Laroche, Habibi, Richard & Sankaranarayanan, 2012; Pentina, Gammoh, Zhang, & Mallin, 2013; Schivinski & Dabrowski, 2016; Zhang, Benyoucef, & Zhao, 2016). Social media allows for a generous audience reach, inciting brand presence over expansive platforms. The networked nature of social media encourages social exchanges within brand communities (Habibi, Laroche, & Richard, 2014; Zaglia, 2013), supporting brand-customer exchange and consumer engagement. Brand-customer relationships through social media have matured into an essential focus within marketing practices (Fournier & Avery, 2011). This chapter focuses on the influence marketing through social media brand communities may induce on Millennial customers.

Knowledge Seeking/Sharing and EWOM

A worldwide infiltration of over 2.4 billion social network users in 2017, with a projected 3 billion users by 2021 (Statista, 2017), demonstrates the possible clout a brand mention on social media is capable of exerting over a global audience of consumers. Social media users are encouraged to engage in worldwide interactive platforms, and brands are ultimately pulled into this environment in reaching customers (Tiago & Veríssimo, 2014). Brand exposure to social media and Internet technologies enriches brand-customer reciprocation allowing for rapid production and distribution of content between parties (Brown, Kozinets, & Sherry, Jr., 2003; Gallaugher & Ransbotham, 2010). Rich and inviting brand communities are founded based on availability of customers, brands, and content circulating social platforms. Social media provides an additional source for unbiased information generated by consumers, known as electronic word-of-mouth (eWOM) (Hennig-Thurau et al., 2004; Trusov, Buckin, & Pauwels, 2009). As consumers seek more genuine reviews in gathering brand or product knowledge, brands have recognised the importance of preserving eWOM as a marketing tool (Cheung & Thadani, 2012; Chevalier & Mayzlin, 2006; Dellarocas, 2003; Duan, Gu, & Whinston, 2008). The travel of eWOM through social media networks can contribute to the attention a consumer gives a brand (Daugherty & Hoffman, 2014), and extend beyond mere attention to act as an influence of purchasing decisions among customers (Godes & Mayzlin, 2004; Park, Lee & Han, 2007).

The ease of accessibility through network means marks the positive reception of eWOM among individual Millennials and collective brand communities alike (Gruen, Osmonbekov, & Czaplewski, 2006; Taken Smith, 2012; Veloutsou and McAlonan, 2012). Online social interactions prompt an exchange of information and consumer input that serve brands and customers (Tikkanen, Hietanen, Henttonen & Rokka, 2009). Consumers may seek to engage in eWOM within online communities for different motives (Balasubramanian & Mahajan, 2001; Hennig-Thurau et al., 2004). Balasubramanian and Mahajan (2001) identified three utility types that rationalise eWOM in communities: *focus-related utility* involves the satisfaction a customer acquires when contributing value to the community. *Consumption utility* considers the value customers attain from directly absorbing the inputs of other community members. *Approval utility* reflects on the satisfaction received when other community members consume and approve of a member's contribution (Balasubramanian & Mahajan, 2001). The following utility types derive the motivation behind consumers sharing and receiving eWOM and information within online brand communities. Hennig-Thurau et al. (2004) add a further two utility types: *moderator-related utility*, which comprises a moderator handling complaints within a consumer-to-consumer interactive setting, and *homeostase utility*, which is constructed on the idea of balance theory (Heider, 1946; Newcomb, 1953) that individuals strive to inject balance in their lives, thus encouraging consumers to express both positive and negative experiences as a way of reinforcing a neutral state (Hennig-Thurau et al., 2004). Brands are intimidated by the notion of diminished control of brand information due to the flexibility of user-generated content in the form of eWOM, yet the impact of negative eWOM can be monitored and handled accordingly (Brown, Broderick, & Lee, 2007; Kozinets, de Valck, Wojnicki, & Wilner, 2010). Some studies argue that publicity via eWOM, positive or negative, can produce optimistic results as the volume of eWOM contributes to brand awareness (Berger, Sorensen, & Rasmussen, 2010; Duan, Gu, & Whinston, 2008; Liu, 2006). Partaking in online communities, through knowledge posting and viewing actions, is an imperative course for community members to dispense information (Butler, 2001; Koh & Kim, 2004). Fashion brands can experience positive aftermaths through consumer circulation of eWOM across social media since information is viewed as authentic (Kulmala, Mesiranta, & Tuominen, 2013; Wolny & Mueller, 2013), even more so within worldwide brand communities of large-scale user-generated information.

Community Participation and Consumer Engagement

Online users are further inclined to share information upon being motivated to participate as community members in brand communities (Woisetschlager, Hartleb, & Blut, 2008). Brand communities unite members around a mutual interest (Muniz & O'Guinn, 2001) that grants members an appeal of participating to that community (Royo-Vela & Casamassima, 2011). Participation extends paramount support for the growth and continuity of online communities (Casalo, Flavián, & Guinalíu, 2007). Recurrent member participation ensures the long-term sustainability of a community (Koh & Kim, 2004). In a study investigating the knowledge shared in online communities, Koh and Kim (2004) demonstrated a parallel relationship between knowledge shared and community participation. Greater degrees of participation in virtual communities allowed for a vaster amount of knowledge distributed (Koh & Kim, 2004). Continuous participation ultimately results in the development of emotional ties such as trust and loyalty to the community and brand (Casalo, Flavián, & Guinalíu, 2007; Holland & Baker, 2001; Koh & Kim, 2004).

The shift to consumer power through social media means has empowered customer-centric techniques in advancing brands (Sashi, 2012). Marketing professionals have embraced the importance of consumer engagement among the advent of digital social platforms encouraging interaction (Baldus, Voorhees, & Calantone, 2014; Dessart, Veloutsou, & Morgan-Thomas, 2015; Sashi, 2012; Wirtz et al., 2013). Social media users are incited to engage in virtual channels, and brands are ultimately pulled into this environment in reaching customers (Tiago & Veríssimo, 2014). Hollebeek, Glynn and Brodie (2014) define consumer brand engagement as "a consumer's positively valenced cognitive, emotional and behavioural brand-related activity during, or related to, specific consumer/brand interactions" (Hollebeek, Glynn & Brodie, 2014). Baldus et al. (2015) define online brand community engagement as "the compelling, intrinsic motivations to continue interacting with an online brand community" (Baldus et al., 2015, p. 2). Consumers may engage in social media communities through interactive activities such as posting photos, stories, commenting or liking other members' posts. A greater extent of engagement is attributed to greater cooperation and interaction, and the ensuing optimistic effects of rich brand-customer and customer-customer relationships (Habibi, Laroche, & Richard, 2014). Social media's interactivity paves the route for continual instant contact that bears the potential to elicit deeper ties among community members.

Sashi (2012) considers the development of customer engagement through a customer engagement cycle consisting of seven stages. The first stage, *connection*, acts as a preliminary step of customers establishing connections with brands or other customers in their search for products that meet their needs. The second stage, *interaction*, is a consequence of regular dialogue and a contributing factor in consumers and brands co-creating value (Prahalad & Ramaswamy, 2004; Sashi, 2012). Sashi (2012) holds *satisfaction* to be the third stage in which customers continue to interact in a community based on the satisfaction achieved from interactions. Satisfaction over a period of time induces *customer retention*, the fourth stage, which results in the following fifth stage, *commitment.* Commitment consists of calculative commitment, a realistic approach that is a product of the absence of alternative choices, and affective commitment, which is based on an emotional stance that develops from reciprocity in a relationship (Gounaris, 2005; Kumar, Hibbard, & Stern, 1994; de Ruyter, Moorman, & Lemmink,

2001). As emotions materialise, customers may feel more motivated to engage in social media brand communities in the sixth stage of *advocacy*. Customers feel an impulse to share experiences of a brand with the community (Sashi, 2012). Finally, through the stages of interacting, committing and advocating a brand, the last stage of *engagement* is reached. This stage progresses community relationships and enforces consumers' role as co-creators of value (Sashi, 2012). Fashion labels have transposed to visual social networking sites such as Instagram and Snapchat in creating posts that engage consumers in the identity of a brand and its establishment in the market.

Customer Equity

Customer equity is regarded as a crucial financial asset that organisations should handle in running and expanding customer value, similar to other assets (Blattberg, Getz, & Thomas, 2001; Kumar & George, 2007; Rust, Lemon, & Zeithaml, 2004). Lemon, Rust, and Zeithaml (2001) and Rust, Lemon, and Zeithaml (2004) explore three drivers of customer equity: value, brand and relationship equity. Value equity comprises the customer's evaluation of a brand's utility depending on what is forgone in exchange for what is gained. Brand equity surpasses the objective value of a brand to consider the subjective evaluation customers form of a brand. Relationship equity highlights the relationship between a brand and customer regardless of the objective and subjective views of a brand (Rust, Lemon, & Zeithaml, 2000).

Brand Equity

Lemon, Rust, and Zeithaml (2001) interpret brand equity as a customer's intangible outlook of what a brand offers. Keller (1993) explores *customer-based brand equity* as the influence of brand knowledge on a consumer's reaction to that brand's promotion. Keller (1993) further investigates brand knowledge as a brand node in customers' minds connected to brand associations, made up of brand awareness and brand image. Brand awareness deliberates the strength of the brand with regard to consumers being able to identify and recognise it (Rossiter & Percy, 1987). Brand awareness may consist of brand *recognition*, which involves consumers identifying a brand, and brand *recall*, which acknowledges consumers' ability to recollect a brand from memory (Keller, 1993). Brand awareness denotes the initial and simple brand recognition on a scale of brand knowledge (Hoyer & Brown, 1990). Wider brand recognition through exposure triggers reassurance among customers as the presumed risk of interacting with, and purchasing from, the brand is reduced (Huang, Schrank, & Dubinsky, 2004). Brand image encompasses the perceptions of a brand drawn from brand associations in a customer's memory (Keller, 1993). Brand associations represent a customer's impression of a brand as part of a brand node kept in mind. Positive and inimitable brand associations assist a customer in distinguishing among different brands, forming brand equity (Keller, 1993).

In a study on the management of brand equity within a multimedia retail environment, Keller (2009) uses the brand resonance model (Keller, 2001) to outline the appropriate experiences that effectively reach customers and strengthen brand-customer relationships. The employment of online interactive marketing communications has enabled resonating benefits among consumers and contributed to brand equity. The first, *brand awareness*, is heightened via online channels as consumers seek interactive outlets to gather information in determining purchase decisions. The second, *brand associations*, are amplified by imagery associations through a brand's creative content, which expresses brand personality. *Brand attitudes* involve meaningful experiences that are expressed via interactive communication settings such as in brand communities. *Brand activity* is especially significant within online interactive environments as it embodies active consumer engagement that expresses informative content and symbolic commitment and brand loyalty (Keller, 2009). Interactive brand communities on social media can bring about singular elements that co-operatively build brand equity among the engaged community as well as outsider observers. Millennials are exposed to brand experiences through social media brand communities that contribute to the collective perception and equity shaped around a brand.

Relationship Equity

Relationship equity considers the aspects that bind a brand and customer beyond brand and value equity (Richards & Jones, 2008; Rust, Lemon, & Zeithaml, 2000). A brand can preserve relationship equity by creating specialised emotional bonds with customers through loyalty programmes or brand communities that encourage interaction (Rust, Zeithaml, & Lemon, 2000). Brand-customer relationships undergo a shift from transactional to emotional when trust and commitment are present (Morgan & Hunt, 1994). As consumers become more engaged in brand communities, trust, commitment and loyalty ensue among the parties. Trust is argued to be an antecedent of loyalty (Chaudhuri & Holbrook, 2001; Chiu, Huang, & Yen, 2010; Kim, Chung, & Lee, 2011). Social media brand communities encourage interaction that fosters social structure and strengthens brand trust and loyalty (Ba, 2001; Walden, 2000; Zheng, Cheung, Lee, & Liang, 2015). Habibi, Laroche, and Richard (2014) assume two ways in which improvement of connections between brand-customer components could escalate brand trust. First, recurring interactions over a prolonged period of time act as the basis of prospering trust as enhanced relationships within a brand community result in positive trust outcomes. The second considers the parallel improvement of relationships and information sharing. The abundance of information disseminated via brand communities appeals to consumers as uncertainty is decreased and trust is developed (Habibi, Laroche, & Richard, 2014; Ba, 2001). Positive engagement on social media contributes to positive functional and emotional experiences that influence brand loyalty (Bruhn, Schnebelen, & Schafer, 2014; Schivinski & Dabrowski, 2016). Online brand community engagements may include non-interactive actions such as reading comments, which are just as effective in ensuring loyalty (Shang et al., 2006).

MOTIVATOR FOR SOCIAL MEDIA BRAND COMMUNITIES

Millennial social media users may gain information, be encouraged to engage and form brand perceptions and relationships as a result of online brand communities. However, Millennials may feel compelled to resort to social media brand communities for self-expression. A consumer may seek to identify with a brand community to belong to a social collective (Algesheimer, Dholakia, & Herrmann, 2005).

Social Media and Social Identity

Social media networks have provided users with an expansive reach in publicly conveying identities (Bagozzi & Dholakia, 2002; Bargh & McKenna, 2004; Dholakia, Bagozzi, & Pearo, 2004; Hogg & Reid, 2006; Pentina, Prybutok, & Zhang, 2008; Hennig-Thurau, Gwinner, Walsh, & Gremler, 2004; Kane, Alavi, Labianca, & Borgatti, 2014; Schivinski & Dabrowski, 2016; Veletsianos, 2013). With the aid of webs of connections entwining into communes around brands and mutual social interests, brand admirers are encouraged to enrich the self through brand affiliation. Customers exercise their presence in overt social media brand communities as a way of shaping and showcasing identity. Aside from sparking knowledge sharing and consumer engagement (Ma & Agarwal, 2007), brand communities aid in augmenting a customer's self-worth by providing social interactions based on the individual he/she believes to be and seeks to be perceived as (Donath, 1999). Social interactions among members mature to relationships as such bonds offer customers the immaterial profit of social placement (Ma & Agarwal, 2007; Ren et al., 2012; Zhu & Chen, 2015). Customers are drawn to associate with brands that potentially advance their social placement through a desired identity.

Social identity theory holds that people are apt to classify themselves and others into social groupings (Ashforth & Mael, 1989; Tajfel & Turner, 1985). Turner (1985) sites groupings or categories as members' prototypical attributes. Social classification allows individuals to cognitively section other individuals into definitive settings while defining themselves; it thus entails the notion of inclusion in an aggregate (Ashforth & Mael, 1989). An individual characterises him/herself according to groups that possess the social categories that individual seeks (Hogg & Abrams, 1988; Hogg, Terry, & White, 1995). Such social categories are pursued on the basis that they pertain to a social consensus from being associated to that group (Jenkins, 2008; Trepte, 2008). Acquiring social consent among a group grants an individual 'belonging' that bolsters self-identity. Social identification is used interchangeably with group identification as the social identity is derived from identifying with a group (Tolman, 1943; Tajfel, 1982). Tajfel (1978) outlines social identity as "that part of an individual's self-concept which derives from his knowledge of his membership of a social group (or groups) together with the value and emotional significance attached to that membership" (Tajfel, 1978, p. 62). Three components add to social identity: a *cognitive* factor (awareness of membership within a group), an *evaluative* factor (awareness of membership is connected to a positive or negative value connotation), and an *emotional* factor (an emotional immersion in the group) (Tajfel, 1978, 1982). Group identification is achieved through a combination of the following components. Individuals are driven to associate with a group that offers the mental and emotional benefits they seek (Fisher & Wakefield, 1998). Affiliation to a group elicits the desired social perspective and instigates a sense of self-worth that advances identity.

While social categorisation draws members into a group based on mutual similarities (in-group), it comparably accentuates the differences between members of different groups (out-group) (Tajfel, 1959, 1969). This is referred to as *depersonalisation* as members are not regarded as individuals but rather as affiliates of a group. Depersonalisation weighs on an individual's self-perception, causing him/her to adapt to attitudes and behaviours that align with the overall perspective of the desired group (Hogg, 2001; Hogg & Terry, 2000). Social identity theory concerns both a personal view of oneself and a social outlook of the collective an individual belongs to (Luhtanen & Crocker, 1992; Nowak, Szamrej, & Latané, 1990). Individuals pursue personal and social identities through actions that personally appeal to their individuality while pertaining to the prototypical qualities of the group they socially embrace. Customers comparably consume brands to express personal character that also appropriates their status within their social group. Personal identity is subdued and dominated by the social identity an individual desires to embody, particularly during settings of high salience (Onorato & Turner, 2004; Turner 1982). Visible consumption of products or brands may induce individuals to exert behaviour that is compliant with a salient identity they socially express. At times of uncertainty, individuals may seek in-group identification to adjust perceptions, behaviour and interaction according to conformed group knowledge that validate an individual's sense of self (Hogg et al., 2006). A variety of activities in daily life can be applied to further an individual's self-expression, including communicating the self through brand consumption (Belk, 1988; Schembri, Merrilees, & Kristiansen, 2010; Stokburger-Sauer & Teichmann, 2013). Symbolic consumption represents individuals with a means to inflate identity that emotionally pertains to the social circle they presently do or aim to share a similar lifestyle to (Gabriel & Lang, 1995; Wattanasuwan, 2005). Customers chase brands that fulfil the symbolic connection of inclusion to a societal circle or brand community that aids their social presence. According to Bhattacharya and Sen (2003), customers are triggered to identify with brands that indulge in consumers' production of the self.

The publicity of social media bears a social influence that may sway individuals' verbalisation. Global social media platforms offer networks of users the potential to voice a free-flow of personal expression across any topic. However, as personal identity is communicated under the basis that it complements the salient social identity (Clement & Krueger, 2002; Haslam, Oakes, Reynolds, & Turner, 1999; Hogg & Turner, 1987; Kietzmann, Hermkens, McCarthy, & Silvestre, 2011), individuals may seek to utilise social media as a means to exert behaviour that adheres to a preferred social group and allows for social inclusion. Kleine, Kleine & Kernan (1993) revealed the degree of identity salience that grants individuals self-fulfilment is dependent on the extent of social links that commend that identity; thus the greater the social response, the more significant that identity becomes. Salience is increasingly prominent via the existence of brand communities that have been transposed to social media platforms to become virtual global communes of brand admirers. Such online communities are regarded as groups gathered with the intention of achieving individual and collective goals (Rheingold, 2002; Bagozzi & Dholakia, 2002). Tajfel's (1978) three components, previously mentioned, can be revisited through *cognition*, as an individual becomes aware of his/her presence within a conspicuous brand community, and this sense of belonging matures into *emotional* attachment to a network of users, which fosters loyalty and relationships (Ashforth & Mael, 1989; Bagozzi & Dholakia, 2002; Bergami & Bagozzi, 2000; Bhattacharya & Sen, 2003). Online community members experience the *evaluative* component as the community members evaluate social identity based on the collective self-placement and self-worth from engaging with that group (Dholakia, Bagozzi, & Pearo, 2004).

The aspiration of ascertaining social consensus among a desired society pushes consumers to manipulate brand association through social media brand communities. Within the fashion industry, social media users connect to brands and communities on social networking platforms that conspicuously allow consumers to depict brand affiliation and ground their presence in a particular social collective.

MANAGERIAL IMPLICATIONS AND RECOMMENDATIONS

This chapter aims to provide an understanding of how social media brand communities have exerted influence on Millennials in the fashion industry (Godey et al., 2016; Gummerus, Liljander, Weman, & Pihlstrom, 2012; Habibi, Laroche, Richard, 2014; Kim & Ko, 2012; Laroche, Habibi, Richard & Sankaranarayanan, 2012; Zheng, Cheung, Lee, & Liang, 2015). As social media advances as the underlying network for modern-day communication, Millennials proceed to interact with such platforms in self-expression over an array of manners including flaunting brand affiliations. This chapter explores the potential of employing brand communities through widespread social media platforms to produce collectively symbolic experiences that further consumers' social identities. Consumers may aspire to publicly engage with a brand and its respective community that fulfils the social prestige they are seeking.

Brands profit from engaging social media communities that bring together global users, allowing brands to deliver information in real-time. Loyal community members accelerate the spread of information as each interaction, 'like', comment or share further exploits a brand message to a new network of users. Consumers' brand devotion grows as they experience a sense of responsibility in contributing to brand information across the community (Algesheimer, Dholakia, & Herrmann, 2005; Fournier & Lee, 2009; Hatch & Schultz, 2010; Muniz & O'Guinn, 2001). Social media marketing efforts ensure customer reach and enrichment of brand awareness and image (Godey et al., 2016). Fashion brands have successfully applied the dynamic nature of social media in documenting live feeds of fashion weeks, promotional campaign events, product launches and celebrity/blogger endorsements that contribute to a brand's equity over an expansive viewing. As a result, brand followers are exposed to a richer experience representative of a lifestyle that accompanies consumption of a brand. Consumers interact in social media brand communities in demonstrating resemblance and self-identification to what that brand symbolises. This study can be used as groundwork for future research to build on.

As marketing principles evolve to accommodate for consumer power shifts and a significance of creating value and relationships with customers (Grönroos & Voima, 2012; Prahalad & Ramaswamy, 2000), the notion of social media has further empowered consumers with a voice to widely proclaim (Hanna, Rohm, & Crittenden, 2011; Kaplan & Haenlein, 2010). Brands are given universal platforms to interact with customers in co-creating value and experiences. This research considers how social media brand communities have exerted a presence among Millennials in the fashion industry. The fashion world was built on a rigid structure of top-to-bottom delivery of tangible products presented within a brick-and-mortar experience. However, brand-customer interactions have been transposed to online means as social media paves the way to tap into experiences providing brands direct real-time access to consumers, and consumers greater insight into brands. Brands and customers are granted leeway to create value through engaging social media brand communities that produce symbolic relationships among community parties. This study demonstrates, within a fast-paced industry abundantly saturated with comparable brands, the importance of reaching Millennial consumers using channels Millennials use and environments Millennials relate to in expressing themselves. This study adds to the literature on marketing to the Millennial cohort (Moore, 2012; Taken Smith, 2011), with the application of social media means that this age has grown with. It is important to note that with the liberation of social media comes diminished brand control over information communicated about the brand. Management of customer experiences gains greater relevance within an online brand community that can be accessed by users across the world. Moreover, the ease and immediacy of consumer interaction exerts an implication for brands to maintain a tone that is in keeping with the brand personality and characterises an inclusive brand image. Social media is a promotional tool that must be run parallel to offline operations as part of an exhaustive marketing strategy that communicates a brand's DNA across multiple channels, eliciting an omni-channel experience.

This research explores the manifestation of social identity theory in social media platforms and brand communities (Bagozzi & Dholakia, 2002; Dholakia, Bagozzi, & Pearo, 2004; Hogg & Reid, 2006; Pentina, Prybutok, & Zhang, 2008). This study recognises the incentives for Millennials to engage in social media brand communities to achieve a desired social identity. The potential to connect with individuals of similar or aspired lifestyles enforces a customer's social placement. Continuous informal contact between brand and customers, centred on the mutual devotion to that brand, develops a sense of belonging that augments the symbolic importance of brand association. Customers are motivated to consume brands and interact in respective communities for the aspirational intention of being grouped into the desired social circle. Brands profit from cultivating a brand image that fits into a particular lifestyle, inducing its community to uphold this perception through group identification that unifies members while dissociating the collective from other groups. Social media brand communities allow self-expression through brand association to be witnessed by a wider network of connections that may or may not belong to the community, allowing social identity to be expressed on a larger scale.

REFERENCES

Algesheimer, R., Dholakia, U., & Herrmann, A. (2005). The Social Influence of Brand Community: Evidence from European Car Clubs. *Journal of Marketing*, *69*(3), 19–34. doi:10.1509/jmkg.69.3.19.66363

Arnett, D., German, S., & Hunt, S. (2003). The Identity Salience Model of Relationship Marketing Success: The Case of Nonprofit Marketing. *Journal of Marketing*, *67*(2), 89–105. doi:10.1509/jmkg.67.2.89.18614

Arora, P. (2014). *The Leisure Commons*. New York: Routledge.

Ashforth, B., & Mael, F. (1989). Social Identity Theory and the Organization. *Academy of Management Review*, *14*(1), 20–39. doi:10.5465/amr.1989.4278999

Ashmore, R., Deaux, K., & McLaughlin-Volpe, T. (2004). An Organizing Framework for Collective Identity: Articulation and Significance of Multidimensionality. *Psychological Bulletin*, *130*(1), 80–114. doi:10.1037/0033-2909.130.1.80 PMID:14717651

Ba, S. (2001). Establishing online trust through a community responsibility system. *Decision Support Systems*, *31*(3), 323–336. doi:10.1016/S0167-9236(00)00144-5

Bagozzi, R., & Dholakia, U. (2002). Intentional social action in virtual communities. *Journal of Interactive Marketing*, *16*(2), 2–21. doi:10.1002/dir.10006

Bagozzi, R., & Dholakia, U. (2006). Open Source Software User Communities: A Study of Participation in Linux User Groups. *Management Science*, *52*(7), 1099–1115. doi:10.1287/mnsc.1060.0545

Balasubramanian, S., & Mahajan, V. (2001). The Economic Leverage of the Virtual Community. *International Journal of Electronic Commerce*, *5*(3), 103–138. doi:10.1080/10864415.2001.11044212

Baldus, B., Voorhees, C., & Calantone, R. (2015). Online brand community engagement: Scale development and validation. *Journal of Business Research*, *68*(5), 2. doi:10.1016/j.jbusres.2014.09.035

Bargh, J., & McKenna, K. (2004). The Internet and Social Life. *Annual Review of Psychology*, *55*(1), 573–590. doi:10.1146/annurev.psych.55.090902.141922 PMID:14744227

Barron, L. (2012). *Social theory in popular culture*. Basingstoke, UK: Palgrave Macmillan.

Belk, R. (1988). Possessions and the Extended Self. *The Journal of Consumer Research*, *15*(2), 139. doi:10.1086/209154

Bergami, M., & Bagozzi, R. (2000). Self-categorization, affective commitment and group self-esteem as distinct aspects of social identity in the organization. *British Journal of Social Psychology*, *39*(4), 555–577. doi:10.1348/014466600164633 PMID:11190685

Berger, J., Sorensen, A., & Rasmussen, S. (2010). Positive Effects of Negative Publicity: When Negative Reviews Increase Sales. *Marketing Science*, *29*(5), 815–827. doi:10.1287/mksc.1090.0557

Berry, L. (1995). Relationship Marketing of Services--Growing Interest, Emerging Perspectives. *Journal of the Academy of Marketing Science*, *23*(4), 236–245. doi:10.1177/009207039502300402

Berthon, P., Pitt, L., & Campbell, C. (2008). Ad Lib: When Customers Create the Ad. *California Management Review*, *50*(4), 6–30. doi:10.2307/41166454

Bhattacharya, C., & Sen, S. (2003). Consumer-Company Identification: A Framework for Understanding Consumers' Relationships with Companies. *Journal of Marketing*, *67*(2), 76–88. doi:10.1509/jmkg.67.2.76.18609

Blackshaw, P., & Nazzaro, M. (2006). *Consumer- Generated Media (CGM) 101: Word-of-Mouth in the Age of the Web-Fortified Consumer*. New York: Nielsen.

Blattberg, R., Getz, G., & Thomas, J. (2001). *Customer Equity: Building and Managing Relationships as Valuable Assets*. Boston: Harvard Business School Press.

BOF & McKinsey & Co. (2018). *The State of Fashion*. McKinsey& Co. Retrieved from https://cdn.businessoffashion.com/reports/The_State_of_Fashion_2018_v2.pdf

Bolton, R., Parasuraman, A., Hoefnagels, A., Migchels, N., Kabadayi, S., Gruber, T., ... Solnet, D. (2013). Understanding Generation Y and their use of social media: A review and research agenda. *Journal of Service Management*, *24*(3), 245–267. doi:10.1108/09564231311326987

Brown, J., Broderick, A., & Lee, N. (2007). Word of mouth communication within online communities: Conceptualizing the online social network. *Journal of Interactive Marketing*, *21*(3), 2–20. doi:10.1002/dir.20082

Brown, S., Kozinets, R., & Sherry, J. Jr. (2003). Teaching Old Brands New Tricks: Retro Branding and the Revival of Brand Meaning. *Journal of Marketing*, *67*(3), 19–33. doi:10.1509/jmkg.67.3.19.18657

Bruhn, M., Schnebelen, S., & Schäfer, D. (2014). Antecedents and consequences of the quality of e-customer-to-customer interactions in B2B brand communities. *Industrial Marketing Management*, *43*(1), 164–176. doi:10.1016/j.indmarman.2013.08.008

Butler, B. (2001). Membership Size, Communication Activity, and Sustainability: A Resource-Based Model of Online Social Structures. *Information Systems Research*, *12*(4), 346–362. doi:10.1287/isre.12.4.346.9703

Casalo, L., Flavián, C., & Guinalíu, M. (2007). The Influence of Satisfaction, Perceived Reputation and Trust on a Consumer's Commitment to a Website. *Journal of Marketing Communications*, *13*(1), 1–17. doi:10.1080/13527260600951633

Chappuis, B., Gaffey, B., & Parvizi, P. (2011). *Are your customers becoming digital junkies?* Retrieved from https://www.mckinsey.com/business-functions/marketing-and-sales/our-insights/are-your-customers-becoming-digital-junkies

Chaudhuri, A., & Holbrook, M. (2001). The Chain of Effects from Brand Trust and Brand Affect to Brand Performance: The Role of Brand Loyalty. *Journal of Marketing*, *65*(2), 81–93. doi:10.1509/jmkg.65.2.81.18255

Cheung, C., & Thadani, D. (2012). The impact of electronic word-of-mouth communication: A literature analysis and integrative model. *Decision Support Systems*, *54*(1), 461–470. doi:10.1016/j.dss.2012.06.008

Chevalier, J., & Mayzlin, D. (2006). The Effect of Word of Mouth on Sales: Online Book Reviews. *JMR, Journal of Marketing Research*, *43*(3), 345–354. doi:10.1509/jmkr.43.3.345

Chiu, C., Huang, H., & Yen, C. (2010). Antecedents of trust in online auctions. *Electronic Commerce Research and Applications*, *9*(2), 148–159. doi:10.1016/j.elerap.2009.04.003

Christodoulides, G., Jevons, C., & Bonhomme, J. (2012). Memo to Marketers: Quantitative Evidence for Change. *Journal of Advertising Research*, *52*(1), 53–64. doi:10.2501/JAR-52-1-053-064

Clement, R., & Krueger, J. (2002). Social Categorization Moderates Social Projection. *Journal of Experimental Social Psychology*, *38*(3), 219–231. doi:10.1006/jesp.2001.1503

Cova, B. (1997). Community and consumption. *European Journal of Marketing*, *31*(3/4), 297–316. doi:10.1108/03090569710162380

Cova, B., & Cova, V. (2002). Tribal Marketing: The tribalisation of society and its impact on the conduct of marketing. *European Journal of Marketing*, *36*(5/6), 595–620. doi:10.1108/03090560210423023

Cova, B., & Pace, S. (2006). Brand community of convenience products: New forms of customer empowerment – the case "my Nutella The Community". *European Journal of Marketing*, *40*(9/10), 1087–1105. doi:10.1108/03090560610681023

Daugherty, T., & Hoffman, E. (2014). eWOM and the importance of capturing consumer attention within social media. *Journal of Marketing Communications*, *20*(1-2), 82–102. doi:10.1080/13527266.2013.797764

de Ruyter, K., Moorman, L., & Lemmink, J. (2001). Antecedents of Commitment and Trust in Customer–Supplier Relationships in High Technology Markets. *Industrial Marketing Management*, *30*(3), 271–286. doi:10.1016/S0019-8501(99)00091-7

Dellarocas, C. (2006). Strategic Manipulation of Internet Opinion Forums: Implications for Consumers and Firms. *Management Science*, *52*(10), 1577–1593. doi:10.1287/mnsc.1060.0567

Deloitte. (2017). *The 2017 Deloitte Millennial Survey*. Deloitte. Retrieved from https://www2.deloitte.com/content/dam/Deloitte/global/Documents/About-Deloitte/gx-deloitte-millennial-survey-2017-executive-summary.pdf

Dessart, L., Veloutsou, C., & Thomas, A. (2015). Consumer engagement in online brand communities: A social media perspective. *Journal of Product and Brand Management*, *24*(1), 28–42. doi:10.1108/JPBM-06-2014-0635

Dewing, M. (2010). *Social Media: An Introduction*. Ottawa: Library of Parliament.

Dholakia, U., Bagozzi, R., & Pearo, L. (2004). A social influence model of consumer participation in network- and small-group-based virtual communities. *International Journal of Research in Marketing*, *21*(3), 241–263. doi:10.1016/j.ijresmar.2003.12.004

Donath, J. (1999). Identity and Deception in the Virtual Community. In P. Kollack & M. Smith (Eds.), *Communities in Cyberspace* (pp. 27–58). New York: Routledge.

Duan, W., Gu, B., & Whinston, A. (2008). The dynamics of online word-of-mouth and product sales—An empirical investigation of the movie industry. *Journal of Retailing*, *84*(2), 233–242. doi:10.1016/j.jretai.2008.04.005

Edelman, D. (2010). Branding in the digital age: You're spending your money in all the wrong places. *Harvard Business Review*, (88), 62–69.

Elliott, R., & Wattanasuwan, K. (1998). Brands as Symbolic Resources for the Construction of Identity. *International Journal of Advertising*, *17*(2), 131–144. doi:10.1080/02650487.1998.11104712

Escalas, J., & Bettman, J. (2003). You Are What They Eat: The Influence of Reference Groups on Consumers' Connections to Brands. *Journal of Consumer Psychology*, *13*(3), 339–348. doi:10.1207/S15327663JCP1303_14

Evans, D. (2012). *Social Media Marketing* (2nd ed.). Indianapolis, IN: John Wiley & Sons Publishing, Inc.

Fischer, E., & Reuber, A. (2011). Social interaction via new social media: (How) can interactions on Twitter affect effectual thinking and behavior? *Journal of Business Venturing*, *26*(1), 1–18. doi:10.1016/j.jbusvent.2010.09.002

Fisher, R., & Wakefield, K. (1998). Factors leading to group identification: A field study of winners and losers. *Psychology and Marketing*, *15*(1), 23–40. doi:10.1002/(SICI)1520-6793(199801)15:1<23::AID-MAR3>3.0.CO;2-P

Fournier, S., & Avery, J. (2011). The Uninvited Brand. *Business Horizons*, *54*(3), 193–207. doi:10.1016/j.bushor.2011.01.001

Fournier, S., & Lee, L. (2009, April). Getting Brand Communities Right. *Harvard Business Review*, 2–8.

Fromm, J., & Garton, C. (2013). *Marketing to Millennials*. Barkley, Inc.

Fuchs, C. (2014). *Social Media: A Critical Introduction*. London: Sage Publications, Ltd.

Gabriel, Y., & Lang, T. (1995). *The Unmanageable Consumer*. London: Sage Publications.

Gainer, B., & Fischer, E. (1994). Community and consumption. *Advances in Consumer Research. Association for Consumer Research (U. S.)*, *21*, 137.

Gallaugher, J., & Ransbotham, S. (2010). Social Media and Customer Dialog Management at Starbucks. *MIS Quarterly Executive*, *9*(4), 197–212.

Gillies, J., & Cailliau, R. (2000). *How the Web was born*. Oxford, UK: Oxford University Press.

Godes, D., & Mayzlin, D. (2009). Firm-Created Word-of-Mouth Communication: Evidence from a Field Test. *Marketing Science*, *28*(4), 721–739. doi:10.1287/mksc.1080.0444

Godey, B., Manthiou, A., Pederzoli, D., Rokka, J., Aiello, G., Donvito, R., & Singh, R. (2016). Social media marketing efforts of luxury brands: Influence on brand equity and consumer behavior. *Journal of Business Research*, *69*(12), 5833–5841. doi:10.1016/j.jbusres.2016.04.181

Gounaris, S. (2005). Trust and commitment influences on customer retention: Insights from business-to-business services. *Journal of Business Research*, *58*(2), 126–140. doi:10.1016/S0148-2963(03)00122-X

Grönroos, C., & Voima, P. (2013). Critical service logic: Making sense of value creation and co-creation. *Journal of the Academy of Marketing Science*, *41*(2), 133–150. doi:10.100711747-012-0308-3

Gruen, T., Osmonbekov, T., & Czaplewski, A. (2006). eWOM: The impact of customer-to-customer online know-how exchange on customer value and loyalty. *Journal of Business Research*, *59*(4), 449–456. doi:10.1016/j.jbusres.2005.10.004

Gummerus, J., Liljander, V., Weman, E., & Pihlström, M. (2012). Customer engagement in a Facebook brand community. *Management Research Review*, *35*(9), 857–877. doi:10.1108/01409171211256578

Gusfield, J. (1978). *Community: A Critical Response* (2nd ed.). New York: Harper Collophon Books.

Habibi, M., Laroche, M., & Richard, M. (2014). Brand communities based in social media: How unique are they? Evidence from two exemplary brand communities. *International Journal of Information Management*, *34*(2), 123–132. doi:10.1016/j.ijinfomgt.2013.11.010

Hanna, R., Rohm, A., & Crittenden, V. (2011). We're all connected: The power of the social media ecosystem. *Business Horizons*, *54*(3), 265–273. doi:10.1016/j.bushor.2011.01.007

Hansen, D., Schneiderman, B., & Smith, M. (2011). *Analyzing social media networks with NodeXL*. Amsterdam: Elsevier.

Haslam, S., Oakes, P., Reynolds, K., & Turner, J. (1999). Social Identity Salience and the Emergence of Stereotype Consensus. *Personality and Social Psychology Bulletin*, *25*(7), 809–818. doi:10.1177/0146167299025007004

Hatch, M., & Schultz, M. (2010). Toward a theory of brand co-creation with implications for brand governance. *Journal of Brand Management*, *17*(8), 590–604. doi:10.1057/bm.2010.14

Heere, B., Walker, M., Yoshida, M., Ko, Y., Jordan, J., & James, J. (2011). Brand Community Development Through Associated Communities: Grounding Community Measurement Within Social Identity Theory. *Journal of Marketing Theory and Practice*, *19*(4), 407–422. doi:10.2753/MTP1069-6679190404

Heider, F. (1946). Attitudes and Cognitive Organization. *The Journal of Psychology*, *21*(1), 107–112. doi:10.1080/00223980.1946.9917275 PMID:21010780

Helal, G., & Ozuem, W. (2017). Social Identity Matters: Social Media and Brand Perceptions in the Fashion Apparel and Accessories Industries. In W. Ozuem & Y. Azemi (Eds.), *Digital Marketing Strategies for Fashion and Luxury Brands* (pp. 326–361). Hershey, PA: IGI Global.

Hennig-Thurau, T., Gwinner, K., Walsh, G., & Gremler, D. (2004). Electronic word-of-mouth via consumer-opinion platforms: What motivates consumers to articulate themselves on the Internet? *Journal of Interactive Marketing*, *18*(1), 38–52. doi:10.1002/dir.10073

Hennig-Thurau, T., Malthouse, E., Friege, C., Gensler, S., Lobschat, L., Rangaswamy, A., & Skiera, B. (2010). The Impact of New Media on Customer Relationships. *Journal of Service Research*, *13*(3), 311–330. doi:10.1177/1094670510375460

Hoffman, D., & Fodor, M. (2016). Can you measure the ROI of your social media marketing? *Sloan Management Review*, *52*(1), 41–49.

Hoffman, D., & Novak, T. (1996). Marketing in Hypermedia Computer-Mediated Environments: Conceptual Foundations. *Journal of Marketing*, *60*(3), 50–68. doi:10.2307/1251841

Hogg, M. (2001). A Social Identity Theory of Leadership. *Personality and Social Psychology Review*, *5*(3), 184–200. doi:10.1207/S15327957PSPR0503_1

Hogg, M., & Abrams, D. (1988). *Social identifications*. London: Routledge.

Hogg, M., & Reid, S. (2006). Social Identity, Self-Categorization, and the Communication of Group Norms. *Communication Theory*, *16*(1), 7–30. doi:10.1111/j.1468-2885.2006.00003.x

Hogg, M., Sherman, D., Dierselhuis, J., Maitner, A., & Moffitt, G. (2006). Uncertainty, entitativity, and group identification. *Journal of Experimental Social Psychology*, *43*(1), 135–142. doi:10.1016/j.jesp.2005.12.008

Hogg, M., & Terry, D. (2000). Social Identity and Self-Categorization Processes in Organizational Contexts. *Academy of Management Review*, *25*(1), 121–140. doi:10.5465/amr.2000.2791606

Hogg, M., Terry, D., & White, K. (1995). A Tale of Two Theories: A Critical Comparison of Identity Theory with Social Identity Theory. *Social Psychology Quarterly*, *58*(4), 255–269. doi:10.2307/2787127

Hogg, M., & Turner, J. (1987). Intergroup behaviour, self-stereotyping and the salience of social categories. *British Journal of Social Psychology*, *26*(4), 325–340. doi:10.1111/j.2044-8309.1987.tb00795.x

Holland, J., & Baker, S. (2001). Customer participation in creating site brand loyalty. *Journal of Interactive Marketing*, *15*(4), 34–45. doi:10.1002/dir.1021

Hollebeek, L., Glynn, M., & Brodie, R. (2014). Consumer Brand Engagement in Social Media: Conceptualization, Scale Development and Validation. *Journal of Interactive Marketing*, *28*(2), 149–165. doi:10.1016/j.intmar.2013.12.002

Houman Andersen, P. (2001). Relationship development and marketing communication: An integrative model. *Journal of Business and Industrial Marketing*, *16*(3), 167–183. doi:10.1108/08858620110389786

Howe, N., & Strauss, W. (2000). *Millennials Rising: The Next Great Generation*. New York: Vintage Books.

Hoyer, W., & Brown, S. (1990). Effects of Brand Awareness on Choice for a Common, Repeat-Purchase Product. *The Journal of Consumer Research*, *17*(2), 141–148. doi:10.1086/208544

Huang, W., Schrank, H., & Dubinsky, A. (2004). Effect of brand name on consumers' risk perceptions of online shopping. *Journal of Consumer Behaviour*, *4*(1), 40–50. doi:10.1002/cb.156

Hudson, S., Huang, L., Roth, M., & Madden, T. (2016). The influence of social media interactions on consumer–brand relationships: A three-country study of brand perceptions and marketing behaviors. *International Journal of Research in Marketing*, *33*(1), 27–41. doi:10.1016/j.ijresmar.2015.06.004

Hunt, S., & Madhavaram, S. (2015). The Service-Dominant Logic of Marketing: Theoretical Foundations, Pedagogy, and Resource-Advantage Theory. In R. Lusch & S. Vargo (Eds.), *The Service-dominant Logic of Marketing: Dialog, Debate, and Directions* (2nd ed.; pp. 67–84). New York: Routledge.

Hutter, K., Hautz, J., Dennhardt, S., & Füller, J. (2013). The impact of user interactions in social media on brand awareness and purchase intention: The case of MINI on Facebook. *Journal of Product and Brand Management*, *22*(5/6), 342–351. doi:10.1108/JPBM-05-2013-0299

Huy, Q., & Shipilov, A. (2012). The key to social media success within organisations. *Sloan Management Review*, *54*(1), 73–81.

Iacobucci, D. (1994). Analysis of Experimental Data. In R. P. Bagozzi (Ed.), *Principles of Marketing Research*. Cambridge, MA: Blackwell Publishing.

Jayachandran, S., Gimeno, J., & Varadarajan, P. (1999). The Theory of Multimarket Competition: A Synthesis and Implications for Marketing Strategy. *Journal of Marketing*, *63*(3), 49. doi:10.2307/1251775

Jenkins, R. (2008). *Social identity (Key Ideas)* (3rd ed.). London: Routledge.

Kane, G., Alavi, M., Labianca, G., & Borgatti, S. (2014). What's Different About Social Media Networks? A Framework and Research Agenda. *Management Information Systems Quarterly*, *38*(1), 274–304. doi:10.25300/MISQ/2014/38.1.13

Kaplan, A., & Haenlein, M. (2010). Users of the world, unite! The challenges and opportunities of Social Media. *Business Horizons*, *53*(1), 59–68. doi:10.1016/j.bushor.2009.09.003

Karpinski, R. (2005). The next phase: Bottom-up marketing. *BtoB Magazine, 90*(5), 38.

Keller, K. (1993). Conceptualizing, Measuring, and Managing Customer-Based Brand Equity. *Journal of Marketing*, *57*(1), 1–22. doi:10.1177/002224299305700101

Keller, K. (2001). Building Customer-Based Brand Equity: A Blueprint for Creating Strong Brands. Marketing Science Institute, 3-23.

Keller, K. (2009). Building strong brands in a modern marketing communications environment. *Journal of Marketing Communications*, *15*(2-3), 139–155. doi:10.1080/13527260902757530

Kietzmann, J., Hermkens, K., McCarthy, I., & Silvestre, B. (2011). Social media? Get serious! Understanding the functional building blocks of social media. *Business Horizons*, *54*(3), 241–251. doi:10.1016/j.bushor.2011.01.005

Kilian, T., Hennigs, N., & Langner, S. (2012). Do Millennials read books or blogs? Introducing a media usage typology of the Internet generation. *Journal of Consumer Marketing*, *29*(2), 114–124. doi:10.1108/07363761211206366

Kim, A., & Ko, E. (2012). Do social media marketing activities enhance customer equity? An empirical study of luxury fashion brand. *Journal of Business Research*, *65*(10), 1480–1486. doi:10.1016/j.jbusres.2011.10.014

Kim, M., Chung, N., & Lee, C. (2011). The effect of perceived trust on electronic commerce: Shopping online for tourism products and services in South Korea. *Tourism Management*, *32*(2), 256–265. doi:10.1016/j.tourman.2010.01.011

Kleine, R. III, Kleine, S., & Kernan, J. (1993). Mundane Consumption and the Self: A Social-Identity Perspective. *Journal of Consumer Psychology*, *2*(3), 209–235. doi:10.1016/S1057-7408(08)80015-0

Koh, J., & Kim, Y. (2004). Knowledge sharing in virtual communities: An e-business perspective. *Expert Systems with Applications*, *26*(2), 155–166. doi:10.1016/S0957-4174(03)00116-7

Kozinets, R. (1999). E-tribalized marketing?: The strategic implications of virtual communities of consumption. *European Management Journal*, *17*(3), 252–264. doi:10.1016/S0263-2373(99)00004-3

Kozinets, R. (2002). The Field Behind the Screen: Using Netnography for Marketing Research in Online Communities. *JMR, Journal of Marketing Research*, *39*(1), 61–72. doi:10.1509/jmkr.39.1.61.18935

Kozinets, R., de Valck, K., Wojnicki, A., & Wilner, S. (2010). Networked Narratives: Understanding Word-of-Mouth Marketing in Online Communities. *Journal of Marketing*, *74*(2), 71–89. doi:10.1509/jmkg.74.2.71

Kulmala, M., Mesiranta, N., & Tuominen, P. (2013). Organic and amplified eWOM in consumer fashion blogs. *Journal Of Fashion Marketing And Management: An International Journal*, *17*(1), 20–37. doi:10.1108/13612021311305119

Kumar, N., Hibbard, J., & Stern, L. (1994). *The Nature and Consequences of Marketing Channel Intermediary Commitment*. Cambridge, UK: Marketing Science Institute.

Kumar, V., & George, M. (2007). Measuring and maximizing customer equity: A critical analysis. *Journal of the Academy of Marketing Science*, *35*(2), 157–171. doi:10.100711747-007-0028-2

Lam, S., Ahearne, M., Hu, Y., & Schillewaert, N. (2010). Resistance to Brand Switching When a Radically New Brand Is Introduced: A Social Identity Theory Perspective. *Journal of Marketing*, *74*(6), 128–146. doi:10.1509/jmkg.74.6.128

Laroche, M., Habibi, M., Richard, M., & Sankaranarayanan, R. (2012). The effects of social media based brand communities on brand community markers, value creation practices, brand trust and brand loyalty. *Computers in Human Behavior*, *28*(5), 1755–1767. doi:10.1016/j.chb.2012.04.016

Lemon, K., Rust, R., & Zeithaml, V. (2001). What drives customer equity. *Marketing Management*, *10*(1), 20–25.

Liu, Y. (2006). Word of Mouth for Movies: Its Dynamics and Impact on Box Office Revenue. *Journal of Marketing*, *70*(3), 74–89. doi:10.1509/jmkg.70.3.74

Luhtanen, R., & Crocker, J. (1992). A Collective Self-Esteem Scale: Self-Evaluation of One's Social Identity. *Personality and Social Psychology Bulletin*, *18*(3), 302–318. doi:10.1177/0146167292183006

Lusch, R. (2007). Marketing's Evolving Identity: Defining Our Future. *Journal of Public Policy & Marketing*, *26*(2), 261–268. doi:10.1509/jppm.26.2.261

Ma, M., & Agarwal, R. (2007). Through a Glass Darkly: Information Technology Design, Identity Verification, and Knowledge Contribution in Online Communities. *Information Systems Research*, *18*(1), 42–67. doi:10.1287/isre.1070.0113

Mangold, W., & Faulds, D. (2009). Social media: The new hybrid element of the promotion mix. *Business Horizons*, *52*(4), 357–365. doi:10.1016/j.bushor.2009.03.002

Manville, B. (2004). Building Customer Communities of Practice for Business Value: Success Factors Profiled from Saba Software and Other Case Studies. In P. Hildreth & C. Kimble (Eds.), *Knowledge Networks: Innovation through Communities of Practices* (pp. 106–123). Hershey, PA: Idea Group Publishing. doi:10.4018/978-1-59140-200-8.ch010

McAlexander, J., Koenig, H., & Schouten, J. (2006). Building Relationships of Brand Community in Higher Education: A Strategic Framework for University Advancement. *International Journal of Educational Advancement*, *6*(2), 107–118. doi:10.1057/palgrave.ijea.2150015

McAlexander, J., Schouten, J., & Koening, H. (2002). Building Brand Community. *Journal of Marketing*, *66*(1), 38–54. doi:10.1509/jmkg.66.1.38.18451

McKinsey. (2016). *The State of Fashion*. Retrieved from https://www.mckinsey.com/industries/retail/our-insights/the-state-of-fashion

Moore, M. (2012). Interactive media usage among millennial consumers. *Journal of Consumer Marketing*, *29*(6), 436–444. doi:10.1108/07363761211259241

Morgan, R., & Hunt, S. (1994). The Commitment-Trust Theory of Relationship Marketing. *Journal of Marketing*, *58*(3), 20. doi:10.2307/1252308

Muniz, A. Jr, & O'Guinn, T. (2001). Brand Community. *The Journal of Consumer Research*, *27*(4), 412–432. doi:10.1086/319618

Murugesan, S. (2007). Understanding Web 2.0. *IT Professional*, *9*(4), 34–41. doi:10.1109/MITP.2007.78

Naylor, R., Lamberton, C., & West, P. (2012). Beyond the "Like" Button: The Impact of Mere Virtual Presence on Brand Evaluations and Purchase Intentions in Social Media Settings. *Journal of Marketing*, *76*(6), 105–120. doi:10.1509/jm.11.0105

Newcomb, T. (1953). An approach to the study of communicative acts. *Psychological Review*, *60*(6), 393–404. doi:10.1037/h0063098 PMID:13112341

Ng, E., Schweitzer, L., & Lyons, S. (2010). New Generation, Great Expectations: A Field Study of the Millennial Generation. *Journal of Business and Psychology*, *25*(2), 281–292. doi:10.100710869-010-9159-4

Nowak, A., Szamrej, J., & Latané, B. (1990). From private attitude to public opinion: A dynamic theory of social impact. *Psychological Review*, *97*(3), 362–376. doi:10.1037/0033-295X.97.3.362

O'Reilly, T. (2005). Web 2.0: Compact Definition? *O'Reilly Radar*. Retrieved from http://radar.oreilly.com/2005/10/web-20-compact-definition.html

O'Reilly, T., & Battelle, J. (2009). *Web Squared: Web 2.0 Five Years On*. Sebastopol, CA: O'Reilly Media.

Onorato, R., & Turner, J. (2004). Fluidity in the self-concept: The shift from personal to social identity. *European Journal of Social Psychology*, *34*(3), 257–278. doi:10.1002/ejsp.195

Ozuem, W., Howell, K., & Lancaster, G. (2008). Communicating in the new interactive marketspace. *European Journal of Marketing*, *42*(9/10), 1059–1083. doi:10.1108/03090560810891145

Parameswaran, M., & Whinston, A. (2007). Research Issues in Social Computing. *Journal of the Association for Information Systems*, *8*(6), 336–350. doi:10.17705/1jais.00132

Park, D., Lee, J., & Han, I. (2007). The Effect of On-Line Consumer Reviews on Consumer Purchasing Intention: The Moderating Role of Involvement. *International Journal of Electronic Commerce*, *11*(4), 125–148. doi:10.2753/JEC1086-4415110405

Paroutis, S., & Al Saleh, A. (2009). Determinants of knowledge sharing using Web 2.0 technologies. *Journal of Knowledge Management*, *13*(4), 52–63. doi:10.1108/13673270910971824

Pentina, I., Gammoh, B., Zhang, L., & Mallin, M. (2013). Drivers and Outcomes of Brand Relationship Quality in the Context of Online Social Networks. *International Journal of Electronic Commerce*, *17*(3), 63–86. doi:10.2753/JEC1086-4415170303

Pentina, I., Prybutok, V., & Zhang, X. (2008). The role of virtual communities as shopping reference groups. *Journal of Electronic Commerce Research*, *9*(2), 114–136.

Phan, M., Thomas, R., & Heine, K. (2011). Social Media and Luxury Brand Management: The Case of Burberry. *Journal Of Global Fashion Marketing*, *2*(4), 213–222. doi:10.1080/20932685.2011.10593099

Pitta, D., & Fowler, D. (2005). Internet community forums: An untapped resource for consumer marketers. *Journal of Consumer Marketing*, *22*(5), 265–274. doi:10.1108/07363760510611699

Pongsakornrungsilp, S., & Schroeder, J. (2011). Understanding value co-creation in a co-consuming brand community. *Marketing Theory*, *11*(3), 303–324. doi:10.1177/1470593111408178

Prahalad, C., & Ramaswamy, V. (2000). Co-opting Customer Competence. *Harvard Business Review*, *78*(1), 79–87.

Prahalad, C., & Ramaswamy, V. (2004). Co-creating unique value with customers. *Strategy and Leadership*, *32*(3), 4–9. doi:10.1108/10878570410699249

Qualman, E. (2013). *Socialnomics*. Hoboken, NJ: John Wiley & Sons.

Rainer, T., & Rainer, J. (2011). *The Millennials*. Nashville, TN: B & H Publishing Group.

Ramaswamy, V. (2008). Co-creating value through customers' experiences: The Nike case. *Strategy and Leadership*, *36*(5), 9–14. doi:10.1108/10878570810902068

Ren, Y., Harper, M., Drenner, S., Terveen, L., Kiesler, S., Riedl, J., & Kraut, R. (2012). Building member attachment in online communities: Applying theories of group identity and interpersonal bonds. *Management Information Systems Quarterly*, *36*(3), 841–864. doi:10.2307/41703483

Rheingold, H. (2002). *Smart mobs*. Cambridge, MA: Perseus Books Group.

Richards, K., & Jones, E. (2008). Customer relationship management: Finding value drivers. *Industrial Marketing Management*, *37*(2), 120–130. doi:10.1016/j.indmarman.2006.08.005

Romero, D., & Molina, A. (2011). Collaborative networked organisations and customer communities: Value co-creation and co-innovation in the networking era. *Production Planning and Control*, *22*(5-6), 447–472. doi:10.1080/09537287.2010.536619

Ross, C., Orr, E., Sisic, M., Arseneault, J., Simmering, M., & Orr, R. (2009). Personality and Motivations Associated With Facebook Use. *Computers in Human Behavior*, *25*(2), 578–586. doi:10.1016/j.chb.2008.12.024

Rossiter, J., & Percy, L. (1978). *Advertising and Promotion Management*. New York: McGraw Hill.

Royo-Vela, M., & Casamassima, P. (2011). The influence of belonging to virtual brand communities on consumers' affective commitment, satisfaction and word-of-mouth advertising. *Online Information Review*, *35*(4), 517–542. doi:10.1108/14684521111161918

Rust, R., Lemon, K., & Zeithaml, V. (2000). *Driving Customer Equity: How Customer Lifetime Value Is Reshaping Corporate Strategy*. New York: The Free Pree.

Rust, R., Lemon, K., & Zeithaml, V. (2004). Return on Marketing: Using Customer Equity to Focus Marketing Strategy. *Journal of Marketing*, *68*(1), 109–127. doi:10.1509/jmkg.68.1.109.24030

Sashi, C. (2012). Customer engagement, buyer-seller relationships, and social media. *Management Decision*, *50*(2), 253–272. doi:10.1108/00251741211203551

Schau, H., Muñiz, A. Jr, & Arnould, E. (2009). How Brand Community Practices Create Value. *Journal of Marketing*, *73*(5), 30–51. doi:10.1509/jmkg.73.5.30

Schembri, S., Merrilees, B., & Kristiansen, S. (2010). Brand consumption and narrative of the self. *Psychology and Marketing*, *27*(6), 623–637. doi:10.1002/mar.20348

Schewe, C., & Meredith, G. (2004). Segmenting global markets by generational cohorts: Determining motivations by age. *Journal of Consumer Behaviour*, *4*(1), 51–63. doi:10.1002/cb.157

Schivinski, B., & Dabrowski, D. (2016). The impact of brand communication on brand equity through Facebook. *Journal of Marketing Communications*, *22*(2), 189–214. doi:10.1080/13527266.2013.871323

Schouten, J., & McAlexander, J. (1995). Subcultures of Consumption: An Ethnography of the New Bikers. *The Journal of Consumer Research*, *22*(1), 43. doi:10.1086/209434

Shang, R., Chen, Y., & Liao, H. (2006). The value of participation in virtual consumer communities on brand loyalty. *Internet Research*, *16*(4), 398–418. doi:10.1108/10662240610690025

Sheth, J. (2011). Impact of Emerging Markets on Marketing: Rethinking Existing Perspectives and Practices. *Journal of Marketing*, *75*(4), 166–182. doi:10.1509/jmkg.75.4.166

Sheth, J., & Sisodia, R. (1999). Revisiting Marketing's Lawlike Generalizations. *Journal of the Academy of Marketing Science*, *27*(1), 71–87. doi:10.1177/0092070399271006

Simmons, G. (2008). Marketing to postmodern consumers: Introducing the internet chameleon. *European Journal of Marketing*, *42*(3/4), 299–310. doi:10.1108/03090560810852940

Smith, A., & Anderson, M. (2018). *Social Media Use in 2018*. Pew Research Center. Retrieved from http://assets.pewresearch.org/wp-content/uploads/sites/14/2018/03/01105133/PI_2018.03.01_Social-Media_FINAL.pdf

Solomon, G., & Schrum, L. (2007). *Web 2.0: New Tools, New Schools*. Eugene, OR: International Society for Technology in Education.

Statista. (2016a). *Global daily social media usage by age 2016*. Retrieved from https://www.statista.com/statistics/613456/daily-social-media-usage-worldwide-age/

Statista. (2016b). *Fashion brands: social visibility score on social networks 2016 | Statistic*. Retrieved from https://www.statista.com/statistics/729691/fashion-brands-social-visibility-score-social-networks-world/

Statista. (2016c). *Instagram: global brand adoption rate 2016*. Retrieved from https://www.statista.com/statistics/305292/worldwide-instagram-brand-adoption-rate-category/

Statista. (2016d). *Instagram usage during MFW by action Italy 2016*. Retrieved from https://www.statista.com/statistics/676023/instagram-usage-during-mfw-by-action-italy/

Statista. (2017a). *Luxury brands discovery sources among Millennials worldwide 2017 | Statistic*. Retrieved from https://www.statista.com/statistics/441758/sources-for-hearing-about-new-luxury-brands-worldwide/

Statista. (2017b). *Number of worldwide social network users 2010-2021 | Statistic*. Retrieved from https://www.statista.com/statistics/278414/number-of-worldwide-social-network-users/

Statista. (2017c). *Snapchat brand stories by media type and industry 2017 | Statistic*. Retrieved from https://www.statista.com/statistics/753645/snapchat-brand-stories-media-type-industry/

Statista. (2017d). *Social network penetration worldwide 2021*. Retrieved from https://www.statista.com/statistics/260811/social-network-penetration-worldwide/

Statista. (2018). *Social media: worldwide penetration rate 2018*. Retrieved from https://www.statista.com/statistics/269615/social-network-penetration-by-region/

Stokburger-Sauer, N. (2010). Brand community: Drivers and outcomes. *Psychology and Marketing*, *27*(4), 347–368. doi:10.1002/mar.20335

Stokburger-Sauer, N., & Teichmann, K. (2013). Is luxury just a female thing? The role of gender in luxury brand consumption. *Journal of Business Research*, *66*(7), 889–896. doi:10.1016/j.jbusres.2011.12.007

Susarla, A., Oh, J., & Tan, Y. (2012). Social Networks and the Diffusion of User-Generated Content: Evidence from YouTube. *Information Systems Research*, *23*(1), 23–41. doi:10.1287/isre.1100.0339

Tajfel, H. (1959). Quantitative Judgement In Social Perception. *British Journal of Psychology*, *50*(1), 16–29. doi:10.1111/j.2044-8295.1959.tb00677.x PMID:13628966

Tajfel, H. (1969). Cognitive Aspects of Prejudice. *The Journal of Social Issues*, *25*(4), 79–97. doi:10.1111/j.1540-4560.1969.tb00620.x PMID:5373848

Tajfel, H. (1972). Social categorization. English manuscript of 'La catégorisation sociale. In S. Moscovici (Ed.), *Introduction à la Psychologie Sociale* (Vol. 1, pp. 272–302). Paris: Larousse.

Tajfel, H. (1978). The achievement of intergroup differentiation. In H. Tajfel (Ed.), *Differentiation between social groups* (pp. 77–100). London: Academic Press.

Tajfel, H. (1978). The achievement of intergroup differentiation. In H. Tajfel (Ed.), *Differentiation between social groups* (p. 62). London: Academic Press.

Tajfel, H. (1982). Social Psychology of Intergroup Relations. *Annual Review of Psychology*, *33*(1), 1–39. doi:10.1146/annurev.ps.33.020182.000245

Tajfel, H., & Turner, J. (1985). The Social Identity Theory of Intergroup Behaviour. In S. Worchel & W. Austen (Eds.), *Psychology of intergroup relations* (2nd ed.; pp. 7–24). Chicago: Nelson-Hall.

Taken Smith, K. (2012). Longitudinal study of digital marketing strategies targeting Millennials. *Journal of Consumer Marketing*, *29*(2), 86–92. doi:10.1108/07363761211206339

Tiago, M., & Veríssimo, J. (2014). Digital marketing and social media: Why bother? *Business Horizons*, *57*(6), 703–708. doi:10.1016/j.bushor.2014.07.002

Tikkanen, H., Hietanen, J., Henttonen, T., & Rokka, J. (2009). Exploring virtual worlds: Success factors in virtual world marketing. *Management Decision*, *47*(8), 1357–1381. doi:10.1108/00251740910984596

Tolman, E. (1943). Identification and the postwar world. *Journal of Abnormal and Social Psychology*, *38*(2), 141–148. doi:10.1037/h0057497

Trepte, S. (2008). Social Identity Theory. In J. Bryant & P. Vorderer (Eds.), *Psychology of Entertainment* (2nd ed.; pp. 255–271). New York: Routledge.

Trusov, M., Bucklin, R., & Pauwels, K. (2009). Effects of Word-of-Mouth Versus Traditional Marketing: Findings from an Internet Social Networking Site. *Journal of Marketing*, *73*(5), 90–102. doi:10.1509/jmkg.73.5.90

Turner, J. (1982). Towards a cognitive redefinition of the social group. In H. Tajfel (Ed.), *Social Identity and Intergroup Relations* (pp. 15–40). Cambridge, UK: Cambridge University Press.

Turner, J. (1985). Social Categorization and Self-Concept: A Social Cognitive Theory of Group Behavior. In E. Lawler (Ed.), *Advances in Group Process: Theory and Research* (pp. 77–121). Greenwich, CT: JAI Press.

Van Dijck, J. (2013). *The culture of connectivity*. Oxford, UK: Oxford University Press. doi:10.1093/acprof:oso/9780199970773.001.0001

Van Dijck, J., & Poell, T. (2013). Understanding Social Media Logic. *Media And Communication*, *1*(1), 2–14. doi:10.17645/mac.v1i1.70

Vargo, S., & Lusch, R. (2004). Evolving to a New Dominant Logic for Marketing. *Journal of Marketing*, *68*(1), 1–17. doi:10.1509/jmkg.68.1.1.24036

Vargo, S., Lusch, R., & Morgan, F. (2015). Historical Perspectives on Service-Dominant Logic. In R. Lusch & S. Vargo (Eds.), *The Service-dominant Logic of Marketing: Dialog, Debate, and Directions* (2nd ed.; pp. 29–42). New York: Routledge.

Veletsianos, G. (2013). Open practices and identity: Evidence from researchers and educators' social media participation. *British Journal of Educational Technology*, *44*(4), 639–651. doi:10.1111/bjet.12052

Veloutsou, C., & Moutinho, L. (2009). Brand relationships through brand reputation and brand tribalism. *Journal of Business Research*, *62*(3), 314–322. doi:10.1016/j.jbusres.2008.05.010

Vogel, V., Evanschitzky, H., & Ramaseshan, B. (2008). Customer Equity Drivers and Future Sales. *Journal of Marketing*, *72*(6), 98–108. doi:10.1509/jmkg.72.6.98

Walden, E. (2000). Some Value Propositions of Online Communities. *Electronic Markets*, *10*(4), 244–249. doi:10.1080/101967800750050362

Wattanasuwan, K. (2005). The self and symbolic consumption. *The Journal of American Academy of Business, Cambridge*, *6*(1), 179–184.

Weber, M. (1978). *Economy and Society: An Outline of Interpretive Sociology* (2nd ed.). University of California Press.

Whiting, A., & Williams, D. (2013). Why people use social media: A uses and gratifications approach. *Qualitative Market Research*, *16*(4), 362–369. doi:10.1108/QMR-06-2013-0041

Williams, D., Crittenden, V., Keo, T., & McCarty, P. (2012). The use of social media: An exploratory study of usage among digital natives. *Journal of Public Affairs*, *12*(2), 127–136. doi:10.1002/pa.1414

Wirtz, J., den Ambtman, A., Bloemer, J., Horváth, C., Ramaseshan, B., van de Klundert, J., ... Kandampully, J. (2013). Managing brands and customer engagement in online brand communities. *Journal of Service Management*, *24*(3), 223–224. doi:10.1108/09564231311326978

Woisetschläger, D., Hartleb, V., & Blut, M. (2008). How to Make Brand Communities Work: Antecedents and Consequences of Consumer Participation. *Journal of Relationship Marketing*, *7*(3), 237–256. doi:10.1080/15332660802409605

Wolny, J., & Mueller, C. (2013). Analysis of fashion consumers' motives to engage in electronic word-of-mouth communication through social media platforms. *Journal of Marketing Management*, *29*(5-6), 562–583. doi:10.1080/0267257X.2013.778324

Zaglia, M. (2013). Brand Communities Embedded in Social Networks. *Journal of Business Research*, *66*(2), 216–223. doi:10.1016/j.jbusres.2012.07.015 PMID:23564989

Zhang, K., Benyoucef, M., & Zhao, S. (2016). Building Brand Loyalty in Social Commerce: The case of brand microblogs. *Electronic Commerce Research and Applications*, *15*, 14–25. doi:10.1016/j.elerap.2015.12.001

Zheng, X., Cheung, C., Lee, M., & Liang, L. (2015). Building brand loyalty through user engagement in online brand communities in social networking sites. *Information Technology & People*, *28*(1), 90–106. doi:10.1108/ITP-08-2013-0144

Zhu, Y., & Chen, H. (2015). Social media and human need satisfaction: Implications for social media marketing. *Business Horizons*, *58*(3), 335–345. doi:10.1016/j.bushor.2015.01.006

Zinkhan, G., & Hirschheim, R. (1992). Truth in Marketing Theory and Research: An Alternative Perspective. *Journal of Marketing*, *56*(2), 80–88. doi:10.2307/1252044

KEY TERMS AND DEFINITIONS

Brand Association: Brand association involves brand attributes set in consumers' minds upon reflecting on a brand.

Brand Communities: Brand communities comprise collectives formed around an interest/attachment to a brand.

Brand-Customer Relationship: Brand-customer relationships consider the recurring interactions between brand and customer that carry the potential to mature into trust, loyalty, and relationships.

Customer Equity: Customer equity consists of the total value of all a company's customers.

Millennial Generation: Millennial generation is a demographic cohort that is born between the early 1980s up to the early 2000s.

Social Identity Theory: Social identity theory reflects on how a person may evaluate him/herself and other based on groups he/she belongs to.

Social Interaction: Social interaction involves reciprocal exchange and response between individuals.

Social Media: Social media includes Internet-centered platforms that facilitate for the production and circulation of user-generated content.

Chapter 8
Service Failure and Recovery Strategy in Computer-Mediated Marketing Environments (CMMEs)

Samuel Ayertey
University of Plymouth, UK

Kerry Howell
University of Plymouth, UK

ABSTRACT

The success of an online recovery strategy is largely attributed to the provider's response speed. Essentially, engagement in conversation with the customer immediately after he/she complains shortens the pre-recovery phase. Service firms expect complaints from consumers when a service failure occurs. Advances in modern information and communication technologies (ICT) infrastructures have changed the way in which customer-firm interactions take place and the nature of the conduct of services. Computer and internet technologies mean that services can be provided over long distances without the requirement for the physical presence of customers and employees. With the continued rapid development in the field of modern computer-mediated marketing environments (CMME) more and more services will be delivered in technology-mediated environments (TMEs). This chapter provides some insights on failure recovery strategies as competitive tools in computer-mediated marketing environments.

INTRODUCTION AND BACKGROUND

When a firm or service supplier fails to meet customer anticipations it is known as a service failure whereas the actions taken by firms or service suppliers to overcome the occurrences are described as recovery strategies in the service marketing literature (Hazée, Van Vaerenbergh, & Armirotto, 2017). Changing buying activities from physical stores to retail websites has been a shift for a number of customers. Attaining a successful formula for e-commerce is challenging, in spite of numerous advantages

DOI: 10.4018/978-1-5225-7344-9.ch008

of online shopping. Service failures are experienced by many customers. For example, according to the Ombudsman Services' fifth annual CAM 2018 report, there were a total of 173 million issues with services and products in 2017 alone, with 57 per cent of the population affected in the UK. Furthermore, the report shows that the most common sectors for complaints were Retail, registering 25 per cent (Ombudsman Services, 2018). Due to its popularity Torres et al. (2014) argue that social media has also received increasing attention from scholars. Hence, the uncertainty of purchasing online can be reduced by social media. The retail sectors that deal mostly with information products or intangibles have also been affected by digital technology and social media. Now that tablets or smartphones can be used, social media platforms (e.g. Instagram and Facebook) and the Internet offer an instant, easy complaint channel for clienteles (Lopez-Lopez *et al.,* 2014) at no significant cost and a slight effort (Obeidat *et al.,* 2017). Recovering from such failures is one of the most thought-provoking tasks faced by management and companies as service failure is a very common situation in doing business. Service failures have unfavourable consequences on both clients and firms such as complaining and switching providers (Zhang *et al.,* 2017). These unfavourable consequences can be minimised by effective service recovery strategies (Strizhakova, Tsarenko, & Ruth, 2012). However, online service organisations face challenges in providing a successful service recovery. Academics and practitioners have been focusing keenly on online service failure and recovery strategies since 2002 (Albrecht, Walsh, & Beatty, 2017; Ozuem & Lancaster, 2014). The complexity of this area has prompted scholars to consider strategies to restore service failures. These include the airline industry (Park & Park, 2016), online retailers (Wang, Wu, Sh., Lin, & Wang, 2011), restaurant services (Nikbin, Marimuthu, & Hyun, 2016), production and management services (Craighead, Karwan, & Miller, 2004), business in general (Choi & Choi, 2014) and marketing (Sivakumar, Li, & Dong, 2014). Research into online service failure and recovery strategies has succeeded in assigning meaning to online service failures and categorising these into many typologies (Tsai *et al.,* 2014 ; Kuo, Yen, & Chen, 2011; Sparks & Bradley, 2017). Further attention has been given to the effects of online service failure and recovery strategies on lenses of traditional encounters and antecedents, with fewer antecedents in online failures being considered (Kuo *et al.,* 2011; Wang *et al.,* 2011; Sopadjieva *et al.,* 2017). Such epistemological orientations limit the potential opportunities inherent in the selling of goods on the Internet. Understanding service inadequacy depends on individual expectations, so approaching the ontology of customers where failure and recovery processes are concerned should be contextual, rather than generic or standardised. Mental accounting theory (Chuang *et al.*, 2012), the disconfirmation paradigm theories (McCollough, Berry, & Yadav, 2000) and so on have been used to examine service failure and service recovery. Recently, as identified by McColl-Kennedy and Sparks (2003), Tax, Brown, and Chandrasherakan, (1998) and Hazée, Van Vaerenbergh, and Armirotto, (2017), justice and fairness theory has been of service in increasing understanding about service failure and recovery. The principles of justice theory depend on equal fairness assessed from all parties in a society (Mandle, 2009). The recovery evaluation stages and the recovery strategy provision were examined by Siu, Zhang, and Yau (2013). The authors combine recovery assessment with the theory of justice and, specifically, the customers' evaluation of how fairly they were treated in the course of recovery. They further put forward that if a client recognises a fair recovery, his/her prior satisfaction with the firm will be maintained. Zhu, Nakata, Sivakumar, and Grewal (2013) sought to understand customer perceptions of what causes service failure (such as the extent to which it is the customer's or the provider's fault) by means of attribution theory.

Different factors are assigned to the lacuna between customers and the provider when a failure arises. This begins with anonymous customer complaints which hinder providers who seek to comprehend customers' conceptualisations of failure, leading providers to view customers as 'heterogeneous' (Sivakumar *et al.,* 2014) when it comes to recovery strategy expectations. Similarly, Bougie, Pieters, and Zeelenberg (2003) contend that 'most dissatisfied customers generally do not bother to complain' (p. 390), situating providers in a position where they do not comprehend the need to provide any kind of recovery strategy. The issue appears to be even more complex in the context of online encounters. Scholars have undoubtedly enriched the service discipline with research, although no satisfactory definition of service failure and recovery strategies exists. Most research has investigated service failure and recovery in conventional services (Lee, Singh, & Chan, 2011; Xiao & Dong, 2015). Justice theory has also been applied to investigate how customers respond in terms of their satisfaction following recovery. Research into the behavioural intentions of customers in online settings has also been scant (Wang *et al.,* 2011).

Empirical research into consumer perceptions of online service failure and recovery, however, is surprisingly scarce, despite the fact that service failures, both off- and online, are inevitable for service firms. Crucially, online service failures can have a negative impact on profitability. Holloway and Beatty (2003) suggest that customers complain online more than offline. For consumers, the Internet offers a platform that makes complaining effortless yet impactful, and a wide and geographically dispersed audience can be reached. Compared with offline environments, switching is easier on the Internet since customers can browse and look for alternative providers with the click of a mouse. Given this background, gaining an understanding of how to manage online service failures effectively is essential to the success of firms operating in an online environment. Current research mainly concerns customer reactions at brick-and-mortar outlets (i.e. offline) to service analysed systematically through research. Studies in this domain underline the importance of fair (or just) service recovery in restoring customer satisfaction following offline service failures (Roschk & Kaiser, 2013; Azemi, Ozuem, Howell, & Lancaster, 2018). In earlier research into online service failures, Holloway and Beatty (2003) noted that, following recovery attempts by online businesses, some customers feel a sense of injustice specifically related to issues of interaction, distribution, and procedures. More recently, Rosenmayer, McQuilken, Robertson, and Ogden (2018) examine the typologies of service failures and recoveries in the omni-channel setting using complaints on Facebook. The study reveals the most predominant failures to include problems with delivery, 'bricks and mortar' shopping, activities of marketing as well as pricing and communications, problems with customer service and also goods. The authors noted that the distributive, procedural, informational and interpersonal justice dimensions are valid in terms of recoveries on Facebook.

THE FASHION INDUSTRY

Over the past 35 years, fashion retailing, an innovative, dynamic and challenging industry, has undergone immense changes, with the United Kingdom remaining at the forefront. As a result, this phenomenon has received considerable academic scrutiny (Doherty, 2000), particularly, but not exclusively, with reference to branding (Birtwistle & Freathy, 1998). Bhardwaj and Fairhurst (2010), amongst others, have recently studied consumer responses to the fast fashion sector, and have discovered significant issues where its development is concerned. They assert that the fashion clothing industry has evolved significantly, principally during the last two decades (*ibid.*). Christopher, Lowson, and Peck (2004) identified problems with the ways in which fashion is consumed, and they note issues concerning quality and innovation, with the market becoming ever more demanding. This becomes evident in the demand for greater variety and more informed styles, which are more economically priced than ever before (Fernie, Maniatakis, &

Moore, 2009). Further, Doyle, Moore, and Morgan (2006) and Mollá-Descals, Frasquet-Deltoro, and Ruiz-Molina (2011) note the changes to the dynamics and increasing complexity of the fashion industry. Characteristic of such changes is a reduction in requirements for manufacturers of large quantities, and a larger number of fashion 'seasons'. Other features include improved organisation of supply chains, leading businesses to opt for models that can be delivered flexibly and quickly and produced at lower cost.

The internal and global importance of the UK fashion industry is underlined by London, which is amongst the top four world fashion centres along with Paris, New York and Milan (BBC News, 2018; Ayertey & Ozuem, 2018). Jackson and Shaw (2006) particularly commented on London's and Birmingham's fundamental creativity and keenness in pursuing the latest trends. They note that these cities are centres of luxury and fashion, attracting extensive traditional and virtual mass media, keen-eyed followers, enthusiasts and professionals. London Fashion Week, which takes place in February and September, is an example, as is the existence of the London College of Fashion. The show is a city-wide celebration of fashion with Alexander McQueen, Marks & Spencer and Topman among the major British brands and designers. With rising figures each year, media coverage at London Fashion Week alone equals or exceeds major news and international sporting events. In 2018, Instagram stories on the official London Fashion Week account received 871,648 views. In addition, to gain inspiration for looks they can themselves create or purchase, 45 per cent of users of Instagram in Britain say they follow at least one fashion account. The fashion and textile industry is one of the most polluting industries in the world. Overall, the consumption of apparel will increase by 63 per cent, from 62 million tons today to 102 million tons in 2030 – an equivalent of more than 500 billion T-shirts, if the global population increases as projected to 8.5 billion people by 2030, according to the Global Fashion Agenda and The Boston Consulting Group, Inc. (2018). There is a growing awareness among young people that the constant consumption of clothing affects the environment. For instance, after transport, housing, and food industries, in the UK the clothing industry ranks fourth in terms of its impact on the environment, according to a report by WRAP (2017).

In terms of business, the fashion industry represents an important part of the national economy. According to data from Oxford Economics (2018) the fashion industry contributed £32.3 billion to the UK economy in 2017, a 5.4 per cent increase over 2016, with the average adult in the UK spending over £1,000 a year on clothes (Bentley, 2018). This growth is significantly far higher than the figure for the overall UK economy.

Although Brexit is causing uncertainty for the UK fashion industry, according to Mintel (2018) the women's wear clothing market is forecast to grow by 14 per cent between 2018 and 2022 to reach £33.5 billion. Mintel (2015) further predicted that the UK online fashion market would grow to £19 billion by 2019. Oxford Economics (2016) published data produced by the British Fashion Council showing significant increases in the UK fashion industry's contribution to the United Kingdom economy, rising by 22 per cent from £21 billion in 2009 to £26 billion in 2014. High street retailers such as New Look and Next and online shops such as ASOS are among the many prominent brands that have value on the UK market. Internet sales in recent years have been significantly high, with 56 percent of people buying clothes online in 2017. In spite of this growing trend, many consumers still prefer to buy clothing in physical stores while offline purchases are expected to remain accountable for around 71.2 per cent of sales by 2020 (Statista, 2017).

By definition, 'experience' goods, for example clothing and footwear, are characterised by intangibility (Hassanein & Head, 2005; Sender, 2014) as well as difficulty in establishing the characteristics of the product (e.g. quality or price) until it has in fact been sold (Weathers, Sharma, & Wood, 2007). The absence of sales staff in online sales further complicates online service experiences, increasing the scope for service failures. Further important factors in this sense are the wide variety of merchandising mechanisms and demands by customers for online interactive assistance (which may also be psychological) from staff (Kunz, 2005). Yet the wide range of communication mechanisms and technology used by online marketers is required to stimulate clientele to buy before they make their own individual evaluation of the product. Customers can, indeed, go to a physical store, a bricks-and-mortar establishment, to review products for quality, size and fit, particularly if the retailer is a large global concern. However, for pure-play fashion sellers this is not possible – the situation is not the same and represents a serious disadvantage. Marketing visually is very difficult to achieve, and there is no direct contact with store staff. What this means is that, in order to compete with physical stores, pure-play online merchants must evolve perfect presentations of their products for their potential customers. In other words, a clear and thorough understanding of how different media affect customers' shopping experiences is essential.

Yang and Young (2009) affirm that purchasers of fashion are firmly convinced that the only way to buy is in a physical store, since their inspiration is a response to their senses (Sender, 2017). Yang and Young (2009) also assert that, increasingly, fashion e-businesses perceive the necessity of developing features for the online customer to interrelate with the product, thus attempting to remove or reduce the risks associated with purchasing fashion online. Cho and Workman (2011) note that among the aspects that concern online customers are the appearance of the fashion item when worn, including with other items, and a range of information regarding the appeal of the item, as well as the need to appeal to the customers' senses. With only 15 per cent of online shoppers ordering all their fashion items online, the vast majority also shop for shoes and clothes in-store, emphasising the significance of combined shopping (Sender, 2017). These imponderables are the root of concerns about the ability of retailers to be able to sell clothes online. A BBC report (2016) affirms that most online clothes shoppers send something back, thus suggesting that individuals like to feel and see garments before purchasing.

In spite of 'self-service' when shopping online, a company is, in actual fact, responsible for shifting the customer back to the satisfied state. The reception of prompt recovery is thus crucial in reducing the level of stress experienced by the consumer after discontent when shopping online. Overall, three-quarters (73 per cent) of online fashion shoppers want more return options such as collection from home or drop-off at numerous places (Sender, 2017). The World Wide Web is a valuable tool in communicating service and value to consumers, but it also operates in a highly competitive environment. Customers' decisions about entering into and maintaining a long-term relationship with a company are largely driven by their assessment of the core service they will receive (Ozuem & Lancaster, 2014).

Additionally, through the growth of pressure groups, service failure without recovery can be broadcast through social media such as Facebook, Instagram and Twitter. The online community is well informed about company activities (Kerr *et al.,* 2012). Therefore, failing to recover from customer dissatisfaction may lead to potential customers choosing other competitors. Service recovery after failure may be seen as one of the most essential strategies in ensuring sound company reputation, encouraging consumers to communicate positive feelings about a company (Ringberg, Odekerker-Schroder, & Christensen, 2007; Hui *et al.,* 2011).

THEORETICAL CONTEXT

The highly personal and interactive nature of service makes it very susceptible to failures (Hoffman *et al.,* 2016). A review of the literature provides divergent meanings or interpretations of what service failure is

(Bitner *et al.,* 1994; Palmer, 2014; Obeidat *et al.,* 2017). When service is not fulfilled, is delayed, or fails to reach the expected standard, Bitner *et al.* (1994) suggested a service failure has occurred. The authors further proposed four causes or service failure types such as: (a) an improper service provider response to a service delivery failure, (b) an ineffective response of the service provider to customer requests and needs, (c) unwanted service provider actions, and finally (d) inappropriate customer behaviour. Hence as argued by Kelley and Davis (1994) service failure may be different in frequency, severity and time. Lin (2006) also defines service failure as a condition in which a business, i.e. a service provider, fails to meet the customer's expectations regarding its products, or if the customer finds the mode of service unacceptable.

Accordingly, the last definition itself suggests that there are two categories of service encounter failures: outcome-oriented and process-oriented (Chuang *et al.,* 2012; Obeidat *et al.,* 2017). The outcome dimension of a service encounter involves what customers actually receive from the service, whereas the process dimension involves the manner in which service providers handle a service failure during the course of service recovery (i.e. how service is delivered) (Yang & Mattila, 2012). In an outcome failure, the organisation does not fulfil the basic service need or perform the core service. In contrast, where a service process failure occurs, the delivery of the core service is flawed or deficient in some way that is directly derivable from the behaviour of service employees. Four types of service failures in self-service technologies were proposed by Meuter, Ostrom, Roundtree, and Bitner (2000, p. 57) as follows:

(1) Technical failures (for example, if the website is temporarily not working)

(2) Process failures (where the goods the customer ordered online fail to reach him/her)

(3) Poor design (customers have difficulty finding their way through web pages), and

(4) Failures that are customer-originated (such as when login is not successful because a customer forgets to use his/her password).

Technology, employees and even customers themselves are among factors that contribute to service failures (Michel, 2001). Service failures are caused by several factors, not just one cause. For example, a more recent study by Frearson (2016) examined problems customers have when shopping online. The most common service failures ranged from late deliveries, missed deliveries and damaged items; more than half of customers in the UK experience such issues, which reveals how likely service failures are to happen and the vulnerabilities in e-commerce activities.

As a result, it becomes essential to have a strategy for how to recover from such failures, and not just recover but also bounce back when a failure occurs as the image of a firm can be affected overall (Swanson & Hsu, 2011) and customers experience a range of emotions after failure (Tombs *et al.,* 2014). Apologies or compensation to the customer have been presented as recovery strategies after a service failure (Gelbrich, Gäthke, & Grégoire, 2016; Sengupta, Ray, Trendel, & Vaerenbergh, 2018). Additionally, a phenomenon which was first discussed by Etzel and Silverman (1981), branded as the service recovery paradox (Ding, Ho, & Lii, 2015), proposed that remarkably strong attempts at recovery can lead to client evaluations higher than transactions with no supposed failure of any kind. However, studies by Knox and Van Oest (2014) contest its existence, whilst studies by Schminke *et al.* (2014) find evidence of the service recovery paradox.

Zemke and Schaaf (1989) applied the term 'recovery' to service settings, along with Lord Marshall who instigated a pioneering programme in British Airways called the 'Putting People First' campaign. Service recovery becomes absolutely essential when a service failure occurs. Recovery is essentially an effort to increase customer satisfaction. Service recovery is growing in importance, partly because of increasing customer expectations and tougher competition among businesses trying to exceed the expectations of their customers. Studies of service management have hitherto been notably based upon investigating the component measures that comprise service recovery. Cheung and To (2016) reveal that a co-created recovery positively influences perceived justice and customer satisfaction with service recovery.

Miller, Craighead, and Karwan, (2000) identify recovery as an attempt to solve problems and pacify upset clients, and to retain the customer base. This is, in a way, a form of exchange, whereby the customer feels they have suffered a loss (a service failure), and the business attempts to recompense the customer for an incurred loss with service recovery (Smith, Bolton, & Wagner, 1999). Fan, Wu, and Wu (2010) and Crisafulli and Singh (2017) suggest that direct human interaction has been substituted by technology in online environments, but researchers have contended that the use of technology can improve the efficiency of recovery services (Ayertey & Ozuem, 2018; Ding & Lii, 2016). Service failures and recovery in traditional services are distinct from online service failures and recovery. Meanwhile, recovery actions that have been identified in research include apologising, following-up, offering compensation, rapid responses to service failure, favourable employee behaviour and causality acknowledging (Gelbrich, Gäthke, & Grégoire, 2015; Goode, Höehle, Venkatesh, & Brown, 2017). Managers should have available a list of possible recovery strategies or techniques to choose from in the case of needing to rectify a service failure. Studies including those of Bradley and Sparks (2012) and Choi and Choi (2014) show that in altering consumer displeasure, high recovery is more effective and emotion following service failure is more positive. Hence, evidence in the existing literature is inconsistent (Chen, Ma, Bian, Zheng, & Devlin, 2018). Miller *et al.* (2000) were amongst the first to underline the importance of analysing recovery strategies from the perspective of operations management, and they called for further analysis of recovery strategies in operations research. They developed a detailed framework in the domain of elements (i.e. the core elements: service recovery expectations, service recovery types, and follow-up service recovery outcome) compiled within the context of a failed service. They classified prior prototypes of findings as follows: if an appropriate recovery strategy is promptly provided, customers will return even when severe failures are experienced (p. 397). Additional findings show the influence of types of recovery strategies on customers. Kuo and Wu (2012) divided recovery strategies into two distinct groups: psychological strategies and tangible strategies. Miller *et al.* (2000) and Kozub, O'Neill, and Palmer (2014) added that tangible recovery strategies offer compensation for actual and perceived costs, such as free services, refunds, gifts, discounts, and coupons to reduce or mitigate practical losses (Kuo & Wu, 2012; Jung & Seock, 2017). Psychological techniques have been acknowledged as useful where the aim is to pacify the customer by showing concern for their needs. Examples include offering an explanation for service failure, acknowledging mistakes, and expressing regret for errors in a polite, empathetic, and considerate way (Chang & Wang, 2012). The essence of the findings in the context of recovery types suggests that the provision of blended recovery strategies is useful, yet an apology alone will not be enough for the customer. Furthermore, customer perceptions of justice influence their satisfaction after recovery, and ultimately word-of-mouth intentions are improved through customer satisfaction (Jung & Seock, 2017). Meanwhile, any extra compensation can enhance customer perceptions of justice. For instance, Mostafa, Lages, Shabbir, and Thwaites (2015) identify that consumers typically recognise the tangible and monetary compensations and endeavours of employees in addressing problems associated with distributive justice, particularly when attempting to address failures. Timely consideration of service failure is often associated with procedural justice. Courtesy and explanations offered by employees are examples of interpersonal justice. Clients who suffer outcome-related service failures respond favourably to tangible recovery, in contrast to those who have experienced process-related service failures. The latter are typically more satisfied with psychological recovery efforts (Chuang, Cheng, Chang, & Yang, 2012). A considerable amount of research supports the idea that customers who receive an apology following a service failure are more satisfied than customers who receive no apology (Roschk & Kaiser, 2013). At the same time, the authors provided empirical evidence to suggest that the presence or absence of an apology is just as important as how an apology is given, and this is crucial for enhancing customer satisfaction. They argue that the more empathetic and strong an apology is in its delivery, the more pacified the customers will be.

In another study by Mattila, Cho, and Ro (2011), it is suggested that human involvement (such as interacting with frontline staff) is more effective when the failure was caused by a human being rather than by a machine. In comparison, human involvement was less effective when a failure was caused by self-service technology. This is because consumers who choose to use self-service technologies to interact with service providers seek to avoid customer–employee interactions. A more recent study by Collier, Breazeale, and White (2017) also found that clients want employees to support a transaction after a breakdown if it occurs in isolation. When other customers are present, customers prefer it when employees resolve the issue and allow them to finish the transaction. In terms of online shopping service failure, previous studies have widely discussed recovery strategies. Kelley, Hoffman, and Davis (1993) explain that the 12 recovery strategies they identified fall into two categories – those that are successful, resulting in increased customer satisfaction, and those that are not. They argue that the severity of the failure should determine the nature of the recovery. Miller *et al.* (2000) contend that their framework shows a clear link between a successful recovery and customer loyalty, satisfaction and retention. Forbes *et al.* (2005) conclude from their survey that the kind of service failure experienced by online clients differs from that experienced by clients in traditional situations. They also affirm that e-tail organisations utilise a different series of recovery strategies to those employed in traditional settings. Despite successful recovery, switching after failure recovery can occur frequently among e-customers. Chang and Wang (2012) note that the most significant beneficial features of service recovery are compensation, the speed with which their service failure was attended to, the nature of the apology, and contact channels. Kuo and Wu's (2012) study concentrated on the effects of recovery strategies in terms of online service failure, using perceived justice theory, in line with Holloway and Beauty (2003) and McCollough, Berry, and Yadav (2000) who also underscored the effectiveness of recovery strategies for dealing with online service failures.

However, instances of repeat purchases remain very rare, regardless of the service recovery strategy used to remedy service failure. Failures are unavoidable, whatever steps a firm may take to prevent mistakes when a service is rendered. As Boshoff (1997, p. 110) asserts: 'Mistakes are an unavoidable feature of all human endeavour and thus also of service delivery'. Therefore, service failure seems to be inevitable, particularly in the fashion industry because of the difficulty of translating the in-store experience into the online environment. In addition, because of the intangibility of service, service failure is difficult to resolve when it occurs.

In the online fashion industry context, the problem associated with the intangibility of services is magnified because consumers cannot directly interact with service personnel. Instead, consumers have to interact with web interfaces, which requires competent management of the technology. Clothing is considered to be a high involvement product category, related to personal ego and products that need to be seen, felt, touched (Ioniţă, 2017; Spence & Gallace, 2011), and tried on because they are difficult to evaluate (Sender, 2014). Chahal and Devi (2015) state that service failure occurs when the expectations of the customer are not met through the initial delivery. Subsequently, a customer may be lost, and may not return to a particular company (Piha & Avlonitis, 2015). Negative word-of-mouth can also lead to dissatisfaction and defection, as suggested by Crisafulli and Singh (2017) and Helm, Moulard, and Richins, (2015). Researchers such as Fatma, Khan, and Rahman (2016) define service failure as a condition in which a business, i.e. a service provider, fails to live up to the customer's expectations regarding its products. Service failure also occurs if the customer finds the mode of service unacceptable. In addition, service failure is the service provider's failure to meet a customer's expectations, as identified by Hoffman, Kelley, and Rotalsky, (2016). For that reason, it is also suggested by Hoffman *et al.* (2016) and Keaveney (1995) that service failures can be separated into two categories: outcome-oriented and process-oriented. The former includes the product customers receive from the business. Process-oriented failure is concerned with the method of provision of the service. Furthermore, Smith *et al.* (1999) and Fu, Wu, Huang, Song, and Gong (2015) argue that outcome-orientated service failures occur when the most important or core services ordered from the company are not delivered. Process-oriented service failures, however, can be defined as the way in which the core service process is undertaken by the provider. This can include errors in specific areas, such as rude or unresponsive employees. By applying these terms in the context of the online fashion industry, an example of a process failure would be a scenario in which technical problems arise when ordering products online, while an outcome failure could occur in the event of failure of a core services such as the incorrect size of a delivered dress that had been purchased online (Ayertey, 2018). Keaveney (1995) and Ghatak and Pal (2016) found that core service failures, which include errors in billing, are amongst the major reasons why customers defect. Therefore, in the case of core service failures customers expect the provider of the service in question to put the matter right (Shin, Ellinger, Mothersbaugh, & Reynolds, 2017). Conversely, Smith *et al.* (1999) and Vakeel, Sivakumar, Jayasimha, and Dey (2018) showed that process failures have a greater impact on dissatisfaction than product failures. As confirmed by Israeli, Lee, and Karpinski (2017), clients are less understanding when the service failure has occurred as a result of process dimensions. Duffy, Miller, and Bexley (2006) and Ringberg, Odekerken-Schröder, and Christensen (2007) argue that the customer's primary concern is the outcome aspect of service recovery, while the service recovery process is internal to the customer, who is not interested in it as such. It is further argued that Outcome-Related Service Failure (ORSF) is associated with an economic loss and Process-Related Service Failure (PRSF) causes social or psychological loss for the customer (Smith *et al.,* 1999; Cheng, Chang, Chuang, & Liao, 2015). Thus, ORSF typically involves a utilitarian exchange which includes money, goods and time, while PRSF involves symbolic exchanges which include status, esteem, respect, sympathy and empathy, amongst others (Hur & Jang, 2016). Therefore, a requirement of service recovery is a high level of communication between the provider and its customer in order to deliver an appropriate response to the disappointed, dissatisfied customer (Meyer, Gremler, & Hogreve, 2014). Hoffman *et al.* (2016) underscored the frequently critical importance of employees in the provision of an effective service recovery. Considering that a 100 per cent satisfaction guarantee promises total customer satisfaction, this would suggest that a high quality service will be delivered (Meyer *et al.,* 2014). According to McColl-Kennedy and Sparks (2003), given that service failures are common in the service industry, and that customers may experience dissatisfaction following such failure, it is important that firms attempt to recover dissatisfied customers through an appropriate set of actions known as 'the customer recovery process'. Learning from service failure, therefore, depends to a considerable extent on establishing the main cause(s) and identifying the fundamental processes that have contributed to the issue, with the aim of finding effective solutions to the client's problems.

MANAGERIAL IMPLICATIONS

The success of an online recovery strategy is largely attributed to the provider's response speed (Pang, Hasan, & Chong, 2014). Essentially, engagement in conversation with the customer immediately after he/she uploads the complaint shortens the pre-recovery phase. Service firms expect complaints from consumers when a service failure occurs. Therefore, companies should prepare strategies for the process of service recovery to deal with difficulties. As BBC Business Editor, Weber (2010) presciently noted serious consequences of negative opinions expressed on the Internet: 'These days, one witty tweet, one clever blog post, one devastating video forwarded to hundreds of friends at the click of a mouse can snowball and kill a product or damage a company's share price'. Of course, positive reactions on the Internet can also have dramatic consequences and social media has enormous influence. If certain businesses are not interested in identifying strategies or devoting time, energy, staff and financial resources to engage effectively with social media, they may well be ignoring or misusing favourable opportunities. They might be failing to deal with negativity amongst the customers upon whom their existence depends. The powerful effects of negative eWOM can affect a firm's performance. Kim and Lee (2015), Chevalier and Mayzlin (2006) and Park and Lee (2009), among others, have all acknowledged the power of negative eWOM on the performance of firms in their research, asserting that negative eWOM is much more effective than positive eWOM. Consumers share negative experiences for three key reasons (Verhagen, Nauta, & Feldberg, 2013). Firstly, sharing negative experiences can serve to mitigate frustration and reduce the anxiety associated with the event. Secondly, negative experiences are shared to warn and prevent others from enduring similar events. Thirdly, consumers can share their negative experiences in order to help companies improve their practices. In sum, eWOM is more often negative than positive (Hornik, Satchi, Cesareo, & Pastore, 2015). Social media has empowered consumers to voice negative experiences and opinions about products or services with reduced physical and psychological costs (Istanbulluoglu, 2017).

As consumers desire experiences in the 21st century, online retailers will also need to elevate the online shopping experience and make it more enjoyable through the use of technology, such as live video on social media platforms, virtual reality and personalised customer service.

REFERENCES

Albrecht, A. K., Walsh, G., & Beatty, S. E. (2017). Perceptions of group versus individual service failures and their effects on customer outcomes: The role of attributions and customer entitlement. *Journal of Service Research*, *20*(2), 188–203. doi:10.1177/1094670516675416

Ayertey, S. B. (2018). *An evaluation of online service failures and recovery strategies in the UK fashion industry* (PhD thesis). University of Plymouth.

Ayertey, S., & Ozuem, W. (2018). Developing Compelling Online Recovery Strategies: Implications for the Fashion Clothing Industry. In Digital Marketing Strategies for Fashion and Luxury Brands (pp. 264-288). IGI Global.

Azemi, Y., Ozuem, W., Howell, K. E., & Lancaster, G. (2018). An exploration into the practice of online service failure and recovery strategies in the Balkans. *Journal of Business Research.*

BBC News. (2016). Available at: http://www.bbc.co.uk/news/business-36395719

BBC News. (2018). *London Fashion Week 'turns collections into commerce'.* Retrieved October 1, 2018 from https://www.bbc.co.uk/news/av/business-26185198/london-fashion-week-turns-collections-into-commerce

Bentley, C. (2018). *Let fashion be your servant not your master says Christian who ran London Fashion Week.* Retrieved October 17, 2018 from https://www.premier.org.uk/News/UK/Let-fashion-be-your-servant-not-your-master-says-Christian-who-ran-London-Fashion-Week

Bhardwaj, V., & Fairhurst, A. (2010). Fast fashion: Response to changes in the fashion industry. *International Review of Retail, Distribution and Consumer Research, 20*(1), 165–173. doi:10.1080/09593960903498300

Birtwistle, G., & Freathy, P. (1998). More than just a name above the shop: A comparison of the branding strategies of two UK fashion retailers. *International Journal of Retail & Distribution Management, 26*(8), 318–323. doi:10.1108/09590559810231788

Bitner, M. J., Booms, B. H., & Mohr, L. A. (1994). Critical service encounters: The employee's viewpoint. *Journal of Marketing, 58*(4), 95–106. doi:10.2307/1251919

Boshoff, C. (1997). An experimental study of service recovery options. *International Journal of Service Industry Management, 8*(2), 110–130. doi:10.1108/09564239710166245

Bougie, R., Pieters, R., & Zeelenberg, M. (2003). Angry customers don't come back, they get back: The experience and behavioural implications of anger and dissatisfaction in services. *Journal of the Academy of Marketing Science, 31*(4), 377–393. doi:10.1177/0092070303254412

Bradley, G., & Sparks, B. (2012). Explanations: If, when, and how they aid service recovery. *Journal of Services Marketing, 26*(1), 41–51. doi:10.1108/08876041211199715

British Fashion Council. (2016). *The British Fashion Industry & London Fashion Week Facts & Figures.* Retrieved October 6, 2018, available at: www. britishfashioncouncil.co.uk

Chahal, H., & Devi, P. (2015). Consumer attitude towards service failure and recovery in higher education. *Quality Assurance in Education, 23*(1), 67–85. doi:10.1108/QAE-07-2013-0029

Chang, D. S., & Wang, T. H. (2012). Consumer preferences for service recovery options after delivery delay with shopping online. *Social Behaviour and Personality: An International Journal, 40*(6), 1033–1044. doi:10.2224bp.2012.40.6.1033

Chen, T., Ma, K., Bian, X., Zheng, C., & Devlin, J. (2018). Is high recovery more effective than expected recovery in addressing service failure? – A moral judgment perspective. *Journal of Business Research, 82*, 1–9. doi:10.1016/j.jbusres.2017.08.025

Cheng, Y. H., Chang, C. J., Chuang, S. C., & Liao, Y. W. (2015). Guilt no longer a sin: The effect of guilt in the service recovery paradox. *Journal of Service Theory and Practice*, *25*(6), 836–853. doi:10.1108/JSTP-12-2013-0296

Cheung, F. Y. M., & To, W. M. (2016). A customer-dominant logic on service recovery and customer satisfaction. *Management Decision*, *54*(10), 2524–2543. doi:10.1108/MD-03-2016-0165

Chevalier, J., & Mayzlin, D. (2006). The effect of word of mouth on sales: Online book reviews. *JMR, Journal of Marketing Research*, *63*(3), 345–354. doi:10.1509/jmkr.43.3.345

Cho, S., & Workman, J. (2011). Gender, fashion innovativeness and opinion leadership, and need for touch: Effects on multi-channel choice and touch/non-touch preference in clothing shopping. *Journal of Fashion Marketing and Management: An International Journal*, *15*(3), 363–382. doi:10.1108/13612021111151941

Choi, B., & Choi, B. J. (2014). The effects of perceived service recovery justice on customer affection, loyalty, and word-of-mouth. *European Journal of Marketing*, *48*(1/2), 108–131. doi:10.1108/EJM-06-2011-0299

Christopher, M., Lowson, R., & Peck, H. (2004). Creating agile supply chains in the fashion industry. *International Journal of Retail & Distribution Management*, *32*(8), 367–376. doi:10.1108/09590550410546188

Chuang, S. C., Cheng, Y. H., Chang, C. J., & Yang, S. W. (2012). The effect of service failure types and service recovery on customer satisfaction: A mental accounting perspective. *Service Industries Journal*, *32*(2), 257–271. doi:10.1080/02642069.2010.529435

Collier, J. E., Breazeale, M., & White, A. (2017). Giving back the "self" in self service: Customer preferences in self-service failure recovery. *Journal of Services Marketing*, *31*(6), 604–617. doi:10.1108/JSM-07-2016-0259

Craighead, C. W., Karwan, K. R., & Miller, J. L. (2004). The effects of severity of failure and customer loyalty on service recovery strategies. *Production and Operations Management*, *13*(4), 307–321. doi:10.1111/j.1937-5956.2004.tb00220.x

Crisafulli, B., & Singh, J. (2017). Service failures in e-retailing: Examining the effects of response time, compensation, and service criticality. *Computers in Human Behavior*, *77*, 413–424. doi:10.1016/j.chb.2017.07.013

Ding, M. C., & Lii, Y. S. (2016). Handling online service recovery: Effects of perceived justice on online games. *Telematics and Informatics*, *33*(4), 881–895. doi:10.1016/j.tele.2016.02.001

Ding, M. C., Ho, C. W., & Lii, Y. S. (2015). Is corporate reputation a double-edged sword? Relative effects of perceived justice in airline service recovery. *International Journal of E-Business Research*, *10*(1), 1–17.

Doherty, A. M. (2000). Factors influencing international retailers" market entry mode strategy: Qualitative evidence from the UK fashion sector. *Journal of Marketing Management*, *16*(1-3), 223–245. doi:10.1362/026725700785100514

Doyle, S. A., Moore, C. M., & Morgan, L. (2006). Supplier management in fast moving fashion retailing. *Journal of Fashion Marketing and Management: An International Journal*, *10*(3), 272–281. doi:10.1108/13612020610679268

Duffy, J. A. M., Miller, J. M., & Bexley, J. B. (2006). Banking customers' varied reactions to service recovery strategies. *International Journal of Bank Marketing*, *24*(2), 112–132. doi:10.1108/02652320610649923

Etzel, M. J., & Silverman, B. I. (1981). A managerial perspective on directions of retail customer dissatisfaction research. *Journal of Retailing*, *57*(3), 124–136.

Fan, Y. W., Wu, C. C., & Wu, W. T. (2010). The impacts of online retailing service recovery and perceived justice on consumer loyalty. *International Journal of Electronic Business Management*, *8*(3), 239.

Fatma, M., Khan, I., & Rahman, Z. (2016). The effect of CSR on consumer behavioural responses after service failure and recovery. *European Business Review*, *28*(5), 583–599. doi:10.1108/EBR-11-2015-0134

Fernie, J., Maniatakis, P. A., & Moore, C. M. (2009). The role of international hubs in a fashion retailer"s sourcing strategy. *International Review of Retail, Distribution and Consumer Research*, *19*(4), 421–436. doi:10.1080/09593960903331428

Forbes, L. P., Kelley, S. W., & Hoffman, K. D. (2005). Typologies of e-commerce retail failures and recovery strategies. *Journal of Services Marketing*, *19*(5), 280–292. doi:10.1108/08876040510609907

Frearson, J. (2016). *Half of consumers experience problems with online shopping*. Assessed October 15, 2018 from https://www.business-reporter.co.uk/2016/06/14/half-consumers-experience-problems-online-shopping-says-report/#gsc.tab=0

Fu, H., Wu, D. C., Huang, S. S., Song, H., & Gong, J. (2015). Monetary or nonmonetary compensation for service failure? A study of customer preferences under various loci of causality. *International Journal of Hospitality Management*, *46*, 55–64. doi:10.1016/j.ijhm.2015.01.006

Gelbrich, K., Gäthke, J., & Grégoire, Y. (2015). How much compensation should a firm offer for a flawed service? An examination of the nonlinear effects of compensation on satisfaction. *Journal of Service Research*, *18*(1), 107–123. doi:10.1177/1094670514543149

Gelbrich, K., Gäthke, J., & Grégoire, Y. (2016). How a firm's best versus normal customers react to compensation after a service failure. *Journal of Business Research*, *69*(10), 4331–4339. doi:10.1016/j.jbusres.2016.04.010

Ghatak, R. R., & Pal, S. S. (2016). Prioritizing the Service Failures of Package Delivery Business: An Analytical Hierarchy Process Analysis. *IUP Journal of Supply Chain Management*, *13*(4), 27.

Global Fashion Agenda and The Boston Consulting Group, Inc. (2018). *Pulse-of-the-fashion-industry-2018*. Accessed October 8, 2018 from https://www.globalfashionagenda.com/pulse-of-the-fashion-industry-2018-report-released/#

Goode, S., Hoehle, H., Venkatesh, V., & Brown, S. A. (2017). User compensation as a data breach recovery action: An investigation of the Sony PlayStation network breach. *Management Information Systems Quarterly*, *41*(3), 703–727.

Hassanein, K., & Head, M. (2005). The impact of infusing social presence in the web interface: An investigation across product types. *International Journal of Electronic Commerce*, *10*(2), 31–55. doi:10.2753/JEC1086-4415100202

Hazée, S., Van Vaerenbergh, Y., & Armirotto, V. (2017). Co-creating service recovery after service failure: The role of brand equity. *Journal of Business Research*, *74*, 101–109. doi:10.1016/j.jbusres.2017.01.014

Helm, A. E., Moulard, J. G., & Richins, M. (2015). Consumer cynicism: Developing a scale to measure underlying attitudes influencing marketplace shaping and withdrawal behaviours. *International Journal of Consumer Studies*, *39*(5), 515–524. doi:10.1111/ijcs.12191

Hoffman, K. D., Kelley, S. W., & Rotalsky, H. M. (2016). Retrospective: Tracking service failures and employee recovery efforts. *Journal of Services Marketing*, *30*(1), 7–10. doi:10.1108/JSM-10-2015-0316

Holloway, B. B., & Beatty, S. E. (2003). Service failure in online retailing: A recovery opportunity. *Journal of Service Research*, *6*(1), 92–105. doi:10.1177/1094670503254288

Hornik, J., Satchi, R. S., Cesareo, L., & Pastore, A. (2015). Information dissemination via electronic word-of-mouth: Good news travels fast, bad news travels faster! *Computers in Human Behavior*, *45*, 273–280. doi:10.1016/j.chb.2014.11.008

Hui, M. K., Ho, C. K., & Wan, L. C. (2011). Prior relationships and consumer responses to service failures: A cross-cultural study. *Journal of International Marketing*, *19*(1), 59–81. doi:10.1509/jimk.19.1.59

Hur, J., & Jang, S. (2016). Toward service recovery strategies: The role of consumer-organization relationship norms. *Journal of Services Marketing*, *30*(7), 724–735. doi:10.1108/JSM-08-2015-0263

Ioniţă, I. M. (2017). Digitalization influence on shopping centers strategic management. *Proceedings of the International Conference on Business Excellence, 11*(1), 750-758.

Israeli, A. A., Lee, S. A., & Karpinski, A. C. (2017). Investigating the dynamics and the content of customers' social media reporting after a restaurant service failure. *Journal of Hospitality Marketing & Management*, *26*(6), 606–626. doi:10.1080/19368623.2017.1281193

Istanbulluoglu, D. (2017). Complaint handling on social media: The impact of multiple response times on consumer satisfaction. *Computers in Human Behavior*, *74*, 72–82. doi:10.1016/j.chb.2017.04.016

Jackson, T., & Shaw, D. (2006). *The fashion handbook*. Oxon, UK: Routledge.

Jung, N. Y., & Seock, Y. K. (2017). Effect of service recovery on customers' perceived justice, satisfaction, and word-of-mouth intentions on online shopping websites. *Journal of Retailing and Consumer Services*, *37*, 23–30. doi:10.1016/j.jretconser.2017.01.012

Keaveney, S. M. (1995). Customer switching behaviour in service industries: An exploratory study. *Journal of Marketing*, *59*(2), 71–82. doi:10.2307/1252074

Kelley, S. W., & Davis, M. A. (1994). Antecedents to customer expectations for service recovery. *Journal of the Academy of Marketing Science*, *22*(1), 52–61. doi:10.1177/0092070394221005

Kelley, S. W., Hoffman, K. D., & Davis, M. A. (1993). A typology of retail failures and recoveries. *Journal of Retailing*, *69*(4), 429–452. doi:10.1016/0022-4359(93)90016-C

Kerr, G., Mortimer, K., Dickinson, S., & Waller, D. S. (2012). Buy, boycott or blog: Exploring online consumer power to share, discuss and distribute controversial advertising messages. *European Journal of Marketing*, *46*(3/4), 387–405. doi:10.1108/03090561211202521

Kim, E. E. K., & Lee, C. H. (2015). How do consumers process online hotel reviews? The effects of eWOM consensus and sequence. *Journal of Hospitality and Tourism Technology*, *6*(2), 113–126. doi:10.1108/JHTT-09-2014-0045

Knox, G., & Van Oest, R. (2014). Customer complaints and recovery effectiveness: A customer base approach. *Journal of Marketing*, *78*(5), 42–57. doi:10.1509/jm.12.0317

Kozub, K. R., O'Neill, M. A., & Palmer, A. A. (2014). Emotional antecedents and outcomes of service recovery: An exploratory study in the luxury hotel industry. *Journal of Services Marketing*, *28*(3), 233–243. doi:10.1108/JSM-08-2012-0147

Kunz, G. I. (2005). *Merchandising: Theory, principles, and practice* (3rd ed.). New York: Fairchild Books.

Kuo, Y. F., & Wu, C. M. (2012). Satisfaction and post-purchase intentions with service recovery of online shopping websites: Perspectives on perceived justice and emotions. *International Journal of Information Management*, *32*(2), 127–138. doi:10.1016/j.ijinfomgt.2011.09.001

Kuo, Y. F., Yen, S. T., & Chen, L. H. (2011). Online auction service failures in Taiwan: Typologies and recovery strategies. *Electronic Commerce Research and Applications*, *10*(2), 183–193. doi:10.1016/j.elerap.2009.09.003

Lee, M. J., Singh, N., & Chan, E. S. (2011). Service failures and recovery actions in the hotel industry: A text-mining approach. *Journal of Vacation Marketing*, *17*(3), 197–207. doi:10.1177/1356766711409182

Lin, W. B. (2006). Correlation between personality characteristics, situations of service failure, customer relation strength and remedial recovery strategy. *Services Marketing Quarterly*, *28*(1), 55–88. doi:10.1300/J396v28n01_04

Lopez-Lopez, I., Ruiz-de-Mayal, R., & Warlop, L. (2014). When sharing consumption emotions with strangers is more satisfying than sharing them with friends. *Journal of Service Research*, *17*(4), 475–488. doi:10.1177/1094670514538835

Mandle, J. (2009). *Rawls's A Theory of Justice: An Introduction*. New York: Cambridge University Press. doi:10.1017/CBO9780511814099

Mattila, A. S., Cho, W., & Ro, H. C. (2011). The role of self-service technologies in restoring justice. *Journal of Business Research*, *64*(4), 348–355. doi:10.1016/j.jbusres.2010.02.014

McColl-Kennedy, J. R., & Sparks, B. A. (2003). Application of fairness theory to service failures and service recovery. *Journal of Service Research*, *5*(3), 251–266. doi:10.1177/1094670502238918

McCollough, M. A., Berry, L. L., & Yadav, M. S. (2000). An empirical investigation of customer satisfaction after service failure and recovery. *Journal of Services Research*, *3*(2), 121–137. doi:10.1177/109467050032002

Meuter, M. L., Ostrom, A. L., Roundtree, R. I., & Bitner, M. J. (2000). Self-service technologies: Understanding customer satisfaction with technology-based service encounters. *Journal of Marketing*, *64*(3), 50–64. doi:10.1509/jmkg.64.3.50.18024

Meyer, J., Gremler, D. D., & Hogreve, J. (2014). Do service guarantees guarantee greater market value? *Journal of Service Research*, *17*(2), 150–163. doi:10.1177/1094670513505359

Michel, S. (2001). Analyzing service failures and recoveries: A process approach. *International Journal of Service Industry Management*, *12*(1), 20–33. doi:10.1108/09564230110382754

Miller, J. L., Craighead, C. W., & Karwan, K. R. (2000). Service recovery: A framework and empirical investigation. *Journal of Operations Management*, *18*(4), 387–400. doi:10.1016/S0272-6963(00)00032-2

Mintel. (2015). *Online Clothing Retailing*. Accessed March 30 2018, from http://oxygen.mintel.com

Mintel. (2018). *UK Womenswear Market Report*. Accessed October 15 2018, from https://store.mintel.com/uk-womenswear-market-report

Mollá-Descals, A., Frasquet-Deltoro, M., & Ruiz-Molina, M. E. (2011). Internationalization patterns in fashion retail distribution: Implications for firm results. *Service Industries Journal*, *31*(12), 1979–1993. doi:10.1080/02642069.2011.540754

Mostafa, R. B., Lages, C. R., Shabbir, H. A., & Thwaites, D. (2015). Corporate image: A service recovery perspective. *Journal of Service Research*, *18*(4), 468–483. doi:10.1177/1094670515584146

Nikbin, D., Marimuthu, M., & Hyun, S. S. (2016). Influence of perceived service fairness on relationship quality and switching intention: An empirical study of restaurant experiences. *Current Issues in Tourism*, *19*(10), 1005–1026. doi:10.1080/13683500.2013.801407

Obeidat, Z. M. I., Xiao, S. H., Iyer, G. R., & Nicholson, M. (2017). Consumer revenge using the internet and social media: An examination of the role of service failure types and cognitive appraisal processes. *Psychology and Marketing*, *34*(4), 496–515. doi:10.1002/mar.21002

Ombudsman Services. (2018). *Consumer action monitor*. Retrieved October 13, 2018 from https://www.ombudsman-services.org/docs/default-source/downloads/cam-2018-report.pdf?sfvrsn=0

Oxford Economies. (2018). *How Fashion Fuels the Economy*. Retrieved October 7, 2018, from http://www.thecreativeindustries.co.uk/industries/fashion/fashion-facts-and-figures/how-fashion-fuels-the-uk-economy

Ozuem, W., & Lancaster, G. (2014). Recovery strategies in on-line service failure. In *Marketing in the cyber era: Strategies and emerging trends* (pp. 143–159). IGI Global. doi:10.4018/978-1-4666-4864-7.ch010

Palmer, A. (2014). *Principles of services marketing* (7th ed.). Maidenhead, UK: McGraw-Hill Education.

Pang, A., Hasan, N. B. B. A., & Chong, A. C. Y. (2014). Negotiating crises in the social media environment. *Corporate Communications*, *19*(1), 96–118. doi:10.1108/CCIJ-09-2012-0064

Park, C., & Lee, T. M. (2009). Information direction, website reputation and eWOM effect: A moderating role of product type. *Journal of Business Research*, *62*(1), 61–67. doi:10.1016/j.jbusres.2007.11.017

Park, J. J., & Park, J. W. (2016). Investigating the effects of service recovery quality elements on passengers' behavioural intention. *Journal of Air Transport Management*, *53*, 235–241. doi:10.1016/j.jairtraman.2016.03.003

Piha, L. P., & Avlonitis, G. J. (2015). Customer defection in retail banking: Attitudinal and behavioural consequences of failed service quality. *Journal of Service Theory and Practice*, *25*(3), 304–326. doi:10.1108/JSTP-04-2014-0080

Ringberg, T., Odekerken-Schröder, G., & Christensen, G. L. (2007). A cultural models approach to service recovery. *Journal of Marketing*, *71*(3), 194–214. doi:10.1509/jmkg.71.3.194

Roschk, H., & Kaiser, S. (2013). The nature of an apology: An experimental study on how to apologize after a service failure. *Marketing Letters*, *24*(3), 293–309. doi:10.100711002-012-9218-x

Rosenmayer, A., McQuilken, L., Robertson, N., & Ogden, S. (2018). Omni-channel service failures and recoveries: Refined typologies using Facebook complaints. *Journal of Services Marketing*, *32*(3), 269–285. doi:10.1108/JSM-04-2017-0117

Schminke, M., Caldwell, J., Ambrose, M. L., & McMahon, S. R. (2014). Better than ever? Employee reactions to ethical failures in organizations, and the ethical recovery paradox. *Organizational Behavior and Human Decision Processes*, *123*(2), 206–219. doi:10.1016/j.obhdp.2013.10.002

Sender, T. (2014). *Top of the online shops: Online fashion clicks with 70% of Brits*. Retrieved April 4, 2018 from http://www.mintel.com/press-centre/retail-press-centre/top-of-the-online-shops-online-fashion-clicks-with-70-of-brits

Sender, T. (2017). *Brits hung up on online fashion: Online sales of clothing, fashion accessories and footwear grow by 17% in 2017*. Retrieved October 5, 2018 from http://www.mintel.com/press-centre/fashion/uk-online-sales-of-clothing-fashion-accessories-and-footwear-grow-by-17-in-2017

Sengupta, S., Ray, D., Trendel, O., & Vaerenbergh, Y. V. (2018). The effects of apologies for service failures in the global online retail. *International Journal of Electronic Commerce*, *22*(3), 419–445. doi:10.1080/10864415.2018.1462951

Shin, H., Ellinger, A. E., Mothersbaugh, D. L., & Reynolds, K. E. (2017). Employing proactive interaction for service failure prevention to improve customer service experiences. *Journal of Service Theory and Practice*, *27*(1), 164–186. doi:10.1108/JSTP-07-2015-0161

Siu, N. Y., Zhang, T. J., & Yau, C. J. (2013). The roles of justice and customer satisfaction in customer retention: A lesson from service recovery. *Journal of Business Ethics*, *114*(4), 675–686. doi:10.100710551-013-1713-3

Sivakumar, K., Li, M., & Dong, B. (2014). Service quality: The impact of frequency, timing, proximity, and sequence of failure and delights. *Journal of Marketing*, *78*(1), 41–58. doi:10.1509/jm.12.0527

Smith, A. K., Bolton, R. N., & Wagner, J. (1999). A model of customer satisfaction with service encounters involving failure and recovery. *JMR, Journal of Marketing Research*, *36*(3), 356–372. doi:10.2307/3152082

Sopadjieva, E., Dholakia, U. M., & Benjamin, B. (2017). A study of 46,000 shoppers shows that omnichannel retailing works. *Harvard Business Review*, 3.

Sparks, B. A., & Bradley, G. L. (2017). A 'triple A' typology of responding to negative consumer-generated online reviews. *Journal of Hospitality & Tourism Research (Washington, D.C.)*, *41*(6), 719–745. doi:10.1177/1096348014538052

Spence, C., & Gallace, A. (2011). Multisensory design: Reaching out to touch the consumer. *Psychology and Marketing*, *28*(3), 267–308. doi:10.1002/mar.20392

Statista. (2017). *Apparel market in the United Kingdom (UK) – Statistics & facts*. Retrieved October 5, 2018 from https://www.statista.com/topics/3348/apparel-market-in-the-uk/

Strizhakova, Y., Tsarenko, Y., & Ruth, J. A. (2012). I'm mad and I can't get that service failure off my mind: Coping and rumination as mediators of anger effects on customer intentions. *Journal of Service Research*, *15*(4), 414–429. doi:10.1177/1094670512443999

Swanson, S. R., & Hsu, M. K. (2011). The effect of recovery locus attributions and service failure severity on word-of-mouth and repurchase behaviors in the hospitality industry. *Journal of Hospitality & Tourism Research (Washington, D.C.)*, *35*(4), 511–529. doi:10.1177/1096348010382237

Tax, S. S., Brown, S. W., & Chandrasherakan, M. (1998). Customer evaluations of service complaint experiences: Implication for relationship marketing. *Journal of Marketing*, *62*(2), 60–76. doi:10.1177/002224299806200205

Tombs, A. G., Russell-Bennett, R., & Ashkanasy, N. M. (2014). Recognising emotional expressions of complaining customers: A cross-cultural study. *European Journal of Marketing*, *48*(7/8), 1354–1374. doi:10.1108/EJM-02-2011-0090

Torres, E. N., Adler, H., & Behnke, C. (2014). Stars, diamonds, and other shiny things: The use of expert and consumer feedback in the hotel industry. *Journal of Hospitality and Tourism Management*, *21*, 34–43. doi:10.1016/j.jhtm.2014.04.001

Tsai, C. T., & Su, C. S. (2009). Service failures and recovery strategies of chain restaurants in Taiwan. *Service Industries Journal*, *29*(12), 1779–1796. doi:10.1080/02642060902793599

Vakeel, K. A., Sivakumar, K., Jayasimha, K. R., & Dey, S. (2018). Service failures after online flash sales: Role of deal proneness, attribution, and emotion. *Journal of Service Management*, *29*(2), 253–276. doi:10.1108/JOSM-08-2017-0203

Verhagen, T., Nauta, A., & Feldberg, F. (2013). Negative online word-of-mouth: Behavioural indicator or emotional release? *Computers in Human Behavior*, *29*(4), 1430–1440. doi:10.1016/j.chb.2013.01.043

Wang, Y., Wu, Sh., Lin, H., & Wang, Y. (2011). The relationship of service failure severity, service recovery justice and perceived switching costs with customer loyalty in the context of e-tailing. *International Journal of Information Management*, *31*(4), 350–359. doi:10.1016/j.ijinfomgt.2010.09.001

Weathers, D., Sharma, S., & Wood, S. L. (2007). Effects of online communication practices on consumer perceptions of performance uncertainty for search and experience goods. *Journal of Retailing*, *83*(4), 393–401. doi:10.1016/j.jretai.2007.03.009

Weber, T. (2010). *Why companies watch your every Facebook, YouTube, Twitter move*. Retrieved January 5, 2018 from http://www.bbc.co.uk/news/business-11450923

WRAP. (2017). *Valuing our clothes: The cost of UK fashion report*. Retrieved October 8, 2018 from http://www.wrap.org.uk/sustainable-textiles/valuing-our-clothes

Xiao, S., & Dong, M. (2015). Hidden semi-Markov model-based reputation management system for online to offline (O2O) e-commerce markets. *Decision Support Systems*, *77*, 87–99. doi:10.1016/j.dss.2015.05.013

Yang, K., & Young, A. P. (2009). The effects of customized site features on internet apparel shopping. *Journal of Fashion Marketing and Management: An International Journal*, *13*(1), 128–139. doi:10.1108/13612020910939923

Yang, W., & Mattila, A. S. (2012). The role of tie strength on consumer dissatisfaction responses. *International Journal of Hospitality Management*, *31*(2), 399–404. doi:10.1016/j.ijhm.2011.06.015

Zemke, R., & Schaaf, R. (1989). *The service edge: 101 companies that profit from customer care*. New York: NAL Books.

Zhang, T. T., Omran, B. A., & Cobanoglu, C. (2017). Generation Y's positive and negative eWOM: Use of social media and mobile technology. *International Journal of Contemporary Hospitality Management*, *29*(2), 732–761. doi:10.1108/IJCHM-10-2015-0611

Zhu, Z., Nakata, C., Sivakumar, K., & Grewal, D. (2013). Fix it or leave it? Customer recovery from self-service technology failures. *Journal of Retailing*, *89*(1), 15–29. doi:10.1016/j.jretai.2012.10.004

KEY TERMS AND DEFINITIONS

Customer Satisfaction: Signifies clients' happiness with a product or service based on the difference between the expected and perceived performance of the product or service.

Fashion: The expression of social status, lifestyle and taste through the use of objects by individuals.

Information and Communication Technologies: These include everyday usage of digital technology such as mobile phones, or tablets, and browsing the Internet, which enables easy communication among its users.

Justice Theory: A leading theoretical framework from academia to service recovery in the service marketing literature based on the theory in social and organizational psychology.

Recovery Strategy: The actions taken by firms or service suppliers to overcome occurrences with standards that fall below the needs and expectations of the customer are described as recovery strategies in the service marketing literature.

Service Failure: When a firm or service supplier fails to meet customer anticipations resulting in displeasure during service delivery.

Service Recovery Paradox: A phenomenon that suggests that remarkably strong attempts at recovery can lead to client evaluations higher than transactions with no supposed failure of any kind.

Chapter 9
User-Generated Content and Consumer Brand Engagement

Muhammad Naem
University of Worcester, UK

Sebastian Okafor
University of Cumbria, UK

ABSTRACT

Debates on the importance of user-generated content (UGC) and consumer brand engagement have increasingly gained attention amongst researchers, practitioners, marketing managers, and business leaders. UGC is a concept popularized in the 21st century with the advent and rise of Web 2.0 technology. Web 2.0 has gained recognition due to its novel features that include openness, participation, and the facilitation of the creation and sharing of content. It revolutionized interactions amongst people, and users are now able to share and create personalized content on the internet instead of merely using the content available. The primary objective of this chapter is to evaluate the influence of UGC on consumer brand engagement and discuss its impact on customers and organizational marketing practices.

INTRODUCTION

User Generated Content (henceforth UGC) which is alternatively known as 'user created content' is content published by users on various online platforms (Shneiderman, Preece & Pirolli, 2011). UGC has been described as content created by a consortium or an individual and published through diverse online platforms (McNally et al., 2012). Leung (2009) notes that UGC is any form of content that is developed by users of a service or system and published openly on an associated online platform or system. Most traditional UGC definitions describe the importance of online platforms and technologies that support the generation of such content. These online platforms and technologies are forms of social media, social computing, Web 2.0, collective action tools, social Web, read/write Web, consumer-generated media, virtual communities, computer-mediated communication, online communities, and socio-technical systems (Shneiderman, Preece & Pirolli, 2011). However, prior research presents a clear restriction upon the definition of UGC: when any user copies any content and uploads or posts it on a social media

DOI: 10.4018/978-1-5225-7344-9.ch009

application then he/she is not creating new content or fulfilling the criteria for UGC. UGC is something which generates the content with transformativity or originality or a combination of both (Kaplan and Haenlein 2010). Other researchers have highlighted the fact that UGC became popular in 2005. UGC comprises various forms of media content that should meet three conditions. The content must be published on any social networking sites or website; it must be created outside professional practices and routines and it needs to highlight some unique or creative effort (Kumar et al., 2016). However, most social media applications are used with the purpose of forwarding the copied content of others. All types of social media have their own culture, norms, architectures and unique features. Users visit social media sites with different intentions and interact in diverse ways. McNally et al. (2012) describe the various forms of UGC such as audio, multimedia productions, individual texts, images, and videos. These are distributed through Flickr, Facebook, YouTube, and personal blogs. They are also distributed across software applications or modifications that are generated to operate within hardware platforms or in existing databases (e.g. game or virtual world modifications, iPhone apps, and utilities that influence publicly available databases); and informal or formal groups that generate and disseminate UGC (such as Linex or Apache, open source software, and Wikipedia).

It has become necessary for nations to make a policy framework in order to create and distribute UGC because these contents can bring creative expressions, innovation, and economic growth (Tang, Fang & Wang, 2014). In certain situations, UGC can bring revenue for its creators though voluntary donations, direct payments, content licensed to third parties and advertising revenues. About 80.7 percent of US internet users are seriously consider product reviews before making a purchase decision (eMarketer, 2016). Marketing communication using social media tools such as Facebook, YouTube, Twitter, and Flicker has increasingly gained the attention of many fashion brands, service providers and consumers.

The recent past has witnessed the advent of a new capability acquired by humans. The internet has become omnipresent, enabling users to share newly generated content with other users by delineating their buying intentions, product, and transaction-based experiences (Chaffey & Ellis-Chadwick, 2016; Ozuem, 2016). Content generated by users can be accessed via applications ('apps') or websites viewed by visitors with an internet connection. Such content can include textual comments, video, images, profiles, votes, usernames, 'hearts' and likes and other media (Ryan & Jones, 2012). Adverts however are not considered to be examples of the type of User Generated Content (UGC) seen on social media platforms (Ryan, 2014). Voluntary contributors contribute UGC to increase numbers and support each other, generating new content that involves a wide range of creative media. Other users co-create such content beyond the prevailing professional traditional environments. UGC as a concept was popularised in the early 21st century with the advent of "Web 2.0" (Charlesworth, 2014).

Web 2.0 has brought about dramatic changes, often characterised by participation, openness, and sharing. This has revolutionised interactions amongst people and users are now able to share and create personalised content on the internet instead of simply using content already available (Weiger et al., 2011). UGC has rapidly evolved as a result of Web 2.0 and has also increased the participation of users in creating such content (Wan & Ren, 2017; Ozuem et al., 2016). Its popularity is increasing because users can create audio, video, text, and other files on the internet and share content with each other on platforms like YouTube, Blogs, Twitter and Facebook, amongst others (Goh et al., 2013). Due to the growth in popularity of sophisticated mobile phone cameras, the creation of video content on the internet has increased exponentially (Kim et al. 2010; Ozuem & Mulloo, 2016).

UGC in the context of social media can be defined as the sum of all ways of supporting the sharing of unique content by using social media applications (Kumar et al., 2016; Kim & Johnson, 2016).

Kaplan and Haenlein (2010) have highlighted the importance of social media for UGC, noting that ten hours of content is uploaded on YouTube every minute. Social media and UGC are closely related and complement each other. Various types of UGC exist on online platforms such as on Twitter, YouTube, Flicker, Wikipedia, Facebook, Tumblr, Pinterest, google+, LinkedIn, Reddit, and Instagram. UGC is generated by many online communities on platforms such as google business TripAdvisor and Zagat, Yelp, and OpenTable, and is also generated by corporate websites such as eBay, and Amazon (Kaplan and Haenlein 2010; Shneiderman, Preece & Pirolli, 2011), according to whom the nature of UGC can vary based on the diverse online applications. UGC can also appeal to corporations who integrate it into their websites and third party selling websites. Less attractive to the commercial world are cross-platform applications such as Viber, WhatsApp, WeChat, Imo, and Tango.

THEORETICAL CONTEXT

UGC is content published on social media or is publicly accessible via networking websites and is created exclusively through amateur practices and routines. It therefore depends on creative effort to some extent (Evans, 2012). UGC in marketing refers to brand-related content created by anyone who does not officially represent the business at issue. UGC can take many forms including podcasts, videos, reviews or social networking updates (Thomsett-Scott, 2014; Ozuem et al., 2016). Barefoot & Szabo, (2010) identify UGC across different media formats including digital video, question-answer debates, wikis, blogging, forums, podcasting social networking, review sites, mobile-phone photography and social media. Content-based sharing sites like Buzzfeed are popular UGC formats.

Any kind of content can be regarded as UGC provided three criteria are met. First, content must have been published, otherwise it cannot be regarded as UGC. (Willis & Wang, 2016) Secondly, the content created must be original; i.e. it must be the work of the content creator (Jiao et al., 2018). Thirdly, content must be created without reward, i.e. it must not be paid content. It must be created by the user voluntarily (Chari et al., 2016). Moreover, Smith & Chaffey (2012), indicate that online communities provide a platform of communication to internet users to enable people to interact with friends and family and discuss a wide array of topics. They exchange pictures, videos, texts, and other materials which are called UGC, which also includes content generated by consumers with respect to their shopping experiences, and is therefore content which consumers share with each other online (Kumar et al., 2016; Jin & Phua, 2016).

UGC can be produced and then shared by an end user of any website or online service (Sterne, 2010). It includes content produced or shared by users who are subscribers or members of an online service rather than produced and shared by the online service or website itself (Herrero et al., 2015; Ozuem & Lancaster, 2014). Other common alternative terms used in place of UGC are conversational media or Consumer Generated Media (CGM) (Stareva, 2014; Ryan & Jones, 2014; Ozuem & Lancaster, 2015). Typically, UGC is created online as it can be easily uploaded and shared with family and friends through social media websites (Brown, 2012). In other words, content that is produced and shared by fans or unpaid contributors qualifies as UGC. Many of these posts, videos and photos are part of what can be termed UGC (Odden, 2012). UGC is a source of that content created by consumers, influencers, social media followers or fans that follow and support various brands (Carvão, 2010; Akehurst, 2009; Tirunillai & Tellis, 2012). Such content, whether in the form of a blog, Wiki, podcast, social image, video or social media post created by a third-party user is then used by businesses on their social media networking or websites for the promotion of their brand(s) (Powell et al., 2011). Such content typically acts as a free source of advertising because it comes at no, or little cost (Cha et al., 2009). Simply put, UGC is content that is not produced by the company itself but by consumers or users (Scott, 2015). Although there exists no single universally accepted definition of UGC, the OECD (2006) defines UGC as having three distinct characteristics: "*i) content made publicly available over the Internet, ii) which reflects a certain amount of creative effort., and iii) which is created outside of professional routines and practices*" (OECD, 2007, p. 4). If these characteristics are present, the content qualifies as UGC. First, the content must be published online. If it is not published online, then it does not qualify as UGC. Secondly, the content must be innovative in nature. Lastly, it must be a personal creation rather than a professional creation.

UGC came into being as a result of content contributed by consumers in the form of audio, video, digital images, blogs, and arguments extracted from posts and other media contributions across the spectrum of social media. Content that is contributed by voluntary donators posted in the form of posts, podcasts, wikis, tweets, pics, videos or audio files or images, blog posts and testimonials is created with the aim of promoting brands that consumers follow on social media (Rodgers & Thorson, 2017). In other words, third party users create the content. UGC offers the option to share content with other networks posted by users in relation to a brand (Dodson, 2016).

At present, the most popular UGC content is available in the form of videos and photos, to the extent that some 44% of adult internet users generate such content (Ryan, 2014). According to Statista, (2017) millennials quite commonly create photos as a form of UGC. Product reviews are also popular, constituting some 29% of UGC content on the web. The new options generated in relation to media drive, more through consumer-created content in the online world, and less through publishers, are called 'user-generated content (UGC)' (Dodson, 2016). UGC is defined as media that is produced as a result of a contribution made through Web 2.0 online technologies. The content is created by the user instead of by professionals receiving regular funding (Smith & Chaffey, 2012). From this definition, it is evident that it is the general public that creates UGC. However, there has been some debate about the uses of UGC in business. In the field of marketing for example, UGC is taken to be content that has an 'unofficial' capacity (Mathieson, 2010) and is created in relation to a brand. This content may take the form of reviews, social media posts, podcasts and videos amongst others. A brand is considered to be based on content generated by a user if followers, associates or colleagues have not had a hand in creating it. UGC refers to media contributed and shared by people online. The Interactive Advertising Bureau (IAB) suggests UGC must have the capacity to engage people and to cultivate conversation. Since marketing now implicates people as users, UGC has given rise to terms like "peer-created content" and "Consumer-Generated Content" (CGC) quite outside of traditional industrial classifications (Schaffer et al., 2013).

Any matter that is selected, prepared and distributed in written and graphical form constitutes publishing activity. Matter is available in the form of magazines, books and newspapers, although UGC content does not come under this purview (Martínez-Navarro & Bigné, 2017). Research has identified that UGC is bound within groups as well as in media, whereas published books are not. (Sheldrake et al., 2011). Traditionally, publishing is intended for published material. However, books available electronically and newspapers available online are considered as examples of publishing, therefore printing does not necessarily require publishing (Evans, 2012). Roberts et al., (2016) following a history of two published editions in about two hundred and forty years is now solely available online. However digital publishing has made its way into the sphere of printed publishing and so the definition of publishing has increasingly blurred boundaries. Technological innovations, in particular, have altered ideas about publishing.

There is now a need to review the concept of publishing in the context of new conditions that have emerged with the dawn of social media. In this context, publishing refers to the dissemination of information to the public (Mahoney & Tang, 2016). However, the public exists at a number of different levels, and in order to understand this, the concept above needs to be examined in closer detail. "General public" indicates that a contributing user does not specify any particular receiver (Agresta et al., 2011). Online content is accessible by a vast and unlimited audience. Limited public access indicates that the contributing user does not specify explicitly a particular receiver but addresses a limited audience. Platforms establish limitations that need e-registration before accessing the reading (Brake, 2014). For instance, if the content is offered to registered users only but registration is open for everyone, the audience will remain confined to users who are already registered. This limited public is bifurcated into "known limited public" and "unknown limited public" (Thomsett-Scott, 2014). The "known limited public" has no particular specified receiver despite the fact the audience is limited to known people. One example of this is the sharing of content between friends as a group on social networks. This is evidence of similarity of 'known-limited public' with private platforms (Barefoot & Szabo, 2010).

The "unknown limited" public denotes an audience that is not limited to known people. The sharing of content within a close community of friends in social networks is a pertinent example of this. If specified receivers are taken to be a limited audience, this is referred to as **private**. In the light of the above, private communication does not fall within the purview of UGC that encompasses the transmission of messages on an individual or group basis on platforms like WhatsApp, email, Viber, WeChat and Imo. This suggests that messages transmitted through email and SMS as well as instantaneous messages, faxes, written letters and telephone calls fall beyond the jurisdiction of UGC (Barefoot & Szabo, 2010). However, communication that takes place at a private level is considered an element akin to activity on social media platforms. For example, social networks enable the general public to create and publish content. They allow private messages to be shared between a limited public. One thing peculiar to social media is that users who develop and contribute content are not bound to delineate their audience except by limiting it (Smith & Zook, 2011).

Reach indicates the tally of individuals that receive a message. When a contributor limits the audience to a lesser extent, the message will likely gain the maximum potential to reach the audience. With lemmatising the audience, the extent of increased intimacy is expected to grow (Evan, 2012). Features are highlighted with reference to the varying degrees of intimacy and reach. This phenomenon of content generated by the general public can be adapted to replace the age-old conception of sender-receiver at contributor and audience levels. Based on such a connection, a user that publishes a message is regarded as a contributor. It is not imperative that contributors are involved in the creation of content. Whether a contributor is involved in content creation or not, in social media, a contributor is seen in the capacity of author and is denoted as such (Evan, 2012).

UGC refers to content that users publish online using an online platform such as social media that contains content generated by users who are not required to possess any specialised programming skills. A company contributes content on a platform like social media encompassing the category of user. Generally, a 'user' refers to a social media user (Brown, 2012). When companies contribute content to a platform like social media this is called UGC (Odden, 2012). A user may be an individual, either skilled or unskilled and is not necessarily acting in a professional or corporate capacity. In this context, a company that contributes content to social media is not considered to be developing UGC. This suggests that an individual who utilises a social media platform is called a user (Powell et al., 2011).

A URL is used as an identifier on search engines to conduct a search of web pages rather than specific content. This does not resonate with the concept of UGC. A single web page carries a single URL but also carries a number of entries from social media contributed by diverse authors (Scott, 2015). In terms of social media, UGC is the smallest unit of contribution made by a single author at a specific time. Content created on the basis of collaboration is generally contributed by many authors (Brown, 2012).

Volunteers regularly contribute content in the form of information, data or media on the web in a presentable, meaningful form. Examples are wikis, restaurant ratings and videos (Kim & Lee, 2017). Moreover, Simon, (2016) noted that when it comes to finding a product rating or a service, customer views make voluntary entries difficult. Recent research found that business-generated content is brand-related quite contrary to user-generated (Schulz et al., 2013). Furthermore, Smith et al., (2012) added that UGC is the outcome of professional work carried out behind the scenes. Such content is inexpensive and has generally undergone development, and users provide it without any charge. The phenomenon of supplying content proves rewarding when it is recognised (Marine-Roig & Anton Clavé, 2016). Content that has the capacity to entertain or inform, gives the impression of real data contributed by others without influence from other media channels (Susarla et al., 2012).

A content unit generated by a user comprises staple data along with metadata. Core data provides staple data information as the content. Metadata is based on information in relation to a core area (Chung, Han & Koo, 2015). Metadata involves the publication date, author ranking in society and expert opinions while still constituting UGC. This work includes expressions obtained through one click as UGC. Examples include 'likes' recorded on Facebook, thumbs up comments on YouTube and 'plus one' ratings on Google. Other users' score ratings based on content units generated by users are called peer ratings (Lu & Stepchenkova, 2015). Social media as well as UGC features represent "Web 2.0" which is also called the "participative web". Web 2.0 is not a new web era. Rather, it is viewed as a leaning propensity trend (Wilson et al., 2012).

The influx of blogs in the contemporary online world as well as videos from YouTube, podcasts and comments on blogs or news articles highlights this dimension (Zhan et al., 2017). Anyone can create content on the internet provided s/he is computer-literate and has access to the internet. Many years ago, corporations and individuals with technical know-how tended to create web content in subjective areas online (Flanagin et al., 2014). Different web forums, chat rooms (Internet Relay Chat), online games and multi-user domains were developed as examples (Fox et al., 2012). Many users have subsequently come to realise that participatory facets pertain to the web. Users are free to make and rate comments while viewing the news, although most encounter an overlap of comments from communities watching on- and offline on social digital networks such as Facebook (Kim, 2012).

UGC is any type of media crafted by consumers or end users that is made publicly available to other users via industry databases and websites or via social media (Roberts et al., 2016). It can include written materials such as forum posts, blog entries and reviews or audio-visual or image-based files (photographs, video clips, audio recordings or GIFs). UGC is essentially any material created outside professional marketing practices and publicised online (Adler & Sillars, 2011). It takes various forms but most relevant and common are consumer-produced recommendations and reviews (Sheldrake & Sheldrake, 2011). Webster et al. (2014), make a comparison between UGC and marketer-generated content. Consumers have become pivotal authors of brand stories since content is easily shared on the social media network and is dynamic (Seadle & Greifender, 2014). Every type of UGC has a different impact on the minds of consumers, so gaining a better understanding of the taxonomy of UGC is essential (Pan & Zhang, 2011). UGC may also be regarded as User Created Content (UCC). However, there does not exist any universal definition of UGC. Research into UGC is ongoing and is considered a growth area in marketing academia (Davis, 2015).

Three characteristics are the subject of debate amongst various scholars. Li et al. (2016), observed that UGC represents the experience and comments of consumers in relation to the products and services delivered to them by brands or companies. Moreover, Granitz, N. & Forman, (2015) observed that UGC represents any content which the public creates online. It is a personal form of content and not a professional one. Heba et al., (2018) indicates that the main feature of UGC is that it is generated voluntarily and by amateurs who are not generating content professionally online. Moreover, Chow & Shi, (2015) observed that self-creation is the most central feature of UGC. It is created without any external or professional help. Xie & Lee, (2015) observed that due to sophisticated online platforms, it is now increasingly difficult to distinguish between UGC and professional content. Bao (2017) argued that many professionals have taken to the internet to generate content which looks like UGC. Such content is used for product reviews and personal experiences about products, but there is a recognised need to develop a classification of UGC that might make it easier for marketers to use it in their marketing activities (Chaffey et al., 2016; Ryan & Jones, 2012; Charlesworth, 2014). Therefore, the ensuing discussion will review the overall taxonomy of UGC and how it relates to marketing objectives.

Switching Focus: Traditional Media to Online Social Media

Nowadays, businesses are switching their focus from traditional media to online social media and they are using sources such as blogs, social networking websites, viral marketing and wikis (Ozuem & Azemi, 2017; Hutton and Fosdick, 2011). Due to this advancement in technology many opportunities have been created for businesses (Ozuem & Lancaster, 2012; Ozuem et al., 2018). For instance, customer communication can be achieved through these media and relationships between businesses and consumers have been strengthened (Abed et al., 2015a, b; Ozuem, 2004). Social media is essentially an internet-enabled platform facilitating a flow of information in the form of decentralised user content through public memberships (Abrahams et al., 2012). In other words, social media can be defined as a group of applications that are based on internet, building on foundations such as the ideology and technology of Web 2.0. This allows the creation and exchange of content that is generated by users (Kaplan and Haenlein, 2010, p. 60). Social media is also referred to as a content-generating network. This involves reviewing content online, obtaining real-time feedback, building customer relationships and facilitating discussions (Rodriguez et al., 2012). In addition, user networks and communities can also increase their presence on social media networking sites (Curran and Lennon, 2011). Abrahams et al. (2012), explain that through social media networking sites, propagating information is easier and has led to decentralised levels of content amongst users. However, there are many other networks that provide the opportunity for users to share their views on products. There is therefore a need to discuss the similarities and differences between social media and other UGC networks.

UGC and social media share the same strong relationship (Rodgers & Thorson, 2017). When they are combined, something magical is created based on the individual strength of each element. Marketers can build strong customer relationships and can strengthen their brands by executing UGC campaigns on social media. The concept of UGC is not new; it was introduced several years ago. However, this phenomenon has recently gained momentum because of the rapid growth of the internet and the easy accessibility this provides, based on instant connectivity and intelligent software (Clark et al., 2017; Hansen & Lee, 2013). Since the internet and technology are at everyone's fingertips, consumers have been granted new powers to make themselves heard and to influence ideas such as sales and marketing

(Hansen & Lee, 2013; Ozuem & Azemi, 2018). Three types of UGC exist in the online environment. First, social media UGC can be found on social media websites such as Facebook, Wikipedia, Twitter, YouTube, Tumblr, Pinterest, Instagram, Reddit, google+ and LinkedIn. Secondly, UGC is created by online communities that rate and review products. Such online communities include Yelp, OpenTable, google business, Zagat and Trip Advisor. Thirdly UGC can be created on corporate websites and third-party sales websites such as Amazon and eBay. Online review websites like Zagat, Trip Advisor, OpenTable and Yelp are common platforms for consumers to express opinions and share experiences about purchasing products and services (Leibtag, 2014).

Users consider UGC information to be more trustworthy and relatable compared to information generated by marketers (Seadle & Greifender, 2014). However, it is necessary to understand the difference between the nature UGC among different networks because the nature of UGC is quite different on company own website, third party selling websites (eBay, Amazon) and on instant messages networks (WhatsApp, Viber, WeChat, Imo etc). To address this issue, a definition of social media should be considered. Charlesworth, (2015;1) stated that *"what is understood by social media is still open to some debate"*, furthermore defining (2015;1) social media as a *"collective term for the various social network and community sites including such online application as blogs, podcasts, reviews and wikis"*. According to this definition, both online communities and social media websites are examples of social media networks. Regarding the use of both kinds of online network, it is obvious that social media networking is not only used for rating and reviewing products (Rossmann et al., 2018) but also to socialise with friends and family. However, online communities such as Zagat, Trip Advisor, OpenTable and Yelp are used particularly to review and rate products. Based on this observation, community websites and social media sites are quite different.

Brands' own websites and third party selling websites such as Amazon and eBay are other sources that amass UGC (Chen & Lurie, 2013). Once again, the question arises as to whether or not to consider UGC created by brands and third-party websites as examples of UGC and social media. Any website where users can add content but cannot control the site is defined as a social media site (Han, 2018). Based on this definition of social media, community websites, third-party selling websites and social media sites are very similar, and differences are difficult to highlight. However, it can be argued that all media can be considered as qualifying as social media, so there is need to more strictly define social media and UGC for the purposes of this research.

From the above definitions of social media, it can be concluded that it existed long before the digital revolution (Chaffey & Ellis-Chadwick, 2016). In the early days, social media was used as source of connection among communities of like-minded people who used to share views on all issues from politics and the latest trends to the best way to cultivate tomatoes (Charlesworth, 2015). However, these connections were strongly limited by location and by the available communications technology of the past (Ryan, 2017; Ozuem et al., 2008). If users at that time wanted to discuss a brand, organisation or product they could do so only with close associates, family or friends (Ryan, 2017; Estrella-Ramón & Ellis-Chadwick, 2017). The digital generation has removed these restrictions (Charlesworth, 2014). In the digital world people can spread UGC across the globe instantly via hand-held devices, tablets, watches, wearables, PCs and laptops (Dodson, 2016; Zhang et al., 2016; Davis, 2015). The above definition of a social circle suggests that UGC created in the form of product ratings on review websites (community websites) and on corporate websites cannot be considered examples of social media enabled UGC. According to Tirunillai & Tellis, (2012), a discussion about conventional social circles is not restricted to any specific topic. However, people cannot communicate easily on Amazon, eBay, Yelp, Zagat, and Trip

Advisor because community websites and third party selling websites like eBay or Amazon only allow product ratings to be generated. Community websites, selling websites and corporate websites cannot therefore be considered as examples of social media for the purposes of this research. Estrella-Ramón & Ellis-Chadwick, (2017) indicate that people can freely communicate and share their views about anything on social media networks such as Twitter, YouTube and Facebook. This research therefore only looks at UGC created on social media sites such as Twitter and Facebook, but it will nonetheless take a detailed look at the nature of UGC on social media sites.

Definitions of social media offer mixed perceptions regarding the difference between UGC on social media and UGC on corporate and community websites. Kaplan and Haenlein (2010) associate social media sites with digital technology by describing social media as a group of internet-based applications that build on the technological and ideological foundation of Web 2.0. These applications facilitate the exchange and creation of UGC. Furthermore, social media is defined by Gensler et al., (2013) as Web 2.0 which is the sum of open-sourced user-controlled, and interactive online applications used to expand the knowledge, market power and experience of users as participants in social and business processes. These Web 2.0 applications support the creation of networked informal users and they facilitate a flow of knowledge and ideas by allowing the efficient generation, sharing, editing, refining and dissemination of informational content (Evans, 2012; Zhang et al., 2016; Schaffer et al., 2014; Agresta et al., 2011). Based on this definition it is clear that corporate websites, social media sites and third-party selling websites all are considered as examples of UGC. The argument here is that company websites, third-party selling websites (eBay, Amazon) and community website cannot be considered examples of UGC. Therefore, community websites such as Zagat, TripAdvisor, OpenTable, Yelp and third party selling websites such as Amazon and eBay are not considered to be examples of social media sites. Moreover, Statista statistics (2018) suggest the penetration of social media in the UK has taken place on social websites only (see Chart 2.1 below). Therefore, due to the restrictions placed on discussion types on third party websites (e.g. eBay, Amazon), corporate websites and community networks (e.g. Trip Advisor, Yelp) these can be rejected as examples of social media UGC (see Figure 2-2 of the Pyramid of UGC Sources). This study specifically considers social media networks as examples of UGC. Pinterest, Twitter and Facebook are amongst the most high-profile examples of social media, and they operate, and work entirely or mostly based on UGC. Moreover, online forums, product reviews and rating websites as well as classified websites also depend on UGC, but these should not be considered as forms of social media UGC. UGC includes blog posts, tweets, testimonials, videos, pictures and everything in between. Peer-reviewed endorsements of brands rather than brand-endorsed messages count as UGC.

Brand-Related User-Generated Content (UGC)

Brand-oriented UGC represents content which is created with reference to a brand and is intended to be brought to the notice of other users as well (Tang et al. 2014). It provides useful information to consumers who are in the process of arriving at a decision about buying products or services (Yadav et al., 2016). eMarketer (2016) report highlighted that 80.7% of internet users in the US regard product reviews by other consumers as influential factors for arriving at a purchasing decision. The importance, relevance and influence of UGC related to brands is increasingly enabling potential customers to make decisions about brands (Munar & Jacobsen, 2013)

Positive responses from consumers can be generated by brand-oriented UGC which includes favourable attitudes with respect to a brand if the brand-oriented UGC is in favour of the brand (Ryan, 2014). It is also important to note that the influence of UGC also depends on the person who generates it. Social media has enabled users to generate and share content with each other. Among those who are in the social circle of consumers it is easier to get within the reach of UGC (Ransbotham et al., 2012). This is also referred to as creating eWOM and brings people together who share the interests of those within their personal network (Yadav et al., 2016). Consumers are also increasingly being exposed to UGC shared by celebrities on their social media pages. Twitter is increasingly becoming a source for politicians and celebrities to share information about what they like or dislike (Ransbotham et al., 2012; Munar, A.M. & Jacobsen, 2013). Existing research has shown that posts by celebrities can influence followers, even if the content is brand-related (Schultz, 2017). However, the extent to which such posts influence consumers who are making a buying decision and the extent to which brand perceptions are affected are not clear. In this, study the relative effectiveness of celebrities and friend posts on social media in relation to brands is examined (Ransbotham et al., 2012). Furthermore, with regard to the fact that brand-related UGC influences other consumers (such as observed by Lu et al. 2014), it is worth noting the nature of responses from recipients of UGC towards these two constructs (Ryan & Jones, 2012).

Sources of Brand-Oriented UGC

Information is an important feature of social media, as everyone is informed about others due to social media (Shao, 2009). The UGC which users usually encounter is the one shared by their friends. Friends represent the major social circle of a person present on social media. People have brought real-life friendships and relationships online (Liu et al., 2011).

Existing research shows that the buying decisions of people are influenced by views shared by their friends. This is called referent power and describes a situation in which people like to identify with popular views held by their friends (Williams et al., 2010). It is supplemented by reward power whereby people believe that by sharing popular views they are rewarding each other. Further, coercive power also underpins this idea in the sense that people believe they are rendered socially isolated if they go against the popular view (Barreda & Bilgihan, 2013). Apart from the venues of traditional marketing, the factor which most influences people is that of friendship affecting the decisions of people through the power of social media (Zeng et al., 2016). Nearly 60% of consumers note their buying decisions were influenced by friends' posts on social media (Diffley et al., 2018).

However, it is important to distinguish between casual friends and close friends. Close friends enjoy influential power with respect to each other. They also interact with each other more frequently than with casual friends and have reciprocal relationships with each other (Malthouse et al., 2016). They are likely to share their feelings and experiences more closely, and more openly and frequently with each other (Merrilees, 2016). Close friends are also likely to share promotional messages with each other. The intensity of relationships is higher and better in close friendships, which is why people attach importance to information passed on by close friends (Kamboj & Sarmah, 2018).

The variations in UGC types are endless. Some major examples include Podcasts, Forums, user-created blog posts, user-created videos, reviews, Facebook posts or comments and blog comments (Dempster & Lee, 2015; Weber & Henderson, 2014; Statista, 2018). Customer feedback is an open-ended type of feedback that comes in the form of FAQs, Q&As or any other direct feedback that directs a brand social media team (Armstrong et al., 2017). Certain platforms that not only allow customers to ask questions, but also to answer them, providing additional integrity to responses because they are produced by the end users of products. Reviews and ratings are comparatively straightforward and include the number of 'likes' on a product Facebook page (Brake, 2014). This is a clear example of UGC as it allows consumers to create direct feedback about products depending on the system being used. Nielsen (2017), showed that peer reviews are long-lasting and durable. The sites on which they appear are highly credible and feature reviews from other customers. The filter options that are a feature of some systems ensure that only verified customers can review, while others are open-ended platforms (Chaffey, 2006; Schultz, 2016). Marketers can enhance current levels of transparency and trust in brands by allowing user-generated images. Beyond fashion, it is exciting for customers to receive mail about a new product and to see others unboxing products (Zahay, 2015). However, the authenticity of UGC does not rely only on the fact that it is user-generated. More crucial is that UGC is unpaid and also serves the purposes of marketing brands (King et al., 2014; Weber & Henderson, 2014). This renders UGC a version of online WOM marketing, although the content is not necessarily generated with the intention of promotion, particularly because modern users are cautious about marketing messages (Armstrong & Kotler, 2014). For example, a satisfied consumer at a restaurant or Samsung/Apple service centre can generate voluntary posts about their experience, on, for example, Instagram – which of course counts as UGC. However, the brand can take advantage of this activity, but it remains necessary for the brand to be aware of response strategies to address both positive and negative customer feedback. Thus, the next section explores how UGC stimulates customer behaviour in diverse ways.

UGC and Consumer Behaviour

The nature of interactions between people is increasingly changing due to the enhanced democratisation of content available online (Scott, 2015). The focus of companies is shifting from influencing the consumers to playing the role of mediator between consumers for the content they are generating (Wen, 2009). Nevertheless, UGC is a legitimate source of feedback from consumers. Consumers provide opinions and feedback as a result of UGC that can help business in terms of customer relationship management and product development (Gu, Tang & Whinston, 2013). This can occur in both a structured and an unstructured manner. This has resulted in the expansion of consumer-oriented intelligence online. The advent of the internet enabled people to discuss their experiences with industry or companies (Stoel & Muhanna, 2016). They became able to interact with countless numbers of other consumers and able to highlight their personal experiences with the brand, bringing into the limelight their experience before other consumers (Chern et al., 2015). UGC is also becoming an addiction that gives users a sense of recognition and status. When they are appreciated, or their views are welcomed on the basis of their experience they feel a sense of recognition within their circle. That is why UGC is increasingly becoming a source of eWOM (Estrella-Ramón et al., 2017) and positive eWOM has a direct positive influence on customer relationships and buying behaviour (Luo et al., 2016; Zhang et al., 2013; Chern et al., 2015; Gu, Tang & Whinston, 2013)

Nevertheless, consumers are increasingly empowered by the internet, particularly in light of Web 2.0 and they can create content and influence brands and other consumer opinions with the content they are creating. Consumers are not passive anymore; they are becoming increasingly active. The internet has also facilitated two-way communication between consumers and brands. Therefore, UGC has the effect of influencing brand loyalty (Kizgin et al., 2018; Ozuem & Thomas, 2015). Previously, business marketers were able to influence the opinions of consumers (Viswanathan et al., 2018). Today, this is achieved by consumers as they can interact without the constraints of geographical boundaries, and they can influence opinion, which is considered a form of UGC. They can opine freely about the products and services they consume from various brands (Kao et al., 2016; Roberts & Kraynak, 2008). With the help of social media, consumers are able to generate, create, exchange, and edit information online and they can support or critique a particular brand overtly via UGC on social media (Du Plessis, 2017). Peer review feedback is regarded as a more reliable source of marketing as compared to online marketing campaigns (Kao et al., 2016; Hautz et al., 2014). This has the effect of driving brand loyalty amongst customers (Ozuem et al., 2016). The profitability of business is also notably influenced by UGC (Akar & Topcu, 2011; Hautz et al., 2014).

Customer satisfaction increases in line with the quality of customer online reviews and this ultimately leads to higher customer purchasing intentions since positive discussion about brands improves customer confidence because they feel they are dealing with a reliable brand (Yadav et al., 2016). As online reviews are easily understandable and objective in nature, they strongly influence the intentions of customers based on reviews that are subjective and emotive (Leibtag, 2014). Detailed videos and written content provide information to people on various products and in imaginative ways (Goodman et al., 2013). The impact of online reviews on consumer behaviour has become an interesting topic for both practitioners and researchers (Ozuem & O'Keeffe, 2015; Seadle & Greifender, 2014). Online stores and brands publish rich information (Yeh, 2015; Prendergast et al., 2010) that has made it easy for customers to access multiple sources of information about brands and products. This is particularly the case in terms of customer reviews about online shopping on social media (Chakravarty et al., 2010). Although positive reviews are generally appreciated, negative reviews cannot be ignored (Feng & Liu, 2018). Regardless of whether the product or brand is of a supreme quality, an unsatisfied customer will post negative reviews that might have a negative impact on the brand and might influence new customers. These negative reviews can influence other consumers to perceive that the product is of lower quality, thus damaging buying intentions and brand trust (Lee & Choeh, 2018). All types of UGC on social media sites impact on customer trust, which will be discussed in the next section.

Customer Trust

Online reviews of consumers on social media in relation to products or services can be highly influential. A number of studies suggest that online reviews strongly influence product choices and risk perception (Sparks et al., 2016: Palmer, 2009; Matzat & Snijders, 2012). Although all consumer reviews are not equally valued, reviews by family members and close friends on social media are highly influential in terms of driving purchase decisions (Wen, 2009; Hsu et al., 2013; Lee, 2017). The value of UGC as feedback can be measured on the basis of the extent to which it is influential and useful. In terms of the usefulness of UGC, negative feedback has a great impact on brand trust amongst new customers and existing customers (Yan & Du, 2016) since it damages perceptions of trustworthiness (Kandampully et al., 2015). For sellers it is very important to understand how to react to negative reviews. The next section will discuss this aspect in detail. However, it should be acknowledged that if a business attracts only positive reviews this attracts suspicion. Brands, however, cannot satisfy everyone (Liang & Corkindale, 2016; Lee & Wu, 2015; Zhou & Duan, 2015). Negative reviews suggest that brands hide nothing, and positive reviews create high trust relationships with customers (Zhang et al., 2015). Online feedback can benefit brands as they add elements of transparency and truth to the brand image that eventually lead to customer trust (Sun, 2013; Wang & Li, 2016; Munar & Jacobsen, 2013).

Moreover, online reviews on social media are considered new forms of recommendations similar to traditional communications by means of word of mouth (Zheng et al., 2015). Customers who contribute content to social media reviews tend to be previous customers who intend to remain anonymous, whereas sources of traditional WOM are generally known and therefore not anonymous (Ryan & Jones, 2012). The number of customer reviews is another concern in terms of online customer reviews as it is useful for identifying reputation. It also holds clues as to the market performance of specific products or services (Mayzlin and Chevalier, 2006; Ozuem et al., 2017). Moreover, Charlesworth, (2014) suggests that the quantity of online reviews also acts as a reference point in winning the confidence of online customers. These ideas will be discussed in future sections of this chapter.

Customers form expectations about a specific product or service on the basis of multiple sources of information such as the brand name and the price of products or services (Mathieson, 2010). Previous experiences of products also have a bearing (Mayzlin et al., 2016). Moreover, Kaur et al., (2018) focused on determining how consumer social media reviews post-purchase can determine levels of both expectations and uncertainty. Customers form pre-purchase expectations about products partly based on online reviews which influence their later buying decisions. Online consumer reviews are generally characterised by volume, variance and valence (Homburg et al., 2015; Richard & Habibi, 2016). Numerous studies have explored how social media consumer reviews influence customer buying decisions. According to recent meta-analysis, the volume and valence of reviews positively influences customer trust and this in turn impacts on buying decisions (Saboo et al., 2016; Floyd et al., 2014). Following a purchase, expectation-confirmation leads to high levels of the post-purchase satisfaction and reduces return probabilities. Similarly, review volumes mitigate return probabilities ((Seadle & Greifender, 2014). This suggests that positive social media reviews also impact on customer buying return decisions.

MANAGERIAL IMPLICATIONS AND CONCLUSION

It is evident from previous studies that UGC is dynamic and complex, as is the impact of UGC on other consumers (Nielsen Company, 2014; Ayeh et al. 2013). Moreover, Tafesse, (2016) observed that consumer choice is influenced by UGC that consumers encounter on social media because people are more influenced by their friends and family. Furthermore, he observed that UGC is more effective in terms of influencing consumer decision making as compared to media campaigns and advertisements, because customers place more trust in their friends than in marketers. Furthermore, Herrero et al., (2015) observed that the product ratings provided on social media are regarded as more reliable by other consumers; certainly, more so than the ratings provided by industry experts. Moreover, Kamboj et al., (2018) observed that negative UGC is more influential than positive UGC because it consists of in-depth information about products. As such, negative comments are the principal reason why customers switch brands in certain circumstances. However, UGC is keenly followed in some industries such as in the travel industry which is heavily influenced by customer reviews and ratings (Ayeh et al. 2013). Moreover, Ye et al., (2010), observed that where UGC acts in support of a particular travel company and increases by 10%, subsequent bookings increased by 5%. Moreover, Yang et al., (2017) observed that UGC provides weak brands with a stronger position in the market. UGC is also regarded by various researchers as a source of eWOM. However, eWOM might be positive or negative (Renton & Simmonds, 2017; Sabate et al., 2014; Pfeffer et al., 2014). These ideas will be discussed in detail further on in this chapter.

There are two-fold repercussions of the new environments that have supported the growth in social media (Hu et al. 2014). Consumer behaviour is highly influenced by UGC as it amounts to eWOM for other consumers (Ring et al. 2016). This has the effect of influencing buying decisions. Hong et al.

(2017), observed that social media UGC is increasingly becoming a prominent source of influencing the decisions of consumers to transact with a particular brand. Gao (et al. 2015) observed that UGC might take the form of a negative or positive comment about a product or service. These comments are made through social media channels. There are different manners and forms of UGC such as those generated in discussion forums online. Examples include blogs, Tweets and Facebook pages. This content has the effect of influencing buying decisions online and offline (Hong et al. 2017). UGC can also amount to a boycott of a brand or company whereby other consumers realise that their fellow consumers were severely affected by the brand's policies or products and services (Fay & Larkin, 2017). UGC can also take the form of mailbags, personal emails, electronic mailings, blog posts, comments on social media, instant messaging, and social media reviews (Gao et al., 2015). However, this research considers social media UGC only. An important feature of UGC is that it is generated by consumers and is not therefore created professionally. Further, UGC on social media is often regarded as more trustworthy by consumers compared with the narratives they find on other media platforms. This is perhaps because people trust their friends and families over marketers (Fay & Larkin, 2017). Sandars and Walsh (2009) observed that since UGC is generated by consumers it is considered reliable and trustworthy by other consumers. Smith (et al. 2012) observed that UGC is equivalent to eWOM and is thus considered reliable by both brands and consumers. Floyd et al. (2014), observed that social influence is a crucial factor behind purchasing decisions and that is why UGC is influential in purchases made by other consumers. The results of research conducted by Geissinger & Laurell, (2016) showed that 70% of consumers looked for consumer reviews before making a buying decision. They typically carried out a search on social media beforehand. Besides, Labrecque, (2014) observed that 78% of consumers believe in the content that is shared by other consumers and value this over industry data. Moreover, Breitsohl et al., (2015) observed that 60% of consumers trust posts by other consumers when it comes to products or services. Some 49% of consumers shape their buying behaviour in the light of such content. Additionally, Breitsohl et al., (2015) observed that those consumers who employed social media platforms arrived at better decisions in terms of product purchases compared with those who did not rely on such a platform. This suggests that UGC on social media impacts customer behaviour in many ways.

REFERENCES

Abed, S., Dwivedi, Y. K., & Williams, M. D. (2015a). Social media as a bridge to e-commerce adoption in SMEs: A systematic literature review. *The Marketing Review*, *15*(1), 39–57. doi:10.1362/146934715X14267608178686

Abrahams, A. S., Jiao, J., Wang, G. A., & Fan, W. (2012). Vehicle defect discovery from social media. *Decision Support Systems*, *54*(1), 87–97. doi:10.1016/j.dss.2012.04.005

Adler, L., & Sillars, R. (2011). *2010; The Linked Photographers' Guide to Online Marketing and Social Media*. Cengage Learning.

Agresta, S., Bough, B. B., & Miletsky, J. I. (2011). *Perspectives™ on Social Media Marketing*. Boston: Cengage Learning.

Akehurst, G. (2009). User generated content: The use of blogs for tourism organisations and tourism consumers. *Service Business*, *3*(1), 51–61. doi:10.100711628-008-0054-2

Armstrong, G., & Kotler, P. (2014). *Marketing: an introduction (12th ed.)*. Harlow: Pearson Education Limited.

Armstrong, G., Kotler, P., & Opresnik, M. O. (2017). *Marketing: an introduction (13th ed.)*. Harlow: Pearson Education Limited.

Ayeh, J. K., Au, N., & Law, R. (2013). "Do we believe in TripAdvisor?" Examining credibility perceptions and online travelers' attitude toward using user-generated content. *Journal of Travel Research*, *52*(4), 437–452. doi:10.1177/0047287512475217

Bao, T. T., & Chang, T. S. (2016). The product and timing effects of eWOM in viral marketing. *International Journal of Business*, *21*(2), 99.

Barefoot, D., & Szabo, J. (2009). *Friends with Benefits: A Social Media Marketing Handbook, 1;1st; edn*. San Francisco, CA: No Starch Press.

Barreda, A., & Bilgihan, A. (2013). An analysis of user-generated content for hotel experiences. *Journal of Hospitality and Tourism Technology*, *4*(3), 263–280. doi:10.1108/JHTT-01-2013-0001

Brake, D. (2014). *Sharing our lives online: risks and exposure in social media*. Basingstoke, UK: Palgrave Macmillan. doi:10.1057/9781137312716

Breitsohl, J., Kunz, W. H., & Dowell, D. (2015). Does the host match the content? A taxonomical update on online consumption communities. *Journal of Marketing Management*, *31*(9-10), 1040–1064. doi:10.1080/0267257X.2015.1036102

Brown, E. (2012). *Working the Crowd - Social media marketing for business* (2nd ed.). Swindon, UK: British Informatics Society Ltd.

Brown, J., Broderick, A. J., & Lee, N. (2007). Word of mouth communication within online communities: Conceptualizing the online social network. *Journal of Interactive Marketing*, *21*(3), 2–20. doi:10.1002/dir.20082

Carvão, S. (2010). Embracing user generated content within destination management organisations to gain a competitive insight into visitors' profiles. *Worldwide Hospitality and Tourism Themes*, *2*(4), 376–382. doi:10.1108/17554211011074038

Cha, M., Kwak, H., Rodriguez, P., Ahn, Y. & Moon, S. (2009). Analyzing the video popularity characteristics of large-scale user generated content systems. *IEEE/ACM Transactions on Networking, 17*(5), 1357-1370.

Chaffey, D. (2006). *Internet marketing: strategy, implementation and practice* (3rd ed.). Prentice Hall/ Financial Times.

Chaffey, D., & Ellis-Chadwick, F. (2016). *Digital marketing* (6th ed.). Harlow: Pearson Education.

Chakravarty, A., Liu, Y., & Mazumdar, T. (2010). The Differential Effects of Online Word-of-Mouth and Critics' Reviews on Pre-release Movie Evaluation. *Journal of Interactive Marketing*, *24*(3), 185–197. doi:10.1016/j.intmar.2010.04.001

Chan-Olmsted, S. M., Cho, M., & Lee, S. (2013). User perceptions of social media: A comparative study of perceived characteristics and user profiles by social media. *Online Journal of Communication and Media Technologies*, *3*(4), 149–178.

Chari, S., Christodoulides, G., Presi, C., Wenhold, J., & Casaletto, J. P. (2016). Consumer Trust in User-Generated Brand Recommendations on Facebook. *Psychology and Marketing*, *33*(12), 1071–1081. doi:10.1002/mar.20941

Charlesworth, A. (2014). *Digital marketing: a practical approach* (2nd ed.). London: Routledge. doi:10.4324/9780203493717

Chen, H., & Huang, C. (2013). An Investigation into Online Reviewers' Behaviour. *European Journal of Marketing*, *47*(10), 1758–1773. doi:10.1108/EJM-11-2011-0625

Chen, Z., & Lurie, N. H. (2013). Temporal contiguity and negativity bias in the impact of online word of mouth. *JMR, Journal of Marketing Research*, *50*(4), 463–476. doi:10.1509/jmr.12.0063

Chern, C., Wei, C., Shen, F., & Fan, Y. (2015). A sales forecasting model for consumer products based on the influence of online word-of-mouth. *Information Systems and e-Business Management*, *13*(3), 445–473. doi:10.100710257-014-0265-0

Chow, W. S., & Shi, S. (2015). Investigating Customers' Satisfaction With Brand Pages In Social Networking Sites. *Journal of Computer Information Systems*, *55*(2), 48–58. doi:10.1080/08874417.2015.11645756

Chu, S. C., & Kim, Y. (2011). Determinants of consumer engagement in electronic word-of-mouth (eWOM) in social networking sites. *International Journal of Advertising*, *30*(1), 47–75. doi:10.2501/IJA-30-1-047-075

Chung, N., Han, H., & Koo, C. (2015). Adoption of travel information in user-generated content on social media: The moderating effect of social presence. *Behaviour & Information Technology*, *34*(9), 902–919. doi:10.1080/0144929X.2015.1039060

Clark, M., Black, H. G., & Judson, K. (2017). Brand community integration and satisfaction with social media sites: A comparative study. *Journal of Research in Interactive Marketing*, *11*(1), 39–55. doi:10.1108/JRIM-07-2015-0047

Curran, J., & Lennon, R. (2011). Participating in the conversation: Exploring adoption of online social media. *Academy of Marketing Studies Journal*, *15*(1), 21–38.

Davis, K. (2015). *Offerpop sifts gold from user-generated content: platform aggregates rich social data with an emphasis on visuals for the entire customer journey*. Haymarket Media, Inc.

Dempster, C., & Lee, J. (2015). *The Rise of the Platform Marketer: Performance Marketing with Google, Facebook, and Twitter, Plus the Latest High-Growth Digital Advertising Platforms*. John Wiley & Sons Inc. doi:10.1002/9781119153863

Diffley, S., McCole, P., & Carvajal-Trujillo, E. (2018). Examining social customer relationship management among Irish hotels. *International Journal of Contemporary Hospitality Management*, *30*(2), 1072–1091. doi:10.1108/IJCHM-08-2016-0415

Dodson, I. (2016). *The Art of Digital Marketing: The Definitive Guide to Creating Strategic, Targeted, and Measurable Online Campaigns* (1st ed.). Hoboken, NJ: John Wiley & Sons Inc.

Dodson, I. (2016). *The digital marketing playbook*. Wiley-Blackwell.

Du Plessis, C. (2017). The role of content marketing in social media content communities. *South African Journal of Information Management*, *19*(1), e1–e7. doi:10.4102ajim.v19i1.866

Duan, W., Gu, B., & Whinston, A. B. (2008). The dynamics of online word-of-mouth and product sales—An empirical investigation of the movie industry. *Journal of Retailing*, *84*(2), 233–242. doi:10.1016/j.jretai.2008.04.005

Dutot, V., & Bergeron, F. (2016). From strategic orientation to social media orientation: Improving SMEs' performance on social media. *Journal of Small Business and Enterprise Development*, *23*(4), 1165–1190. doi:10.1108/JSBED-11-2015-0160

Dwivedi, Y. K., Kapoor, K. K., & Chen, H. (2015). Social media marketing and advertising. *The Marketing Review*, *15*(3), 289–309. doi:10.1362/146934715X14441363377999

eMarketer. (2016). *Internet users rely on reviews when deciding which products to purchase*. Available at: www.emarketer.com/Article/Internet-Users-Rely-on-Reviews-Deciding-Which-Products-Purchase/1014465

Estrella-Ramón, A., & Ellis-Chadwick, F. (2017). Do different kinds of user-generated content in online brand communities really work? *Online Information Review*, *41*(7), 954–968. doi:10.1108/OIR-08-2016-0229

Evans, D. (2008). *Social Media Marketing*. Sybex.

Evans, D. (2012). *Social Media Marketing: An Hour a Day* (2nd ed.). Sybex.

Feng, J., & Liu, B. (2018). Dynamic Impact of Online Word-of-Mouth and Advertising on Supply Chain Performance. *International Journal of Environmental Research and Public Health*, *15*(1), 69. doi:10.3390/ijerph15010069 PMID:29300361

Feng, J., & Papatla, P. (2012). Is Online Word of Mouth Higher for New Models or Redesigns? An Investigation of the Automobile Industry. *Journal of Interactive Marketing*, *26*(2), 92–101. doi:10.1016/j.intmar.2012.01.001

Flanagin, A. J., Hocevar, K. P., & Samahito, S. N. (2014). Connecting with the user-generated Web: How group identification impacts online information sharing and evaluation. *Information Communication and Society*, *17*(6), 683–694. doi:10.1080/1369118X.2013.808361

Floyd, K., Freling, R., Alhoqail, S., Cho, H. Y., & Freling, T. (2014). How Online Product Reviews Affect Retail Sales: A Meta-analysis. *Journal of Retailing*, *90*(2), 217–232. doi:10.1016/j.jretai.2014.04.004

Fox, A. K., Bacile, T. J., Nakhata, C., & Weible, A. (2018). Selfie-marketing: Exploring narcissism and self-concept in visual user-generated content on social media. *Journal of Consumer Marketing*, *35*(1), 11–21. doi:10.1108/JCM-03-2016-1752

Gao, G., Greenwood, B. N., Agarwal, R., & McCulllough, J. (2015). Vocal Minority and Silent Majority: How Do Online Ratings Reflect Population Perceptions of Quality? *Management Information Systems Quarterly*, *39*(3), 565–589. doi:10.25300/MISQ/2015/39.3.03

Geissinger, A., & Laurell, C. (2016). User engagement in social media – an explorative study of Swedish fashion brands. *Journal of Fashion Marketing and Management*, *20*(2), 177–190. doi:10.1108/JFMM-02-2015-0010

Gensler, S., Völckner, F., Liu-Thompkins, Y., & Wiertz, C. (2013). Managing Brands in the Social Media Environment. *Journal of Interactive Marketing*, *27*(4), 242–256. doi:10.1016/j.intmar.2013.09.004

Ghose, A., Ipeirotis, P. G., & Li, B. (2012). Designing Ranking Systems for Hotels on Travel Search Engines by Mining User-Generated and Crowdsourced Content. *Marketing Science*, *31*(3), 493–520. doi:10.1287/mksc.1110.0700

Goh, K., Heng, C., & Lin, Z. (2013). Social Media Brand Community and Consumer Behavior: Quantifying the Relative Impact of User- and Marketer-Generated Content. *Information Systems Research*, *24*(1), 88–107. doi:10.1287/isre.1120.0469

Goodman, G. F., Schaffer, N., Korhan, J., & Safko, L. (2013). *2014; Social Marketing Digital Book Set*. John Wiley & Sons Inc.

Granitz, N., & Forman, H. (2015). Building self-brand connections: Exploring brand stories through a transmedia perspective. *Journal of Brand Management*, *22*(1), 38–59. doi:10.1057/bm.2015.1

Gu, B., Tang, Q., & Whinston, A. B. (2013). The influence of online word-of-mouth on long tail formation. *Decision Support Systems*, *56*, 474–481. doi:10.1016/j.dss.2012.11.004

Hansen, S. S., & Lee, J. K. (2013). What Drives Consumers to Pass Along Marketer-Generated eWOM in Social Network Games? Social and Game Factors in Play. *Journal of Theoretical and Applied Electronic Commerce Research*, *8*(1), 53–10.

Hautz, J., Füller, J., Hutter, K., & Thürridl, C. (2014). Let Users Generate Your Video Ads? The Impact of Video Source and Quality on Consumers' Perceptions and Intended Behaviors. *Journal of Interactive Marketing*, *28*(1), 1–15. doi:10.1016/j.intmar.2013.06.003

He, S., & Wen, N. (2015). A Cautious Pursuit of Risk in Online Word-Of-Mouth: The Effect of Truncated Distribution on Consumer Decisions. *Advances in Consumer Research. Association for Consumer Research (U. S.)*, *43*, 736.

Herrero, Ã., Martín, H. S., & Hernández, J. M. (2015). How online search behavior is influenced by user-generated content on review websites and hotel interactive websites: 1. *International Journal of Contemporary Hospitality Management*, *27*(7), 1573–1597. doi:10.1108/IJCHM-05-2014-0255

Homburg, C., Ehm, L., & Artz, M. (2015). Measuring and managing consumer sentiment in an online community environment. *JMR, Journal of Marketing Research*, *52*(5), 629–641. doi:10.1509/jmr.11.0448

Hong, H., Xu, D., Xu, D., Wang, G. A., & Fan, W. (2017). An empirical study on the impact of online word-of-mouth sources on retail sales. *Information Discovery and Delivery*, *45*(1), 30–35. doi:10.1108/IDD-11-2016-0039

Hsu, C., Chuan-Chuan Lin, J., & Chiang, H. (2013). The effects of blogger recommendations on customers' online shopping intentions. *Internet Research*, *23*(1), 69–88. doi:10.1108/10662241311295782

Huang, Y., Chen, C. H., & Khoo, L. P. (2012). Products classification in emotional design using a basic-emotion based semantic differential method. *International Journal of Industrial Ergonomics*, *42*(6), 569–580. doi:10.1016/j.ergon.2012.09.002

Hutton, G., & Fosdick, M. (2011). The globalisation of SM, consumer relationships with brand evolve in the digital age. *Journal of Advertising Research*, *51*(4), 564–570. doi:10.2501/JAR-51-4-564-570

Jiao, Y., Ertz, M., Jo, M., & Sarigollu, E. (2018). Social value, content value, and brand equity in social media brand communities: A comparison of Chinese and US consumers. *International Marketing Review*, *35*(1), 18–41. doi:10.1108/IMR-07-2016-0132

Jiao, Y., Gao, J., & Yang, J. (2014). Social value and content value in social media: Two ways to flow. *Journalof Advanced Management Science*, *3*(4), 299–306.

Jin, S. V., & Phua, J. (2016). Making Reservations Online: The Impact of Consumer-Written and System-Aggregated User-Generated Content (UGC) in Travel Booking Websites on Consumers' Behavioral Intentions. *Journal of Travel & Tourism Marketing*, *33*(1), 101–117. doi:10.1080/10548408.2015.1038419

Kamboj, S., & Sarmah, B. (2018). Construction and validation of the customer social participation in brand communities scale. *Internet Research*, *28*(1), 46–73. doi:10.1108/IntR-01-2017-0011

Kamboj, S., Sarmah, B., Gupta, S., & Dwivedi, Y. (2018). Examining branding co-creation in brand communities on social media: Applying the paradigm of Stimulus-Organism-Response. *International Journal of Information Management*, *39*, 169–185. doi:10.1016/j.ijinfomgt.2017.12.001

Kandampully, J., Zhang, T., & Bilgihan, A. (2015). Customer loyalty: A review and future directions with a special focus on the hospitality industry. *International Journal of Contemporary Hospitality Management*, *27*(3), 379–414. doi:10.1108/IJCHM-03-2014-0151

Kao, T., Yang, M., Wu, J. B., & Cheng, Y. (2016). Co-creating value with consumers through social media. *Journal of Services Marketing*, *30*(2), 141–151. doi:10.1108/JSM-03-2014-0112

Kaplan, A. M., & Haenlein, M. (2010). Users of the world, unite! The challenges and opportunities of Social Media. *Business Horizons*, *53*(1), 59–68. doi:10.1016/j.bushor.2009.09.003

Kaur, P., Dhir, A., Rajala, R., & Dwivedi, Y. (2018). Why people use online social media brand communities: A consumption value theory perspective. *Online Information Review*, *42*(2), 205–221. doi:10.1108/OIR-12-2015-0383

Kim, A. J., & Johnson, K. K. (2016). Power of consumers using social media: Examining the influences of brand-related user-generated content on Facebook. *Computers in Human Behavior*, *58*, 98–108. doi:10.1016/j.chb.2015.12.047

Kim, J. (2012). The institutionalisation of YouTube: From user-generated content to professionally generated content. *Media Culture & Society*, *34*(1), 53–67. doi:10.1177/0163443711427199

Kim, M., & Lee, M. (2017). Brand-related user-generated content on social media: The roles of source and sponsorship. *Internet Research*, *27*(5), 1085–1103. doi:10.1108/IntR-07-2016-0206

Kim, S. H., Park, N., & Park, S. H. (2013). Exploring the Effects of Online Word of Mouth and Expert Reviews on Theatrical Movies' Box Office Success. *Journal of Media Economics*, *26*(2), 98–114. doi:10.1080/08997764.2013.785551

King, C., So, K. K. F., & Sparks, B. (2014). Customer Engagement with Tourism Brands: Scale Development and Validation. *Journal of Hospitality & Tourism Research (Washington, D.C.)*, *38*(3), 304–332. doi:10.1177/1096348012451456

King, C., So, K. K. F., Sparks, B. A., & Wang, Y. (2016). The Role of Customer Engagement in Building Consumer Loyalty to Tourism Brands. *Journal of Travel Research*, *55*(1), 64–78. doi:10.1177/0047287514541008

King, R.A., Racherla, P. & Bush, V.D. (2014). What We Know and Don't Know About Online Word-of-Mouth: A Review and Synthesis of the Literature. *Journal of Interactive Marketing, 28*(3), 167-183.

Kizgin, H., Jamal, A., Dey, B. L., & Rana, N. P. (2018). The Impact of Social Media on Consumers' Acculturation and Purchase Intentions. *Information Systems Frontiers*, *20*(3), 503–514. doi:10.100710796-017-9817-4

Kumar, A., Bezawada, R., Rishika, R., Janakiraman, R., & Kannan, P. K. (2015). From Social to Sale: The Effects of Firm Generated Content in Social Media on Customer Behavior. *Journal of Marketing*, *80*(1), 7–25. doi:10.1509/jm.14.0249

Kuo, Y., & Hou, J. (2017). Oppositional Brand Loyalty in Online Brand Communities: Perspectives on Social Identity Theory and Consumer-Brand. *Journal of Electronic Commerce Research*, *18*(3), 254.

Labrecque, L. I. (2014). Fostering Consumer–Brand Relationships in Social Media Environments: The Role of Parasocial Interaction. *Journal of Interactive Marketing*, *28*(2), 134–148. doi:10.1016/j.intmar.2013.12.003

Le, T. D. (2018). Influence of WOM and content type on online engagement in consumption communities: The information flow from discussion forums to Facebook. *Online Information Review*, *42*(2), 161–175. doi:10.1108/OIR-09-2016-0246

Lee, I. (2017). A study of the effect of social shopping deals on online reviews. *Industrial Management & Data Systems*, *117*(10), 2227–2240. doi:10.1108/IMDS-09-2016-0378

Lee, K., & Carter, S. (2011). Global marketing management. *Strategic Direction*, *27*(1). doi:10.1108d.2011.05627aae.001

Lee, S., & Choeh, J. Y. (2018). The interactive impact of online word-of-mouth and review helpfulness on box office revenue. *Management Decision*, *56*(4), 849–866. doi:10.1108/MD-06-2017-0561

Lee, T. Y., & Bradlow, E. T. (2011). Automatic marketing research using online customer reviews. *JMR, Journal of Marketing Research*, *48*(October), 881–894. doi:10.1509/jmkr.48.5.881

Lee, Y., & Wu, W. (2015). Effects of Medical Disputes on Internet Communications of Negative Emotions and Negative Online Word-of-Mouth. *Psychological Reports*, *117*(1), 251–270. doi:10.2466/21.PR0.117c13z1 PMID:26226491

Leibtag, A. (2014). *2013; The Digital Crown: Winning at Content on the Web*. Morgan Kaufmann Publishers Inc.

Leung, L. (2009). User-generated content on the internet: An examination of gratifications, civic engagement and psychological empowerment. *New Media & Society*, *11*(8), 1327–1347. doi:10.1177/1461444809341264

Li, Y. M., Chen, H. M., Liou, J. H., & Lin, L. F. (2014). Creating social intelligence for product portfolio design. *Decision Support Systems*, *66*, 123–134. doi:10.1016/j.dss.2014.06.013

Li, Y. M., & Shiu, Y. (2012). A diffusion mechanism for social advertising over microblogs. *Decision Support Systems*, *54*(1), 9–22. doi:10.1016/j.dss.2012.02.012

Liang, W. K., & Corkindale, D. (2016). The Effect of Online Word-of-Mouth on Risk Assessment for an Experience Service as Price Acceptability Changes. *Services Marketing Quarterly*, *37*(3), 156–170. doi:10.1080/15332969.2016.1184540

Liu, Q., Karahanna, E., & Watson, R.T. (2011). Unveiling user-generated content: Designing websites to best present customer reviews. Elsevier Inc.

Liu, X., Burns, A. C., & Hou, Y. (2017). An Investigation of Brand-Related User-Generated Content on Twitter. *Journal of Advertising*, *46*(2), 236–247. doi:10.1080/00913367.2017.1297273

Lu, Q., Ye, Q., & Law, R. (2014). Moderating Effects of Product Heterogeneity Between Online Word-Of-Mouth and Hotel Sales. *Journal of Electronic Commerce Research*, *15*(1), 1.

Lu, W., & Stepchenkova, S. (2015). User-Generated Content as a Research Mode in Tourism and Hospitality Applications: Topics, Methods, and Software. *Journal of Hospitality Marketing & Management*, *24*(2), 119–154. doi:10.1080/19368623.2014.907758

Luo, B., Zhang, Z., Liu, Y., & Gao, W. (2016). What does it say and who said it? The contingent effects of online word of mouth in China. *Nankai Business Review International*, *7*(4), 474–490. doi:10.1108/NBRI-12-2015-0035

Mahoney, L. M., & Tang, T. (2016). *Strategic Social Media: From Marketing to Social Change* (1st ed.). Hoboken, NJ: Wiley-Blackwell. doi:10.1002/9781119370680

Malthouse, E. C., Calder, B. J., Kim, S. J., & Vandenbosch, M. (2016). Evidence that user-generated content that produces engagement increases purchase behaviours. *Journal of Marketing Management*, *32*(5-6), 427–444. doi:10.1080/0267257X.2016.1148066

Marine-Roig, E., & Anton Clavé, S. (2016). A detailed method for destination image analysis using user-generated content. *Information Technology & Tourism*, *15*(4), 341–364. doi:10.100740558-015-0040-1

Martínez-Navarro, J., & Bigné, E. (2017). The Value Of Marketer-generated Content On Social Network Sites: Media Antecedents and Behavioral Responses. *Journal of Electronic Commerce Research*, *18*(1), 52.

Mathieson, R. (2010). *The On-Demand Brand: 10 Rules for Digital Marketing Success in an Anytime, Everywhere World* (1st ed.). Amacom, Saranac Lake.

Matzat, U. U., & Snijders, C. C. (2012). Rebuilding trust in online shops on consumer review sites: Sellers' responses to user-generated complaints. *Journal of Computer-Mediated Communication*, *18*(1), 62–79. doi:10.1111/j.1083-6101.2012.01594.x

McNally, M. B., Trosow, S. E., Wong, L., Whippey, C., Burkell, J., & McKenzie, P. J. (2012). User-generated online content 2: Policy implications. *First Monday*, *17*(6). doi:10.5210/fm.v17i6.3913

Merrilees, B. (2016). Interactive brand experience pathways to customer-brand engagement and value co-creation. *Journal of Product and Brand Management*, *25*(5), 402–408. doi:10.1108/JPBM-04-2016-1151

Moon, S., Park, Y., & Seog Kim, Y. (2014). The impact of text product reviews on sales. *European Journal of Marketing*, *48*(11/12), 2176–2197. doi:10.1108/EJM-06-2013-0291

Munar, A. M., & Jacobsen, J. K. S. (2013). Trust and Involvement in Tourism Social Media and Web-Based Travel Information Sources. *Scandinavian Journal of Hospitality and Tourism*, *13*(1), 1–19. doi:10.1080/15022250.2013.764511

Odden, L. (2012). *Optimise: How to Attract and Engage More Customers by Integrating SEO, Social Media, and Content Marketing*. Somerset: Wiley.

OECD. (2006). *OECD Information Technology Outlook, 2006*. OECD. Available at www.oecd.org/sti/ito

OECD. (2007). *Communication Outlook, 2007*. Paris: OECD.

Ozuem, W. (Ed.). (2016). *Competitive social media marketing strategies*. IGI Global. doi:10.4018/978-1-4666-9776-8

Ozuem, W., & Azemi, Y. (Eds.). (2017). *Digital Marketing Strategies for Fashion and Luxury Brands*. IGI Global.

Ozuem, W., & Azemi, Y. (2018). Online Service Failure and Recovery Strategies in Luxury Brands: A View from Justice Theory. In Digital Marketing Strategies for Fashion and Luxury Brands (pp. 108-125). IGI Global. doi:10.4018/978-1-5225-2697-1.ch005

Ozuem, W., Howell, K. E., & Lancaster, G. (2008). Communicating in the new interactive marketspace. *European Journal of Marketing*, *42*(9/10), 1059–1083. doi:10.1108/03090560810891145

Ozuem, W., & Lancaster, G. (2012). Technology-induced customer services in the developing countries. In *Service science research, strategy and innovation: Dynamic knowledge management methods* (pp. 185–201). IGI Global. doi:10.4018/978-1-4666-0077-5.ch012

Ozuem, W., & Lancaster, G. (2014). Recovery strategies in on-line service failure. In A. Ghorbani (Ed.), *Marketing in the cyber era: Strategies and emerging trends* (pp. 143–159). Hershey, PA: IGI Global. doi:10.4018/978-1-4666-4864-7.ch010

Ozuem, W., & Lancaster, G. (2015). Examining the Dynamics of Value Propositions in Digital Books: A Social Constructivist Perspective. In Handbook of Research on Scholarly Publishing and Research Methods (pp. 295-311). IGI Global. doi:10.4018/978-1-4666-7409-7.ch015

Ozuem, W., & Mulloo, B. N. (2016). Basics of mobile marketing strategy. In *Competitive Social Media Marketing Strategies* (pp. 155–172). IGI Global. doi:10.4018/978-1-4666-9776-8.ch008

Ozuem, W., & O'Keeffe, A. (2015). Towards Leadership Marketing: An Exploratory and Empirical Study. In Marketing and Consumer Behavior: Concepts, Methodologies, Tools, and Applications (pp. 1570-1590). IGI Global.

Ozuem, W., Patel, A., Howell, K. E., & Lancaster, G. (2017). An exploration of consumers' response to online service recovery initiatives. *International Journal of Market Research*, *59*(1), 97–115.

Ozuem, W., Pinho, C. A., & Azemi, Y. (2016). User-generated content and perceived customer value. In *Competitive Social Media Marketing Strategies* (pp. 50–63). IGI Global. doi:10.4018/978-1-4666-9776-8.ch003

Ozuem, W., Prasad, J., & Lancaster, G. (2018). Exploiting online social gambling for marketing communications. *Journal of Strategic Marketing*, *26*(3), 258–282. doi:10.1080/0965254X.2016.1211728

Ozuem, W., & Thomas, T. (2015). Inside the Small Island Economies: Loyalty Strategies in the Telecommunications Sector. In Handbook of Research on Global Business Opportunities (pp. 316-349). IGI Global.

Ozuem, W., Thomas, T., & Lancaster, G. (2016). The influence of customer loyalty on small island economies: An empirical and exploratory study. *Journal of Strategic Marketing*, *24*(6), 37–41. doi:10.1080/0965254X.2015.1011205

Ozuem, W. F. (2004). *Conceptualising marketing communication in the new marketing paradigm: A postmodern perspective*. Universal-Publishers.

Palmer, A. (2009). *Study: Online Shoppers Trust Customer Reviews More than Friends*. Progressive Grocer.

Palmer, R., Cockton, J., Cooper, G., & Sc, M. (2007). *Managing marketing*. London: Butterworth-Heinemann.

Pan, Y., & Zhang, J. Q. (2011). Born Unequal: A Study of the Helpfulness of User-Generated Product Reviews. *Journal of Retailing*, *87*(4), 598–612. doi:10.1016/j.jretai.2011.05.002

Papthanassis Rodgers, S. L., & Thorson, E. (2017). *Digital advertising: theory and research* (3rd ed.). Abingdon, UK: Routledge. doi:10.4324/9781315623252

Pfeffer, J., Zorbach, T., & Carley, K. M. (2014). Understanding online firestorms: Negative word-of-mouth dynamics in social media networks. *Journal of Marketing Communications*, *20*(1-2), 117–128. doi:10.1080/13527266.2013.797778

Powell, G., Groves, S., & Dimos, J. (2011). *ROI of Social Media: How to Improve the Return on Your Social Marketing Investment, 1* (1st ed.). Hoboken, NJ: Wiley.

Prendergast, G., Ko, D., & Siu Yin, V. Y. (2010). Online word of mouth and consumer purchase intentions. *International Journal of Advertising*, *29*(5), 687–708. doi:10.2501/S0265048710201427

Ransbotham, S., Kane, G. C., & Lurie, N. H. (2012). Network Characteristics and the Value of Collaborative User-Generated Content. *Marketing Science*, *31*(3), 387–405. doi:10.1287/mksc.1110.0684

Rathore, A. K., Ilavarasan, P. V., & Dwivedi, Y. K. (2016). Social media content and product co-creation: An emerging paradigm. *Journal of Enterprise Information Management*, *29*(1), 7–18. doi:10.1108/JEIM-06-2015-0047

Renton, M., & Simmonds, H. (2017). Like is a verb: Exploring tie strength and casual brand use effects on brand attitudes and consumer online goal achievement. *Journal of Product and Brand Management*, *26*(4), 365–374. doi:10.1108/JPBM-03-2016-1125

Richard, M., & Habibi, M. R. (2016). Advanced modeling of online consumer behavior: The moderating roles of hedonism and culture. *Journal of Business Research*, *69*(3), 1103–1119. doi:10.1016/j.jbusres.2015.08.026

Ring, A., Tkaczynski, A., & Dolnicar, S. (2016). 2014; "Word-of-Mouth Segments: Online, Offline, Visual or Verbal? *Journal of Travel Research*, *55*(4), 481–492. doi:10.1177/0047287514563165

Roberts, M. L., Barker, M. S., Zahay, D. L., Bormann, N. F., & Barker, D. (2016). *Social media marketing: a strategic approach* (2nd ed South-Western.

Rodgers, S. L. & Thorson, E. (2017). Digital advertising: theory and research (3rd ed.). Routledge.

Rossmann, A., Ranjan, K. R., & Sugathan, P. (2016). Drivers of user engagement in eWoM communication. *Journal of Services Marketing*, *30*(5), 541–553. doi:10.1108/JSM-01-2015-0013

Ryan, D. (2014). *Understanding digital marketing: marketing strategies for engaging the digital generation* (3rd ed.). London: KoganPage.

Ryan, D. (2017). *Understanding digital marketing: marketing strategies for engaging the digital generation* (4th ed.). London: KoganPage.

Ryan, D., & Jones, C. (2012). *Understanding digital marketing: marketing strategies for engaging the digital generation* (2nd ed.). London: Kogan Page.

Ryan, D., & Jones, C. (2014). *The Best Digital Marketing Campaigns in the World II, Second* (1st ed.). London: Kogan Page Ltd.

Sabate, F., Berbegal-Mirabent, J., Cañabate, A., & Lebherz, P. R. (2014). Factors influencing popularity of branded content in Facebook fan pages. *European Management Journal*, *32*(6), 1001–1011. doi:10.1016/j.emj.2014.05.001

Saboo, A. R., Kumar, V., & Ramani, G. (2016). Evaluating the impact of social media activities on human brand sales. *International Journal of Research in Marketing*, *33*(3), 524–541. doi:10.1016/j.ijresmar.2015.02.007

Sadek, Elwy, & Eldallal. (2018). The impact of social media brand communication on consumer-based brand equity dimensions through Facebook in fast moving consumer goods: The case of Egypt. *Journal of Business and Retail Management Research, 12*(2).

Sandars, J., & Walsh, K. (2009). 2008; "The use of online word of mouth opinion in online learning: A questionnaire survey. *Medical Teacher*, *31*(4), 325–327. doi:10.1080/01421590802204403 PMID:18937096

Schaffer, N., Safko, L., Korhan, J., Goodman, G. F., Stratten, S., & Zarrella, D. (2013). *Social Marketing Digital Book Set* (1st ed.). Hoboken, NJ: John Wiley & Sons Inc.

Schultz, C. D. (2016). Insights from consumer interactions on a social networking site: Findings from six apparel retail brands. *Electronic Markets*, *26*(3), 203–217. doi:10.100712525-015-0209-7

Schultz, C. D. (2017). Proposing to your fans: Which brand post characteristics drive consumer engagement activities on social media brand pages? *Electronic Commerce Research and Applications*, *26*, 23–34. doi:10.1016/j.elerap.2017.09.005

Schulz, S., Pauw, G., Clercq, O., Desmet, B., Hoste, V., Daelemans, W., & Macken, L. (2016). Multimodular Text Normalisation of Dutch User-Generated Content. *ACM Transactions on Intelligent Systems and Technology*, *7*(4), 1–22. doi:10.1145/2850422

Scott, D. M. (2015). *The New Rules of Marketing and PR: How to Use Social Media, Online Video, Mobile Applications, Blogs, News Releases, and Viral Marketing to Reach Buyers Directly* (5th ed.). New York: John Wiley & Sons Inc. doi:10.1002/9781119172499.ch02

Seadle, M. & Greifender, E. (2014). *Structuring the digital domain*. Emerald Group Publishing Ltd.

Shao, G. (2009). Understanding the appeal of user-generated media: A uses and gratification perspective. *Internet Research*, *19*(1), 7–25. doi:10.1108/10662240910927795

Sheldrake, P., & Sheldrake, P. P. I. (2011). *The Business of Influence: Reframing Marketing and PR for the Digital Age, 1* (1st ed.). New York: Wiley.

Shneiderman, B., Preece, J., & Pirolli, P. (2011). Realizing the value of social media requires innovative computing research. *Communications of the ACM*, *54*(9), 34–37. doi:10.1145/1995376.1995389

Simon, J.P. (2016). User generated content – users, community of users and firms: toward new sources of co-innovation? *Info, 18*(6), 4-25.

Smith, A. N., Fischer, E., & Yongjian, C. (2012). How Does Brand-related User-generated Content Differ across YouTube, Facebook, and Twitter? *Journal of Interactive Marketing*, *26*(2), 102–113. doi:10.1016/j.intmar.2012.01.002

Smith, P., & Chaffey, D. (2012). *Emarketing excellence*. St. Louis, MO: Taylor and Francis. doi:10.4324/9780080504896

Smith, P. R., & Zook, Z. (2011). *Marketing communications: integrating offline and online with social media* (5th ed.). London: Kogan Page.

Sparks, B. A., So, K. K. F., & Bradley, G. L. (2016). Responding to negative online reviews: The effects of hotel responses on customer inferences of trust and concern. *Tourism Management*, *53*, 74–85. doi:10.1016/j.tourman.2015.09.011

Stareva, I. (2014). *Social Media and the Rebirth of PR: The Emergence of Social Media as a Change Driver for PR* (1st ed.). Hamburg: Anchor Academic Publishing.

Statista. (2018). *How do online customer reviews affect your opinion of a local business?* Available at https://www.statista.com/statistics/315751/online-review-customer-opinion/

Sterne, J. (2010). *Social media metrics: how to measure and optimise your marketing investment*. Hoboken, NJ: John Wiley & Sons.

Stoel, M. D., & Muhanna, W. A. (2016). Online word of mouth: Implications for the name-your-own-price channel. *Decision Support Systems*, *91*, 37–47. doi:10.1016/j.dss.2016.07.006

Sun, H. (2013). Moderating Role of Online Word of Mouth on Website Attributes and Consumer Trust in E-commerce Environment. *Journal of Applied Sciences (Faisalabad)*, *13*(12), 2316–2320. doi:10.3923/jas.2013.2316.2320

Susarla, A., Oh, J., & Tan, Y. (2012). Social Networks and the Diffusion of User-Generated Content: Evidence from YouTube. *Information Systems Research*, *23*(1), 23–41. doi:10.1287/isre.1100.0339

Tafesse, W. (2016). An experiential model of consumer engagement in social media. *Journal of Product and Brand Management*, *25*(5), 424–434. doi:10.1108/JPBM-05-2015-0879

Tang, C., Mehl, M. R., Eastlick, M. A., He, W., & Card, N. A. (2016). A longitudinal exploration of the relations between electronic word-of-mouth indicators and firms' profitability: Findings from the banking industry. *International Journal of Information Management*, *36*(6), 1124–1132. doi:10.1016/j.ijinfomgt.2016.03.015

Tang, L. (2017). Mine Your Customers or Mine Your Business: The Moderating Role of Culture in Online Word-of-Mouth Reviews. *Journal of International Marketing*, *25*(2), 88–110. doi:10.1509/jim.16.0030

Tang, T., Fang, E., & Wang, F. (2014). Is neutral really neutral? The effects of neutral user-generated content on product sales. *Journal of Marketing*, *78*(4), 41–58. doi:10.1509/jm.13.0301

Thomsett-Scott, B. C. (2014). *Marketing with Social Media: A LITA Guide*. Chicago: ALA TechSource.

Tirunillai, S., & Tellis, G. J. (2012). Does Chatter Really Matter? Dynamics of User-Generated Content and Stock Performance. *Marketing Science*, *31*(2), 198–215. doi:10.1287/mksc.1110.0682

Viswanathan, V., Malthouse, E. C., Maslowska, E., Hoornaert, S., & Van den Poel, D. (2018). Dynamics between social media engagement, firm-generated content, and live and time-shifted TV viewing. *Journal of Service Management*, *29*(3), 378–398. doi:10.1108/JOSM-09-2016-0241

Wan, F., & Ren, F. (2017). The Effect Of Firm Marketing Content On Product Sales: Evidence From a Mobile Social Media Platform. *Journal of Electronic Commerce Research*, *18*(4), 288–302.

Wang, P., Sun, L., & Peng, L. (2013). Modeling product attitude formation process in online word-of-mouth. *Nankai Business Review International*, *4*(3), 212–229. doi:10.1108/NBRI-07-2013-0025

Wang, X., & Li, Y. (2016). How Trust and Need Satisfaction Motivate Producing User-Generated Content. *Journal of Computer Information Systems*, *57*(1), 49–57. doi:10.1080/08874417.2016.1181493

Weber, L., & Henderson, L. L. (2014). *The Digital Marketer: Ten New Skills You Must Learn to Stay Relevant and Customer-Centric*. John Wiley & Sons Inc.

Webster, J. G. (2014). *Marketplace of Attention: How Audiences Take Shape in a Digital Age*. MIT Press.

Weiger, W. H., Wetzel, H. A., & Hammerschmidt, M. (2017). Leveraging marketer-generated appeals in online brand communities: An individual user-level analysis. *Journal of Service Management*, *28*(1), 133–156. doi:10.1108/JOSM-11-2015-0378

Wen, I. (2009). Factors affecting the online travel buying decision: A review. *International Journal of Contemporary Hospitality Management*, *21*(6), 752–765. doi:10.1108/09596110910975990

Williams, R., van der Wiele, T., van Iwaarden, J., & Eldridge, S. (2010). The importance of user-generated content: The case of hotels. *The TQM Journal*, *22*(2), 117–128. doi:10.1108/17542731011024246

Willis, E., & Wang, Y. (2016). Blogging the brand: Meaning transfer and the case of Weight Watchers' online community. *Journal of Brand Management*, *23*(4), 457–471. doi:10.1057/bm.2016.16

Wood, N. T., & Burkhalter, J. N. (2014). Tweet this, not that: A comparison between brand promotions in microblogging environments using celebrity and company-generated tweets. *Journal of Marketing Communications*, *20*(1-2), 129–146. doi:10.1080/13527266.2013.797784

Xie, K., & Lee, Y. (2015). Social Media and Brand Purchase: Quantifying the Effects of Exposures to Earned and Owned Social Media Activities in a Two-Stage Decision Making Model. *Journal of Management Information Systems*, *32*(2), 204–238. doi:10.1080/07421222.2015.1063297

Xie, K. L., Zhang, Z., Zhang, Z., Singh, A., & Lee, S. K. (2016). Effects of managerial response on consumer eWOM and hotel performance: Evidence from TripAdvisor. *International Journal of Contemporary Hospitality Management*, *28*(9), 2013–2034. doi:10.1108/IJCHM-06-2015-0290

Xue, F., & Zhou, P. (2010). 2011; "The Effects of Product Involvement and Prior Experience on Chinese Consumers' Responses to Online Word of Mouth. *Journal of International Consumer Marketing*, *23*(1), 45–58. doi:10.1080/08961530.2011.524576

Yadav, M., Kamboj, S., & Rahman, Z. (2016). Customer co-creation through social media: The case of 'Crash the Pepsi IPL 2015'. *Journal of Direct, Data and Digital Marketing Practice*, *17*(4), 259–271. doi:10.1057/dddmp.2016.4

Yan, Y. & Du, S. (2016). Empirical Study for the Influence Factors of Customer Satisfaction Based on B2C Online Shopping. *Revista Ibérica de Sistemas e Tecnologias de Informação, E14*, 300.

Yang, J., Zheng, R., Zhao, L., & Gupta, S. (2017). Enhancing customer brand experience and loyalty through enterprise microblogs: Empirical evidence from a communication framework perspective. *Information Technology & People*, *30*(3), 580–601. doi:10.1108/ITP-09-2015-0219

Yeh, C. (2015). Online word-of-mouth as a predictor of television rating. *Online Information Review*, *39*(6), 831–847. doi:10.1108/OIR-01-2015-0033

Yoo, B., Donthu, N., & Lee, S. (2000). An examination of selected marketing mix elements and brand equity. *Journal of the Academy of Marketing Science*, *28*(2), 195–211. doi:10.1177/0092070300282002

Yoon, S., & Han, H. (2012). Experiential approach to the determinants of online word-of-mouth behavior. *Journal of Global Scholars of Marketing Science*, *22*(3), 218–234. doi:10.1080/21639159.2012.699219

Zahay, D. (2015). *The impact of digital shopping channels on multi-channel marketing and attribution in the changing retail landscape*. Emerald Group Publishing Ltd.

Zhan, Y., Liu, R., Li, Q., Leischow, S. J., & Zeng, D. D. (2017). Identifying Topics for E-Cigarette User-Generated Contents: A Case Study From Multiple Social Media Platforms. *Journal of Medical Internet Research, 19*(1), e24. doi:10.2196/jmir.5780 PMID:28108428

Zhang, X., Yu, Y., Li, H., & Lin, Z. (2016). Sentimental interplay between structured and unstructured user-generated contents. *Online Information Review, 40*(1), 119–145. doi:10.1108/OIR-04-2015-0101

Zhang, Z., Ye, Q., Song, H., & Liu, T. (2015). The structure of customer satisfaction with cruise-line services: An empirical investigation based on online word of mouth. *Current Issues in Tourism, 18*(5), 450–464. doi:10.1080/13683500.2013.776020

Zheng, X., Cheung, C. M. K., Lee, M. K. O., & Liang, L. (2015). Building brand loyalty through user engagement in online brand communities in social networking sites. *Information Technology & People, 28*(1), 90–106. doi:10.1108/ITP-08-2013-0144

Zhou, W., & Duan, W. (2015). An empirical study of how third-party websites influence the feedback mechanism between online Word-of-Mouth and retail sales. *Decision Support Systems, 76*, 14–23. doi:10.1016/j.dss.2015.03.010

KEY TERMS AND DEFINITIONS

Brand-Oriented UGC: Brand-oriented UGC is any content related to a brand and created by a user with the purpose of sharing content with others using social media tools.

Consumer Buying Behavior: The total buying behavior of the ultimate consumer when purchasing a product or service.

Consumer Engagement: Consumer engagement is an action-oriented relationship and commitment that extends beyond purchasing.

Customer Trust: A belief in the given content of a social commerce organisation that enhances e-word-of-mouth and the purchase intentions of customers. Customers are more likely to buy from people they trust or purchase a product or service that performs what it claims.

E-Word-of-Mouth: E-word-of-mouth can be described as a deliberate influencer of customer-to-customer interactions using online social networking tools. Consumers can generate online content and share such content with their online networks with the purpose of creating word-of-mouth reviews for brands.

Social Media Networks/Platforms: Groups of internet-based applications that facilitate the creation and exchange of personal information or contents or participating in a social networking User-Generated Content

User-Generated Content: UGC is any form of digital content users generated and shared online with other users. These contents produced can be viewed and shared by other users of the service or websites.

Chapter 10
The Impacts of Omni-Channel Purchasing Behavior on Service Quality

Elena Patten
Corvinus University, Budapest

ABSTRACT

In omni-channel retailing, the combination of different retail channels along the different customer touchpoints has become the predominant purchasing pattern for customers. The consumers´ purchasing behavior has changed tremendously with the development of e-commerce. The so-called omni-channel customers tend to switch retail channels during their purchasing process. In order to address changing consumer behavior, omni-channel fashion retailing companies still need to learn how to be able to provide an excellent service to these customers. This chapter aims to investigate this phenomenon from the perspective of omni-channel customers.

INTRODUCTION

Retailing has changed fundamentally during the last decade (Neslin et al., 2006; Piotrowicz & Cuthbertson, 2014; Zhang et al., 2010). This development was mainly driven by technological and societal factors (Emrich, 2011; Hsieh & Tseng, 2018). In this context, the Internet was probably the most important technological invention (Patten & Rashid, 2015).

Several different kinds of leisure activities nowadays take place in the Internet. The use of social media websites, such as Facebook, Twitter or Instagram, has become an important activity of everyday life (Stokinger & Ozuem, 2015). The permanent usage of mobile devices together with the dominance of Social Media has created the situation, that customers virtually bring their whole social network to a store (Piotrowicz & Cuthbertson, 2014). The borders between offline and online activities are blurred, and retailers use Social Media as an important instrument of communication (Ozuem, Helal, Howell and Lancaster, 2018).

DOI: 10.4018/978-1-5225-7344-9.ch010

The result is that retailers are continuing to develop their online shops. Over the past few years, several different online retailing business models have developed in the market (for a review, see Bächle & Lehmann, 2010). During the initial phase, 'pure online players,' such as Amazon and eBay, launched their online shops. In the next phase, 'shopping comparison' websites appeared on the market. These players allowed customers to compare products on a single page and to read recommendations and critiques written by previous users. The 'optimization and scale-up' phase, which started from 2005, offered new system solutions and service providers. Since 2008, many brick-and-mortar retailers have been launching online shops as an addition to their offline channels and so have become multichannel retailers (Heinemann, 2013). Then, these retailers focussed on the integration of the different retail channels and offered 'cross-channel'- services, such as 'click and collect', the ability to order and return or exchange goods in-store, ordering while in-store, using own mobile device or self-service technology provided by the retailer (Piotrowicz & Cuthbertson, 2014). Ultimately, 'clicks and mortar' retailers aim to offer fully integrated channels to become omni-channel retailers (Saghiri, Wilding, Mena, & Bourlakis, 2017; Verhoef, Kannan, & Inman, 2015). This chapter will focus on omni-channel retailing. It will, therefore, aim to investigate the concept of integration in omni-channel retailing by considering the different elements of the retail mix. Furthermore, it will elaborate the key drivers of perceived omni-channel service quality.

THEORETICAL CONTEXT: THE CONCEPT OF INTEGRATION

Research about omni-channel retailing embraces the concept of "integration" of the different operated channels within an organization (Ailawadi & Farris, 2017). Channel integration initially meant that a retailer should provide a 'seamless' customer experience between stores and online shops; customers should be able to easily switch channels during their interaction with the retailer (Goersch, 2002; Seck, 2013). However, important questions remain unanswered yet: Does a seamless customer experience automatically mean a full integration? In other words, does it mean the more integrated the better? For retailers, the level of integration is a difficult managerial decision. They face various challenges since channels might be different regarding purposes and features, cost structure and competitors (Berry et al., 2010). Studies have investigated the optimal level of integration in certain areas. Related literature has devoted to several aspects of the retail-mix. Mainly, a special focus has been set on integration of assortment (Emrich, Paul, & Rudolph, 2015; Mantrala et al., 2009), pricing and promotions (Vogel & Paul, 2015; Wolk & Ebling, 2010), fulfilment (Agatz, Fleischmann, & Van Nunen, 2008; Lang & Bressolles, 2013; Wolk & Ebling, 2010; Xing, Grant, McKinnon, & Fernie, 2010), and web- and store design integration (Emrich & Verhoef, 2015). However, none of the aforementioned areas have been completely resolved yet. Quite the contrary, there are still several areas for further investigation (Verhoef et al., 2015).

With regard to the assortment strategy of a retailer, it is deemed necessary to overcome the complex duty to offer an attractive assortment on the one hand side but avoid choice difficulty on the other hand side (Mantrala et al., 2009). There is a controversy in the reviewed literature about the degree of assortment integration in omni-channel retailing. Some researchers argue, that the assortment does not necessarily need to be integrated, when the target customer of the two channels is different (Berry et al., 2010; Neslin & Shankar, 2009). This is not the case for omni-channel customers, who switch retail channels during their purchases. However, other researchers argue that product consistency is crucial to provide a seamless shopping experience for the customer (Berman & Thelen, 2004). In practice, most of 'clicks and mortar' retailers nowadays apply an asymmetrical assortment strategy, which means, that they offer a larger assortment online than offline (Emrich et al., 2015). Emrich et al. (2015) investigated the impact of assortment integration on underlying assortment relations. They classified three different assortment relations. Either, assortments are substitutive (for instance, when a retailer sells two different kinds of similar shoes), or complementary (shoes and shoe crème), or independent (shoes and sun lotion). Emrich et al. found out that in any of the three assortment structures no integration of assortment is detrimental. However, they argued, that for an omni-channel retailer with a substitutive assortment, the perceived variety is lower when the assortment strategy is asymmetrical, because customers tend to disesteem the decreased channel choice and autonomy.

Regarding pricing and promotions, 'clicks and mortar' retailers often need to find a way out of a dilemma: Generally, customers expect products online to be equally or even less expensive than in-store (Zhang et al., 2010). But at the same time, customers expect integrated channels with a consistence pricing strategy among channels (Seck, 2013). How can retailers overcome this dilemma without loosing market share and unsatisfied customers? In practise, retailers mostly tend towards a partial integration of their pricing (Wolk & Ebling, 2010). They charge the same-posted prices among their different channels, because they fear that different prices might lead to customers' confusion and resentment. But, at the same time many retailers apply channel specific price promotions or charging handling and shipping costs (Neslin et al., 2006). In the reviewed literature, most of the researchers argue in favour of a consisting pricing strategy for all channels of a retailer (Berman & Thelen, 2004; Vogel & Paul, 2015; Wolk & Ebling, 2010).

Wolk and Ebling (2010) developed a conceptual framework on the factors, which might influence a pricing strategy across channels, namely competition, offline reach, online reach, number of distribution channels, size of company, product type, and brand power. They argued, that the lower the level of competition in one segment is, the higher the extent of price differentiation is. Thus, market power has an impact on price differentiation. For Wolk and Ebling, physical distance is a criterion, which determines if customers have an easy access to a product or if they need to spend high transaction costs to get access. For retailers that operate multiple channels this means, that if he operates just few stores and apart from that sells his products online, the retailer will be able to operate both channels more separable. As a consequence, this retailer is more in a position that he can apply price differentiation online and offline. The increasing number of customers who buy online and furthermore use different channels of one retailer during their purchase process leads customers to easily have access to a retailer's overall offer. This will lead retailers to offer the same prices among their different retail channels. Regarding the number of distribution channels, the two researchers argue, that a customized operation of each channel means an increase of transaction costs and effort for the retailer. Concluding, the more channels a retailer operates, the less channel-based price differentiation he will apply. The size of company is therefore pivotal, that retailers, which face lower cost when engaging in price differentiation, will apply it more often. Normally big companies can leverage on strategic advantages such as an efficient organization, cheaper purchases or superior technologies. Thus, bigger retailing companies will more likely apply channel-based price differentiation. For certain product types, customers prefer one channel over another. For instance, customers prefer to buy clothing in-store, since they want to try it on and physically see and touch the item. So, if one channel is superior for the customer than another, it is more likely that customers will accept channel-based price differentiation and pay a higher price in that channel, which they prefer. Generally, branding decreases the customer's price sensitivity. But channel-based price differentiation might lead also to confusion and in turn decreases brand power (Wolk & Ebling, 2010).

Wolk and Ebling`s conceptual framework gives a valuable contribution to the debate of channel-based price differentiation. It is the first framework to conceptualize the different influencing factors considering customer (market), retailer and product characteristics.

However, channel-based price differentiation has certain positive and negative impacts on customer satisfaction: It positively affects their perceptions of value, increases relationship quality, and enhances repurchase intentions, but it also leads to perceptions of price unfairness and limits customer self-determination, which negatively affect retention outcomes (Vogel & Paul, 2015). It remains questionable, which of the mentioned criteria affect more the final choice of shopping location and furthermore the long-term relationship with the retailer: Would customers rather buy at a retailer with a higher perception of value or would they tend to buy at a competitor, where they find the pricing fairer?

A possible pricing strategy for omni-channel retailers, which embraces both- a high perception of value and price fairness, is considered as "self-matching pricing" (Kireyev, Kumar, & Ofek, 2015): Here, the retailer can set different prices across channels, but he will offer the lower price to the customer when he can supply evidence. Thus, 'self-matching policies, by design, offer retailers the flexibility of setting different prices across channels, while affording consumers the possibility of a consistent experience, presumably in line with the omni-channel philosophy' (Kireyev et al., 2015, p. 29).

Price promotions at omni-channel retailers have several within and across channel implications: Offline price promotions can reduce category sales online during the promotion period; furthermore, online promotions can reduce category sales offline during the promotion period; negative cross-channel effects are higher for loyal customers than for opportunists; and, the impact of online promotions on offline sales within the promoted category is higher than vice versa (Breugelmans & Campo, 2016).

One can conclude, that a successful management of pricing and promotions is a complex field in omni-channel retailing. It is deemed necessary to consider effects within and across channels and set a coherent pricing and promotion strategy.

Regarding fulfilment, a coherent omni-channel strategy should concern both the marketing mix and operations management (Agatz et al., 2008). In this respect fulfilment is an important component of a retailer's operations strategy. According to the reviewed fulfilment literature, omni-channel e-fulfilment can be considered as fulfilling online or in-store orders including warehousing, picking and order preparation, distribution, purchasing, delivery and returns (Agatz et al., 2008; Lang & Bressolles, 2013). For omni-channel customers, four dimensions of fulfilment can be considered as predominantly important, namely timeliness, availability, condition and return (Xing & Grant, 2006; Xing et al., 2010). Timeliness refers to several aspects, such as speed of delivery, choice of delivery date, or delivery within a certain time slot. Availability refers to the confirmation of availability, order tracking, or waiting time. Condition refers to order accuracy, order completeness, or order damage. Return refers to return policies, such as ease of return and return channel options, the promptness of collection and of replacement (Lang & Bressolles, 2013). For omni-channel retailers this means, that their supply chain management needs to be adapted to these specific customer needs. This has several impacts: (1) an online channel not only provides a physical product but also several related services, most notably delivery. The delivery service may range from making the product available for pick-up to time-specific home delivery. The management of this service component of e-fulfilment gives rise to novel planning issues. (2) The flexibility of an omni-channel retailer with respect to order promising and pricing, makes it necessary to imply an appropriate strategy. (3) The integration of different channels raises issues in inventory deployment, since different channels may require different service levels (Agatz et al., 2008). (4) E-fulfilment requirements are different across different product categories (Hu, Kumar, & Sumit, 2014).

THE OMNI-CHANNEL CUSTOMER JOURNEY

In omni-channel retailing, the combination of different retail channels along the different customer touchpoints has become the predominant purchasing pattern for customers (Mahrdt, Lessing, Wagner, & Geissler, 2013; Neslin et al., 2006).

The so-called 'research-shopper' phenomenon is described as a common tendency among customers to use one channel for search and another for purchase (Verhoef, Neslin, & Vroomen, 2007).

Shankar (2011) and Heinemann (2013) call the switch between different channels 'ropo', which basically has two meanings:

1. 'Research online and purchase offline' means that Internet users research online before making any purchase decision. They compare prices online, obtain information from the producer's webpage or read comments of other users of the same product. This trend is called "web-rooming", a wordplay of "show-rooming", where customers shop online, but use the store before they physically interact with the product (Verhoef et al., 2015). This purchase pattern has an important impact on the overall purchase process: In the past, a customer first decided about the retailer and then decided about the product that he wanted to buy from this retailer. Then, he went to the store to get information about different products in the assortment of this retailer. Most probably, he also frequented other retailers in order to compare the offer and afterwards made their purchase decision. Nowadays, the customer primarily decides about the product and then chooses an adequate retailer. Thus, when the customer—after the initial phase of product decision— frequents a retail store, he has already collected several information, such as product features, prices, online availability and opinions from other users (Verhoef et al., 2007). The 'point of decision' is nowadays often relocated to the Internet, while the store is only perceived as the 'point of sale' (Heinemann, 2013; Shankar, 2011). The customer increasingly trusts the opinions of other product users more than the recommendations made by in-store sales people or advertisements. When the customer enters a retail store, he already possesses high knowledge about products and feature. Hence, the customer nowadays has high expectations regarding product availability, immediate accessibility to information, products and service delivery.
2. Customers can also 'research offline and purchase online'. In this context, the store can be seen as a 'show-room', where customers can physically touch their product, interact with sales people, gather information and enjoy a shopping experience (Verhoef et al., 2015). A survey reveals that over 50% of non-food online customers use stores as the pre-purchase channel. Customers try a product in-store, especially when high 'mispurchase risks' are associated with buying the product (Heinemann, 2013).

Verhoef et al. (2007) explain that there are three reasons for this phenomenon: First, customers prefer the channel that offers them the most advantages in each part of the purchase process- and they switch among channels during the purchase process if another channel offers more advantages ("Attribute-based decision-making). Second, it is seen as unlikely that customers generally purchase via the channel with the most research advantages ("Lack of channel lock-in"). Third, customers carry out research shopping when a channel switch increases their overall shopping experience ("Cross-channel synergy").

Another study focussed on retention and free-riding behaviour: Customers search at one channel from a certain retailer and buy at a different channel but stay with the same retailer ("cross-channel retention") or they search at a channel at one retailer, but then purchase at a different channel of another retailer ("cross-channel free-riding") (Heitz-Spahn, 2013). Chiu et al. (2011) identified two major reasons for cross-channel free riding: Customers who have a high level of self-efficacy tend to switch channels and retailers during their purchasing process. Second, customers will buy at the retailer who offers good quality and a low risk. Furthermore they investigated, that within-firm lock-in decreases cross-channel free-riding. This means, that retailers can install switching barriers, which reduce the customers' intention to switch channels. Heitz-Spahn (2013) however elaborated shopping convenience, flexibility and price comparisons as the three major cross-channel free-riding motives. It is arguable, if these motives are similar in any industry or if there are major differences regarding the purchasing pattern. Regarding that, Heitz-Spahn (2013) argued, that for products, which customers buy in a low frequency but have a high financial value, cross-channel free-riding behaviour is more likely than for other product categories. Kushwaha and Shankar (2013) also found out, that customer behaviour is different among product categories. They clustered these different product categories in hedonic and utilitarian ones. Kushwaha and Shankar investigated, that customers of hedonic products, such as apparel, tend more towards impulse purchase and variety-seeking behaviour and switch the channel more often than customers of utilitarian products (Kushwaha & Shankar, 2013). Besides a different purchasing behaviour across product categories, the degree of maturity plays an important role in omni-channel purchasing behaviour: Melis et al. (2015) conducted research in the UK grocery omni-channel market. They found out, that at the beginning of purchasing online, customers tend to buy at the retailer first, which they prefer when purchasing offline. When they become more convenient with purchasing online, they start switching channels (Melis, 2015).

PERCEIVED SERVICE QUALITY IN OMNI-CHANNEL RETAILING

In the context of omni-channel retailing, the evaluation and understanding of service quality has become a topic of major interest both for academics and practitioners (Badrinarayanan, Becerra, & Madhavaram, 2014; Banerjee, 2014; Seck & Philippe, 2013; Swaid & Wigand, 2012; Van Birgelen, De Jong, & Ruyter, 2006). "Owing to the intangible, heterogeneous and inseparable nature of services" (Martinez & Martinez, 2010, p. 30), several definitions of service quality have been built over the years. Zeithaml (1988), for instance, sees service quality as "...the consumer´s judgment about a product´s overall excellence or superiority" (Zeithaml, 1988, p.3), Bitner and Hubbert (1994) view service quality as "...the consumer´s overall impression of the relative inferiority/superiority of the organization and its services" (Bitner & Hubbert, 1994, p.77). The academic debate about how to evaluate service quality has developed extensively since the 1980. In essence, the service quality literature can be divided into two streams: Some researchers use a performance-only approach to evaluate service quality (Boulding, Kalra, Staelin, & Zeithaml, 1993; Cronin & Taylor, 1992; Teas, 1993). In contrast, the majority of researchers evaluate service quality based on the disconfirmation paradigm as a gap between expected service and perceived service (Carr, 2007; Dabholkar, Thorpe, & Rentz, 1996; Grönroos, 1984; Parasuraman, Zeithaml, & Berry, 1988). These studies draw extensively on the work of Oliver (1990). Oliver sees himself in the tradition of Sherif´s and Hovland´s "assimilation theory" (Sherif & Hovland, 1961) and Festinger´s "dissonance theory" (Festinger, 1957), whereby "customers are posited to perceptually distort expectation- discrepant performance so as to coincide with their prior expectation level" and "post exposure ratings are primarily a function of the expectation level because the task of recognizing disconfirmation is believed to be psychologically uncomfortable" (Oliver, 1980, p. 460).

Several different service quality gap models, such as "The Service Quality Model" (Grönroos, 1984), "SERVQUAL" (Parasuraman et al., 1988), "E-SQUAL" (Parasuraman, Zeithaml, & Malhorta, 2005) or "WEBQUAL" (Loiacono, Watson, & Goodhue, 2002) have been developed to conceptualize service quality and consumers' perception of it. But most of the approaches tend to take a single-channel perspective and do not consider omni-channel settings (Seck & Philippe, 2013; Sousa & Voss, 2012). But, it is deemed necessary to view omni-channel service quality from a different perspective than traditional (for instance retail stores) and electronic (for instance the Internet) service settings, since perceived service quality results from all moments of contact between a retailer and its customers- across all channels (Sousa & Voss, 2006).

Regarding a **conceptual framework** for omni-channel service quality, Sousa and Voss (2006) were the first researchers to develop framework that did not take a single channel approach. In their 'Service Delivery System (SDS)', they aim to consider all moments of contact between a firm and its customers. Sousa and Voss distinguish between a physical and a virtual component of service delivery. In the physical component non-automated operations take place and humans are directly involved. In the virtual component, operations are automated and humans do not play an active role. Sousa and Voss also distinguish between back office and front office operations. Back office operations are not directly visible to the customer whilst front office operations are visible. The researchers argue that existing service quality research has a single channel, which is a front office process. In their framework, the physical and the virtual service components (front office and back office) are linked with each other by integration mechanisms. These mechanisms function to integrate 'the several service components and associated parts of the SDS' (Sousa & Voss, 2006, p. 359). According to Sousa and Voss, all front and back office physical and virtual operations enriched with integration mechanisms lead to overall perceived service quality. Sousa and Voss argue for a separate examination of physical, virtual and integration quality: First of all they emphasize the different nature of the three quality dimensions. Second, they forecast a rapid technological development for the virtual dimension and they see advantages in examining it separately from the other two, more constant dimensions of physical and integration quality.

Service quality attributes, the so-called **'dimensions'** play a predominant role in service quality research, as perceived service quality is a function of different dimensions (Zeithaml & Berry, 1990). In the reviewed literature there is agreement that the key distinction between omni-channel and single channel service quality conceptualizations is the 'integration quality' dimension.

In their 'Multichannel Service Delivery System (SDS)' framework Sousa and Voss established the integration quality dimension. They defined integration quality as providing a "seamless service experience across channels" (Sousa & Voss, 2006, p. 359). Sousa and Voss surmised that in a omni-channel service system, even when the service quality of each channel is very high, the overall perception of service could be very low when the integration quality is perceived as low. Sousa and Voss presented two sub dimensions for integration quality: "Channel-service configuration" and "integrated interactions": Channel-service configuration is the degree of choice a customer has regarding a service offer in each of the channel ('service breadth'). When introducing integrated interactions Sousa and Voss refer to "the consistency of interactions across channels" (Sousa & Voss, 2006, p. 366). The researchers emphasize two aspects of integrated interactions: Content and process consistency. Content consistency means that customers receive the same information from the company when communicating through different channels. Process consistency means that customers expect the same handling of comparable processes.

Banerjee (2014) built up on Sousa and Voss´s framework and extended their findings about the integration quality dimensions into a new concept, consisting of three additional sub-dimensions. First, "the appropriateness of channel service configuration" refers to the degree to which a channel is suitable for different functions as a sub- dimension of channel-service configuration. Second, "transaction data and interaction data integration" refers to the degree to which customer transaction information and inbound and outbound interaction information are synthesized within and across channels. Third, "within channel and across channel integration" refers to the degree to which content and process information is integrated within parts of a channel and across channels (Sousa & Voss, 2006, p. 359).

Swaid and Wigand added "integrated pick-up" as another omni-channel service quality sub-dimenison, which means "the extend of smooth and easy pickup of products purchased online using a physical outlet/touchpoint" (Swaid & Wigand, 2012, p. 306). Swaid and Wigand concluded that integrated pick-up is one of the key dimensions of omni-channel service quality.

Next to integration quality, Sousa and Voss (2006) investigated virtual and physical quality as two other primary dimensions of omni-channel service quality (Sousa & Voss, 2006). The definition of virtual quality can be considered as the equivalent of electronic service quality based on single channel conceptualizations (for a review, see Ladhari, 2010). In an electronic setting, service quality means general perceived service in the virtual marketplace- with human intervention and without (Santos, 2003).

Furthermore, physical service quality can be considered as equivalent of traditional service quality based on single channel conceptualizations (for a review, see Martinez & Martinez, 2010).

Thus, from the reviewed literature, the extant knowledge about service quality dimensions can be synthesized as follows:

- Omni-channel service quality is a multidimensional construct, which consists of primary dimensions and corresponding sub dimensions.
- There is evidence in the reviewed literature that the existing dimensions have not fully grasped the customer´s perception of omni-channel service quality yet since studies consistently investigate new dimensions.
- Omni-channel service quality consists of the quality that each channel can provide for the customer. However, omni-channel service quality is not a simple summation between service quality perceptions in each channel. Even when physical and electronic qualities are very high, the overall service quality perception from the customer can be very low when the integration of each service channel is missing. Thus, the service quality dimensions that are experienced in any channel during the purchase process should be congruent on and offline and should provide a seamless shopping experience for the customer.
- The key distinction between omni-channel and single channel service systems is the integration quality dimension. The integration quality dimension has the purpose to provide a "seamless service experience across channels" (Sousa & Voss, 2006, p. 359).

Regarding different **methods**, the research of service quality in omni-channel settings is still in its early stages and few studies have examined service quality in a omni-channel context. The reviewed omni-channel service quality studies applied different methods including a literature review (Sousa & Voss, 2006), qualitative methods (Banerjee, 2014) and mixed methods (Swaid & Wigand, 2012) (Seck

& Philippe, 2013). There are several implications of method choices: With their literature review, Sousa and Voss set the foundation for developing a framework of service quality in omni-channel services. At the time of their research, there was an absence of a sound conceptual foundation for the research topic called omni-channel service quality. Sousa and Voss's study aimed to develop the theory (Sousa & Voss, 2006). Banerjee (2014) selected qualitative methods and conducted in-depth interviews in order to develop a service quality conceptualization and to gain an in-depth understanding of the omni-channel service quality phenomenon. Generally, the qualitative research method has a non-numeric manner and helps to observe a phenomenon in depth (Saunders, Lewis, & Thornhill, 2009). It provides answers to 'how' and 'why' questions. In contrast, the quantitative method embraces a positivistic research paradigm and is applied either to analyse covariance or to test whether hypotheses are wrong or right (Guba & Lincoln, 1994). In the field of omni-channel service quality research, some researchers have applied mixed methods. They developed their theories applying a qualitative approach first before testing them in a quantitative manner.

Basically, there are two different **perspectives** regarding omni-channel service quality, namely the organizational and the customer ones. The perspective in the reviewed service quality literature is the customer´s perspective. Grönroos argued that it is particularly important to understand how the customer evaluates service, because "if we know this and the components of service quality, we will be able to develop service-oriented concepts and models more successfully" (Grönroos, 1984, p. 36). Impacts related to high service quality can be considered as customer satisfaction (Bitner & Hubbert, 1994), customer loyalty (Grönroos, 1984, p. 37), purchase intention (Bolton & Drew, 1991; Bressolles, Durrieu, & Senecal, 2014; Cronin, Brady, & Hult, 2000; Cronin & Taylor, 1992; Spreng & Mackoy, 1996), profitability (Collier & Bienstock, 2006; Cox & Dale, 2001; Cristobal, Flavian, & Guinaliu, 2007; Gummerus, Liljander, Pura, & Van Riel, 2004; Ozuem et al 2018), and purchase retention (Cai & Jun, 2003; Parasuraman et al., 1988; Zeithaml, 2000). One can conclude from this, that studies with a customer perspective help retailers improve their service strategy and the performance of their service offer (Cristobal et al., 2007; Fassnacht & Köse, 2007; Zeithaml, 2000).

In the reviewed literature, three different **industry** contexts of service quality can be identified: 'pure' service industries (such as banking), the retail industry (such as clothing stores) and a mix of pure service and retail industries. The distinction between pure service and retail industries is that the pure service industry is an industry, where service is the actual 'product', and the retail industry is an industry, in which stores offer a mix of merchandise and service (Dabholkar et al., 1996; Kaynama, Black, & Keesling, 2000). The early service quality models were researched in the pure service industry (Kaynama et al., 2000). Later, researchers argued for a distinction to be made between different industries as in, for instance, retail shopping which accounts for unique aspects of service. These aspects include store image (Thang & Tan, 2003), store environment (Baker, Grewal, & Parasuraman, 1994; Dabholkar et al., 1996), in-store experiences (Dabholkar et al., 1996) and experiences related to the merchandise (Dabholkar et al., 1996) (Bishop Gagliano & Hathcote, 1994). Mostly, these criteria can be translated to the online world (Kim & Stoel, 2004). Even though online and offline shopping provides for a different shopping experience: Online customers pay more attention to privacy/ security; they appreciate some distinctive online capabilities such as interactivity, community, content, personalized experiences, increased product selection and information (Wolfinbarger & Gilly, 2003). Offline customers however value the personal contact with sales people in- store and the physical interaction with merchandise (Dabholkar et al., 1996).

AN OMNI-CHANNEL RETAILING SERVICE QUALITY CONCEPTUALIZATION

This paper builds on extant literature regarding omni-channel retailing and perceived service quality. It suggests that omni-channel service quality conceptualization consists of different ingredients. It is an interplay between omni-channel customer interaction with the retailer and the omni-channel retailer`s integration of assortment, pricing & promotions, fulfilment and web & store design. Ultimately, omni-channel service quality involves three dimensions, namely physical, electronic and integration quality. Or, as an equation: Omni-channel service quality = Integration quality – (physical channels quality + electronic channels service quality).

MANAGERIAL IMPLICATIONS AND RECOMMENDATIONS

This chapter provides a number of managerial implications. Nowadays, customers use the Internet for many cultural activities everyday. The borders between activities like socializing, communicating and purchasing get blurred. That is why it is important for omni-channel retailers to set up coherent and integrated sales and communication strategies across channels. Omni-channel customers expect a seamless shopping experience. Against this background, it is a strategic managerial decision for omni-channel retailers to find the 'right' level of integration regarding assortment, pricing and promotions, fulfilment, and web and store design. Omni-channel customers expect a high degree of product availability, immediate accessibility to information, products and service delivery. They will choose the channel and retailer who is able to provide him the best solutions.

Omni-channel retailers need to be aware of the fact that the customer's journey has changed fundamentally in the context of omni-channel retailing. Basically, two different phenomena emerged, namely 'web-rooming' and 'show-rooming'. It is crucial for omni-channel retailers to adequately respond to the new customer purchasing behaviour. First and foremost they need to train their sales force to be more competent than their customers in every respect. Otherwise they lose an important competitive advantage. Customers then rather stay online and buy on the Internet, or buy at someone else's store. Whichever journey customers choose, managers of omni-channel retailers should find ways to avoid 'cross-channel free-riding' behaviour, which means that customers do not just switch the channel, but also the retailer. It might be necessary to install switching barriers. For instance, customers might find it costly when they need to provide their information again or when it is laborious to express their concerns every time they switch between retailers. Furthermore omni-channel retailers need to train the empathy of their sales force. Nowadays it is crucial that sales people have a feeling of what the each customer actually expects. Does this customer at all wish consultancy? Does this customer already have some knowledge about the product he requires? How can the sales person support customer loyalty at this client? Sales force is supposed to address to the various requests of an individualistic buyership.

Thus, the changed behaviour of omni-channel customers makes it necessary to elaborate a new approach towards service quality. At present, omni-channel retailers still take a single-channel approach, and do not consider the distinctive requirements of multiple-channel systems. Here, it is important to bear in mind that even when the service quality of each channel is very high, the overall perception of service could be very low when the integration quality is perceived as low. So, managers of omni-channel retailers should not only put their emphasis on enhancing and improving physical and/or electronic service quality, but also shift towards the integration of both channels` service offers. The overall purchasing experience needs to be consistent for the customer at all moments of contact between the retailer and him/her in order to receive a seamlessly perceived service quality. Then, omni-channel customers can take advantage of both online and offline channels and experience a congruent shopping experience across channels.

REFERENCES

Agatz, N., Fleischmann, M., & Van Nunen, J. (2008). E-fulfilment and multichannel distribution- a review. *European Journal of Operational Research, 187*(2), 339–356. doi:10.1016/j.ejor.2007.04.024

Ailawadi, K. L., & Farris, P. (2017). Managing multi- and omni-channel distribution: Metrics and research directions. *Journal of Retailing*, *93*(1), 120–135. doi:10.1016/j.jretai.2016.12.003

Bächle, M., & Lehmann, F. (2010). *E-business: Grundlagen elektronischer Geschäftsprozesse im Web 2.0*. Oldenburg: Oldenburg Verlag. doi:10.1524/9783486709834

Badrinarayanan, V., Becerra, E., & Madhavaram, S. (2014). Influence of congruity in store-attribute dimensions and self-image on purchase intentions in online stores of multichannel retailers. *Journal of Retailing and Consumer Services*, *21*(6), 1013–1020. doi:10.1016/j.jretconser.2014.01.002

Baker, J., Grewal, D., & Parasuraman, A. (1994). The influence of store environment on quality inferences and store image. *Journal of the Academy of Marketing Science*, *22*(4), 328–339. doi:10.1177/0092070394224002

Banerjee, M. (2014). Misalignment and its influence on integration quality in multichannel services. *Journal of Service Research*, *17*(4), 460–474. doi:10.1177/1094670514539395

Berman, B., & Thelen, S. (2004). A guide to developing and managing a well-integrated multi-channel retail strategy. *International Journal of Retail & Distribution Management*, *32*(3), 147–156. doi:10.1108/09590550410524939

Berry, L., Bolton, R., Bridges, C., Meyer, J., Parasuraman, A., & Seiders, K. (2010). Opportunities for innovation in the delivery of interactive retail services. *Journal of Interactive Marketing*, *24*(2), 155–167. doi:10.1016/j.intmar.2010.02.001

Bishop Gagliano, K., & Hathcote, J. (1994). Customer expectations and perceptions of service quality in retail apparel specialty stores. *Journal of Services Marketing*, *8*(1), 60–69. doi:10.1108/08876049410053311

Bitner, M. J., & Hubbert, A. R. (1994). Encounter satisfaction versus overall satisfaction versus quality. In R. T. Rust & R. L. Oliver (Eds.), *Service Quality: New Directions in Theory and Practice* (pp. 72–94). London: Sage. doi:10.4135/9781452229102.n3

Bolton, R., & Drew, J. (1991). A multistage model of customers' assessments of service quality and value. *The Journal of Consumer Research*, *17*(4), 375–384. doi:10.1086/208564

Boulding, W., Kalra, A., Staelin, R., & Zeithaml, V. (1993). A dynamic process model of service quality: From expectations to behavioral intentions. *JMR, Journal of Marketing Research*, *30*(1), 7–27. doi:10.2307/3172510

Bressolles, G., Durrieu, F., & Senecal, S. (2014). A consumer typology based on e-service quality and e-satisfaction. *Journal of Retailing and Consumer Services*, *21*(6), 889–896. doi:10.1016/j.jretconser.2014.07.004

Breugelmans, E., & Campo, K. (2016). Cross-channel effects of price promotions: An empirical analysis of the multi-channel grocery retail sector. *Journal of Retailing*, *92*(3), 333–351. doi:10.1016/j.jretai.2016.02.003

Cai, S., & Jun, M. (2003). Internet users' perceptions of online service quality: A comparison of online buyers and information searchers. *Managing Service Quality*, *13*(6), 504–519. doi:10.1108/09604520310506568

Carr, C. (2007). The FAIRSERV model: Consumer reactions to services based on a multidimensional evaluation of service fairness. *Decision Sciences*, *38*(1), 107–130. doi:10.1111/j.1540-5915.2007.00150.x

Collier, J., & Bienstock, C. (2006). Measuring service quality in e-retailing. *Journal of Service Research*, *8*(3), 260–275. doi:10.1177/1094670505278867

Cox, J., & Dale, B. G. (2001). Service quality and e-commerce: An explanatory analysis. *Managing Service Quality*, *11*(2), 121–131. doi:10.1108/09604520110387257

Cristobal, E., Flavian, C., & Guinaliu, M. (2007). Perceived e-service quality: Measurement validity and effects on consumer satisfaction and web site loyalty. *Managing Service Quality*, *17*(3), 317–340. doi:10.1108/09604520710744326

Cronin, J. Jr, Brady, M., & Hult, G. (2000). Assessing the effects of quality, value, and customer satisfaction on consumer behavioral intentions in service environments. *Journal of Retailing*, *76*(2), 193–218. doi:10.1016/S0022-4359(00)00028-2

Cronin, J., & Taylor, S. (1992). Measuring service quality: A reexamination and extension. *Journal of Marketing*, *56*(3), 55–68. doi:10.2307/1252296

Dabholkar, P., Thorpe, D., & Rentz, J. (1996). A measure of service quality for retail stores: Scale development and validation. *Journal of the Academy of Marketing Science*, *24*(1), 3–16. doi:10.1007/BF02893933

Emrich, O. (2011). *Cross Channel Management- Kompetenzen, Instrumente und Erfolgspotenziale* (Dissertation). University St. Gallen, St. Gallen.

Emrich, O., Paul, M., & Rudolph, T. (2015). Shopping benefits of multichannel assortment integration and the moderating role of retailer type. *Journal of Retailing*, *91*(2), 326–342. doi:10.1016/j.jretai.2014.12.003

Emrich, O., & Verhoef, C. P. (2015). The impact of a homogenous versus a prototypical web design on online retail patronage for multichannel providers. *International Journal of Research in Marketing*, *32*(4), 363–374. doi:10.1016/j.ijresmar.2015.04.002

Fassnacht, M., & Köse, I. (2007). Consequences of web-based service quality: Uncovering a multi-faceted chain of effects. *Journal of Interactive Marketing*, *21*(3), 35–54. doi:10.1002/dir.20084

Festinger, L. (1957). *A theory of cognitive dissonance*. New York: Harper & Row.

Goersch, D. (2002). *Multi-Channel integration and its implications for retail web sites*. Paper presented at the 10th European Conference on Information Systems, Gdansk.

Grönroos, C. (1984). A service quality model and its marketing implications. *European Journal of Marketing*, *18*(4), 36–44. doi:10.1108/EUM0000000004784

Gummerus, J., Liljander, V., Pura, M., & Van Riel, A. (2004). Customer loyalty to content-based web sites: The case of an online health-care service. *Journal of Services Marketing*, *18*(3), 175–186. doi:10.1108/08876040410536486

Heinemann, G. (2013). *No-Line-Handel*. Wiesbaden: Gabler Verlag. doi:10.1007/978-3-658-00851-2

Heitz-Spahn, S. (2013). Cross-channel free-riding consumer behavior in a multichannel environment: An investigation of shopping motives, sociodemographics and product categories. *Journal of Retailing and Consumer Services*, *20*(6), 570–578. doi:10.1016/j.jretconser.2013.07.006

Hsieh, J., & Tseng, C. (2018). Exploring social influence on hedonic buying of digital goods- online games' virtual items. *Journal of Electronic Commerce Research*, *19*(2), 164–185.

Hu, M., Kumar, R., & Sumit, C. (2014, March). Best practices in strategic multichannel fulfillment. *Ivey Business Journal,* 1-6.

Kaynama, S., Black, C., & Keesling, G. (2000). Impact of the internet on internal service quality factors: The travel industry case. *Journal of Applied Business Research*, *19*, 135–146.

Kim, S., & Stoel, L. (2004). Apparel retailers: Website quality dimensions and satisfaction. *Journal of Retailing and Consumer Services*, *11*(2), 109–117. doi:10.1016/S0969-6989(03)00010-9

Kireyev, P., Kumar, V., & Ofek, E. (2015). *Match your own price? Self-matching as a multichannel retailer's pricing strategy. Harvard Business Review*.

Kushwaha, T., & Shankar, V. (2013). Are multichannel customers really more valuable? The moderating role of product category characteristics. *Journal of Marketing*, *77*(4), 67–102. doi:10.1509/jm.11.0297

Ladhari, R. (2010). Developing e-service quality scales: A literature review. *Journal of Retailing and Consumer Services*, *17*(6), 464–477. doi:10.1016/j.jretconser.2010.06.003

Lang, G., & Bressolles, G. (2013). Economic performance and customer expectation in e-fulfillment systems: a multichannel retailer perspective. *Supply Chain Forum, 14*(1), 16-27.

Loiacono, E., Watson, R., & Goodhue, D. (2002). WEBQUAL: A measure of website quality. *Journal of Marketing*, *60*, 432–438.

Mahrdt, N., Lessing, M., Wagner, W., & Geissler, H. (2013). *Herausforderung Multi - Channel - Neue Wege zum Markterfolg*. Bad Homburg: Gemini.

Mantrala, M., Levy, M., Kahn, B., Fox, E., Gaidarev, P., Dankworth, B., & Shah, D. (2009). Why is assortment planning so difficult for retailers? A framework and research agenda. *Journal of Retailing*, *85*(1), 71–83. doi:10.1016/j.jretai.2008.11.006

Martinez, J., & Martinez, L. (2010). Some insights on conceptualizing and measuring service quality. *Journal of Retailing and Consumer Services*, *17*(1), 29–42. doi:10.1016/j.jretconser.2009.09.002

Melis, K., Campo, K., Breugelmans, L., & Lamey, L. (2015). The impact of the multuchannel retail mix on online store choice: Does online experience matter? *Journal of Retailing*, *91*(2), 272–288. doi:10.1016/j.jretai.2014.12.004

Neslin, S., Grewal, D., Leghorn, R., Shankar, V., Teerlin, M., Thomas, J., & Verhoef, P. (2006). Challenges and opportunities in multichannel customer management. *Journal of Service Research*, *9*(2), 95–112. doi:10.1177/1094670506293559

Neslin, S., & Shankar, V. (2009). Key issues in multichannel customer management: Current knowledge and future directions. *Journal of Interactive Marketing*, *23*(1), 70–82. doi:10.1016/j.intmar.2008.10.005

Oliver, R. L. (1980). A cognitive model of the antecedents and consequences of satisfaction decisions. *JMR, Journal of Marketing Research*, *17*(4), 460–469. doi:10.2307/3150499

Ozuem, W. (forthcoming). Social media brand perceptions of millennials in the fashion apparel and accessories industries: A social identity perspective. *International Journal of Retail & Distribution Management*.

Ozuem, W., Howell, K. E., & Lancaster, G. (2018). Developing technologically induced environments: The case of the Nigerian banking sector. *Journal of Financial Services Marketing*, *23*(1), 50–61. doi:10.105741264-018-0043-z

Parasuraman, A., Zeithaml, V., & Berry, L. (1988). SERVQUAL: A multiple-item scale for measuring consumer perceptions of service quality. *Journal of Retailing*, *64*(1), 12–40.

Parasuraman, A., Zeithaml, V., & Malhorta, A. (2005). E-S-QUAL: A multiple-item scale for assessing electronic service quality. *Journal of Service Research*, *7*(3), 213–233. doi:10.1177/1094670504271156

Patten, E., & Rashid, T. (2015). CRM in a German multichannel retailing company: Investigating and evaluating the sales peoples' role. *International Journal of Sales. Retailing and Marketing*, *4*(2), 22–34.

Piotrowicz, W., & Cuthbertson, R. (2014). Introduction to the special issue: information technology in retail: toward omnichannel retailing. *International Journal of Electronic Commerce*, *18*(4), 5–16. doi:10.2753/JEC1086-4415180400

Saghiri, S., Wilding, R., Mena, C., & Bourlakis, M. (2017). Toward a three-dimensional framework for omni-channel. *Journal of Business Research*, *77*, 53–67. doi:10.1016/j.jbusres.2017.03.025

Santos, J. (2003). E-service quality: A model of virtual service quality dimensions. *Managing Service Quality*, *13*(3), 233–246. doi:10.1108/09604520310476490

Seck, A. (2013). The issue of multichannel integration, a key challenge for service firms in a context of multichannel services distribution. *International Business Research*, *6*(2), 160–169.

Seck, A., & Philippe, J. (2013). Service encounter in multi-channel distribution context: Virtual and face-to-face interactions and consumer satisfaction. *Service Industries Journal*, *33*(6), 565–579. doi:10.1080/02642069.2011.622370

Shankar, V., Inman, J. J., Mantrala, M., Kelley, E., & Rizley, R. (2011). Innovations in shopper marketing: Current insights and future research issues. *Journal of Retailing*, *87*(1), 29–43. doi:10.1016/j.jretai.2011.04.007

Sherif, M., & Hovland, C. I. (1961). *Social judgment: assimilation and contrast effects in communication and attitude change*. Yale University Press.

Sousa, R., & Voss, C. (2006). Service quality in multichannel services employing virtual channels. *Journal of Service Research*, *8*(4), 356–371. doi:10.1177/1094670506286324

Sousa, R., & Voss, C. (2012). The impacts of e-service quality on customer behavior in multi-channel services. *Total Quality Management & Business Excellence*, *23*(7), 769–787.

Spreng, R., & Mackoy, R. (1996). An empirical examination of a model of perceived service quality and satisfaction. *Journal of Retailing*, *72*(2), 201–214. doi:10.1016/S0022-4359(96)90014-7

Stokinger, E., & Ozuem, W. (2015). Social media and customer retention: implications for the luxury beauty industry. In G. Bowen & W. Ozuem (Eds.), *Marketing strategies: Social media and online brand communities*. Hershey, PA: IGI Global. doi:10.4018/978-1-4666-6595-8.ch009

Swaid, S., & Wigand, R. (2012). The effective of perceived site-to-store service quality on perceived value and loyalty intentions in multichannel retailing. *International Journal of Management*, *29*(3), 301–313.

Teas, K. (1993). Expectations, performance evaluation, and consumers' perceptions of quality. *Journal of Marketing*, *57*(4), 18–34. doi:10.2307/1252216

Thang, D., & Tan, B. (2003). Linking consumer perception to preference of retail stores: An empirical assessment of the multi-attributes of store image. *Journal of Retailing and Consumer Services*, *10*(4), 193–200. doi:10.1016/S0969-6989(02)00006-1

Van Birgelen, M., De Jong, A., & Ruyter, K. (2006). Multi-channel service retailing: The effects of channel performance satisfaction on behavioral intentions. *Journal of Retailing*, *82*(4), 367–377. doi:10.1016/j.jretai.2006.08.010

Verhoef, P., Kannan, P. K., & Inman, J. J. (2015). From multi-channel retailing to omni-channel retailing: Introduction to the special issue on multi-channel retailing. *Journal of Retailing*, *91*(2), 174–181. doi:10.1016/j.jretai.2015.02.005

Verhoef, P., Neslin, S., & Vroomen, B. (2007). Multichannel Customer Management: Understanding the Research Shopper Phenomenon. *International Journal of Research in Marketing*, *24*(2), 129–148. doi:10.1016/j.ijresmar.2006.11.002

Vogel, J., & Paul, M. (2015). One firm, one product, two prices: Channel-based price differentiation and customer retention. *Journal of Retailing and Consumer Services*, *27*, 126–139. doi:10.1016/j.jretconser.2015.07.007

Wolfinbarger, M., & Gilly, M. (2003). eTailQ: Dimensionalizing, measuring and predicting etail quality. *Journal of Retailing*, *79*(3), 183–198. doi:10.1016/S0022-4359(03)00034-4

Wolk, A., & Ebling, C. (2010). Multichannel price differentiation: An empirical investigation of existence and causes. *International Journal of Research in Marketing*, *27*(2), 142–150. doi:10.1016/j.ijresmar.2010.01.004

Xing, Y., & Grant, D. (2006). Developing a framework for measuring physical distribution service quality of multichannel and 'pure player' Internet retailers. *International Journal of Retail & Distribution Management*, *34*(4), 278–289. doi:10.1108/09590550610660233

Xing, Y., Grant, D., McKinnon, A., & Fernie, J. (2010). Physical distribution service quality in online retailing. *International Journal of Physical Distribution & Logistics Management*, *40*(5), 415–432. doi:10.1108/09600031011052859

Zeithaml, V. (1988). Consumer perceptions of price, quality, and value: A means-end model and synthesis of evidence. *Journal of Marketing*, *52*(3), 2–22. doi:10.1177/002224298805200302

Zeithaml, V. (2000). Service quality, profitability, and the economic worth of customers: What we know and what we need to learn. *Journal of the Academy of Marketing Science*, *28*(1), 67–85. doi:10.1177/0092070300281007

Zeithaml, V., & Berry, L. (1990). *Delivering Quality Service*. New York: The Free Press.

Zhang, J., Farris, P., Irvin, J., Kushwaha, T., Steenburgh, T., & Weitz, B. (2010). Crafting integrated multichannel retailing strategies. *Journal of Interactive Marketing*, *24*(2), 168–180. doi:10.1016/j.intmar.2010.02.002

KEY TERMS AND DEFINITIONS

Cross-Channel Free Riding: A customer first selects one retail channel to search for information about a product and then switches the retailer and the channel to purchase it.

Cross-Channel Retailing: A multichannel retailing system with a given degree of channel integration and customer interaction across different retail channels.

Integration Quality: The distinctive dimension of service quality in a multichannel system, which provides a seamless service experience for multichannel customers.

Multichannel Service Quality: A construct, which consists of the three dimensions physical, electronic and integration quality.

Omni-Channel Retailing: A multichannel retailing system with full channel integration and/or customer interaction across different retail channels.

Show-Rooming: Customers use an offline-mediated environment to gather information about a product, physically touch and see it, but then purchase it in an online-mediated environment.

Web-Rooming: Customers use an online-mediated environment to gather information about products, but then purchase it in an offline-mediated environment.

Chapter 11
Smartphones:
Resource Dimensions and Uses

Ibelema Sam-Epelle
University of Gloucestershire, UK

Kenneth Appiah
University of Cumbria, UK

ABSTRACT

Understanding the adoption of technologies is crucial for researchers and practitioners, as identifying key factors helps to predict and explain users' attitude towards adopting or rejecting technology. However, as smartphones are well-diffused technologies, there is contention that research efforts shift to understanding their usage comprehensively. As personal technologies that users make meaning of, smartphone usage is assumed to be more comprehensive than that of previous generation mobile phones. This chapter examines how the usage of smartphones is redefining and increasingly adding value to consumer consumption processes.

INTRODUCTION

The continually evolving usage of smartphones suggests that they are both consumer and prosumer devices used for both personal and business purposes. Individuals pursue goals with their smartphones and construct meaning regarding their devices, hence the smartphone as an extension of self (Arbore, Graziani, & Venturini, 2014; Jung, 2014). However, while a significant body of work informs on the personal use of smartphones globally, the business orientation of smartphone use is lacking from an individualistic standpoint. Value and use are complementaries; perception of smartphone value influences adoption and experiential value is resultant of usage. The proliferation of smartphones comes with dependency, as people increasingly hinge on smartphones for varying reasons. One of such reasons appears to be the ability of the smartphone to serve as a business administration resource, wherein it is used to mediate business activities and processes.

DOI: 10.4018/978-1-5225-7344-9.ch011

This occurrence is evident in the United Kingdom (UK). A 2013 study reports that 85 per cent of the adult population would not leave home without smartphones; and smartphone penetration is projected to be at 90 per cent of the population by 2020 (Deloitte, 2017; Google Confidential and Proprietary, 2013). Another recent nationwide study by the country's telecom regulator, Ofcom (2016), which aimed to investigate how heavy reliance on a smartphone could affect digital behaviour and media literacy, found interestingly that micro-business owners choose to use the smartphone to run their businesses. This suggests that the business use of smartphones transcends the organisational context in which it has been predominantly studied. Considering the rising trend of entrepreneurialism in the country, as a result of people valuing autonomy and creativity over linear career progressions, rather than a response to a recent recession or a waning job market (Yoshioka, 2016), it is surprising that smartphones are still generally viewed as technological products users consume, rather than resources used to facilitate business administration. In fact, there is a consensus amongst market experts that smartphone use for leisure and enjoyment is likely to exceed its use for productivity purposes (Yang & Kim, 2012). The adoption of workflow apps, when compared to communication apps, was found to be modest among UK workers in a recent survey (Deloitte, 2017).

To advance understanding with respect to the usage and the resource dimension of smartphones in the *adoption of technologies context*, this enquiry utilises the concept of the business actor. In the context of this study, business actors are individuals involved in business activities who use their smartphones actively for business administration. Hence their use is assumed to be different from both the broad consumer archetype and business users within the enterprise. Research shows that these users are likely to be 'digital daters' (Forbes, 2010); i.e. they own and use more than one mobile device. It is of theoretical importance to gain more insights into the deployment of smartphones specifically for business purposes. The variety of technological platforms, multiple operating systems and therefore different application designs are the most significant drawbacks to ensuring the future success of m-business (Burger, 2007). In the case of these business actors, what rationales guide the use of a smartphone for business purposes? What impedes smartphone usage in this context? What unique values does smartphone use offer in this context? What influences the preference of smartphones amongst other available mobile devices?

THEORETICAL CONTEXT

Physically, the smartphone is a technological convergence that can be understood objectively through device specifications; the effect of human interaction facilitates values that are intrinsic and individualistic. The subjective view of smartphones regards them as an extension of self (Arbore *et al.*, 2014; Jung, 2014). Analysis of the definitions provided by publications since 2007, when the iPhone changed the paradigm of the platform (Sarwar & Rahim Soomro, 2013), indicates that smartphones are defined by what they are physically, and the potential and implications of their application through human interaction.

There is agreement that smartphones are mobile devices: a categorisation of mobile technologies (which include a network infrastructure that facilitates connectivity) and Information Systems (IS) scholars have contended that smartphone technology deserves investigation in its own right (Chen & Park, 2007; Y. M. Kang, Lee, & Lee, 2014); yet the term lacks a standard definition in the literature (Kim, Chun, & Lee, 2014). Cumulatively, smartphone definitions include 'technicality', 'socio-technicality', or 'contradiction'-oriented approaches within two broad perspectives of 'user/personal/consumer' and 'business/enterprise' vantage points.

Within the literature, the dominant view in describing smartphones focuses on the object itself: the artefact and the technological innovation. Hence, technicality has been a route to defining smartphones. Technicality defines the degree to which the perception of a mobile service is technologically excellent in the process of providing services; users' perceptions of ease of use, system reliability, connectivity and efficiency determine it (Kim *et al.*, 2007; Verkasalo, López-Nicolás, Molina-Castillo, & Bouwman, 2010). From this standpoint, the smartphone is a 'convergence of PDA and mobile phone technologies, with multiple capabilities akin to computerlike functionality' (Chen & Park, 2007; Gill, Kamath, & Gill, 2012; Kang, Cho, & Lee, 2011; Kang, Lee, & Lee, 2014; Kim *et al.*, 2014; Putzer & Park, 2010). Publications concurrently describe the smartphone as an enterprise- or prosumer-focused device that incorporates an operating system capable of enterprise applications such as mobile e-mail, Personal Information Management (PIM) synchronisation, security and device management features (Beurer-Zuellig & Meckel, 2008); suggesting they are potential business resources.

Cumulatively, the technical-oriented definitions indicate that smartphones differ not only from static Information Technology (IT) but also from the previous generation of telephony: mobile (feature) phones (Calvosa, 2015; Y. M. Kang *et al.*, 2011, 2014). Beyond being mobile, smartphones can multi-task as they run advanced mobile operating systems. Additionally, smartphones can run apps, and provide the user with the ability to personalise the device (Jung, 2014). The technical-centric approach to defining the smartphone as being mainly artefact/architecture-oriented accommodates a passivity towards the application and implications of the technology.

The socio-technicality viewpoint partially addresses this limitation about the implications of smartphone technology; thus, it is defined beyond mere technical architecture. For instance, Yang and Kim (2012) define smartphones as programmable phones that provide their users with advanced capabilities and features to enhance their daily work and personal lives, insinuating that smartphones are user-empowering information technology (IT) (Jung, 2014).

While this view embraces the implication of applying the technology, its shortcoming lies in its optimism. In other words, it downplays the less desirable consequences of usage, such as addiction (Ahn, Wijaya, & Esmero, 2014), distraction-related concerns (Gill *et al.*, 2012), and younger generation social disorders that affect broader society, such as phubbing and nomophobia (Anshari *et al.*, 2016), which have resulted from smartphone dependency. Phubbing is a term that refers to people snubbing others around them as they concentrate on their phones. Nomophobia is a common social phobia that may develop if an individual is obsessed with their smartphone and begins to show uncomfortable behaviour when faced with a situation where they have no access to their phone (Anshari *et al.*, 2016).

In agreement with Feenberg (2002) that 'a complete definition must show how the orientation toward reality characteristic of technology is combined with the realisation of technology in the social world' (p. 175), in the reviewed literature, Deloitte's (2017) report on the 'state of the smart', presents the most robust description of the smartphone:

... a multi-purpose device the likes of which has never existed before. It is a digital Swiss army knife with a set of tools that is millions of apps deep. It can be a powerful productivity tool, which can also goad users into obsessing over inbox size, rather than effective communication. It can be used to work when away from the office, and not to work while in it (p. 8).

This approach to viewing the smartphone is a critical evaluation of the socio-technical perspective, as it accounts for technicality and both ends of the implication spectrum. The device can hence be a blessing or curse; research indeed shows that smartphone use involves numerous paradoxes (Bruzzi & Joia, 2015; Lipman, 2013). The consumerisation of IT shows the appeal of personal device use for work purposes. The descriptions of the smartphone above indicate both 'product' and 'resource' orientations of the technology within society.

SMARTPHONE USE

In exploring the business use of smartphones, understanding smartphone use entailment is crucial, as it links back to 'system use', which IS scholars have understood traditionally as the frequency of using a system (DeLone & McLean, 2003; Venkatesh, Morris, Davis, & Davis, 2003). Indicative of the existing IS literature, the 'adoption' and 'use' of the smartphone are complementary research areas. The latter mainly concerns the post-adoption stage, wherein successful adoption has taken place as resistance is overcome (Choi & Yoo, 2015; M.-K. Kim, Chang, Wong, & Park, 2013). Concerning smartphone value, two distinct dimensions provide an explanation for values users derive and those they perceive, which influence adoption. Experiential values have been demonstrated to be the outcome of using smartphones, from the user standpoint (referred to as user values) (Bødker, Gimpel, & Hedman, 2009, 2014; Jung, 2014) – which can lead to broader life values (Park & Han, 2013).

However, studies have mainly focused on the general consumer standpoint and thus limit the extent to which they inform on the business usage (and associated value) of the smartphone. Aldhaban (2012) found that smartphone studies relating to business and marketing are lacking compared to those on adoption and software/security issues. The consumer-centric orientation of smartphone issues might be a reason for the relatively low interest from scholarship regarding the business use. Being personal devices, studying the typical use of the consumer would hardly reveal the resource dimension of smartphones; mundane usage makes up a significant amount of the average users' smartphone usage (Ahn *et al.*, 2014; Meeker & Wu, 2013). Employing the distinction of 'time-in' and 'time-out' usage, Bødker, Gimpel, and Hedman (2010; 2014) demonstrate how technology use evolves over time and provide theoretical explanation of this change[1]; they show how smartphones go from having 'representative meaning that was greater than functional value to being merited according to the ability to blend in with other activities' (p. 11).

Understanding the adoption of technologies is becoming crucial for researchers and practitioners, as identifying key factors helps to predict and explain users' attitude towards adopting or rejecting technology (Aldhaban, 2012; Davis, 1989; Venkatesh, 2000). However, as smartphones are well-diffused technologies, there is contention that research efforts shift to understanding its usage comprehensively – being personal technologies that users make meaning of, smartphone usage is assumed to be more comprehensive than previous generation mobile phones (Jung, 2014; Tossell, Kortum, Shepard, Rahmati, & Zhong, 2012). IS Scholars have detailed some factors that influence individuals' adoption of smartphones, albeit mainly from a consumer standpoint. Aldhaban (2012) proposes a taxonomy of smartphone adoption factors to identify and explain key factors influencing the adoption of smartphones. Each main factor has sub-factors that contribute to its influence on adoption (see Figure 1).

In the existing literature, the adoption process suggests two perspectives of the adopter: a passive responder to technology or an active agent in the adoption process.

Figure 1. Taxonomy and critical factors of smartphone adoption (Adapted from Aldhaban, 2012)

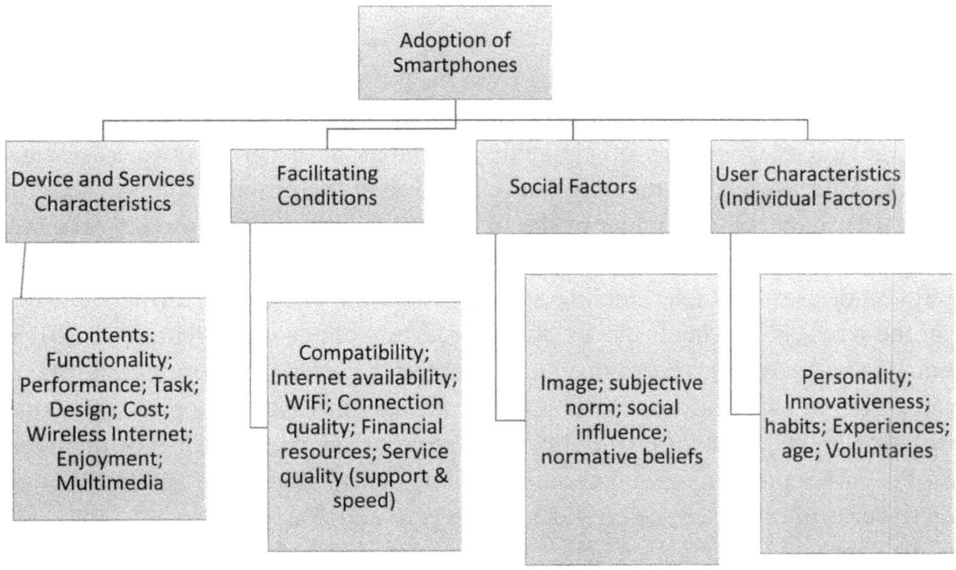

Smartphone Value: Perceived and Experiential

Smartphone use is indicated to be the result of adoption and results in values for the smartphone user – these can be both positive and negative. From an adoption standpoint, the perceived values of the technology, which are judged by the potential adopter, influence the adoption or rejection of the technology. For instance, the Technology Acceptance Model (TAM), which is arguably the most influential IS theory, regards two key variables – perceived usefulness (PU) and perceived ease of use (PEOU) – as central to individuals' decision to adopt a given technology (Davis, 1989; Li, 2010). The value-oriented approach challenges this, contending that the presumptions of the model consider the potential adopter a passive responder to technology, as opposed to an active agent in the adoption process (Bagozzi, 2007; Jung, 2014; Lamb & Kling, 2003). Consequently, studies have investigated the experiential values users pursue and achieve by using smartphones (Bødker *et al.*, 2009; Jung, 2014), as they are experiential computers.

Figure 2. Smartphone use entailment: adoption, use, user and values relations of smartphones

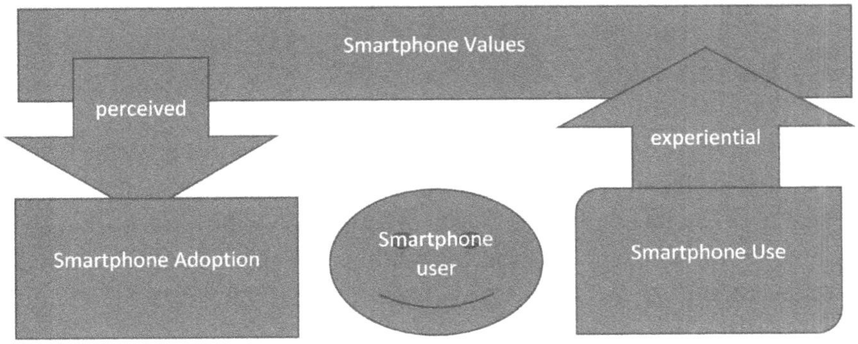

The Disparity Between Consumer and Business Perspectives

The notion of the smartphone user is crucial in the smartphone usage framework, as the user is the agent who adopts and uses, pursues and derives value from the technology. Segmenting technology users has provided insights into the nuances of technology value and has been a means of approaching smartphone adoption and usage studies. One means of segmenting considers the disparity between users and non-users of the technology. Alternatively, segmenting can be based solely on different kinds of smartphone users. Kang *et al.*'s (2014) study is an exemplar of the first route and reports that service-oriented functional attributes – *'wireless Internet'* and *'mobile applications'* – are consistent with the adoption of smartphones, regardless of user. However, mobile apps are more important to smartphone users, while the availability of the wireless Internet is more critical for feature phone users. Kim *et al.* (2013) examined the perceived risks and switching barriers on non-adopters' intention to use smartphones, arguing that consumer perception of usefulness does not always translate into actual adoption. The study suggests that *perceived usefulness, financial risk and cost-effectiveness* generally influence the intention to use smartphones. Put differently, those who choose to avoid smartphones have additional concerns about the non-attractiveness of other service providers (Kim *et al.*, 2013).

Based on the alternative segmenting approach, Canio *et al.* (2016) segment smartphone consumers using activities they perform on personal mobile devices; identifying users regarding *demographics, smartphone owned, hours of usage, and reason to use*. Five main profiles of users emerge from their study: *utility users, gamers, unfriendly users, moderator users, and supersmartphoners*. Using similar segmenting tactics, Arbore *et al.* (2014) focused on multifaceted motives for adopting personal technologies, providing an analysis of the drivers of overall perceptions and the role of individual differences among potential users in forming these attitudes. The research identifies three smartphone user types: *pragmatic segment* – driven by expected functional value; *symbolic segment* – driven mainly by symbolic value; and *IT worried* – which represents individuals concerned with the hedonic value of technology. Their study result indicates that *value drivers*, *control beliefs*, and *normative beliefs* play different roles in determining smartphone acceptance depending on three individual characteristics: *playfulness, public self-consciousness, and innovativeness*. An earlier study on the impact of personality traits on smartphone ownership and used by Lane and Manner (2011), applied logistic regression and hierarchical linear regression to analyse results from 312 participants. The study found that extraverted individuals were more likely to own a smartphone and reported greater importance for the texting function of the device.

Cumulatively, these studies provide insights into smartphone use, as they demonstrate nuances of 'collective' usage. They also present a shift from what makes users adopt the technology, to what ownership usage reflects. However, while smartphone studies have providing insights about smartphone users, they mainly centre on the archetypical consumer, who might consider smartphones as mainly a product.

From a Business Perspective

Existing IS literature indicates two broad categorisations of smartphone users; within these categorisations, some delineations exist. Broadly, smartphone business users include organisational and non-organisational users. Organisational users include individuals such as employees who work within a firm; these could be mobile or non-mobile workers (e.g. Bao, Pierce, Whittaker, & Zhai, 2011; Beurer-Zuellig & Meckel, 2008). The consumerisation of IT has made studying such users paramount.

Non-organisational users include business actors like micro-business administrators, proprietors, entrepreneurs and knowledge workers. These business actors use smartphones for work but do not function within an organisational setting; rather, the business in this context operates within a dynamic 'service system' (Maglio & Spohrer, 2007). Between the two broad categorisations of business users, nuances exist in their adoption and usage of smartphones for business. For one, the organisational user is mainly an acceptor of technology, i.e. passive in the adoption process. Mostly these users have their smartphones handed down by the employer. Where such is not the case, there are still organisational boundaries that limit the usage of smartphone for such users, such as IT policies that limit how, when and where these users utilise these devices for work. Additionally, device affordances and environmental context can serve as constraints to business use of smartphones (Bao *et al.*, 2011). [1]

MANAGERIAL IMPLICATIONS

The 'use' construct links back to the notion of system use, which has traditionally been assessed based on the frequency of using a technological system within the organisational context. Venkatesh, Morris, Davis, and Davis (2003) define 'system use' as the frequency, duration, and intensity of an employee's interactions with a particular system. This viewpoint considers use regarding an acceptor, within an adopting organisation. Moreover, scholars have critiqued the construct of 'use' as being too simplistic and needing further development to include both the 'extent' (i.e. used features) and 'nature' (mechanism of used features) (Bødker *et al.*, 2009; DeLone & McLean, 2003). Smartphone use is assumed to be more comprehensive than the previous generation static IT (Jung, 2014; Tossell *et al.*, 2012). The descriptions of the smartphone suggest dual perspectives of 'product' and 'resource'. While they are platforms for consuming services, they equally are platforms for rendering service. The resource dimension is evident in one such practitioner view of the smartphone:

A smartphone is a mobile communications device that uses an identifiable open OS ... Third-party applications can be installed and removed, and they can be created for the device's OS and application programming interfaces (APIs) ... The OS must support a multitasking environment and user interface that can handle multiple applications simultaneously ... (Gartner, 2018).

Such portrayal of a smartphone, significantly based on its technicality, suggests that the multi-tasking ability and availability of apps are critical for smartphone use. However, the transformational abilities of mobile applications are not comprehensive enough (Pratap & Srivastava, 2013). While apps are becoming strategic and marketing tools for companies, individuals' usage suggests a mainly regular use for activities such as media consumption, browsing and social networking.

Following the dual perspectives of smartphones, business use mainly reflects the resource dimension. However, this dimension is understood mainly in organisational terms. IT business value, particularly concerning m-business usage of IT and research concerning the consumerisation of IT and concurrent trend of BYOD (Bring Your Own Device) enrich this use dimension. Smartphone use from a business perspective indicates various values including collaboration, efficiency, cost reductions and productivity gains (Bao, Pierce, Whittaker, & Zhai, 2011).

In this context, Beurer-Zuellig and Meckel's (2008) is a seminal study on the resource usage of smartphones to meet the need of workforce mobilisation. The study elicits the influence of e-mail on work processes and communication amongst sixteen German companies and finds that smartphones have the potential to improve and accelerate work processes through timely provision of information, enhanced reachability and the simplification of coordination processes. In an organisational context as well, Chen, Yen, and Chen (2009) provide empirical evidence on the possible influences of attitude towards smartphone use, including organisational culture, policy and the external environment. Context is shown to be impactful on smartphone use in different ways (Chow & Ma, 2017; Müller, Gove, Webb, & Cheang, 2015; Tri Do, Blom, & Gatica-Perez, 2011).

Within the organisational setting, nuances exist when juxtaposing mobile and non-mobile workers' use of smartphones. Bao, Pierce, Whittaker, and Zhai's (2011) study provides a snapshot of smartphone use which helps explain why even highly capable phones are not yet substitutable for computers, concerning non-mobile workers. Implicitly, the scholars' conclusions bolster the 'conditional value' of smartphones (cf. Bødker *et al.*, 2009; Ofcom, 2016). When compared to other mobile devices, usage of the smartphone is demonstrated to be more varied than tablets. Therefore, it is increasingly important to investigate how smartphone usage unfolds concerning different types of context. The disparity of mobile device use is unique in different contexts, hence the need for different design solutions (Müller *et al.*, 2015).

Generally, the outcomes of using IT have been traditionally examined through approaches limited mainly to the context of system use itself (e.g. system satisfaction, usage intention, and intention to return) (Jung, Pawlowski, & Kim, 2017). This study differentiates from previous studies in the way it approaches context, i.e. it is sensitive to the context in which the system is used, not solely the context of system use itself. While we know that people pursue goals with smartphones (Jung, 2014), it is unclear how the smartphone facilitates the business goals of individuals and the challenges associated with the materialisation. Moreover, user values of the smartphone (Bødker *et al.*, 2009; Jung, 2014) alone do not fully explain the impact and potential business value of the technology.

REFERENCES

Ahn, H., Wijaya, M. E., & Esmero, B. C. (2014). A systemic smartphone usage pattern analysis: Focusing on smartphone addiction issue. *International Journal of Multimedia and Ubiquitous Engineering*, *9*(6), 9–14. doi:10.14257/ijmue.2014.9.6.02

Aldhaban, F. (2012). Exploring the Adoption of Smartphone Technology : Literature Review. In *2012 Proceedings of PICMET '12: Technology Management for Emerging Technologies* (pp. 2758–2770). PICMET.

Anshari, M., Alas, Y., Hardaker, G., Jaidin, J. H., Smith, M., & Ahad, A. D. (2016). Smartphone habit and behavior in Brunei: Personalization, gender, and generation gap. *Computers in Human Behavior*, *64*, 719–727. doi:10.1016/j.chb.2016.07.063

Arbore, A., Graziani, R., & Venturini, S. (2014). Personal mobile technologies: Decomposing and de-averaging the value of a smartphone. *Journal of Information Systems*, *28*(1), 167–185. doi:10.2308/isys-50668

Bagozzi, R. P. (2007). The Legacy of the Technology Acceptance Model and a Proposal for a Paradigm Shift. *Journal of the Association for Information Systems*, *8*(4), 244–254. doi:10.17705/1jais.00122

Bao, P., Pierce, J., Whittaker, S., & Zhai, S. (2011). Smart phone use by non-mobile business users. *Proceedings of the 13th International Conference on Human Computer Interaction with Mobile Devices and Services – MobileHCI '11*, 445–455. 10.1145/2037373.2037440

Beurer-Zuellig, B., & Meckel, M. (2008). Smartphones enabling mobile collaboration. *Proceedings of the Annual Hawaii International Conference on System Sciences*, 1–10.

Bødker, M., Gimpel, G., & Hedman, J. (2009). *The user experience of smart phones : A consumption values approach.* In Global Mobility Roundtable, Cairo, Egypt.

Bødker, M., Gimpel, G., & Hedman, J. (2010). Technology use: Time-in or time-out. *18th European Conference on Information Systems.* Retrieved from http://aisel.aisnet.org/ecis2010/135

Bødker, M., Gimpel, G., & Hedman, J. (2014). Time-out/time-in: The dynamics of everyday experiential computing devices. *Information Systems Journal*, *24*(2), 143–166. doi:10.1111/isj.12002

Bruzzi, P., & Joia, L. A. (2015). Detecting and sorting the paradoxes associated with smartphone use by Brazilian professionals. *Twenty-first Americas Conference on Information Systems*, 1–12. Retrieved from https://aisel.aisnet.org/cgi/viewcontent.cgi?article=1345&context=amcis2015

Burger, A. K. (2007). M-commerce hot spots, Part 2: Scaling walled gardens. *E-Commerce Times, 5.*

Calvosa, P. (2015). Cycles of convergence and dynamics of growth in the smartphone industry. *European Scientific Journal, 11*(19), 1–28. Retrieved from https://eujournal.org/index.php/esj/article/view/5925/5710

Chen, J. V., & Park, Y. (2007). Acceptance and adoption of the innovative use of smartphone. *Industrial Management & Data Systems*, *107*(9), 1349–1365. doi:10.1108/02635570710834009

Chen, J. V., Yen, D. C., & Chen, K. (2009). The acceptance and diffusion of the innovative smart phone use: A case study of a delivery service company in logistics. *Information & Management*, *46*(4), 241–248. doi:10.1016/j.im.2009.03.001

Choi, S., & Yoo, J. (2015). Roles of user resistance and social influence in continued use of smartphone. In *International Conference on Advanced Communication Technology, ICACT* (pp. 287–291). Academic Press. 10.1109/ICACT.2015.7224805

Chow, T. C.-L., & Ma, W. W. K. (2017). Do we really know what people are using their smartphone for? *2017 International Symposium on Educational Technology (ISET)*, 34–38. 10.1109/ISET.2017.16

Davis, F. D. (1989). Perceived usefulness, perceived ease of use, and user acceptance of information technology. *Management Information Systems Quarterly*, *13*(3), 319–339. doi:10.2307/249008

De Canio, F., Pellegrini, D., & Aramendia-muneta, M. E. (2016). The smartphoners: Consumer segmentation by smartphone usage. *Mercati e Competitivita*, *1*(1), 125–146.

DeLone, W. H., & McLean, E. R. (2003). The DeLone and McLean model of information systems success : A ten-year update. *Journal of Management Information Systems*, *19*(4), 9–30. doi:10.1080/07421222.2003.11045748

Feenberg, A. (2002). *Transforming technology: A critical theory revisited* (2nd ed.). Oxford University Press.

Forbes. (2010). *The untethered executive: Business information in the age of mobility*. Retrieved from https://images.forbes.com/forbesinsights/StudyPDFs/The_Untethered_Executive.pdf

Gartner. (2018). *Smartphone*. Retrieved June 3, 2018, from https://www.gartner.com/it-glossary/smart-phone

Gill, P. S., Kamath, A., & Gill, T. S. (2012). Distraction: An assessment of smartphone usage in health care work settings. *Risk Management and Healthcare Policy*, *5*, 105–114. doi:10.2147/RMHP.S34813 PMID:22969308

Goodwin, E., Babin, L., & Cole, H. (2014). The impact of mobile apps on small business revenues. *Journal of Business and Economics*, *5*(4), 437–442.

Google Confidential and Proprietary. (2013). *Our mobile planet: United Kingdom Understanding the mobile consumer*. Author.

Jung, Y. (2014). What a smartphone is to me: Understanding user values in using smartphones. *Information Systems Journal*, *24*(4), 299–321. doi:10.1111/isj.12031

Jung, Y., Pawlowski, S. D., & Kim, H.-W. (2017). Exploring associations between young adults' Facebook use and psychological well-being: A goal hierarchy approach. *International Journal of Information Management*, *37*(1), 1391–1404. doi:10.1016/j.ijinfomgt.2016.10.005

Kang, Y. M., Cho, C., & Lee, S. (2011). Analysis of factors affecting the adoption of smartphones. In *International Technology Management Conference (ITMC)* (pp. 919–925). IEEE.

Kang, Y. M., Lee, M., & Lee, S. (2014). Service-oriented factors affecting the adoption of smartphones. *Journal of Technology Management & Innovation*, *9*(2), 98–117. doi:10.4067/S0718-27242014000200008

Kim, D., Chun, H., & Lee, H. (2014). Determining the factors that influence college students' adoption of smartphones. *Journal of the Association for Information Science and Technology*, *65*(3), 578–588. doi:10.1002/asi.22987

Kim, H. W., Chan, H. C., & Gupta, S. (2007). Value-based adoption of mobile internet: An empirical investigation. *Decision Support Systems*, *43*(1), 111–126. doi:10.1016/j.dss.2005.05.009

Kim, M.-K., Chang, Y., Wong, S. F., & Park, M.-C. (2013). The effect of perceived risks and switching barriers on the intention to use smartphones among non-adopters in Korea. *Information Development*, 1–12.

Lamb, R., & Kling, R. (2003). reconceptualizing users as social actors in information systems research. *Management Information Systems Quarterly*, *27*(2), 197–235. doi:10.2307/30036529

Lane, W., & Manner, C. (2011). The impact of personality traits on smartphone ownership and use. *International Journal of Business and Social Science*, *2*(17), 22. Retrieved from http://www.ijbssnet.com/journals/Vol_2_No_17/4.pdf

Li, L. (2010). A critical review of technology acceptance literature. *Southwest Decisino Sciences Institute*, 22. Retrieved from http://www.swdsi.org/swdsi2010/SW2010_Preceedings/papers/PA104.pdf

Lipman, V. (2013, July). Are smartphones a hidden drag on the economy? *Forbes*.

Maglio, P. P., & Spohrer, J. (2007). Fundamentals of service science. *Journal of the Academy of Marketing Science*, *36*(1), 18–20. doi:10.100711747-007-0058-9

Meeker, M., & Wu, L. (2013). *Internet Trends D11 Conference*. Retrieved from https://www.slideshare.net/kleinerperkins/kpcb-internet-trends-2013

Müller, H., Gove, J. L., Webb, J. S., & Cheang, A. (2015). Understanding and comparing smartphone and tablet use. In *Proceedings of the Annual Meeting of the Australian Special Interest Group for Computer Human Interaction on - OzCHI '15* (pp. 427–436). New York: ACM Press. 10.1145/2838739.2838748

Ofcom. (2016). *'Smartphone by default' internet users: A qualitative research report*. Ofcom.

Park, J., & Han, S. H. (2013). Defining user value: A case study of a smartphone. *International Journal of Industrial Ergonomics*, *43*(4), 274–282. doi:10.1016/j.ergon.2013.04.005

Pratap, U., & Srivastava, R. (2013). Transforming business with mobile enterprise apps. *International Journal of Engineering And Computer Science, 2*(6), 2057–2066. Retrieved from http://ijecs.in/issue/v2-i6/54 ijecs.pdf

Putzer, G. J., & Park, Y. (2010). The effects of innovation factors on smartphone adoption among nurses in community hospitals. *Perspectives in Health Information Management*, *7*. Retrieved from http://www.ncbi.nlm.nih.gov/pubmed/20697467 PMID:20697467

Deloitte. (2017). State of the smart consumer and business usage patterns. Global Mobile Consumer Survey 2017. Retrieved from https://www.deloitte.co.uk/mobileuk/assets/img/download/global-mobile-consumer-survey-2017_uk-cut.pdf#page=16

Sarwar, M., & Rahim Soomro, T. (2013). Impact of smartphones on society. *European Journal of Scientific Research*, *98*(2), 216–226. Retrieved from http://www.europeanjournalofscientificresearch.com

Tossell, C. C., Kortum, P., Shepard, C., Rahmati, A., & Zhong, L. (2012). An empirical analysis of smartphone personalisation: Measurement and user variability. *Behaviour & Information Technology*, *31*(10), 995–1010. doi:10.1080/0144929X.2012.687773

Tri Do, T. M., Blom, J., & Gatica-Perez, D. (2011). Smartphone usage in the wild: a large-scale analysis of applications and context. In *ICMI '11 Proceedings of the 13th international conference on multimodal interfaces* (pp. 353–360). Alicante, Spain: ACM. Retrieved from https://infoscience.epfl.ch/record/192383/files/Do_ICMI_2011.pdf

Venkatesh, V. (2000). Determinants of perceived ease of use: Integrating control, intrinsic motivation, and emotion into the technology acceptance model. *Information Systems Research*, *11*(4), 342–365. doi:10.1287/isre.11.4.342.11872

Venkatesh, V., Morris, M., Davis, G., & Davis, F. (2003). User acceptance of information technology: Toward a unified view. *Management Information Systems Quarterly*, *27*(3), 425–478. doi:10.2307/30036540

Verkasalo, H., López-Nicolás, C., Molina-Castillo, F. J., & Bouwman, H. (2010). Analysis of users and non-users of smartphone applications. *Telematics and Informatics*, *27*(3), 242–255. doi:10.1016/j.tele.2009.11.001

Yang, K., & Kim, H.-Y. (2012). Mobile shopping motivation: An application of multiple discriminant analysis. *International Journal of Retail & Distribution Management, 40*(10), 778–789. doi:10.1108/09590551211263182

Yoshioka, M. (2016). *How entrepreneurial was the UK in 2015?* Retrieved from https://centreforentrepreneurs.org/how-entrepreneurial-was-the-uk-in-2015/

KEY TERMS AND DEFINITIONS

Business Actor: Individuals who actively carry out business administration functions with the aid of personally owned mobile devices.

Digital Daters: Individuals (mainly business actors) who own and use more than one personal mobile computer for varying purposes.

Product (Use): An experiential good manufactured to meet market needs. Hence smartphone as a product reflects a category which encompasses an ecosystem of manufacturers, app developers, suppliers and users. From a service reference point, product-use emphasizes the consumption of services on smartphones.

Resource (Use): Assets that possess unique capabilities, hence can be employed to reach individuals' goals. From a service perspective, resource-use hence emphasizes the smartphone as a service rendering device; a crucial aspect of work, and user empowering technologies.

Smartphone: A product-service system used by individuals for service consuming and service rendering purposes.

Chapter 12
Online Service Failure:
Understanding the Building Blocks of Effective Recovery Strategy

Yllka Azemi
Indiana University Northwest, USA

Wilson Ozuem
University of Cumbria, UK

ABSTRACT

Digital media literature suggests that social media has eased the process of conceptualizing the customer, inclusive of their perception of fairness in the recovery provision. This is because individuals in social media reveal personal information and engage in online conversation and online communities. However, the inherited risk in social media such as the rapid spread of online negative word-of-mouth and the ease of switching behavior to other online providers no longer permits superficial understanding of customers' perception of failure-recovery experiences. Drawing on extant conceptual theories, the current chapter examines online failure and recovery strategies and argues that effective recovery strategies not only enhance the development of marketing communication programs but act as an effective tool for customer retention.

INTRODUCTION

The online environment has revealed the advantages of mass marketing, permitting extended customer targeting (Poddar et al., 2009; Azemi & Ozuem, 2016). While a growing number of businesses are adopting e-tailing to expand beyond isolated markets, luxury businesses are still debating over a brick-and-mortar versus online approach (Gu & Ye, 2014; Felix et al., 2016; Ozuem & Azemi, 2018). Quach and Thaichon (2018) describe luxury brands across four resources (love, status, information, services), highlighting customers' affection (i.e., love) for the product and the prestige (i.e., status) they gain from luxury product ownership as two main resources to evaluate customers' satisfaction. They define information and services as means to support the customers' buying process. Online provider-customer

DOI: 10.4018/978-1-5225-7344-9.ch012

collaboration acknowledges a human-free interaction, recognizing customers' structured online purchasing behavior (Weitzl & Hutzinger, 2017). This conveys skepticism that e-tailing could serve an environment that reaches affection and love. It implies an increased risk of dissatisfaction among online luxury customers, defined by services marketing scholars as the service failure phenomenon (Choi & Mattila, 2008; Chuang et al., 2012). While there is an established conceptual clarification of the recovery strategy types applicable to service failures, a favorable application of recovery strategies seems yet to be recognized (Hess et al., 2003; Ringberg et al., 2007). As Hazée et al. (2017) argue, 'the literature seems to have taken for granted that organizations could apply the same recovery options' (pp. 101-102). This leads to the double deviation scenario, which represents customers' extended dissatisfaction with the company after the recovery strategy is experienced (Casado-Diaz & Nicolau-Gonzalbez, 2009). Luxury companies' efforts to alter customer dissatisfaction into the service recovery paradox (i.e.,customers' increased satisfaction with the company after the recovery rather than prior to the failure) seem evident (Matos et al., 2007). However, driven by the high product quality and impulsive purchasing novelties, the detriments of online service failure in online luxury businesses seem to foster the awakening of a double deviation scenario over the service recovery paradox. That being said, online luxury customers have higher recovery expectations, calling for providers to maximize the recovery effort.

Recently, Azemi et al. (2018) posited the reasoning of customer expectation to be customers' necessity for online banking. They described occupation status as the source of the online banking need, utilizing it as the mediator to a threefold customer typology, i.e., exigent customers, solutionist customers, and impulsive customers. Exigent customers posit online banking as the origin of their jobs' functioning, whereas solutionist customers use online banking in an effort to facilitate the operation of their jobs. Impulsive customers capture online banking as a function independent of their job-related usage, employing online banking for their personal purposes. For exigent customers a service recovery paradox is identified with prompt compensation, co-creation, and customer recovery strategy. They appreciate a prompt apology, whereas explanation and downward social comparison result in a double deviation scenario. With a lower perceived risk from the failure, solutionist customers are satisfied with an apology and explanation, and a prompt compensation maximizes their happiness. If granted the recovery responsibility (i.e., customer recovery strategy), solutionist customers' aggressiveness increases, leading to the double deviation scenario. Being labeled with the trait of patience, the service recovery paradox among impulsive customers is constructed if explanation is used jointly with any of the following recovery strategies: downward social comparison, apology, and empathy. Although this study provides no evidence of a double deviation scenario, impulsive customers are prone to switching to other brands if advised by family and friends. The study does not optimize conceptualization of online failure-recovery among online luxury brands, yet it serves to prove heterogeneity among online luxury customers.

Focusing on emerging markets, Azemi et al.'s (2018) study maximizes understanding of customers with a higher degree of sensitivity towards the provider. This is in line with luxury customers, who essentially allocate responsibility for the selling-buying encounter and the recovery to the provider. Additional supporting evidence to reinforce the existence of such customers is found in Schoefer and Diamantapolous' (2009) study. They present the 'negativists' group of customers for whom providers are antagonists that use profit generation as the determinant of the success of customer-provider collaboration. This contradicts the relational customer-provider marketing philosophy, which sets the customer at the core of the transaction the outcome of which is a long-lasting customer-provider relationship (Farrell & Hartline, 2014). That being said, luxury e-tailing and e-tailing activities that emphasize a sales marketing approach lead to service failures. While this section has revealed the sensitivity of online luxury consumers, emphasizing the necessity to further decipher the online luxury failure-recovery phenomenon as a paradox that is yet to be conceptualized, the following section provides conceptual explanation of online service failure and recovery strategy types as proof of a mutually satisfactory experience among the luxury e-tailers and consumers.

THEORETICAL CONTEXT: SERVICE FAILURES AND ONLINE SERVICE FAILURES

A chronological reflection of the extant literature provides some elucidation of types of service failures. In the context of self-service technologies (SST), and incorporating to some degree online services, subject to an analysis of customer dissatisfaction, Meuter, Ostrom, Roundtree & Bitner (2000) introduced the four-grounded service failure typology. The model is related to the virtual provider-customer encounter, and it includes the following types of service failures: *(1) technology failure, (2) process failure, (3) poor design, and (4) customer-driven failure* (p. 57). These authors suggested delineations with examples of each failure type as follows (see page 57): (1) Technology failure—the interface of the medium fails to work and obstructs the use of services (for example, 'a broken ATM'). (2) Process failure—a failure that emerges after the customer has completed an interaction with a technological service medium. Most likely the customer will recognize the failure after some time has passed (for example, a customer has ordered and paid online for a product but has not received it). (3) Poor design—a technological failure occurs (for example, on a website or with an ATM) because there is a lack of clarity in terms of how to use it, and there is a service design problem with the service itself, rather than with the medium (for example, a prolonged period is required for the money to be transferred from an ATM to a customer's account). (4) Customer-driven failure—failures can occur when the customer is 'at fault' (for example, a customer does not recall the personal identification number required to make an online transaction) (see page 57). The study identifies the first failure type (i.e., technology failure) as the most frequent kind, although it suggests that they all represent customers' perceptions of self-service technology incidents. Further, it emphasizes the lack of recoveries in self-services (i.e., online services), implying an increased risk from encountering failures (Meuter et al. 2000). Based on these ideas, customers are strict observers of online providers, and the provider must understand how customers assign meaning to service failures to develop effective online recovery strategies.

An additional construct that categorizes online service failures is the six-fold typology advanced by Holloway & Beatty (2003). The authors reviewed the first two types of failure in parallel with the process, technology, and poor design failures of Meuter et al. (2000). They tackled the issue of online versus traditional service encounters and suggested that service failures also differ within these encounters. The failure typology suggested by them incorporates the following: *(1) delivery, (2) website design, (3) payment, (4) security, (5) product quality, and (6) customer service problems* (p. 95). This hierarchy of failure types has been set based on the frequency of occurrence—from the most frequent to the least frequent failure type. In analyzing these failure types, the delivery problems that the authors emphasized include complaints such as 'the product arrived later than promised, the wrong product was delivered, and merchandise was delivered to the wrong address' (p. 95). Website design problems include the following: the website did not open, the content was not user-friendly, and the website was only available in one language (see p. 96). Payment problems refer to customer perceptions of paying more than they have gain from the service (see p. 96). Security problems include fraud issues (see p. 96). Problems with product quality are associated with customers' perception that they have received a quality lower than they have thought they would get (see p. 96), and customer service problems occur because the provider does not respond to customer requests (see p. 96). The authors considered the behavior of customers after online failure and suggested that they did not seem to be happy with the online recovery. Further, they emphasize customers' perception of being unfairly treated by the provider. This delineation, besides enriching the theoretical background of online research, provides an informative guide for the provider to identify their fallacies and a source to provide meaning to customer expectations. Additionally, to be able to perceive as much information as possible from the customer, the authors accentuate the importance of providing both online and offline means of customer-provider interaction such as 'toll-free numbers, e-mail addresses, and real-time chat rooms' (Holloway & Beatty, 2003, p. 102).

JUSTICE THEORY: THE MEDIATOR OF THE LUXURY BRANDING PROVIDER-CUSTOMER INTERACTION

Failure-recovery literature has traditionally identified customer satisfaction as being his/her perception fairly recovered (Smith & Bolton, 2002; Wirtz & Mattila, 2004; Wang et al. 2011). Justice theory, inclusive of its three components (distributive, procedural and interactional justice) dominates the theoretical background to explain such phenomena. Smith et al. (1999) defined distributive justice as customers' evaluation of recovery fairness on grounds of 'the perceived outcome of exchange', and procedural justice in terms of the evaluation of the fairness of procedures/strategies that the provider uses to deal with the failure-recovery experience (p. 357). Wirtz & Mattila (2004) identify interactional justice with customer judgment of the fair recovery of an employee's behavior, largely defined in terms of the 'apology, perceived helpfulness, courtesy, and empathy' (p. 151). The literature in the justice theory and services recovery reveals contradictory findings. This is also evident for the online luxury brands. For example, Wirtz & Mattila (2004) suggest that all three justice dimensions (i.e., distributive, procedural, and interactional) have impact on generating satisfaction in the recovery. However, customers are more satisfied with an immediate response and apology (i.e., with procedural and interactional justice) than with compensation (i.e., distributive justice). Yet the latter seems to generate satisfaction when the provider is ineffective in meeting customers' expectations in one of the former two (Wirtz & Mattila, 2004). Kau & Loh (2006) dispute the work of Wirtz & Mattila (2004) and suggest that rather than procedural and interactional justice, distributive justice is the main attributor of customer satisfaction. Later, Rio-Lanza et al. (2009) proclaimed that procedural justice is the justice dimension with the greatest influence in generating customer satisfaction. Both Kau & Loh (2006) and Rio-Lanza et al. (2009) consider mobile phone services. The very different outcomes suggested by these studies with the same research focus (the same industry used) raise the question of why these different findings have occurred. The uniqueness within the study of Rio-Lanza et al. (2009) is that of examining emotions as an element that mediates customers' perception of justice. Following this, one may argue that emotion is a key factor justifying the findings.

Having stated that customers of online luxury branding are more emotionally than rationally driven (Heine, 2009; Okonkwo, 2010), one might suggest that Rio-Lanza et al.'s (2009) work represents the reality of luxury customers' perception of fairness in the failure-recovery experience. This is in line with Ozuem & Lancaster (2014) who state that prompt recoveries make luxury fashion customers believe that the provider dealt fairly with the customer. Later, Ozuem et al. (2017) argued that customers are happy if the provider apologizes for the failure. Both these studies were conducted in United Kingdom. The variation across findings implies customers' heterogeneity in assigning meaning. Subsequently, Ozuem et al. (2017) called for personalized recovery strategies, suggesting that structured recovery platforms might undermine customers' specific recovery requests.

Piff et al. (2010) support this, arguing that the wealth positioning of an individual describes his/her stance towards others. Yet luxury customers who are not millionaires might be happier with the distributive (i.e., compensatory) rather than procedural or interactional justice. Herrmann, Xia, Monroe & Huber (2007) argue that customers of top automobile companies (i.e., luxury ones) evaluate the encounter on grounds of the price (i.e., distributive justice). If these customers (who are not necessarily millionaires) are happy with the compensation, the procedures of the encounter and the employee behavior are of a lower importance. Cultural background seems to be another factor to determine customers' recovery requests. Bian & Forsythe (2012) explain how Chinese customers' purchase of luxury products is driven by the purpose of being socially accepted. In contrast, consumers in the United States seem to buy luxury products as a means to feel unique (Bian & Forsythe, 2012). Bian & Forsythe (2012) did not examine the cultural background of luxury customers in terms of justice theory. However, their findings imply the influence of others or personal individuality traits to evaluate one justice dimension over the other.

Digital media literature suggests that social media has eased the process of conceptualizing the customer (Kietzmann et al., 2011; Gruber et al. 2015; Rauschnabel et al. 2016), inclusive of their perception of fairness in the recovery provision. This is because individuals in social media reveal personal information and engage in online conversation and online communities (Brogi et al. 2013; Ozuem, Howell & Lancaster, 2016). However, the inherited risk in social media such as the rapid spread of online negative word of mouth, and the ease of switching behavior to other online providers, no longer permits superficial understanding of customers' perception of failure-recovery experiences (Barwise & Meehan, 2010; Gu & Ye, 2014). Consequently, both academics and practitioners seek understanding and effective use of social media throughout the failure-recovery experience. The difficulty of achieving this seems to be greater in the luxury industry due to customers being emotionally rather than rationally driven. The following section provides theoretical explanation and conceptual cases to illustrate luxury branding customer-provider interaction in social media in cases of failure-recovery encounters.

SOCIAL MEDIA: THE MEDIUM OF THE FAILURE-RECOVERY ENCOUNTER

Customers of luxury fashion products appear to use Twitter over the other social media platforms to approach brands (Opitz, 2016). According to Opitz (2016) Twitter is followed by Instagram, and the latter is particularly powerful if luxury fashion influencers reveal the message to the audience. The author discusses the cases of two leading luxury fashion brands, Gucci and Prada, that have used fashionista public figures to reach audiences. The former used Chiara Ferragni and the latter used Arielle Noa Charnas, through whom Gucci and Prada reached thousands of engagement (Opitz, 2016). This suggests that influencers should be used as a means of online recovery strategies. Facebook is another social media platform to mediate provider-customer communication throughout the luxury branding failure-recovery process. In this context, digital marketing literature identifies social media with different platforms, which inclusively permit simultaneous failure and recovery experiences (Kuo et al. 2011; Gu & Ye, 2014).

In social media, the provider might deliver the recovery in the form of the *comment*, as a response to a customer's online complaint. Secondly, the provider might approach the complainant with *personal messages*, turning the communication and recovery provision from a community one into a provider-complainant experience. Thirdly, providers could go to *live streaming* in developing a realistic recovery provision. The advantage here is that the host in real time might read customer comments, identify possible criticisms (i.e., failure), and provide an immediate response (i.e., deliver a recovery). Live streaming is also used by Armani, which has organized online interviews with leading people in fashion brands (Stocker, 2012). This again suggests that in cases of customer dissatisfaction, live streaming interviews with knowledgeable people on the issue could be used as form of explanation recovery strategy. The failure-recovery literature has traditionally identified explanation with a satisfactory recovery strategy (Barwise & Meehan, 2010; Pang et al. 2014), in particular when the customer believes that the person involved possesses adequate information.

According to Andjelic (2015), the majority of luxury brands are utilizing contemporary digital marketing strategies (including live streaming); however, they are failing to reveal the original message of the luxury product. From this viewpoint, live streaming would be an unsuccessful recovery strategy if the authentic message of the luxury brand were not revealed. A recent example of a successful use of the live streaming is the Balmain luxury fashion company (Andjelic, 2015). The host in the live streaming was the designer of Balmain products, Oliver Rousteing. In this example, the host was the one to develop the message of the brand, and subsequently it was not difficult for the customer to conceptualize its authenticity (Andjelic, 2015).

Both live streaming (such as the case of Armani, and Balmain) and use of public figures as means to communicate with customers (e.g., Gucci and Prada) are effective recovery strategies if a sincere message is revealed. If customers interpret an online message as one that does not present the reality, a minor failure turns into a major one (Barwise & Meehan, 2010; Xia, 2013). In such a situation, customers feel that the company is trying to take advantage of them (Ringberg et al. 2007). Regardless of the means of online delivery of the message, its inappropriate content might lead to the double deviation scenario. Jin (2012) suggests that dissatisfaction with the content of a Facebook page not only reduces customers' online repurchase tendency but also leads to customers' complete ignorance of luxury brands' Facebook pages. The author used Louis Vuitton, which is one of the leading luxury brands, as a case study to understand this phenomenon and found that regardless of how well a brand is positioned, a customer's discontent experience with the Facebook page leads to switching behavior and loyalty reduction. The author suggests that such an outcome is evident across both hedonic and utilitarian customer types, although the risk seems to be greater within the former group. Further, customers whose purchasing decision is motivated by others rather than by personal desire seem to be stricter in evaluating the company through Facebook lenses (Jin, 2012). Additionally, the content of the message should be relevant to the targeted customers. For example, Coach, which is a U.S. luxury brand, used public figures from China as a means to facilitate online communication with Chinese customers (Ng, 2014). The risk of failure to provide a satisfactory online experience in general and a recovery strategy in particular does not seem to be isolated to the online means of customer-provider interaction. An unsatisfactory online experience with a provider seems to lead to reduction of offline purchases too (Piercy & Archer-Brown, 2014).

Further, the failure-recovery process in the offline environment might require one or more steps, each step consisting of a face-to-face employee-customer interaction. The time gap between steps prolongs the recovery completion, increasing the risk of dissatisfaction. Customer-provider online interaction is a twenty-four hour communication process. Even if the provider does not complete the recovery provision at once, the provider's online presence controls the customer. This does not mean that the provider should ignore the customer request (Azemi & Ozuem, 2016). Indeed, in such cases the online customer feels that he/she was not treated fairly, spreading negative word-of-mouth and harming the company respectively (Kietzmann et al., 2011; Xia, 2013; Brogi et al. 2013). However, it is recommended that the provider uses numerous media platforms simultaneously to communicate messages to the audience. In this way, the customer would consider that the provider has not reneged on its responsibilities. Rather, he/she would acknowledge the provider's continued online relationship as its strategic approach.

Harris et al. (2006) suggest that online customers are more tolerant of failures compared to offline ones. In contrast, social media literature (Kuo et al. 2011; Gruber et al. 2015) emphasizes customers' firm stance of revenge in cases of failure experience. Social media platforms such as Facebook and Twitter in particular are used to spread online negative word-of-mouth (Kietzmann et al. 2011; Gregoire et al. 2015). The risk embedded in online negative WOM is explained on two grounds. First, other customers become aware that a company has failed to provide a satisfactory experience. Second, competitors make use of the unsatisfactory experience to increase their target groups. In the latter context, Gregoire et al. (2015) talk about the '*feeding the vultures*' (p. 175), which refers to competitors' engagement with online complaints about other providers.

Negative online word-of-mouth is of a greater risk if the complaint triggers online conversation (Xia, 2013; Brogi et al. 2013). Gu & Ye (2014) suggest that almost half of customers consider other complaints before communicating their own or becoming engaged in online negative word-of-mouth. The risk seems higher within the luxury branding industry. Zheng et al. (2009) suggest that 55 per cent of luxury branding customers consider other customers' reviews (p. 724). The authors argue that luxury companies ignore online comments, emphasizing that such a strategy leads to customers' perception of injustice in their recovery approach. This calls for recovery platforms that treat the customers inclusively. Such platforms should be customized to individual recovery requests (Ozuem et al. 2017) as a means to enhance satisfaction in general and to trigger positive word of mouth. Similarly to offline customers and those of other industries, luxury customers that are satisfied with the recovery have a low tendency to spread positive word of mouth (Zheng et al. 2009). However, if they do, they enhance other customers' trust towards the provider (Brogi et al. 2013).

Prada has also used customization as a means to enhance customer satisfaction, developing apps that could be used by customers to customize their preferred products (Stocker, 2012). A recent study to consider such contexts is that of Yoo & Park (2016). These authors propose that customization generates credibility for luxury customers in a four-fold scheme of values. This typology includes 'hedonic, utilitarian, social, and creative achievement value' (p. 4) and is defined respectively as follows: the product has made the customer satisfied, the product met the customer's need, the customer has received what other individuals value, and the product that the customer has received makes him/her feel worthy (p. 2). The authors further suggest that mass customization generates loyalty.

In the broadest terms, in the context of recovery strategy, customization might help the provider in a two-fold continuum: (1) providers would be able understand customer recovery requests better, and (2) a customized product could be used as a replacement for the one that generated the failure. That is, such a digital marketing strategy might assist in meeting customer expectations and in overcoming service failures, respectively (Stocker, 2012). For example, Christian Louboutin developed apps to facilitate customer online store visits and purchases (Stocker, 2012). The customer-app interaction might be identified with the co-creation recovery strategy. As Roggeveen et al. (2012) explain, co-creation might have the same impact as financial recovery strategies in generating customer satisfaction. On the other side, Hermès has developed an app that teaches customers 'how to tie their scarves' (Heine & Berghaus, 2014, p. 230). Customers might use such an informative online section when not happy with their Hermès scarf due to lack of knowledge on tying it.

MANAGERIAL IMPLICATIONS

Following Kim & Ko's (2012) suggestion, providers could overcome online service failures if the following two are achieved: (1) *brand equity,* and (2) *relationship equity*. Brand equity refers to the influence that social media has on constructing a luxury brand that stands out from others in the market. This could be accomplished through successfully revealing the authentic message inherited in the brand. This additionally helps towards reaching the stance presented by the second concept, relationship equity, which is identified with the impact that the online interaction has in triggering a long-lasting relationship (see Kim and Ko, 2012, p. 1481). The latter concept is supported by numerous services marketing scholars (Hess et al. 2003; Hui et al. 2011) who suggest that if customers were happy with the prior long relationship they would be less strict in judging the service failure experience. However, as Finocchiaro (2010) suggests, online luxury brands should acknowledge the risk of online failure. This is in line with services marketing literature, which has traditionally emphasized that service failures are inevitable (Smith et al. 1999; Craighead et al. 2004; Ringberg et al. 2007). This implies the urge of online luxury branding to go online.

Guillory's, (2016) two-fold failure typology proposes that luxury-branding providers could avoid failure on grounds of (1) *failure in ordering* (i.e., issues with the website) and (2) *failure in shipping* (issues with the delivery). According to Riley and Lacroix (2003), luxury branding is identified with the 'spontaneity of shopping', which is generated by the perceived 'pleasure of touching and feeling' the product (p. 103). This does not seem to restrict Guillory' s, (2016) *failure in ordering* to the technical aspect of the website. Indeed, it suggests that providers should develop websites that visually stand out, rather than merely presenting informative content. It is recommended that prior to creating websites and social media content, a provider's marketing representatives should develop focus groups of luxury branding customers asking them about the features that would trigger emotional linkage with these platforms. The foundation to such a suggestion lies in the work of Ridgway & Myers (2014), who examined customers' perception of the quality of fashion products on grounds of the color of the logo. The authors suggest that blue, green, and purple colors represent *competence*, *ruggedness*, and *sophistication* respectively. This implies that any deviation from such linkage between the color and customer's perception of the quality lead to luxury-branding service failure.

However, the challenge remains of how to develop recovery platforms that generate customer satisfaction in general and service recovery in particular (e.g., Maxham & Netemeyer, 2002; Matos et al. 2007) even after technical issues such as the aforementioned happen. Academics and practitioners highlight that customers are heterogeneous in their perception of service failure and recovery strategy experiences (Ringberg et al. 2007; Schoefer & Diamantopoulos, 2009). To our greatest knowledge, there is no luxury branding customer typology that would guide recovery provision. However the extant empirical evidence explains how customers in general develop failure-recovery perception. Such information should lay the foundation for the providers to develop recovery strategies and utilize them, respectively. For example, Kim et al. (2016) reveal a seven-fold typology of attributes that customers use to evaluate a luxury product. This includes: (1) 'status aspiration', (2) 'romance and seduction', (3) 'involvement with a fantasy world or adventure', (4) 'other-directedness', (5) 'self-esteem, power and success', (6) 'sensory world of beauty, nature, body and feelings', and (7) 'activation' (p. 308). In the broadest terms, they are identified with the feelings of being emotionally well, powerful, and well positioned in the society, since customers subjectively evaluate luxury products. As qualitative scholars explain, subjectivity leads to multiple realities (Saunders et al. 2009; Maxwell, 2013; Ozuem, Thomas & Lancaster 2016). This again emphasizes the importance of developing multiple recovery programs. Thus providers should utilize strategies that can be customized to meet the requests of every customer.

It is suggested that luxury brands should be part of social media to be able to understand and evaluate customers' very personal failure-recovery requests (Ozuem, Howell & Lancaster, 2016). Their social media presence is greatly identified with customer-provider communication through messages such as those on Facebook or Twitter. The consensus remains that customers' online messages reveal a lot about them (Barwise & Meehan, 2010; Gregoire et al. 2015). That is, social media overcomes the main challenge that marketers have in providing a successful recovery (i.e., understanding of customers' failure-recovery requirements). To take advantage of such benefits, luxury companies should have digital marketing representatives that continually follow customer messages, for if a message took the form of a complaint or online negative word-of-mouth. Stokinger & Ozuem (2015) emphasize that communication through social media generates trust among luxury customers. Further, social media permits a prompt recovery. Customers who receive prompt recoveries seem to believe that the provider was fair throughout the recovery process (e.g., Smith et al. 1999).

Further, it is important that providers become part of online communities. Online communities seem to generate more information than personal messages. Members of online communities share the same interests, implying a tendency to generate more talk. One's talk seems to 'provide value to [other] members' (Schau et al., 2009, p. 30). Schau et al. (2009) explain the close relationship of online community members with the concept of '*social network*', inclusive of the following: '(1) welcoming, (2) empathizing, and (3) governing' (p. 34). In the broadest terms, these elements are defined as members' support of each other both psychologically and from a decision-making perspective. Subsequently, customers seem to stick to such communities for a long period of time. Schau et al. (2009) illustrate such a stance with the online community of BMW Minis, which are considered luxury cars. Moreover, rather than customers alone, providers themselves should initiate online communities. Heine & Berghaus (2014) use the Lancome Rose Beauty Community as an example of a success story. Lancome opened and named this online community after a very satisfied customer (see p. 232). This illustrates the will of the company to appreciate its customers. Under such circumstances, there is a greater tendency of customers to engage in online communities. It is recommended that luxury companies have specialists who know how to collect and analyze data from communities regardless of its origin. Additionally, digital marketing experts must be able to use the data as a means to develop recovery programs and generate customer satisfaction.

Regardless of the emphasis in customizing recovery approaches, there is a set of golden recovery rules applicable to all types of customers. These include: (1) apology (Bell & Zemke, 1987; Kuo et al. 2011), (2) acknowledgement, and (3) provision of a sincere explanation of the issue (Barwise & Meehan, 2010). Jones (2015) provides examples of luxury companies including Saint Laurent and Tom Ford that have used advertisements that do not adequately present females. In these cases, the golden recovery rules might have controlled customer dissatisfaction. Additionally, to overcome the risk of an escalation of online negative word-of-mouth, it is recommended that luxury companies transfer the recovery process to the offline environment. This is essential in two scenarios: first, if a major failure occurs, second, if the recovery process does not end with the golden recovery rules. Further, providers should develop digital marketing strategies that include multiple social media platforms (Heine and Berghaus, 2014). Approaching the dissatisfied customer as a follow- up to the recovery on numerous platforms could enhance his/her trust in the provider, particularly if the recovery was successful, thus illuminating the service recovery paradox. However, as Okonkwo (2009) proposes, the overall luxury branding strategy should embed policies on the use of online media. This would enhance the coordination between a luxury brand's online business and other departments within the company, which in turn would generate a better use of recovery strategies and satisfactory customer recovery experiences.

CONCLUSION AND FUTURE RESEARCH

The online competition and the enhanced customer power (Chaffey & Ellis-Chadwick, 2012) have directed luxury brands towards social media (Kim & Ko, 2012; Stocker, 2012). However, luxury brands seem to have engaged in e-commerce at a slower pace compared to other industries (Meuter et al. 2000; Harris et al. 2006). The increased risk that the provider would not be able to develop an emotional link with the customer, thus generating failure, justifies the luxury brand's skepticism. The digital environment in general and social media in particular have turned failure-recovery into a co-created experience between the provider and the customer (Kietzmann et al. 2011; Gregoire et al. 2015; Gruber et al. 2015). The advantages inherent in social media such as the ease of conceptualizing customers' failure-recovery perception have overcome the main challenge to providing a just recovery (Ozuem, Howell & Lancaster, 2016). However, it is suggested that the majority of recovery attempts in a brick-and-mortar context lead to customer irritation (Casado-Diaz & Nicolau-Gonzalbez, 2009). The risk seems to be greater in online services, where the ease to spreading negative word-of-mouth and switching are 'one second' activities. Indeed, this sensitivity is more acute in the luxury branding industry, where the customer is greatly influenced by emotional linkage with the product (Okonkwo, 2010; Ozuem & Lancaster, 2014).

REFERENCES

Andjelic, A. (2015). Luxury brands are failing in their storytelling. *The Guardian*. Retrieved November 10, 2016, from https://www.theguardian.com/media-network/2015/nov/23/luxury-brands-marketing-failing-storytelling

Azemi, Y., & Ozuem, W. (2016). Online service failure and recovery strategy: The mediating role of social media. In Competitive social media marketing strategies. Hershey, PA: IGI Global.

Azemi, Y., Ozuem, W., Howell, K. E., & Lancaster, G. (in press). An exploration into the practice of online service failure and recovery strategies in the Balkans. *Journal of Business Research*.

Barwise, P., & Meehan, S. (2010). The one thing you must get right when building a brand. *Harvard Business Review*, *88*(12), 80–84.

Bell, C. R., & Zemke, R. E. (1987). Service breakdown the road to recovery. *Management Review*, *76*(10), 32–35.

Bian, Q., & Forsythe, S. (2012). Purchase intention for luxury brands: A cross cultural comparison. *Journal of Business Research*, *65*(10), 1443–1451. doi:10.1016/j.jbusres.2011.10.010

Brogi, S., Calabrese, A., Campisi, D., Capece, G., Costa, R., & Pillo, F. D. (2013). The effects of online brand communities on brand equity in the luxury fashion industry. *International Journal of Engineering Business Management*, *5*, 32. doi:10.5772/56854

Casado-Diaz, A. B., & Nicolau-Gonzalbez, J. L. (2009). Explaining consumer complaining behaviour in double deviation scenarios: The banking services. *Service Industries Journal*, *29*(12), 1659–1668. doi:10.1080/02642060902793524

Chaffey, D., & Ellis-Chadwick, F. (2012). *Digital marketing: strategy, implementation and practice* (5th ed.). Harlow: Pearson Education Limited.

Choi, S., & Mattila, A. S. (2008). Perceived controllability and service expectations: Influences on customer reactions following service failure. *Journal of Business Research*, *61*(1), 24–30. doi:10.1016/j.jbusres.2006.05.006

Chuang, S. C., Cheng, Y. H., Chang, C. J., & Yang, S. W. (2012). The effect of service failure types and service recovery on customer satisfaction: A mental accounting perspective. *Service Industries Journal*, *32*(2), 257–271. doi:10.1080/02642069.2010.529435

Craighead, C. W., Karwan, K. R., & Miller, J. L. (2004). The effects of severity of failure and customer loyalty on service recovery strategies. *Production and Operations Management*, *13*(4), 307–321. doi:10.1111/j.1937-5956.2004.tb00220.x

Felix, R., Rauschnabel, P. A., & Hinsch, C. (2017). Elements of strategic social media marketing: A holistic framework. *Journal of Business Research*, *70*, 118–126. doi:10.1016/j.jbusres.2016.05.001

Ferrell, O. C., & Hartline, M. D. (2014). *Marketing Strategy* (6th ed.). Chicago: Cengage Learning.

Finocchiaro, P. (2010). Luxury brands must risk failure to succeed in new media. *Luxury Daily*. Retrieved September 14, 2016, from https://www.luxurydaily.com/luxury-brands-must-risk-failure-to-succeed-in-new-media-morpheus-exec/

Gregoire, Y., Salle, A., & Tripp, T. M. (2015). Managing social media crises with your customers: The good, the bad, and the ugly. *Business Horizons*, *58*(2), 173–182. doi:10.1016/j.bushor.2014.11.001

Gruber, D. A., Smerek, R. E., Thomas-Hunt, M. C., & James, E. H. (2015). The real-time power of twitter: Crises management and leadership in an age of social media. *Business Horizons*, *58*(2), 163–172. doi:10.1016/j.bushor.2014.10.006

Gu, B., & Ye, Q. (2014). First step in social media: Measuring the influence of online management responses on customer satisfaction. *Production and Operations Management*, *23*(4), 570–582. doi:10.1111/poms.12043

Guillory, S. (2016) *Top five customer complaints with fashion retailers*. Retrieved October 12, 2016, from: http://apparel.edgl.com/news/Top-Five-Customer-Complaints-With-Fashion-Retailers105498

Harris, K. E., Grewal, D., Mohr, L. A., & Bernhardt, K. L. (2006). Consumer responses to service recovery strategies: The moderating role of online versus offline environment. *Journal of Business Research*, *59*(4), 425–431. doi:10.1016/j.jbusres.2005.10.005

Hazée, S., Vaerenbergh, Y. V., & Armirotto, V. (2017). Co-creating service recovery after service failure: The role of brand equity. *Journal of Business Research*, *74*, 101–109. doi:10.1016/j.jbusres.2017.01.014

Heine, K. (2009). Using personal and online repertory grid methods for the development of a luxury brand personality. *Electronic Journal of Business Research Methods*, *7*(1), 25–38.

Heine, K., & Berghaus, B. (2014). Luxury goes digital: How to tackle the digital luxury brand-consumer touchpoints. *Journal of Global Fashion Marketing*, *5*(3), 223–234. doi:10.1080/20932685.2014.907606

Herrmann, A., Xia, L., Monroe, K. B., & Huber, F. (2007). The influence of price fairness on customer satisfaction: An empirical test in the context of automobile purchases. *Journal of Product and Brand Management*, *16*(1), 49–58. doi:10.1108/10610420710731151

Hess, R. L. Jr, Ganesan, S., & Klein, N. M. (2003). Service failure and recovery: The impact of relationship factors on customer satisfaction. *Journal of the Academy of Marketing Science*, *31*(2), 127–145. doi:10.1177/0092070302250898

Holloway, B. B., & Beatty, Sh. E. (2003). Service failure in online retailing: A recovery opportunity. *Journal of Service Research*, *6*(1), 92–105. doi:10.1177/1094670503254288

Hui, M. K., Ho, C. K. Y., & Wan, L. C. (2011). Prior relationships and consumer responses to service failures: A cross-cultural study. *Journal of International Marketing*, *19*(1), 59–81. doi:10.1509/jimk.19.1.59

Jin, S. A. A. (2012). The potential of social media for luxury brand management. *Marketing Intelligence & Planning*, *30*(7), 687–699. doi:10.1108/02634501211273805

Jones, S. (2015). *How should luxury brands navigate advertising controversies?* Retrieved August 19, 2016, from https://www.luxurydaily.com/how-should-luxury-brands-navigate-advertising-controversies/

Kau, A., & Loh, E. W. (2006). The effects of service recovery on consumer satisfaction: A comparison between complainants and non-complainants. *Journal of Services Marketing*, *20*(2), 101–111. doi:10.1108/08876040610657039

Kietzmann, J. H., Hermkens, K., McCarthy, I. P., & Silvestre, B. S. (2011). Social media? Get serious! Understanding the functional building blocks of social media. *Business Horizons*, *54*(3), 241–251. doi:10.1016/j.bushor.2011.01.005

Kim, A. J., & Ko, E. (2012). Do social media marketing activities enhance customer equity? An empirical study of luxury fashion brand. *Journal of Business Research*, *65*(10), 1480–1486. doi:10.1016/j.jbusres.2011.10.014

Kim, J. E., Lloyd, S., & Cervellon, M. C. (2016). Narrative-transportation storylines in luxury brand advertising: Motivating consumer engagement. *Journal of Business Research*, *69*(1), 304–313. doi:10.1016/j.jbusres.2015.08.002

Kuo, Y., Yen, S., & Chen, L. (2011). Online auction service failures in Taiwan: Typologies and recovery strategies. *Electronic Commerce Research and Applications*, *10*(2), 183–193. doi:10.1016/j.elerap.2009.09.003

Matos, C. A., Henrique, J. L., & Rossi, C. A. V. (2007). Service recovery paradox: A meta-analysis. *Journal of Service Research*, *10*(1), 60–77. doi:10.1177/1094670507303012

Maxham, J. G. III, & Netemeyer, R. G. (2002). A longitudinal study of complaining customers' evaluations of multiple service failures and recovery efforts. *Journal of Marketing*, *66*(4), 57–71. doi:10.1509/jmkg.66.4.57.18512

Maxwell, J. A. (2013). Qualitative research design: an Interactive approach (3rd ed.). Thousand Oaks, CA: Sage Publications, Inc.

Meuter, M. L., Ostrom, A. L., Roundtree, R. I., & Bitner, M. J. (2000). Self-service technologies: Understanding customer satisfaction with technology-based service encounters. *Journal of Marketing*, *64*(3), 50–64. doi:10.1509/jmkg.64.3.50.18024

Ng, M. (2014). Social media and luxury fashion brands in China: The case of Coach. *Journal of Global Fashion Marketing*, *5*(3), 251–265. doi:10.1080/20932685.2014.907607

Okonkwo, U. (2009). Sustaining the luxury brand on the Internet. *Journal of Brand Management*, *16*(5/6), 302–310. doi:10.1057/bm.2009.2

Okonkwo, U. (2010). *Luxury online: styles, systems, strategies*. Basingstoke, UK: Palgrave Macmillan. doi:10.1057/9780230248335

Opitz, L. (2016). *Luxury fashion meets social media: Gucci vs. Prada*. Retrieved September 10, 2016, from https://www.talkwalker.com/blog/luxury-fashion-social-listening

Ozuem, W., & Azemi, Y. (2018). Online service failure and recovery strategies in luxury brands: A view from justice theory. In Digital Marketing Strategies for Fashion and Luxury Brands. Hershey, PA: IGI Global. doi:10.4018/978-1-5225-2697-1.ch005

Ozuem, W., Howell, K. E., & Lancaster, G. (2016). Understanding technologically-induced customer services in the Nigerian banking sector: The internet as a post-modern phenomenon. *International Journal of Information Technology and Management*, *15*(3), 272–290. doi:10.1504/IJITM.2016.077349

Ozuem, W., & Lancaster, G. (2014). Recovery strategies in on-line service failure. In A. Ghorbani (Ed.), *Marketing in the cyber era: Strategies and emerging trends* (pp. 143–159). Hershey, PA: IGI Global. doi:10.4018/978-1-4666-4864-7.ch010

Ozuem, W., Patel, A., Howell, K. E., & Lancaster, G. (2017). An exploration of customers' response to online service recovery initiatives. *International Journal of Market Research*, *59*(1), 97–116.

Ozuem, W., Thomas, T., & Lancaster, G. (2016). The influence of customer loyalty on small island economies: An empirical and exploratory study. *Journal of Strategic Marketing*, *24*(6), 37–41. doi:10.1080/0965254X.2015.1011205

Pang, A., Hasan, N. B. B. A., & Chong, A. C. Y. (2014). Negotiating crises in the social media environment. *Corporate Communications*, *19*(1), 96–118. doi:10.1108/CCIJ-09-2012-0064

Piercy, N., & Archer-Brown, C. (2014). Online service failure and propensity to suspend offline consumption. *Service Industries Journal*, *34*(8), 659–676. doi:10.1080/02642069.2014.886192

Piff, P. K., Kraus, M. W., Cote, S., Cheng, B. H., & Keltner, D. (2010). Having less, giving more: The influence of social class on prosocial behavior. *Journal of Personality and Social Psychology*, *99*(5), 771–784. doi:10.1037/a0020092 PMID:20649364

Poddar, A., Donthu, N., & Wei, Y. (2009). Web site customer orientations, web site quality, and purchase intentions: The role of web site personality. *Journal of Business Research*, *62*(4), 441–450. doi:10.1016/j.jbusres.2008.01.036

Quach, S., & Thaichon, P. (2017). From connoisseur luxury to mass luxury: Value co-creation and co-destruction in the online environment. *Journal of Business Research*, *81*, 163–172. doi:10.1016/j.jbusres.2017.06.015

Rauschnabel, P. A., Kammerlander, N., & Ivens, B. S. (2016). Collaborative brand attacks in social media: Exploring the antecedents, characteristics, and consequences of a new form of brand crises. *Journal of Marketing Theory and Practice*, *24*(4), 381–410. doi:10.1080/10696679.2016.1205452

Ridgway, J., & Myers, B. (2014). A study on brand personality: Consumers' perceptions of colours used in fashion brand logos. *International Journal of Fashion Design. Technology and Education*, *7*(1), 50–57.

Riley, F. D., & Lacroix, C. (2003). Luxury branding on the Internet: Lost opportunity or impossibility? *Marketing Intelligence & Planning*, *21*(2), 96–104. doi:10.1108/02634500310465407

Ringberg, T., Odekerken-Schroder, G., & Christensen, G. L. (2007). A cultural models approach to service recovery. *Journal of Marketing*, *71*(3), 194–214. doi:10.1509/jmkg.71.3.194

Rio-Lanza, A. B. D., Vazquez-Casielles, R., & Diaz-Martin, A. M. (2009). Satisfaction with service recovery: Perceived justice and emotional responses. *Journal of Business Research*, *62*(8), 775–781. doi:10.1016/j.jbusres.2008.09.015

Roggeveen, A. L., Tsiros, M., & Grewal, D. (2012). Understanding the co-creation effect: When does collaborating with customers provide a lift to service recovery? *Journal of the Academy of Marketing Science*, *40*(6), 771–790. doi:10.100711747-011-0274-1

Saunders, M., Lewis, P., & Thornhill, A. (2009). *Research methods for business students* (5th ed.). Harlow: Pearson Education Limited.

Schau, H. J., Muniz, A. M. Jr, & Arnould, E. J. (2009). How brand community practices create value. *Journal of Marketing*, *73*(5), 30–51. doi:10.1509/jmkg.73.5.30

Schoefer, K., & Diamantopoulos, A. (2009). A typology of consumers' emotional response style during service recovery encounters. *British Journal of Management*, *20*(3), 292–308. doi:10.1111/j.1467-8551.2008.00589.x

Smith, A. K., & Bolton, R. N. (2002). The effect of customers' emotional responses to service failures on their recovery effort evaluations and satisfaction judgments. *Journal of the Academy of Marketing Science*, *30*(1), 5–23. doi:10.1177/03079450094298

Smith, A. K., Bolton, R. N., & Wagner, J. (1999). A model of customer satisfaction with service encounters involving failure and recovery. *JMR, Journal of Marketing Research*, *36*(3), 356–372. doi:10.2307/3152082

Stocker, K. (2012). *A look back: How luxury brands made an impact online.* Retrieved September 7, 2016, from https://www.drapersonline.com/retail/ecommerce/a-look-back-how-luxury-brands-made-an-impact-online/5038955.article

Stokinger, E., & Ozuem, W. (2015). Social media and customer retention: Implications for the luxury beauty industry. In Computer-mediated marketing strategies: Social media and online brand communities. Hershey, PA: IGI Global.

Wang, Y., Wu, S., Lin, H., & Wang, Y. (2011). The relationship of service failure severity, service recovery justice and perceived switching costs with customer loyalty in the context of e-tailing. *International Journal of Information Management*, *31*(4), 350–359. doi:10.1016/j.ijinfomgt.2010.09.001

Weitzl, W., & Hutzinger, C. (2017). The effects of marketer-and-advocate-initiated online service recovery responses on silent bystanders. *Journal of Business Research*, *80*, 164–175. doi:10.1016/j.jbusres.2017.04.020

Wirtz, J., & Mattila, A. S. (2004). Consumer responses to compensation, speed of recovery and apology after a service failure. *International Journal of Service Industry Management*, *15*(2), 150–166. doi:10.1108/09564230410532484

Xia, L. (2013). Effects of companies' responses to consumer criticism in social media. *International Journal of Electronic Commerce*, *17*(4), 73–99. doi:10.2753/JEC1086-4415170403

Yoo, J., & Park, M. (2016). The effects of e-mass customization on consumer perceived value, satisfaction, and loyalty toward luxury brands. *Journal of Business Research*, *69*(12), 5775–5784. doi:10.1016/j.jbusres.2016.04.174

Zheng, T., Youn, H., & Kincaid, C. S. (2009). An analysis of customers' e-complaints for luxury resort properties. *Journal of Hospitality Marketing & Management*, *18*(7), 718–729. doi:10.1080/19368620903170240

KEY TERMS AND DEFINITIONS

Double Deviation Scenario: Customer dissatisfaction with the company is greater after the recovery experience than prior to it.

Luxury Product: A high-priced product with specific attributes that trigger customers' emotions and emotional purchase respectively.

Online Recovery Strategy: The activity or activities that the provider utilizes online to make the customer satisfied after a service failure experience.

Online Service Failure: If the customer's expectation from the online purchase is not met, an online service failure occurs.

Service Failure Recovery Paradox: The customer's satisfaction with the company is greater after the recovery than prior to the service failure.

Socially Constructed Online Experience: An experience that is developed by more than one party, inclusive of the context, with the online failure recovery strategy seen as a three-fold construct of (1) customer, (2) provider, and (3) online platform.

Section 3
Opportunities and Challenges in Designing Computer-Mediated Marketing Strategies

Chapter 13
Competing Through Online Service Failures and Recovery Strategies

Dipen Rai
University of the West of Scotland, UK

Dominic Appiah
Arden University, UK

ABSTRACT

The ideas of service failure and recovery strategies have been transformed, due to the internet environment, from a consumer-provider perspective to a multifaceted web quality activity. The research on service failure and recovery strategies has been well-developed in terms of the consumer's viewpoint of service as well as the responsibility for recovery conventionally expected to be allotted to the marketer. On the contrary, existing research indicates that there is a limited range of understanding of consumer-website interactivity relating to online service failure and recovery strategies as well as less understanding of the highly diverse characteristics of computer-mediated marketing environments (CMMEs). The perspectives of CMMEs relate to online customer behavior as distinct from conventional behavior. In fact, providers are involved in intense activity in the online environment in terms of market competition, as customers are positioned just a click away from switching providers in the case of service failure.

INTRODUCTION AND CONTEXT

The literature on service failures and recovery strategies is focussed on understanding the perspectives of customers' explanations viewed from the provider's viewpoint (Parasuraman *et al.*, 2005; Zhu *et al.*, 2013). The provider's outlook appears to have been anticipated, being mainly approached as two different performers, in order to excel consumer's explanations (Grewal *et al.*, 2008; Huang *et al.*, 2013). Consumers have been conceptualised as experiencing entirely the same treatment with service failures and recovery strategies, with limited exceptions affecting the subjective view of the occurrence (Maxham & Netemeyer, 2002). A review of the literature describes the experience of service failure-recovery

DOI: 10.4018/978-1-5225-7344-9.ch013

as a five-stage procedure: a service failure occurs, recovery expectations arise, recovery strategies are provided, and recovery and post-recovery behaviour is evaluated. Conversely, forming an understanding of the consumer is predominantly related to particular processes, affecting explanations succeeded to the missing stage (Mohr *et al.*, 2006). Accordingly, consumer experience accounts for particular backgrounds which exceed the possibility of further descriptive factors (Rio-Lanza et al., 2009; Mattila Choi, 2008). Much of io-Lanza et al., 2009; Mattila & Choi, 2008). Much of the relevant literature has been developed using context-free methods and positivist ontological views and consumers responses are typically concentrated and organised. This would suggest that service failure and recovery strategies are related as iterative experiences. Moreover, the customer's experience is anticipated during service failure-recovery. Consequently, Miller *et al.* (2000) demonstrated that the literature on service failure and recovery strategies is recognised through the attempts of academics to assign customer perceptions in service failures and recovery to objective facts.

Nevertheless, the literature underscores a number of contrasting and contradictory outcomes. It advises that consumers are heterogeneous and need to be managed subjectively (Diaz-Martin *et al.*, 2008; Wang *et al.*, 2011; Azemi & Ozuem, 2016). The existing literature on service failures and recovery strategies resonates significantly with the perceived advantages of service recovery which have been the subject of research. However, Rust & Oliver (2000) described the suggestive outcomes as affirming that acceptable recoveries might be harmful to the service provider. This indicates how distinctive the consumers are in reality and advises a contextual method for handling service failures and recovery strategies phenomena in general and consumers in a specific context. The literature in electronic media is highly reinforced by an espistemological orientation (McCarthy *et al.*, 2011). Electronic media literature appears to have established the underpinnings to research into service failures and recovery strategies while the onset of the internet has exposed offline service failures and recovery strategies as distinct from traditional offline practice traits (Salle *et al.*, 2015; Ozuem, Thomas and Lancaster, 2016). It is suggested that computer-mediated marketing environments (CMMEs) have become empowered, allowing consumers to develop insights and act on means of highly individual orientation (Ellis-Chadwick & Chaffey, 2012). It underlines the subjectivity of consumers' insights and relates the service failures and recovery strategies occurrences to experience with uncertain resultsrategies occurrences to experience. Moreover, vendor observation of consumers is highlighted, relating the service failures-recovery occurrence to a combined experience between the customer and the provider.

Research appears to have established the foundation of a comprehensive framework on the literature of service failures and recovery strategy (Ringberg *et al.*, 2007). Scholars perceive consumers as heterogeneous on the basis of positioning existing positivist ontological literature and advise that consumers' perceptions cause personalised, unique service failures and recovery strategies stem from their cultural backgrounds. Therefore, in order to develop the empirical data considering cultural backgrounds, customers' perspectives have been subject to attention. According to Howell (2012), the distinction between 'real' and 'ideal', as stated by Arthur Schopenhauer, has not been isolated. Academics have explained that the 'real' (considered as consumer behaviour and perception) is a reflection of the 'ideal' (considered as consumer's inherited cultural backgrounds). This type of epistemological orientation supported scholars in conceptualising their interpretation of customers' perceptions towards service failure perspectives, recovery expectancy and appraisal as well as after-recovery action (Schwandt, 2000). The reactions of consumers do not restrict the failure-recovery experience to specific antecedents and particular processes. They realised that service failure-recovery has the five phases and provides a unique experience after its occurrence. Developing the study of Ringberg *et al.* (2007), inherited cultural features identify likenesses within heterogeneous social actors and scholars have categorised consumers as falling into three groups: (a) an opposition cultural framework which considers consumers who ally in their contentions with the provider and wish to profited from them, (b) a rational cultural framework which considers consumers who are involved in a good association with the provider, despite failures, and (c) a utilitarian cultural framework which considers consumers who calculate the losses of the service failures against any remuneration from the recovery.

Ringberg *et al.*'s study (2007) advises that service failures and recovery strategies can be described more precisely when the mental states of the social actors are comprehended. Moreover, it claims that the mental states of the customers are formulated to include the mutual culture. It shows that this study supports the the ontological orientation and contradicts the epistemological position. It further affirms that Ringberg *et al.* (2007) have attempted the cultural background in an apparent method. They have provided no description in its regard by defining the cultural context very simply. Their descriptions on service failure perspectives, recovery expectations and appraisal are limited to utility and emotion theory. The present study relates to the epistemological position of Ringberg *et al.* (2007). Interpretivism pursues theorising one's subjective (experience???) to the occurrence (Schwandt, 2000). Scholars have termed qualities in one's perception as 'permanent' and 'learned in a single trial', Lincoln & Denzin (2000) stated that their position appears to mislead at the start, with indistinct phases of qualitative research. Positivism highlighted the fact that academics' orientations to one's own perception was in process and the limitations on the contextual method were visible. Brown (1954) stated that these limitations had been interrogated in the context of culture since the 90s because of the association of culture with learning theory. Learning is related to the collaboration of other social actors and occurrences as well as taking place in order to adjust to social occurrence and increasing satisfaction. Academics associate the above-mentioned qualitative methodology with social constructivism (Collins & Young, 2004; Gubrium & Holstein, 2007; Cunliffe, 2008).

Ozuem & Lancaster (2013) presented the service failure-recovery experience as interaction of the consumers with others by commencing with social constructivitism in the literature of service failures and recovery strategies. The present study focuses on the service failures perspective, recovery expectancy and appraisal as well as after-recovery action, formed by the interaction between consumers and the provider. It means the perception of individuals constantly accepts the latest information that matches and substitutes inherited characteristics. It is divergent from Ringberg *et al.*'s study (2007), as present research does not segregate descriptions of customers' perceptions and inherited characteristics before service failures. This present study will integrate service failures and recovery strategies as a combined experience between the providers and consumers. It will evaluate the service failure-recovery from the perspectives of both customers and providers in order to enrich understanding on the topic. It seeeks to allow a contextual and inclusive conceptualisation of consumers during the service failure-recovery procedure. The reseacher is not isolated from the research context because of implementation of social constructivism. Instead, Strauss (1988) stated that it links data enrichment to the researcher's empirical data. Maxwell (2012) illustrated the point that empirical data indicates the personal and professional experience of the researcher with the studied phenomenon. Personal, professional experiences and background of the researcher have directed the present study in Nepal, relating to online service failures and recovery strategies in the banking sector. Since Nepal is a developing nation and Ringberg *et al.*'s study is limited to only the developed nations, investigating online service failures and recovery strategies in the Nepalese banking industry reveals an inadequacy in the existing literature.

Defining Failure and Online Failure

Scholars have provided definitions and concepts of service in various contexts. Most of the scholars have considered services as actions, events and interactions (Lovelock, 1991; Vargo & Lusch, 2004; Zeithaml *et al.*, 2012). It can be defined as a change in the condition of a customer or of a good position in some financial unit, that is carried out as an outcome of an action of another financial unit, after prior negotiation with the customer or financial unit (Hill, 1977). A service is defined as a procedure or performance, for instance: banking, accounting, or hospitality activities are considered service-based (Lovelock, 1991). Services are the series of activities that usually have an intangible character. They do not essentially occur in interaction between the consumer and service provider or goods or physical resources that are provided as a solution to the consumer's difficulties (Grönroos, 2016). Similarly, Timm (2011, p. 13) believed that *"Business benefits from good service, service skills are crucial for success at all organisational levels. A commitment to using customer service skills ignites a growth process."*

Customers purchase a product which provides services rather than goods or services for creating value (Barrows *et al.*, 2011). Service is the activity of the business and its performance from the customers' perspective. In addition, services are considered as economic activities which create "added value" as well as providing advantages to cutomers or businesses (Gilmore, 2003). Furthermore, most scholars have cited the characteristics of service: intangibility, heterogeneity, inseparability and perishability, that significantly affect its delivery and marketing (Kotler, 2009). What service provides to consumers and what they receive, it can be illustrated from a consumer's perspective regarding service and its concept (Gummesson, 2002). The service provider needs to develop a uniform system of associated activities which provides the solution to consumer problems or offers exclusive experiences. Moreover, it underlines the consumers' perspective that service activities can assist the consumer in resolving their problems (Johnson & Gustafsson, 2003).

Service as an institution is the entire business or non-profitable organisation that belongs within the service industry such as a financial institute or a charity (Gilmore, 2003). Service as a main product is the trading outputs of service enterprises, like insurance policies or bank accounts. Service as product development is an outlying activity proposed to augment the delivery of a main product such as a loyalty program or complimentary drinks in a restaurant. Service as product support is consumer-oriented activity which occurs after the delivery of a product such as updating services or repair facilities.

The service industry comprises various sectors like hospitality, finance and tourism. Most of the sectors include various sub-sectors such as the tourism sector, which involves a range of enterprises from large hotels and airline companies to small restaurants, cabs and local travel agents. It can be said that the service sector occupies a diverse field with various enterprises in distinct frameworks (Gilmore, 2003).

Acoording to Vargo & Lusch (2004, p. 2), an alternative method to define the service is *"the application of specialised competences through deeds, processes and performances for the benefit of another entity or the entity itself"*. The authors consider that this definition covers a fundamental function of entire businesses and organisations. The definition of the term service has various interpretations. The meanings of processes, activites, performance, solutions and experiences are not clearly linked by researchers to customers' problems. It is essential that more specific perspectives and definitions from the customers' point of view be developed as research development into service (Vargo & Lusch, 2004).

The definition of service as act-based is that acts are implemented after confirming a deal between traders and customers. Acts are implemented by traders or their negotiators and are objective in nature (Kayastha, 2011). Traders allow access to their acts or they undertake performances to transform customers' products or they undertake performances and transfer ownership of products to customers in negotiations such as insurance, leasing, or lending. Service can be defined as marketing transactions *"where the object of the market transaction is other than the transfer of ownership of a tangible commodity"* (Judd, 1964 p. 58). This definition categorises all act-based exchanges in the form of services, except where traders transfer ownership of tangible products to the customers. Moreover, it also categorises various sorts of exchanges as services, where traders do not perfrom acts such as insurance, licensing and sales of intangible products, or leasing. Services are also recognised from their characteristics which are considered exceptional in services (Moeller, 2010; Zeithaml, 2014). Intangibility, heterogeneity, inseparability and perishability are generally considered exceptional characteristics of services. These four characteristics, which do not occur simultaneously are not present in many services such as manufacture and utilisation of repair services. Consumers can utilise the machines and equipment when it is delivered after repair.

Conventionally, the definition of services focuses on the distinctions between services and products. The notion of services is described as "IHIP" as intangible, heterogeneous, inseparable and perishable (Zeithaml *et al.*, 2012). Even so, online services are generally patterned, tangible, non-heterogeneous, and advanced, independent of their utilisation. They are also non-perishable (Tate & Evermann, 2010). Therefore, a novel concept and definition is necessary. Online services are defined as *"services delivered via information and communication technologies where the customer interacts solely with an appropriate user interface in order to retrieve desired benefit"* (Fassnacht & Koese, 2006, p. 23). As a result, according to DeLone & McLean (2004), e-commerce events are also incorporated in online services and are defined as constituting usage of the internet in order to enable, execute as well as process, commercial transactions.

Online services are different from conventional services because of technology mediation creating a novel concept in terms of online experience and an information service:

1. **Online experience:** Online experience is considered a self-service experience (Zhu *et al.*, 2002). It is also conceptualised as *"a customer's experience that results from purchase through or engagement with information technology mediated service delivery"* (Rowley, 2006, p. 342);
2. **Information service:** Online service is described as an information service when the primary value exchanges information between the service provider and the consumer (Rust & Lemon, 2001).

A comprehensive definition is needed to cover the entire range of prompts and encounters which occur before, during and after the delivery of online service (Parasuraman *et al.*, 2005; Bauer *et al.*, 2006). Online service is defined as delivering an excellent experience to customers as regards the interactive course of knowledge (Rust & Lemon, 2001). The delivery of effective online services needs to be scheduled and implemented carefully to make online services more strategic and valuable channels (Boyer *et al.*, 2002). Deliberately, the service provider ought to attempt to involve the consumer in designing the complete online process which implements certain aspects of online operations. Moreover, a service provider needs to be familiar with the requirements of the consumer until s/he receives responses from them after delivery of the service to accomplish the necessary amendments to the processes of the online services. Some scholars suggest that online services ought to be delivered over an electronic means and acknowledge that the web should be the channel for an online service network system (Rust & Lemon, 2001; Voss, 2003). The online service encounter can be described as *"the initial landing on the home page until the requested service has been completed or the final product has been delivered and is fit for use"* (Boyer et al., 2002, p. 178). It leads to a novel idea termed 'virtual operations' in the field of operations management, described as online opreations which frequently involve commercial transactions by the use of the internet. Even so, not only the internet is an electronic network for online services (Madu & Madu, 2002).

The definition of online services can be extended to encompass all the characteristics of online networks. Therefore, online service can be defined as delivering the service through ICT (Information and Communication Technology) in which the consumer interacts individually with an apprpriate user interface to access preferred advantages such as websites and Automated Teller Machines (Fassnacht & Koese, 2006). Accordingly, a comprehensive definition of the online service is: the delivery of service via interactive networks by means of computers, mobile phones, the internet between the consumer's databank and the service provider to access essential information as well as to perform the relevant tasks at any place and at any time when required. Resources such as computers, mobile phones and internet access are accessible to the consumer who are prepared to use them.

The Concept of Service Failures and Online Service Failures

Service failures take place whenever the consumer's perceptions drop below their expectations in the performance of initial service delivery (Holloway & Beatty, 2005; Zeithaml, 2014). It is virtually impossible for organisations to avoid service failures, which could conceivably result from human error while the service is being delivered as well as from inherent general features of the service (Brown *et al.*, 1994).

Most companies emphasise consumer satisfaction with the delivery of high quality service. However mistakes occur in all service systems as service failures are unavoidable(Hart *et al.*, 1990; Schneider & Bowen, 1999). In addition, some scholars affirm that *"even the companies with the strategic plans and the tightest quality control procedures cannot avoid mistakes in all interactions with customers"* (Webster & Sundaram, 1998, p. 153, cited in Bradley & Sparks, 2009).

Service failures can be defined as a faulty result which reflects a breakdown in consistency (Berry & Parasuraman, 1992). Similarly, it is defined as *"service performances that fall below customer expectation"* (Hoffman & Bateson, 2010, p. 327). It is also described as any service-associated calamities, or real as well as alleged troubles which occur during the consumer's experience with a company (Maxham J., 2001). In the view of some researchers, it could be expensive if the service provider does not manage the service failures expeditiously, which could also lead to consumer refusal (Liu *et al.*, 2000; Maxham, 2001; Kotler & Keller, 2011). Service failures can occur due to the distinctive characteristics of the services (Lewis & Spyrakopoulos, 2001). Moreover, service failures transpire while service is unable to meet the expectation of the consumer due to a fault in any of the steps during the delivery of the services (Sparks & Fredline, 2007). Similarly, service failures occur when the consumer is not pleased with his/her service experience from the service provider (Liao H., 2007). In addition, other scholars believe that service failures can be caused by consumer behaviour while delivering the service (Armistead *et al.*, 1995).

Researchers need to focus on service failure, as the outcome can be a loss in profitability and/or of the consumer (Schlesinger & Heskett, 1991; Bejou & Palmer, 1998). Similarly, service failure can lead to a decrease in consumer confidence, accompanied by adverse word-of-mouth marketing, in addiotion to the direct expense of redelivering the service (Parasuraman *et al.*, 2005). In addition, the effect of service failure and consumer repurchasing behaviour has been investigated in order to reflect the importance service quality in airline service industry. The research revealed that service failure had an adverse influence on consumer repurchasing behaviour (Petrick *et al.*, 2017). Moreover, similar research examining baking services showed that service failure had an adverse impact on consumer loyalty, repurchasing behaviours and intentions (Jones & Farquhar, 2007; Kalamas *et al.*, 2008; Sousa & Voss, 2009).

Earlier studies indicated that the severity of the failure and critical failure had a substantial effect on consumer satisfaction, adverse word-of-mouth messages and consumer loyalty. Jones *et al.*'s study, (2004), investigated the effect of severe service failure on trust, loyalty, consumer satisfaction and adverse word-of-mouth messaging, and established that it had a substantial effect on consumer trust, loyalty and adverse word-of-mouth message. Likewise, Kim & Ulgado's study, (2012) investigated consumer perspectives on service failure severity, repurchasing behaviour and recovery satisfaction in hospitality services. They similarly discovered that service failure severity had a substantial adverse effect on consumer repurchasing behaviour.

It is argued that only a small range, from 5% to 10% of disappointed consumers, want to complain to the firms when they experience service failures. (Tax & Brown, 1998). In fact, an average of eleven customers out of hundred complain to their service provider when experiencing service failures whereas an average of praise their service provider for a good service experience (Hart *et al.*, 1990). Thus, service providers may perceive that only a limited number of the consumer complain directly to the firm regarding their bad experience of the service failure. However, it is essential for them to be aware that these consumer recommendations or complaints to their family and friends can significantly influence their impressions when they have adverse service experiences. The idea of online service failures is based on ECT (Expectation Confirmation Theory) and can be defined on the basis of the conventional "gap" framework of service quality (Oliver, 1980; Parasuraman *et al.*, 2005). Online service failure is defined as *"the gap that occurs when customers' perceived quality of service delivery does not match their service expectations"* (Tate *et al.*, 2014. p. 2). E-tail consumers experience various online service failures as compared with their conventional retail counterparts (Kelley *et al.*, 2005). Consequently, novel failure recovery strategies are essential in order to deal with online service failures.

Online service failures can lead to an adverse effect on profitability despite both online and offline service failures being inevitable incidents in the service industry. However, consumers complain online more about online service failures as compared with offline. It is because customers have a platform of internet where they can complain easily but effectively and can be reached by geographically disseminated spectators (Holloway & Beatty, 2005). It is easier to switch the service provider online compared with offline, since consumers can find alternative providers with just a click. Therefore, managing online service failures efficiently is crucial for companies operating online to succeed.

Types of Online Service Failures

Relevant current literature provides illustrations of the types of online service failures. Meuter *et al.* (2000, p. 57) presented four types of service failures in terms of SST (Self-service Technologies), account to an analysis of consumer discontent, including to some extent of online services. The framework is associated with virtual provider-consumer encounters that comprise the subsequent forms of online service failures:

1. **Technology Failure:** It is the failures of the interface of the channel that obstruct consumers from exploiting service such as a website if it is not functioning correctly or not available, or a faulty ATM;

2. **Process Failure:** It is a failure that occurs after the completion of the consumer's interaction with a technological service channel such as a website by obstructing the accomplishment of the current service. For instance: a consumer places an order and pays for an item online but never receives it. However, the consumer would find the failure most likely after concluding the order;
3. **Poor Design:** This failure occurs because of technology design problems due to the lack of clarity regarding its use for instance, difficulty in navigating the website and service design problems which are beyond the users' interface. For instance, a long time is needed to transfer money from an ATM to the consumer's account;
4. **Consumer-driven Failure:** This failure occurs when a consumer makes 'a mistake'. For instance, consumers cannot recall their passwords or private identification numbers in order to conclude the online transaction and/or access the service.

This study has determined that technology failure occurs frequently. However it represents the perceptions of the consumers in self-service technology events (Meuter *et al.*, 2000). Moreover, it focuses the lack of recoveries in online services by indicating an increased threat resulting from failures encountered. Consumers are critical spectators of online service providers, based on these ideas. Therefore, a service provider needs to comprehend why consumers take the trouble to indicate online service failures, in order to improve the efficiency of recovery strategies.

Accordingly, Holloway & Beatty, (2005, p. 95) categorised online service failures into a six-fold typology. These service failures were reviewed in parallel with the failures advanced by Meuter *et al.* (2000) and the following types of failures by undertaking the issues between traditional against online service events were suggested (Ozuem & Azemi, 2017, p. 111):

1. **Delivery:** This problem involves complaints, such as 'the items arrived late', 'incorrect items were delivered' or 'the items were delivered to the incorrect address';
2. **Website design:** This problem involves website content that is not user-friendly, or the website fauils to open, and/or is not available in other languages;
3. **Payment:** It refers to the consumer's insights regarding paying more as compared with what was received from the service;
4. **Security:** This problem involves issues regarding fraud;
5. **Product quality:** It is also associated with the consumer's impression that s/he has received a lower quality product than expected;
6. **Customer service:** This problem occurs when service providers do not respond to requests sent by customers.

Customers may not seem delighted with the service recovery after online failures. In addition, their perception may not be treated fairly by the service provider. Besides underpinning the theoretical context of online service, this description delivers a useful guide for the service provider in order to recognise their misconceptions and a source for offering value to consumer anticipation (Holloway & Beatty, 2005). Moreover, it is essential to provide both offline and online routes of consumer-provider communication; for instance, real-time chat, emails and toll-free telephone numbers in order to receive more information from the consumers.

A conception of the types of online service failures introduced by Meuter et al. (2000) and Holloway & Beatty (2005) is illustrated in Figure 1 below, created by the author. Sets A and set B indicate the types of online service failures developed by Meuter *et al.* (2000) and Holloway & Beatty (2005) respectively. The two sets provided signify types of online service failures. The intersection of Set A and Set B indicates the components of the two types of online service failures which are similar to one another. The intersected segment indicates the most frequent service failures documented by both research sources and provides suitable guidelines that might improve online services (Holloway & Beatty 2005, p. 101).

Online Service Failures in Banking Sector

A research on online service failures in the banking sector reveals a three types failures- (a) Functional failures, (b) Informational failures and (c) System failures (Tan et al., 2011). The types of online service failures developed by Meuter et al. (2000) and Holloway & Beatty (2005) are indicated as an intersected section (Figure 1). System failures appear to be recognised with technology failure, poor design and website design problems. Functional failures refer to the process failure (Figure 2). The author described that online service failures in the banking sector dominate the offline because consumers are transferring their banking activities to online.

When the types of online service failures are evaluated on a macro level, service failures researched by the scholars can be merged to a large extent and interconnected to online services and online banking services. Service failures are considered as a 'triangle' which comprises the interruption of service, service encounter and the deviance from consumer expectations (Wirtz & Mattila, 2004; Vazquez-Casielles et al., 2008). The construction of categories looks easier based on equivalence of service and service encounter interruptions compared to simply concentrating on consumer expectations. The insights of consumer anticipation become more difficult while contemplating ideas relevant to recovery service failure.

Recovery Strategies

According to Grönroos (2007, p. 13), "*service recovery refers to the actions a service provider takes in response to service failures.*" This typical definition encompasses the concept that creating gratitude

Figure 1. Types of online service failures
Source: Meuter et al. (2000) & Holloway & Beatty (2005)

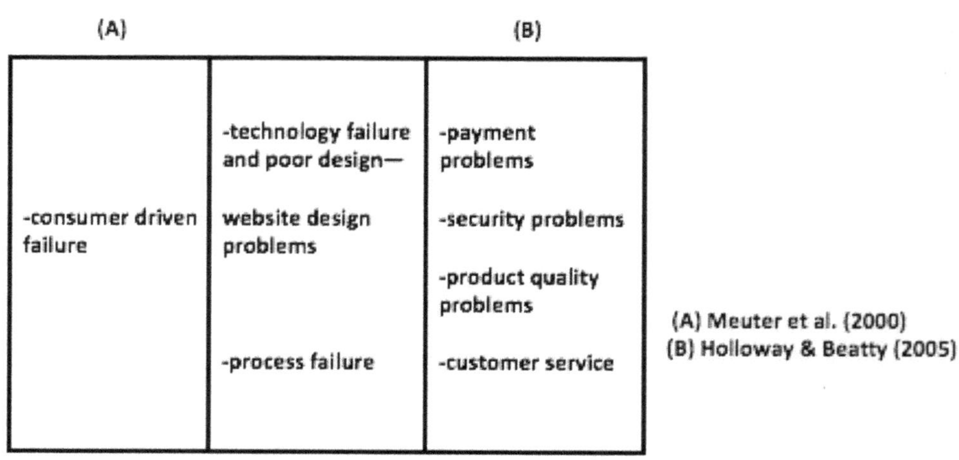

Figure 2. Types of online service failures online banking system
Sources: Meuter et al. (2000), Holloway & Beatty (2005) & Tan et al. (2011)

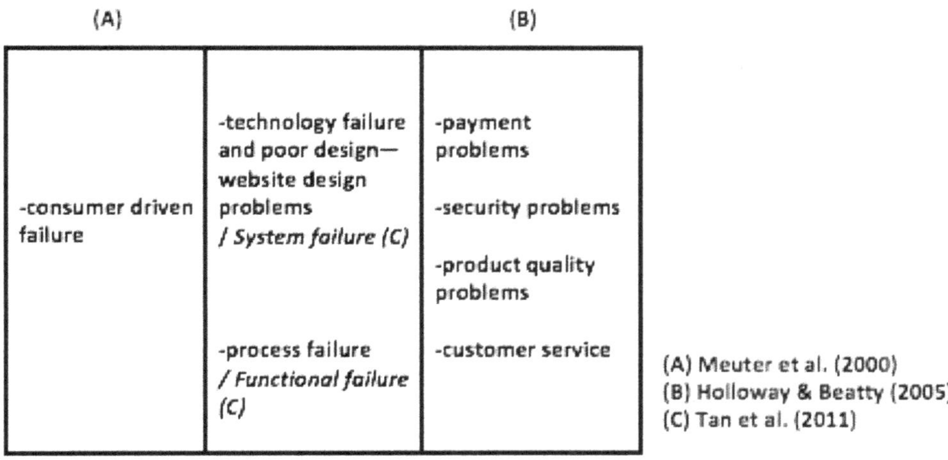

for. and understanding of, service recovery is crucial, as firms must endeavour to discover methods to recover from service failures. A service recovery should be able to eliminate or minimise the negative feelings of disappointed consumers (Hart *et al.*, 1990; Bowen & Johnston, 2009). Thus, effective implementation of a service recovery strategy can be anticipated as good, compared with managing consumer complaints since an appropriate recovery strategy aims to solve a consumer's troubles in order to prevent disappointment, while handling complaints with a view to upgrading systems (Lewis & Spyrakopoulos, 2001). Therefore, it can be anticipated that service providers can create brand equity in consumers by implementing appropriate recovery strategies (Chandrashekaran *et al.*, 2007).

Hocutt *et al.* (2007) recommend that compensation and an apology can be crucial elements for a service recovery. The eight recovery measures proposed by Gremler *et al.*, (2014) for treating every consumer fairly, involve management having to provide explanations after the occurrence of failures, punctuality, encouraging complaints to discover customers' adverse feelings, receiving information from the experienced consumers, opposing of failures and learning from recovery experiences by creating and retaining relationships with consumers. Service recovery is crucial after the occurrence of service failures in order to increase consumer satisfaction. It has been growing due to higher customer expectations and tougher rivalry among companies attempting to exceed their consumers' expectations. Service recovery is identified as efforts to resolve problems, to calm disappointed customers and hopefully to retain them as the firm's customers (Miller *et al.*, 2000). Similarly, it is a mode of exchange, as consumers feel they have suffered a loss due to the service failures and firms attempt to compensate customers' losses with service recovery (Smith *et al.*, 1999).

Apologising, recompense, confirming a speedy response to the consumers and following-up have been acknowledged as recovery actions in research (Smith *et al.*, 1999; Gelbrich & Roschk, 2011). Businesses should have possible recovery strategies that they may implement in order to resolve service failures. The impact of recovery strategies on the revenue of the firm can be important and maintaining decent relationships with existing customers is a crucial strategy (Ozuem *et al.*, 2017). Furthermore, it highlights the importance of evaluating the recovery strategies at the beginning from the operation management's perception (Miller *et al.*, 2000). They introduced a comprehensive framework in the domain of components, such as core components, follow-up, service recovery types, expectations and results collated within the outline of the service failures. The framework categorises earlier patterns of findings as: "*if an appropriate recovery strategy is promptly provided, customers will return even when severe failures are experienced*" (Miller *et al.* 2000; p. 397). Other findings illustrate the impact of kinds of recovery strategies on consumers.

Recovery strategies can be categorised into two groups: tangible recovery strategies and psychological recovery strategies (Kuo & Wu, 2012). In addition, tangible recovery strategies provide recompense for real and perceived expenses like refunds, free services, discounts, gifts and vouchers in order to reduce losses. On the other hand, psychological recovery strategies attempt to calm the consumers by showing concern for their requirements, for example explaining details after a failure, confessing to a mistake and expressing disappointment for a fault in a polite, compassionate and concerned manner (Chang & Wang, 2012). The provision of mixed recovery strategies is beneficial in terms of recovery types as an apology itself is not enough for the consumer. At the same time, any additional recompense can increase the consumer's perception of justice. Customers who experience outcome-oriented service failures react satisfactorily to tangible recovery, while those clients who experience process-oriented service failures are happier with psychological recovery efforts (Cheng *et al.*, 2012).

A substantial number of studies indicates that clients who receive an apology after the occurrence of service failures are more satisfied than those who do not receive an apology from the service providers (Roschk & Gelbrich, 2014). Meanwhile, this study (??) proposes that the absence or presence of the apologies is just as essential as the way they are given and it is important to increase consumer satisfaction. More customers are satisfied with the delivery of a more sympathetic, convincing apology (Ayertey & Ozuem, 2018). It is advised that human participation is more effective after the occurrence of failures caused by human beings rather than by machines, for instance, interaction with frontline employees. In comparison human participation is less effective when the failures are caused by self-service technology. It is because a customer who prefers to use self-service technology to cooperate with service providers is attempting to avoid interaction between employees and consumers (Mattila *et al.*, 2011).

Earlier studies have extensively reviewed recovery strategies in the context of online service failures. Kelley *et al.* (2005) described twelve recovery strategies, categorised into two groups - one those that are successful with greater consumer satisfaction and others that are not. The nature of the recovery should be decided by the seriousness of the failures. Worth highlighting is the fact that the framework indicates a connection between an effective recovery and consumer satisfaction, loyalty and retention (Miller *et al.*, 2000). A survey conducted by Kelley *et al.* (2005) concluded that the type of service failures experienced by offline customers varies from the online environment. Moreover, online-based firms implement different sets of recovery strategies as compared with those engaged in offline settings. However, switching to another service provider can take place often among those customers who are based online despite successful failure recovery.

Compensation and apology are considered as the most important beneficial characters of service recovery after the occurrence of service failures (Chang & Wang, 2012). The study conducted by Kuo & Wu (2012) focussed on the impact of recovery strategies in the context of online service failures by implementing the apparent justice theory as proposed by McCollough *et al.* (2000). Holloway & Beatty (2005) highlighted the significance of recovery strategies in order to deal with online service failures. Repurchasing, however, would be exceptional despite the service recovery strategy implemented to rectify service failures. Whatever steps an organisations may take in order to prevent failures while service is concentrated, failures are inevitable. "*Mistakes are an unaviodable feature of all human endeavour and thus also of service delivery*" (Boshoff, 1997, p. 110). Thus, service failures appears to be inescapable, especially in the banking sector due to the difficulty of rendering face-to-face service experience in an online context. Moreover, service failures are difficult to rectify after their occurrence due to the intangible nature of the service.

Discussion has focussed on the primary concern of consumers being result-oriented service recovery whereas process-oriented service recovery is internal for consumers who are not very interested (Duffy *et al.*, 2006; Ringberg *et al.*, 2007). It is further claimed that outcome-oriented service failures are related to financial loss while process-oriented service failures create psychological loss (Gelbrich & Roschk, 2011) for consumers. Therefore, outcome-oriented service failures usually include a utilitarian strategy that involves possessions, time and money whereas process-oriented service recovery includes a symbolic strategy that involves respect, prestige, sympathy and appreciation (Smith *et al.*, 1999). Thus, a high level of interaction is essential for service recovery between a customer and his/her service provider regarding delivery of an appropriate response to dissatisfied, unhappy consumers (Casado-Díaz & Nicolau-Gonzálbez, 2009). The often critical significance of workforces in the provision of a successful service recovery is highlighted. Furthermore, service failure is usual and consumers may experience disappointments in the service industry after failure occurs. It is essential that orgnisations attempt to respond to disappointed consumers with a suitable series of actions called "the customer recovery process" (Sparks *et al.*, 2003). Achieving success from service failure relies to a substantial extent on determining the key causes and recognising the basic processes that have led to the problem.

Some studies argue that an optimum recovery strategy can be based on the synthesis of the consumer assessments and cost structures of an organisation, whereas several scholars agree with the perception of matching service failures with recovery strategies (Smith *et al.*, 1999; McColl-Kennedy & Sparks, 2003; Parasuraman *et al.*, 2005). Different organisations can have different cost structures that lead them to select different results or methods for recovery strategies. In such cases, the matching recovery strategy might not be a consistent optimum for all organisations (Zhu *et al.*, 2013). The integration of the three dimensions of justice supports resolving criticism of the general insights of justice and their successive behaviours (Blodgett *et al.*, 1997). Similarly, organisations can implement both recovery strategies concurrently to alter service failures encounters. This two-fold approach is commonly termed a 'mixed strategy'. When organisations implement mixed strategies, it is an indication of willingness to put extra effort into recovery for a failure instead of using the matching strategy (Zhu *et al.*, 2013).

When outcome failures occur (for example, service providers deliver the wrong product to a customer), a utilitarian strategy is implemented (for example, replacing the product) with an additional strategy (for example, an apology or the offer of a guarantee). Such service providers implement a mixed strategy rather than just one, similar to the research by Blodgett *et al.* (1997) illustrating maximum levels of interactional and procedural justice can equalise minimum levels of distributive justice. Similarly, while process failures take place (for example, front-line staff are unkind to a consumer), service providers would implement a symbolic strategy (for example, an apology) with a utilitarian strategy (for example, compensation). The effective recovery must concentrate more on outcome failures in the retail sector rather than process failures (Lockshin & McDougall, 1998; Bienstock *et al.*, 2008). This study is further reinforced by Yanamandram & White (2006) who stipulated that the firm's identification of the trouble and reassurance that it would not occur again have higher significance in business-to-business services than apologising. Service providers must recover outcome failures employing greater effort since they often involve core services and have a crucial effect on a specific transaction (Parasuraman *et al.*, 2005; Gronroos, 2007).

MANAGERIAL IMPLICATIONS AND CONCLUSION

Online service failure and service recovery strategies have only recently come into focus in service management literature. (Boroumand *et al.*, 2008; Fan *et al.*, 2010). Academics have derived research orientations to transfer the complications and conflicts from offline failure recovery literature to online (2014). Descriptions of service failures and recovery strategies emerge as they affect the risks and opportunities accredited to the multifaceted nature of digital backgrounds (Piercy & Archer-Brown, 2014). The existing literature on service failure and recovery strategies shows that understanding consumers is important and requires further examination by academics and specialists (Netemeyer & Maxham, 2002; Lo & Wu, 2012; Zhu *et al.*, 2013). This indicates that comprehending service failures and recovery experience from an online perspective is essential to positive recovery platforms. The discussion above emphasises the need to comprehend and relate the service failure-recovery to hypothetical explanations, leading the present study to explore the phenomenon on a broad spectrum.

The current study offers significants pointers for managers in the services sector. The findings suggest that service providers benefit from having a set of service recovery strategies in place to deploy when failures occur. One effective recovery strategy indicated in the literature is offering compensation to customers following a failure (Grewal et al., 2008; Crisafulli & Singh, 2017). Findings from this study indicates that compensation is an effective recovery strategy; however, this strategy is most effective if the compensation is perceived by customers as being benevolently offered, hence, managers should train frontline employees to offer customers recovery compensation in a manner that demonstrates sincere regret for the service failure (Lastner et al, 2016).

Another practical implication, emerging from this study have in response to service failures is the use of apologies, which are not just expected by affected customers, but are also beneficial in restoring organizational reputation especially in the context of service failure. On a long term, such an appreciation may enrich and facilitate the process of managerial decisionmaking involving communication choices aimed at repairing or fortifying relationships with customers (Salvador et al., 2012).

REFERENCES

Armistead, C., Clark, G., & Stanley, P. (1995). *Managing Service Recovery.* Cranfield, UK: Cranfield School of Management.

Ayertey, S., & Ozuem, W. (2018). *Developing Compelling Online Recovery Strategies: Implications for the Fashion Clothing Industry*. Hershey, PA: IGI Global. doi:10.4018/978-1-5225-2697-1.ch013

Barrows, C. W., Powers, T., & Reynolds, D. R. (2011). *Introduction to Management in the Hospitality Industry* (10th ed.). John Wiley & Sons.

Bauer, H. H., Falk, T., & Hammerschmidt, M. (2006). eTransQual: A transaction process-based approach for capturing service quality in online shopping. *Journal of Business Research, 59*(7), 866–875. doi:10.1016/j.jbusres.2006.01.021

Bejou, D., & Palmer, A. (1998). Service failure and loyalty: An exploratory empirical study of airline customers. *Journal of Services Marketing, 12*(1), 7–22. doi:10.1108/08876049810202339

Berry, L. L., & Parasuraman, A. (1992). Marketing Services: Competing Through Quality. *Journal of Marketing*, *56*(2), 132–134. doi:10.2307/1252050

Bienstock, C. C. B., Royne, M., Sherrell, D., & Stafford, T. F. (2008). An expanded model of logistics service quality: Incorporating logistics information technology. *International Journal of Production Economics*, *113*(1), 205–222. doi:10.1016/j.ijpe.2007.03.023

Blodgett, G., Hill, D. J., & Tax, S. S. (1997). The effects of distributive, procedural, and interactional justice on postcomplaint behavior. *Journal of Retailing*, *73*(2), 185–210. doi:10.1016/S0022-4359(97)90003-8

Boroumand, L., Aghdasi, M., Albadvi, A., Jamshidian, M., & Perzon, H. (2008). Service Failure-Recovery in Online Shops in Iran. *International Journal of Information Science and Technology*, *6*(2), 61–75.

Boshoff, C. (1997). An experimental study of service recovery options. *International Journal of Service Industry Management, 8*(2), 110-130.

Bowen, D., & Johnston, R. (2009). Why service recovery fails: Tensions among customer, employee, and process perspectives. *Journal of Service Management*, *20*(3), 253–273. doi:10.1108/09564230910964381

Boyer, K. K., Hallowell, R., & Roth, A. V. (2002). E-services: Operating strategy—a case study and a method for analyzing operational benefits. *Journal of Operations Management*, *20*(2), 175–188. doi:10.1016/S0272-6963(01)00093-6

Bradley, G. L., & Sparks, B. A. (2009). Dealing with service failures: The use of explanations. *Journals of Travel & Toursim Markeing*, *26*(2), 129–143. doi:10.1080/10548400902862010

Brown, M. (1954). On a definition of culture. *Psychological Review*, *60*(3), 215. doi:10.1037/h0059520 PMID:13056118

Casado-Díaz, A. B., & Nicolau-Gonzálbez, J. L. (2009). Explaining consumer complaining behaviour in double deviation scenarios: The banking services. *Service Industries Journal*, *29*(12), 1659–1668. doi:10.1080/02642060902793524

Chandrashekaran, M., Rotte, K., Tax, S. S., & Grewal, R. (2007). Satisfaction Strength and Customer Loyalty. *JMR, Journal of Marketing Research*, *44*(1), 153–163. doi:10.1509/jmkr.44.1.153

Chang, D.-S., & Wang, T.-H. (2012). Consumer preferences for service recovery options after delivery delay when shopping online. *Social Behavior and Personality*, *40*(6), 1033–1044. doi:10.2224bp.2012.40.6.1033

Cheng, Y.-H., Chuang, S.-C., & Chang, C.-J. (2012). The effect of service failure types and service recovery on customer satisfaction: A mental accounting perspective. *Service Industries Journal*, *32*(2), 257–271. doi:10.1080/02642069.2010.529435

Choi, B., & Choi, B.-J. (2014). The effects of perceived service recovery justice on customer affection, loyalty, and word-of-mouth. *European Journal of Marketing*, *48*(1/2), 108–131. doi:10.1108/EJM-06-2011-0299

Chou, F. S., & Lai, M. C. (2015). The Relationships among Involvement Level, Service Failure, Service Recovery Disconfirmation and Customer Lifetime Value. *Journal of Economics. Business and Management*, *3*(4), 452–456.

Collin, A., & Young, R. A. (2004). Introduction: Constructivism and social constructionism in the career field. *Journal of Vocational Behavior*, *64*(3), 373–388. doi:10.1016/j.jvb.2003.12.005

Crisafulli, B., & Singh, J. (2017). Service failures in e-retailing: Examining the effects of response time, compensation, and service criticality. *Computers in Human Behavior*, *77*, 413–424. doi:10.1016/j.chb.2017.07.013

Cunliffe, A. L. (2008). Orientations to Social Constructionism: Relationally Responsive Social Constructionism and its Implications for Knowledge and Learning. *SAGE Journals*, *39*(2), 123–136.

DeLone, W. H., & McLean, E. R. (2004). Measuring e-Commerce Success: Applying the DeLone & McLean Information Systems Success Model. *International Journal of Electronic Commerce*, *9*(1), 31-47.

Duffy, J. A., Miller, J. M., & Bexley, J. B. (2006). Banking customers' varied reactions to service recovery strategies. *International Journal of Bank Marketing*, *24*(2), 112–132. doi:10.1108/02652320610649923

Ellis-Chadwick, F., & Chaffey, D. (2012). *Digital Marketing: Strategy, Implementation and Practice* (5th ed.). London: Pearson Education Ltd.

Fan, Y.-W., Wu, C.-C., & Wu, W.-T. (2010). The impacts of Online Retailing Service Failure Recovery and Perceived Justice on Consumer Loyalty. *International Journal of Electronic Business Management*, *8*(3), 239–249.

Fassnacht, M., & Koese, I. (2006). Quality of Electronic Services: Conceptualizing and Testing a Hierarchical Model. *Journal of Service Research*, *9*(1), 19–37. doi:10.1177/1094670506289531

Gelbrich, K., & Roschk, H. (2011). A Meta-Analysis of Organizational Complaint Handling and Customer Responses. *Journal of Service Research*, *14*(1), 24–43. doi:10.1177/1094670510387914

Gilmore, A. (2003). *Services Marketing and Management* (1st ed.). London: SAGE Publications Ltd.

Gremler, D. D., Hogreve, J., & Meyer, J. (2014). Do Service Guarantees Guarantee Greater Market Value? *Journal of Service Research*, *17*(2), 150–163. doi:10.1177/1094670513505359

Grewal, D., Roggeveen, A. L., & Tsiros, M. (2008). The Effect of Compensation on Repurchase Intentions in Service Recovery. *Journal of Retailing*, *84*(4), 424–434. doi:10.1016/j.jretai.2008.06.002

Grönroos, C. (2007). *Service Management and Marketing: Customer Management in Service* (3rd ed.). Chichester, UK: John Wiley & Sons.

Grönroos, C. (2016). Internationalization strategies for services: A retrospective. *Journal of Services Marketing*, *30*(2), 129–132. doi:10.1108/JSM-11-2015-0354

Gubrium, J. F., & Holstein, J. A. (2007). *Handbook of Constructionist Research* (1st ed.). New York: Guilford Press.

Gummesson, E. (2002). Relationship marketing: Its role in the service economy. *Understanding Services Management*, *16*(7), 224–268.

Hart, C. W., Heskett, J. L., & Sasser, W. E. (1990). The Profitable Art of Service Recovery. *Harvard Business Review*, *68*(4), 148–156. PMID:10106796

Hill, T. P. (1977). On Goods and Services. *Review of Income and Wealth*, *23*(4), 315–318. doi:10.1111/j.1475-4991.1977.tb00021.x

Hocutt, M. A., Bowers, M. R., & Donavan, T. (2007). The art of service recovery: Fact or fiction? *Journal of Services Marketing*, *20*(3), 199–207. doi:10.1108/08876040610665652

Hoffman, K. D., & Bateson, J. E. (2010). *Services Marketing: Concepts, Strategies, & Cases*. Mason, OH: Cengage Learning.

Holloway, B. B., & Beatty, S. E. (2005). Customer Retention Online: The Influence of Switching Barriers. *Asia Pacific Advances in Consumer Research*, *6*, 104.

Howell, K. (2012). *An Introduction to the Philosophy of Methodology* (1st ed.). London: Sage Publications Ltd.

Huang, M., Zhou, Y., Tsang, A. S., & Zhou, N. (2013). Recovery strategy for group service failures The interaction effects between recovery modes and recovery dimensions. *European Journal of Marketing*, *47*(8), 1133–1156. doi:10.1108/03090561311324255

Huang, M., Zhou, Y., Tsang, A. S., & Zhou, N. (2014). Group service recovery strategies effectiveness: The moderating effects of group size and relational distance. *Journal of Business Research*, *67*(11), 2480–2485. doi:10.1016/j.jbusres.2014.03.008

Johnson, M. D., & Gustafsson, A. (2003). *Competing in a Service Economy: How to Create a Competitive Advantage Through Service Development and Innovation*. San Francisco, CA: John Wiley & Sons.

Jones, H., & Farquhar, J. D. (2007). Putting it right: Service failure and customer loyalty in UK banks. *International Journal of Bank Marketing*, *25*(3), 161–172. doi:10.1108/02652320710739869

Jones, M. A., Weun, S., & Beatty, S. E. (2004). The impact of service failure severity on service recovery evaluations andpost-recovery relationships. *Journal of Services Marketing*, *18*(2), 133–146. doi:10.1108/08876040410528737

Kalamas, M., Laroche, M., & Makdessian, L. (2008). Reaching the Boiling Point: Consumers' Negative Affective Reactions to Firm-Attributed Service Failures. *Journal of Business Research*, *61*(8), 813–824. doi:10.1016/j.jbusres.2007.09.008

Kayastha, S. (2011). Defining Service and Non-Service Exchanges. *Service Science*, *3*(4), 313–324. doi:10.1287erv.3.4.313

Kelley, S. W., Forbes, L. P., & Hoffman, K. D. (2005). Typologies of e-commerce retail failures and recovery strategies. *Journal of Services Marketing*, *19*(5), 280–292. doi:10.1108/08876040510609907

Kim, N., & Ulgado, F. M. (2012). The effect of on-the-spot versus delayed compensation: The moderating role of failure severity. *Journal of Services Marketing*, *26*(3), 158–167. doi:10.1108/08876041211223960

Kotler, P. (2009). *Marketing Management* (1st ed.). Harlow: Pearson Education.

Kotler, P., & Keller, K. L. (2011). *Marketing Management* (14th ed.). Pearson Education.

Kuo, Y.-F., & Wu, C.-M. (2012). Satisfaction and post-purchase intentions with service recovery of online shopping websites: Perspectives on perceived justice and emotions. *International Journal of Information Management*, *32*(2), 127–138. doi:10.1016/j.ijinfomgt.2011.09.001

Lastner, M. M., Folse, J. A. G., Mangus, S. M., & Fennell, P. (2016). The road to recovery: Overcoming service failures through positive emotions. *Journal of Business Research*, *69*(10), 4278–4286. doi:10.1016/j.jbusres.2016.04.002

Lewis, B. R., & Spyrakopoulos, S. (2001). Service failures and recovery in retail banking: The customers' perspective. *International Journal of Bank Marketing*, *19*(1), 37–48. doi:10.1108/02652320110366481

Liao, H. (2007). Do it right this time: The role of employee service recovery performance in customer-perceived justice and customer loyalty after service failures. *The Journal of Applied Psychology*, *92*(2), 475–489. doi:10.1037/0021-9010.92.2.475 PMID:17371092

Liu, B. S.-C., Sudharshan, D., & Hamer, L. O. (2000). After-service response in service quality assessment: A real-time updating model approach. *Journal of Services Marketing*, *14*(2), 160–177. doi:10.1108/08876040010321000

Lo, Y. H., & Wu, C.-C. (2012). Customer reactions to encountering consecutive service failures. *Journal of Consumer Behaviour*, *11*(3), 217–224. doi:10.1002/cb.1376

Lockshin, L., & McDougall, G. (1998). Service problems and recovery strategies: An examination of the critical incident technique in a business-to-business market. *International Journal of Retail & Distribution Management*, *26*(11), 429–438. doi:10.1108/09590559810246395

Lovelock, C. (1991). *Services Marketing*. Prentice Hall.

Madu, C. N., & Madu, A. A. (2002). Dimensions of e-quality. *International Journal of Quality & Reliability Management*, *19*(3), 246–258. doi:10.1108/02656710210415668

Mattila, A., & Choi, S. (2008). Perceived Controllability and Service Expectations: Influences on Customer Reactions Following Service Failure. *Journal of Business Research*, *61*(1), 24–30. doi:10.1016/j.jbusres.2006.05.006

Mattila, A. S., Cho, W., & Ro, H. C. (2011). The role of self-service technologies in restoring justice Author links open overlay panel. *Journal of Business Research*, *64*(4), 348–355. doi:10.1016/j.jbusres.2010.02.014

Maxham, J. III. (2001). Service recovery's influence on consumer satisfaction, positive word-of-mouth, and purchase intentions. *Journal of Business Research*, *54*(1), 11–24. doi:10.1016/S0148-2963(00)00114-4

Maxham, J. G. III, & Netemeyer, R. G. (2002). A Longitudinal Study of Complaining Customers' Evaluations of Multiple Service Failures and Recovery Efforts. *Journal of Marketing*, *66*(4), 57–71. doi:10.1509/jmkg.66.4.57.18512

Maxwell, J. A. (2012). *Qualitative Research Design: An Interactive Approach* (3rd ed.). London: SAGE Publications, Inc.

McCarthy, I. P., Kietzmann, J. H., Hermkens, K., & Silvestre, S. (2011). Social media? Get serious! Understanding the functional building blocks of social media. *Business Horizons*, *54*(3), 241–251. doi:10.1016/j.bushor.2011.01.005

McCollough, M. A., Berry, L. L., & Yadav, M. S. (2000). An Empirical Investigation of Customer Satisfaction After Service Failure and Recovery. *Journal of Service Research*, *3*(2), 121–137. doi:10.1177/109467050032002

Meuter, M. L., Ostrom, A. L., Roundtree, R. I., & Bitner, M. J. (2000). Self-Service Technologies: Understanding Customer Satisfaction with Technology-Based Service Encounters. *Journal of Marketing*, *64*(3), 50–64. doi:10.1509/jmkg.64.3.50.18024

Migacz, S. J., Zou, S., & Petrick, J. F. (2017). The "Terminal" Effects of Service Failure on Airlines: Examining Service Recovery with Justice Theory. *Journal of Travel Research*, 1–16.

Miller, J. L., Craighead, C. W., & Karwan, K. R. (2000). Service recovery: A framework and empirical investigation. *Journal of Operations Management*, *18*(4), 387–400. doi:10.1016/S0272-6963(00)00032-2

Moeller, S. (2010). Characteristics of services – a new approach uncovers their value. *Journal of Services Marketing*, *24*(5), 359–368. doi:10.1108/08876041011060468

Mohr, L. A., Harris, K. E., & Bernhardt, K. L. (2006). Online service failure, consumer attributions and expectations. *Journal of Services Marketing*, *20*(7), 453–458. doi:10.1108/08876040610704883

Oliver, R. L. (1980). A Cognitive Model of the Antecedents and Consequences of Satisfaction Decisions. *JMR, Journal of Marketing Research*, *17*(4), 460–469. doi:10.2307/3150499

Ozuem, W., & Azemi, Y. (2017). Online Service Failure and Recovery Strategies in Luxury Brands: A View From Justice Theory. IGI Global.

Ozuem, W., Howell, K. E., & Lancaster, G. (2008). Communicating in the new interactive marketspace. *European Journal of Marketing*, *42*(9), 1059–1083. doi:10.1108/03090560810891145

Ozuem, W., & Lancaster, G. (2013). Recovery strategies in on-line service failure. *Marketing in the Cyber Era: Strategies and Emerging Trends*, 143-159.

Ozuem, W., Patel, A., Howell, K. E., & Lancaster, G. (2017). An exploration of consumers' response to online service recovery initiatives. *International Journal of Market Research*, *59*(1), 97–112.

Parasuraman, A., Zeithaml, V. A., & Malhotra, A. (2005). A Multiple-Item Scale for Assessing Electronic Service Quality. *Journal of Service Research*, *7*, 1–21. doi:10.1177/1094670504271156

Piercy, N., & Archer-Brown, C. (2014). Online service failure and propensity to suspend offline consumption. *Service Industries Journal*, *34*(8), 659–676. doi:10.1080/02642069.2014.886192

Rao, K. R. (2004). *Services Marketing*. Pearson Education.

Ringberg, T., Odekerken-Schröder, G., & Christensen, G. L. (2007). A Cultural Models Approach to Service Recovery. *Journal of Marketing*, *71*(3), 194–214. doi:10.1509/jmkg.71.3.194

Rowley, J. (2006). An analysis of the e-service literature: Towards a research agenda. *Internet Research, 16*(3), 339–359. doi:10.1108/10662240610673736

Rust, R. T., & Lemon, K. N. (2001). E-Service and the Consumer. *International Journal of Electronic Commerce, 5*(3), 85–101. doi:10.1080/10864415.2001.11044216

Rust, R. T., & Oliver, R. L. (2000). Should We Delight the Customer? *Journal of the Academy of Marketing Science, 28*(1), 86–94. doi:10.1177/0092070300281008

Salle, A., Tripp, T. M., & Grégoire, Y. (2015). Managing social media crises with your customers: The good, the bad, and the ugly. *Business Horizons, 58*(2), 173–182. doi:10.1016/j.bushor.2014.11.001

Salvador, R. O., Folger, R., & Priesemuth, M. (2012). Article. *Journal of Managerial Issues, 24*(2), 124–139.

Schlesinger, L. A., & Heskett, J. (1991). Breaking the Cycle of Failure in Services. *MIT Sloan Management Review, 32*(3), 17–28.

Schneider, B., & Bowen, D. E. (1999). Understanding Customer Delight and Outrage. *Sloan Management Review, 41*(1), 35–45.

Schwandt, T. A. (2000). *Three epistemological stances for qualitative inquiry: Interpretivism, hermeneutics and social constructivism* (2nd ed.). London: SAGE Publication Ltd.

Smith, A. K., Bolton, R. N., & Wagner, J. (1999). A model of customer satisfaction with service encounters involving failure and recovery. *JMR, Journal of Marketing Research, 36*(3), 356–372. doi:10.2307/3152082

Sousa, R., & Voss, C. A. (2009). The effects of service failures and recovery on customer loyalty in e-services: An empirical investigation. *International Journal of Operations & Production Management, 29*(8), 834–864. doi:10.1108/01443570910977715

Sparks, B., & Fredline, L. (2007). Providing an Explanation for Service Failure: Context, Content, and Customer Responses. *Journal of Hospitality & Tourism Research (Washington, D.C.), 31*(2), 241–260. doi:10.1177/1096348006297292

Strauss, A. L. (1988). Qualitative Analysis for Social Scientists. *European Sociological Review, 4*(3), 276–277.

Tan, C.-W., Bebasat, I., & Cenfetelli, R. T. (2011). Understanding E-Service Failures: Formation, Impact and Recovery. *SIGHCI Proceedings.*

Tate, M., & Evermann, J. (2010). The end of SERVQUAL in online services research: Where to from here? *e-Service Journal, 7*(1), 60–85. doi:10.2979/esj.2010.7.1.60

Tate, M., Nili, A., & Gable, G. G. (2014). A typology of technological enablers of website service failure prevention. *Pacific Asia Conference on Information Systems (PACIS).*

Tax, S. S., & Brown, S. W. (1998). Recovering and Learning from Service Failure. *Sloan Management Review, 40*(1), 70.

Timm, P. R. (2011). Customer Service: Career Success Through Customer Satisfaction (Illustrated ed.). Prentice Hall.

Vargo, S. L., & Lusch, R. F. (2004). Evolving to a New Dominant Logic for Marketing. *Journal of Marketing*, *68*(1), 1–17. doi:10.1509/jmkg.68.1.1.24036

Vazquez-Casielles, R., Rio-Lanza, A. B., & Diaz-Martin, A. M. (2008). Satisfaction with service recovery: Perceived justice and emotional responses. *Journal of Business Research*, *62*, 775–781.

Wang, Y.-S., Wu, S.-C., Lin, H.-H., & Wang, Y.-Y. (2011). The relationship of service failure severity, service recovery justice and perceived switching costs with customer loyalty in the context of e-tailing. *International Journal of Information Management*, *31*(4), 350–359. doi:10.1016/j.ijinfomgt.2010.09.001

Wirtz, J., & Mattila, A. S. (2004). Consumer responses to compensation, speed of recovery and apology after a service failure. *International Journal of Service Industry Management*, *15*(2), 150–166. doi:10.1108/09564230410532484

Yanamandram, V., & White, L. (2006). Switching barriers in business-to-business services: A qualitative study. *International Journal of Service Industry Management*, *17*(2), 158–192. doi:10.1108/09564230610656980

Zeithaml, V. A., Bitner, M. J., & Gremler, D. D. (2012). *Services Marketing* (6th ed.). McGraw-Hill Education.

Zhu, F. X., Wymer, W. J., & Chen, I. (2002). IT-based services and sevice quality in consumer banking. *International Journal of Service Industry Management*, *13*(1), 69–90. doi:10.1108/09564230210421164

Zhu, Z., Nakata, C., Sivakumar, K., & Grewal, D. (2013). Fix It or Leave It? Customer Recovery from Self-service Technology Failures. *Journal of Retailing*, *89*(1), 15–29. doi:10.1016/j.jretai.2012.10.004

KEY TERMS AND DEFINITIONS

Online Service Failure: Online service failure is a break that appears when the quality of service delivered is not what customers expected in the internet platform.

Recovery Strategy: Recovery strategy refers to the provision of recompense in the forms of real and perceived expenses, both tangible and psychological.

Service Failure: Service failure occurs when the perceptions of the customer fall below their expectations in the delivery of service.

Service Recovery: Service recovery is used to define the activities taken by service providers in order to recover the service failure.

Chapter 14
Calculation of Facebook Marketing Effectiveness in Terms of ROI

Tereza Semerádová
Technical University of Liberec, Czech Republic

Petr Weinlich
Technical University of Liberec, Czech Republic

ABSTRACT

This chapter demonstrates how to assess the performance of organic and sponsored activities on Facebook using the data available in Facebook Ads Manager, Facebook Page Insights, and Google Analytics. The main aim of the proposed ROI calculation model is to connect common social media marketing objectives with the analytical information available. The main emphasis is put on the technical aspect of ad performance assessment. The authors explain how the Facebook attribution system and post-impression algorithm work, describe the relation between advertising goals and metrics displayed as achieved campaign results, and demonstrate how to derive ROI indexes from different Facebook conversions. The chapter also includes a practical example how to calculate current and future value of ongoing ads.

INTRODUCTION

The digital advertising has become a key instrument for reaching marketing and business goals of many companies. This sector is rapidly growing reaching 281.407 billion USD in 2018. Even though the Search advertising still represents the largest segment with a market volume of 127.546 billion USD, Social media advertising is not far behind. With the annual growth of 10.5% this segment is expected to reach a market volume of 76.561 billion USD in 2022 (Statista, 2018a). Ad revenues of Facebook, the leading company on the field of social media advertising, stood at more than 39.9 billion USD in 2017 which is almost a 22 billion increase in comparison to 2015. In addition, the current statistics imply another potential for expansion for mobile advertising. According to Statista (2018b), mobile advertising seems to be the most promising form of revenue generation for the company. It is expected that Facebook mobile advertising revenues will reach 60.68 billion USD in 2021.

DOI: 10.4018/978-1-5225-7344-9.ch014

The growing importance of social advertising in terms of online marketing activities is undoubtable. Big brands such as Samsung, Proter&Gambler, Coca Cola or Oreo embraced Facebook advertising as a key part of their marketing strategies. Samsung, who is one the Facebook biggest clients, spent 10 million USD in three weeks on Facebook just to launch its Galaxy S III phone. Also, Procter & Gamble, the world's largest advertiser, has a massive presence on Facebook and spends yearly about 60 million USD on sponsored posts. Brand´s Facebook influence does not have to be expressed only by the amount spent on online advertising. For instance, Coca-Cola has 76 million fans on Facebook, making it the most-liked brand on the planet, while Starbucks with 37 million fans occupies the fourth rank (Business Insider, 2018).

It can thus be assumed that greater effectiveness of online advertising contributes to improving business activities of companies that use it. Current studies show that online advertising, by making use of proper expertise and technologies, may help to change customer buying behavior (Abayi & Khoshtinat, 2016). Results of the previous surveys and studies supported the assumption that Facebook seems to be an effective medium for customer relationship management and the promotion of new products. Businesses are very keen to harvest all the benefits offered by this network. Facebook activities help to build awareness, inform, promote the brand and its product consistently with the business goals. However, understanding the targeted group of customers and the technical and contextual characteristics of the online media in use represent a crucial prerequisite for achieving all the online marketing objectives. Companies need to understand what are the correlations between their social media activities, online advertising and the benefits gained from such efforts (Ertugan, 2017).

One of the biggest issues in terms of assessing the effectiveness of Facebook marketing efforts is the quantification of the achieved results. Only some of the advertising efforts may be directly expressed as revenues. The remaining processes such as raising awareness and community building,contribute to the generation of profit indirectly. However, companies invest significant amounts of money in order to expand their fan bases, promote their company culture or engage in communication with their current customers. All of these partial steps contribute to creating the brand´s image and finally selling the promoted products. These activities, in particular, are causing considerable problems when it comes to calculating their contribution to the final revenues. Nevertheless, knowing the performance of all the marketing efforts on Facebook helps to effectively allocate the marketing ressources.

In this chapter, the researchers are going to focus on the calculation of return on Facebook marketing investments, hereinafter referred to as ROI-FM, including the proposition of Facebook advertising effectiveness evaluation models for individual goals reachable via this network. Thanks to the sophisticated tracking systems offered by Facebook and their connection to website analytical applications such as Google Analytics, the companies have numerous possibilities how to monitor the impact of their Facebook (and other) advertisements. It is important to understand the advertising system and the metrics related to it. Choosing the right metrics and interpreting them correctly with regards to the marketing goals is the only way how to assess the effectiveness of Facebook activities and optimize the settlement of online advertisements.

The following paragraphs are going to explain how Facebook attribution system and post impression algorithm work, describe the relation between advertising goals and metrics displayed as achieved campaign results, and demonstrate how to derive ROI-FM indexes from different Facebook conversions. Aim of this chapter is to connect common social media marketing objectives with analytical information available in Facebook Insights and Facebook Ads Manager. The authors believe that the proposed perspective could help the marketers to take full advantage of the possibilities offered by this networking platform.

FACEBOOK POST AND AD PERFORMANCE

Corvi and Bonera (2010) define advertising effectiveness as the extent to which advertising brings the desired effects. The authors also add that this effectiveness is not easy to measure due to its connection to marketing, financial, environmental, competition and other variables and that cannot always be expressed with quantitative measures. Aslam & Karjaluoto (2017) made a synthesis of previous papers discussing the topic of online advertising. In their paper they make difference between paid advertising and online marketing since the last one may include organic elements such as friend referrals or search engine optimization. The effectiveness assessment thus should not be restricted only to sponsored posts but also to other Facebook activities with organic (unpaid) reach and with other objectives than just increasing the number of product orders. Accordingly, the activities may be generalized by dividing them into two groups: customer relationship management and product promotion.

Customer Engagement

Customer engagement is generally defined as the relationship users have with the brand, advertisement or post (Kuvykaitė & Tarutė, 2015). However, universal definition of this concept is still missing. Engagement is in terms of social networks expressed as a range of metrics while contextual relevance remains a critical aspect. According to a survey organized by Deloitte (2015), consumers do not use Facebook to look for new products or to engage with brands. Their primary motivation is to look for social information and entertainment.

Brands should therefore go beyond evelatuating just the purchases, but also examine other engagement parameters such as consumer's comments (Fulgoni, 2016). Research results presented by Brettel et al. (2015) indicate that in long term customers that like the brand page and interact with it (liking posts, commenting) are more likely to bring sales benefits.

However, many companies tend to misinterpret the achieved results and overestimate the effects of their Facebook activities. According to Heller Baird and Parasnis (2011), 38% of consumers feel social media interactions with a brand will not increase their loyalty to a brand. In addition, not all interactions may be considered as having the same value since for instance liking a brand page can occur for utilitarian reasons such as winning in a competition or getting a discount (Wallace et al., 2014).

The relevancy of shared content influences the way how consumers perceive marketing communication of the brand. Individual features that have the most significant impact on the consumer's perception are described by the Elaboration Likelihood Model (ELM). This model covers also disruptive effects that may result in negative attitudes toward the post or advertisement and as consequence in lower engagement rate (Petty & Cacioppo, 1986).

Heinonen (2011) suggested that consumer´s behavior is not influenced by a single motivation but rather by a variety of factors. He also adds that due to the growing portion of user generated content, traditional marketing strategies are less effective. Consumers are becoming active producers of business values.

User experience may be viewed as a composite variable consisting of extrinsic and intrinsic factors. Extrinsic factors are connected to utilitarian value which describes the level of satisfaction with the information gained on products, specific problems or areas of interest. Whereas intrinsic factors correspond to hedonic value. Hedonic factors represent entertainment, fun, and sensory stimulation (Gutiérrez-Cillán et al., 2017). The main objective of social media marketers should thus be to satisfy both extrinsic and intrinsc factors. Whereas the primary impuls of the brand´s pages would be to focus on supplying required information on the products they sell, they should not neglect the intrinsic experience the users of social networks are looking for. The level of satisfaction with the dimensions described above conditions consumer´s motivation to stay in the community and possibly becoming a more active member (Bicen et al., 2011).

Zhou et al. (2013) studied the predeterminants of successful conversion from visitors to active members in online brand communities. They came to conclusion, that if the user by viewing the branded posts perceives them as having satisfactory informational value and realizes the benefits of belonging to this particular community his intention to participate will grow stronger.

Dehghani & Tumer (2015) studied the link between brand image, brand equity and purchase intention. They found high correlations between the examined factors and confirmed that Facebook may enhance brand image and brand equity leading to increased purchase intention.The authors describe a new phenomenon they refer to as trust advertising. Trust advertising is based on such features as participation, realization, personalization and feedback that should be developed all along the entire purchase cycle. Harris and Dennis (2011) in their paper studied factors influencing customer trust and engagement when it comes to Facebook branded content. They found out that social network users have a hierarchy of trust that goes as follows in the descending order Facebook friends, expert blogs, independent review sites and lastly celebrities and e-retailer sites.

Dehghani & Tumer (2015) also suggest that user´s willingness to purchase products increases with the growing number of "like"s and "share"s that possibly reflect the reputability of the brand in the eyes of the consumer. LaPointe (2012) came to different conclusions. He thinks that the membership of branded pages on Facebook and likelihood to click on advertising are not necessarily correlated. Banelis et al. (2013) argue that many buyers that frequently purchase goods from one category probably have larger brand repertoires and they are more likely to be 'fans' of multiple Facebook pages from this category.

In their experiment, Beukeboom et al. (2015) proved that there is a positive relationship between brand equity, purchase intention, brand attitudes and becoming a fan of a brand page. In a one month period the authors observed how engagement parameters changed for the users that became followers of a selected brand.The parameters increased in all the observed cases.

Many brands assume, that sharing large amounts of branded content will lead to the growth in sales and increased fan commitment and content sharing. However, only small fraction of the branded content is shared by the fans. Yuki (2015) claims that only 7% of the brand's activites are forwarded. Even Facebook´s own statistics support the assumption that posting too much branded content and pushing the fans to interact with it may chase them away and negatively react to advertised content (Brettel et al., 2015). There is also no significant correlation between the People Talking About This (PTAT) metric and brand´s sales of profit (Smallwood, 2016).

Some studies suggest that the strength of the fan base influence may differ across the product categories. For instance, fashion products content has a bigger potential to be shared by the social network users rather then financial services. Promoting products may therefore be slightly problematic for some categories that offer rather professional services. Facebook marketing is best suited for the promotion of consumer goods and products that are connected with entertainment and lifestyle. Even though, despite these barriers, neglecting company presence on Facebook may lead to missed opportunities to gain new customers. Companies thus should not abandon social networks but actively communicate with their potential customers, assess the impact of their activities and carefully consider the investments in Facebook advertising. For some categories, Facebook may be only used just as an indirect marketing support channel. Being able to measure the performance of individual media used, and understand them correctly represent a building stone of an effective social media marketing. Based on the results described in the Harvard Business Review study of 2100 companies, only 7% of the respondents were able to fully embrace the potential of social networks and were trying to understand the effectiveness of their advertising and marketing activities (Kohli et al., 2015).

When it comes to assessing the effectiveness of Facebook content, it is necessary to make a distinction between „brand posts“ and „user posts“. Through branded posts companies try to influence the experience of their followers. However, not all posts have the same impact and not all post generate the same value. Since Facebook posts are designed to allow the sharing of many types of content and to trigger various responses, measuring the user experience and reaction is very difficult due to the high number of possible permutations (Gutiérrez-Cillán et al., 2017).

Advertising Performance

Thanks to the personal details on all their users that Facebook and other social media store, they represent a superior channel to other advertising media since they allow the marketers to use this information to reach their target audiences (Curran et al., 2011). Advertising on Facebook is specific in that the advertiser may choose what advertising model he wants use and what metrics will be calculated to measure the performance of the advertisement. However, Facebook does not use the Flat Fee (FF) model. The advertising costs depend on the engagement rate, which measures how much the ads are relevant for the target audiences. The bigger the engagement is, the lower the costs will decrease (Tikno, 2017).

In the FF model, the marketing costs depend on the advertisement size and the impression time. In this advertising model, the advertiser pays for the time his advertising unit is being displayed regardless of the number of conversions generated during that period. While the CPM (from Latin Cost Per Mille), also known as the CPT (Cost Per Thousand) model is based on the calculation of the cost needed to pay by the advertiser to reach 1000 recipients. Just as the FF, neither the CPM model takes into account the number of actions (website visits, purchases made in the eshop, etc.) gained thanks to the advertisement. An other model that is used by Facebook advertising system is the CPC model (Cost per Click). Unlike the previous two models, CPC is based on the number of interactions with the ad. The advertiser is charged an exact sum that is determined as the number of actual clicks leading the advertisers website multiplied by the CPC index which determines the cost per click on an advertisement unit. Advertisers ordering campaigns in this model assess the effectiveness of their ads using the CTR index (click through rate) that indicates what percentage of the impressions resulted in the user interaction with the ad. Similar principle is used in the CPA model (Cost Per Action) where the advertiser pays not just for a click and a lead to his website, but rather for any action that is relevant to him. Advertising costs are drawn only when the action defined by the advertiser occurs such as filling the order form, providing contact details etc. The effectiveness of the CPA model is usually assessed via the conversion rate that stands for the percentage of users reacting to the advertisement performed the desired action.

In her paper, Magdalena Rzemieniak (2015) assessed the effectiveness and frequency of use of three types of online campaign settlements models: impression models, effectiveness models and hybrid models. Her survey comprising 50 entrepreneurs revealed that 80% of the respondents use the CPC model for most of their ads that over 60% of them also consider the most effective.

All of these advertising models have in common the need to captivate the viewer's attention and induce his interaction with the post. The marketers thus need to learn how to earn higher engagement rates. Tikno (2017) investigated the performance of different media types used on Facebook. The author used as control variables the gender, age and product type to define the interest group. The results showed that video based posts lead to higher engagement compared to images.

Dehghani and Tumer (2015) studied on the sample of 100 student from Cypriot universities the students´perception of branded content on Facebook. Their results indicate that in order to achieve a high level of effectiveness, the ads should include features such as personalization, participation and realization.

Despite all the undeniable benefits of sponsored content, users do not come to Facebook to browse through the advertisements. Ad placements are therefore susceptible to avoidance and may easily be ignored. Van den Broeck et al. (2018) analyzed the level of avoidance for the newsfeed and for the right sidebar. The avoidance level for the newsfeed was significantly higher. The authors also find out that product involvement and right audience targeting had positive moderating effect on intention to skip advertisements.

Research presented by Bang and Lee (2016) suggests that ad avoidance is more related to the habitual appearance than information processing. These results are in compliance with findings presented by Van den Broeck et al. (2018). Visual characteristics, timing, placement and audience targeting have been found to be key determinants of user interaction with the ad. According to Fan et al. (2017), placement is not a sufficient reason to ad avoidance. If the content of the ad is consistent with the interests of the user and fits within the social media context, the advertisement may actually provide positive experience to the user and lead to desired interaction.

The term "ad placement" is used to describe all advertising spaces provided by Facebook such as the newsfeed, righ side bar, Instagram, Audience Network, instream videos or messenger. The individual placements have different potential for reaching the Facebook users and perform differently when comes to the type of content chosen for the advertisement. Facebook newsfeed (with the possibility of distinction for desktop and mobile devices) represents the most popular placement on Facebook (Campbell and Marks, 2015). Thanks to their resemblance to the user generated content, sponsored posts provide a consistent reading experience (eMarketer, 2016).

Research related to the effectiveness of ad placements on social networks is very limited (Bang and Lee, 2016; Van den Broeck et al., 2017). The scarceness of information may be caused by the lack of nonexperimental data collected from real life campaigns and web traffic. Nevertheless, the evidence for website ad placements suggests that user´s reaction in terms of ad processing, attention, attitudes and clicks depend very strongly on the chosen ad placement (Mulhern, 2013). Feeling of intrusiveness is one of the other frequently mentioned causes of ad avoidance (Ying et al., 2009). Sponsored content is often perceived by the users as obstructing since it intervenes with the browsing goals of the consumers. Van den Broeck et al. (2017) presumes that newsfeed ads are more likely to be ignored than ads placed in the right column. Moreover, statistics report that there is also a different cost per conversion for different placements on Facebook. This only confirms the assumption of distinct effectiveness levels for advertising spaces (Loomer, 2013). In addition, the conversion cost and final campaign results are also determined by the price and optimization models.

Many researchers agree that advertising blindness may be avoided by achieving higher product involvement (Cho, 2003; Rejón-Guardia and Martínez-López, 2014; Kelly et al., 2010). The term product involvement is defined as "[…] perceived relevance of the object based on inherent needs, values, and interests" (Zaichkowsky, 1985, p. 342). Becker-Olsen (2003) found that adjusting the ad content to match the interests of the target audience may lead to higher effectiveness of newsfeed ads over the right column placements. The author argues that thanks to the better fit of the ad with the audience the cognitive effort increases leading to a greater engagement. Cowley and Barron (2008) came to similar conclusions. They believe that the persuasion ability of the advertisements is related to the context where the ad is placed. If the post is not consistent with the expected content in the newsfeed, the users find it less entertaining, brand attitude decreases and ad avoidance increases.

Bleier et al. (2015), Chi (2011) and Taylor et al. (2011) believe that the motivation to use Facebook may as well influence the attitudes toward online advertising. Smock et al. (2011) identified nine user motivations to be part of Facebook community: Habitual pass time, Relaxing entertainment, Expressive information sharing, Escapism, Cool new trend, Companionship, Professional advancement, Social interaction, To meet new people. All these motives may be divided into two categories: goal-oriented search motives and playful surfing motives. For search tasks online ads are perceived as irritating and lead to lower attitude towards the ad (Duff and Faber, 2011).

Some authors emphasize the need to assess the effectiveness of advertising more systematically. According to Knoll (2015), there is no systematic empirical overview setting the guidelines on how to measure the performance of social media campaigns. Many research studies tend to focus on the identification of the relation between attitudes, perception and online advertising, but they provide no practical insights for advertisers.

COLLECTING PERFORMANCE DATA

The benefits of advertising in an online environment include large array of benefits. In addition to easy targeting of selected customer groups and flexible communication with potential customers, easy traceability of user´s actions represents the key prerequisite to accurately measure the performance of Facebook marketing activities. Conveniently, Facebook has its own tracking system that is able to evaluate user behavior, divide users into customer segments based on multiple selection criteria and precisely measure the level of user engagement with the post in the form of likes, shares, clicks and other metrics. The assesssment of ad / post effectiveness and the calculation of ROI-FM strongly depend on the quality of available data. Based on the previously described findings, ad effectiveness assessment requires information about the target audience, user engagement and interaction with the post, user behavior and attitudes toward the ad. In order to calculate the return of marketing investements, the company also needs to keep track of its advertising and ad processing expenses.

Advertising Costs

Companies of all sizes resort to social media as to a less expensive option compared to offline advertisement media. Facebook advertising is suitable even for restricted budgets. Advertisers decide how much they want to spend per each campaign. Whether the ad will be shown to a user from a target group depends on the evaluation of the two objectives that Facebook defines as its priority in terms of sponsored content. Firstly, Facebook's efforts to help advertisers reach the target audience and reach marketing goals. Secondly, the company strives to create for the people who use its applications and services a positive and relevant environment. For this reason, ads are delivered based on an auction that takes into account the interests of both advertisers and users. The aim of these auctions is to offer the right person the right ad at the right time. The winner of the auction is not the highest bid, but the ad with the highest total value.

The total value is calculated as a combination of three factors: the advertiser's bid, the estimated response rate, the quality and relevance of the ad. An advertiser's bid is the amount he is willing to pay for displaying his ads to the target audience. The estimated response rate is calculated by Facebook based on the previous responses of the audience the advertiser is trying to reach, taking into account the type of reaction the ad is optimized for. This estimated response rate includes also the historical effectiveness of your ad. The quality and relevance of the sponsored content is judged by the actual user response. If the advertised post does not generate any clicks or if it receives negative reactions, the quality and thus the total value may decrease. On the other hand, in the case of positive reactions, the quality and relevance score of the ad is growing. Relevance score for each ad is always displayed in the Ads Manager. This score ranges from 1-10 points, 10 representing the highest quality ranking.

During every auction, these three factors are recalculated in relation to the goals of the ad optimization. An ad with a higher total value wins and is finally displayed to the user. Thanks to the combination of multiple factors, better advertising can defeat an advertiser with a higher bid. The advertiser pays only when a conversion action for which he is optimizing the ad occurs. For example, the compan´s goal is to make the customers visit the company´s website, the conversion action will be a click on the web. This is the so-called PPC (pay-per-click, pay-per-click) system. The amount that Facebook will charge the advertisers is the minimum amount he neededs to win the auction.

The costs of Facebook advertising may vary considerably depending on the industry and the target group the company wants to offer their product. The total budget spend on a campaign is determined by the advertiser. This amount may range from 5 USD a week to 500 USD a day. The ad and campaign investment is not limited. It is up to the advertiser to decide how much money from the corporate budget he wants to spend on advertising. For advanced ad types, there is a minimum amount set to ensure their functionality.

Based on the budget, the bid, and targeting parameters, Facebook estimates the number of people the ad may potentially reach and who represent the target group corresponding the best to your advertising objectives.

Profiling the Target Audience

All the ads a company may order on Facebook always have the same structure, regardeless the advertising objectives. A Facebook advertising order consists of a campaign, a set of ads, and the ad itself. Different parameters are set for each of these levels. By structuring the campaign, companies may gain a better insight into the promotions that are currently running. Also all of these steps are part of the target group definition process and help to collect detailed information about the ad performance.

At the campaign level the advertiser selects the appropriate goal / purpose of the ads. In this step, there is a limited number of options the advertiser may choose from. The most frequently selected campaign goals include, for example, earning more fans for the company page, getting reactions for the posts, or achieving a higher website traffic. The advertiser should select such campaign goals that correspond the best the marketing objectives of the company. Campaign goal selection is important for Facebook optimization. Based on the chosen purpose, the algorithm selects the group of users that is most likely to perform the desired action.

On the ad set level, the exact requirements for the target audience are specified. These include geographic, demographic and interest parameters. Next, the budget, the way of drawing it, the start and duration of the campaign, the placement of the ads, and the type of connection to Facebook company page are specified. Within a single campaign, it is possible to have multiple sets that differ from each other in terms of targeting parameters. For example, if the company wants to target women aged 18-24 and 40-54 it has to address each of these two segments differently (different slogan, creative). It is thus best for the advertiser to set up two ad sets.

The final element of the advertising Facebook structure are the ads. This last step consists in setting the visual parameters and the content of the advertisement. At this point, the advertiser is choosing whether the company should present itself through an image or video, or what text to add to make the most of the sponsored post.

Choosing the wrong campaign goal may negatively affect the performance of the advertisement. Based on the various Facebook marketing activities, the campaign goals and targeting strategies may be divided into three groups: Awareness, Consideration and Conversion (Table 1). These three groups describe the main stages of the new customer acquisition. Structuring marketing efforts in accordance with the acquisition stages may contribute to easier estimation of the value assigned to individual conversions (likes, shares, clicks, etc.).

If the advertiser´s goal is to let people know about the existence of the company and what its value lies in, the best option is to optimize the ads for raising awareness. Imagine promoting a small craft firm specializing in the production of wooden fashion accessories such as brooches, wooden business card cases or wooden bowties. In the ads, you want to emphasize that all goods are handcrafted and that you put a lot of care in every single piece you made. By emphasizing these qualities of your products, you will help your customers better understand why this company stands out over competition. In this case, it is the best to optimize the campaign for reach. When selecting as campaign goal the reach, Facebook will strive to show the ad to as many people as possible, but it will not consider whether these users will click on your ads or not.

When selecting a targeting category Consideration, the ads are primarily served to users who are likely to make a response (click, page markup as I like it, video viewing, etc.). The first goal in this group is "Traffic". The Traffic destination is selected by the advertiser. It depends on whether he want the users to visit the website, app or messenger. Campaign goal "Engagement" helps to increase the user interaction with the post, event or the number of followers of the company page. Another interesting targeting goal in this category is "Lead generation". This option serves to collect information about the potential customers. With this type of advertising, you can offer customers, for example, a newsletter registration, a discount on selected goods, or the possibility of early registration at your event.

Table 1. Facebook targeting strategies

<table>
<tr><td>Awareness
Objectives that generate interest in your product or service:
• Brand awareness
• Reach</td><td rowspan="2">Consideration
Objectives that get people to start thinking about your business and look for more information about it:
• Traffic
• App instals
• Engagement
• Video views
• Lead generation
• Messages</td></tr>
<tr><td>Conversion
Objectives that encourage people interested in your business to purchase or use your product or service:
• Conversions
• Catalog sales
• Store visits</td></tr>
</table>

Source: (the authors)

Conversion targeting is meant to reach a narrower set of users who are most likely to perform the desired action (for example, buying goods). Facebook includes into this target audience users who have already reacted in a similar way to other ads. With the help of the ads from this category the advertiser may also create so-called dynamic ads. Dynamic ads allow to automatically promote products from the selected catalog. Catalog products are displayed to those users who have visited the company website at least once. If the user has viewed a particular product on the website, he will see an ad containing the image of this particular product or of a product from a similar category. The product catalog combined with dynamic ads is the most powerful remarketing tool.

Another category of advertising objectives is represented by "Store visits". This kind of ad is suitable for companies with multiple stores. Similarly to products, the advertiser may create dynamic ads for the company stores locations. These ads are delivered based on the geographic location of the user. If the user is in a location near your local store, you'll see a relevant ad.

Tracking User Behavior

Just prior to ordering Facebook advertisements, the advertiser should consider what are the business goals of the company. Depending on these goals, the company should choose appropriate tracking tools to help evaluate the performance of the advertising campaigns. If one of the goals is to redirect potential customers to the website, the company will need to integrate Facebook pixel to optimize its ads. Additionally, if the advertiser seeks more accurate monitoring of your customers' behavior, it is required to install analytical software such as Google Analytics on the company website and use UTM links.

Facebook pixel represents a specific Facebook-generated fraction of code that is created specifically for the company advertising account. After uploading this code to the website, Facebook is able to monitor whether the customer has made the requested actions. A properly installed Facebook allows not only to track conversion events, but also to optimize the ads, and to use remarketing. Remarketing tools are used to reach all the users that visited the company website, or just those customer segments that have visited specific pages, products, or made specific actions, but have not completed them (for example, saving goods into a shopping cart but not making a purchase). With the pixel, it is possible to track specific conversions across devices that the user owns, search for new customers and create remarketing ads.

One of the key steps leading to effective measurement of website traffic is to add UTM parameters to the links shared on social networks and other online spaces. However, this tool will not bring any results if the company does not use any analytical software on the web. UTM parameters are text fragments that are attached in the specified format to the web link. Attaching these textual segments does not change anything about the landing page but it will allow the analytical software to exactly identify from what source, campaign, or advertisement the users come to the website. UTM parameters represent a way of communicating between the web and the analytical web application.

UTM parameters generally contain the following 5 elements:

utm_source = source name (the name of the linked site)

utm_medium = media name = type of marketing channel (cpc = paid search, organic = unpaid search, referral = link, etc.)

utm_campaign = campaign = campaign name (for example, in Sklie) or other modulation (eg Facebook date or newsletter)

utm_content = ad name = another sub-level, for example, the name of the ad group in the PPC ad

utm_term = keyword = another sub-level, for example, keyword in PPC ad

Advertisers should mark using the UTM parameters all links uploaded as posts, as well as advertisements. This marking system significantly contributes to better segmentation of website traffic and helps to predict the behavior of visitors coming from different online sources (Direct, Social, Organic search, and Refferal).

Facebook Metrics

As mentioned in the previous paragraphs, one of the big advantages of online marketing tools lies in the possibility to precisely measure the impact and performance of individual ads. However, evaluating the return of your marketing investments (ROI) may not be an easy task. In the online environment and specifically on Facebook, you will find a great deal of data (metrics), whose value may be judged differently depending on your marketing goals. In addition, in the online environment, there are two types of content: organic and sponsored. Organic reach includes all the results achieved without having to use facebook advertising. Even though these posts do not require funds for advertising they still generate marketing costs in the form of content production expenses. Evaluating the performance of the Facebook activities contributes to the increase of ROI-FM, and helps identify new customer groups, test creatives, and optimize the marketing strategies.

Facebook provides several applications through which the advertiser may access the collected data. Administrators of Facebook company pages can get the general review of posts organic and paid performance through the Insights tab. If the company manages ads directly from the Facebook page,advertising results will appear under the Promotion tab. However, the most comprehensive set of reporting tools is offered by the Ad Manager and Business Manager.

The Business Manager provides multiple reporting features, such as Ads Manager; Testing and Learning tool; Facebook Analytics; Pixel, Offline events, Application events, and Conversion managers. From the point of view of advertising effectiveness, the first three of the above, are the most relevant.

When seeing the Facebook ads in Newsfeed, Instagram, or Audience Network, the user can do several actions, including giving likes, sharing, viewing videos, visiting the website, or purchasing a product. All of these actions are recorded and displayed in the reporting columns for each ad in the Ads Manager. Hovever, not all conversions are recorded and displayed instantly. Conversions made on the web are attributed to the ads when they occur, which may be within a few days. For example, When browsing Facebook, thanks to a sponsored post, the user gets interested in a new mobile phone. Through the ad, he is redirected to the dealer's website and puts the phone in the shopping cart, but he does not complete the purchase. After three days of thinking he decides that he will buy the mobile phone. Even though he reacted to the ad earlier, the measurable result happened after three days. This action can be reflected as two different metrics in the Ads Manager, both as impression attribution and click attribution. Impression attribution means that the user saw your ad and subsequently made a purchase without clicking on that ad. Click attribution refers to the situation where the click was made directly from the ad.

Nevertheless, the number of interactions with the post cannot be confused with the advertising results. The results column only records the values that match the campaign target. Generally, every advertisement gets more reactions than results. If the objective of the ad is to gain more web traffic, ale click leading on the website will be recorded as results and all the likes, shares and comments will be registered as interactions. In detailed ad reports, these events are held in separate columns. Tracking the interactions, not just the results, provides additional insights into the ad's performance. It is possible that the ad received only 10 results (e.g. web clicks) but it could have contributed to 50 new followers of the company Facebook page.

Due to the growing number of channels and devices used by individual users, Facebook is gradually introducing new attribution models and switching from cookie-based to person-based monitoring. Currently, two types of attribution models can be distinguished, taking into account user behavior across devices: Last used channel model and Touch point model.

Facebook currently (May 2018) uses the model of the last channel when assigning ad conversions. Conversion then attributes the last ad the user has clicked on. If he does not click on any ad, the conversion is credited to the last displayed ad. The default conversion count is set to 28 days. Conversion events outside of this conversion window are not counted. In the near future, Facebook is getting ready to move to the Touch Point Model. This approach to monitoring divides the final value of the conversion and assigns it to the individual channels and ads that contributed throughout the process (Figure 1).

The result metrics depend on the selected Facebook campaign goals and include the following variables: reach, engagement, link click, mobile app install, 3s video views, potential customers on the web, shopping on the web, and the value of site purchase conversion.

The first of the metrics is reach. Reach describes the size of the audience the post was displayed to. After defining demographic and geographic data for the advertisement targeting, Facebook estimates the daily reach based on the information about the active users who use Facebook daily. However, this estimated reach is also affected by the placement, budget, and campaign goal. For example, if the advertiser decides to remove the right column placement, the reach will decrease due to the loss of potential views in this part of interface on desktop computers and laptops. The overall reach of the campaign is expressed as the number of unique users who saw the campaign. One user can see the ad multiple times, but nothing changes in reach. The "reach optimization" goal allows the advertiser to control the frequency of viewing the same ad by one user.

There are two types of "click" metrics in Facebook reports: link-click metric and an all-clicks metric. The all-clicks metric encompasses all clicks on the ad and its parts including the likes, shares, comments, or the clicks to view a full screen image or video. While link-click counts only the clicks on links leading to external websites or other parts of Facebook. Based on these two metrics, Facebook calculates other derived metrics: CPC (all), CPC (link clicks), CTR (all), and CTR (link clicks). CPC represents the average cost per click, while the CTR indicates the average clickthrough rate. CPC is expressed as the total campaign costs divided by the number of clicks. CTR refers to the number of times people clicked on the link in the ad compared to how many times they saw the ad.

Engagement reflect whether the ads are interesting (relevant) for the target audience the advertiser choose. The higher the relevance, the higher the chance that the target audience will take action. Engagement is calculated as the sum of all actions performed in connection with the ad. The average cost per engagement is calculated as the ratio of the amount issued and the level of engagement.

In the Ads manager and in the page Insights it is possible to find another metric describing all video views longer than 3 seconds. In Facebook reports, you may also find 10s video views and viewing the

Figure 1. Facebook attribution models
Source: (the authors)

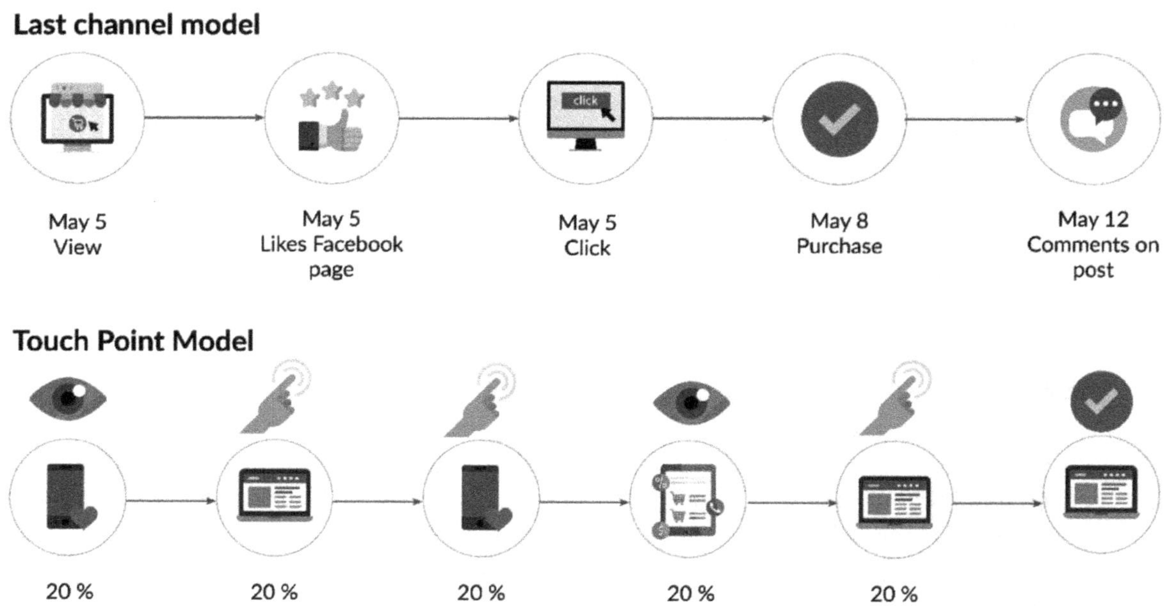

entire video metrics. However, the issue of video metrics is that about 90% of videos are triggered automatically and only 10% is played by the user. A similar situation concerns the impressions of the video. If the user views one video multiple times, each of these views is counted as one impression. For this reason, additional video metrics, such as the percentage of the video viewed (how many percent of the video the users saw) and the number of unique impressions, are worth evaluating. Impression provides an overview of how many times the advertisement has been displayed on Facebook. However, impression does not represent a unique view. That is way along with impressions the Facebook reports also the Frequency indicator that indicates how many times the average user has already seen the ad, and the CPM index describing the average cost per 1000 impressions.

The advertiser has a plethora of variables to evaluate the individual campaigns and advertisements. Facebook offers over 50 different metrics with varying levels of detail that help to shed some light on the effectiveness of posts and ads. Nevertheless, not all metrics are suitable for all purposes and advertising goals. The advertiser must choose which indexes are relevant for his ads and which are redundant since they offer unnecessarily detailed information.

The Costs of the Content Processing

In addition to the price payed for the advertising space and the impressions of the ads, the companies should also consider the expenses needed for the creation of the marketing content. Now, Facebook supports the distribution of almost all type of multimedia including photo, gif files, videos, photo presentations and 3D product models. The audience at social networks has quite high expectations when it comes to the content they usually engage with. Due to the increasing number of brands and advertisers who compete to gain the users attention, the quality of the sponsored content is growing, turning Facebook advertising into highly competitive environment. However, creating quality content requires time, skill and a good technical background. At this point, it is necessary to decide whether the advertiser is able to produce such a content with the company resources or whether he should use the services of a digital agency. The advertiser may choose both. Many of the big brands have their own creative departments that take care of the visual design of the regular posts but for bigger campaigns they resort to professional assistance. It is not possible to objectively demonstrate which of the options is more profitable. The realization of the benefits is strongly individual and depends on many internal characteristics of the company such as the frequency with which the company produces creative content, available equipment and human resources.

The price of the creative content cannot be neglected since it generally represents significant percentage of the company´s marketing budget. Each of the online and offline communication channels has different requirements on size, format, resolution and sound the processing of sound elements that are an integral part of multimedia advertisements. When creating promotional material, these aspects must be taken into account to ensure that the resulting material can be distributed without any problems to the end-viewer. Notwithstanding, the calculation of the content processing costs is not the main objective of this chapters, the authors believe that understanding the creative design process will help to clarify the economic demands on online advertising.

The graphic designer works with graphical software editors to process vector and bitmap graphics. He often needs to use paid graphical elements from photo stocks, illustrative images, vector graphics, and / or icons, sounds and pythographs. Another distinctive graphic element is the typography used. The fonts used often provide the graphs with a certain mood and atmosphere and should of course always be selected with regard to the target audience of the advertiser and to the need for text readability on various devices. One design is generally used for many advertising formats (flyer, poster, banners, slideshow, newsletter graphics). The graphic designer must re-lay the required formats, modify them, and eventually export them to suitable output variants (pdf, jpeg, esp, png, gif). All of these steps require investments. The price of content varies of course depending on the required quality. Thanks to the technological development of media content processing, the technological level is rising even for low end devices. The development of both audio and video recorders has progressed considerably, and over the past decade, high-quality audiovisual material can be created with relatively cheap technical tools. The following list of equipment is divided into 3 price ranges for each area (graphics, audio, video) - from the cheapest possible equipment, through the middle quality class to the professional equipment (Table 2). The price range is only indicative. Obviously, equipment is not replaced after every campaign made but nevertheless there is 2 to 3 years amortization for most of the technological devices.

It is difficult generalize the time needed for the creation of an advertisement. The time allowance is very fluctuating and may, of course, vary according to the complexity of the project. Also, an experienced worker who can efficiently and appropriately use modern technological processes and software tools can produce the resulting product in less time than an employee with less practical experience. A web banner can take about 5 hours to create. Making an audio record composed of an actor's commentary along with audiobook and FX sound effects can take a range of 3 to 20 hours. It is thus up to each advertiser to estimate these costs for his advertisements and product promotion. Generally, the company use two ways how to express the content processing costs – as the part of marketing costs or as the part of the product costs. Before starting to track the ROI of Facebook advertisements it is crucial to decide what is the costs structure. For the purposes of further calculations described in this chapter, the authors include content production costs in the product costs as a flat rate.

Table 2. Average content processing costs

Quality Category	Informative Price of the Devices	Price Range
	Graphics Processing - Image Recording	
Low end	Smartphone with Camera application	100 - 300 €
Middle class	Compact camera (500 €)	400 - 600 €
Profi class	DSLR Cameras - body (2.000 €) + lenses (2.0000 €) + accessories - flash lights, stands, filters (1.500 €)	5.000 - 10.000 €
	Graphics processing - postproduction	
Low end	Filters in the Camera application on the smartphone	100 - 300 €
Middle class	Freeware + free plugins	400 - 600 €
Profi class	Software tools for the processing of raster and vector graphics (1.000 €), graphical interface - tablet (1.000 €)	1.500 - 5.000 €
	Sound processing - recording	
Quality category	**Informative price of the devices**	**Price range**
Low end	Smartphone with sound recording application	100 - 300 €
Middle class	Condenser microphone (150 €), sound card (300 €)	300 - 600 €
Profi class	Stereo pair of condenser microphones (1.000 €) + microphone preamp (1.5000 €) + AD/DA convertor (1.500 €) + accessories (500 €)	4.000 - 6.000 €
	Sound processing - postproduction	
Low end	Mobile application on the smartphone	0 €
Middle class	Freeware + free plugins	0 €
Profi class	Software tools (1.000 € + professional postproduction plugins (3.000 €) + hardware - compressors, EQ, mastering chain (20.000 €)	20.000 - 50.000 €
	Video processing - recording	
Quality category	**Informative price of the devices**	**Price range**
Low end	Smartphone with Camera application	100 - 300 €
Middle class	Handheld video camera (400 €)	300 - 600 €
Profi class	Professional video camera (10.000 €), lenses (2.000 €), accessories (1.000 €)	12.000 - 50.000 €
	Video processing - postproduction	
Low end	Smartphone video editor	0 €
Middle class	Freware + free plugins	0 €
Profi class	Software tools for video data editation (1.500 €), hardware for color correction (10.000), HW work station (4.000 €)	15.00 - 50.000 €

Source: (the authors)

ROI-FM DETERMINATION MODEL

The effectiveness of Facebook ads is generaly measured by the level of user engagement. According to Tikno (2017) the engagement rate represents … *the proportion of action taken by the Facebook user to displaying ads with how many times the ads is showed*:

$$E = A / R \quad (1)$$

which:

E = Engagement Rate

A = Action taken (Amount of People who liked, commented, shared, or clicked on the ad)

R = Reach (Amount of People who saw the ad)

This formula allows to measure the post performance and compare posts (both organic and sponsored) between each other and to monitor the development of the relative Facebook marketing effectiveness over time. Nevertheless, this formula does not reflect the financial aspects of the marketing activities and thus does not provide complete information in terms of marketing investments. Eventhough, marketing costs may seem irrelevant for organic (unpaid) posts, there are still costs associated with the creation of the visual content. Moreover even the organic posts may generate financial value. For this reason, financial variables should be incorporated in the effectiveness assessment model.

The definition of this model will partly depend on the goals the company is trying to achieve. Are the company's objectives to increase the brand awareness, revenues, customer satisfaction, or other? Let's start with a simple ROI calculation model modified for the social media purposes. In broader sense, the return on investment in social media represents the sum of all social media actions that create value taking into account all the resources invested in their implementation. This simplified formula would look like this:

Simple ROI Calculation = [(Total revenue - Marketing investment) / Marketing ivestment] * 100 (2)

However, this formula is very simplified, since it only operates with revenue from sales rather than actual profits. To accurately measure the ROI, it is desirable to know the cost of the goods sold:

ROI Calculation for direct activities = [(Total revenue - Total COGS - Marketing Investment) / Marketing investment] * 100 (3)

where:

Total revenue = sales generated by the marketing campaign such as ecommerce transactions

Total COGS = cost of goods sold

The problem with this formula is that for many Facebook activities the contribution to the revenu is indirect. Only data available for these activities are Facebook metrics such as the reach, the number of interactions, page view, etc. The effectiveness model should thus also reflect this reality. Therefore:

ROI Calculation for Indirect Contribution = [(Total value of the actions taken - Total COGS - Marketing Investment) / Marketing investment] * 100 (4)

The most difficult step consists in the calculation of the Total value of the actions taken. Not all interactions have the same value and except for the posts / ads optimized for purchases it is not possible to directlly measure the revenue generated by the advertisement. Taking into consideration the Facebook attribution models described above, all of the conversions contribute to the final result. The revenues coming from purchases should thus be distributed between the others conversions with appropriates weights. If the advertisers desires to assess the effectiveness of individual ads, they need to know what these bring them in terms of likes, shares, clicks etc.The average revenue contribution of the conversions may be calculated based on the historical data the company managed to collect and should reflect the targetting characteristics of the audience. It is likely that different customer segments will have different average revenues since some target groups require more marketing effort and respond to ads more conservatively. Before calculation the average revenu contibution per conversion, the advertiser should firstly analyze data available in the GA and find out what is the conversion rate per visitor and what actions lead to the final purchases. Combining these data with the post information provided by Facebook is the only way to get the entire profile of user behavior and estimate the real value of each conversion.

Looking back the attribution model described in the section 2.4, the conversion process goes from the less engaging actions such as likes, comments and shares to the actions that require more cognitive effort from the consumer. Generally, there is decreasing tendency along the conversion processes. This tendency is being referred to as marketing funnel. The stages customer usually travel through are post views, reactions (likes, comments, shares), click on the link and web visit, registration to the newsletter, purchase. There maybe other stages included depending on the business model the company applies. Due to the marketing funnel the contribution of the conversion to the revenue increases toward the and of the buying process. Therefore, the revenu contribution per metric may be expressed as:

$$ARMS = (P/M) * TR \tag{5}$$

where:

ARMS = Average revenue per metric per customer segment

P = Number of purchases per segment for a monitored period of time

M = Number of the metrics conversions per segment for a monitored period of time

TR = Total revenue

The adjusted formula for the individual advertisements is thus defined as follows:

$$\text{ROI Calculation for individual advertisements} = (\{[(n_{WCK}*AR_{WCK} + n_{RE}*AR_{RE} + n_{AD}*AR_{AD} + n_{LCS}*AR_{LCS} + n_F*AR_F + n_{VW}*AR_{VW} + n_M*{}_{ARM} + TPC) - \text{Total COGS} - \text{Advertisement costs}]\} / \text{Advertisement costs}) * 100 \tag{6}$$

where:

- **AR_{WCK}:** Average revenue of website clicks per customer segment;

- **AR_{RE}:** Average revenue of registration per customer segment;
- **AR_{AD}:** Average revenue of application download per customer segment;
- **AR_{LCS}:** Average revenue of reactions (likes, comments, shares) per customer segment;
- **AR_{F}:** Average value of fans per customer segment;
- **AR_{VW}:** Average value of video views per customer segment;
- **AR_{M}:** Average value of other metric per customer segment chosen by the company;
- **TPC:** Total purchase value per campaign - calculated based on the acctual data related to the specific campaign retrieved from the website analytical software;
- **nM:** Number of conversions for the observed metric.

In the formula above, it is possible to replace the observed metrics or to ad others such as video views, reach, etc. The average values expressed in the aformentionned relationship represent future value of the campaign, not the current value which is expressed by the revenu generated by the purchases. The authors believe that this model could help to improve the evaluation of the indirect activities that are more difficult to judge since they not produce enough instant revenue but could lead to purchases in the future.

To properly estimate the profit from certain consumer actions (purchase, page views, app downloads, newsletter registration, etc.), setting up the tracking systems described above (Google Analytics, Facebook pixel, etc.) to identify which conversions can be assigned to Facebook campaigns is crucial. Because of the short life cycle of social networking campaigns, unsuccessful campaigns should be optimized or turned off as soon as possible. Understanding the available metrics and what value they represent is the only way how to judge Facebook effectiveness properly.

Interpreting the Advertising Results

In the following paragraphs, the authors are going to demonstrate how to use the aformentionned formula with the organic and advertising results. Data presented in this chapter was collected by a Czech company selling home accessories and interior decorations. In the course of the two weeks, the company ran eight advertisements and published three posts from which one were sponsored. Each of the posts was sponsored for three days. For all the posts and ads, the company kept track of these variables if they were relevant: number of web clicks, reactions (likes and comments), purchases, newsletter registration, and campaign costs. The final data was exported from Facebook Ads Manager and completed with data collected via Google Analytics and UTM enhanced web filtering (Tables 3 and 4).

Based on the historical data collected for this customer segment, the company estimated the average value for each of the monitored metric. From Google Analytics, the company extracted the revenues generated by the purchases by the Facebook campaigns, and estimated the total costs of the goods sold. Ad effectiveness was then calculated using the ROI formula for individual marketing campaigns (Tables 5 and 6).

Looking more closely on the previous results it is possible to see that the campaign value significantly increased for the majority of ads. This increased value represents current revenue and the value that the ads / posts could bring in the future. However, these results cannot be used for reporting purposes, they better describe the performance of the ads. If the ad performance would be judged just based on the number of purchases, most of the posts would be described as ineffective. On the other hand, assum-

Table 3. Advertising results

Advertisements							
Campaign Name	**Optimization Goals**	**Type of the Content**	**Website Clicks**	**Reactions**	**Number of Purchases**	**Newsletter Registration**	**Campaign Costs**
Campaign 1	Engagement: fans	Photo	28	382	2	15	63 USD
Campaign 2	Engagement: fans	Video	48	647	9	27	77 USD
Campaign 3	Lead generation	Photo	215	93	82	29	35 USD
Campaign 4	Lead generation	Video	301	124	151	14	48 USD
Campaign 5	Conversions	Product carousel	355	82	263	27	54 USD
Campaign 6	Conversions	Photo	276	133	189	42	39 USD
Campaign 7	Catalog sales	Photo	115	25	97	34	22 USD
Campaign 8	Catalog sales	Product carousel	184	18	164	58	28 USD

Source: (the authors)

Table 4. Results for the posts on the company page

Posts on the Company Page							
Campaign Name	**Optimization Goals**	**Type of the Content**	**Website Clicks**	**Reactions**	**Number of Purchases**	**Newsletter Registration**	**Campaign Costs**
Post 1 organic	not defined	Photo	2	21	0	0	0
Post 2 organic	not defined	Video	1	39	0	0	0
Post 3 organic	not defined	Video	3	52	0	0	0
Post 3 sponsored	Engagement	Video	29	631	4	0	61 USD

Source: (the authors)

Table 5. ROI and average revenues for the advertisements

Advertisements						
Campaign Name	**AR_{WCK} (USD)**	**AR_{LCS} (USD)**	**AR_{RE} (USD)**	**TPC (USD)**	**42% COGS (USD)**	**Campaign ROI**
Campaign 1	0,6	0,1	0,8	85	35,7	145,24
Campaign 2	0,6	0,1	0,8	382	160,44	421,25
Campaign 3	0,6	0,1	0,8	3432	1441,4	6075,43
Campaign 4	0,6	0,1	0,8	6127	2573,3	7754,79
Campaign 5	0,6	0,1	0,8	10522	4419,24	11666,22
Campaign 6	0,6	0,1	0,8	7638	3207,96	11838,05
Campaign 7	0,6	0,1	0,8	3751	1575,4	10249,09
Campaign 8	0,6	0,1	0,8	6493	2727,1	13922,5

Source: (the authors)

Table 6. ROI and average revenues for page posts

Posts on the Company Page						
Campaign Name	**AR_{WCK} (USD)**	**AR_{LCS} (USD)**	**AR_{RE} (USD)**	**TPC (USD)**	**42% COGS (USD)**	**Campaign ROI**
Post 1 organic	0,6	0,1	0,8	0	0	5,4
Post 2 organic	0,6	0,1	0,8	0	0	8.4
Post 3 organic	0,6	0,1	0,8	0	0	12,2
Post 3 sponsored	0,6	0,1	0,8	0	0	135,4098361

Source: (the authors)

ing that the ad that is having the highest number of reactions is more successful than the ads that has only few is equally as misleading. Tracking the conversions all along the buying process is necessary to understand the ad effectiveness and the behavior of the consumers.

CONCLUSION

The benefits of Facebook advertisements in terms of reaching marketing goals of the company have been proven by many researchers and practitioners (Abayi et al., 2016; Bang et al., 2016; Dehghani et al., 2015). However, the effects of the activities on social networks may have both positive and negative impacts on consumer behavior (Ertugan, 2017; Taylor, 2011). Current literature does not provide enough evidence about the relationship between Facebook advertising, brand awareness and customer attitudes toward the brand. Research suggests that there might be significant differences in ad effectiveness when it comes to contextual setting and industrial orientation of the company (Kohli et al., 2015). Despite the inability to directly quantify the effectiveness of Facebook activities, scientists and practitioners agree that companies should not abandonne this social network and rather focus on testing which activities are suitable for their objectives.

Thanks to the tracking possibilities provided by Facebook advertising systems and website analytical software, the companies have a great opportunity to observe almost instantly what is the impact of their marketing efforts. Regular assessment of Facebook and website metrics may contribute to identification of types of content and posting strategies work with the targeted audience. It is important to keep in mind that the success of a company post or sponsored advertising depends on many factors. These factors include visual processing, post type, content, and targeting parameters. All of the aforementioned variables require testing and adjustments over time.

The calculation of ROI for Facebook marketing activities represents a continuous process whose accuracy depends on the quality of the available data. In addition to ad performance data, ROI calculation requires also the information about the costs incurred to create the visual content of the ad and the costs needed to produce the goods and services offered by the company.

Although the revenue component of the ROI formula may seem easy to extract from the company system, there are many Facebook activities that generate revenues indirectly such as building online community or motivating the followers to engage more with the content shared by the company. This indirect value is generally calculated based on the historic data the company managed to collect during a certain time period. In order to obtain a solid ROI estimate that could be used as the basis for further marketing decision-making, marketers need to carefully select the advertising metrics that will be used for the effectiveness assessment.

ACKNOWLEDGMENT

This research was supported by the Technical University of Liberec [project SGS-EF-3320-21230 Impact of technical and aesthetic parameters of web design on user satisfaction and online shopping behavior of the customer].

REFERENCES

Abayi, M., & Khoshtinat, B. (2016). Study of the Impact of Advertising on Online Shopping Tendency for Airline Tickets by Considering Motivational Factors and Emotional Factors. *Procedia Economics and Finance*, *36*, 532–539. doi:10.1016/S2212-5671(16)30065-X

Aslam, B., & Karjaluoto, H. (2017). Digital advertising around paid spaces, E-advertising industry's revenue engine: A review and research agenda. *Telematics and Informatics*, *34*(8), 1650–1662. doi:10.1016/j.tele.2017.07.011

Banelis, M., Riebe, E., & Rungie, C. (2013). Empirical evidence of repertoire size. *Australasian Marketing Journal*, *21*(1), 59–65. doi:10.1016/j.ausmj.2012.11.001

Bang, H., & Lee, W. (2016). Consumer Response to Ads in Social Network Sites: An Exploration into the Role of Ad Location and Path. *Journal of Current Issues and Research in Advertising*, *37*(1), 1–14. doi:10.1080/10641734.2015.1119765

Becker-Olsen, K. (2003). And Now, A Word from Our Sponsor--A Look at the Effects of Sponsored Content and Banner Advertising. *Journal of Advertising*, *32*(2), 17–32. doi:10.1080/00913367.2003.10639130

Beukeboom, C., Kerkhof, P., & de Vries, M. (2015). Does a Virtual Like Cause Actual Liking? How Following a Brand's Facebook Updates Enhances Brand Evaluations and Purchase Intention. *Journal of Interactive Marketing*, *32*, 26–36. doi:10.1016/j.intmar.2015.09.003

Bicen, H., & Cavus, N. (2011). Social network sites usage habits of undergraduate students: Case study of Facebook. *Procedia: Social and Behavioral Sciences*, *28*, 943–947. doi:10.1016/j.sbspro.2011.11.174

Bleier, A., & Eisenbeiss, M. (2015). Personalized Online Advertising Effectiveness: The Interplay of What, When, and Where. *Marketing Science*, *34*(5), 669–688. doi:10.1287/mksc.2015.0930

Brettel, M., Reich, J., Gavilanes, J., & Flatten, T. (2015). What Drives Advertising Success on Facebook? An Advertising-Effectiveness Model. *Journal of Advertising Research*, *55*(2), 162–175. doi:10.2501/JAR-55-2-162-175

Campbell, C., & Marks, L. (2015). Good native advertising isn't a secret. *Business Horizons*, *58*(6), 599–606. doi:10.1016/j.bushor.2015.06.003

Chi, H. H. (2011). Interactive digital advertising vs. virtual brand community: Exploratory study of user motivation and social media marketing responses in Taiwan. *Journal of Interactive Advertising*, *12*(1), 44–61. doi:10.1080/15252019.2011.10722190

Cho, C. H. (2003). The effectiveness of banner advertisements: Involvement and click-through. *Journalism & Mass Communication Quarterly*, *80*(3), 623–645. doi:10.1177/107769900308000309

Corvi, E., & Bonera, M. (2010, October). The effectiveness of advertising: a literature review. *Xth Global Conference on Business and Economics*, 3-6.

Cowley, E., & Barron, C. (2008). When Product Placement Goes Wrong: The Effects of Program Liking and Placement Prominence. *Journal of Advertising*, *37*(1), 89–98. doi:10.2753/JOA0091-3367370107

Curran, K., Graham, S., & Temple, C. (2011). Advertising on Facebook. *International Journal of E-Business Development*, *1*, 26–33.

Dehghani, M., & Tumer, M. (2015). A research on effectiveness of Facebook advertising on enhancing purchase intention of consumers. *Computers in Human Behavior*, *49*, 597–600. doi:10.1016/j.chb.2015.03.051

Dehghani, M., & Tumer, M. (2015). A research on effectiveness of Facebook advertising on enhancing purchase intention of consumers. *Computers in Human Behavior*, *49*, 597–600. doi:10.1016/j.chb.2015.03.051

Deloitte. (2015). *Facebook's global economic impact: A report for Facebook.* Retrieved from www2.deloitte.com/content/dam/Deloitte/uk/Documents/technology-media-telecommunications/deloitte-uk-global-economic-impact-of-facebook.pdf

Duff, B., & Faber, R. (2011). Missing the Mark. *Journal of Advertising*, *40*(2), 51–62. doi:10.2753/JOA0091-3367400204

EMarketer. (2016). *US Digital Video ad Spending will Continue to Grow at a Pace that Exceeds TV Advertising Growth Through 2020*. Retrieved from https://www.emarketer.com/Article/Digital-Video-Advertising-Grow-Annual-Double-Digit-Rates/1014105

Ertugan, A. (2017). Using statistical reasoning techniques to describe the relationship between Facebook advertising effectiveness and benefits gained. *Procedia Computer Science*, *120*, 132–139. doi:10.1016/j.procs.2017.11.220

Fulgoni, G. (2016). In the Digital World, Not Everything That Can Be Measured Matters. *Journal of Advertising Research*, *56*(1), 9–13. doi:10.2501/JAR-2016-008

Gutiérrez-Cillán, J., Camarero-Izquierdo, C., & San José-Cabezudo, R. (2017). How brand post content contributes to user's Facebook brand-page engagement. The experiential route of active participation. *BRQ Business Research Quarterly*, *20*(4), 258–274. doi:10.1016/j.brq.2017.06.001

Harris, L., & Dennis, C. (2011). Engaging customers on Facebook: Challenges for e-retailers. *Journal of Consumer Behaviour, 10*(6), 338–346. doi:10.1002/cb.375

Heinonen, K. (2011). Consumer activity in social media: Managerial approaches to consumers' social media behavior. *Journal of Consumer Behaviour, 10*(6), 356–364. doi:10.1002/cb.376

Heller Baird, C., & Parasnis, G. (2011). From social media to social customer relationship management. *Strategy and Leadership, 39*(5), 30–37. doi:10.1108/10878571111161507

Insider, B. (2018). These Are The 35 Biggest Advertisers On Facebook. *Business Insider*. Retrieved 1 May 2018, from http://www.businessinsider.com/top-advertisers-on-facebook-2013-11

Kelly, L., Kerr, G., & Drennan, J. (2010). Avoidance of Advertising in Social Networking Sites. *Journal of Interactive Advertising, 10*(2), 16–27. doi:10.1080/15252019.2010.10722167

Knoll, J. (2015). Advertising in social media: A review of empirical evidence. *International Journal of Advertising, 35*(2), 266–300. doi:10.1080/02650487.2015.1021898

Kohli, C., Suri, R., & Kapoor, A. (2015). Will social media kill branding? *Business Horizons, 58*(1), 35–44. doi:10.1016/j.bushor.2014.08.004

Kuvykaitė, R., & Tarutė, A. (2015). A Critical Analysis of Consumer Engagement Dimensionality. *Procedia: Social and Behavioral Sciences, 213*, 654–658. doi:10.1016/j.sbspro.2015.11.468

LaPointe, P. (2012). Measuring Facebook's Impact on Marketing. *Journal of Advertising Research, 52*(3), 286–287. doi:10.2501/JAR-52-3-286-287

Loomer, J. (2013). *How to Measure Facebook Advertising Success: Monitor These 5 Metrics*. Academic Press.

Mulhern, F. (2013). Integrated marketing communications: From media channels to digital connectivity. In *The Evolution of Integrated Marketing Communications* (pp. 19–36). Routledge.

Petty, R., & Cacioppo, J. (1986). The Elaboration Likelihood Model of Persuasion. *Communication and Persuasion*, 1-24. doi:10.1007/978-1-4612-4964-1_1

Rejón-Guardia, F., & Martínez-López, F. J. (2014). Online advertising intrusiveness and consumers' avoidance behaviors. In *Handbook of strategic e-business management* (pp. 565–586). Berlin: Springer. doi:10.1007/978-3-642-39747-9_23

Rzemieniak, M. (2015). Measuring the Effectiveness of Online Advertising Campaigns in the Aspect of e-entrepreneurship. *Procedia Computer Science, 65*, 980–987. doi:10.1016/j.procs.2015.09.063

Sitta, D., Faulkner, M., & Stern, P. (2018). What can the brand manager expect from Facebook? *Australasian Marketing Journal, 26*(1), 17–22. doi:10.1016/j.ausmj.2018.01.001

Smock, A., Ellison, N., Lampe, C., & Wohn, D. (2011). Facebook as a toolkit: A uses and gratification approach to unbundling feature use. *Computers in Human Behavior, 27*(6), 2322–2329. doi:10.1016/j.chb.2011.07.011

Statista. (2018a). Social Media Advertising - worldwide. *Statista Market Forecast*. Retrieved 1 May 2018, from https://www.statista.com/outlook/220/100/social-media-advertising/worldwide#

Statista. (2018b). Facebook ad revenue 2009-2017. *Statista*. Retrieved 1 May 2018, from https://www.statista.com/outlook/220/100/social-media-advertising/worldwide#

Taylor, D. G., Lewin, J. E., & Strutton, D. (2011). Friends, fans, and followers: Do ads work on social networks? How gender and age shape receptivity. *Journal of Advertising Research*, *51*(1), 258–275.

Tikno. (2017). Measuring performance of facebook advertising based on media used: a case study on online shops in indonesia. *Procedia Computer Science, 111*, 105-112. doi:10.1016/j.procs.2017.06.016

Van den Broeck, E., Poels, K., & Walrave, M. (2018). An experimental study on the effect of ad placement, product involvement and motives on Facebook ad avoidance. *Telematics and Informatics*, *35*(2), 470–479. doi:10.1016/j.tele.2018.01.006

Wallace, E., Buil, I., de Chernatony, L., & Hogan, M. (2014). Who "Likes" You … and Why? A Typology of Facebook Fans. *Journal of Advertising Research*, *54*(1), 92–109. doi:10.2501/JAR-54-1-092-109

Ying, L., Korneliussen, T., & Grønhaug, K. (2009). The effect of ad value, ad placement and ad execution on the perceived intrusiveness of web advertisements. *International Journal of Advertising*, *28*(4), 623–638. doi:10.2501/S0265048709200795

Yuki, T. (2015). What Makes Brands' Social Content Shareable on Facebook? *Journal of Advertising Research*, *55*(4), 458–470. doi:10.2501/JAR-2015-026

Zaichkowsky, J. (1985). Measuring the Involvement Construct. *The Journal of Consumer Research*, *12*(3), 341. doi:10.1086/208520

Zhou, Z., Wu, J., Zhang, Q., & Xu, S. (2013). Transforming visitors into members in online brand communities: Evidence from China. *Journal of Business Research*, *66*(12), 2438–2443. doi:10.1016/j.jbusres.2013.05.032

ADDITIONAL READING

Beuckels, E., Cauberghe, V., & Hudders, L. (2017). How media multitasking reduces advertising irritation: The moderating role of the Facebook wall. *Computers in Human Behavior*, *73*, 413–419. doi:10.1016/j.chb.2017.03.069

Boerman, S., Willemsen, L., & Van Der Aa, E. (2017). This Post Is Sponsored. *Journal of Interactive Marketing*, *38*, 82–92. doi:10.1016/j.intmar.2016.12.002

Celebi, S. (2015). How do motives affect attitudes and behaviors toward internet advertising and Facebook advertising? *Computers in Human Behavior*, *51*, 312–324. doi:10.1016/j.chb.2015.05.011

Fatehkia, M., Kashyap, R., & Weber, I. (2018). Using Facebook ad data to track the global digital gender gap. *World Development*, *107*, 189–209. doi:10.1016/j.worlddev.2018.03.007

Lin, C., & Kim, T. (2016). Predicting user response to sponsored advertising on social media via the technology acceptance model. *Computers in Human Behavior*, *64*, 710–718. doi:10.1016/j.chb.2016.07.027

Liu, S., & Mattila, A. (2017). Airbnb: Online targeted advertising, sense of power, and consumer decisions. *International Journal of Hospitality Management*, *60*, 33–41. doi:10.1016/j.ijhm.2016.09.012

Shareef, M., Mukerji, B., Alryalat, M., Wright, A., & Dwivedi, Y. (2018). Advertisements on Facebook: Identifying the persuasive elements in the development of positive attitudes in consumers. *Journal of Retailing and Consumer Services*, *43*, 258–268. doi:10.1016/j.jretconser.2018.04.006

Tran, T. (2017). Personalized ads on Facebook: An effective marketing tool for online marketers. *Journal of Retailing and Consumer Services*, *39*, 230–242. doi:10.1016/j.jretconser.2017.06.010

KEY TERMS AND DEFINITIONS

Ad Placement: All the advertising spaces, mostly payed, offered by online publishers, websites and social networks to advertisers to display their advertisements. The individual placements have different potential for reaching the users and perform differently when comes to the type of content chosen for the advertisement.

Ad Targeting: Selection of potential customer groups to which an advertisement is going to be displayed. This specification of the ad´s audience is done via targeting parameters including demographic and geographic information, interests, or device preferences.

Conversion: Desired action performed by a consumer as a reaction to an advertisement or other marketing effort. The desired action can take many forms including the purchases, membership registrations, newsletter subscriptions, application downloads, etc.

Facebook Ads Manager: Tool developed by Facebook to manage advertisements on this social network, Instagram and ads displayed in the Audience network. This application allows the advertiser to create and target the ads, set campaign budget, view history, and collect data about previous and ongoing ads.

Marketing Funnel: Set of actions a consumer, website visitor, needs to go through before he makes the desired conversion (usually purchase). The actions customer usually travel through are post views, reactions (likes, comments, shares), click on the link and web visit, registration to the newsletter, purchase. Since the conversion process goes from the less engaging actions such as likes, comments and shares to the actions that require more cognitive effort from the consumer, the number of users willing to do the actions decreases.

Organic Reach: Number of people who viewed unpaid content on their screen. Generally, this term is used in association with social networks. Inversely, sponsored reach describes the number of people who viewed a paid advertisement.

UTM Parameters: Text fragments that are attached in the specified format to the web link. Attaching these textual segments allows the analytical software to exactly identify from what source, campaign, or advertisement the users come to the website. UTM parameters generally contain the following five elements: utm_source, utm_medium, utm_campaign, utm_content, utm_term.

Chapter 15
E-WOM:
The New Consumer Megaphone - Underlying Reasons and Related Factors

Esra Güven
Manisa Celal Bayar University, Turkey

Özlem Işık
Manisa Celal Bayar University, Turkey

ABSTRACT

Together with the internet, social networking sites provide the consumers and the companies with a new marketing channel. In these online platforms, people make groups and come together for specific purposes. This new vivid and productive environment attracts the consumers seeking for product information and the companies trying to be in close contact with the customers. So the traditional WOM (word of mouth) has gained a new momentum and transformed into a new form in this online environment, called e-WOM (electronic word of mouth). Setting out from this recent fact, the chapter aims to give a general review of word of mouth communication starting with the traditional word of mouth and then elaborating e-WOM. It tries to tell about what e-WOM is and how it functions in online environments. As well as the definitions and the explanations of e-WOM, the chapter also aims to give the underlying reasons and the related factors during the process of e-WOM communication, thus putting a general framework for the companies and brands about this new marketing communication.

INTRODUCTION

In today's world, consumers face an excessive amount of message from the brands and companies and they are fed up with all this mess. So the consumers are seeking ways to save time during their purchase process. At that point word of mouth, WOM, is regarded as the ultimate and effective solution for the consumers. Thanks to the internet, millions of people from different parts of the world are engaged in the conversations about the brands and companies. These informal conversations between consumers allow them to get the right product information from the right people such as the experienced customers, opinion leaders and market mavens.

DOI: 10.4018/978-1-5225-7344-9.ch015

The growth of internet as a large scale information database allows people to participate in online communications for an exchange of information beyond time and space (Bechina & Husta, 2011:82). Especially because of its potential to remove the time and space limitations, this extraordinary communication opportunity has had a profound impact on many scientific communication-based fields. Like many other fields, marketing has also been affected deeply from both the content and the strategic importance of these new communication platforms.

Together with the internet, social networking sites are coming to the fore more and more. The social networking sites, getting rid of the apathy of technology, create a similar effect in online environments just as the traditional face-to-face communications do in real environments. Internet users and consumers are increasingly participating in and adopting social networking sites because these sites allow consumers to be engaged in personal connections in a cooperation-based structure, thus leading to common and widespread social networks (Akar, 2010:108). These platforms provide the consumers and the companies with a new marketing channel. In these online platforms, people make groups and come together for specific purposes. This vivid and efficient environment also attracts the consumers seeking for product information and the companies trying to be in close contact with the customers. So the traditional WOM has gained a new form in this online environment, called e-WOM.

Social media is regarded as the most popular media of communication today, so people use social media platforms widely in our century. Especially because of the lack of time people suffer in modern world, social media functions as a bridge to connect people to each other. Millions of people use social media to be in contact with their peers and acquaintances and also to share about their lives and opinions as well as collecting information about others. These social media users, at the same time a consumer each, attract companies and brands. So, many brands and companies are in an effort to be able to use social media effectively to develop an understanding of these new platforms in order to answer the needs of consumers (He et al.,2013).

This chapter has been prepared to give a general review of traditional WOM and its online counterpart, e-WOM. The chapter also aims at the underlying reasons, the potential impact, the measurement and the basic factors affecting word of mouth in online environments.

WOM AND E-WOM

In our increasingly competitive environment, though it is possible to reach each individual through electronic communication devices, the significance WOM, known as word of mouth, has remained the same over the years and it has gained a new importance together with the introduction of internet and Web 2.0 technology. Today businesses need to know and benefit from the potential of word of mouth communications and prepare strategical plans in accordance with this new version of word of mouth communication.

The concept WOM is a far older concept than the marketing itself. From the beginning of civilization on, people have taken advice from other people as regards many different things in their daily lives. Even, it is known that early people took advice from each other about foods and commodities informally (Arora, 2007:52).

In the early 1950s, B.E Asch mentioned 'crowd physchology' in his work, and then in 1957 Jr.Brooks and C.Roberts published an article in the *Journal of Marketing*. This article is regarded as the first study emphasizing the significance of WOM in the introduction of new products (Kanning, 2008:62).

Even if WOM has been attracting researchers for a few decades, the founder of the earliest WOM theories is known to belong to Arndt (1967). According to Arndt, WOM is an interpersonal communication about the goods and services without any commercial aim. Another researcher, Dichter (1966) elaborated the issue and mentioned four motivation factors for communicators. These factors are the stimulants about the products, the communicator, the message and others. Of these four, the stimulants about the message are still of great importance. Again, in those years, some significant interpersonal factors about WOM such as tie strength, perceived risk and homophily are known to have been discussed (Kanning, 2008:62).

According to Kanning, (2008) WOM is known as two-way communication created by the individual or the group about the products, services or the organizations. Known also as 'zero-media', this kind of marketing communication has a potential to reduce the cost to the minimum. WOM communication occurs as an information flow between the sender and the receiver, the main actors of communication. So, during the process of WOM, the reciprocity of these main actors is needed. As shown in Figure 1, the flow of the WOM messages is conducted from the sender to the receiver, and then the purchase decision, as buying or giving up buying, is made. During this purchase decision process, there occurs a filtering in a black box and certain factors affect the filtering in this box (Voyer, 1999:6).

As WOM is a communicational process, all the factors affecting communication also affect the WOM itself. For example, the problems related with nuisance, encoding and decoding will be able to contribute to different and sometimes problematic evaluations of WOM messages (Tax et al.,1993:75).

Together with the advance in technology and internet, a new breakthrough has been started and the e-WOM in online environments- has come into being in an unexpected speed. Consumers today use internet to share experience and opinions, and also they have a valuable opportunity to to follow other consumers' product evaluations through social networks, blogs, consumer review websites (Lee & Koo, 2012:1974). This unexpected breakthrough has caught the marketing environments unprepared and therefore the theoretical studies have gained an urgent importance and need.

The related literature mentions a communication of consumers via internet, which occurs as a result of the demand for the information about the products or services, and this kind of online consumer communication is regarded as e-WOM. Some researchers deal with e-WOM in terms of relationship marketing, and while doing that they discuss the opportunities and threats resulting from the increase in online consumer behaviours. Such kinds of research lines also mention an internet consumer communication and they handle this kind of communication in terms of traditional WOM. According to the definition given by Hennig-Thurau (2004),e-WOM is the positive or negative reviews of the former or

Figure 1. Communication model of WOM
Source: Duncan and Moriarty 1998 modified by Voyer, 1999:6

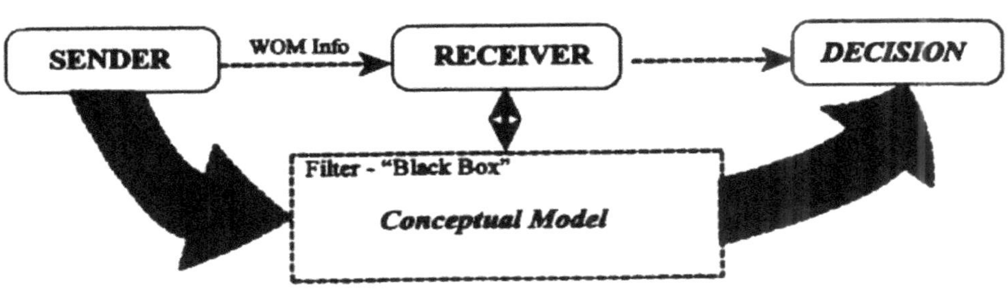

actual consumers about the product or company, which has the potential to reach too many people via internet (p.39).

Bickart and Schindler (2001) previously stated that, whereas typical WOM communication consists of exchange of oral words between friends or acquaintances, online WOM (e-WOM) are made up of ideas and experiences shared through written words in online environments. The advantage of written words is that they allow people to follow the information within their own pace. The written language also transmits the information more precisely and put it in a more formal way (Sun et al., 2006:1107). Marshall McLuhan states that written communication is a more logical way as the letters and words follow each other in a linear model. In recent days, Lopez and Sicilia (2014) also had a research about the difference between WOM e-WOM. As seen in Figure 2, the authors focus on the dissimilarity between these two channels. Whereas the traditional WOM has as a simultaneous and bidirectional characteristic, e-WOM doesn't necessarily occur simultaneously and bidirectionally. The messages written by the source has a characteristic to stay there for a long time. This difference enables the consumers searching for information to reach the former messages as well as the new ones, thus making the communication moe effective (p.30).

The fact that e-WOM messages are independent of company or brands and they are based upon the experiences of consumers themselves puts e-WOM messages in a different place. As seen in a lot of research, the credibility of e-WOM messages is higher than several other advertisement methods, leading trust to develop and consumer decisions to be affected. Another important factor that makes e-WOM messages valuable is that these messages are not limited to the time they were written, and at the same time they have a potential to reach many people many times. Yet another important point is that the intonations, body language, physical environment in which the communication occurs and many other perceptual factors are reduced to minimum in written communication. This difference can also help e-WOM messages be perceived as unbiased.

e-WOM has a long life span because of the fact that it is stored on net and so is always available when needed. While in real life people can get information only their friends and acquaintances, e-WOM in online environments can give the consumers an opportunity to reach thousands of opinions from many other consumers.

Figure 2. WOM and e-WOM communication
Source: Lopez & Sicilia (2014)

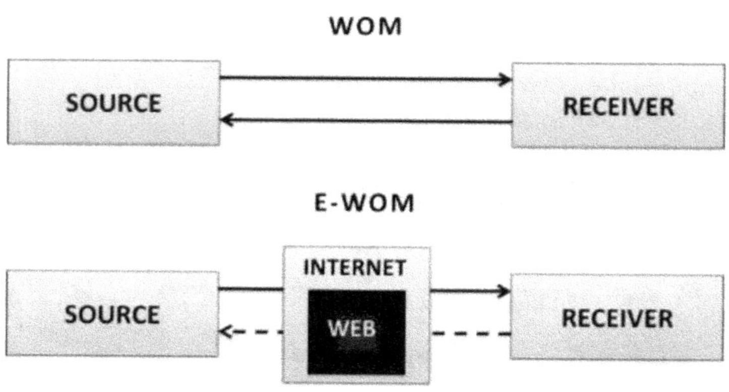

As the significance of creating information grows, the information itself becomes a valuable product and service. In modern world, companies and brands not only need to acquire the right information, but they also need to transmit the information about themselves to the target consumer rightly. e-WOM, at that point, is useful for the companies and brands as well as the consumers themselves (Xiuqing & Haiqing, 2007:77).

WHY DO THE CONSUMERS PARTICIPATE IN WORD OF MOUTH?

There are many underlying motives to participate in e-WOM communication. Studying these motives and underlying reasons, Hennig-Thurau and Walsh (2003) have put some reasons forward. These are reducing risk, saving time, learning about how to use a product, reducing cognitive dissonance, making up for the dissonance among online people, searching for new products and increasing social status. Of all these factors put forward by the researchers, reducing risk and saving time are regarded as the most efficient ones.

Cantallops and Salvi (2014) has done research about the underyling reasons of customers and put nine basic reasons forward. These are given in Figure 3 as service quality, failure and recovery, helping companies, helping other vacationers, pre-purchase expectations, social identity, sense of community belonging, customer dissatisfaction and satisfaction.

On the other hand, some research about wom communication indicate that WOM is performed in the following conditions:

1. The conditions in which the consumer feels themselves insufficient about the knowledge needed for a reasonable decision;
2. The conditions in which the product is a complex one and evaluations by using objective criteria are difficult (In such sitıations, the experiences of others function as experience by observation);

Figure 3. Main review-generating factors
Source: Cantallops & Salvi (2014)

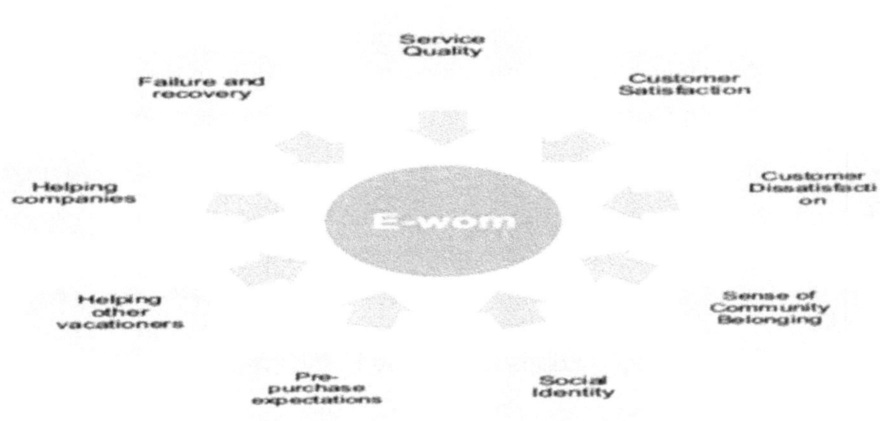

3. The conditions in which the consumer lacks the ability to evaluate the product or service;
4. The conditions in which the credibility of other sources are perceived as low;
5. The conditions in which reaching opinion leaders are easier than reaching other sources, thus helping the consumer save time;
6. The conditions in which there are strong social ties between the receiver and the source;
7. The conditions in which the individuals' need of social approval is high.

As seen above, the factors such as credibility, trust and interpersonal relationships play determinant roles in applying to WOM communication. In addition to the factors mentioned, the self perception of the individual and his/her social environments is of valuable importance for participating in WOM communication.

Mowen (1990:551) and Fill (2001:53) also give some underlying reasons for WOM communication. These are shown below.

Product Involvement

When the consumers are highly involved in a purchase decision, they tend to do a detailed research about the product or the service. Some parts of this research can be done through listening to the opinions and experiences of the friends and the mavens. In such cases with high involvement, personal effect can have a higher frequency than usual. Further, consumers have a higher tendency to talk about the high level satisfaction and dissatisfaction. These kinds of conversations allow the consumers to have more experiences in a short time.

Showing Themselves

This factor points to an adoption of product or service, gaining prestige, and the status level of the consumer. More importantly, as the consumer is seeking for a guarantee about the purchase decision, the dissonance can be reduced by this way.

Other Necessities

Products can help to utter the emotions of love, friendship and interest, and so sharing experiences about the products through WOM can help the consumers spread the benefits of the products.

Message Content

Another factor to motivate the conversation about the products are, according to Dichter, the messages surrounding the product itself. The advertisements messages, the seminars triggering sharing and WOM, exhibitions and commercial publishings can be mentioned in this group. The people identifying themselves with the product strongly, called brand advocates, participate in WOM communications commonly. The brand advocacy can be exhibited not only by WOM but by wearing and using the the products of the brand, as well.

THE ELEMENTS HAVING IMPACT ON WORD OF MOUTH

Whether they are in real or online environments, word of mouth communications are affected by some factors. When the related literature is reviewed, seven basic factors are mentioned as the factors having a potential impact on word of mouth communications, and these are tie-strength, homophily, trust, interpersonal communication and personal effect, source credibility, expertise, and perceived risk. Bewaring of these factors would be beneficial for the companies to use WOM as a competitive advantage.

Tie Strength

The features of the ties between the couple of communicators independent of certain contents are of critical importance for understanding of WOM process (Brown & Reingen, 1987:351). All WOM communications take place in a social relationship. This relationship can be categorized according to the the intimacy between the receiver and the source. This structural intimacy can be represented by 'tie strength'. This concept points to the quality of the ties between the members of a network (Brown & Reingen, 1987:352). Tie strength is a multidimensional structure closely related with the strength of the interpersonal relationship in a social network environment (Money et al., 1998:79). When it comes to the fact that communication is a social phenomenon and in the center of sociability are the interpersonal relationship, tie strength which represents the strength of these relationships comes to the fore as an efficient element in social relationships.

Social ties can be classified as strong and weak. The strong ties such as families and friends make up of the strong and closer relationship in the personal network of the individual, and provide them with emotional support. On the other hand, weak ties are generally the relationships consisting of a larger group such as acquaintances and colleagues. This kind of relationship is the one having a facilitating effect during the information search for different subjects (Granovetter, 1973:1363). In their study, Brown and Reingen (1987) showed that weak ties function as a vital bridge which allows the information to spread among distinctive groups. But in micro level (between the individuals and small groups), strong ties are more likely to function in referral behaviour.

Some research shows that tie strength has an impact on information flow and transmission. When compared to the individuals with weak tie strength, the individuals with strong tie strength communicate more often and exhibit a more often information exchange (Brown & Reingen, 1987:357).

Through the personal networks available in social networking sites, the product choices of consumers are affected both by the strong ties and by the weak ties. Whereas the strong ties are more effective on the communications between individuals and in small group levels, the weak ties have a more widespread effect as the social networking sites have no time restrictions and are more attractive. Social networking sites achieve this impact by opening the personal networks of the individuals to the groups and communities outside. Such an enlargement accelerates e-WOM in large scale networks because the tie strength perception encourages the communication and information flow between the consumers (Chu & Kim, 2011:54). Through a literature review, it can be seen that in this information flow, strength ties and some other times weak ties sometimes come one step forward. So it wouldn't be wise to regard one of them superior to the other.

Homophily

Source similarity or homophily refers to the similarity levels of the individuals in terms of certain shared traits (Rogers, 1983:274). The social comparison theory (1954) offers a mechanism to explain how homophily affects the persuasion. This theory suggests that individuals tend to compare their attitude and abilities with others. The tendency of an individual to compare himself/herself increases as the compared one is seen as similar. Because, according to Festinger, individuals have an assumption that similar people have similar preferences, a source perceived similar by the receiver may have a stronger persuasion impact on the receiver (Festinger, 1954 cited by Prendergast et al., 2010:690).

The similarity in homophily gains function through strong tie strength. According to the findings, people have a tendency to look for advice from the the people such as friends and other people with close relationship with themselves (Brown & Reingen, 1987:356), so the stronger the ties are, the more likely it would be to start the e-WOM communication (Armelini, 2011:207).

When it comes to the application of homophily factor to the e-WOM platforms, the people with similar interest come together in online environments, and even in the same online groups, some individuals with more similar interests tend to have a closer relationship, which is regarded as a function of homophily in online environments. These kinds of similarities and thus close relationships in online environments may have an effect to increase the likelihood of individuals to persuade each other about the goods and services.

Trust

The sum of one's expectations that other(s) will behave in a proper way is termed as trust (Farrel & Knight, 2003:541). The term trust that represents this sum of expectations is regarded as an invaluable factor that determines the structure of the relationship between the people both in real and online environments.

The main point that determines the relationship between social media and opinion receivers and followers is the benefits of web 2.0 and the trust towards them. All online opinion receivers (users) are aware of the basic benefits of the online applications such as social networks. About seventy percent of these people believe that social media is effective in being in relation with friends and acquaintances, and thus being aware of the new products. But the factor that inhibits all these potential benefits is the trust factor, and thus this factor always occupies the minds of the users of web 2.0 (Yao, 2011:62).

Trust, known as being willing to get support from a communication partner, is directly related to e-WOM behaviour. Trust is an important element to be taken into consideration in the conceptualization of involving in e-WOM in social networking sites (Moorman et al., 1993:82). When the anonymity of virtual environments is taken into consideration, the significance of trust can be seen more precisely. In the e-WOM communication largely consisting of the communication between the people not knowing each other, trust shouldn't be neglected while trying to determine the effect of e-WOM messages. According to the recent research, consumers regard social media as a more reliable source than the content created by the marketers (Mangold & Fauld, 2009:360).

When compared to the reviews shared by anonymous sources through other e-WOM channels (consumer review websites, forums and etc.,), the connections in social networking sites are closely interrelated with the actual networks of the consumers. As a result of this close interrelationship, social connections in online networks are more trustworthy than other sources such as advertisers or other anonymous sources. Furthermore, social networking websites facilitate the information exchange with the real world by supporting these real world relationship, and trust in real environments is transmitted to the online environments. This kind of transmitted trust affects the willingness of the consumers to be involved in e-WOM communications (Chu & Kim, 2011:56).

Interpersonal Communication and Personal Effect

The research having been done about traditional shopping and buying behaviour demonstrates that consumers are affected and directed by the people they interact. The impact of personal information sources on consumer choice is another well-established fact (King & Summers, 1970:43).

One of the most powerful categories of personal effect in the market is e-WOM. The power of e-WOM to motivate the attitude and behaviours is widely appreciated among academicians and the practitioners. The research by Richins (1983) on e-WOM, for example, points out that sixty percent of the dissatisfied customers share their dissatisfaction with a friend or an acquaintance (Kiecker & Cowles, 2002:312). Accordingly, the sensitivity of consumers to interpersonal effect is regarded as a valuable structure to explain the effect of e-WOM in online environments as well as in offline ones.

In online social networks, both the normative and informative effects are able to direct the behaviours of the consumers. The consumers exposed to informative effect exhibit a need to get information and guidance, which facililates the participation in e-WOM communications. On the other hand, the consumers exposed to normative effect are more likely to behave in accordance with the expectations of the people they respect. Because these individuals are in dire need of social approval through using the products approved by the people they respect, they actively search for information from the online sources (Chu & Kim, 2011:56).

Source Credibility

The most important determinant regarding the effect of the source who is communicated is the credibility of this source. The credibility here refers to the trust for the source about his or her unbiased information and also seeing the source as an expert and experienced one (Belch & Belch, 2003:168). As seen here, source credibility has got two dimensions, trust and expertise. The qualifications such as knowledge, skill, ability, intelligence and social status provide the source with expertise. An information source with high expertise can be more persuasive than the one with less expertise, but expertise is not sufficient alone and needs to be accompanied by trustworthiness and reliability (Kiecker & Cowles, 2002:314).

Crebility has a significant effect on the reception and decoding of the message. The perceived integrity and impartiality of the message source are of great importance for the way the receiver is affected by the message. The credibility of the message will likely be higher when the receiver respects and is of high opinion about source (Schiffmann & Kanuk, 2000:281).

Online communications about the products are largely based on the independent sources such as the experienced and unbiased consumers, so the credibility of these sources especially when they are opinion leaders and mavens will be higher than usual. e-WOM messages, due to the impartial sources sharing reviews, are likely to have a stronger persuasive power on consumers.

Expertise

Another important factor in e-WOM is the expertise. When it comes to expertise in e-WOM communication, opinion leaders and market mavens whose opinions are more effective than other consumers will come to the fore (Richins & Root-Shaffer, 1988:32). The potential receivers in e-WOM communications ask an expert when they need information or review about the products or services.

Here, when the expert is the receiver, the expertise level can affect not only the purchase decision but also the perceived risk (Armelini, 2011:208). According to the findings of a lot of research, when the receiver is completely ignorant or expert, the likelihood of searching for information will be lower than usual. The fact behind these findings are that experts decide about the products or services on their own because they have an adequate knowledge and experience to overcome the risk in purchase decision. As for the completely ignorant individuals, they don't ignore the advice and suggestions, because they don't have adequate knowledge or experience to make a comparison and so they buy the product without thinking when they have the opportunity (Voyer, 1999:63-64). The individuals with the ability and interest to arrange the information are the ones who have the potential to start e-WOM process (Armelini, 2011:208).

Perceived Risk

Perceived risk is essentially a concept of physchology which is introduced into marketing by Bauer in 1960s. Consumers, especially because of the lack of direct contact in online environments, have a potential risk about the qualifications of the product. According to research by Arndt, the people with high risk perception are more likely to take place in an information search than the ones with lower perceptions Murray (1991). Word of mouth is an important information source which reduces the risk and allows the consumers to give feedback, so it has a larger effect on consumers than many other sources (Zhenquan & Xueyin, 2009:2034).

Risk perception can be divided into two categories as social risk and financial risk. Social risk refers to negative outputs likely to come from the consumers'social environment while financial risk refers to the financial loss experienced after a dissatisfying purchase. Both of these risks are the results of normative and informative effect. The former occurs when the individuals try to behave in accordance with the expectations of others, and the latter results from the fact the consumers regard the information as a medium to enrich their knowledge about the product, and this in turn will determine from whom they will get advice (Wangenheim & Bayón 2004 cited by Armelini, 2011:208). In this context, it can be easily said that perceived risk is of a complex structure and even of importance for determining the information sources.

THE POTENTIAL POWER AND THE MEASUREMENT OF WOM

In today's world in which the effectiveness of advertisement diminishes, and people get more advice from their friends and acquaintances, it has become significant that to what extent e-WOM has an effect on the productivity of marketing (Armelini, 2011:206).

WOM has a great potential to have an effect on consumers thanks to some of its characteristics. First, it has a high credibility and this credibility is the most essential characteristics underlying its power.

Next, the flow of WOM information occurs in two-way flow rather than one way. That is, consumer is able to ask questions at every point in the communication process and get the required information. Further, WOM has a dynamic structure to allow the consumers to remember their experiences more easily. Finally, when compared to other marketing communication types, WOM is a marketing strategy with lower cost, larger outputs, higher efficiency and lower risk (Xiuqing & Haiqing, 2007:76).

A lot of research shows that personal effect is a more determining factor than advertisement or other sources. The high perceived credibility here is the most striking element, because there is a general tendency to believe that the consumers sharing information in the process of WOM have no commercial aims (Engel et al., 2005:731). This general tendency not only causes these messages to be more valuable on the eyes of consumers but offers significant opportunities for the companies trying to take advantage of WOM, as well. In the research done by Local Review Survey, as in Figure 4, only seven percent of the consumers are not interested in online communications, and the larger ninety three percent usually have a look at online messages in different platforms.

The value of WOM as a marketing communication is increasing every other day because of two basic reasons. First, consumers have lost their interest towards the advertisement and traditional media. Second, the information and telecommunication technologies are causing the effect of WOM to increase. For example, Jeff Bezos, the CEO of Amazon, says 'we don't advertise on TV and transfer all the money -we would otherwise spend on TV commercials- to the shipping system we call 'supersaver shipping'. Our customers talk to each other about this free shipping system and we earn more. WOM is really a very efficient communication method, I believe' (Armelini, 2011:205).

As regards the effects on consumer purchase decision, the power of WOM is well-established in marketing literature (Gilly et al., 1998:83). WOM is known as the exchange of marketing information by the consumers, and plays a vital role in changing attitudes towards the products and services. WOM messages are created by a more reliable information source than the messages of the companies, and thus consumers largely prefer WOM to get information about their potential purchase (Feick & Price, 1987 cited by Chua & Kim, 2011:48). Regarding these preferences, Marketing Charts (2017) offers some figures as in Figure 5.

Figure 4. Trust and influence on online reviews
Source: Local Consumer Survey (2017)

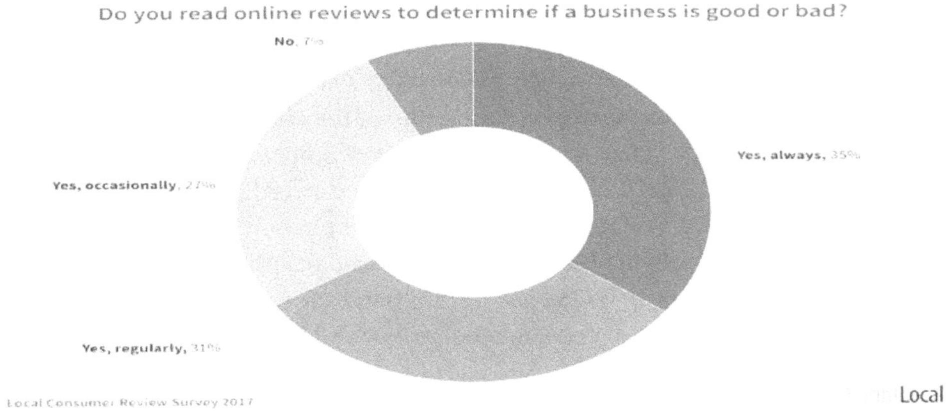

Figure 5. Most trusted ınfluential advertising media
Source: Marketing Charts.com (2017)

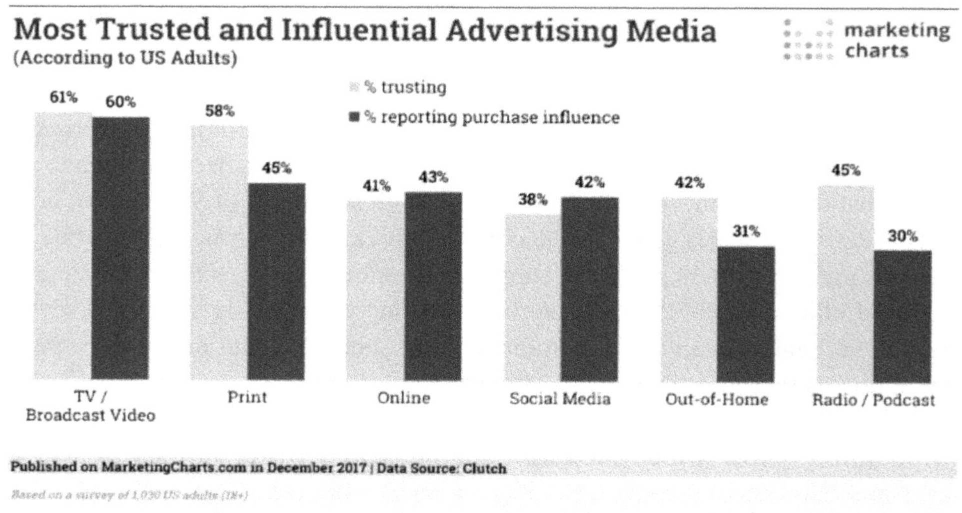

An important factor to make WOM communication more valuable is that WOM has an interpersonal nature. This communication often occurs between the individuals who have already had a social relationship other than sharing marketing experiences. This former relationship may affect the perception of the receiver about the similarity, motivation, credibility and reliability of the source, thus enriching these kinds of communications (Jun et al., 2011:264).

WOM messages in consumer review websites sometimes take over more important marketing roles than other product reviews in different platforms. So marketers need to develop strategic reactions in accordance with WOM messages especially shared in independent consumer review platforms. Marketers need to adopt a proactive strategy to apply just before the WOM communications in these environments. They also need to take the expertise power of their target consumers into consideration while deciding to create suitable platforms for the consumers to share their experiences. Because the expertise of the target consumers in brand controlled environments may have an unwanted damage on the brand (Chen & Xie, 2008:488-489).

Word of mouth can have an ability to affect the customers more than any other promotion effort. It can change the opinions of the customers and the new beliefs it created can be more permanent and strong in the mind of the customers. Mentioned as the 'two-edged sword', WOM is regarded as a means of communication having a power to increase the profitability of the company but at the same time having an incredible power to damage the financial conditions of the companies (Richins, 1983:68).

To be able to control and not to get harm from this two-edged sword,, companies are seeking ways to measure it. Being able to measure WOM communications will provide an important market advantage for the companies. When looked into the literature, it can be said that there are not enough studies about the measurement of WOM. Although WOM has been around for long years, the academicians focus more on the detemining role of WOM in consumer behaviour and less on the measurement of this communication (Goyette et al., 2010:9).

There are several factors that limit to reach the former experience or information in the memory. The three basic factors to understand the measurement of WOM are the length of time that has passed since the last experience (Brown & Beltramini, 1989:9); the amount of the material in the same common content group (Feldman & Lynch, 1988:421); the special characteristics of the information itself such as vividness (Herr et al., 1991:454). These three factors may allow the researchers to reach the information in the consumer's mind. As you can easily see in the advertisements, the main efforts named as repetition, intensity and frequency and originality are directly related to the above mentioned three factors.

Because of the fact that WOM can be measured through the purchase intention or just after the purchase, the chance of some factors known as belief, attitude, intention and behaviour to direct WOM communciations will be likely to increase (Tax et al., 1993:76).

An important point in the measurement of WOM is that many studies focus on only one dimension of WOM and doesn't determine in what dimension the mesasurement is done (Goyette et al., 2010:9). As WOM communications consist of many various factors and elements, and the one dimensional studies will cause a lack of comprehensiveness, the multidimensional scales will surely increase the reliability and validity of the measurement.

The most popular method to measure WOM communications in literature is the questionnaire method. In the research done by many researchers, such as Bowman and Narayandas (2001), Brown and Reingen (1987), the researchers ask a direct and one dimensional question to the participants: Have you ever told anything to anyone about the product X? (Godes & Mayzlin, 2004:548).

Another scale used to measure word of mouth communications is the Net Promoter Score (Scale) by Reicheld (2003) as seen in Figure 6. This scale has been designed to measure the number of the people who like or dislike about the brand. Many companies and brands these days use this scale to measure the satisfaction or dissatisfaction of customers.

NPS is one of the most widely used scales in the consumer relationship management and marketing research (Reichheld, 2003:53). This scale is of a simple structure to get an understanding about the consumers. Contrary to the market conditions, NPS measures the conditions the companies can change. The consumer is given a scale based the values between 0 and 1, and is asked about the likelihood of recommendation about the product or the service (Samson, 2006:648).

Figure 6. The net promoter score scale
Source: Reicheld (2003)

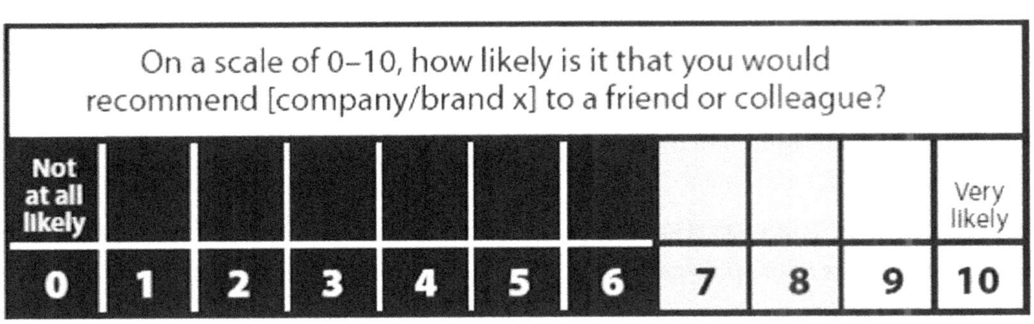

CONCLUSION

Together with the rapid transformation in internet and information technologies, consumers have experienced a transformation from a passive information receivers to active seekers and providers. Such an evolution has caused the effect of traditional advertisement to start to be questioned as the individuals are searching for product information from either their environments or social media platforms that are gainining popularity rapidly these days.

This increasing popularity of social media and the enourmous information exchange in these platforms have caused the traditional WOM to gain a new and faster dimension. This new concept that points out to the marketing communication between the consumers and comes true via the social media tools is called as e-WOM. This new concept requires many related traditional phenomena ranging from tie strength to opinion leaders to be revisited.

The individuals now socialize through social media platforms such as blogs, consumer websites and social networks, thus shaping their purchase decisions. The consumers in these platforms are involved in the communications sometimes as an opinion leader and some other times as just a follower, and spread negative or positive messages about products or services. In other words, the communications with high persuasive power in social media platforms between millions of people are sometimes positive and sometimes negative and damaging. At that point, companies need to benefit from the power of social media and use it for their own advantage. The companies which succeed in using these platforms effectively have a greater advantage over their competitors. So the marketing communicators should analyze these communications meticulously. What is important here is to perform a good analysis and understand the e-WOM communication process in social media platforms.

To sum up, to analyse word of communications and how it functions especially in online environments is extremely important for the companies seeking ways to be in contact with their customers. So, companies or brands need to know about the transformation process from WOM to e-WOM, the underlying reasons of these online communications, all the related factors ranging from tie-strength to perceived risk, and also the measurements of these communications. This profound awareness will provide the companies with efficient stretagies in their marketing activities.

REFERENCES

Akar, E. (2010). *Sosyal medya pazarlaması: Sosyal web de pazarlama stratejileri*. Ankara: Efil Yayınevi.

Armelini, G. (2011). *The Effect of Word of Mouth in Customer Equity and Brand Equity*. Chinese Business Review.

Arora, H. (2007). Word of Mouth in the World of Marketing. *The Icfai Journal of Marketing Management, VI, 4*, 51–65.

Bechina, A. A., & Husta, E. (2011). The Role of Social Networking Tools on Purchasing Decision Making Process. *Proceedings of the International Conference on Intellectual Capital*, 81-87.

Belch, B. (2003). *Advertising and promotion an integrated marketing communications perspective (6th ed.)*. McGraw-Hill/Irwin.

Bickart, B., & Schindler, R. M. (2001). Internet forum as influential sources of consumer information. *Journal of Interactive Marketing*, *1*(3), 31–40. doi:10.1002/dir.1014

Brown, J. J., & Reingen, P. H. (1987). Social ties and word-of-mouth referral behavior. *The Journal of Consumer Research*, *14*(3), 350–362. doi:10.1086/209118

Brown, S. P., & Beltramini, R. F. (1989). Consumer complaining and word of mouth activities: Field evidence. *Advances in Consumer Research. Association for Consumer Research (U. S.)*, *16*(1), 9–16. Retrieved from http://www.acrwebsite.org/search/view-conference-proceedings.aspx?Id=6872

Chen, Y., & Xie, J. (2008). Online consumer review: Word-of-mouth as a new element of marketing communication mix. *Management Science*, *54*(3), 477–491. doi:10.1287/mnsc.1070.0810

Chu, S.-C., & Kim, Y. (2011). Determinants of consumer engagement in electronic word-of mouth (eWOM) in social networking sites. *International Journal of Advertising*, *30*(1), 47–75. doi:10.2501/IJA-30-1-047-075

Engel, J. F., Blackwell, R. D., & Miniard, P. W. (2005). *Consumer Behaviour*. Thompson South Western Company.

Farrell, H., & Knight, J. (2003). Trust, institutions, and institutional change: Industrial districts and the social capital hypothesis. *Politics & Society*, *31*(4), 537–566. doi:10.1177/0032329203256954

Feldman, J. M., & Lynch, J. G. (1988). Self-generated validity and other effects of measurement on belief, attitude, intention, and behavior. *The Journal of Applied Psychology*, *73*(3), 421–435. doi:10.1037/0021-9010.73.3.421

Festinger, L. (1954). A theory of social comparison processes. *Human Relations*, *7*(2), 117–140. doi:10.1177/001872675400700202

Gilly, M. C., Graham, J. L., Wolfinbarger, M. F., & Yale, L. J. (1998). A dyadic study of interpersonal information search. *Journal of the Academy of Marketing Science*, *26*(2), 83–100. doi:10.1177/0092070398262001

Godes, D., & Mayzlin, D. (2004). Using Online Conversations to Study Word-of-Mouth Communication. *Marketing Science*, *23*(4), 545–560. doi:10.1287/mksc.1040.0071

Goyette, I., Ricard, L., Bergeron, J., & Marticotte, F. (2010). e-WOM Scale: Word-of-Mouth Measurement Scale for e-Services Context. *Canadian Journal of Administrative Sciences*, *27*(01), 5–23. doi:10.1002/cjas.129

Granovetter, M. S. (1973). The strength of weak ties. *American Journal of Sociology*, *78*(6), 1360–1380. doi:10.1086/225469

He, W., Zha, S., & Li, L. (2013). Social media competitive analysis and text mining: A case study in the pizza industry. *International Journal of Information Management*, *33*(3), 464–472. doi:10.1016/j.ijinfomgt.2013.01.001

Hennig-Thurau, T., Gwinner, K. P., Walsh, G., & Gremler, D. D. (2004). Electronic word-of-mouth via consumer-opinion platforms: What motivates consumers to articulate themselves on the Internet? *Journal of Interactive Marketing*, *18*(1), 38–52. doi:10.1002/dir.10073

Hennig-Thurau, T., Walsh, G., & Walsh, G. (2003). Electronic word-of-mouth: Motives for and consequences of reading customer articulations on the Internet. *International Journal of Electronic Commerce*, *8*(2), 51–74. doi:10.1080/10864415.2003.11044293

Herr, P. M., Kardes, F. R., & Kim, J. (1991). Effects of word-of-mouth and product-attribute information on persuasion: An accessibility-diagnosticity perspective. *The Journal of Consumer Research*, *17*(4), 454–462. doi:10.1086/208570

Jun, S.-Y., Cha, T., & Aggarwal, P. (2011). How Much Better? The Effect Of Tensile Information On Word-Of-Mouth Effectiveness. *Journal of Marketing Theory and Practice*, *19*(3), 263–276. doi:10.2753/MTP1069-6679190301

Kanning, L. (2008). *Evolvement and Prospect of Study on Word-of-Mouth Communication*. Working paper.

Kiecker, P., & Cowles, D. (2002). Interpersonal Communication and Personel Influence on the Internet. *Journal of Euromarketing*, *11*(2), 310–321. doi:10.1300/J037v11n02_04

King, C. W., & Summers, J. O. (1970). Overlap of opinion leadership across consumer product categories. *JMR, Journal of Marketing Research*, *7*(1), 43–50. doi:10.2307/3149505

Lee, K. T., & Koo, D. M. (2012). Effects of attribute and valence of e-WOM on message adoption: Moderating roles of subjective knowledge and regulatory focus. *Computers in Human Behavior*, *28*(5), 1974–1984. doi:10.1016/j.chb.2012.05.018

López, M., & Sicilia, M. (2014). Determinants of E-WOM influence: The role of consumers' internet experience. *Journal of Theoretical and Applied Electronic Commerce Research*, *9*(1), 28–43. doi:10.4067/S0718-18762014000100004

Mangold, W. G., & Faulds, D. J. (2009). Social media: The new hybrid element of the promotion mix. *Business Horizons*, *52*(4), 357–365. doi:10.1016/j.bushor.2009.03.002

Money, R. B., Gilly, M. C., & Graham, J. L. (1998). Explorations of national culture and word-of-mouth referral behavior in the purchase of industrial services in the United States and Japan. *Journal of Marketing*, *62*(4), 76–87. doi:10.1177/002224299806200406

Prendergast, G., Ko, D., & Yuen, S. Y. (2010). Online Word of Mouth and Consumer Purchase Intentions. *International Journal of Advertising*, *29*(5), 687–708. doi:10.2501/S0265048710201427

Reichheld, F. F. (2003). The one number you need to grow. *Harvard Business Review*, *81*(12), 46–55. PMID:14712543

Richins, M. L. (1983). Negative word-of-mouth by dissatisfied consumers: A pilot study. *Journal of Marketing*, *47*(1), 68–78. doi:10.1177/002224298304700107

Richins, M. L., & Root-Shaffer, T. (1988). The role of evolvement and opinion leadership in consumer word-of-mouth: An implicit model made explicit. *Advances in Consumer Research. Association for Consumer Research (U. S.)*, *15*(1), 32–36. Retrieved from http://www.acrwebsite.org/search/view-conference-proceedings.aspx?Id=6790

Rogers, E. M. (1983). *Diffusion of innovations*. New York: Free Press.

Samson, A. (2006). Understanding the buzz that matters: Negative vs positive word of mouth. *International Journal of Market Research*, *48*(6), 647–657. doi:10.1177/147078530604800603

Schiffmann, L. G., & Kanuk, L. L. (2000). *Consumer Behaviour* (7th ed.). Upper Saddle River, NJ: Prentice Hall.

Sun, T., Youn, S., Wu, G., & Kuntaraporn, M. (2006). Online Word-of-Mouth (or Mouse): An Exploration of Its Antecedents and Consequences. *Journal of Computer-Mediated Communication*, *11*(1), 1104–1127. doi:10.1111/j.1083-6101.2006.00310.x

Tax, S.S., Chandrashekaran, M., & Christiansen, T. (1993). Word of Mouth in consumer decision making: An agenda for research. *Journal of Consumer Satisfaction and Complaining Behaviour*, *6*(10), 74-80.

Voyer, P. A. (1999). *Word-of-mouth processes within a services purchase decision context* (Dissertation thesis). The University of New Brunswick.

Xiuqing, S., & Haiqing, G. (2007). *Online WOM Marketing and the Application of Its Strategy*. Academic Press.

Yao, P. (2011). Research on WOM Marketing of Forest Products Based on Web 2.0. *Journal of Chinese Marketing*, *4*(2), 61–66.

Zhenquan, S., & Xueyin, X. (2009). The Processes of Online Word-of-Mouth on the Purchase Decision. *Proceedings of the 7th International Conference on Innovation & Management*, 2033-2036.

Chapter 16
The Challenges of Nation Branding in the Digital Age:
Case of Spain's Nation Branding Project, Marca España

Mario Ciutad
Northumbria University London, UK

Hamid Jahankhani
Northumbria University London, UK

Jim O'Brien
Northumbria University London, UK

ABSTRACT

The concept of nation branding, the origins of the term, and how brand management is applied to obtain the expected results are investigated. Governments are driving nation branding projects, but some, like in the case of the Spanish project Marca España (ME), fail in detailing their objectives. Even when the objectives are weak, it is necessary to evaluate the performance of these projects. This is why some studies and indexes have been created. The indexes distinguish how a country ranks in various areas of study (economic, social, cultural, etc.), and the results are used to measure the efficiency of nation branding. Certain methodologies are used in this study together with various sets of data: from economic indicators and reputation indexes to the digital relevance of Spain.

INTRODUCTION

Nation branding (NB) is alive. On November 7th, 2017 an article was published in The Guardian titled "How to sell a country: the booming business of nation branding". It has been over twenty years now that the concept of NB started being studied through different disciplines: from marketing to political science. One of the consequences of its' multidisciplinary approaches is that there is no unanimous

DOI: 10.4018/978-1-5225-7344-9.ch016

consensus about a unique definition of NB. This paper wants to review the different definitions of NB and deepen into the concepts that converged to make it possible: the country of origin effect (COO), place branding and public diplomacy.

It is widely accepted that without globalization NB would have never existed. According to Dinnie the "challenge of distinguishing their product offerings from those of the competition has assumed critical importance for nations competing for both domestic and foreign consumers" (2007). NB was born to brand countries so they would acquire a competitive advantage respect its' competitors. Establishing a link between countries and brands brought scepticism to the concept. Many of the authors reviewed are perfectly aware of the differences between a brand and a nation (Anholt 2007, Olins 2005, Fan 2006). However, they agree that countries can adopt marketing techniques to brand themselves and improve or enhance their image and reputation. Through NB they expect to achieve economic and/or political outcomes. Porter (1990) first wrote about the competitive advantage of certain products or services based on the country that produced them. A good country image is the ticket to business and political influence. Most governments know that and have decided to start NB projects. To coordinate all the actors involved (ministries, agencies, tourism boards...) they have relied on marketing agencies or consultants like Simon Anholt.

Yet, many NB projects fail, and it can happen for multiple reasons: from a weak coordination of its' participants to a poor branding strategy or the rejection of its citizens because of its' exclusiveness, as Fan claims happened with Cool Britannia´s failure (2006). Nevertheless, it is widely accepted that some of the NB strategies work. Spain is cited multiple times as a country with a solid brand due to a good branding strategy since Franco's death (Anholt, 2008, Gilmore, 2002). This chapter focus on the (possible) effects of Spain's branding project Marca España (ME) since 2012, when the country's image was seriously damaged after the banking crisis and the spread of corruption cases.

Even if NB can work, it is difficult to quantify the success of a NB project. Is it possible to quantify the impact of NB when attracting tourists, foreign direct investment, talent, increasing exports or having a more influential role in the international scene due to NB? This research wants to study the plausible effect of ME in these years, focusing on tourism. In the last decade some indices have been ranking nations after considering various areas of study, one of them being tourism. The aim is to analyse if there are any patterns which indicate that Marca España has succeeded enhancing Spain's image or reputation according to the different Indices. Has the position of Spain in the Indices improved while Marca España has taken place? Is there a correlation between ME and some of Spain´s economic indicators?

All big countries in the world need to be very active digitally if they want to try to influence, like USA and UK which both have a strong public diplomacy (PD) or to improve or maintain their reputation. What about Spain? Does the country have a strong presence in the internet? Is it among the highest searches? The research will have a deep look at the Digital Country Index, a study of countries' worldwide searches which can help to determine the strengths and weaknesses of Spain in the internet.

Nation Branding

Since the first time that the term "nation branding" was used, the concept has been the object of multiple studies and research. However, according to Fan (2006), the efforts of theorizing what NB is have not produced a commonly accepted single definition of the notion because of "concerns applying branding and marketing communications techniques to promote a nation's image" (2006). One of the reasons which has been strongly pointed out as the cause of the scepticism around the theory of NB is the inclusion of the term "brand". As Dinnie (2007) claims, if instead of the word "brand", "reputation" would have been used, there would not have been such a controversy. Some academics argue that NB is just a semantic evolution of what has been known for decades as the country of origin (COO) effect, while for others it is just place branding. Instead, there are those who believe in NB as a developed and coordinated strategy to enhance a country´s image and reputation (Fan, 2006). Despite the different criteria everyone must agree that a country's image and reputation affect not only economically but also in terms of influence, the base of a country's soft power. The economic consequences for a country with bad image can be devastating and as Kotler and Gertner, (2002) claims "confronting a negative image can be an arduous challenge" because being able to change a country image or even a stereotype takes a long time.

Origins and Country of Origin Effect

Simon Anholt allegedly coined the term "nation branding" in 1996 but, however, in 2007, when Anholt first approached the idea of treating a nation as a brand he was associating NB to the concept of COO (2007). According to Dinnie (2007) COO is the effect, positive or negative, produced by the image of the country of origin of a product or service. Authors Jaffe and Nebenzahl (2001) would rather call it country image effect (CIE). The perception of the COO on the consumer can lead to purchasing an item or service just because the country has a positive reputation in that field. If a consumer is offered a TV produced in Japan or the same model produced in Morocco it is highly probable that the consumer will end up purchasing the Japanese television, due to the association of Japan with high-quality technology. The same could happen with Scotch whisky, German cars or Italian fashion. For the O'Shaughnessy brothers, the effect can be extended not only to products belonging to the same field but it "becomes a factor in the image of any product from that country" (2000). However, as Anholt (2007) suggests it is almost impossible that a country, even a rich one, can set the highest standard of quality to all the products or services they offer. So even if a consumer has the COO perception in his mind and purchases partly because of the good reputation it does not mean that the product acquired is the best.

So, the COO theory reveals few paradoxes. First, in a globalized world where companies outsource to other companies in different countries part of the work, and the shareholders might belong to different countries. Therefore, is the consumer aware of the real origin of what is being purchased? Second, if the COO has such an impact, then how to explain that it is possible to have a negative country image whereas having an excellent product brand image. Fan (2006) claims that such is the case of Chinese consumers when facing Japanese products. Even if Japan still carries a negative image among Chinese people, they admire their high-quality products and brands. Despite the paradoxes, many studies have proved that COO influences the consumer and so trade authorities admit that "their country's reputation constitutes an important asset to be managed" (Kotler and Gertner, 2002).

Country as Brand

Despite some criticisms, the association between countries and brands crystallized in the first years of the 21st century. The publication of the Journal Brand Management dedicated to NB for the first time increased the interest in this theory. In fact, by then, as Papadopoulos and Heslop (2002) stated most marketers, economists and politicians were already aware that nations behaved similarly to brands and understood its importance. One of the first researches about NB placed Spain as a good example. By publishing "A country –can it be repositioned? Spain –the successful story of country branding" (2002)

Gilmore attempted to prove the fact that NB existed and could work. She claimed that a coordinated nation brand strategy had increased Spain´s image and reputation, from a poor and isolated country to a modern and opened one, therefore enhancing its' economic indicators (argued as "exaggerated" by Fan in 2007). So, the perception that a country's branding strategy could pay satisfactory results enforced many governments to plan strategies, successfully or not. That helped to deepen the research of the links between countries and brands, although the scepticism continued. Olins' (2002) research defended that there was awareness of the big differences between branding a country or a product, but the link between them was the use of similar marketing techniques. Fan (2007) also highlighted the differences but reached a similar conclusion: marketing techniques could help a country to "sell" goods and places as well as to identify target audiences.

Yet, Anholt suggests that brand management could provide a strong means to improve a country's competitiveness. For that, Anholt (2007) redefined the concept as Competitive Identity, which as used to "describe the synthesis of brand management (BM) with public diplomacy, trade, investment, tourism and export promotion" (2007). Competitive identity is the way Anholt describes how a country forges its' reputation through six different channels, Tourism, Brand, Policy, Investment, Culture, People.

Place Branding

The evolution of NB cannot be understood without the concept of place branding. According to Moilanen (2009) place branding implies applying marketing techniques to places, no matter if it is a country, region or city being branded. Since NB was coined it has been debated whether NB was in the end just place branding (Jaffe, 2001) or place branding a form of NB (Fan, 2006). Place branding means the promotion of a nation, or a city or region in the country, as a tourist destination according to Fan (2006). Yet, it is a too simple approach because, as it happens to a country, regions and cities compete not only to attract tourists but also FDI, talent, the hosting of major events etc.

Brand Management

Doyle defines brand management as "a range of marketing disciplines focused on treating the brand as a managed asset" (2011). In NB the brand would be the country and the techniques implemented should enhance the brand's image among the consumers. Every brand needs a sustained BM not only to achieve positive outcomes but also to survive in such a competitive market. Moreover, BM can be helpful after unexpected situations happen. For instance, like recently in UK or Spain, a country (brand) will have to find how to maintain its' reputation after a terrorist attack. BM can keep the unity of the country by sending a positive message in and out of its' borders. In a tourist destination like Spain, BM can also help to fix a tourism strategy for the country. Through the opening of new resorts or high-standard establishments, BM can help a country to make a qualitative step. Those are few reasons why BM is so relevant to NB. Moreover, due to the analogy between countries and brands, the theory of NB has adapted some of the terminology used in branding.

Brand Identity

Nandan, 2005 explain that brand identity "originates from the company" and is the way a company wants to identify itself. Through branding, a company will display its' identity while differentiating its' product from others. Anholt (2011) describes brand identity as perceptible through the senses. Nation-brand identity, what the country wants to be identified for, can include a logo, an anthem or a slogan and is based on history, folklore, language, art. However, as Dinnie (2007) explains, a nation's identity will never be able to include the vast variety of elements forming the national identity of a country. That could be the case of Spain and Catalonia or UK and Scotland, because a nation is not a unitary entity in which all members think, feel and act as one. That is the reason why it is difficult that the brand identity of Spain or UK can reflect the national identity of Catalonia or Scotland. In that case, the feeling of not being included can produce rejection for Spain's NB project, as will be confirmed in this research.

Brand Image

The brand image is a set of principles about a certain brand, in other words, the perceptions that a consumer has of a brand. Similarly, for Jaffe and Nebenzahl (2001) a nation´s image is made of perceptions that any individual has of a country's products or brands. Nevertheless, hardly anyone has an unclouded vision of all the countries in the world or even, many countries have negative images in the eyes of many consumers. On many occasions a country's image can be just formed of stereotypes and it is commonly accepted that it takes a long time to change that. For Anholt (2011) these clichés, no matter if positive or not, if true or untrue, condition everyone´s attitude towards places, products or brands. So, can the stereotypes of a nation be changed through NB? Depending on the source the answer could either be positive (Gilmore, 2002), negative (Anholt, 2008) or unclear (Fan, 2007). Dinnie reflects the conceptual model which goes from nation-brand identity to nation- brand image, and defines who the communicators of the nation-brand identity are.

The process pursues that both internal and external audiences, enhance or even improve their perception of the country. A key role is that of the communicators because they are the ones spreading a nation-brand's identity. In the case of Spain some of them have been: As brand ambassadors the tennis-player Rafael Nadal in 2011 or actor Antonio Banderas in 2013 but also sporting achievements like the World Cup championship in 2010. Sport can make an impact on a country's image and so must be strategically used in NB projects.

Brand Equity

Doyle (2011) describes Brand equity as the additional value of a variety of products and services that is higher than the net book value of a company, which implies that a high brand equity can make the company value much more than what the book accounts reflect. Regarding a nation's brand equity Papadopoulos defines it as the "value of perceptions embedded by various target markets about the country" (2002). The concept is clear but, is a nation brand equity measurable? Since the term NB appeared there have been few attempts to rank a country's image and reputation or even quantify a nation brand's equity, one of them the "Nation Brands" index from Brand Finance. However, assigning monetary value to a country using marketing equity instruments has been extendedly criticized. Rasmussen and Merkelsen (2012) explain that the validity is questionable" (2012). The extent to which a nations brand even should be measured in monetary terms is a subject of some debate.

THE IMPACT OF NATION BRANDING

The competition between nations to acquire a competitive advantage has generated a momentum and motivation for many governments to devote resources to develop NB. Kotler and Gertner, (2002) points out why governments should manage and supervise their branding: it is the urge for tourists, FDI, factories, exports, talented individuals and foreign markets that makes them use marketing techniques to fulfil the objectives. However, as later developed, it is not only the economic benefits that matter. This is the case of soft power, defined by Pamment (2014) as the power of attract and influence to favour collaboration standing "from the attractiveness of a nation's values, culture, and policies".

Economic Factors

Tourism

Tourism is considered one of the major benefits of a good nation-brand strategy as it plays a huge role, as an economic objective (rising the quantity and quality of tourists visiting) and also as the communicator of the nation´s brand because, as Anholt claims "it has permission to brand the country directly" (2007) through its' tourism boards and actors. A good image as a tourist destination can also boost exports or FDI with a good NB strategy and the correct use of data and Business Intelligence.

According to Dinnie (2007) the fact that many countries compete as tourist destinations urges them to create a unique "product" and look for a niche which makes them more attractive than their competitors. Countries like Croatia, Greece or Spain have succeeded in branding themselves and acquiring a competitive advantage to become top holiday destinations. However, as Kotler and Gertner, (2002) points out tourism is not the panacea: despite being a major income source a country might need to solve their problems first to manage to attract tourists and income. The image of a country does not change in short-term from negative to positive so even if a nation's tourist promotion image is seducing, if it does not match reality will not be successful.

One of the risks for some countries is that they fall into the traditional holiday field, just offering "sun and sea" which in the end can attract many low-spender tourists by forcing tourism actors to lower their prices. As Olins (2005) states, a country will differentiate from others by promoting the art, culture, history, architecture and other unique features to attract tourists looking for something else rather than beach vacations, and who will probably spend more. This has been one of the objectives of the Spanish governments and all the tourism actors. ME has tried to promote more than just sun and sand but also the culture, heritage, gastronomy and drinks to attract specific tourists and not just low-spender holiday-goers. The results of this research will try to find out if it has been achieved or not.

Foreign Direct Investment (FDI)

The total amount of FDI in the world ascended to $1.8 trillion (UNCTAD, 2015) so there is little doubt that there is a fierce rivalry between countries to receive the investments and therefore, jobs and new opportunities. However, despite being present in all NB studies and with the vast amount of literature about FDI, Papadopoulos et al (2016) claims that there has not been much research about NB from an FDI approach. Dinnie (2007) categorized four major features that are valued by those companies eager to invest overseas: a stable economic and political environment, skilled workforce, streamlined administrative procedures and infrastructure. The better a country scores in those aspects, the highest options to be allocated the resources. The launch of "Creative France" in 2015 aimed, among others, to increase FDI in the country by highlighting its' positive features and fight against the perception of being a "more complicated country" according to François Hollande, (2014) than others. However, in 2016 FDI inflows in France decreased 39% (UNCTAD).

Exports

Like nation-branding with FDI purposes, the objective in this case is to increase the country's export power and maintain or gain a reputation for its' products and services. Partly due to the COO effect some "Made in.." labels are much more successful than others even if the latter offer better goods. Anholt states that a nation's export brands "act as powerful ambassadors of each country's image abroad, but only where their country of origin is explicit" (2007). The COO effect may not produce results if a product has been made in various countries or even, if a consumer is not able to associate a powerful brand to its' COO. Some brands prefer having the appeal of a different COO and so name their products in other languages, for example Japanese car manufacturer Toyota naming its cars under Italian names because they sound more attractive. Olins (2005) also reinforces this view by saying that having a powerful COO effect in one field can eclipse the attempts of products from other sectors, as happens with German fashion.

Soft Power and Public Diplomacy

As opposed to hard power, which implies coercion, soft power is a country's ability to overcome objectives by influencing and persuading, rather than threatening or imposing. Soft power as an influence tool is compulsory in the IT era and as Melissen (2005) states, due to the existence of strong transnational connections, a decrease in soft power can carry consequences. Through NB a country will try to enhance its' image and reputation to gain influence (soft power) and one of the tools used will be public diplomacy (PD). Rasmussen affirms that it is commonly agreed that PD is "a strategic communication instrument aimed at foreign publics" (2012). PD will use communication as a mean to influence others through "communicative practices such as culture, advocacy and branding" (Pamment, 2014). Complementing the traditional diplomacy, more based in relations between states, PD focuses on "non-official groups, organizations and individuals" (Melissen, 2005). And for Zaharna (2016) PD might be facing a new impulse, the second after the 9/11 attacks, when PD was used to influence foreign audiences to favour USA's policies and decisions. The new call for PD has been made by the globalization of the internet and the growth of social media and the term has evolved into what has been called "Public Diplomacy 2.0".

Public Diplomacy (PD) 2.0

Such is the importance given to the new PD that authors like Mytko (2012) highlight the enormous disadvantage for those states which do not recognize the value of PD 2.0. Other authors like Iosifidis and Wheeler (2016) claim that the evolution of the IT age has urged many nations (including USA and UK) to use digital instruments to receive positive opinion in the international scene. In their words "digital communication has revolutionized the practice of public diplomacy" (2016). According to Melissen (2011) countries realized that the one-way communication to foreign audiences had ended with the development of new technologies and the new PD. It is no more a one-way dialogue and hierarchy is substituted for a more horizontal approach. Iosifidis and Wheeler define the new PD as the "construction of horizontal webs to engage the public, NSA and civil society organizations that are relevant for foreign policy objectives" (2016). PD tries to use well-known and influential organizations, individuals and NGO's so that they give support to the country and its' policies. However, as Dinnie (2007) claims, these kinds of touchpoints between a brand/country and an audience are not controllable so, even if unintentionally, something positive could turn into negative and spread like a virus.

The Power of Social Media

Our global societies are eager to be informed and communicate, through many different channels, and the number of social media users increases daily due to the incorporation of less developed countries. Harris (2013) claims that social media "are effective for conveying any message to a given public, whether it is from a corporation, a public figure, or a government". Governments understood that they could not miss the chance given by social media to reach their target audiences and one of the first exploiting it was President Obama in his 2008 campaign. Since his election the use of social media boosted to engage audiences and improve the country's image after Bush's presidency. With the use of social media and fake news, governments like Russia have tried to influence in foreign affairs such as the Catalan separatist movement, Brexit or Trump's election. The power that social media offer is being used by governments and organizations to try to influence. Also, governments, diplomats, Royal Houses and other governmental actors embrace social media to send their messages but also listen and interact with the audiences. It is a way of branding the nation no matter the distance, as in the case of UK with some of the members of the Commonwealth. NB projects rely on the use of social media to reach and engage audiences around the world. The question is whether they succeed or not.

MARCA ESPAÑA (ME)

The NB project Marca España was born in 2012 and it defines itself as a long-term governmental policy developed to enhance the country's image inside and outside its' borders. Marca España Council unites all the actors who take part in the project, ranging from several official agencies to tourism boards, local and regional governments or Spanish public television RTVE. The Council works in different workshops, depending on the field (PD, Economic diplomacy, Sport diplomacy, regional and local administrations…).

The first plan was implemented in 2013 and it established the general priorities of the project. Geographical priorities, as 15 countries were targeted, sectorial priorities like tourism, renewable energies, sport, biotechnology among others, as well as the horizontal priorities, focused on employment, increase of exports, FDI or the promotion of the Spanish language. After defining its' general purposes (although never in detail) the second plan focused on communication and some economic features (internationalization of companies, FDI, etc). The 2015 plan aimed at improving coordination and established ways to communicate the distinctive characteristics (history, culture, food, sports.etc). Finally, in 2016 the plan was dedicated to critically analyse the actions in the 2012-2015 period and evaluate the results. It has been the duty of Real Instituto El Cano, with its' annual Barometer of Spain's image to study the country's perception. A summary of the different activities developed by ME can be found in Figure 1.

Figure 1. Marca España activities in the period 2012-2016. Data source from Marca España, un proyecto hecho realidad (2012/2016).

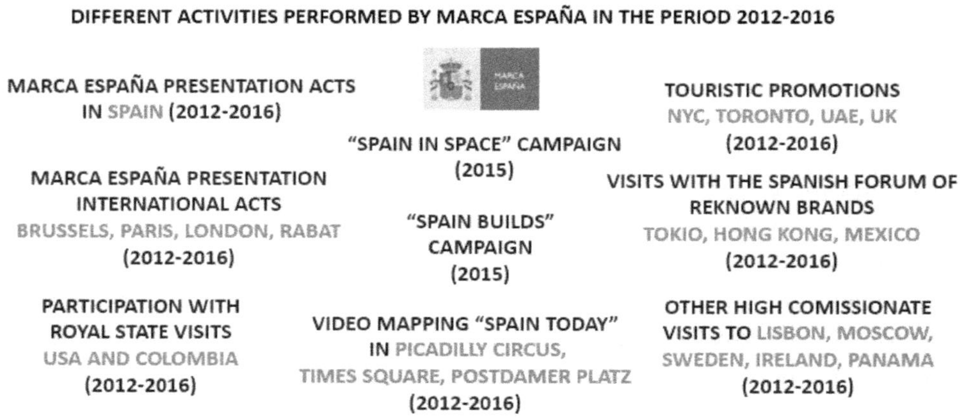

One of the countries in the world which academics cite as an example of having performed a successful NB is Spain (Anholt, 1998; Gilmore, 2002; Olins, 2005). Yet, this success in rebranding a nation with a turbulent history has been the result of decades of NB's implementation.

Olins (2005) described Spain before Franco's death as an "isolated, autarkic, poverty-stricken, authoritarian anachronism, hardly part of modern Europe at all". Those were the consequences of a 40-year dictatorship which deepened the stereotypes that the country already had gained through history: an ultra-catholic, savage and obscure country, home-born of the Spanish Inquisition. So how could Spain change its image and become a respected country in the international arena?

After Franco's death, Spain was merely seen as an affordable place for holidays, "a poverty-stricken country of no cultural or commercial influence" (Olins, 2005). However, during the 1980s and 1990s Spain invested in a NB strategy, one of its' symbols being Joan Miro's sun drawing (Moilanen, 2009). As Gilmore points out, the sun "graphically unified a myriad of activities, publicity events and ads" (2002). These campaigns were implemented in a context of modernization and aperture to the world which lead to the acceptance in the European Economic Community in 1986. During the 1990s the privatization and globalization of Spanish multinationals in Latin America (Repsol, Telefonica, BBVA…) contributed to enhance Spain´s image as a modern country with economic opportunities and brands which could compete internationally. Other events such as the 1992 Barcelona Olympic Games helped to put Spain on the map. Additionally, as Olins states "the reality has changed but so have perceptions" (2005).

So why NB in Spain can be considered a success according to most academics in the field? No matter how much a country invests in NB, if the image trying to project on their audiences does not correspond with reality the project will fail. As Gilmore (2002) states, what is being branded must be an intensification of what is there already, not an invention, and Spain has successfully done it by capturing its' people spirit.

While the number of tourists grew exponentially there was the risk that Spain was still seen as a cheap holiday destination for low-spenders. As Olins (2005) suggests, to differentiate itself to other similar competitors a country must emphasize other features like culture, gastronomy or nature "through sophisticated imagery" as a way to attract less tourists but who will spend more. The growth, even if slow, of other non-beach destinations in Spain and the fact that Spain has good positions in the cultural aspects of the different Indices (Figure 2) are a positive sign but everyone should admit that Spain is still too associated to low-cost holidays.

However, Spain's NB faces other challenges, like being considered more than just a tourist powerful brand or the recent decrease of its' image due to the separatist tensions in the region of Catalonia, as can be seen in a recent study (Figure 3).

In different rankings and Indices studied Spain usually hits the top-10 in tourism and culture, while in those aspects related to business, the digital economy or the best places to work in, the country usually

Figure 2. Spain's cultural position in different Indices. Data sources from Digital country index, Reputation Institute, 2017and Soft power 30 (2017).

SPAIN'S CULTURAL POSITION IN THE INDEXES

THE SOFT POWER 30 (2017)	6
THE SOFT POWER 30 (2015)	5
DIGITAL COUNTRY INDEX (2017)	8
COUNTRY REP TRACK (2013)	8
COUNTRY REP TRACK (2011)	8

Figure 3. How the Catalan separatist movement affects Spain's image. Data source from a Report on the Spain brand reputation in the European context by Reputation Institute (2017).

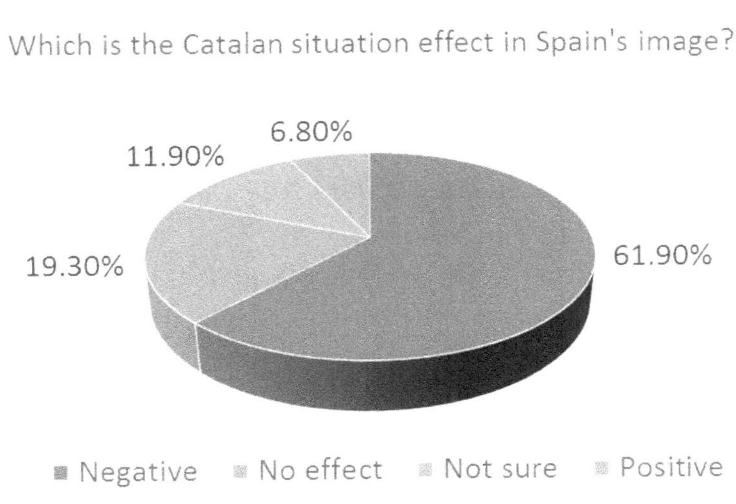

**For a more accurate representation see the electronic version.*

does not stand out. As the academics state, all the citizens should know and identify themselves with the project and the national identity projected. Yet, according to the research by Rius and Zamorano (2014) about Marca España, the project tends to focus on the Spanish nation, a Spanish identity which is not inclusive with other nationalities in Spain, like the Catalan or the Basque, (The Real Instituto Elcano, 2017). They criticize the use of ME to project a uniformed image of Spanish culture, without considering the different regions. Melissen (2011) claims that some regions in contemporary cracked countries like Belgium or Spain "have been practising their own assertive public diplomacy". So, if ME is not able to engage all Spanish citizens and many do not feel identified with it, it will hardly achieve its' objectives.

Spain's Indicators

One of the objectives of ME is not only receiving more international visitors annually but also receiving visitors looking for more than cheap sun and sea holidays. Analysing the number of tourists and linking it on the income spent in Spain will give a clue on the performance of Spanish tourism. As can be seen in figures 4 and 5, the number of international tourists has increased during the period 2012-2016.

Figure 4. Spain indicators 2012- 2016. Data source from the World Bank 2017.

YEAR	Population (M)	GDP (current Billion US$)	International tourism, number of arrivals (M)	GDP Growth	GDP per capita €	Unemploy-ment rate	Exports of goods and services (M US$)	FDI Outflows (M US$)	FDI Inflows (M US$)	High Education Students
2012	46,818,216	$1.30	57.5	-2.9%	24,100	25.77%	214,094,097	-2,479	24,667	72,488
2013	46,727,890	$1.36	60.6	-1.7%	23,300	25.73%	253,799,183	12,823	37,436	73,639
2014	46,512,199	$1.37	64.9	1.4%	22,780	23,70%	243,659,858	36,325	25,655	71,533
2015	46,449,565	$1.19	68.2	3.4%	22,518	20.90%	238,752,264	44,489	11,910	76,057
2016	46,440,099	$1.23	75.3	3.3%	22,562	18.63%	229,374,120	41,789	18,659	N/A
AVERAGE (2012-2016)	**46,589,594**	**$1.29**	**65**	**0.70%**	**23,052**	**22.76%**	**235,935,904**	**26,589**	**23,665**	**73,429**

**For a more accurate representation see the electronic version.*

Figure 5. Number of international tourists to Spain, 2012-2016. Data source from the World Bank 2017.

Yet, this research cannot establish a direct link between the increase in the number of tourists and the influence of ME campaigns. However, the positive trend does not discard a possible impact of Spanish tourist campaigns under the project ME. In figure 6, the expenditure per visitor is shown and it has not improved in the period 2013-2016. In this case, the objective of ME for attracting visitors who would spend more during their visit has not been successful.

Another of the main objectives of a NB project is to increase the amount of FDI in the country. Figure (7) shows the amount of FDI outflows and inflows: while the outflows show a very positive trend, the inflows seem to decrease since they peaked in 2013.

The results reveal that if ME was trying to increase the FDI inflows, the strategy has not yet worked out. However, data from 2017 would help to determine if the trend continues being negative or not.

Image and Reputation Indices and Rankings

As mentioned before, governments tend to use the results in the reputation rankings to accept or reject the success of a NB project. When trying to determine if ME has succeeded in improving the country' s

Figure 6. Expenditure per visitor in Spain. Data source from Bank of Spain (2017).

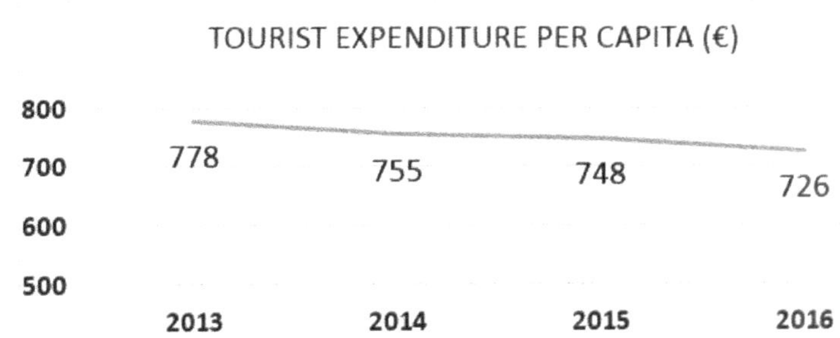

Figure 7. Amount of foreign direct investment, outflows and inflows, 2012-2016. Data source from UNCTAD, 2017.

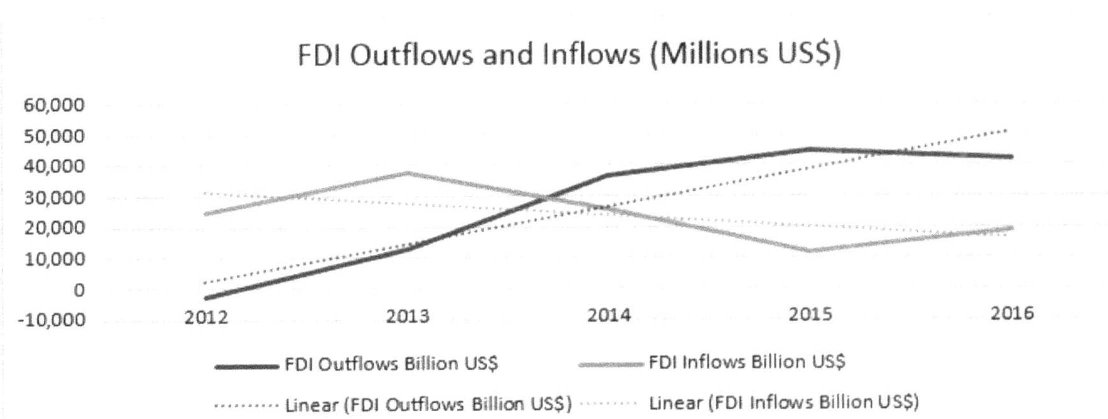

**For a more accurate representation see the electronic version.*

image it is compulsory to observe the position of Spain in those indices in the period 2012-2017. A positive trend could confirm that ME has had a role on the improvement of Spain´s image. On the contrary, a negative result would instantly undermine the capacity of ME to achieve its purposes.

The position of Spain in the different Indices is shown in figure 8. Information from six indices has been gathered. It is important to note that not all Indices are published annually.

In three out of six indices (Nation Brand, Digital Country Index and Country RepTrack) the position of Spain has improved in the period going from 2012 to 2016. Meanwhile, in other two the position of Spain has remained the same (Anholt-GFK) or has improved one position (Good Country Index). The only ranking in which Spain has lost positions is in the Soft Power 30 index, from the 14th position in 2014 to the 15th in 2017.

All in all, it can be confirmed that the image of Spain, according to the Indices, has improved in the period when ME has taken place. The Spanish government has published the results of some Indices in Marca España's annual reports and has used the positive results to strongly support the continuity of the project.

This research has also look at the position of Spain in the "Tourism" aspect of the Indices. The ranking was compared to the classification of two other major competitor countries: France and Italy. This should provide a more accurate approach to the performance and attractiveness of Spain as a tourist destination, in comparison to France, the country with more visitors in the world and one of the highest in expenditure per tourist, Figure 9.

The missing data has not been collected because the Indices are not published annually. Examining the table, the three countries are top-ranked, being Spain the 1st positioned in the Digital Country Index while Italy is the 1st ranked in the Anholt-GFK. France obtains the 3d position in the Soft Power 30, while Spain is 6th. In the Country Brand ranking dedicated to Tourism Spain achieved the 3rd place, although fell from the 2nd in 2014. The three countries have comparable results in the Indices and the position of Spain remains very stable in all of them, with no changes at all in some cases. Spain should

Figure 8. The position of Spain in the reputation Indices. Data sources are from - NBI Anholt-GFK Index, Brand Finance Nation Brands, Digital Country Index (Bloom Consulting), Country RepTrack (reputation Institute), The Soft Power 30 (Portland Communications) and The Good Country Index (Anholt).

	ANHOLT- GFK	NATION BRANDS	DIGITAL COUNTRY INDEX	COUNTRY REP TRACK	SOFT POWER 30	GOOD COUNTRY INDEX	
2012		13		16			15
2013	11	18		18			16
2014	12	18		18		19	17
2015	12	16	15	17	14		15
2016	11	14	9	17	12	21	14
2017		12	7	13	15	18	13
	12	15	10	17	14	19	

**For a more accurate representation see the electronic version.*

Figure 9. The position of France, Spain and Italy in the "Tourism" area of the Indices. Data sources from Anholt- GFK NBI, digital country index, country brand tourism ranking, Country RepTrack and Soft Power 30.

YEAR	ANHOLT-GFK NATION BRANDS INDEX			DIGITAL COUNTRY INDEX			COUNTRY BRAND RANKING TOURISM			COUNTRY REP TRACK			SOFT POWER 30		
	FR	SP	ITA	FR	SP	ITA	FR	SP	ITA	FR	SP	ITA	FR	SP	ITA
2012							3	2	12						
2013		5					4	2	7		8	2			
2014		5					5	2	10	10		3			
2015				4	1	2					9	2	3	6	8
2016				4	1	2						4	3	6	7
2017	2	4	1	3	1	2	6	3	10		10	5	3	6	7

take into consideration the results from France in some indices to develop ideas to help increase the quality of its' visitors.

With these results it is difficult to accept or discard the relevance of ME because a clear results and solid conclusions cannot be extracted.

Digital Performance (PD) of Spain

Today, every country intending to have a reputation in the world must have a digital strategy, as the internet is one of the most influencing tools nowadays. A country with a poor image abroad or even, almost no image at all, will not achieve many search results in Google while countries which are also strong brands will achieve high amount of results. The Digital Country Index is a study based on the online searches (social media is being excluded) according to five parameters: tourism, talent, investment, exports and national prominence. This was published in 2015 and 2017 by Bloom Consulting. and its' results gives an idea of how Spain is performing in the digital world, Figure 10.

According to the Index (figure 11), Spain has improved its' results in 2017, comparing to 2015. In 2015 Spain was ranked in 19th position in "Exports", while in 2017 it escalated to the 10th position. It means that there has been a major increase in the searches for Spain exports. In "Investment" where keywords like "stock exchange" or "invest in Spain" are searched, the rank also improved, from the 15th to the 11th position in just 2 years. For the areas of "talent" and "prominence" Spain won one position in 2017.

Looking more in detail the results in the different areas (figure 12) indicate that the importance of arts, culture and sports in the searches too. Those aspects are major assets to increase the interest of potential consumers/visitors. The "export from Spain" accounted 48% of the searches related to exports.

The most positive figure would be the one related to "Tourism" where Spain maintains the 1st position in the ranking, meaning that it is the country with more online searches. The researcher has found more details of the 2015 Index: Spain ranked 2nd in the world when the searches were related to visiting

Figure 10. Digital performance of Spain. Data source from digital country index by Bloom Consulting, 2015 and 2017.

	GOOGLE SEARCHES (M)	GOOGLE SEARCH TOURISM (M)	GOOGLE SEARCH CULTURE	GOOGLE SEARCH REPUTATION	TRIPADVISOR TOTAL SEARCH RESULTS	TRIPADVISOR LOCATIONS SEARCH	TRIPADVISOR ATTRACTIONS SEARCH	GOVERNMENT'S FACEBOOK FOLLOWERS	
FRANCE	1,120	23.1	29	53	340,546	20,468	41,868	FRANCE	411,488
GREECE	170	6.17	359	4	85,886	3,132	10,154	GREECE	8,140
ITALY	537	11.8	31	36	520,540	12,103	80,344	ITALY	32,150
SPAIN	340	10.1	80	28	318,757	9,085	38,013	**SPAIN**	21,524
TURKEY	252	6.08	14	15	79,749	893	8,743	TURKEY	62,516
UK	1,300	24.7	21	6	362,191	11,148	58,571	UK	479,437
USA	1,490	11.8	27	14	1,328,972	33,609	198,774	USA	8,530,419
	744	13	80	22	433,806	12,920	62,352		

**For a more accurate representation see the electronic version.*

Figure 11. Spain's position in the five parameters of digital country index. Data source from digital country index by Bloom Consulting.

	DIGITAL COUNTRY INDEX				
	EXPORTS	INVESTMENT	TOURISM	TALENT	PROMINENCE
2015	19	15	1	8	9
2017	10	11	1	7	8

Figure 12. Percentages of searches of the different sub-aspects in the digital country index 2017. Data source Bloom Consulting.

the country, 3rd in searches for cultural assets (after Italy and France), 6th in nature and 7th in leisure and entertainment. The combination of the scores gave Spain the 1st position in "Tourism".

However, even if Spain is ranked first, in 2017 the searches for general information took 78% of the total searches, while "outdoor & nature" (5%) or "cultural assets" (4%) were minority. Online searches on these aspects must improve if Spain want to receive visitors who are not just looking for low-cost holidays.

Figure 13. Percentage of searches regarding Spain's "Tourism" in the digital country index 2017. Data source from Bloom Consulting.

To enhance its' PD, all governments, ministries, agencies, tourism boards have social media accounts. It is a way to maintain interest from the audience (possible customers). The Figure 14 shows the number of followers of different state governments.

However, in light of the Facebook and Cambridge analytica where large scale information harvesting was exercised, many researches are now asking for data regulations because there is concern about the ethics and the privacy implications where companies and may be some governments use private data/information in order to plan strategic future direction, (Seargeant and Tagg, 2018).

By comparing the number of followers of the Spanish government with those of other countries, it is obvious that Spain is not performing in that front. With just 21,500 followers, it seems not to be generating enthusiasm, while French government is 20 times higher and USA, with 8.5 million followers dominates the list.

Figure 14. Number of followers of different state accounts. Data source from Facebook, 2017.

GOVERNMENT'S FACEBOOK FOLLOWERS	
FRANCE	411,488
GREECE	8,140
ITALY	32,150
SPAIN	21,524
TURKEY	62,516
UK	479,437
USA	8,530,419

CRITICAL DISCUSSION

The purpose of NB is to improve a country´s image and reputation. By doing so, some results are expected, becoming more influential (soft power) and an increase in economic indicators such as exports, visitors and FDI. This research aimed at identifying whether NB has achieved its' objectives in the case of Spain or not. ME is a NB project started in 2012 to mitigate the loss of reputation after the banking crisis. However, the opacity of the Spanish government regarding the project is major. There are general information but not many details about the specific activities, budget or implementation. The activities developed can be found in the internet, but without much content. No information can be found regarding the budget of the project and without knowing the expenditure of each activity it is difficult to measure its' impact. Furthermore, ME has not specified specifically the objectives that the project is seeking. There are no figures available on explicit targets, just general statements, which makes it easier for the government to defend the impact of ME. For all these reasons being able to evaluate the performance of ME is an almost impossible task.

In 2012 the Real Instituto El Cano, a Spanish institution specialized in sociological studies, started the annual Barometer of the image of Spain. One of the main reasons for its' creation was to evaluate the performance of ME. By analysing annually the image of Spain and its' different aspects (culture, goods, sport, governance…) the government not only wanted to know lean and know the country image but also try to establish the weaknesses, and reverse them, figure 15. Spain aimed at collecting primary data about many distinctive features to extract conclusions and work on them. The initiative is positive because having that kind of data, if analysed correctly, can help to establish strengths and weaknesses and implement measures to improve results. Nevertheless, Spain could work much more with first hand data to improve the results in some areas such as exports. The use of Business Intelligence is a must in a country receiving 80 million visitors in 2017. Each visitor in Spain produces a big amount of data which should be thoroughly analysed to understand what the tourist seeks, their expectations, where

Figure 15. Spain's image. Data source from the Real Instituto El Cano, 2017.

BAROMETER SPAIN'S IMAGE BY REAL INSTITUTO EL CANO

YEAR	GLOBAL VALUE (0/10)	ECONOMY	CULTURE/ CULTURAL PRODUCTION	GOVERNANCE	SOCIETY/ CITIZENS	SPANISH COMPANIES ABROAD	SPAIN, COUNTRY TO INVEST	SPORT
2012	6.5	5	7.3	5.2	6.7	N/A	N/A	N/A
2013	6.7	5.7	7.6	5.9	7	N/A	N/A	7.8
2015	6.9	5.9	6.9	6.2	7.2	6.3	6.3	7.5
2016	7.2	5.8	6.8	6.1	7	6.2	6.1	7.2
2017	7.1	5.7	6.6	6.1	6.9	6	5.9	7
AVERAGE	6.9	5.6	7.0	5.9	7.0	6.2	6.1	7.4

**For a more accurate representation see the electronic version.*

they go, their favourite attractions or the products they buy. If one of the objectives of NB is the export of goods, why not analysing the best-selling products among tourists? Knowing the specific brands or the origin of the wine and oil that tourists buy could help target countries for Spanish products. For a country like Spain, tourism is a major source of income and the more visitors spend during their stay, the better for the economy, for example creating more jobs. However, the "sun and sea" tourism is not giving Spain an added value.

As seen in Figures 5 and 6 the number of tourists visiting Spain has gradually increase in the period 2012-2016. However, the expenditure per visitor has dropped. With such a fierce competition on low-cost holidays from countries like Greece, Portugal or Turkey, Spain needs to offer the customers much more. The aim is to target countries with big-spender tourists (Russia, Asia, USA, Middle East) and, after analysing the behaviour of visitors from those countries with the data that they have produced, try to offer potential customers the holidays they desire. Word of mouth is still vital in tourism because visitors will talk about the stay, the attractions and the products to their friends and families, creating new potential visitors. This is of course a very important factor in the digital age as visitors not only provide real time information about their stay through social medias, but also their blugs written after their stay can reach many million other potential visitors. Obviously, the process that leads to the final decisions is not easy because storing data from 80 million customers will require a huge budget, as well as professionals capable of analysing and transforming the data to be understandable to those making decisions, from a senior management level to lower management level.

A national brand project can only be successful if achieves the purposes for which it was created. However, evaluating the impact of a NB project in some indicators is virtually impossible, especially in the case of ME. Proving that the campaigns have resulted in an increase of exports or FDI seems impossible without having detailed data from the campaigns ME executed (budget, target countries etc.). Therefore, a positive trend could not be confirmed that ME has worked. Instead, if the indicators have had a negative trend, it should confirm that the project has not accomplished its' purposes. This research has taken some of Spain's indicators in the period 2012-2016 to determine if they had a positive or negative tendency. The tourist indicator, even if positive, reflected less expenditure from visitors, which is one of the objectives of Spanish tourism. The FDI graph has showed that FDI outflows have boosted, while FDI inflows have even descended in the period 2012-2016. The number of exports of goods and services do show a slight rise in the figures, although it is decreasing since 2014. These two indicators are critical for a NB project as they are two of the objectives that every academic cites (Anholt, 2008; Dinnie, 2011). In the case of Spain, the figures show quite a positive trend, but no research will be able to confirm that ME had influence on them. Carrying out a comprehensive regular survey through questionnaires would result in valuable data and would help Spain to identify channels to influence decision.

The development of NB created the need to quantify a country' s image and reputation. That is why some Indices were created with the purpose to rank the countries according to different parameters. The Spanish government publishes some of the results to evaluate ME and that is why this research has collected data from some Indices and compared the trend in the period 2012-2016. A decrease in Spain's position in the rankings would not be positive for ME, while having better results could be used by the government to defend the influence of ME. After analysing the positions in the rankings, it can be confirmed that the trend is positive, because in five out of six indices Spain gained positions or remained the same. So even if the impact of NB is not measurable, it is valid to say that the image of Spain slightly improved between 2012 and 2016.

This research does not doubt neither the objectivity of the results nor the methodology used and in fact, Spain's position in the rankings is quite similar, usually being in the top 20. Yet, how objective are these results? Quantifying the image of a nation according to some parameters does not seem an easy task. Most of the studies publish the methodology used, as well as the percentage of each parameter and sub-parameter but who determines what the percentage of each aspect should be? Some indices give parameters such as tourism or environment (which helps to increase Spain's position) more weight than the economy.

The Good Country Index, created by Simon Anholt, is believed to be one of the most complete rankings and one with respect to this research in which Spain could see in detail which aspects could give the country a better position. This Index gives a country a position based on areas such as contribution to science, peace order, climate change combat, world order etc. giving this Index a different approach than other indices. Those states with an image of being open-minded, pacifist, green and solidary usually top many of the reputation indices. Countries like Switzerland, Sweden or Iceland frequently obtain high positions. Spain should also play the card of the environment and market nature as one of the most important assets in the country. With 48 biosphere reserves accredited by UNESCO in 2017, the same as USA, Spain tops the rank in that area. However, the image of Spain is much more related to words like "sun" and "beach". Marketing nature could attract many different kind of tourists, from ski-goers to sports looking for a place to train. The same happens with cultural holidays or religious stays.

Another aspect in which Spain had a very good score in 2012 was sport with 7.8/10. However, the score has been descending and it was 7/10 in 2017. Sport can become the best of the promotions for a country, as it happened when Spain won the football World Cup in 2010. The repercussion of events like that one is not measurable. Including top ranked athletes can promote the image of a country in such a way that Spain designated some well-known athletes as ambassadors of ME. Football player from FC Barcelona Andres Iniesta became a ME ambassador, opening the door to rising the promotion of Spain in Asia, where FCB and Real Madrid are followed enthusiastically.

The Digital Country Index of 2015 and 2017, analyses the interest of worldwide searches for all countries in the world, detailing several aspects. The results are very positive in the five areas considered. It confirms the interest of digital users in Spain. However, the government should exploit the data to turn these results into economic advantages by implementing measures and making information in the web more available. Also, the tourism detailed results show that the government and tourism agencies should apply their own BI system to identify tourists looking for something different than sun holidays.

NB and PD are two concepts related to each other. This research also looked at the impact of digital performace and after analysing the number of followers of the Spanish government in Facebook as well as other data such as the social media followers of ME, the views of ME videos in YouTube this research concludes that its' performance is very low. For example, compared to other governments the Spanish has a small number of followers, and the same happens to ME. With hardly 2,400 subscribers in YouTube and the same number in Facebook it does not look like the project ME has digital relevance. One of the promotional videos in YouTube reached 150,000 views, yet the rest have been watched 3,000 times on average. Not very satisfactory results, especially when some videos have millions of viewers.

All in all, the analysis of the different areas (economic, Indices, Image Barometer, Digital Spain) throw different results and it is not possible to conclude that ME had an impact on Spain's image or on consumers. Similarly, this researcher doubts that NB campaigns can be adequately evaluated.

CONCLUSION

This research started by questioning if the expected effects of a nation branding campaign are measurable. Through a set of objectives and methodologies the aim was to conclude if, in the case of Spain, the nation branding project Marca España has had an impact in the country' s image and has influenced some indicators. Even if confirming the hypothesis is not possible due to many limitations, nation branding in Spain and other countries will continue because the quest for a good country image is vital in a globalized world with so many competitors.

A quick search for "nation branding" in Google produces 14 million results and "public diplomacy" achieves 17 million. It cannot be denied that have awakened the interest of different audiences, from academics to governments and marketing agencies or consultants. Countries like France, Poland, Switzerland, Belgium and many others have undertaken NB projects, not all of them being successful. Yet, who determines if a NB project is successful or not? What kind of evaluations take place?

Many Indices have been published since the boom of NB to measure a country's image as a way of analysing the performance of a NB project. Since NB was coined by Anholt in 1997, other institutions and consultancy agencies have now started creating their own rankings and nowadays some of the studies have been available for a decade. As NB does not pay results in the short-term, being able to analyse the trends during a considerable period of time can help to increase the trust in NB.

The digital area has been analysed through the study of Spain's results in the Digital Country Index. Spain has been able to improve its' position and data shows that in non-economic aspects (like tourism) the country is very attractive for the internet users. Despite that, the Spanish government should start using the data from the visitors to enhance other indicators, like exports.

New consumers of Spanish high-quality products would open new markets. Public diplomacy 2.0 also needs a bigger push, with the Ministries, regional governments, tourism agencies, diplomats playing a more active role and adopting strategies to target better audiences or, in other words, a better marketing.

Offering a critical vision of NB, it seems that every country needs to have NB but no one is able to scientifically prove its' success. However, failure is easier to prove. If a country is losing position in the indices and the economic indicators have a negative trend the project will have failed without doubt.

REFERENCES

Anholt, S. (1998). Nation-brands of the twenty-first century. *Journal of Brand Management*, *5*(6), 395–406. doi:10.1057/bm.1998.30

Anholt, S. (2007). *Competitive identity: The new brand management for nations, cities and regions.* Basingstoke, UK: Palgrave Macmillan. doi:10.1057/9780230627727

Anholt, S. (2011). *Beyond the nation brand: The role of image and identity in international relations.* Academic Press.

Anholt, S. (2017). *The Good Country Index*. Retrieved from https://goodcountry.org/index/results?p=overall

Anholt-GfK Nation Brands Index. (2017). Retrieved from http://nation-brands.gfk.com

Bank of Spain. (2017). *Expenditure per visitor in Spain*. Retrieved from https://www.bde.es/bde/en/

Brand Finance. (2017). *Brand finance Nation Brands, the annual report on the world's most valuable nation brands*. Retrieved from http://brandfinance.com/images/upload/bf_nation_brands_2017.pdf

Dinnie, K. (2007). *Nation branding: concepts, issues, practice, Butterworth Heinemann Digital Country Index, 2017*. Bloom Consulting. Retrieved from https://www.digitalcountryindex.com/country-index-results

Doyle, C. (2011). *Brand management*. A Dictionary of Marketing.

Fan, Y. (2006). Branding the nation: What is being branded? *Journal of Vacation Marketing*, *12*(1), 1, 5–14. doi:10.1177/1356766706056633

Gilmore, F. (2002). A country –can it be repositioned? Spain –the successful story of country branding. *Journal of Brand Management*, *9*(4/5), 281–293. doi:10.1057/palgrave.bm.2540078

Harris, B. (2013). Diplomacy 2.0: The future of social media in nation branding. *The Journal of Public Diplomacy*, *4*(1). Retrieved from http://surface.syr.edu/exchange/vol4/iss1/3

Hollande, F. (2014). France Tries to Tempt In More Foreign Investment. *International Business*, p. B1. Retrieved from https://www.nytimes.com/2014/02/18/business/international/hollande-throws-open-frances-doors-to-business.html

Iosifidis, P., & Wheeler, M. (2016). *Public spheres and mediated social networks in the western context and beyond*. Retrieved from https://ebookcentral.proquest.com

Jaffe, E. D., & Nebenzahl, I. D. (2001). *National Image & Competitive Advantage: The Theory and Practice of Country-of-Origin Effect*. Copenhagen Business School Press.

Kotler, P., & Gertner, D. (2002). Country as brand, product, and beyond: A place marketing and brand management perspective. *Journal of Brand Management*, *9*(4/5), 249–261. doi:10.1057/palgrave.bm.2540076

Marca España. (2017). *Activities in the period of 2012-2016*. Retrieved from http://marcaespana.es/actualidad/marca-espa%C3%B1a/marca-espa%C3%B1a-un-proyecto-hecho-realidad

Melissen, J. (2005). *The New Public Diplomacy: Soft Power in International Relations (Studies in Diplomacy and International Relations)*. London: Palgrave Macmillan UK. doi:10.1057/9780230554931

Melissen, J. (2011). Beyond the New Public Diplomacy. The Hague: Netherlands Institute of International Relations 'Clingendael'.

Moilanen, T., & Rainisto, S. (2009). *How to brand nations, cities and destinations: A planning book for place branding*. New York: Palgrave Macmillan. doi:10.1057/9780230584594

Mytko, G. (2012). The United Kingdom and the Rise of Digital Public Diplomacy. *Exchange: The Journal of Public Diplomacy*.

Nandan, S. (2005). An exploration of the brand identity–brand image linkage: A communications perspective. *Journal of Brand Management*, *12*(4), 264–278. doi:10.1057/palgrave.bm.2540222

O'Shaughenssy, N. J. (2000). Testing the nation as a brand: Some neglected issues. *Journal of Macromarketing*, *20*(1), 56–64. doi:10.1177/0276146700201006

Olins, W. (2002). Branding the nation - the historical context. *Journal of Brand Management*, *9*(4F0020004), 241–248. doi:10.1057/palgrave.bm.2540075

Olins, W. (2005). Making a National Brand. In J. Melissen (Ed.), *The New Public Diplomacy. Studies in Diplomacy and International Relations*. London: Palgrave Macmillan. doi:10.1057/9780230554931_9

Pamment, J. (2014). Articulating influence: Toward a research agenda for interpreting the evaluation of soft power, public diplomacy and nation brands. *Public Relations Review*, *40*(1), 50–59. doi:10.1016/j.pubrev.2013.11.019

Papadopoulos, N., Hamzaoui-Essoussi, L., & El Banna, A. (2016). Nation branding for foreign direct investment: An Integrative review and directions for research and strategy. *Journal of Product and Brand Management*, *25*(7), 615–628. doi:10.1108/JPBM-09-2016-1320

Papadopoulos, N., & Heslop, L. (2002). Country equity and country branding: problems and prospects. *Journal of Brand Management, 9*(4-5), 294-314.

Porter, M. (1990). *The competitive advantage of nations*. Free Press. doi:10.1007/978-1-349-11336-1

Rasmussen & Merkelsen. (2012). The new PR of states: How nation branding practices affect the security function of public diplomacy. *Public Relations Review, 38*(5), 810-818.

Reputation Institute. RepTrack. (2017). *Digital country index*. Retrieved from https://www.reputation-institute.com

Rius Ulldemolins, J., & Zamorano, M. (2014). Spain's nation branding project Marca España and its cultural policy: The economic and political instrumentalization of a homogeneous and simplified cultural image. *International Journal of Cultural Policy*, 1–21.

Seargeant, P., & Tagg, C. (2018). Social media and the future of open debate: A user-oriented approach to Facebook's filter bubble conundrum. *Discourse, Context & Media Journal*.

Soft Power 30. (2017). A global ranking of soft power. *Portland Communications*. Retrieved from https://softpower30.com/wp-content/uploads/2017/07/The-Soft-Power-30-Report-2017-Web-1.pdf

The Organisation for Economic Co-operation and Development (OECD). (2017). *Selected indicators for Spain*. Retrieved from https://data.oecd.org/spain.htm

The Real Instituto El Cano. (2017). Retrieved from http://www.realinstitutoelcano.org/wps/portal/rielcano_en

United Nations Trade and Development (UNCTAD). (2017). *Amount of Foreign direct investment*. Retrieved from http://unctad.org/en/pages/PublicationWebflyer.aspx?publicationid=1555

World Bank. (2017). Retrieved from https://data.worldbank.org/country/spain

World Travel and Tourism Council. (2017). *Travel and Tourism Economic impact – Spain*. Retrieved from https://www.wttc.org/-/media/files/reports/economic-impact-research/countries-2017/spain2017.pdf

Zaharna & Uysal. (2016). Going for the jugular in public diplomacy: How adversarial publics using social media are challenging state legitimacy. *Public Relations Review, 42*(1), 109-119.

Chapter 17
Disruptive Technology in the Smartphones Industry:
Identity Theory Perspective

Dominic Appiah
Arden University, UK

Wilson Ozuem
University of Cumbria, UK

Kerry E. Howell
University of Plymouth, UK

ABSTRACT

The impact of identity on brand loyalty has taken precedence as an area of focus in recent marketing research. This has occurred in an era defined by technological revolution, which has created market disruptions, and there are implications for customer-brand relationships. Nonetheless, existing research has failed to acknowledge the impact of socio-psychological attributes and functional utility maximization. Knowledge that illuminates how firms can reposition themselves to sustain brand loyalty when disruptions occur in today's complex and globalized business environment is also required. The chapter presents an empirical investigation into the phenomenon of brand switching behavior among consumers in a specific competitive market, particularly in the smartphone industry. It explores how resistance could be built from an identity theory perspective, as emphasis has historically been placed on the functional utility of products at the expense of social meanings. This chapter provides consideration for market disruptions in the smartphone industry. It confirms that the literature does not capture other non-utilitarian factors such as socio-psychological benefits; hence, there are underlying factors that motivate consumers to continue buying brands they buy.

DOI: 10.4018/978-1-5225-7344-9.ch017

BACKGROUND AND RATIONALE

The plethora of research on brand switching covers customer motivations to review available alternatives due to changes in competitive activities as a means to maximise the functional utility of product attributes and the marketing mix (Guadagni & Little, 1983; Seiders & Tigerts, 1997). Nonetheless, extant literature in this stream of research fails to acknowledge the impact of socio-psychological attributes besides functional utility maximisation. This chapter presents an empirical investigation into the phenomenon of brand switching behaviour of consumers in a competitive market, with implications for how resistance can be built from an identity theory perspective (Tajfel & Turner, 1979; Swait & Erdem 2007; Lam *et al.*, 2013; Hsu & Liou, 2017; Appiah & Ozuem, 2017).

Much emphasis has been placed on the functional utility of products at the expense of social meanings. With the exceptions of product function, insufficient attention has been paid to socio-psychological attributes and personal and social meanings of brands. The assumption is that people are continually involved in social interactions and interpreting their constantly changing world. This chapter deviates from the conventional economic perspective of treating brand switching as functional utility maximisation (Guadagni & Little, 1983; Seiders & Tigerts, 1997), to treating brand switching as a consequence of social mobility between brand identities amongst consumers (Lam *et al.*, 2013). The chapter seeks to investigate consumer identification with brands in the Smartphone industry across the United Kingdom. The Smartphone industry was chosen as the product category for this chapter because it represents a context in which brand switching is most likely to occur due to multiple alternatives and short inter-purchase frequencies (Campo *et al.*, 2000; Goldsmith, 2000). Notably, the market for Smartphones is exceptionally dynamic, considering the degree and rate of change in technology. The extent of product innovation disrupting the Smartphone market is staggering (Azize Sahin *et al.*, 2013; Cecere *et al.*, 2015).

Existing literature on brand loyalty and identity theory is explored to examine the effects of identity on customer loyalty. Despite extensive studies on brand loyalty (Ozuem, Thomas & Lancaster, 2016; Appiah, Ozuem, & Howell, 2016; Giovanisa & Athanasopouloub, 2018), there has been little research on how market disruptions affect customer–brand relationships and how firms can reposition themselves to sustain brand loyalty when disruptions occur in today's complex and globalised business environment (Lam *et al.*, 2010; Appiah & Ozuem, 2017). Although loyalty literature provides rich and useful insight into customer–brand relationships, two limitations warrant further investigation:

1. Sustainability of brand loyalty predictors refers to resisting both time and market disruptions (*ibid.*). However, brand loyalty literature has mainly focused on how brands perform under normal market conditions (Keller & Lehmann, 2006). Yet, as the business environment grows more complex and globalised, market disruptions become more prevalent;
2. Another limitation arises when we consider the perceived value of brands when conceptualised and operationalised as functional utilitarian values. This is prevalent in brand loyalty literature, which does not capture other non-utilitarian factors such as socio-psychological benefits that might motivate customers to continue buying (Holbrook & Corfman, 1985; Richins, 1994; Sheth *et al.*, 1991; Lam *et al*, 2013; Hsu & Liou, 2017).

The chapter considers identified limitations to propose and develop a conceptual customer–brand identity (CBI) model framework to examine the issue of brand switching in a specific market disruption, namely the introduction of a radically new brand due to innovation in the Smartphone industry, and to support the antecedents of consumer identification at a more matured and competitive stage. This sector was selected as the product category because it represents a context in which brand switching is most likely to occur due to multiple alternatives and short inter-purchase frequencies (Campo *et al.*, 2000; Goldsmith, 2000; Appiah, 2014; Jung, Hun, & Oh, 2017).

Little research has been conducted to explore further the phenomenon of brand switching from an identity theory perspective that utilises grounded theory methodology. This could provide useful insights and serve as a basis for future research, as well as benefiting practitioners, especially brand and customer relationship managers who must devise customer relationship strategies to achieve sustainable competitive advantage (Sirgy, 1982; Lam *et al.*, 2010; Appiah, Ozuem, & Howell, 2017)

Overview of the Smartphones Industry

There has been massive escalation in the number of Smartphone users recently as it is widely used as a communication tool that connects users through voice calls, text messages, emails and social networking sites for entertainments (Wang, Xiang, & Fesenmaier, 2014; Tan, Hsiao, Tseng, & Chang, 2017). The Smartphone is a multi-functional device which apart from its telephone functionalities has a wide range of applications such as email, Internet, calendar, notepads and in-built cameras (Norazah, 2013; Wang *et al.*, 2014; Jeong, Kim, Yum, & Hwang, 2016). The Smartphone is a significant shift from the traditional mobile phone and a major difference between the two is that various applications can be added after the purchase of the Smartphone device, whereas the same cannot be said of the mobile phone. Hence Smartphones are considered radically innovative products due their additional features which are similar to computers.

The evolution of the Smartphone has significantly impacted consumer behaviour and choice. Mobile phone technology was initially used only for communication purposes but has recently advanced to include additional features that have created a greater market and altered the purchase behaviour of the consumers (Slawsby *et al.*, 2003; Appiah & Ayertey, 2018; Dwivedi, 2015). In this modern era of technological advancement, users of mobile phones expect other features such as media support, Internet connectivity and special applications (Jones, 2002; Hansen, 2003; Norazah, 2013; Jeong *et al.*, 2016; Tan *et al.*, 2017).

There is the need to emphasise that recently, Smartphones have attracted the attention of all age groups from teenagers to the older generation, and special features in terms of both hardware and software have largely contributed to the impact on customer choice and purchase intentions (Tussyadiah, 2015), enabling manufacturers to innovate new services that have created a competitive environment.

The dramatic growth in the usage of Smartphones has attracted researchers and academics (Park & Yang, 2006; Wang *et al.*, 2014; Kim *et al.*, 2016; Jeong *et al.*, 2016; Tan *et al.*, 2017), and special features in Smartphones have created greater perception and expectations (Aaker, 1997; Dickinson, Ghali, Cherret, Speed, Davis, & Norgate, 2014; Wang *et al.*, 2014; Tan *et al.*, 2017). The significant component of the Smartphone that drives demand and helps manufacturers maintain a strong influence in the Smartphone market is the operating system (OS). There are major software operating systems such as iOS (Apple), Android (Google), Windows (Microsoft), Symbian (Nokia), and RIM (Blackberry). Innovations in hardware and software have triggered enormous growth in the Smartphone market, since the multi-functional operations in these devices generate the trust in technology that consumers expect. Trust in Smartphone devices and their features ultimately adds brand recognition and this is the primary factor that affects intentions to purchase (Nah *et al.*, 2003; Tussyadiah, 2015).

Smartphones Market Structure

The Smartphone market has experienced sturdy growth in recent years mainly due to technological advancement in the industry (Kim *et al.*, 2016; Tan *et al.*, 2017; Jeong *et al.*, 2016). A MarketLine (2017) report confirmed an impressive volume of 1,349.6 million sales of Smartphone units in 2016, which according to the report represents 92.7 per cent of the market's overall volume in the mobile phone industry as compared to ordinary mobile devices with a sales volume of 106.3 million units, which constituted 7.3 per cent of the market total in the same year.

The current global Smartphone market continues to be dominated by a small number of large technology firms such as Apple, Samsung and Huawei. Apple's Smartphone market share continues to grow across the globe, after consumers increasingly turn their backs on competing Android devices. It realised $215,639 million in revenue in 2016. Samsung, in particular, has seen its market share dropping across the world, retaining revenues of $172,840 million in the year 2015, a decrease of 2.7 per cent compared to fiscal 2014. Huawei's consumer business segment develops, manufactures and sells a range of Smartphone devices, with the company recording $59,453 million revenue in 2015 (MarketLine, 2017).

In spite of the significant growth in the industry (Kim, Nam, Oh, & Kan, 2016), the Smartphone market is changing with severe threats facing the industry (Felix, 2015; Tan *et al.*, 2017). Manufacturers with high demand leverage their competitive advantage to enable them to maintain their position in the market and a positive brand image, to explore new revenue streams and most importantly achieve a sustainable product differentiation to drive sales (Gartner, 2016; Jeong *et al.*, 2016).

THEORETICAL AND CONCEPTUAL FOUNDATIONS

Switching Behaviour

Switching occurs when a customer is motivated to review available alternatives in a marketplace due to a change in competitive activity in the marketplace (Seiders & Tigert, 1997; Appiah, Ozuem, & Howell, 2017). Similarly, Hogan and Armstrong (2001) posited that brand switching is about replacing an incumbent resource with a more valuable one to achieve competitive advantage. Sathish, Kumar, Naveen, & Jeevanantham (2011) indicated that brand switching is a consumer behaviour that sees the behaviour of consumers differ based on the satisfaction level of consumers with providers or companies. Hence brand switching can be defined as the process of being loyal to one product or service, and switching to another, due to dissatisfaction or any other problems. They further argue that even if a consumer is loyal to a particular brand, if the brand does not satisfy his/her needs the consumer may switch to a competing brand. Therefore, management needs to constantly evaluate and redirect its resources and capabilities in order to maintain a strong position relative to competitors (Itami & Roehl, 1987).

Product characteristics are likely to affect exploratory tendencies such as brand switching proponents (BSP) and innovation in product contexts with a large number of available alternatives and a short inter-purchase frequency (Hoyer & Ridgway, 1984). These characteristics include product involvement, perceived risk, brand loyalty, perceived brand differentiation/similarity, hedonism (or pleasure) and strength of preference (Hoyer & Ridgway, 1984; Van Trijp, Hoyer, & Inman, 1996). When individuals are highly involved with a product and loyal to a brand, their propensity to switch is likely to be lower (Hoyer & Ridgway, 1984; Sloot, Verhoef, & Franses, 2005).

Individuals who are involved with a product have 'a narrow latitude acceptance' (Sherif & Sherif, 1967); thus, they are unlikely to be persuaded to switch. Similarly, according to Sloot *et al.* (2005), loyal consumers are less likely to switch to another brand. Persuasion to switch may be manifested in the form of sales promotions such as offers and discounts, which have been found to encourage switching across various product contexts (Kahn & Louie, 1990).

Further, high perceived risk indicates that individuals are concerned with losses resulting from their purchases (Mitchell, 1999). High perceived risk leads to avoidance tendencies and behaviours (e.g. commitment to a brand, repeat purchase behaviour) as consumers are 'more often motivated to avoid mistakes than to maximise utility in purchasing' (Mitchell, 1999, p. 163). Moreover, perceived similarity between brands within a product class indicates that individuals are likely to exhibit switching tendencies, such as alternating among familiar brands within a product class (Hoyer & Ridgway, 1984).

Hedonism may also encourage switching within specific categories of products (Hoyer & Ridgway, 1984; Van Trijp *et al.*, 1996). Hedonism is associated with enjoyment or pleasure that an individual derives from specific products (Griffin, Babin, & Modianos, 2000). Consumers are more intrinsically motivated with products that are associated with affective (hedonic) sensations (Hirschman & Holbrook, 1982); thus the repeated consumption of such products is likely to elicit switching tendencies (Van Trijp *et al.*, 1996).

Market disruptions are the major cause of brand switching. Market disruptions are major events occurring in a market that threaten customer–brand relationships (Fournier, 1998; Stern, Thompson, & Arnould, 1998; Appiah, Ozuem, & Howell, 2016). Disruption is defined as a situation where markets cease to function in a regular manner, typically characterised by rapid and large market declines. For instance, disruptions in the financial markets are caused by a glut of sellers willing to trade at any price, combined with the near or total absence of buyers at a particular time. In these circumstances, prices can decline precipitously (Shapiro, 2010).

In the financial market, disruptions can result from both physical threats to the stock exchange or unusual trading. According to a report by Shapiro (2010), concerns over the financial situation in Greece and uncertainty concerning elections in the United Kingdom, among other things, constrained the financial market of that time with implications for trading.

Innovations and Disruptions in Brand Switching

The ultimate causes of brand switching are market disruptions. Market disruptions are key happenings in a market which more often than not impede customer–brand relationships (Fournier, 1998; Christensen, 2013; Jung *et al.*, 2017). Disruption is therefore a state where markets cease to operate in their usual routine, characteristically by steep and huge market declines.

This chapter focuses on disruptions that occur within product markets. As noted by McGrath (2011), the concept of 'market disruption' that occurs in a product market directly harkens to research in two significant areas (technology and innovation), which in recent time have attracted significant attention and development by firms placed in the Smartphone industry. Disruptions displace and alter how we think, behave, transact business, learn and go about our daily undertakings. This is echoed by Christensen (2013), who states that disruptions displace existing markets, industries and technology that develop something unique, more efficient and more worthwhile.

The theory of disruptive innovation introduced by Christensen (2013) provides clarification for the displacement of industry giants by lesser competitors, opening a channel for new entrants (Bower &

Christensen, 1995; Christensen, 2013; Giovanisa & Athanasopouloub, 2018). Disruptive innovation creates a new market, apart from disrupting existing ones. The term is used in business and technology literature to describe innovations that improve products or services in ways that markets do not expect; first by generating a different set of consumers in the new market (Ozuem, Howell, & Lancaster, 2008; Christensen, 2013; Giovanisa & Athanasopouloub, 2018), and later by lowering prices in the existing market.

According to McGrath (2011), the concept's explanatory power is derived from the belief that industry incumbents and new entrants rely on technological trajectories. Industry front-runners tend to lay more emphasis on and invest in sustaining innovations that constantly improve their leading products and increase their overall performance in attributes that are perceived as being important for their existing customer base. Over time, the performance increase achieved through sustaining innovations begins to overshoot the needs of the best customers who pay the most, whereas the new entrants' disruptive products become good enough to meet the needs of the dominant incumbents' customers.

Christensen (2013) identified a number of industries in which the pattern of disruption closely fits with his theory. These include retail, computers, hospitals and automobiles but there has been little research into how these disruptions impact upon and affect the perceived value of brands in disruptive times. There are different factors and determinants which affect consumers in switching from one product to another. The next section looks at two main switching behaviours for the purpose of this chapter.

The function of identity in loyalty literature and its causal effects on brand switching proponents (BSP) in the context of Smartphone purchases is considered in this section. Contextually, the Smartphone was utilised as a relevant product category mainly because it denotes an industry within which brand switching is expected due to the multiple alternatives and short inter-purchase frequency that define the setting for innovative disruptions (Campo *et al.*, 2000; Goldsmith, 2000; Jung *et al.*, 2017).

Switching is likely to happen at any time a customer is motivated to review available alternatives of the same product within the same marketplace due to variations in competitive activity (Seiders & Tigert, 1997; Jung *et al.*, 2017). Similarly, Hogan and Armstrong (2001) insisted that brand switching is the act of replacing an incumbent brand with a favoured one from the same category in order to achieve satisfaction. Sathish *et al.* (2011) indicated that brand switching is a consumer behaviour that depicts differences centred on consumers' satisfaction levels. Hence, brand switching is the process of being loyal to one product or service for a period of time but deciding to swap for another, due to dissatisfaction or a change in preferences. They further suggest that even if a consumer is loyal to a selected brand but subsequently establishes dissatisfaction, he/she may switch to a competing brand. Therefore, brand managers must consistently evaluate and redirect resources and capabilities into a product to ensure a strong position (Itami & Roehl, 1987; Appiah & Ozuem, 2018).

Losing a consumer is a serious setback for a firm as it can have severe implications both financially and for its market position. Reinvesting resources in attracting new consumers can have huge costs in advertising and promotions. Peters (1987) confirms that it may cost a firm five times more to obtain fresh customers than to keep present ones.

Product features may likely affect exploratory behaviours such as BSPs and innovation in product contexts with a wider options and a short inter-purchase frequency (Hoyer & Ridgway, 1984). The characteristics named above may comprise perceived risk, brand loyalty, perceived brand differentiation/similarity, hedonism (desire) and strength of preference (Van Trijp *et al.*, 1996; Hoyer & Ridgway, 1984). Consumers who become extremely engaged with a brand are less likely to switch (Sloot *et al.*, 2005; Hoyer & Ridgway, 1984).

Consumers with high involvement with a product have slim latitude of acceptance (Sherif & Sherif, 1967; Giovanisa & Athanasopouloub, 2018); they remain doubtful to be persuaded to other alternatives, and on the same issue Sloot *et al.* (2005) agree that loyal customers may be highly unlikely to switch to an alternative. Activities to persuade consumers to switch are usually demonstrated as sales promotions, typically as offers and discounts that most often encourage switching across numerous product categories (Kahn & Louie, 1990).

Perceived risk is an indicator that consumers are worried about potential losses as a result of their purchases (Mitchell, 1999; Jung *et al.*, 2017). High perceived risk creates avoidance behaviours such as commitment and repeat buying, as consumers are usually motivated not to commit mistakes instead of to maximise utility in purchase activity (Mitchell, 1999). Perceived similarity amongst brands in the product category also reflects a high tendency of consumers to possibly switch.

Hedonism encourages switching in certain product categories (Van Trijp *et al.*, 1996; Hoyer & Ridgway, 1984). Hedonism is related to the pleasure that a consumer gains from a selected product (Griffin *et al.*, 2000), as consumers are innately inspired by products that provide (hedonic) feelings (Hirschman & Holbrook, 1982; Giovanisa & Athanasopouloub, 2018) and are consequently expected to trigger repeat purchase intentions and elicit switching inclinations (Van Trijp *et al.*, 1996).

Embodied Practices: Identity Theory and Brand Switching

Identity theory is principally a micro-sociological theory that sets out to explain individual role-related behaviour. The theory places major theoretical emphasis on a multifaceted and dynamic self that mediates the relationship between social structure and individual behaviour.

Identity theory (Stryker, 1987; Stryker & Serpe, 1982; Burke, 1980; McCall & Simmons, 1978; Yeh *et al.*, 2016) explains social behaviour in terms of the reciprocal relations between self and society. Turner (2007) posits that identity theory seeks to explain why, where choice is possible, one role-related behavioural choice is consistently made rather than another (Yeh *et al.*, 2016; Da Silveira, 2013; He *et al.*, 2012).

Brand switching occurs when a customer is motivated to review their available alternatives in the marketplace due to a change in competitive activities in the market (Seiders & Tigerts, 1997). Socially, switching occurs when a customer's belief in a brand is externally influenced within the social setting (Appiah & Ozuem, 2018). The customer's belief then impacts his or her attitude towards using a particular brand, which leads to changes in the purchase intention (Li, 2013).

Identity theory (Stryker, 1968) lays emphasis on the social roles of individuals in several social settings. Hence, marketing research based on identity theory concentrates on how consumers perceive a brand as 'me' or 'not me' (Kliene *et al.*, 1995) and how they behave in agreement with the most salient identity (Arnet, German, & Hunt, 2003; Bolton & Americus, 2004; Oyserman, 2009).

Burke and Stets (2009) affirm that one of the early views of identity that grew out of the symbolic interaction framework, with its emphasis on symbols and meanings, is that identities provide 'meaning' for individuals' lives. They stress that a life without meaning has no purpose, no structure, and no framework. Consistent with this view, Thoits (1986) suggests that identities provide a sense of purpose and meaning in life, defining who we are, as well as why we behave in specified ways in society, integrating us with the actions and expectations of others. Identities thus increase self-esteem and reduce depression and anxiety (Thoits, 1986).

Consumer research from an identity point of view has recognised for some time that people consume in many ways that are consistent with their sense of self (Sirgy, 1982). Academics agree that successful brands are designed to satisfy not only the functional needs of consumers but also their symbolic needs (Kapferer, 1997; Yeh *et al.*, 2016; Da Silveira, 2013; He *et al.*, 2012; O'Keeffe, Ozuem, & Lancaster, 2016; Giovanisa & Athanasopouloub, 2018).

Consumers often use the 'self' as a reference category for understanding their surroundings (Rogers, Kuiper, & Kirker, 1977; He *et al.*, 2012), especially when they judge other people. Customers can develop strong relationships with the unique identities of brands for their own unique identity (Fournier, 1998; Yeh *et al.*, 2016; Stokburger-Sauer *et al.*, 2012; Da Silveira, 2013; He *et al.*, 2012; Ozuem, Thomas, & Lancaster, 2016; Giovanisa & Athanasopouloub, 2018). In support of Fournier's view, Tian *et al.* (2001) insist that individuals have different levels of motivation and needs for distinctiveness in their identities (Yeh *et al.*, 2016).

Identity theory is closely linked to the self-concept; both examine the interrelation between the self and social entities (Belk, 1988, Sirgy, 1982; He *et al.*, 2012). These theories have many similar concepts that have been introduced into the marketing literature. Hence this chapter draws from such theory to conceptualise CBI (Yeh *et al.*, 2016; Lam *et al.*, 2013), and in doing so, a brand is perceived as a relationship partner that is significant to the private self. Thus the individual customer uses the brand to define who they are (including the social self), such that these customers consider themselves to be part of a group of customers who identify with a particular brand.

Drawing from the above, it can be said that shoppers re-purchase specific brands that carry meanings for them, as opposed to just offering product utility. Hence, it can be argued that particular brands that possess distinctive identities have the potential to win the attention of consumers and, ultimately, their loyalty. For that reason, brand managers need to create and sustain a clearer and consistent identity, to ensure brands serve stable references for consumers (Aaker, 1996; Kapferer, 2008; Chaplin & Roedder, 2005; O'Keeffe *et al.*, 2016). This supports a widely-held belief that a stable brand identity may assist firms to adapt to market variations (Collins & Porras, 1994). Practically, and consistent with this principle, firms strive to stabilise the identity of their brands over a long term.

Resistance Through Consumer–Brand Identification (CBI)

Although it is only in recent years that the concept of CBI has gained momentum within the marketing literature, the idea that consumers may identify with companies has earlier origins. The notion of company identification has since transferred to the brand domain. In Bhattacharya and Sanker (2003) seminal work, the authors suggest that customers may have their self-definitional needs partially satisfied by companies and thus they identify with the company (O'Keeffe *et al.*, 2016).

Ahearne *et al.* (2005) elaborate upon earlier ideas in suggesting that customers identify with companies and that identification has an impact on both in-role and extra-role behaviour. More specifically, consumers who identify with a company exhibit greater product utilisation, which in itself serves as an act of self-expression. Consumers also exhibit stronger extra-role behaviours such as positive word-of-mouth when they identify with the company. In accordance with Bhattacharya and Sanker (2003), brands may be meaningful social categories for consumers to identify with where identification is defined as a dynamic, selective and volitional act driven by satisfaction of one or more self-definitional needs.

Similarly, social identification theory suggests that the more consumers identify with brands, the more likely they are to engage in brand-supportive behaviours such as brand reputation protection and brand loyalty (Bhattacharya & Sanker, 2003; Ahearne *et al.*, 2005). Bhattacharya and Sanker (2003) suggest that when a consumer identifies with a company they receive more than typically thought-of utilitarian benefits such as product value, consistency and convenience. Additionally, they receive company-based value at a higher level in the form of social identities which help consumers satisfy specific self-definitional needs. Brands as 'concrete actualisations' of firms represent social categories with which consumers are able to identify, since meaning may be transferred between brands and the self (Belk, 1988; Fournier, 1998; McCracken, 1986).

In their conceptualisation of CBI, Lam *et al.* (2010) suggest that the brand serves as a relationship partner to both the 'private self' (i.e. such that individuals use the brand to define who they are) and the 'social self', such that individuals consider themselves part of an in-group identifying with the brand. CBI is a psychological state that goes beyond just the cognitive overlap between the brand and the self; it also includes the affective and evaluative facets of psychological oneness with the brand. It can be argued that CBI is at a higher level of abstraction than the less abstract concept of self–brand congruity (Lam *et al.*, 2012). More specifically, CBI is the customers' psychological state of perceiving, feeling, and valuing their belongingness with a particular brand, which thus illuminates CBI as a formative construct consisting of three dimensions, namely the cognitive, emotional and evaluative dimensions.

Belongingness refers to the psychological oneness resulting from an actual membership of a brand community. In accordance with Stokburger-Sauer *et al.* (2012) who support the use of the three aforementioned components, CBI may be more extensively defined as the extent to which the brand is incorporated into one's self-concept through the development of cognitive connection with the brand, valuing this connection with the brand, and the emotional attachment to the brand (Yeh *et al.*, 2016; Stokburger-Sauer *et al.*, 2012; Da Silveira *et al.*, 2013). As a result of self-categorisation a cognitive connection is formed between the individual and the brand. The evaluative component is the degree to which consumers value their connection with the brand and the value placed on this connection by others. It describes the consumer's feelings towards the brand and towards others' evaluations of the brand. The emotional component is the emotional attachment to the group and to the evaluations associated with the group.

CBI suggests that the consumption domain identification is driven by the need for self-continuity or self-verification, self-distinctiveness and self-enhancement (Bhattacharya & Sanker, 2003; Chernev *et al.*, 2011; Yeh *et al.*, 2016; Stokburger-Sauer *et al.*, 2012; Da Silveira *et al.*, 2013). Thus, identification with a brand is likely to be related to the extent to which a person perceives the brand: 1) to have a personality that is similar to his or her own, 2) to be distinctive, and 3) to be prestigious. Specifically, CBI identifies the extent to which consumers: 1) feel that their interactions with a brand help them connect with important others, 2) perceive a brand in warm, emotional terms rather than cold and rational ones, and 3) have fond memories of brand consumption experiences. Our need for self-continuity goes hand in hand with our need for self-enhancement, which encompasses the maintenance and affirmation of positive self-views that subsequently lead to greater self-esteem (Da Silveira *et al.*, 2013). Such identity-related needs are also met through identification with prestigious entities such as brands (Thomson *et al.*, 2005; Yeh *et al.*, 2016; Stokburger-Sauer *et al.*, 2012).

Hughes and Ahearne (2010) define brand identification as the degree to which a person defines his or her self by the same attributes as he or she believes define a brand. The authors expand on this definition to include the concept of the integration of brand identity with self-identity, describing brand identity as 'the set of brand associations from which a person derives functional, emotional and self-expressive benefits'. Other authors highlight how CBI is distinct from other constructs in the branding literature, describing CBI as distinct from the emotional bond that is central to concepts of emotional brand attachment (Malär *et al.*, 2011) and distinct from brand love (Batra *et al.*, 2012).

The extent to which the brand expresses and enhances one's identity is determined by the level of brand identification and this has a positive effect on word-of-mouth reports (Kim *et al.*, 2001). Identification is often linked to the causes and aims of the organisation; in instances where the organisation is known to stand for a particular cause, consumers are likely to identify with the mission of the company and furthermore to demonstrate loyalty to its products (Bhattacharya *et al.*, 1995; O'Keeffe *et al.*, 2016). Findings support this idea and illustrate how consumers of a brand are more likely to identify with the brand and be loyal to the brand when it is perceived to be a socially responsible brand (Du *et al.*, 2007). Furthermore, social identity with a brand community impacts the consumer's brand identification, where brand identification describes the 'extent to which the consumer sees his or her own self-image as overlapping with the brand's image'. The consumer's social identity with the brand community strengthens through greater involvement in the community that subsequently promotes the assimilation of the brand image into the consumer's identity (He *et al.*, 2012; Yeh *et al.*, 2016; Stokburger-Sauer *et al.*, 2012; Da Silveira *et al.*, 2013).

Bhattacharya and Sanker (2003) suggest that self–brand congruity is an antecedent of CBI. Since self–brand congruity captures only a symbolic driver of CBI, it is a necessary but not a sufficient condition for developing CBI. Functional drivers also play an important role in CBI formation (Lam *et al.*, 2012). Ahearne *et al.* (2005) posit that as an extension of the identification occurring within the context of formal memberships (such as those of academic institution alumni and members of museums), identification does necessarily occur in the consumer-company relationship. In particular, their empirical evidence points towards outcomes of identification in the form of in-role behaviours such as product utilisation and extra-role behaviours such as positive word-of-mouth.

Functional congruity between the brand and the expectations of the consumer leads to clearer identification with a brand. Homburg *et al.* (2009) report a strong influence of customer-company identification on customer loyalty. Park *et al.* (2013) propose that the more the brand is incorporated into the self, the more likely consumers are to expend social, financial and time resources on the brand to maintain the brand relationship. For example, consumers are more likely to support the brand with which they identify by repurchasing associated products and services, thereby exhibiting a long-term preference for the brand and a willingness to pay a price premium. Lam *et al.* (2010) claimed that CBI inhibits consumers from switching brands. CBI produces brand advocacy in the form of positively promoting the brand to social others. CBI is positively related to brand advocacy, that is, positive word-of-mouth and recommendation behaviour (Ahearne *et al.*, 2005). A number of positive outcomes of identification have been empirically identified, such as loyalty (Bhattacharya & Sanker, 2003), commitment (Bergami & Bagozzi, 2000) and brand advocacy (Badrinarayanan & Laverie, 2011).

According to Badrinarayanan and Laverie (2011), when individuals identify with a brand they form a psychological relationship with it, and consequently demonstrate favouritism and work to the benefit of the brand. Consumer–brand identification is positively associated with consumer–brand relationship quality. People who identify with a particular brand experience a positive psychological outcome in the form of enhanced self-esteem, and they engage in positive action strategies towards the brand (Donavan *et al.*, 2006). As mentioned previously, identification is driven by the need for self-continuity, self-distinctiveness and self-enhancement. The necessity for self-continuity suggests that to try to understand themselves and their social worlds, people are motivated to maintain a consistent sense of self (Bhattacharya & Sanker, 2003; He *et al.*, 2012; Yeh *et al.*, 2016; Stokburger-Sauer *et al.*, 2012; Da Silveira *et al.*, 2013; O'Keeffe *et al.*, 2016). Consumers are therefore expected to consume and identify with those brands which match their own sense of which they are, and in so doing, satisfy their need for self-expression.

Brand Loyalty

Imperatively, firms focus much attention and investment to develop stronger brands (He *et al.*, 2012). A much stronger brand in today's competitive market is inevitably influential in establishing a sustainable competitive advantage (Bhattacharya & Lordish, 2000; Aaker, 1995; Mizerski & Soh, 2012). The shift to a relationship marketing paradigm positions brand loyalty at a relational focal point (Oliver, 1999; He *et al.*, 2012; Ozuem *et al*, 2016; Giovanisa & Athanasopouloub, 2018). Brand loyalty has conventionally been regarded as a behavioural construct linking to repeat purchase intentions (Nam *et al.*, 2011).

Brand loyalty has been defined as an extreme commitment to repurchase or re-patronise a particular product or service on a consistent basis, triggering repetitive same-brand purchases, irrespective of other influence and marketing efforts aiming to cause switching (Oliver, 1999). Similarly, Dimitriades (2006) shares this view and specifies that satisfied consumers are less sensitive to changes in prices, less persuaded by competitor attacks, and most importantly loyal to a particular brand or firm for longer than dissatisfied ones.

In line with Dimitriades (2006) and Oliver (1999) above, loyalty to a brand is expressed with a positive attitude, which motivates a consumer to repetitively demand goods or services of a certain brand over a considerable period of time (Dwivedi, 2015; Liu *et al*, 2012). Those with the same viewpoint insist that consumers might have a strong attitude that potentially has an effect on their behaviour towards a specific brand. This phenomenon is denoted as brand insistence (Copeland, 1923; Leckie *et al.*, 2016). Brand insistence is further described in terms of recognition, preference and insistence.

Customer Satisfaction and Loyalty

Customer satisfaction refers to the psychological state ensuing when the emotion surrounding disconfirmed expectations is combined with the consumer's prior feelings about the brand experience (Oliver, 1981). Consistent with this view, Shankar *et al.* (2003) define satisfaction as the perception of a service or product providing pleasurable fulfilment.

Elaborating on the positive relationship between customer satisfaction and loyalty discussed by Shankar *et al.* (2003), Taylor and Baker (1994) also confirm that customer satisfaction is widely recognised as a key influence in the formation of consumers' future purchase intentions. Similarly, satisfied customers are more likely to tell others of their favourable experience and thus engage in positive word-of-mouth advertising (Badrinarayanan & Laverie, 2011; He *et al.*, 2012; Yeh *et al.*, 2016).

Rodriguez del Bosque and San Martin (2008) are of the view that consumer satisfaction is not only cognitive but also emotional. Consumers show satisfaction with a brand when brand identification augments their positive image within a social group, or when a sense of belonging to that social group is achieved (Kim *et al.*, 2001; He *et al.*, 2012). Brand identification encourages symbolic interaction, emotional bonding and brand loyalty. As indicated by Peter and Olson (1993), 94 per cent of Harley-Davidson buyers are emotionally attached to the brand. They not only enjoy the quality of the motorbikes but also enjoy the experience of being part of the brand community, and so they remain loyal. From this notion the current chapter proposes that stronger consumer identification with a brand translates into consumer satisfaction.

Satisfaction is theoretically referred to as an affective-oriented assessment of the services provided and as such is the emotive aspect of loyalty (Cronin *et al.*, 2000; Oliver, 1999). When deciding whether to switch to a competing retailer, customers are often guided by their feelings of satisfaction/dissatisfaction with the retailer (He *et al.*, 2012; Yeh *et al.*, 2016).

Solomon (2002) suggests that lifestyles comprise shared values, tastes and consumption patterns. Hence he perceives brands and brand settings as a communication of lifestyles. The more a brand image fits a consumer's lifestyle, the higher the level of satisfaction with the brand experience. Therefore, marketers ensure they are able to develop consumer satisfaction with brands by creating a brand which equals the identified lifestyle (Badrinarayanan & Laverie, 2011; He *et al.*, 2012; Solomon, 2002; Yeh *et al.*, 2016).

There is positive relationship between consumer satisfaction and brand loyalty (e.g. Back & Parks, 2003) and this is supported by Rust and Zahorik (1993), when they demonstrated a connection between consumer satisfaction and brand loyalty. McDougall and Levesque (1994) show that customer satisfaction impacts positively on brand loyalty. Hence, consumer satisfaction with brand experience has a positive effect on brand loyalty (Badrinarayanan & Laverie, 2011).

CONCLUSION AND MANAGERIAL IMPLICATIONS

In the marketing context, the narrative analysis of marketing relationships by Stern, Thomson & Arnold (1998) implies that customers may switch to a brand they used to dislike by revising their view of the brand's identity and reference group. Research into cultural assimilation also reports that immigrants swap their cultural identities in consumption as they assimilate into the mainstream culture (Oswald, 1999). Similarly, Chaplin and Roedder (2005) suggest that as children mature into adolescents, their self-concept becomes more sophisticated and so do their connections with brands. When the boundary between the in-group and the out-group is impermeable and changing group membership is not realistic, social mobility is not a viable strategy to cope with identity threats. For example, people rarely change their political affiliation, as social identity theory suggests that under such circumstances people will engage in social creativity (Tajfel & Turner, 1979). Tajfel and Turner (1979, p. 43) posit that social creativity can take multiple forms, such as (1) comparing the in-group with the out-group based on some new dimensions, (2) changing the values assigned to the attributes of the group such that previously negative comparisons are now cast in a positive light, and (3) avoiding using the high-status out-group as a comparative frame of reference. In other words, social creativity is a form of identity-based comparison that is based on in-group biases, and defined as a strong belief in the superiority of the group with which a person identifies. It is a form of prejudice against the non-identified group. Brewer (1979) posits that such in-group biases are both cognitive and motivational because these biases motivate in-group members (e.g. brand identifiers) to attend only to elements that the in-group will evaluate more positively than the out-group.

Managerial implications based on findings indicate that innovative brands, such as Smartphones, are susceptible to disruption in their initial stages. This drives huge interest that may interrupt consumer–brand relationships, yet with time this interest may become fragile (Fournier, 1998). Brand managers must allocate investment to build stronger customer–brand identification/relationship at the maturity stage of the product life cycle to resist switching during disruptions. First, in order to extend the maturity stage of a brand, brand managers should invest in activities that enhance consumers' perceived quality and self–brand congruity. Smartphone manufacturers must commit investment to symbolic drivers such as self–brand congruity at maturity stages of the brand life cycle rather than instrumental drivers such as quality (functional utility). This strategy is effective as brand loyalty and resilience to market disruptions are sustained.

REFERENCES

Aaker, D. A. (1995). *Building Strong Brands*. New York: The Free Press.

Aaker, D. A. (1996). *Building Strong Brands*. New York: The Free Press.

Aaker, J. (1997). Dimensions of Brand Personality. *JMR, Journal of Marketing Research*, *34*(3), 347–356. doi:10.2307/3151897

Ahearne, M., Bhattacharya, C. B., & Gruen, T. (2005). Antecedents and Consequences of Customer–Company identification: Expanding the Role of Relationship Marketing. *The Journal of Applied Psychology*, *90*(3), 574–585. doi:10.1037/0021-9010.90.3.574 PMID:15910151

Appiah, D. (2014). *Building Brand Loyalty: Identity Theory Perspective. Seventh International Scientific Conference*. Institute of Economic Research.

Appiah, D., & Ayertey, S. (2018). Towards Understanding the Moderating Roles Of Smartphones On Brand Switching. In *Annual International Conference*. Global Business and Technology Association.

Appiah, D., & Ozuem, W. (2017). Issues and the Importance of Branding, Brand Personality and Symbolic Meaning of Brands to the Consumer. In Global Information Diffusion and Management in Contemporary Society. IGI Global.

Appiah, D., & Ozuem, W. (2018). The Dynamics of Resistance to Brand Switching in the Smartphones Industry. In *Managing Diversity, Innovation, and Infrastructure in Digital Business*. Hershey, PA: IGI Global.

Appiah, D., Ozuem, W., & Howell, E. K. (2016). Towards a Sustainable Brand Loyalty*: Attitudinal Loyalty Perspective. Eighteenth Annual International Conference*. Global Business and Technology Association.

Appiah, D., Ozuem, W., & Howell, K. E. (2017). Brand Switching in the Smartphone Industry: A Preliminary Study. *Global Business and Technology Association Conference*, Vienna, Austria.

Arnett, D. B., German, S. D., & Hunt, S. D. (2003). The Identity salience Model of Relationship Marketing success: The case of Non-profit Marketing. *Journal of Marketing*, *67*(4), 89–105. doi:10.1509/jmkg.67.2.89.18614

Azize, S., Hakan, K., & Cemal, Z. (2013). Creating Commitment, Trust and Satisfaction for a Brand: What is the Role of Switching Costs in Mobile Phone Market? *Procedia: Social and Behavioral Sciences*, *99*, 496–502. doi:10.1016/j.sbspro.2013.10.518

Back, K. J., & Parks, S. C. (2003). A brand loyalty model involving cognitive, affective, and conative brand loyalty and customer satisfaction. *Journal of Hospitality & Tourism Research (Washington, D.C.)*, *27*(4), 419–435. doi:10.1177/10963480030274003

Badrinarayanan, V., & Laverie, D. A. (2011). Brand advocacy and Sales effort by retail Salespeople: Antecedents and influence of identification with Manufacturers' Brands. *Journal of Personal Selling & Sales Management*, *31*(2), 123–140. doi:10.2753/PSS0885-3134310202

Badrinarayanan, V., & Laverie, D. A. (2011). Brand advocacy and Sales effort by retail Salespeople: Antecedents and influence of identification with Manufacturers' Brands. *Journal of Personal Selling & Sales Management*, *31*(2), 123–140. doi:10.2753/PSS0885-3134310202

Batra, R., Lehmann, D. R., & Singh, D. (1993). The Brand Personality Component of Brand Goodwill: Some Antecedents and Consequences. In Brand Equity and Advertising. Hillsdale, IL: Lawrence Erlbaum Associates.

Belk, R. W. (1988). Possessions and the Extended Self. *The Journal of Consumer Research*, *15*(9), 139–168. doi:10.1086/209154

Bhattacharya, C. B., & Lordish, L. (2000). *Towards a System for Monitoring Brand Health from Store Scanner Data*. MSI working Paper, Report No. 00-111.

Bhattacharya, C. B., & Sanker, S. (2003). Consumer-Company Identification: A Framework for Understanding Consumers' Relationship with Companies. *Journal of Marketing*, *67*(4), 76–88. doi:10.1509/jmkg.67.2.76.18609

Bolton, L. E., & Americus, R. I. I. (2004). Sticky Priors: The Perseverance of Identity Effects on Judgements. *JMR, Journal of Marketing Research*, *41*(11), 397–410. doi:10.1509/jmkr.41.4.397.47019

Bower, J. L., & Christensen, C. M. (1995). Disruptive Technologies: Catching the Wave. *Havard Business Review*, (2-3), 43-53.

Brewer, M. B. (1979). In-group Bias in the Minimal Intergroup Situation: A Cognitive–Motivational Analysis. *Psychological Bulletin*, *86*(2), 307–324. doi:10.1037/0033-2909.86.2.307

Burke, P., & Stets, J. E. (2009). *Identity Theory*. Oxford, UK: Oxford University Press. doi:10.1093/acprof:oso/9780195388275.001.0001

Burke, P. J. (1980). The Self: Measurement Implications from a Symbolic Interactionist Perspective. *Social Psychology Quarterly*, *43*, 18–29. doi:10.2307/3033745

Campo, K., Gijsbrechts, E., & Nisol, P. (2000). Towards understanding consumer Response to Stock outs. *Journal of Retailing*, *76*(2), 219–242. doi:10.1016/S0022-4359(00)00026-9

Cecere, G., Corrocher, N., & Battaglia, R. D. (2015). Innovation and Competition in the Smartphone Industry: Is there a Dominant Design? *Journal of Telecommunications Policy*, (39) 162-175.

Chaplin, L. N., & Roedder, D. J. (2005). The Development of Self-Brand Connections in Children and Adolescents. *The Journal of Consumer Research*, *32*(1), 119–129. doi:10.1086/426622

Christensen, C. M. (2013). *The Innovators Dilema: When New Technologies Cause Great Firms to Fail.* Boston: Harvard Business School Press.

Copeland, M. T. (1923). Relation of Consumer's Buying Habits to Marketing Methods. *Harvard Business Review*, *1*, 282–289.

Cronin, J. J. Jr, Brady, M. K., & Hult, G. T. M. (2000). Assessing the Effects of Quality, Value, and Customer Satisfaction on Consumer Behavioral Intentions in Service Environments. *Journal of Retailing*, *76*(2), 193–218. doi:10.1016/S0022-4359(00)00028-2

Da Silveira, C., Lages, C., & Simões, C. (2013). Reconceptualizing brand identity in a dynamic environment. *Journal of Business Research*, *66*(1), 28–36. doi:10.1016/j.jbusres.2011.07.020

Dickinson, J. E., Ghali, K., Cherrett, T., Speed, C., Davies, N., & Norgate, S. (2014). Tourism and the smartphone app: Capabilities, emerging practice and scope in the travel domain. *Current Issues in Tourism*, *17*(1), 84–101. doi:10.1080/13683500.2012.718323

Dimitriades, Z. S. (2006). Customer Satisfaction, Loyalty and commitment in service organisations: Some evidence from Greece. *Management Research News*, *29*(12), 782–800. doi:10.1108/01409170610717817

Dimitriadis, S., & Papista, E. (2011). Linking Consumer-Brand Identification to Relationship Quality. An Integrated Framework. *Journal of Consumer Behaviour*, *10*(3), 271–289. doi:10.1362/147539211X602513

Donavan, D. T., Janda, S., & Suh, J. (2006). Environmental Influences in Corporate Brand Identification and Outcomes. *Journal of Brand Management*, *14*(1/2), 125–136. doi:10.1057/palgrave.bm.2550057

Du, S., Bhattacharya, C. B., & Sen, S. (2007). Reaping Relational Rewards from Corporate Social Responsibility: The Role of Competitive Positioning. *International Journal of Research in Marketing*, *24*(3), 224–241. doi:10.1016/j.ijresmar.2007.01.001

Dwivedi, A. (2015). A higher-order model of consumer brand engagement and its impact on loyalty intentions. *Journal of Retailing and Consumer Services*, *24*, 100–109. doi:10.1016/j.jretconser.2015.02.007

Felix, R. (2015). The state of the Global Smartphone Market. *Statista Infographics.* Retrieved from: https://www.statista.com/charts/2512/smartphone-market-share

Fournier, S. (1998). Consumers and Their Brands: Developing Relationship Theory in Consumer Research. *The Journal of Consumer Research*, *24*(3), 343–373. doi:10.1086/209515

Giovanisa, A. N., & Athanasopouloub, P. (2018). Consumer-Brand Relationships and Brand Loyalty in Technology-Mediated Services. *Journal of Retailing and Consumer Services*, *40*(1), 287–294. doi:10.1016/j.jretconser.2017.03.003

Goldsmith, R. E. (2000). Characteristics of the Heavy User of Fashionable Clothing. *Journal of Marketing Theory and Practice*, *8*(4), 21–28. doi:10.1080/10696679.2000.11501877

Griffin, M., Babin, B. J., & Modianos, D. (2000). Shopping Values of Russian Consumers: The Impact of Habituation in a Developing Economy. *Journal of Retailing*, *76*(1), 33–52. doi:10.1016/S0022-4359(99)00025-1

Guadagni, P. M., & Little, J. D. C. (1983). A Logit Model of Brand Choice Calibrated on Scanner Data: A Logit Model of Brand Choice Calibrated on Scanner Data. *Journal of Marine Science*, *2*(3), 203–238. doi:10.1287/mksc.2.3.203

Hansen, L. (2003). Service Layer Essential for Future Success. *Ericsson Mobility World*. Available at: http://www.ericsson.com

He, H., Yan, L., & Lloyd, H. (2012). Social identity perspective on brand Loyalty. *Journal of Business Research*, *65*(5), 648–657. doi:10.1016/j.jbusres.2011.03.007

Hirschman, E. C., & Holbrook, M. B. (1982). Hedonic consumption: Emerging Concepts, Methods and Propositions. *Journal of Marketing*, *46*(3), 92–101. doi:10.1177/002224298204600314

Hogan, E. J., & Armstrong, G. (2001). Toward a Resource Based Theory of Business Exchange Relationships: The Role of Relational Asset Value. *Journal of Business-To-Business Marketing*, *8*(4), 3–28. doi:10.1300/J033v08n04_02

Holbrook, M. B., & Corfman, K. P. (1985). Quality and Value in the Consumption Experience: Phaedrus Rides Again. In C. V. S. How, J. J. Merchandise, & J. C. Olson (Eds.), *Perceived Quality*. Lanham, MD: Lexington Books.

Homburg, C., Wieseke, J., & Hoyer, W. D. (2009). Social Identity and the Social Profit chain. *Journal of Marketing*, *73*(2), 38–54. doi:10.1509/jmkg.73.2.38

Hoyer, W. D., & Ridgway, N. M. (1984). Variety seeking as an explanation for exploratory behaviour: A theoretical model. In T. C. Kinnear (Ed.), *Advances in Consumer Research* (Vol. 11, pp. 114–119). Provo, UT: Association for Consumer Research.

Hsu, L. C., & Liou, D. K. (2017). Maintaining Customer-Brand Relationships in the Mobile Industry: The Mediation Effects of Brand Relationship Benefits and Quality. *International Journal of Mobile Communications*, *15*(4), 388. doi:10.1504/IJMC.2017.084861

Hughes, D. E., & Ahearne, M. (2010). Energizing the Reseller's Sales Force: The Power of Brand Identification. *Journal of Marketing*, *74*(4), 81–96. doi:10.1509/jmkg.74.4.81

Itami, H., & Roehl, W. T. (1987). Mobilizing Invisible Assets. Harvard University Press.

Jeong, S. H., Kim, H. J., Yum, J. Y., & Hwang, Y. R. (2016). What Type of Content are Smartphone Users Addicted to? SNS vs Games. *Journal of Computers in Human Behavior*, *54*, 10–17. doi:10.1016/j.chb.2015.07.035

Jones, S. (2002). *3G Launch Strategies, Early Adopters, Why & How to make them yours*. Tarifica report.

Jung, J., Hun, H., & Oh, M. (2017). Travellers Switching Behaviour in the Airline Industry from the Perspective of the Push-Pull-Mooring Framework. *Journal of Torurism Management.*, *59*, 139–153. doi:10.1016/j.tourman.2016.07.018

Kahn, B. E., & Louie, T. A. (1990). Effects of Retraction of Price Promotions on Brand Choice Behaviour for Variety-Seeking and Last-purchase Loyal Consumers. *JMR, Journal of Marketing Research*, *27*(3), 279–289. doi:10.2307/3172586

Kapferer, J. N. (1997). *Strategic Brand Management: Creating and Sustaining Brand Equity Long Term*. London: Kogan Page Ltd.

Kapferer, J. N. (2008). *The New Strategic Brand Management, Creating and Sustaining Brand Equity Long Term*. London: Kogan Page.

Keller, K. L., & Lehmann, D. R. (2006). Brands and Branding: Research Findings and Future Priorities. *Journal of Marine Science*, *25*(6), 740–759. doi:10.1287/mksc.1050.0153

Kim, C. K., Han, D. C., & Park, S. B. (2001). The Effect of Brand Personality and Brand Identification on Brand Loyalty: Applying the Theory of Social Identification. *The Japanese Psychological Research*, *43*(4), 195–206. doi:10.1111/1468-5884.00177

Kim, D., Nam, J. K., Oh, J. S., & Kang, M. C. (2016). A Latent Profile Analysis of the Interplay between PC and Smartphone in Problematic Internet Use. *Journal of Computers in Human Behavior*, *56*, 360–368. doi:10.1016/j.chb.2015.11.009

Kleine, S. S., Kleine, R. E. III, & Allen, C. T. (1995). How is a Possession 'Me' or 'Not Me'? Characterizing Types and Antecedents of Material Possession Attachment. *The Journal of Consumer Research*, *22*(12), 327–343. doi:10.1086/209454

Lam, S. K., Ahearn, M., Hu, Y., & Schillewaert, N. (2010). Resistance to Brand Switching When a Radically New Brand Is Introduced: A Social Identity Theory Perspective. *Journal of Marketing*, *74*(6), 128–146. doi:10.1509/jmkg.74.6.128

Lam, S. K., Ahearne, M., Mullins, R., Hayati, B., & Schillewaert, N. (2013). Exploring the Dynamics of Antecedents to Consumer–Brand Identification with a New Brand. *Journal of the Academy of Marketing Science*, *41*(2), 243–252. doi:10.100711747-012-0301-x

Leckie, C., Munyaradzi, W. N., & Johnson, L. W. (2016). Antecedents of Consumer Brand Engagement and Brand Loyalty. *Journal of Marketing Management*, *32*(5-6), 5–6, 558–578. doi:10.1080/0267257X.2015.1131735

Liu, S., Moizer, J., Megicks, P., Kasturiratne, D., & Jayawickrama, U. (2014). A Knowledge Chain Management Framework to Support Integrated Decisions in Global Supply Chains. *Journal of Production Planning and Control*, *25*(8), 639–649. doi:10.1080/09537287.2013.798084

Malär, L., Krohmer, H., Hoyer, W. D., & Nyffenegger, B. (2011). Emotional Brand Attachment and Brand Personality: The Relative Importance of the Actual and the Ideal Self. *Journal of Marketing*, *75*(4), 35–52. doi:10.1509/jmkg.75.4.35

McCall, G. J., & Simmons, J. L. (1978). *Identities and Interactions* (Revised edition). New York: Free Press.

McCracken, G. (1986). Culture and Consumption: A Theoretical Account of the Structure: A Theoretical Account of the Structure and Movement of the Cultural Meaning of Consumer Goods. *The Journal of Consumer Research*, *13*(1), 71–84. doi:10.1086/209048

McDougall, G., & Levesque, T. (1994). A Revised View of Service Quality Dimensions: An Empirical Investigation. *Journal of Professional Services Marketing*, *11*(1), 189–210. doi:10.1080/15332969.1994.9985149

McGrath, R. G. (2011, January). When your Business Model is in Trouble. *Harvard Business Review*, 96–98.

Mintel Group. (2017). *Smartphone Purchasing Process*. London.

Mitchell, V.-W. (1999). Consumer Perceived Risk: Conceptualisations and Models. *European Journal of Marketing*, *33*(1/2), 163–195. doi:10.1108/03090569910249229

Nah, F. F.-H., Zhao, F., & Zhu, W. (2003). Factors influencing Users' Adoption of Mobile Computing. In J. Mariga (Ed.), *Managing E-commerce and Mobile Computing Technologies Book*. Hershey, PA: Idea Group Inc.

Norazah, M. S. (2013). Students' dependence on smart phones: The influence of social needs, social influences and convenience. *Campus-Wide Information Systems*, *30*(2), 124–134. doi:10.1108/10650741311306309

O'Keeffe, A., Ozuem, W., & Lancaster, G. (2016). Leadership Marketing: An Exploratory Study. *Journal of Strategic Marketing*, *24*(5), 418–443. doi:10.1080/0965254X.2014.1001867

Oliver, R. L. (1981). Measurement and Evaluation of Satisfaction Processes in Retail Settings. *Journal of Retailing*, *57*(3), 25–48.

Oliver, R. L. (1999). Whence Consumer Loyalty? *Journal of Marketing*, *63*(10), 33–44. doi:10.2307/1252099

Oswald, L. R. (1999). Culture Swapping: Consumption and the Ethnogenesis of Middle-Class Haitan Immigrants. *The Journal of Consumer Research*, *25*(3), 303–318. doi:10.1086/209541

Oyserman, D. (2009). Identity-Based Motivation: Implications for Action-Readiness, procedural Readiness and Consumer Behaviour. *Journal of Consumer Psychology*, *19*(3), 250–260. doi:10.1016/j.jcps.2009.05.008

Ozuem, W., Howell, K. E., & Lancaster, G. (2008). Communicating in the New Interactive Marketplace. *European Journal of Marketing*, *42*(9/10), 1059–1083. doi:10.1108/03090560810891145

Ozuem, W., Thomas, T., & Lancaster, G. (2016). The Influence of Customer Loyalty on Small Island Economies: An empirical and Exploratory Study. *Journal of Strategic Marketing*, *24*(6), 447–469. doi:10.1080/0965254X.2015.1011205

Park, C. W., Eisingerich, A. B., & Park, J. W. (2013). Attachment–Aversion (AA) Model of Customer–Brand Relationships. *Journal of Consumer Psychology*, *23*(2), 229–248. doi:10.1016/j.jcps.2013.01.002

Park, J. K., & Yang, S. (2006). The Moderating Role of Consumer Trust and Experiences: Value Driven Usage of Mobile Technology. *International Journal of Mobile Marketing*, *1*(2), 24–32.

Peter, J., & Olson, C. (1993). *Consumer Behaviour and Marketing Strategy* (European Edition). London: McGraw Hill.

Peters, T. (1987). *Thriving on Chaos*. New York: Alfred A. Knopf.

Richins, M. L. (1994). Valuing Things: The Public and Private Meanings of Possessions. *The Journal of Consumer Research, 21*(10), 504–521. doi:10.1086/209414

Rodriguez del Bosque, I., & San Martin, H. (2008). Tourist Satisfaction a Cognitive Affective Model. *Annals of Tourism Research, 35*(2), 551–573. doi:10.1016/j.annals.2008.02.006

Rogers, T. B., Kuiper, N. A., & Kirker, W. S. (1977). Self-Reference and Encoding of Personal Information. *Journal of Personality and Social Psychology, 35*(9), 677–688. doi:10.1037/0022-3514.35.9.677 PMID:909043

Rust, R. T., & Zahorik, A. J. (1993). Customer Satisfaction, Customer Retention, and Market Share. *Journal of Retailing, 69*(2), 193–215. doi:10.1016/0022-4359(93)90003-2

Sathish, M., Kumar, K. S., Naveen, K. J., & Jeevanantham, V. (2011). A Study on Consumer Switching Behaviour in Cellular Service Provider: A Study with reference to Chennai. *Far East Journal of Psychology and Business, 2*(2), 72.

Seiders, K., & Tigert, D. J. (1997). Impact of Market Entry and Competitive Structure on Store Switching/Store Loyalty. *International Review of Retail, Distribution and Consumer Research, 7*(3), 227–247. doi:10.1080/095939697343003

Shankar, V., Smith, A. K., & Rangaswamy, A. (2003). 'Customer Satisfaction and Loyalty in Online and Offline Environments'. *International Journal of Research in Marketing, 20*(2), 153–175. doi:10.1016/S0167-8116(03)00016-8

Shapiro, L. M. (2010). *Severe Market Dissruption on 6th May, 2010: Congressional Testimony*. Collingdale, PA: Diane Publishing Co.

Shapiro, L. M. (2010). *Severe Market Dissruption on 6th May, 2010: Congressional Testimony*. Collingdale, PA: Diane Publishing Co.

Sherif, C. W., & Sherif, M. (1967). *Attitude, Ego-involvement, and Change*. Westport, CT: Green Wood Press.

Sheth, J. N., Newman, B. I., & Gross, B. L. (1991). Why We Buy What We Buy: A Theory of Consumption Values. *Journal of Business Research, 22*(2), 159–170. doi:10.1016/0148-2963(91)90050-8

Sirgy, M. J. (1982). Self-Concept in Consumer Behaviour: A Critical Review. *The Journal of Consumer Research, 9*(3), 287–300. doi:10.1086/208924

Sirgy, M. J., Grewal, D., & Mangleburg, T. (2000). Retail Environment, Self-Congruity, and Retail Patronage: An Integrative Model and a Research Agenda. *Journal of Business Research, 49*(2), 127–138. doi:10.1016/S0148-2963(99)00009-0

Slawsby, A., Leibovitch, A. M., & Giusto, R. (2003). *Worldwide Mobile Phone Forecast and Analysis, 2003-2007*. IDC Report, No. 29586.

Sloot, L. M., Verhoef, P. C., & Franses, P. H. (2005). The Impact of Brand Equity and the Hedonic Level of Products on Consumer Stock-Out Reactions. *Journal of Retailing*, *81*(1), 15–34. doi:10.1016/j.jretai.2005.01.001

Stern, B. B., Thompson, J. C., & Arnould, E. J. (1998). Narrative Analysis of a Marketing Relationship: The Consumer's Perspective. *Journal of Psychology and Marketing*, *15*(3), 195–214. doi:10.1002/(SICI)1520-6793(199805)15:3<195::AID-MAR1>3.0.CO;2-5

Stokburger-Sauer, N., Ratneshwar, S., & Sen, S. (2012). Drivers of Consumer-Brand Identification. *International Journal of Research in Marketing*, *29*(4), 406–418. doi:10.1016/j.ijresmar.2012.06.001

Stryker, S. (1968). Identity Salience and Role Performance: The Relevance of Symbolic Interaction Theory for Family Research. *Journal of Marriage and the Family*, *30*(40), 558–564. doi:10.2307/349494

Stryker, S. (1987). *The Interplay of Affect and Identity: Exploring the Relationships of Social Structure, Social Interaction, Self, and Emotion*. Presented at the *annual meetings of the American Sociological Association*, Chicago, IL.

Stryker, S., & Serpe, R. T. (1982). Commitment, Identity Salience, and Role Behavior: A Theory and Research Example. In W. Ickes & E. S. Knowles (Eds.), *Personality, Roles, and Social Behavior* (pp. 199–218). New York: Springer-Verlag. doi:10.1007/978-1-4613-9469-3_7

Swait, J., & Erdem, T. (2007). Brand Effects on Choice and Choice Set Formation under Uncertainty. *Journal of Marine Science*, *26*(5), 679–697. doi:10.1287/mksc.1060.0260

Tajfel, H., & Turner, J. C. (1979). The Social Identity Theory of Inter-Group Behaviour. In *Psychology of Intergroup Relations*. Chicago: Nelson-Hall.

Tan, W., Hsiao, Y., Tseng, S., & Chang, C. (2017). Smartphone Application Personality and its Relationship to Personalities of Smartphone Users and Social Capital Accrued through use of Smartphone Social Applications. *Journal of Telematics and Informatics*, *35*(1), 255–26. doi:10.1016/j.tele.2017.11.007

Taylor, S. A., & Baker, T. L. (1994). An Assessment of the Relationship between Service Quality and Customer Satisfaction in the Formation of Consumers' Purchase Intentions. *Journal of Retailing*, *70*(2), 163–178. doi:10.1016/0022-4359(94)90013-2

Thoits, P. A. (1986). Multiple Identities: Examining Gender and Marital Status differences in Distress. *American Sociological Review*, *51*(2), 259–272. doi:10.2307/2095520

Tian, K. T., Bearden, W. O., & Hunter G. L. (2001). Consumers Need for Uniqueness: Scale Development and Validation. *Journal of Consumer Research, 28*(1), 50-56.

Turner, H. J. (2007). *Handbook of Sociological Theory*. New York: Springer.

Tussyadiah, I. P. (2015). The Influence of Innovativeness on On-Site Smartphone Use among American. *Journal of Travel & Tourism Marketing*. doi:10.1080/10548408.2015.1068263

Van Trijp, H. C. M., Hoyer, W. D., & Inman, J. J. (1996). Why Switch? Product Category-Level Explanations for True Variety-Seeking Behaviour. *JMR, Journal of Marketing Research*, *33*(3), 281–292. doi:10.2307/3152125

Wang, D., Xiang, Z., & Fesenmaier, D. R. (2014). Adapting to the Mobile World: A Model of Smartphone Use. *Journal of Tourism Research*, *48*, 11–26.

Yeh, C., Wang, Y., & Yieh, K. (2016). Predicting smartphone brand loyalty: Consumer value and consumer-brand identification perspectives. *International Journal of Information Management, 36*(3), 245–257. .2015.11.013 doi:10.1016/j.ijinfomgt

Compilation of References

Aaker, D. (1991). *Managing Brand Equity: Capitalizing on the Value of a Brand Name*. New York: Free Press.

Aaker, D. (1996). Measuring Brand Equity Across Products and Markets. *California Management Review*, *38*(3), 102–120. doi:10.2307/41165845

Aaker, D. (2004). Leveraging the Corporate Brand. *California Management Review*, *46*(3), 6–18. doi:10.1177/000812560404600301

Aaker, D. A. (1995). *Building Strong Brands*. New York: The Free Press.

Aaker, D., & Joachimsthaler, E. (2000). *Brand leadership*. New York: Free Press.

Aaker, D., & Keller, K. (1990). Consumer Evaluations of Brand Extensions. *Journal of Marketing*, *54*(1), 27–41. doi:10.2307/1252171

Aaker, J. (1997). Dimensions of Brand Personality. *JMR, Journal of Marketing Research*, *34*(3), 347. doi:10.2307/3151897

Abayi, M., & Khoshtinat, B. (2016). Study of the Impact of Advertising on Online Shopping Tendency for Airline Tickets by Considering Motivational Factors and Emotional Factors. *Procedia Economics and Finance*, *36*, 532–539. doi:10.1016/S2212-5671(16)30065-X

Abdulwahab, M., & Al-Damen, D. (2015). The Impact of Entrepreneurs' Characteristics on Small Business Success at Medical Instruments Supplies Organizations in Jordan. *International Journal of Business and Social Science*, *6*(8), 164–175.

Abed, S., Dwivedi, Y. K., & Williams, M. D. (2015a). Social media as a bridge to e-commerce adoption in SMEs: A systematic literature review. *The Marketing Review*, *15*(1), 39–57. doi:10.1362/146934715X14267608178686

Abrahams, A. S., Jiao, J., Wang, G. A., & Fan, W. (2012). Vehicle defect discovery from social media. *Decision Support Systems*, *54*(1), 87–97. doi:10.1016/j.dss.2012.04.005

Abu-Saifan, S. (2012, February). Social Entrepreneurship: Definition and Boundaries. *Technology Innovation Management Review*, 22-27.

Adjei, M., Noble, S., & Noble, C. (2009). The influence of C2C communications in online brand communities on customer purchase behavior. *Journal of the Academy of Marketing Science*, *38*(5), 634–653. doi:10.100711747-009-0178-5

Adler, L., & Sillars, R. (2011). *2010; The Linked Photographers' Guide to Online Marketing and Social Media*. Cengage Learning.

Agafonow, A. (2014). Value Creation, Value Capture, and Value Devolution. *Administration & Society*, *47*(8), 1038–1060. doi:10.1177/0095399714555756

Agatz, N., Fleischmann, M., & Van Nunen, J. (2008). E-fulfilment and multichannel distribution- a review. *European Journal of Operational Research*, *187*(2), 339–356. doi:10.1016/j.ejor.2007.04.024

Agresta, S., Bough, B. B., & Miletsky, J. I. (2011). *Perspectives™ on Social Media Marketing*. Boston: Cengage Learning.

Ahearne, M., Bhattacharya, C. B., & Gruen, T. (2005). Antecedents and Consequences of Customer–Company identification: Expanding the Role of Relationship Marketing. *The Journal of Applied Psychology*, *90*(3), 574–585. doi:10.1037/0021-9010.90.3.574 PMID:15910151

Ahlqvist, T., Back, A., Halonen, M., & Heinonen, S. (2008). *Social media roadmaps: exploring the futures triggered by social media*. VTT. Retrieved from http://www.vtt.fi/inf/pdf/tiedotteet/2008/t2454.pdf

Ahmad, S., Abu Bakar, A., Faziharudean, T., & Mohamad Zaki, K. (2014). An Empirical Study of Factors Affecting E-Commerce Adoption among Small- and Medium-Sized Enterprises in a Developing Country: Evidence from Malaysia. *Information Technology for Development*, *21*(4), 555–572. doi:10.1080/02681102.2014.899961

Ahn, H., Wijaya, M. E., & Esmero, B. C. (2014). A systemic smartphone usage pattern analysis: Focusing on smartphone addiction issue. *International Journal of Multimedia and Ubiquitous Engineering*, *9*(6), 9–14. doi:10.14257/ijmue.2014.9.6.02

Aichner, T., & Jacob, F. (2015). Measuring the degree of corporate social media use. *International Journal of Market Research*, *57*(2), 257–276. doi:10.2501/IJMR-2015-018

Ailawadi, K. L., & Farris, P. (2017). Managing multi- and omni-channel distribution: Metrics and research directions. *Journal of Retailing*, *93*(1), 120–135. doi:10.1016/j.jretai.2016.12.003

Ainin, S., Parveen, F., Moghavvemi, S., Noor, I. J., & Nor Liyana, M. S. (2015). Factors influencing the use of social media by SMEs and its performance outcomes. *Industr Mngmnt & Data Systems*, *115*(3), 570–588. doi:10.1108/IMDS-07-2014-0205

Akar, E. (2010). *Sosyal medya pazarlaması: Sosyal web de pazarlama stratejileri*. Ankara: Efil Yayınevi.

Akehurst, G. (2009). User generated content: The use of blogs for tourism organisations and tourism consumers. *Service Business*, *3*(1), 51–61. doi:10.100711628-008-0054-2

Akpinar, E., & Berger, J. (2017). Valuable Virality. *JMR, Journal of Marketing Research*, *54*(2), 318–330. doi:10.1509/jmr.13.0350

Alalwan, A., Rana, N., Dwivedi, Y., & Algharabat, R. (2017). Social media in marketing: A review and analysis of the existing literature. *Telematics and Informatics*, *34*(7), 1177–1190. doi:10.1016/j.tele.2017.05.008

Alarcón, C. N., Sepúlveda, A. N., Valenzuela-Fernández, L., & Gil-Lafuent, J. (2018). Systematic mapping on social media and its relation to business. *European Research on Management and Business Economics*, *24*(2), 104–113. doi:10.1016/j.iedeen.2018.01.002

Albrecht, A. K., Walsh, G., & Beatty, S. E. (2017). Perceptions of group versus individual service failures and their effects on customer outcomes: The role of attributions and customer entitlement. *Journal of Service Research*, *20*(2), 188–203. doi:10.1177/1094670516675416

Aldhaban, F. (2012). Exploring the Adoption of Smartphone Technology : Literature Review. In *2012 Proceedings of PICMET '12: Technology Management for Emerging Technologies* (pp. 2758–2770). PICMET.

Alexander, B., & Levine, A. (2008). *Web 2.0 Storytelling Emergence of a New Game*. EDUCAUSE Review.

Algesheimer, R., Dholakia, U., & Herrmann, A. (2005). The Social Influence of Brand Community: Evidence from European Car Clubs. *Journal of Marketing*, *69*(3), 19–34. doi:10.1509/jmkg.69.3.19.66363

Ali, A. H. (2011). Power of Social Media in Developing Nations: New Tools for Closing the Global Digital Divide and Beyond, The. *Harv. Hum. Rts. J.*, *24*, 185.

Ali, I., Jiménez-Zarco, A. I., & Bicho, M. (2015). Using Social Media for CSR communication and engaging stakeholders. *Developments in Corporate Governance and Responsibility*, *7*, 165–185. doi:10.1108/S2043-052320150000007010

Allan, B. (2005). Social enterprise: Through the eye of consumer. *Social Enterprise Journal*, *1*, 57–77. doi:10.1108/17508610580000707

Alshawi, M., & Goulding, J. (2008). Organisational e-readiness: Embracing IT for sustainable competitive advantage. *Construction Innovation*, *8*(1), ci.2008.33308aaa.001. doi:10.1108/ci.2008.33308aaa.001

Aluri, A., Slevitch, L., & Larzelere, R. (2015). The effectiveness of embedded social media on hotel websites and the importance of social interactions and return on engagement'. *International Journal of Contemporary Hospitality Management*, *27*(4), 670–689. doi:10.1108/IJCHM-09-2013-0415

Alvarez, S., Barney, J., & Anderson, P. (2013). Forming and Exploiting Opportunities: The Implications of Discovery and Creation Processes for Entrepreneurial and Organizational Research. *Organization Science*, *24*(1), 301–317. doi:10.1287/orsc.1110.0727

Alvord, S. H., Brown, L. D., & Letts, C. W. (2004). Social entrepreneurship and societal transformation: An exploratory study. *The Journal of Applied Behavioral Science*, *40*(3), 260–282. doi:10.1177/0021886304266847

Amaldoss, W., & Jain, S. (2008). Research Note —Trading Up: A Strategic Analysis of Reference Group Effects. *Marketing Science*, *27*(5), 932–942. doi:10.1287/mksc.1070.0350

Anderson, M., Sims, J., Price, J., & Brusa, J. (2011). Turning 'like' to 'buy' social media emerges. *Strategy &*, 1–12.

Anderson, E. (1998). Customer Satisfaction and Word of Mouth. *Journal of Service Research*, *1*(1), 5–17. doi:10.1177/109467059800100102

Anderson, P. H. (2001). Relationship development and marketing communication: An integrative model. *Journal of Business and Industrial Marketing*, *16*(3), 167–183. doi:10.1108/08858620110389786

Anderson, S., Hamilton, K., & Tonner, A. (2016). Social labour: Exploring work in consumption. *Marketing Theory*, *16*(3), 383–400. doi:10.1177/1470593116640598

Andjelic, A. (2015). Luxury brands are failing in their storytelling. *The Guardian*. Retrieved November 10, 2016, from https://www.theguardian.com/media-network/2015/nov/23/luxury-brands-marketing-failing-storytelling

Andzulis, J., Panagopoulos, N., & Rapp, A. (2012). A Review of Social Media and Implications for the Sales Process. *Journal of Personal Selling & Sales Management*, *32*(3), 305–316. doi:10.2753/PSS0885-3134320302

Anholt, S. (2011). *Beyond the nation brand: The role of image and identity in international relations*. Academic Press.

Anholt, S. (2017). *The Good Country Index*. Retrieved from https://goodcountry.org/index/results?p=overall

Anholt-GfK Nation Brands Index. (2017). Retrieved from http://nation-brands.gfk.com

Anholt, S. (1998). Nation-brands of the twenty-first century. *Journal of Brand Management*, *5*(6), 395–406. doi:10.1057/bm.1998.30

Anholt, S. (2007). *Competitive identity: The new brand management for nations, cities and regions*. Basingstoke, UK: Palgrave Macmillan. doi:10.1057/9780230627727

Anokhin, S., Grichnik, D., & Hisrich, R. D. (2008). The journey from novice to serial entrepreneurship in China and Germany: Are the drivers the same. *Managing Global Transitions*, *6*(2), 117–142.

Ansarin, M., & Ozuem, W. (2014). Social media and online brand communities. In Computer-Mediated Marketing Strategies: Social Media and Online Brand Communities. IGI Global.

Ansarin, M., & Ozuem, W. (2015). Social media and online brand communities. In Computer-Mediated Marketing Strategies: Social Media and Online Brand Communities (pp. 1-27). IGI Global.

Anshari, M., Alas, Y., Hardaker, G., Jaidin, J. H., Smith, M., & Ahad, A. D. (2016). Smartphone habit and behavior in Brunei: Personalization, gender, and generation gap. *Computers in Human Behavior*, *64*, 719–727. doi:10.1016/j.chb.2016.07.063

Appiah, D. (2014). *Building Brand Loyalty: Identity Theory Perspective. Seventh International Scientific Conference.* Institute of Economic Research.

Appiah, D., & Ozuem, W. (2017). Issues and the Importance of Branding, Brand Personality and Symbolic Meaning of Brands to the Consumer. In Global Information Diffusion and Management in Contemporary Society. IGI Global.

Appiah, D., & Ayertey, S. (2018). Towards Understanding the Moderating Roles Of Smartphones On Brand Switching. In *Annual International Conference*. Global Business and Technology Association.

Appiah, D., & Ozuem, W. (2018). The Dynamics of Resistance to Brand Switching in the Smartphones Industry. In *Managing Diversity, Innovation, and Infrastructure in Digital Business*. Hershey, PA: IGI Global.

Appiah, D., Ozuem, W., & Howell, E. K. (2016). Towards a Sustainable Brand Loyalty*: Attitudinal Loyalty Perspective. Eighteenth Annual International Conference*. Global Business and Technology Association.

Appiah, D., Ozuem, W., & Howell, K. E. (2017). Brand Switching in the Smartphone Industry: A Preliminary Study. *Global Business and Technology Association Conference*, Vienna, Austria.

Arbore, A., Graziani, R., & Venturini, S. (2014). Personal mobile technologies: Decomposing and de-averaging the value of a smartphone. *Journal of Information Systems*, *28*(1), 167–185. doi:10.2308/isys-50668

Argo, J., Dahl, D., & Manchanda, R. (2005). The Influence of a Mere Social Presence in a Retail Context. *The Journal of Consumer Research*, *32*(2), 207–212. doi:10.1086/432230

Armelini, G. (2011). *The Effect of Word of Mouth in Customer Equity and Brand Equity*. Chinese Business Review.

Armistead, C., Clark, G., & Stanley, P. (1995). *Managing Service Recovery*. Cranfield, UK: Cranfield School of Management.

Armstrong, G., & Kotler, P. (2014). *Marketing: an introduction (12th ed.)*. Harlow: Pearson Education Limited.

Armstrong, G., Kotler, P., & Opresnik, M. O. (2017). *Marketing: an introduction (13th ed.)*. Harlow: Pearson Education Limited.

Armstrong, J. S. (2001). *Principles of forecasting: A handbook for researchers and practitioners illustrated* (J. S. Armstrong, Ed.). New York: Springer Science & Business Media. doi:10.1007/978-0-306-47630-3

Arndt, J. (1967). Role of Product-Related Conversations in the Diffusion of a New Product. *JMR, Journal of Marketing Research*, *4*(3), 291–297. doi:10.1177/002224376700400308

Arnett, D., German, S., & Hunt, S. (2003). The Identity Salience Model of Relationship Marketing Success: The Case of Nonprofit Marketing. *Journal of Marketing*, *67*(2), 89–105. doi:10.1509/jmkg.67.2.89.18614

Arnold, M. J., & Reynolds, K. E. (2003). Hedonic shopping motivations. *Journal of Retailing*, *79*(2), 77–95. doi:10.1016/S0022-4359(03)00007-1

Arora, H. (2007). Word of Mouth in the World of Marketing. *The Icfai Journal of Marketing Management, VI, 4*, 51–65.

Arora, P. (2014). *The Leisure Commons*. New York: Routledge.

Arora, P., & Predmore, C. E. (2013). Social media as a strategic tool: Going beyond the obvious. *Advanced Series in Management*, *11*, 115–127. doi:10.1108/S1877-6361(2013)0000011010

Arrigo, E. (2014). Social media opportunities for market-driven firms. In Integrating social media into business practice, applications, management, and models. IGI Global.

Ashforth, B., & Mael, F. (1989). Social Identity Theory and the Organization. *Academy of Management Review*, *14*(1), 20–39. doi:10.5465/amr.1989.4278999

Ashley, C., & Tuten, T. (2015). Creative Strategies in Social Media Marketing: An Exploratory Study of Branded Social Content and Consumer Engagement. *Psychology and Marketing*, *32*(1), 15–27. doi:10.1002/mar.20761

Ashmore, R., Deaux, K., & McLaughlin-Volpe, T. (2004). An Organizing Framework for Collective Identity: Articulation and Significance of Multidimensionality. *Psychological Bulletin*, *130*(1), 80–114. doi:10.1037/0033-2909.130.1.80 PMID:14717651

Aslam, B., & Karjaluoto, H. (2017). Digital advertising around paid spaces, E-advertising industry's revenue engine: A review and research agenda. *Telematics and Informatics*, *34*(8), 1650–1662. doi:10.1016/j.tele.2017.07.011

Atkin, C., & Block, M. (1983). Effectiveness of Celebrity Endorsers. *Journal of Advertising Research*, *23*(1), 57–61.

Austin, J., Stevenson, H., & Wei-Skillern, J. (2006). Social and commercial entrepreneurship: Same, different, or both? *Entrepreneurship Theory and Practice*, *30*(1), 1–22. doi:10.1111/j.1540-6520.2006.00107.x

Ayeh, J. K., Au, N., & Law, R. (2013). "Do we believe in TripAdvisor?" Examining credibility perceptions and online travelers' attitude toward using user-generated content. *Journal of Travel Research*, *52*(4), 437–452. doi:10.1177/0047287512475217

Ayertey, S. B. (2018). *An evaluation of online service failures and recovery strategies in the UK fashion industry* (PhD thesis). University of Plymouth.

Ayertey, S., & Ozuem, W. (2018). Developing Compelling Online Recovery Strategies: Implications for the Fashion Clothing Industry. In Digital Marketing Strategies for Fashion and Luxury Brands (pp. 264-288). IGI Global.

Ayertey, S., & Ozuem, W. (2018). *Developing Compelling Online Recovery Strategies: Implications for the Fashion Clothing Industry*. Hershey, PA: IGI Global. doi:10.4018/978-1-5225-2697-1.ch013

Ayertey, S., Ozuem, W., & Appiah, D. (2018). Service failure and recovery strategy in computer- mediated environments. *Global Business and Technology Association Conference*, Bangkok, Thailand.

Ayertey, S., Ozuem, W., & Appiah, D. (2018). Service Failure and Recovery Strategy in Computer-Mediated Marketing Environments. *Global Business and Technology Association Conference.*

Azemi, Y., & Ozuem, W. (2014). Social media and SMEs in transition countries. In Computer-mediated marketing strategies: social media and online brand communities. IGI Global.

Azemi, Y., & Ozuem, W. (2016). Online service failure and recovery strategy: The mediating role of social media. In Competitive social media marketing strategies. Hershey, PA: IGI Global.

Azemi, Y., Ozuem, W., Howell, K. E., & Lancaster, G. (2018). An exploration into the practice of online service failure and recovery strategies in the Balkans. *Journal of Business Research*.

Azize, S., Hakan, K., & Cemal, Z. (2013). Creating Commitment, Trust and Satisfaction for a Brand: What is the Role of Switching Costs in Mobile Phone Market? *Procedia: Social and Behavioral Sciences*, *99*, 496–502. doi:10.1016/j.sbspro.2013.10.518

Babin, B. J., Darden, W. R., & Griffin, M. (1994). Work and/or fun: Measuring hedonic and utilitarian shopping value. *The Journal of Consumer Research*, *20*(4), 644–657. doi:10.1086/209376

Bächle, M., & Lehmann, F. (2010). *E-business: Grundlagen elektronischer Geschäftsprozesse im Web 2.0*. Oldenburg: Oldenburg Verlag. doi:10.1524/9783486709834

Back, K. J., & Parks, S. C. (2003). A brand loyalty model involving cognitive, affective, and conative brand loyalty and customer satisfaction. *Journal of Hospitality & Tourism Research (Washington, D.C.)*, *27*(4), 419–435. doi:10.1177/10963480030274003

Badrinarayanan, V., Becerra, E., & Madhavaram, S. (2014). Influence of congruity in store-attribute dimensions and self-image on purchase intentions in online stores of multichannel retailers. *Journal of Retailing and Consumer Services*, *21*(6), 1013–1020. doi:10.1016/j.jretconser.2014.01.002

Badrinarayanan, V., & Laverie, D. A. (2011). Brand advocacy and Sales effort by retail Salespeople: Antecedents and influence of identification with Manufacturers' Brands. *Journal of Personal Selling & Sales Management*, *31*(2), 123–140. doi:10.2753/PSS0885-3134310202

Bagozzi, R. P. (2007). The Legacy of the Technology Acceptance Model and a Proposal for a Paradigm Shift. *Journal of the Association for Information Systems*, *8*(4), 244–254. doi:10.17705/1jais.00122

Bagozzi, R. P., & Dholakia, U. M. (2002). Intentional social action in virtual communities. *Journal of Interactive Marketing*, *16*(2), 2–21. doi:10.1002/dir.10006

Bagozzi, R. P., & Lee, K.-H. (2002). Multiple Routes for Social Influence: The Role of Compliance, Internalization, and Social Identity. *Social Psychology Quarterly*, *65*(3), 226–247. doi:10.2307/3090121

Bagozzi, R., & Dholakia, U. (2006). Open Source Software User Communities: A Study of Participation in Linux User Groups. *Management Science*, *52*(7), 1099–1115. doi:10.1287/mnsc.1060.0545

Baker, A., Donthu, N., & Kumar, V. (2016). Investigating How Word-of-Mouth Conversations About Brands Influence Purchase and Retransmission Intentions. *JMR, Journal of Marketing Research*, *53*(2), 225–239. doi:10.1509/jmr.14.0099

Baker, J., Grewal, D., & Parasuraman, A. (1994). The influence of store environment on quality inferences and store image. *Journal of the Academy of Marketing Science*, *22*(4), 328–339. doi:10.1177/0092070394224002

Bakewell, C., & Mitchell, V. (2003). Generation Y female consumer decision-making styles. *International Journal of Retail & Distribution Management*, *31*(2), 95–106. doi:10.1108/09590550310461994

Balaji, M. S., Khong, K. W., & Chong, A. Y. L. (2016). Determinants of negative word-of-mouth communication using social networking sites. *Information & Management*, *53*(4), 528–540. doi:10.1016/j.im.2015.12.002

Balasubramanian, S., & Mahajan, V. (2001). The Economic Leverage of the Virtual Community. *International Journal of Electronic Commerce*, *5*(3), 103–138. doi:10.1080/10864415.2001.11044212

Balasubramanian, S., Raghunathan, R., & Mahajan, V. (2005). Consumers in a multichannel environment: Product utility, process utility, and channel choice. *Journal of Interactive Marketing*, *19*(2), 12–30. doi:10.1002/dir.20032

Baldus, B., Voorhees, C., & Calantone, R. (2015). Online brand community engagement: Scale development and validation. *Journal of Business Research*, *68*(5), 2. doi:10.1016/j.jbusres.2014.09.035

Ballantine, P., & Martin, B. (2005). Forming Parasocial Relationships in Online Communities. *Advances in Consumer Research. Association for Consumer Research (U. S.)*, *32*, 197–201.

Bamberg, S., & Hunecke, M., & Blöhbaum. (2007). Social context, morality and the use of public transportation: Results from two field studies. *Journal of Environmental Psychology*, *27*, 190–203. doi:10.1016/j.jenvp.2007.04.001

Banelis, M., Riebe, E., & Rungie, C. (2013). Empirical evidence of repertoire size. *Australasian Marketing Journal*, *21*(1), 59–65. doi:10.1016/j.ausmj.2012.11.001

Banerjee, M. (2014). Misalignment and its influence on integration quality in multichannel services. *Journal of Service Research*, *17*(4), 460–474. doi:10.1177/1094670514539395

Bang, H., & Lee, W. (2016). Consumer Response to Ads in Social Network Sites: An Exploration into the Role of Ad Location and Path. *Journal of Current Issues and Research in Advertising*, *37*(1), 1–14. doi:10.1080/10641734.2015.1119765

Bank of Spain. (2017). *Expenditure per visitor in Spain*. Retrieved from https://www.bde.es/bde/en/

Bao, P., Pierce, J., Whittaker, S., & Zhai, S. (2011). Smart phone use by non-mobile business users. *Proceedings of the 13th International Conference on Human Computer Interaction with Mobile Devices and Services – MobileHCI '11*, 445–455. 10.1145/2037373.2037440

Bao, T. T., & Chang, T. S. (2016). The product and timing effects of eWOM in viral marketing. *International Journal of Business*, *21*(2), 99.

Barefoot, D., & Szabo, J. (2009). *Friends with Benefits: A Social Media Marketing Handbook, 1;1st; edn*. San Francisco, CA: No Starch Press.

Bargh, J., & McKenna, K. (2004). The Internet and Social Life. *Annual Review of Psychology*, *55*(1), 573–590. doi:10.1146/annurev.psych.55.090902.141922 PMID:14744227

Barnes, D., Clear, F., Dyerson, R., Harindranath, G., Harris, L., & Rae, A. (2012). Web 2.0 and micro-businesses: An exploratory investigation. *Journal of Small Business and Enterprise Development*, *19*(4), 687–711. doi:10.1108/14626001211277479

Barnes, N. G. (2010). Tweeting and blogging to the top. *Marketing Research*, *22*(1), 8–13.

Barreda, A., & Bilgihan, A. (2013). An analysis of user-generated content for hotel experiences. *Journal of Hospitality and Tourism Technology*, *4*(3), 263–280. doi:10.1108/JHTT-01-2013-0001

Barron, L. (2012). *Social theory in popular culture*. Basingstoke, UK: Palgrave Macmillan.

Barrows, C. W., Powers, T., & Reynolds, D. R. (2011). *Introduction to Management in the Hospitality Industry* (10th ed.). John Wiley & Sons.

Barwise, P., & Meehan, S. (2010). The one thing you must get right when building a brand. *Harvard Business Review*, *88*(12), 80–84.

Barwise, P., & Meehan, S. (2010, December). The One Thing You Must Get Right When Building a Brand. *Harvard Business Review*.

Ba, S. (2001). Establishing online trust through a community responsibility system. *Decision Support Systems*, *31*(3), 323–336. doi:10.1016/S0167-9236(00)00144-5

Batra, R., Lehmann, D. R., & Singh, D. (1993). The Brand Personality Component of Brand Goodwill: Some Antecedents and Consequences. In Brand Equity and Advertising. Hillsdale, IL: Lawrence Erlbaum Associates.

Batra, R., & Ahtola, O. T. (1991). Measuring the hedonic and utilitarian sources of consumer attitudes. *Marketing Letters*, *2*(2), 159–170. doi:10.1007/BF00436035

Bauer, H. H., Falk, T., & Hammerschmidt, M. (2006). eTransQual: A transaction process-based approach for capturing service quality in online shopping. *Journal of Business Research*, *59*(7), 866–875. doi:10.1016/j.jbusres.2006.01.021

BBC News. (2016). Available at: http://www.bbc.co.uk/news/business-36395719

BBC News. (2018). *London Fashion Week 'turns collections into commerce'.* Retrieved October 1, 2018 from https://www.bbc.co.uk/news/av/business-26185198/london-fashion-week-turns-collections-into-commerce

Bearden, W., & Etzel, M. (1982). Reference Group Influence on Product and Brand Purchase Decisions. *The Journal of Consumer Research*, *9*(2), 183–194. doi:10.1086/208911

Bechina, A. A., & Husta, E. (2011). The Role of Social Networking Tools on Purchasing Decision Making Process. *Proceedings of the International Conference on Intellectual Capital*, 81-87.

Bechmann, A., & Lomborg, S. (2013). Mapping actor roles in social media: Different perspectives on value creation in theories of user participation. *Sage (Atlanta, Ga.)*, 767–679. doi:10.1177/1461444812462853

Becker-Olsen, K. (2003). And Now, A Word from Our Sponsor--A Look at the Effects of Sponsored Content and Banner Advertising. *Journal of Advertising*, *32*(2), 17–32. doi:10.1080/00913367.2003.10639130

Bejou, D., & Palmer, A. (1998). Service failure and loyalty: An exploratory empirical study of airline customers. *Journal of Services Marketing*, *12*(1), 7–22. doi:10.1108/08876049810202339

Belch, B. (2003). *Advertising and promotion an integrated marketing communications perspective (6th ed.)*. McGraw-Hill/Irwin.

Belk, R. (1988). Possessions and the Extended Self. *The Journal of Consumer Research*, *15*(2), 139. doi:10.1086/209154

Bell, C. R., & Zemke, R. E. (1987). Service breakdown the road to recovery. *Management Review*, *76*(10), 32–35.

Bellenger, D. N., & Korgaonkar, P. K. (1980). Profiling the recreational shopper. *Journal of Retailing*, *56*(3), 77–91. Available at http://connection.ebscohost.com/c/articles/4667116/profiling-recreational-shopper

Bennett, S., Maton, K., & Kervin, L. (2008). The 'digital natives' debate: A critical review of the evidence. *British Journal of Educational Technology*, *39*(5), 775–786. doi:10.1111/j.1467-8535.2007.00793.x

Bentley, C. (2018). *Let fashion be your servant not your master says Christian who ran London Fashion Week.* Retrieved October 17, 2018 from https://www.premier.org.uk/News/UK/Let-fashion-be-your-servant-not-your-master-says-Christian-who-ran-London-Fashion-Week

Bergami, M., & Bagozzi, R. (2000). Self-categorization, affective commitment and group self-esteem as distinct aspects of social identity in the organization. *British Journal of Social Psychology*, *39*(4), 555–577. doi:10.1348/014466600164633 PMID:11190685

Berger, J., & Milkman, K. L. (2012). What makes online content viral? *JMR, Journal of Marketing Research*, *49*(2), 192–205. doi:10.1509/jmr.10.0353

Berger, J., Sorensen, A., & Rasmussen, S. (2010). Positive Effects of Negative Publicity: When Negative Reviews Increase Sales. *Marketing Science*, *29*(5), 815–827. doi:10.1287/mksc.1090.0557

Berman, B., & Thelen, S. (2004). A guide to developing and managing a well-integrated multi-channel retail strategy. *International Journal of Retail & Distribution Management*, *32*(3), 147–156. doi:10.1108/09590550410524939

Bernoff, J., & Li, C. (2008). Harnessing the power of the oh-so-social web. *Sloan Management Review*, *49*(3), 36–42.

Bernritter, S. F., Verlegh, P. W., & Smit, E. G. (2016). Why nonprofits are easier to endorse on social media: The roles of warmth and brand symbolism. *Journal of Interactive Marketing*, *33*, 27–42. doi:10.1016/j.intmar.2015.10.002

Berry, L. (1995). Relationship Marketing of Services--Growing Interest, Emerging Perspectives. *Journal of the Academy of Marketing Science*, *23*(4), 236–245. doi:10.1177/009207039502300402

Berry, L. L., & Parasuraman, A. (1992). Marketing Services: Competing Through Quality. *Journal of Marketing*, *56*(2), 132–134. doi:10.2307/1252050

Berry, L., Bolton, R., Bridges, C., Meyer, J., Parasuraman, A., & Seiders, K. (2010). Opportunities for innovation in the delivery of interactive retail services. *Journal of Interactive Marketing*, *24*(2), 155–167. doi:10.1016/j.intmar.2010.02.001

Berthon, P. R., Pitt, L. F., Plangger, K., & Shapiro, D. (2012). Marketing meets web 2.0, social media, and creative consumers: Implications for international marketing strategy. *Business Horizons*, *55*(3), 261–271. doi:10.1016/j.bushor.2012.01.007

Berthon, P. R., Pitt, L., & Campbell, C. (2008). Ad lib: When customers create the ad. *California Management Review*, *50*(4), 6–31. doi:10.2307/41166454

Bertot, J. C., Jaeger, P. T., & Grimes, J. M. (2010). Using ICTs to create a culture of transparency: E-government and social media as openness and anti-corruption tools for societies. *Government Information Quarterly*, *27*(3), 264–271. doi:10.1016/j.giq.2010.03.001

Bertot, J. C., Jaeger, P. T., & Hansen, D. (2012). The impact of polices on government social media usage: Issues, challenges, and recommendations. *Government Information Quarterly*, *29*(1), 30–40. doi:10.1016/j.giq.2011.04.004

Beukeboom, C. J., Kerkhof, P., & de Vries, M. (2015). Does a virtual like cause actual liking? How following a brand's Facebook updates enhances brand evaluations and purchase intention. *Journal of Interactive Marketing*, *32*, 26–36. doi:10.1016/j.intmar.2015.09.003

Beurer-Zuellig, B., & Meckel, M. (2008). Smartphones enabling mobile collaboration. *Proceedings of the Annual Hawaii International Conference on System Sciences*, 1–10.

Bhardwaj, V., & Fairhurst, A. (2010). Fast fashion: Response to changes in the fashion industry. *International Review of Retail, Distribution and Consumer Research*, *20*(1), 165–173. doi:10.1080/09593960903498300

Bhatli, D., & Mejri, C. A. (2015). The Influence of Social Media on Consumption Practices. In *Ideas in Marketing: Finding the New and Polishing the Old. Developments in Marketing Science: Proceedings of the Academy of Marketing Science*. Springer. 10.1007/978-3-319-10951-0_289

Bhattacharya, C. B., & Lordish, L. (2000). *Towards a System for Monitoring Brand Health from Store Scanner Data*. MSI working Paper, Report No. 00-111.

Bhattacharya, C., & Sen, S. (2003). Consumer-Company Identification: A Framework for Understanding Consumers' Relationships with Companies. *Journal of Marketing*, *67*(2), 76–88. doi:10.1509/jmkg.67.2.76.18609

Bian, Q., & Forsythe, S. (2012). Purchase intention for luxury brands: A cross cultural comparison. *Journal of Business Research*, *65*(10), 1443–1451. doi:10.1016/j.jbusres.2011.10.010

Bicen, H., & Cavus, N. (2011). Social network sites usage habits of undergraduate students: Case study of Facebook. *Procedia: Social and Behavioral Sciences*, *28*, 943–947. doi:10.1016/j.sbspro.2011.11.174

Bickart, B., & Schindler, R. M. (2001). Internet forum as influential sources of consumer information. *Journal of Interactive Marketing*, *1*(3), 31–40. doi:10.1002/dir.1014

Biel, A. (1993). Converting image into equity in the book. In D. Aaker & A. Biel (Eds.), *Brand equity and advertising: Advertising's role in building strong brands* (1st ed.; pp. 67–82). New York: Psychology Press.

Bienstock, C. C. B., Royne, M., Sherrell, D., & Stafford, T. F. (2008). An expanded model of logistics service quality: Incorporating logistics information technology. *International Journal of Production Economics*, *113*(1), 205–222. doi:10.1016/j.ijpe.2007.03.023

Birtwistle, G., & Freathy, P. (1998). More than just a name above the shop: A comparison of the branding strategies of two UK fashion retailers. *International Journal of Retail & Distribution Management*, *26*(8), 318–323. doi:10.1108/09590559810231788

Bishop Gagliano, K., & Hathcote, J. (1994). Customer expectations and perceptions of service quality in retail apparel specialty stores. *Journal of Services Marketing*, *8*(1), 60–69. doi:10.1108/08876049410053311

Bitner, M. J., Booms, B. H., & Mohr, L. A. (1994). Critical service encounters: The employee's viewpoint. *Journal of Marketing*, *58*(4), 95–106. doi:10.2307/1251919

Bitner, M. J., & Hubbert, A. R. (1994). Encounter satisfaction versus overall satisfaction versus quality. In R. T. Rust & R. L. Oliver (Eds.), *Service Quality: New Directions in Theory and Practice* (pp. 72–94). London: Sage. doi:10.4135/9781452229102.n3

Biyalogorsky, E., Gerstner, E., & Libai, B. (2001). Customer Referral Management: Optimal Reward Programs. *Marketing Science*, *20*(1), 82–95. doi:10.1287/mksc.20.1.82.10195

Black, N. J., Lockett, A., Ennew, C., Winklhofer, H., & McKechnie, S. (2002). Modelling consumer choice of distribution channels: An illustration from financial services. *International Journal of Bank Marketing*, *20*(4), 161–173. doi:10.1108/02652320210432945

Blackshaw, P., & Nazzaro, M. (2006). *Consumer- Generated Media (CGM) 101: Word-of-Mouth in the Age of the Web-Fortified Consumer*. New York: Nielsen.

Blattberg, R., Getz, G., & Thomas, J. (2001). *Customer Equity: Building and Managing Relationships as Valuable Assets*. Boston: Harvard Business School Press.

Blazevic, V., Wiertz, C., Cotte, J., de Ruyter, K., & Keeling, D. I. (2014). GOSIP in cyberspace: Conceptualization and scale development for general online social interaction propensity. *Journal of Interactive Marketing*, *28*(2), 87–100. doi:10.1016/j.intmar.2013.09.003

Blázquez, M. (2014). Fashion shopping in multichannel retail: The role of technology in enhancing the customer experience. *International Journal of Electronic Commerce*, *18*(4), 97–116. doi:10.2753/JEC1086-4415180404

Bleier, A., & Eisenbeiss, M. (2015). Personalized Online Advertising Effectiveness: The Interplay of What, When, and Where. *Marketing Science*, *34*(5), 669–688. doi:10.1287/mksc.2015.0930

Blodgett, G., Hill, D. J., & Tax, S. S. (1997). The effects of distributive, procedural, and interactional justice on post-complaint behavior. *Journal of Retailing*, *73*(2), 185–210. doi:10.1016/S0022-4359(97)90003-8

Bødker, M., Gimpel, G., & Hedman, J. (2009). *The user experience of smart phones : A consumption values approach.* In Global Mobility Roundtable, Cairo, Egypt.

Bødker, M., Gimpel, G., & Hedman, J. (2010). Technology use: Time-in or time-out. *18th European Conference on Information Systems*. Retrieved from http://aisel.aisnet.org/ecis2010/135

Bødker, M., Gimpel, G., & Hedman, J. (2014). Time-out/time-in: The dynamics of everyday experiential computing devices. *Information Systems Journal*, *24*(2), 143–166. doi:10.1111/isj.12002

BOF & McKinsey & Co. (2018). *The State of Fashion*. McKinsey& Co. Retrieved from https://cdn.businessoffashion.com/reports/The_State_of_Fashion_2018_v2.pdf

BOF & McKinsey&Co. (2018*). The State of Fashion 2018.* Retrieved from https://cdn.businessoffashion.com/reports/The_State_of_Fashion_2018_v2.pdf

Bogataj Habjan, K., & Pucihar, A. (2017). Cloud Computing Adoption Business Model Factors: Does Enterprise Size Matter? *The Engineering Economist*, *28*(3).

Bojārs, U., Breslin, J. G., Finn, A., & Decker, S. (2008). Using the Semantic Web for linking and reusing data across Web 2.0 communities. *Journal of Web Semantics*, *6*(1), 21–28. doi:10.1016/j.websem.2007.11.010

Bolton, L. E., & Americus, R. I. I. (2004). Sticky Priors: The Perseverance of Identity Effects on Judgements. *JMR, Journal of Marketing Research*, *41*(11), 397–410. doi:10.1509/jmkr.41.4.397.47019

Bolton, R. N., Parasuraman, A., Hoefnagels, A., Migchels, N., Kabadayi, S., Gruber, T., ... Solnet, D. (2013). Understanding Generation Y and their use of social media: A review and research agenda. *Journal of Service Management*, *24*(3), 245–267. doi:10.1108/09564231311326987

Bolton, R., & Drew, J. (1991). A multistage model of customers' assessments of service quality and value. *The Journal of Consumer Research*, *17*(4), 375–384. doi:10.1086/208564

Bone, P. (1995). Word-of-mouth effects on short-term and long-term product judgments. *Journal of Business Research*, *32*(3), 213–223. doi:10.1016/0148-2963(94)00047-I

Bong Na, W., Marshall, R., & Lane Keller, K. (1999). Measuring brand power: Validating a model for optimizing brand equity. *Journal of Product and Brand Management*, *8*(3), 170–184. doi:10.1108/10610429910272439

Bonsón, E., Torres, L., Royo, S., & Flores, F. (2012). Local e-government 2.0: Social media and corporate transparency in municipalities. *Government Information Quarterly*, *29*(2), 123–132. doi:10.1016/j.giq.2011.10.001

Boroumand, L., Aghdasi, M., Albadvi, A., Jamshidian, M., & Perzon, H. (2008). Service Failure-Recovery in Online Shops in Iran. *International Journal of Information Science and Technology*, *6*(2), 61–75.

Boshoff, C. (1997). An experimental study of service recovery options. *International Journal of Service Industry Management, 8*(2), 110-130.

Boshoff, C. (1997). An experimental study of service recovery options. *International Journal of Service Industry Management*, *8*(2), 110–130. doi:10.1108/09564239710166245

Bougie, R., Pieters, R., & Zeelenberg, M. (2003). Angry customers don't come back, they get back: The experience and behavioural implications of anger and dissatisfaction in services. *Journal of the Academy of Marketing Science*, *31*(4), 377–393. doi:10.1177/0092070303254412

Boulding, W., Kalra, A., Staelin, R., & Zeithaml, V. (1993). A dynamic process model of service quality: From expectations to behavioral intentions. *JMR, Journal of Marketing Research*, *30*(1), 7–27. doi:10.2307/3172510

Bowen, D., & Johnston, R. (2009). Why service recovery fails: Tensions among customer, employee, and process perspectives. *Journal of Service Management*, *20*(3), 253–273. doi:10.1108/09564230910964381

Bower, J. L., & Christensen, C. M. (1995). Disruptive Technologies: Catching the Wave. *Havard Business Review*, (2-3), 43-53.

Bowers, M. R., Martin, C. L., & Luker, A. (1990). Trading places: Employees as customers, customers as employees. *Journal of Services Marketing*, *4*(2), 55–69. doi:10.1108/EUM0000000002512

boyd, d., & Ellison, N. (2007). Social Network Sites: Definition, History, and Scholarship. *Journal of Computer-Mediated Communication*, *13*(1), 210-230.

Boyd, D., & Ellison, N. (2008). Social network sites: Definition, history, and scholarship. *Journal of Computer-Mediated Communication*, *13*(1), 211.

Boyer, K. K., Hallowell, R., & Roth, A. V. (2002). E-services: Operating strategy—a case study and a method for analyzing operational benefits. *Journal of Operations Management*, *20*(2), 175–188. doi:10.1016/S0272-6963(01)00093-6

Bradley, G. L., & Sparks, B. A. (2009). Dealing with service failures: The use of explanations. *Journals of Travel & Toursim Markeing*, *26*(2), 129–143. doi:10.1080/10548400902862010

Bradley, G., & Sparks, B. (2012). Explanations: If, when, and how they aid service recovery. *Journal of Services Marketing*, *26*(1), 41–51. doi:10.1108/08876041211199715

Brake, D. (2014). *Sharing our lives online: risks and exposure in social media.* Basingstoke, UK: Palgrave Macmillan. doi:10.1057/9781137312716

Brake, D. K., & Safko, L. (2009). So exactly what is the social media? In *The social media bible: Tactics, tools and strategies for business success* (p. 6). John Wiley & Sons.

Brakus, J., Schmitt, B., & Zarantonello, L. (2009). Brand Experience: What Is It? How Is It Measured? Does It Affect Loyalty? *Journal of Marketing*, *73*(3), 52–68. doi:10.1509/jmkg.73.3.52

Brand Finance. (2017). *Brand finance Nation Brands, the annual report on the world's most valuable nation brands.* Retrieved from http://brandfinance.com/images/upload/bf_nation_brands_2017.pdf

Breitsohl, J., Kunz, W. H., & Dowell, D. (2015). Does the host match the content? A taxonomical update on online consumption communities. *Journal of Marketing Management*, *31*(9-10), 1040–1064. doi:10.1080/0267257X.2015.1036102

Brengarth, L. B., & Mujkic, E. (2016). Web 2.0: How social media applications leverage non-profit responses during a wildfire crisis. *Computers in Human Behavior*, *54*, 589–596. doi:10.1016/j.chb.2015.07.010

Bressolles, G., Durrieu, F., & Senecal, S. (2014). A consumer typology based on e-service quality and e-satisfaction. *Journal of Retailing and Consumer Services*, *21*(6), 889–896. doi:10.1016/j.jretconser.2014.07.004

Brettel, M., Reich, J., Gavilanes, J., & Flatten, T. (2015). What Drives Advertising Success on Facebook? An Advertising-Effectiveness Model. *Journal of Advertising Research*, *55*(2), 162–175. doi:10.2501/JAR-55-2-162-175

Breugelmans, E., & Campo, K. (2016). Cross-channel effects of price promotions: An empirical analysis of the multi-channel grocery retail sector. *Journal of Retailing*, *92*(3), 333–351. doi:10.1016/j.jretai.2016.02.003

Brewer, M. B. (1979). In-group Bias in the Minimal Intergroup Situation: A Cognitive–Motivational Analysis. *Psychological Bulletin*, *86*(2), 307–324. doi:10.1037/0033-2909.86.2.307

British Fashion Council. (2016). *The British Fashion Industry & London Fashion Week Facts & Figures.* Retrieved October 6, 2018, available at: www. britishfashioncouncil.co.uk

Brodie, J. R., Ilic, A., Juric, B., & Hollebeek, L. (2013). Consumer engagement in a virtual brand community: An exploratory research. *Journal of Business Research, 66*(1), 105–114. doi:10.1016/j.jbusres.2011.07.029

Brodie, J. R., Juric, B., & Ilic, A. (2011). Consumer engagement: Conceptual domain, Fundamental propositions and implications for research. *Journal of Service Research, 14*(3), 252–271. doi:10.1177/1094670511411703

Brogi, S., Calabrese, A., Campisi, D., Capece, G., Costa, R., & Pillo, F. D. (2013). The effects of online brand communities on brand equity in the luxury fashion industry. *International Journal of Engineering Business Management, 5*, 32. doi:10.5772/56854

Brown, E. (2012). *Working the Crowd - Social media marketing for business* (2nd ed.). Swindon, UK: British Informatics Society Ltd.

Brown, J. J., & Reingen, P. H. (1987). Social ties and word-of-mouth referral behavior. *The Journal of Consumer Research, 14*(3), 350–362. doi:10.1086/209118

Brown, J., Broderick, A., & Lee, N. (2007). Word of mouth communication within online communities: Conceptualizing the online social network. *Journal of Interactive Marketing, 21*(3), 2–20. doi:10.1002/dir.20082

Brown, M. (1954). On a definition of culture. *Psychological Review, 60*(3), 215. doi:10.1037/h0059520 PMID:13056118

Brown, S. P., & Beltramini, R. F. (1989). Consumer complaining and word of mouth activities: Field evidence. *Advances in Consumer Research. Association for Consumer Research (U. S.), 16*(1), 9–16. Retrieved from http://www.acrwebsite.org/search/view-conference-proceedings.aspx?Id=6872

Brown, S., Kozinets, R., & Sherry, J. Jr. (2003). Teaching Old Brands New Tricks: Retro Branding and the Revival of Brand Meaning. *Journal of Marketing, 67*(3), 19–33. doi:10.1509/jmkg.67.3.19.18657

Bruhn, M., Schnebelen, S., & Schäfer, D. (2014). Antecedents and consequences of the quality of e-customer-to-customer interactions in B2B brand communities. *Industrial Marketing Management, 43*(1), 164–176. doi:10.1016/j.indmarman.2013.08.008

Bruner, G. C. II, & Kumar, A. (2005). Explaining consumer acceptance of handheld internet devices. *Journal of Business Research, 58*(5), 553–558. doi:10.1016/j.jbusres.2003.08.002

Brunswicker, S., & Vanhaverbeke, W. (2013). *Open Innovation in Small and Medium-Sized Enterprises (SMEs): External Knowledge Sourcing Strategies and Internal Organizational Facilitators.* SSRN Electronic Journal.

Bruzzi, P., & Joia, L. A. (2015). Detecting and sorting the paradoxes associated with smartphone use by Brazilian professionals. *Twenty-first Americas Conference on Information Systems*, 1–12. Retrieved from https://aisel.aisnet.org/cgi/viewcontent.cgi?article=1345&context=amcis2015

Bughin, J. (2008). The rise of enterprise 2.0. *Journal of Direct Data and Digital Marketing Practice, 9*(3), 251–259. doi:10.1057/palgrave.dddmp.4350100

Burger, A. K. (2007). M-commerce hot spots, Part 2: Scaling walled gardens. *E-Commerce Times, 5.*

Burke, P. (2006). *Contemporary social psychological theories.* Stanford, CA: Stanford Social Sciences.

Burke, P. J. (1980). The Self: Measurement Implications from a Symbolic Interactionist Perspective. *Social Psychology Quarterly, 43*, 18–29. doi:10.2307/3033745

Burke, P., & Stets, J. E. (2009). *Identity Theory*. Oxford, UK: Oxford University Press. doi:10.1093/acprof:oso/9780195388275.001.0001

Butler, B. (2001). Membership Size, Communication Activity, and Sustainability: A Resource-Based Model of Online Social Structures. *Information Systems Research*, *12*(4), 346–362. doi:10.1287/isre.12.4.346.9703

Buttle, F. (1998). Word of mouth: Understanding and managing referral marketing. *Journal of Strategic Marketing*, *6*(3), 241–254. doi:10.1080/096525498346658

Cai, S., & Jun, M. (2003). Internet users' perceptions of online service quality: A comparison of online buyers and information searchers. *Managing Service Quality*, *13*(6), 504–519. doi:10.1108/09604520310506568

Cai, S., & Xu, Y. (2011). Designing not just for pleasure: Effects of web site aesthetics on consumer shopping value. *International Journal of Electronic Commerce*, *15*(4), 159–188. doi:10.2753/JEC1086-4415150405

Calvosa, P. (2015). Cycles of convergence and dynamics of growth in the smartphone industry. *European Scientific Journal, 11*(19), 1–28. Retrieved from https://eujournal.org/index.php/esj/article/view/5925/5710

Campbell, C., & Marks, L. (2015). Good native advertising isn't a secret. *Business Horizons*, *58*(6), 599–606. doi:10.1016/j.bushor.2015.06.003

Campbell, C., Pitt, L., Parent, M., & Berthon, P. (2011). Understanding Consumer Conversations Around Ads in a Web 2.0 World. *Journal of Advertising*, *40*(1), 87–102. doi:10.2753/JOA0091-3367400106

Campo, K., Gijsbrechts, E., & Nisol, P. (2000). Towards understanding consumer Response to Stock outs. *Journal of Retailing*, *76*(2), 219–242. doi:10.1016/S0022-4359(00)00026-9

Cao, Y., Ajjan, H., & Hong, P. (2013). Using Social Media Applications for Educational Outcomes in College Teaching: A Structural Equation Analysis. *British Journal of Educational Technology*, *44*(4), 581–593. doi:10.1111/bjet.12066

Cardoso, P., & Pinto, S. (2010). Hedonic and utilitarian shopping motivations among Portuguese young adult consumers. *International Journal of Retail & Distribution Management*, *38*(1), 538–558. doi:10.1108/09590551011052124

Carlson, B., Suter, T., & Brown, T. (2008). Social versus psychological brand community: The role of psychological sense of brand community. *Journal of Business Research*, *61*(4), 284–291. doi:10.1016/j.jbusres.2007.06.022

Carlson, J., Rahman, M., Voola, R., & De Vries, N. (2018). Customer engagement behaviours in social media: Capturing innovation opportunities. *Journal of Services Marketing*, *32*(1), 83–94. doi:10.1108/JSM-02-2017-0059

Carmeli, A., & Schaubroeck, J. (2007). The influence of leaders' and other referents' normative expectations on individual involvement in creative work. *The Leadership Quarterly*, *18*(1), 35–48. doi:10.1016/j.leaqua.2006.11.001

Carr, C. (2007). The FAIRSERV model: Consumer reactions to services based on a multidimensional evaluation of service fairness. *Decision Sciences*, *38*(1), 107–130. doi:10.1111/j.1540-5915.2007.00150.x

Carr, C. T., Wohn, Y. D., & Hayes, R. A. (2016). As social support: Relational closeness, automaticity, and interpreting social support from paralinguistic digital affordances in social media. *Computers in Human Behavior*, *62*, 385–393. doi:10.1016/j.chb.2016.03.087

Carvão, S. (2010). Embracing user generated content within destination management organisations to gain a competitive insight into visitors' profiles. *Worldwide Hospitality and Tourism Themes*, *2*(4), 376–382. doi:10.1108/17554211011074038

Casado-Diaz, A. B., & Nicolau-Gonzalbez, J. L. (2009). Explaining consumer complaining behaviour in double deviation scenarios: The banking services. *Service Industries Journal*, *29*(12), 1659–1668. doi:10.1080/02642060902793524

Casalo, L., Flavián, C., & Guinalíu, M. (2007). The Influence of Satisfaction, Perceived Reputation and Trust on a Consumer's Commitment to a Website. *Journal of Marketing Communications*, *13*(1), 1–17. doi:10.1080/13527260600951633

Castells, M. (2011). A network theory of power. *International Journal of Communication*, *5*, 773–787.

Cecere, G., Corrocher, N., & Battaglia, R. D. (2015). Innovation and Competition in the Smartphone Industry: Is there a Dominant Design? *Journal of Telecommunications Policy*, (39) 162-175.

Certo, S., & Miller, T. (2008). Social entrepreneurship: Key issues and concepts. *Business Horizons*, *51*(4), 267–271. doi:10.1016/j.bushor.2008.02.009

Cha, M., Kwak, H., Rodriguez, P., Ahn, Y. & Moon, S. (2009). Analyzing the video popularity characteristics of large-scale user generated content systems. *IEEE/ACM Transactions on Networking, 17*(5), 1357-1370.

Chaffey, D. (2006). *Internet marketing: strategy, implementation and practice* (3rd ed.). Prentice Hall/Financial Times.

Chaffey, D., & Ellis-Chadwick, F. (2012). *Digital marketing: strategy, implementation and practice* (5th ed.). Harlow: Pearson Education Limited.

Chaffey, D., & Ellis-Chadwick, F. (2016). *Digital marketing* (6th ed.). Harlow: Pearson Education.

Chahal, H., & Devi, P. (2015). Consumer attitude towards service failure and recovery in higher education. *Quality Assurance in Education*, *23*(1), 67–85. doi:10.1108/QAE-07-2013-0029

Cha, J. (2009). Shopping on social networking web sites: Attitudes toward real versus virtual items. *Journal of Interactive Advertising*, *10*(1), 77–93. doi:10.1080/15252019.2009.10722164

Chakravarti, A., & Janiszewski, C. (2003). The Influence of Macro-Level Motives on Consideration Set Composition in Novel Purchase Situations. *The Journal of Consumer Research*, *30*(2), 244–258. doi:10.1086/376803

Chakravarty, A., Liu, Y., & Mazumdar, T. (2010). The Differential Effects of Online Word-of-Mouth and Critics' Reviews on Pre-release Movie Evaluation. *Journal of Interactive Marketing*, *24*(3), 185–197. doi:10.1016/j.intmar.2010.04.001

Chandrashekaran, M., Rotte, K., Tax, S. S., & Grewal, R. (2007). Satisfaction Strength and Customer Loyalty. *JMR, Journal of Marketing Research*, *44*(1), 153–163. doi:10.1509/jmkr.44.1.153

Chang, C. C. (2008). Factors influencing visual comfort appreciation of the product form of digital cameras. *International Journal of Industrial Ergonomics*, *38*(11), 1007–1016. doi:10.1016/j.ergon.2008.04.002

Chang, C.-C., Hung, S.-W., Cheng, M.-J., & Wu, C.-Y. (2015). Exploring the intention to continue using social networking sites: The case of Facebook. *Technological Forecasting and Social Change*, *95*, 48–56. doi:10.1016/j.techfore.2014.03.012

Chang, D. S., & Wang, T. H. (2012). Consumer preferences for service recovery options after delivery delay with shopping online. *Social Behaviour and Personality: An International Journal*, *40*(6), 1033–1044. doi:10.2224bp.2012.40.6.1033

Chang, E. (2001). *The mediating role of hedonic shopping value in apparel shopping satisfaction*. Oregon State University.

Chang, H. H., & Wang, I. C. (2008). An investigation of user communication behaviour in computer mediated environments. *Computers in Human Behavior*, *24*(5), 2336–2356. doi:10.1016/j.chb.2008.01.001

Chang, Y. P., & Zhu, D. H. (2011). Understanding social networking sites adoption in China: A comparison of pre-adoption and post-adoption. *Computers in Human Behavior*, *27*(5), 1840–1848. doi:10.1016/j.chb.2011.04.006

Chan, N. L., & Guillet, B. D. (2011). Investigation of Social Media Marketing: How Does the Hotel Industry in Hong Kong Perform in Marketing on Social Media Websites? *Journal of Travel & Tourism Marketing*, *28*(4), 345–368. doi:10.1080/10548408.2011.571571

Chan-Olmsted, S. M., Cho, M., & Lee, S. (2013). User Perceptions of Social Media: A comparative study of perceived characteristics and user Profiles by social media. *Journal of Communication and Media Technologies*, *3*(4).

Chan-Olmsted, S. M., Cho, M., & Lee, S. (2013). User perceptions of social media: A comparative study of perceived characteristics and user profiles by social media. *Online Journal of Communication and Media Technologies*, *3*(4), 149–178.

Chan, Y. Y. Y., & Ngai, E. W. T. (2011). Conceptualising electronic word of mouth activity: An input-process-output perspective. *Marketing Intelligence & Planning*, *29*(5), 488–516. doi:10.1108/02634501111153692

Chaplin, L. N., & Roedder, D. J. (2005). The Development of Self-Brand Connections in Children and Adolescents. *The Journal of Consumer Research*, *32*(1), 119–129. doi:10.1086/426622

Chappuis, B., Gaffey, B., & Parvizi, P. (2011). *Are your customers becoming digital junkies?* Retrieved from https://www.mckinsey.com/business-functions/marketing-and-sales/our-insights/are-your-customers-becoming-digital-junkies

Chari, S., Christodoulides, G., Presi, C., Wenhold, J., & Casaletto, J. P. (2016). Consumer Trust in User-Generated Brand Recommendations on Facebook. *Psychology and Marketing*, *33*(12), 1071–1081. doi:10.1002/mar.20941

Charlesworth, A. (2014). *Digital marketing: a practical approach* (2nd ed.). London: Routledge. doi:10.4324/9780203493717

Chathoth, P. K., Ungson, G. R., Harrington, R. J., & Chan, E. S. W. (2014). Barriers affecting organisational adoption of higher order customer engagement in tourism service interactions. *Tourism Management*, *42*(3), 181–193. doi:10.1016/j.tourman.2013.12.002

Chatterjee, P. (2010). Multiple-channel and cross-channel shopping behavior: Role of consumer shopping orientations. *Marketing Intelligence & Planning*, *28*(1), 9–24. doi:10.1108/02634501011014589

Chaudhuri, A., & Holbrook, M. (2001). The Chain of Effects from Brand Trust and Brand Affect to Brand Performance: The Role of Brand Loyalty. *Journal of Marketing*, *65*(2), 81–93. doi:10.1509/jmkg.65.2.81.18255

Chauhan, K., & Pillai, A. (2013). Role of content strategy in social media brand communities: A case of higher education institutes in India. *Journal of Product and Brand Management*, *22*(1), 40–51. doi:10.1108/10610421311298687

Chau, M., & Xu, J. (2012). Business intelligence in Blogs: Understanding consumer interactions and communities. *Management Information Systems Quarterly*, *36*(4), 1189–1216. doi:10.2307/41703504

Cheng-Hsui Chen, A. (2001). Using free association to examine the relationship between the characteristics of brand associations and brand equity. *Journal of Product and Brand Management*, *10*(7), 439–451. doi:10.1108/10610420110410559

Cheng, Y. H., Chang, C. J., Chuang, S. C., & Liao, Y. W. (2015). Guilt no longer a sin: The effect of guilt in the service recovery paradox. *Journal of Service Theory and Practice*, *25*(6), 836–853. doi:10.1108/JSTP-12-2013-0296

Chen, H., & Huang, C. (2013). An Investigation into Online Reviewers' Behaviour. *European Journal of Marketing*, *47*(10), 1758–1773. doi:10.1108/EJM-11-2011-0625

Chen, J. V., & Park, Y. (2007). Acceptance and adoption of the innovative use of smartphone. *Industrial Management & Data Systems*, *107*(9), 1349–1365. doi:10.1108/02635570710834009

Chen, J. V., Yen, D. C., & Chen, K. (2009). The acceptance and diffusion of the innovative smart phone use: A case study of a delivery service company in logistics. *Information & Management*, *46*(4), 241–248. doi:10.1016/j.im.2009.03.001

Chen, T., Ma, K., Bian, X., Zheng, C., & Devlin, J. (2018). Is high recovery more effective than expected recovery in addressing service failure? – A moral judgment perspective. *Journal of Business Research*, *82*, 1–9. doi:10.1016/j.jbusres.2017.08.025

Chen, X., Li, M., & Fang, Q. (2009). Factors influencing consumption experience of mobile device: A study from experiential view. *Proceedings of the International Conference on Electronic Business (ICEB)*, 701–710.

Chen, Y., & Xie, J. (2008). Online consumer review: Word-of-mouth as a new element of marketing communication mix. *Management Science*, *54*(3), 477–491. doi:10.1287/mnsc.1070.0810

Chen, Z., & Lurie, N. H. (2013). Temporal contiguity and negativity bias in the impact of online word of mouth. *JMR, Journal of Marketing Research*, *50*(4), 463–476. doi:10.1509/jmr.12.0063

Chern, C., Wei, C., Shen, F., & Fan, Y. (2015). A sales forecasting model for consumer products based on the influence of online word-of-mouth. *Information Systems and e-Business Management*, *13*(3), 445–473. doi:10.100710257-014-0265-0

Cheung, C. M. K., & Thadani, D. R. (2010). The state of electronic word-of-mouth research: A literature analysis. In *Proceedings of Pacific Asia Conference on Information Systems.* Taipei, Taiwan: AIS Electronic Library (AISeL).

Cheung, C. M. K., & Thadani, D. R. (2012). The impact of electronic word-of-mouth communication: A literature analysis and integrative model. *Decision Support System, 54*(1), 461-470. doi:org/. doi:10.1010/j.dss.2012.06.008

Cheung, C. M., Chiu, P. Y., & Lee, M. K. (2011). Online social networks: Why do students use facebook? *Computers in Human Behavior*, *27*(4), 1337–1343. doi:10.1016/j.chb.2010.07.028

Cheung, C. M., & Lee, M. K. (2009). Understanding the sustainability of a virtual community: Model development and empirical test. *Journal of Information Science*, *35*(3), 279–298. doi:10.1177/0165551508099088

Cheung, C. M., & Lee, M. K. (2010). A theoretical model of intentional social action in online social networks. *Decision Support Systems*, *49*(1), 24–30. doi:10.1016/j.dss.2009.12.006

Cheung, C., & Thadani, D. (2012). The impact of electronic word-of-mouth communication: A literature analysis and integrative model. *Decision Support Systems*, *54*(1), 461–470. doi:10.1016/j.dss.2012.06.008

Cheung, F. Y. M., & To, W. M. (2016). A customer-dominant logic on service recovery and customer satisfaction. *Management Decision*, *54*(10), 2524–2543. doi:10.1108/MD-03-2016-0165

Chevalier, J., & Mayzlin, D. (2006). The Effect of Word of Mouth on Sales: Online Book Reviews. *JMR, Journal of Marketing Research*, *43*(3), 345–354. doi:10.1509/jmkr.43.3.345

Chiang, W. K., Zhang, D., & Zhou, L. (2006). Predicting and explaining patronage behavior toward web and traditional stores using neural networks: A comparative analysis with logistic regression. *Decision Support Systems*, *41*(2), 514–531. doi:10.1016/j.dss.2004.08.016

Chi, H. H. (2011). Interactive digital advertising vs. virtual brand community: Exploratory study of user motivation and social media marketing responses in Taiwan. *Journal of Interactive Advertising*, *12*(1), 44–61. doi:10.1080/15252019.2011.10722190

Chih, W., & Lin, Y. 2010. The study of the effects and consequences of perceived website attitude. *Proceedings of the 12th International Conference on Electronic Commerce*, 18–20.

Childers, T., & Rao, A. (1992). The Influence of Familial and Peer-Based Reference Groups on Consumer Decisions. *The Journal of Consumer Research*, *19*(2), 198–211. doi:10.1086/209296

Chiu, C., Hsu, M., & Wang, E. (2006). Understanding knowledge sharing in virtual communities: An integration of social capital and social cognitive theories. *Decision Support Systems*, *42*(3), 1872–1888. doi:10.1016/j.dss.2006.04.001

Chiu, C., Huang, H., & Yen, C. (2010). Antecedents of trust in online auctions. *Electronic Commerce Research and Applications*, *9*(2), 148–159. doi:10.1016/j.elerap.2009.04.003

Chiu, C.-M., Wang, E. T. G., Fang, Y.-H., & Huang, H.-Y. (2014). Understanding customers' repeat purchase intentions in B2C e-commerce: The roles of utilitarian value, hedonic value and perceived risk. *Information Systems Journal*, *24*(1), 85–114. doi:10.1111/j.1365-2575.2012.00407.x

Cho, C. H. (2003). The effectiveness of banner advertisements: Involvement and click-through. *Journalism & Mass Communication Quarterly*, *80*(3), 623–645. doi:10.1177/107769900308000309

Choi, S., & Yoo, J. (2015). Roles of user resistance and social influence in continued use of smartphone. In *International Conference on Advanced Communication Technology, ICACT* (pp. 287–291). Academic Press. 10.1109/ICACT.2015.7224805

Choi, B., & Choi, B. J. (2014). The effects of perceived service recovery justice on customer affection, loyalty, and word-of-mouth. *European Journal of Marketing*, *48*(1/2), 108–131. doi:10.1108/EJM-06-2011-0299

Choi, S., & Mattila, A. S. (2008). Perceived controllability and service expectations: Influences on customer reactions following service failure. *Journal of Business Research*, *61*(1), 24–30. doi:10.1016/j.jbusres.2006.05.006

Choi, S., & Rifon, N. (2012). It Is a Match: The Impact of Congruence between Celebrity Image and Consumer Ideal Self on Endorsement Effectiveness. *Psychology and Marketing*, *29*(9), 639–650. doi:10.1002/mar.20550

Chong, A. Y. L., Lacka, E., Boying, L., & Chan, H. K. (2018). The role of social media in enhancing guanxi and perceived effectiveness of E-commerce institutional mechanisms in online marketplace. *Information & Management*, *55*(5), 621–632. doi:10.1016/j.im.2018.01.003

Cho, S., & Workman, J. (2011). Gender, fashion innovativeness and opinion leadership, and need for touch: Effects on multi-channel choice and touch/non-touch preference in clothing shopping. *Journal of Fashion Marketing and Management: An International Journal*, *15*(3), 363–382. doi:10.1108/13612021111151941

Chou, F. S., & Lai, M. C. (2015). The Relationships among Involvement Level, Service Failure, Service Recovery Disconfirmation and Customer Lifetime Value. *Journal of Economics. Business and Management*, *3*(4), 452–456.

Chow, T. C.-L., & Ma, W. W. K. (2017). Do we really know what people are using their smartphone for? *2017 International Symposium on Educational Technology (ISET)*, 34–38. 10.1109/ISET.2017.16

Chow, W. S., & Shi, S. (2015). Investigating Customers' Satisfaction With Brand Pages In Social Networking Sites. *Journal of Computer Information Systems*, *55*(2), 48–58. doi:10.1080/08874417.2015.11645756

Christensen, C. M. (2013). *The Innovators Dilema: When New Technologies Cause Great Firms to Fail*. Boston: Harvard Business School Press.

Christodoulides, G., Jevons, C., & Bonhomme, J. (2012). Memo to marketers: Quantitative evidence for change. How user-generated content really affects brands. *Journal of Advertising Research*, *52*(1), 53–64. doi:10.2501/JAR-52-1-053-064

Christopher, M., Lowson, R., & Peck, H. (2004). Creating agile supply chains in the fashion industry. *International Journal of Retail & Distribution Management*, *32*(8), 367–376. doi:10.1108/09590550410546188

Chuang, S. C., Cheng, Y. H., Chang, C. J., & Yang, S. W. (2012). The effect of service failure types and service recovery on customer satisfaction: A mental accounting perspective. *Service Industries Journal*, *32*(2), 257–271. doi:10.1080/02642069.2010.529435

Chung, N., Han, H., & Koo, C. (2015). Adoption of travel information in user-generated content on social media: The moderating effect of social presence. *Behaviour & Information Technology*, *34*(9), 902–919. doi:10.1080/0144929X.2015.1039060

Chung, Y.-S. (2015). Hedonic and utilitarian shopping values in airport shopping behavior. *Journal of Air Transport Management*, *49*, 28–34. doi:10.1016/j.jairtraman.2015.07.003

Chu, S., & Kim, Y. (2011). Determinants of consumer engagement in electronic word-of-mouth (eWOM) in social networking sites. *International Journal of Advertising*, *30*(1), 47–75. doi:10.2501/IJA-30-1-047-075

Clark, M., Black, H. G., & Judson, K. (2017). Brand community integration and satisfaction with social media sites: A comparative study. *Journal of Research in Interactive Marketing*, *11*(1), 39–55. doi:10.1108/JRIM-07-2015-0047

Clement, R., & Krueger, J. (2002). Social Categorization Moderates Social Projection. *Journal of Experimental Social Psychology*, *38*(3), 219–231. doi:10.1006/jesp.2001.1503

Cohen, J. B., & Golden, E. (1972). Informational Social Influence and Product Evaluation. *The Journal of Applied Psychology*, *56*(1), 54–59. doi:10.1037/h0032139

Colleoni, E. (2013). CSR communication strategies for organizational legitimacy in social media. *Corporate Communications*, *18*(2), 228–248. doi:10.1108/13563281311319508

Colliander, J., & Dahlén, M. (2011). Following the Fashionable Friend: The Power of Social Media. *Journal of Advertising Research*, *51*(1), 313–320. doi:10.2501/JAR-51-1-313-320

Collier, J. E., Breazeale, M., & White, A. (2017). Giving back the "self" in self service: Customer preferences in self-service failure recovery. *Journal of Services Marketing*, *31*(6), 604–617. doi:10.1108/JSM-07-2016-0259

Collier, J., & Bienstock, C. (2006). Measuring service quality in e-retailing. *Journal of Service Research*, *8*(3), 260–275. doi:10.1177/1094670505278867

Collin, A., & Young, R. A. (2004). Introduction: Constructivism and social constructionism in the career field. *Journal of Vocational Behavior*, *64*(3), 373–388. doi:10.1016/j.jvb.2003.12.005

Collin, P., Rahilly, K., Richardson, I., & Third, A. (2011). *The Benefits of Social Networking Services. Research Report.* Melbourne: Cooperative Research Centre for Young People.

Constantinides, E., & Fountain, S. (2008). Web 2.0: Conceptual foundations and marketing issues. *Journal of Direct. Data and Digital Marketing Practice*, *9*(3), 231–244. doi:10.1057/palgrave.dddmp.4350098

Copeland, M. T. (1923). Relation of Consumer's Buying Habits to Marketing Methods. *Harvard Business Review*, *1*, 282–289.

Cornwell, T., Roy, D., & Steinard, E. II. (2001). Exploring Managers' Perceptions of the Impact of Sponsorship on Brand Equity. *Journal of Advertising*, *30*(2), 41–51. doi:10.1080/00913367.2001.10673636

Cornwell, T., Weeks, C., & Roy, D. (2005). Sponsorship-linked Marketing: Opening the Black Box. *Journal of Advertising*, *34*(2), 21–42. doi:10.1080/00913367.2005.10639194

Corvi, E., & Bonera, M. (2010, October). The effectiveness of advertising: a literature review. *Xth Global Conference on Business and Economics*, 3-6.

Cothrel, J. P., & Williams, R. L. (1999). On-Line Communities: Helping Them Form and Grow. *Journal of Knowledge Management*, *3*(1), 54–60. doi:10.1108/13673279910259394

Cottet, P., Lichtlé, M. C., & Plichon, V. (2006). The role of value in services: A study in a retail environment. *Journal of Consumer Marketing*, *23*(4), 219–227. doi:10.1108/07363760610674347

Coursaris, O. W.V., & Constantinos, K. (2013). Organizational Social Media: A Comprehensive Framework and Research Agenda. In *46 Hawaii International Conference on system Sciences*. Michigan State University.

Cova, B. (1997). Community and consumption. *European Journal of Marketing*, *31*(3/4), 297–316. doi:10.1108/03090569710162380

Cova, B., & Cova, V. (2001). Tribal aspects of postmodern consumption research: The case of French in-line roller skaters. *Journal of Consumer Behaviour*, *1*(1), 67–76. doi:10.1002/cb.54

Cova, B., & Cova, V. (2002). Tribal Marketing: The tribalisation of society and its impact on the conduct of marketing. *European Journal of Marketing*, *36*(5/6), 595–620. doi:10.1108/03090560210423023

Cova, B., & Dalli, D. (2009). Working consumers: The next step in marketing theory? *Marketing Theory*, *9*(3), 315–339. doi:10.1177/1470593109338144

Cova, B., & Pace, S. (2006). Brand community of convenience products: New forms of customer empowerment – the case "my Nutella The Community". *European Journal of Marketing*, *40*(9/10), 1087–1105. doi:10.1108/03090560610681023

Cowley, E., & Barron, C. (2008). When Product Placement Goes Wrong: The Effects of Program Liking and Placement Prominence. *Journal of Advertising*, *37*(1), 89–98. doi:10.2753/JOA0091-3367370107

Cox, A.D., Cox, D., & Anderson, R.D. (2005). Reassessing the pleasures of store shopping. *Journal of Business Research, 58*(3), 250–259.

Cox, C., Burgess, S., Sellitto, C., & Buultjens, J. (2008). *Consumer-Generated Web-based Tourism Marketing*. Queensland, Australia: Sustainable Tourism Cooperative Research Centre.

Cox, J., & Dale, B. G. (2001). Service quality and e-commerce: An explanatory analysis. *Managing Service Quality*, *11*(2), 121–131. doi:10.1108/09604520110387257

Coyle, J. R., & Thorson, E. (2001). The effects of progressive levels of interactivity and vividness in web marketing sites. *Journal of Advertising*, *30*(3), 65–77. doi:10.1080/00913367.2001.10673646

Craighead, C. W., Karwan, K. R., & Miller, J. L. (2004). The effects of severity of failure and customer loyalty on service recovery strategies. *Production and Operations Management*, *13*(4), 307–321. doi:10.1111/j.1937-5956.2004.tb00220.x

Crisafulli, B., & Singh, J. (2017). Service failures in e-retailing: Examining the effects of response time, compensation, and service criticality. *Computers in Human Behavior*, *77*, 413–424. doi:10.1016/j.chb.2017.07.013

Cristobal, E., Flavian, C., & Guinaliu, M. (2007). Perceived e-service quality: Measurement validity and effects on consumer satisfaction and web site loyalty. *Managing Service Quality*, *17*(3), 317–340. doi:10.1108/09604520710744326

Cronin, J. Jr, Brady, M., & Hult, G. (2000). Assessing the effects of quality, value, and customer satisfaction on consumer behavioral intentions in service environments. *Journal of Retailing*, *76*(2), 193–218. doi:10.1016/S0022-4359(00)00028-2

Cronin, J., & Taylor, S. (1992). Measuring service quality: A reexamination and extension. *Journal of Marketing*, *56*(3), 55–68. doi:10.2307/1252296

Cunliffe, A. L. (2008). Orientations to Social Constructionism: Relationally Responsive Social Constructionism and its Implications for Knowledge and Learning. *SAGE Journals*, *39*(2), 123–136.

Curran, J., & Lennon, R. (2011). Participating in the conversation: Exploring adoption of online social media. *Academy of Marketing Studies Journal*, *15*(1), 21–38.

Curran, K., Graham, S., & Temple, C. (2011). Advertising on Facebook. *International Journal of E-Business Development, 1*, 26–33.

Da Silva, R., & Alwi, S. (2008). Online brand attributes and online corporate brand images. *European Journal of Marketing, 42*(9/10), 1039–1058. doi:10.1108/03090560810891136

Da Silveira, C., Lages, C., & Simões, C. (2013). Reconceptualizing brand identity in a dynamic environment. *Journal of Business Research, 66*(1), 28–36. doi:10.1016/j.jbusres.2011.07.020

Dabholkar, P., Thorpe, D., & Rentz, J. (1996). A measure of service quality for retail stores: Scale development and validation. *Journal of the Academy of Marketing Science, 24*(1), 3–16. doi:10.1007/BF02893933

Dacin, M., Dacin, P., & Tracey, P. (2011). Social Entrepreneurship: A Critique and Future Directions. *Organization Science, 22*(5), 1203–1213. doi:10.1287/orsc.1100.0620

Dahnil, M. I., Marzuki, K. M., Langgat, J., & Fabeil, N. F. (2014). Factors Influencing SMEs Adoption of Social Media Marketing. *Procedia: Social and Behavioral Sciences, 148*, 119–126. doi:10.1016/j.sbspro.2014.07.025

Dang, Y., Zhang, Y., Hu, P. J.-H., Brown, S. A., Ku, Y., Wang, J.-H., & Chen, H. (2014). An integrated framework for analysing multilingual content in Web 2.0 social media. *Decision Support Systems, 61*, 126–135. doi:10.1016/j.dss.2014.02.004

Dann, S., & Dann, S. (2011). *E-marketing: theory and application*. Basingstoke, UK: Palgrave Macmillan. doi:10.1007/978-0-230-36473-8

Daugherty, T., Eastin, M., & Bright, L. (2008). Exploring Consumer Motivations for Creating User-Generated Content. *Journal of Interactive Advertising, 8*(2), 16–25. doi:10.1080/15252019.2008.10722139

Daugherty, T., & Hoffman, E. (2014). eWOM and the importance of capturing consumer attention within social media. *Journal of Marketing Communications, 20*(1-2), 82–102. doi:10.1080/13527266.2013.797764

Davis, F. D. (1989). Perceived usefulness, perceived ease of use, and user acceptance of information technology. *Management Information Systems Quarterly, 13*(3), 319–339. doi:10.2307/249008

Davis, K. (2015). *Offerpop sifts gold from user-generated content: platform aggregates rich social data with an emphasis on visuals for the entire customer journey*. Haymarket Media, Inc.

Davis, L. (2013). Exploring Chinese consumers' shopping value across retail outlets. *International Journal of China Marketing, 14*(1), 51–64.

De Bruyn, A., & Lilien, G. L. (2008). A multi-stage model of word-of-mouth influence through viral marketing. *International Journal of Research in Marketing, 25*(3), 151–163. doi:10.1016/j.ijresmar.2008.03.004

De Canio, F., Pellegrini, D., & Aramendia-muneta, M. E. (2016). The smartphoners: Consumer segmentation by smartphone usage. *Mercati e Competitivita, 1*(1), 125–146.

de Ruyter, K., Moorman, L., & Lemmink, J. (2001). Antecedents of Commitment and Trust in Customer–Supplier Relationships in High Technology Markets. *Industrial Marketing Management, 30*(3), 271–286. doi:10.1016/S0019-8501(99)00091-7

de Valck, K., van Bruggen, G., & Wierenga, B. (2009). Virtual communities: A marketing perspective. *Decision Support Systems, 47*(3), 185–203. doi:10.1016/j.dss.2009.02.008

De Veirman, M., Cauberghe, V., & Hudders, L. (2017). Marketing through Instagram influencers: The impact of number of followers and product divergence on brand attitude. *International Journal of Advertising*, *36*(5), 798–828. doi:10.1080/02650487.2017.1348035

De Vries, L., Gensler, S., & Leeflang, P. S. (2012). Popularity of brand posts on brand fan pages: An investigation of the effects of social media marketing. *Journal of Interactive Marketing*, *26*(2), 83–91. doi:10.1016/j.intmar.2012.01.003

Dees, J. G. (1998). *The meaning of social entrepreneurship*. Comments and suggestions contributed from the Social Entrepreneurship Funders Working Group.

Dees, J. G., & Anderson, B. B. (2003). For-Profit Social Ventures. *International Journal of Entrepreneurship Education*, *2*, 1–26.

Dehghani, M., & Tumer, M. (2015). A research on effectiveness of Facebook advertising on enhancing purchase intention of consumers. *Computers in Human Behavior*, *49*, 597–600. doi:10.1016/j.chb.2015.03.051

Della Corte, V., Iavazzi, A., & D'Andrea, C. (2015). Customer involvement through social media: The cases of some telecommunication firms. *Journal of Open Innovation: Technology, Market, and Complexity*, *1*(1), 10. doi:10.118640852-015-0011-y

Dellarocas, C. (2006). Strategic Manipulation of Internet Opinion Forums: Implications for Consumers and Firms. *Management Science*, *52*(10), 1577–1593. doi:10.1287/mnsc.1060.0567

Dellarocas, C. (2010). Online reputation systems: How to design one that does what you need. *Sloan Management Review*, *51*(3), 33–38.

Dellarocas, C., Zhang, X., & Awad, N. (2007). Exploring the value of online product reviews in forecasting sales: The case of motion pictures. *Journal of Interactive Marketing*, *21*(4), 23–45. doi:10.1002/dir.20087

Deloitte. (2015). *Facebook's global economic impact: A report for Facebook*. Retrieved from www2.deloitte.com/content/dam/Deloitte/uk/Documents/technology-media-telecommunications/deloitte-uk-global-economic-impact-of-facebook.pdf

Deloitte. (2016). *Global Fashion & Luxury Market. Private Equity and Investors Survey 2016*. Author.

Deloitte. (2017). State of the smart consumer and business usage patterns. Global Mobile Consumer Survey 2017. Retrieved from https://www.deloitte.co.uk/mobileuk/assets/img/download/global-mobile-consumer-survey-2017_uk-cut.pdf#page=16

Deloitte. (2017). *The 2017 Deloitte Millennial Survey*. Deloitte. Retrieved from https://www2.deloitte.com/content/dam/Deloitte/global/Documents/About-Deloitte/gx-deloitte-millennial-survey-2017-executive-summary.pdf

DeLone, W. H., & McLean, E. R. (2004). Measuring e-Commerce Success: Applying the DeLone & McLean Information Systems Success Model. *International Journal of Electronic Commerce*, *9*(1), 31-47.

DeLone, W. H., & McLean, E. R. (2003). The DeLone and McLean model of information systems success : A ten-year update. *Journal of Management Information Systems*, *19*(4), 9–30. doi:10.1080/07421222.2003.11045748

Dempster, C., & Lee, J. (2015). *The Rise of the Platform Marketer: Performance Marketing with Google, Facebook, and Twitter, Plus the Latest High-Growth Digital Advertising Platforms*. John Wiley & Sons Inc. doi:10.1002/9781119153863

Deng, X., Joshi, K., & Li, Y. (2015). Introduction to the Social Media and Enterprise Minitrack: Job and Work Design Issues. In *System Sciences (HICSS), 2015 48th Hawaii International Conference on* (pp. 1818–1818). IEEE.

Dessart, L., Veloutsou, C., & Thomas, A. (2015). Consumer engagement in online brand communities: A social media perspective. *Journal of Product and Brand Management*, *24*(1), 28–42. doi:10.1108/JPBM-06-2014-0635

Dess, G. D., Lumpkin, G. T., & McGee, J. E. (1999). Linking Corporate Entrepreneurship to Strategy, Structure, and Process: Suggested Research Directions. *Entrepreneurship Theory and Practice*, *23*(3), 85–102. doi:10.1177/104225879902300306

Dewing, M. (2010). *Social Media: An Introduction*. Ottawa: Library of Parliament.

Dhar, V., & Chang, E. (2009). Does Chatter Matter? The Impact of User-Generated Content on Music Sales. *Journal of Interactive Marketing*, *23*(4), 300–307. doi:10.1016/j.intmar.2009.07.004

Dholakia, U. M., Bagozzi, R. P., & Pearo, L. K. (2004). A social influence model of consumer participation in network-and small-group-based virtual communities. *International Journal of Research in Marketing*, *21*(3), 241–263. doi:10.1016/j.ijresmar.2003.12.004

Dholakia, U. M., Kahn, B. E., Reeves, R., Rindfleisch, A., Stewart, D., & Taylor, E. (2010). Consumer behavior in a multichannel, multimedia retailing environment. *Journal of Interactive Marketing*, *24*(2), 86–95. doi:10.1016/j.intmar.2010.02.005

Di Gangi, M., & Wasko, M. (2009). The Co-Creation of Value: Exploring User Engagement in User-Generated Content Websites. *Pre-ICIS 8th Annual JAIS Theory Development Workshop.*

Di Gangi, P. M., & Wasko, M. (2009). Open innovation through online communities. In Knowledge management and organizational learning. Springer. doi:10.1007/978-1-4419-0011-1_13

Dickinson, J. E., Ghali, K., Cherrett, T., Speed, C., Davies, N., & Norgate, S. (2014). Tourism and the smartphone app: Capabilities, emerging practice and scope in the travel domain. *Current Issues in Tourism*, *17*(1), 84–101. doi:10.1080/13683500.2012.718323

Diffley, S., McCole, P., & Carvajal-Trujillo, E. (2018). Examining social customer relationship management among Irish hotels. *International Journal of Contemporary Hospitality Management*, *30*(2), 1072–1091. doi:10.1108/IJCHM-08-2016-0415

Dijkmans, C., Kerkhif, P., Buyukcan-Tetic, A., & Beukeboom, C. J. (2015). Online Conversation and Corporate Reputation: A Two-Wave Longitudinal Study on the Effects of Exposure to the Social Media Activities of a Highly Interactive Company. *Journal of Computer-Mediated Communication*, *20*(6), 632–648. doi:10.1111/jcc4.12132

Dimitriades, Z. S. (2006). Customer Satisfaction, Loyalty and commitment in service organisations: Some evidence from Greece. *Management Research News*, *29*(12), 782–800. doi:10.1108/01409170610717817

Dimitriadis, S., & Papista, E. (2011). Linking Consumer-Brand Identification to Relationship Quality. An Integrated Framework. *Journal of Consumer Behaviour*, *10*(3), 271–289. doi:10.1362/147539211X602513

Ding, M. C., Ho, C. W., & Lii, Y. S. (2015). Is corporate reputation a double-edged sword? Relative effects of perceived justice in airline service recovery. *International Journal of E-Business Research*, *10*(1), 1–17.

Ding, M. C., & Lii, Y. S. (2016). Handling online service recovery: Effects of perceived justice on online games. *Telematics and Informatics*, *33*(4), 881–895. doi:10.1016/j.tele.2016.02.001

Dinnie, K. (2007). *Nation branding: concepts, issues, practice, Butterworth Heinemann Digital Country Index, 2017.* Bloom Consulting. Retrieved from https://www.digitalcountryindex.com/country-index-results

Dobele, A., Lindgreen, A., Beverland, M., Vanhamme, J., & van Wijk, R. (2007). Why pass on viral messages? Because they connect emotionally. *Business Horizons*, *50*(4), 291–304. doi:10.1016/j.bushor.2007.01.004

Dodson, I. (2016). *The Art of Digital Marketing: The Definitive Guide to Creating Strategic, Targeted, and Measurable Online Campaigns* (1st ed.). Hoboken, NJ: John Wiley & Sons Inc.

Dodson, I. (2016). *The digital marketing playbook*. Wiley-Blackwell.

Doherty, A. M. (2000). Factors influencing international retailers" market entry mode strategy: Qualitative evidence from the UK fashion sector. *Journal of Marketing Management*, *16*(1-3), 223–245. doi:10.1362/026725700785100514

Dolan, R., & Goodman, S. (2017). Succeeding on social media Exploring communication strategies for wine marketing. *Journal of Hospitality and Tourism Management*, *33*, 23–30. doi:10.1016/j.jhtm.2017.09.001

Donath, J. (1999). Identity and Deception in the Virtual Community. In P. Kollack & M. Smith (Eds.), *Communities in Cyberspace* (pp. 27–58). New York: Routledge.

Donavan, D. T., Janda, S., & Suh, J. (2006). Environmental Influences in Corporate Brand Identification and Outcomes. *Journal of Brand Management*, *14*(1/2), 125–136. doi:10.1057/palgrave.bm.2550057

Dong, B., Evans, K. R., & Zou, S. (2008). The effects of customer participation in co-created service recovery. *Journal of the Academy of Marketing Science*, *36*(1), 123–137. doi:10.100711747-007-0059-8

Doyle, C. (2011). *Brand management*. A Dictionary of Marketing.

Doyle, S. A., Moore, C. M., & Morgan, L. (2006). Supplier management in fast moving fashion retailing. *Journal of Fashion Marketing and Management: An International Journal*, *10*(3), 272–281. doi:10.1108/13612020610679268

Drummond, C., McGrath, H., & O'Toole, T. (2017). The impact of social media on resource mobilisation in entrepreneurial firms. *Industrial Marketing Management*.

Du Plessis, C. (2017). The role of content marketing in social media content communities. *South African Journal of Information Management*, *19*(1), e1–e7. doi:10.4102ajim.v19i1.866

Duan, W., Gu, B., & Whinston, A. B. (2008). The dynamics of online word-of-mouth and product sales—An empirical investigation of the movie industry. *Journal of Retailing*, *84*(2), 233–242. doi:10.1016/j.jretai.2008.04.005

Duff, B., & Faber, R. (2011). Missing the Mark. *Journal of Advertising*, *40*(2), 51–62. doi:10.2753/JOA0091-3367400204

Duffy, J. A. M., Miller, J. M., & Bexley, J. B. (2006). Banking customers' varied reactions to service recovery strategies. *International Journal of Bank Marketing*, *24*(2), 112–132. doi:10.1108/02652320610649923

Duggan, M., Ellison, N., Lampe, C., Lenhart, A., & Madden, M. (2015). Demographics of Key Social Networking Platforms. *PewResearch Center*. Retrieved from http://www.pewinternet.org/2015/01/09/demographics-of-key-social-networking-platforms-2/

Dunne, Á., Lawlor, M. A., & Rowley, J. (2010). Young people's use of online social networking sites–a uses and gratifications perspective. *Journal of Research in Interactive Marketing*, *4*(1), 46–58. doi:10.1108/17505931011033551

Durkin, M., McGowan, P., & McKeown, N. (2013). Exploring social media adoption in small to medium-sized enterprises in Ireland. *Journal of Small Business and Enterprise Development*, *20*(4), 716–734. doi:10.1108/JSBED-08-2012-0094

Du, S., Bhattacharya, C. B., & Sen, S. (2007). Reaping Relational Rewards from Corporate Social Responsibility: The Role of Competitive Positioning. *International Journal of Research in Marketing*, *24*(3), 224–241. doi:10.1016/j.ijresmar.2007.01.001

Dutot, V., & Bergeron, F. (2016). From strategic orientation to social media orientation: Improving SMEs' performance on social media. *Journal of Small Business and Enterprise Development*, *23*(4), 1165–1190. doi:10.1108/JSBED-11-2015-0160

Dutta, S. (2010, November). What's Your Personal Social Media Strategy? *Harvard Business Review*, 1–5. PMID:21049685

Dwivedi, A. (2015). A higher-order model of consumer brand engagement and its impact on loyalty intentions. *Journal of Retailing and Consumer Services*, *24*, 100–109. doi:10.1016/j.jretconser.2015.02.007

Dwivedi, Y. K., Kapoor, K. K., & Chen, H. (2015). Social media marketing and advertising. *The Marketing Review*, *15*(3), 289–309. doi:10.1362/146934715X14441363377999

Eastman, J., Iyer, R., & Thomas, S. (2013). The Impact of Status Consumption on Shopping Style: An Exploratory Look at the Millennial Generation. *The Marketing Management Journal*, *23*(1), 57–73.

Eastman, J., & Liu, J. (2012). The impact of generational cohorts on status consumption: An exploratory look at generational cohort and demographics on status consumption. *Journal of Consumer Marketing*, *29*(2), 93–102. doi:10.1108/07363761211206348

Economic Times. (2016). *Zara Key Statistics: A detailed report on how Zara is using social media*. Retrieved from http://retail.economictimes.indiatimes.com/social-analytics/Fashion/Zara/494

Edelman, D. (2010). Branding in the digital age: You're spending your money in all the wrong places. *Harvard Business Review*, (88), 62–69.

Ekinci, Y., Sirakaya-Turk, E., & Preciado, S. (2011). Symbolic consumption of tourism destination brands. *Journal of Business Research*, *66*(6), 711–718. doi:10.1016/j.jbusres.2011.09.008

Elliott, R., & Wattanasuwan, K. (1998). Brands as Symbolic Resources for the Construction of Identity. *International Journal of Advertising*, *17*(2), 131–144. doi:10.1080/02650487.1998.11104712

Ellis-Chadwick, F., & Chaffey, D. (2012). *Digital Marketing: Strategy, Implementation and Practice* (5th ed.). London: Pearson Education Ltd.

eMarketer. (2016). *Internet users rely on reviews when deciding which products to purchase*. Available at: www.emarketer.com/Article/Internet-Users-Rely-on-Reviews-Deciding-Which-Products-Purchase/1014465

EMarketer. (2016). *US Digital Video ad Spending will Continue to Grow at a Pace that Exceeds TV Advertising Growth Through 2020*. Retrieved from https://www.emarketer.com/Article/Digital-Video-Advertising-Grow-Annual-Double-Digit-Rates/1014105

Emrich, O. (2011). *Cross Channel Management- Kompetenzen, Instrumente und Erfolgspotenziale* (Dissertation). University St. Gallen, St. Gallen.

Emrich, O., Paul, M., & Rudolph, T. (2015). Shopping benefits of multichannel assortment integration and the moderating role of retailer type. *Journal of Retailing*, *91*(2), 326–342. doi:10.1016/j.jretai.2014.12.003

Emrich, O., & Verhoef, C. P. (2015). The impact of a homogenous versus a prototypical web design on online retail patronage for multichannel providers. *International Journal of Research in Marketing*, *32*(4), 363–374. doi:10.1016/j.ijresmar.2015.04.002

Enders, A., Hungenberg, H., Denker, H., & Mauch, S. (2008). The long tail of social networking. *European Management Journal*, *26*(3), 199–211. doi:10.1016/j.emj.2008.02.002

Endress, T. (2014). Digital Governance and Social Media Engagement. In Computer-mediated marketing strategies: social media and online brand communities. IGI Global.

Engel, C., Bell, R., Meier, R., & Rumpel, J. (2011). Young consumers in the new marketing ecosystem: An analysis of their usage of interactive technologies. *Academy of Marketing Studies Journal*, *15*(2), 23–44.

Engel, J. F., Blackwell, R. D., & Miniard, P. W. (2005). *Consumer Behaviour*. Thompson South Western Company.

Englis, B., & Solomon, M. (1995). To Be and Not to Be: Lifestyle Imagery, Reference Groups, and The Clustering of America. *Journal of Advertising*, *24*(1), 13–28. doi:10.1080/00913367.1995.10673465

Erkan, I., & Evans, C. (2016). The influence of eWOM in social media on consumers' purchase intentions: An extended approach to information adoption. *Computers in Human Behavior*, *61*, 47–55. doi:10.1016/j.chb.2016.03.003

Ertugan, A. (2017). Using statistical reasoning techniques to describe the relationship between Facebook advertising effectiveness and benefits gained. *Procedia Computer Science*, *120*, 132–139. doi:10.1016/j.procs.2017.11.220

Escalas, J., & Bettman, J. (2003). You Are What They Eat: The Influence of Reference Groups on Consumers' Connections to Brands. *Journal of Consumer Psychology*, *13*(3), 339–348. doi:10.1207/S15327663JCP1303_14

Escalas, J., & Bettman, J. (2005). Self-Construal, Reference Groups, and Brand Meaning. *The Journal of Consumer Research*, *32*(3), 378–389. doi:10.1086/497549

Escalas, J., & Bettman, J. (2017). Connecting With Celebrities: How Consumers Appropriate Celebrity Meanings for a Sense of Belonging. *Journal of Advertising*, *46*(2), 297–308. doi:10.1080/00913367.2016.1274925

Estrella-Ramón, A., & Ellis-Chadwick, F. (2017). Do different kinds of user-generated content in online brand communities really work? *Online Information Review*, *41*(7), 954–968. doi:10.1108/OIR-08-2016-0229

Etzel, M. J., & Silverman, B. I. (1981). A managerial perspective on directions of retail customer dissatisfaction research. *Journal of Retailing*, *57*(3), 124–136.

Evans, D. (2012). *Social Media Marketing: An Hour a Day* (2nd ed.). Indianapolis: John Wiley & Sons Publishing, Inc.

Faci, N., Maamar, Z., Buregio, V., Uglijanin, E., & Benslimane, D. (2017). Web 2.0. Applications in the workplace: How to ensure their proper use? *Computers in Industry*, *88*, 1–11. doi:10.1016/j.compind.2017.03.003

Falk, J. (2014). *Physical mobile interaction in omni-channel retailing: Using the customers' smartphone to interact with smart objects in a store*. Linköping University.

Fan, Y. (2006). Branding the nation: What is being branded? *Journal of Vacation Marketing*, *12*(1), 1, 5–14. doi:10.1177/1356766706056633

Fan, Y. W., Wu, C. C., & Wu, W. T. (2010). The impacts of online retailing service recovery and perceived justice on consumer loyalty. *International Journal of Electronic Business Management*, *8*(3), 239.

Fan, Y.-W., Wu, C.-C., & Wu, W.-T. (2010). The impacts of Online Retailing Service Failure Recovery and Perceived Justice on Consumer Loyalty. *International Journal of Electronic Business Management*, *8*(3), 239–249.

Farrell, H., & Drezner, D. (2008). The power and politics of blogs. *Public Choice*, *134*(1-2), 15–30. doi:10.100711127-007-9198-1

Farrell, H., & Knight, J. (2003). Trust, institutions, and institutional change: Industrial districts and the social capital hypothesis. *Politics & Society*, *31*(4), 537–566. doi:10.1177/0032329203256954

Fassnacht, M., & Koese, I. (2006). Quality of Electronic Services: Conceptualizing and Testing a Hierarchical Model. *Journal of Service Research*, *9*(1), 19–37. doi:10.1177/1094670506289531

Fassnacht, M., & Köse, I. (2007). Consequences of web-based service quality: Uncovering a multi-faceted chain of effects. *Journal of Interactive Marketing*, *21*(3), 35–54. doi:10.1002/dir.20084

Fatma, M., Khan, I., & Rahman, Z. (2016). The effect of CSR on consumer behavioural responses after service failure and recovery. *European Business Review*, *28*(5), 583–599. doi:10.1108/EBR-11-2015-0134

Feenberg, A. (2002). *Transforming technology: A critical theory revisited* (2nd ed.). Oxford University Press.

Feldman, J. M., & Lynch, J. G. (1988). Self-generated validity and other effects of measurement on belief, attitude, intention, and behavior. *The Journal of Applied Psychology, 73*(3), 421–435. doi:10.1037/0021-9010.73.3.421

Feldwick, P. (1996). Do we really need 'Brand Equity'? *Journal of Brand Management, 4*(1), 9–28. doi:10.1057/bm.1996.23

Felix, R. (2015). The state of the Global Smartphone Market. *Statista Infographics.* Retrieved from: https://www.statista.com/charts/2512/smartphone-market-share

Felix, R., Rauschnabel, P. A., Gallaugher, J., & Ransbotham, J. (2010). Social media and customer dialog management at Starbucks. *MIS Quarterly Executive, 9*(4), 197–212.

Felix, R., Rauschnabel, P. A., & Hinsch, C. (2017). Elements of strategic social media marketing: A holistic framework. *Journal of Business Research, 70,* 118–126. doi:10.1016/j.jbusres.2016.05.001

Feng, J., & Liu, B. (2018). Dynamic Impact of Online Word-of-Mouth and Advertising on Supply Chain Performance. *International Journal of Environmental Research and Public Health, 15*(1), 69. doi:10.3390/ijerph15010069 PMID:29300361

Feng, J., & Papatla, P. (2012). Is Online Word of Mouth Higher for New Models or Redesigns? An Investigation of the Automobile Industry. *Journal of Interactive Marketing, 26*(2), 92–101. doi:10.1016/j.intmar.2012.01.001

Ferguson, R. (2008). Word of mouth and viral marketing: Taking the temperature of the hottest trends in marketing. *Journal of Consumer Marketing, 25*(3), 179–182. doi:10.1108/07363760810870671

Fernández-Olmos, M., & Ramírez-Alesón, M. (2017). How internal and external factors influence the dynamics of SME technology collaboration networks over time. *Technovation, 64-65,* 16–27. doi:10.1016/j.technovation.2017.06.002

Fernie, J., Maniatakis, P. A., & Moore, C. M. (2009). The role of international hubs in a fashion retailer"s sourcing strategy. *International Review of Retail, Distribution and Consumer Research, 19*(4), 421–436. doi:10.1080/09593960903331428

Ferrell, O. C., & Hartline, M. D. (2014). *Marketing Strategy* (6th ed.). Chicago: Cengage Learning.

Festinger, L. (1954). A theory of social comparison processes. *Human Relations, 7*(2), 117–140. doi:10.1177/001872675400700202

Festinger, L. (1957). *A theory of cognitive dissonance.* New York: Harper & Row.

Fill, C. (2009). *Marketing communications: Interactivity, communities and content* (5th ed.). Harlow, UK: Prentice Hall/ Financial Times

Finch, J., Wagner, B., & Hynes, N. (2012). Resources prospectively: How actors mobilize resources in business settings. *Journal of Business Research, 65*(2), 164–174. doi:10.1016/j.jbusres.2011.05.017

Finocchiaro, P. (2010). Luxury brands must risk failure to succeed in new media. *Luxury Daily.* Retrieved September 14, 2016, from https://www.luxurydaily.com/luxury-brands-must-risk-failure-to-succeed-in-new-media-morpheus-exec/

Fiore, A. M. (2002). Effects of experiential pleasure from a catalogue environment on approach responses toward fashion apparel. *Journal of Fashion Marketing and Management: An International Journal, 6*(2), 122–133. doi:10.1108/13612020210429467

Fiore, A., Kim, J., & Lee, H. (2005). Effect of image interactivity technology on consumer responses toward the online retailer. *Journal of Interactive Marketing, 19*(3), 38–53. doi:10.1002/dir.20042

Fischer, E., Bristor, J., & Gainer, B. (1996). Creating or escaping community? An exploratory study of Internet consumers' behaviors. *Advances in Consumer Research. Association for Consumer Research (U. S.), 23,* 178–182.

Fischer, E., & Reuber, A. R. (2011). Social interaction via new social media: (How) can interactions on Twitter affect effectual thinking and behavior? *Journal of Business Venturing*, *26*(1), 1–18. doi:10.1016/j.jbusvent.2010.09.002

Fisher, R., & Wakefield, K. (1998). Factors leading to group identification: A field study of winners and losers. *Psychology and Marketing*, *15*(1), 23–40. doi:10.1002/(SICI)1520-6793(199801)15:1<23::AID-MAR3>3.0.CO;2-P

Flanagin, A. J., Hocevar, K. P., & Samahito, S. N. (2014). Connecting with the user-generated Web: How group identification impacts online information sharing and evaluation. *Information Communication and Society*, *17*(6), 683–694. doi:10.1080/1369118X.2013.808361

Floyd, K., Freling, R., Alhoqail, S., Cho, H. Y., & Freling, T. (2014). How Online Product Reviews Affect Retail Sales: A Meta-analysis. *Journal of Retailing*, *90*(2), 217–232. doi:10.1016/j.jretai.2014.04.004

Flynn, L., Goldsmith, R., & Eastman, J. (1996). Opinion Leaders and Opinion Seekers: Two New Measurement Scales. *Journal of the Academy of Marketing Science*, *24*(2), 137–147. doi:10.1177/0092070396242004

Forbes. (2010). *The untethered executive: Business information in the age of mobility*. Retrieved from https://images.forbes.com/forbesinsights/StudyPDFs/The_Untethered_Executive.pdf

Forbes. (2012). *The Future Of Fashion Retailing -- The H&M Approach (Part 3 of 3)*. Retrieved from http://www.forbes.com/sites/gregpetro/2012/11/05/the-future-of-fashion-retailing-the-hm-approach-part-3-of-3/#49f3d33d6dbf

Forbes. (2015). *H&M Has Largest Audience On Social Media, Latest Data From Sprinklr Shows*. Retrieved from http://www.forbes.com/sites/fionabriggs/2015/12/22/hm-has-largest-audience-on-social-media-latest-data-from-sprinklr-shows/#4ce692054ac0

Forbes. (2016). *The World's Most Valuable Brands*. Retrieved from http://www.forbes.com/powerful-brands/list/#tab:rank_header:oneYearValueChange_industry:Retail

Forbes, L. P., Kelley, S. W., & Hoffman, K. D. (2005). Typologies of e-commerce retail failures and recovery strategies. *Journal of Services Marketing*, *19*(5), 280–292. doi:10.1108/08876040510609907

Fortin, D. R., & Dholakia, R. R. (2005). Interactivity and vividness effects on social presence and involvement with a web-based advertisement. *Journal of Business Research*, *58*(3), 387–396. doi:10.1016/S0148-2963(03)00106-1

Fosso Wamba, S., & Carter, L. (2014). Social Media Tools Adoption and Use by SMEs: An Empirical Study. *Journal of End User and Organizational Computing*, *26*(1), 1–16. doi:10.4018/joeuc.2014040101

Fournier, S. (1998). Consumers and Their Brands: Developing Relationship Theory in Consumer Research. *The Journal of Consumer Research*, *24*(3), 343–373. doi:10.1086/209515

Fournier, S., & Avery, J. (2011). The uninvited brand. *Business Horizons*, *54*(3), 193–207. doi:10.1016/j.bushor.2011.01.001

Fournier, S., & Lee, L. (2009, April). Getting Brand Communities Right. *Harvard Business Review*, 2–8.

Foux, G. (2006). Consumer generated media: Get your consumers involved. *Brand Strategy*, *202*, 38–39.

Fox, A. K., Bacile, T. J., Nakhata, C., & Weible, A. (2018). Selfie-marketing: Exploring narcissism and self-concept in visual user-generated content on social media. *Journal of Consumer Marketing*, *35*(1), 11–21. doi:10.1108/JCM-03-2016-1752

Frearson, J. (2016). *Half of consumers experience problems with online shopping*. Assessed October 15, 2018 from https://www.business-reporter.co.uk/2016/06/14/half-consumers-experience-problems-online-shopping-says-report/#gsc.tab=0

Freling, T., & Forbes, L. (2005). An empirical analysis of the brand personality effect. *Journal of Product and Brand Management*, *14*(7), 404–413. doi:10.1108/10610420510633350

Fromm, J., & Garton, C. (2013). *Marketing to Millennials*. Barkley, Inc.

Fuchs, C. (2014). *Social Media: A Critical Introduction*. London: Sage Publications, Ltd.

Fu, H., Wu, D. C., Huang, S. S., Song, H., & Gong, J. (2015). Monetary or nonmonetary compensation for service failure? A study of customer preferences under various loci of causality. *International Journal of Hospitality Management*, *46*, 55–64. doi:10.1016/j.ijhm.2015.01.006

Fulgoni, G. (2016). In the Digital World, Not Everything That Can Be Measured Matters. *Journal of Advertising Research*, *56*(1), 9–13. doi:10.2501/JAR-2016-008

Fu, P. W., Wu, C. C., & Cho, Y. J. (2017). What makes users share content on Facebook? Compatibility among psychological incentive, social capital focus, and content type. *Computers in Human Behavior*, *67*, 23–32. doi:10.1016/j.chb.2016.10.010

Gabriel, Y., & Lang, T. (1995). *The Unmanageable Consumer*. London: Sage Publications.

Gainer, B., & Fischer, E. (1994). Community and consumption. *Advances in Consumer Research. Association for Consumer Research (U. S.)*, *21*, 137.

Gallaugher, J., & Ransbotham, S. (2010). Social Media and Customer Dialog Management at Starbucks. *MIS Quarterly Executive*, *9*(4).

Galvagno, M., & Dalli, D. (2014). Theory of value co-creation: A systematic literature review. *Managing Service Quality*, *20*(4), 643–683. doi:10.1108/MSQ-09-2013-0187

Gao, G., Greenwood, B. N., Agarwal, R., & McCulllough, J. (2015). Vocal Minority and Silent Majority: How Do Online Ratings Reflect Population Perceptions of Quality? *Management Information Systems Quarterly*, *39*(3), 565–589. doi:10.25300/MISQ/2015/39.3.03

Gartner. (2018). *Smartphone*. Retrieved June 3, 2018, from https://www.gartner.com/it-glossary/smartphone

Gefen, D., & Straub, D. (2003). Managing user trust in B2C e-services. *e-Service Journal*, *2*(2), 7–24. doi:10.2979/esj.2003.2.2.7

Geissinger, A., & Laurell, C. (2016). User engagement in social media – an explorative study of Swedish fashion brands. *Journal of Fashion Marketing and Management*, *20*(2), 177–190. doi:10.1108/JFMM-02-2015-0010

Gelbrich, K., Gäthke, J., & Grégoire, Y. (2015). How much compensation should a firm offer for a flawed service? An examination of the nonlinear effects of compensation on satisfaction. *Journal of Service Research*, *18*(1), 107–123. doi:10.1177/1094670514543149

Gelbrich, K., Gäthke, J., & Grégoire, Y. (2016). How a firm's best versus normal customers react to compensation after a service failure. *Journal of Business Research*, *69*(10), 4331–4339. doi:10.1016/j.jbusres.2016.04.010

Gelbrich, K., & Roschk, H. (2011). A Meta-Analysis of Organizational Complaint Handling and Customer Responses. *Journal of Service Research*, *14*(1), 24–43. doi:10.1177/1094670510387914

Gensler, S., Völckner, F., Liu-Thompkins, Y., & Wiertz, C. (2013). Managing brands in the social media environment. *Journal of Interactive Marketing*, *27*(4), 242–256. doi:10.1016/j.intmar.2013.09.004

Georgescu, M., & Popescul, D. (2015). Social media–the new paradigm of collaboration and communication for business environment. *Procedia Economics and Finance*, *20*, 277–282. doi:10.1016/S2212-5671(15)00075-1

Ghatak, R. R., & Pal, S. S. (2016). Prioritizing the Service Failures of Package Delivery Business: An Analytical Hierarchy Process Analysis. *IUP Journal of Supply Chain Management*, *13*(4), 27.

Ghodeswar, B. (2008). Building brand identity in competitive markets: A conceptual model. *Journal of Product and Brand Management*, *17*(1), 4–12. doi:10.1108/10610420810856468

Ghose, A., Ipeirotis, P. G., & Li, B. (2012). Designing Ranking Systems for Hotels on Travel Search Engines by Mining User-Generated and Crowdsourced Content. *Marketing Science*, *31*(3), 493–520. doi:10.1287/mksc.1110.0700

Gillies, J., & Cailliau, R. (2000). *How the Web was born*. Oxford, UK: Oxford University Press.

Gill, P. S., Kamath, A., & Gill, T. S. (2012). Distraction: An assessment of smartphone usage in health care work settings. *Risk Management and Healthcare Policy*, *5*, 105–114. doi:10.2147/RMHP.S34813 PMID:22969308

Gilly, M., Graham, J., Wolfinbarger, M., & Yale, L. (1998). A Dyadic Study of Interpersonal Information Search. *Journal of the Academy of Marketing Science*, *26*(2), 83–100. doi:10.1177/0092070398262001

Gilmore, A. (2003). *Services Marketing and Management* (1st ed.). London: SAGE Publications Ltd.

Gilmore, F. (2002). A country –can it be repositioned? Spain –the successful story of country branding. *Journal of Brand Management*, *9*(4/5), 281–293. doi:10.1057/palgrave.bm.2540078

Giovanisa, A. N., & Athanasopouloub, P. (2018). Consumer-Brand Relationships and Brand Loyalty in Technology-Mediated Services. *Journal of Retailing and Consumer Services*, *40*(1), 287–294. doi:10.1016/j.jretconser.2017.03.003

Global Fashion Agenda and The Boston Consulting Group, Inc. (2018). *Pulse-of-the-fashion-industry-2018*. Accessed October 8, 2018 from https://www.globalfashionagenda.com/pulse-of-the-fashion-industry-2018-report-released/#

Glover, S., & Benbasat, I. (2011). A comprehensive model of perceived risk of e-commerce transactions. *International Journal of Electronic Commerce*, *15*(2), 47–78. doi:10.2753/JEC1086-4415150202

Gobé, M. (2010). *Emotional Branding* (2nd ed.). New York: Allworth Press.

Godes, D., & Mayzlin, D. (2004). Using Online Conversations to Study Word-of-Mouth Communication. *Marketing Science*, *23*(4), 545–560. doi:10.1287/mksc.1040.0071

Godes, D., & Mayzlin, D. (2009). Firm-Created Word-of-Mouth Communication: Evidence from a Field Test. *Marketing Science*, *28*(4), 721–739. doi:10.1287/mksc.1080.0444

Godey, B., Manthiou, A., Pederzoli, D., Rokka, J., Aiello, G., Donvito, R., & Singh, R. (2016). Social media marketing efforts of luxury brands: Influence on brand equity and consumer behavior. *Journal of Business Research*, *69*(12), 5833–5841. doi:10.1016/j.jbusres.2016.04.181

Goersch, D. (2002). *Multi-Channel integration and its implications for retail web sites*. Paper presented at the 10th European Conference on Information Systems, Gdansk.

Goh, K., Heng, C., & Lin, Z. (2013). Social Media Brand Community and Consumer Behavior: Quantifying the Relative Impact of User- and Marketer-Generated Content. *Information Systems Research*, *24*(1), 88–107. doi:10.1287/isre.1120.0469

Goldfarb, A., & Tucker, C. (2011). Online display advertising: Targeting and obtrusiveness. *Marketing Science*, *30*(3), 389–404. doi:10.1287/mksc.1100.0583

Goldsmith, R. E. (2000). Characteristics of the Heavy User of Fashionable Clothing. *Journal of Marketing Theory and Practice*, *8*(4), 21–28. doi:10.1080/10696679.2000.11501877

Goldsmith, R. E., & Flynn, L. R. (2005). Bricks, clicks, and pix: Apparel buyers' use of stores, internet, and catalogs compared. *International Journal of Retail & Distribution Management*, *33*(4), 271–283. doi:10.1108/09590550510593202

Gomez, L., Alvarado, Y., Bernabe, K., & Melendez, L. (2017). Snapchat As An Influential Tool For Marketing Communication: An Exploratory Analysis Of Brands Usage. In *2017 Academy of Marketing Science Annual Conference*. Coronado, CA: 2017 Academy of Marketing Science Annual Conference.

Goode, S., Hoehle, H., Venkatesh, V., & Brown, S. A. (2017). User compensation as a data breach recovery action: An investigation of the Sony PlayStation network breach. *Management Information Systems Quarterly*, *41*(3), 703–727.

Goodman, G. F., Schaffer, N., Korhan, J., & Safko, L. (2013). *2014; Social Marketing Digital Book Set*. John Wiley & Sons Inc.

Goodrich, K. (2011). Anarchy of effects? Exploring attention to online advertising and multiple outcomes. *Psychology and Marketing*, *28*(4), 417–440. doi:10.1002/mar.20371

Goodwin, E., Babin, L., & Cole, H. (2014). The impact of mobile apps on small business revenues. *Journal of Business and Economics*, *5*(4), 437–442.

Google Confidential and Proprietary. (2013). *Our mobile planet: United Kingdom Understanding the mobile consumer*. Author.

Gordhamer, S. (2009). *4 ways Social media is changing Business*. Retrieved from http://Mashable.com /2009/09/22/Social-Media-Business

Görsch, D. (2002). Multi-channel integration and its implications for retail web sites. *Ecis*, 748–758. Available at: http://aisel.aisnet.org/ecis2002/11

Gounaris, S. (2005). Trust and commitment influences on customer retention: Insights from business-to-business services. *Journal of Business Research*, *58*(2), 126–140. doi:10.1016/S0148-2963(03)00122-X

Goyette, I., Ricard, L., Bergeron, J., & Marticotte, F. (2010). e-WOM Scale: Word-of-Mouth Measurement Scale for e-Services Context. *Canadian Journal of Administrative Sciences*, *27*(01), 5–23. doi:10.1002/cjas.129

Granitz, N., & Forman, H. (2015). Building self-brand connections: Exploring brand stories through a transmedia perspective. *Journal of Brand Management*, *22*(1), 38–59. doi:10.1057/bm.2015.1

Granovetter, M. S. (1973). The strength of weak ties. *American Journal of Sociology*, *78*(6), 1360–1380. doi:10.1086/225469

Gregoire, Y., Salle, A., & Tripp, T. M. (2015). Managing social media crises with your customers: The good, the bad, and the ugly. *Business Horizons*, *58*(2), 173–182. doi:10.1016/j.bushor.2014.11.001

Grewal, D., Roggeveen, A. L., & Tsiros, M. (2008). The Effect of Compensation on Repurchase Intentions in Service Recovery. *Journal of Retailing*, *84*(4), 424–434. doi:10.1016/j.jretai.2008.06.002

Griffin, M., Babin, B. J., & Modianos, D. (2000). Shopping Values of Russian Consumers: The Impact of Habituation in a Developing Economy. *Journal of Retailing*, *76*(1), 33–52. doi:10.1016/S0022-4359(99)00025-1

Grizane, T., & Jurgelane, I. (2017). Social Media Impact on Business Evaluation. *Procedia Computer Science*, *104*, 190–196. doi:10.1016/j.procs.2017.01.103

Grönroos, C. (1984). A service quality model and its marketing implications. *European Journal of Marketing*, *18*(4), 36–44. doi:10.1108/EUM0000000004784

Grönroos, C. (2007). *Service Management and Marketing: Customer Management in Service* (3rd ed.). Chichester, UK: John Wiley & Sons.

Grönroos, C. (2016). Internationalization strategies for services: A retrospective. *Journal of Services Marketing*, *30*(2), 129–132. doi:10.1108/JSM-11-2015-0354

Gronroos, C., & Gummerus, J. (2014). The service revolution and its marketing implications: Service logic versus service–dominant logic. *Managing Service Quality*, *24*(3), 206–229. doi:10.1108/MSQ-03-2014-0042

Gronroos, C., & Voima, P. (2013). Critical service logic: Making sense of value creation and co-creation. *Journal of the Academy of Marketing Science*, *41*(2), 133–150. doi:10.100711747-012-0308-3

Gruber, D. A., Smerek, R. E., Thomas-Hunt, M. C., & James, E. H. (2015). The real-time power of twitter: Crises management and leadership in an age of social media. *Business Horizons*, *58*(2), 163–172. doi:10.1016/j.bushor.2014.10.006

Gruen, T., Osmonbekov, T., & Czaplewski, A. (2006). eWOM: The impact of customer-to-customer online know-how exchange on customer value and loyalty. *Journal of Business Research*, *59*(4), 449–456. doi:10.1016/j.jbusres.2005.10.004

Grunig, J. E. (2009). Paradigms of global public relations in an age of digitalisation. *Prism*, *6*(2).

Guadagni, P. M., & Little, J. D. C. (1983). A Logit Model of Brand Choice Calibrated on Scanner Data: A Logit Model of Brand Choice Calibrated on Scanner Data. *Journal of Marine Science*, *2*(3), 203–238. doi:10.1287/mksc.2.3.203

Gu, B., Tang, Q., & Whinston, A. B. (2013). The influence of online word-of-mouth on long tail formation. *Decision Support Systems*, *56*, 474–481. doi:10.1016/j.dss.2012.11.004

Gu, B., & Ye, Q. (2014). First Step in Social Media: Measuring the Influence of Online Management Responses on Customer Satisfaction. *Production and Operations Management*, *23*(4), 570–582. doi:10.1111/poms.12043

Gubrium, J. F., & Holstein, J. A. (2007). *Handbook of Constructionist Research* (1st ed.). New York: Guilford Press.

Guillory, S. (2016) *Top five customer complaints with fashion retailers*. Retrieved October 12, 2016, from: http://apparel.edgl.com/news/Top-Five-Customer-Complaints-With-Fashion-Retailers105498

Gummerus, J., Liljander, V., Weman, E., & Pihlström M. H. (2011). *Consumer motivations to join a facebook brand community*. Marketing Fields Forever: Academy of Marketing Conference, Liverpool, UK.

Gummerus, J., Liljander, V., Pura, M., & Van Riel, A. (2004). Customer loyalty to content-based web sites: The case of an online health-care service. *Journal of Services Marketing*, *18*(3), 175–186. doi:10.1108/08876040410536486

Gummerus, J., Liljander, V., Weman, E., & Pihlstrom, M. (2012). *Consumer motivations to join a Facebook brand community. In Marketing Fields Forever 2012*. Emeralds.

Gummerus, J., Liljander, V., Weman, E., & Pihlström, M. (2012). Customer engagement in a Facebook brand community. *Management Research Review*, *35*(9), 857–877. doi:10.1108/01409171211256578

Gummesson, E. (2002). Relationship marketing: Its role in the service economy. *Understanding Services Management*, *16*(7), 224–268.

Gummesson, E., Lusch, R. F., & Vargo, S. L. (2010). Transitioning from service management to service-dominant logic: Observations and recommendations. *International Journal of Quality and Service Sciences*, *2*(1), 8–22. doi:10.1108/17566691011026577

Gummesson, E., & Mele, C. (2010). Marketing as value co-creation through network interaction and resource integration. *Journal of Business Market Management*, *4*(4), 181–198. doi:10.100712087-010-0044-2

Gunasekaran, A., McGaughey, R., Ngai, E., & Rai, B. (2009). E-Procurement Adoption in the Southcoast SMEs. *International Journal of Production Economics*, *122*(1), 161–175. doi:10.1016/j.ijpe.2009.05.013

Gupta, A., Su, B. C., & Walter, Z. (2004). Risk profile and consumer shopping behavior in electronic and traditional channels. *Decision Support Systems*, *38*(3), 347–367. doi:10.1016/j.dss.2003.08.002

Gurău, C. (2012). A life-stage analysis of consumer loyalty profile: Comparing Generation X and Millennial consumers. *Journal of Consumer Marketing*, *29*(2), 103–113. doi:10.1108/07363761211206357

Gurol, Y., & Atsan, N. (2006). Entrepreneurial characteristics amongst university students. *Education + Training*, *48*(1), 25–38. doi:10.1108/00400910610645716

Gusfield, J. (1978). *Community: A Critical Response* (2nd ed.). New York: Harper Collophon Books.

Gutiérrez-Cillán, J., Camarero-Izquierdo, C., & San José-Cabezudo, R. (2017). How brand post content contributes to user's Facebook brand-page engagement. The experiential route of active participation. *BRQ Business Research Quarterly*, *20*(4), 258–274. doi:10.1016/j.brq.2017.06.001

H&M. (2017). *The H&M Group's sales development for the full-year 2017 including the fourth quarter 2017*. Retrieved from https://about.hm.com/en/media/news/financial-reports/2017/12/2765961.html

Habibi, M. R., Laroche, M., & Richard, M.-O. (2014). Brand communities based in social media: How unique are they? Evidence from two exemplary brand communities. *International Journal of Information Management*, *34*(2), 123–132. doi:10.1016/j.ijinfomgt.2013.11.010

Habibi, M. R., Laroche, M., & Richard, M.-O. (2014). The roles of brand community and community engagement in building brand trust on social media. *Computers in Human Behavior*, *37*, 152–161. doi:10.1016/j.chb.2014.04.016

Hajli, N. (2015). Social commerce constructs and consumer's intention to buy. *International Journal of Information Management*, *35*(2), 183–191. doi:10.1016/j.ijinfomgt.2014.12.005

Hajli, N., Shanmugam, M., Papagiannidis, S., Zahay, D., & Richard, M. O. (2017). Branding co-creation with members of online brand communities. *Journal of Business Research*, *70*, 136–144. doi:10.1016/j.jbusres.2016.08.026

Hajli, N., & Sims, J. (2015). Social commerce: The transfer of power from seller to buyers. *Technological Forecasting and Social Change*, *94*, 350–358. doi:10.1016/j.techfore.2015.01.012

Hakala, U., Svensson, J., & Vincze, Z. (2012). Consumer-based brand equity and top-of-mind awareness: A cross-country analysis. *Journal of Product and Brand Management*, *21*(6), 439–451. doi:10.1108/10610421211264928

Hamid, N. R, & Akhir, R. M., & Cheng, A. Y. (2013). Social media: An emerging dimension of marketing communication. *Journal of Management and Marketing Research*, *12*, 4–11.

Hammedi, W., Kandampully, J., Zhang, T. T., & Bouquiaux, L. (2015). Online customer engagement: Creating social environments through brand community constellations. *Journal of Service Management*, *26*(5), 777–806. doi:10.1108/JOSM-11-2014-0295

Hanna, R., Rohm, A., & Crittenden, V. L. (2011). We're all connected: The power of the social media ecosystem. *Business Horizons*, *54*(3), 265–273. doi:10.1016/j.bushor.2011.01.007

Hansen, L. (2003). Service Layer Essential for Future Success. *Ericsson Mobility World*. Available at: http://www.ericsson.com

Hansen, D., Dunne, C., & Shneiderman, B. (2010). *Analyzing Social Media Networks with NodeXL.* HCIL University of Maryland.

Hansen, D., Schneiderman, B., & Smith, M. (2011). *Analyzing social media networks with NodeXL.* Amsterdam: Elsevier.

Hansen, S. S., & Lee, J. K. (2013). What Drives Consumers to Pass Along Marketer-Generated eWOM in Social Network Games? Social and Game Factors in Play. *Journal of Theoretical and Applied Electronic Commerce Research, 8*(1), 53–10.

Harding, R. (2007). Understanding social entrepreneurship. *Industry and Higher Education, 21*(1), 73–86. doi:10.5367/000000007780222723

Harrigan, P., Soutar, G., Choudhury, M. M., & Lowe, M. (2015). Modelling CRM in a Social Media Age. *Australasian Marketing Journal, 23*(1), 27–37. doi:10.1016/j.ausmj.2014.11.001

Harris, B. (2013). Diplomacy 2.0: The future of social media in nation branding. *The Journal of Public Diplomacy, 4*(1). Retrieved from http://surface.syr.edu/exchange/vol4/iss1/3

Harris, K. E., Grewal, D., Mohr, L. A., & Bernhardt, K. L. (2006). Consumer responses to service recovery strategies: The moderating role of online versus offline environment. *Journal of Business Research, 59*(4), 425–431. doi:10.1016/j.jbusres.2005.10.005

Harris, L., & Dennis, C. (2011). Engaging customers on Facebook: Challenges for e-retailers. *Journal of Consumer Behaviour, 10*(6), 338–346. doi:10.1002/cb.375

Harris, L., & Rae, A. (2009). Social networks: The future of marketing for small business. *The Journal of Business Strategy, 30*(5), 24–31. doi:10.1108/02756660910987581

Harrysson, M., Metayer, E., & Sarrazin, H. (2012). How 'social intelligence' can guide decisions. *The McKinsey Quarterly*, 1–9.

Hart, C. W., Heskett, J. L., & Sasser, W. E. (1990). The Profitable Art of Service Recovery. *Harvard Business Review, 68*(4), 148–156. PMID:10106796

Haslam, S., Oakes, P., Reynolds, K., & Turner, J. (1999). Social Identity Salience and the Emergence of Stereotype Consensus. *Personality and Social Psychology Bulletin, 25*(7), 809–818. doi:10.1177/0146167299025007004

Hassanein, K., & Head, M. (2005). The impact of infusing social presence in the web interface: An investigation across product types. *International Journal of Electronic Commerce, 10*(2), 31–55. doi:10.2753/JEC1086-4415100202

Hatch, M., & Schultz, M. (2010). Toward a theory of brand co-creation with implications for brand governance. *Journal of Brand Management, 17*(8), 590–604. doi:10.1057/bm.2010.14

Haugh, H. (2005). A research agenda for social entrepreneurship. *Social Enterprise Journal, 1*(1), 1–12. doi:10.1108/17508610580000703

Hautz, J., Füller, J., Hutter, K., & Thürridl, C. (2014). Let Users Generate Your Video Ads? The Impact of Video Source and Quality on Consumers' Perceptions and Intended Behaviors. *Journal of Interactive Marketing, 28*(1), 1–15. doi:10.1016/j.intmar.2013.06.003

Hau, Y. S., & Kim, Y. G. (2011). Why Would Online Gamers Share Their Innovation-Conducive Knowledge in the Online Game User Community? Integrating Individual Motivations and Social Capital Perspectives. *Computers in Human Behavior, 27*(2), 956–970. doi:10.1016/j.chb.2010.11.022

Hazée, S., Van Vaerenbergh, Y., & Armirotto, V. (2017). Co-creating service recovery after service failure: The role of brand equity. *Journal of Business Research, 74*, 101–109. doi:10.1016/j.jbusres.2017.01.014

Hearn, G., Foth, M., & Gray, H. (2009). Applications and implementations of new media in corporate communications: An action research approach. *Corporate Communications*, *14*(1), 49–61. doi:10.1108/13563280910931072

Heere, B., Walker, M., Yoshida, M., Ko, Y., Jordan, J., & James, J. (2011). Brand Community Development Through Associated Communities: Grounding Community Measurement Within Social Identity Theory. *Journal of Marketing Theory and Practice*, *19*(4), 407–422. doi:10.2753/MTP1069-6679190404

He, H., Yan, L., & Lloyd, H. (2012). Social identity perspective on brand Loyalty. *Journal of Business Research*, *65*(5), 648–657. doi:10.1016/j.jbusres.2011.03.007

Heider, F. (1946). Attitudes and Cognitive Organization. *The Journal of Psychology*, *21*(1), 107–112. doi:10.1080/00223980.1946.9917275 PMID:21010780

Heine, K. (2009). Using personal and online repertory grid methods for the development of a luxury brand personality. *Electronic Journal of Business Research Methods*, *7*(1), 25–38.

Heine, K., & Berghaus, B. (2014). Luxury goes digital: How to tackle the digital luxury brand-consumer touchpoints. *Journal of Global Fashion Marketing*, *5*(3), 223–234. doi:10.1080/20932685.2014.907606

Heinemann, G. (2013). *No-Line-Handel*. Wiesbaden: Gabler Verlag. doi:10.1007/978-3-658-00851-2

Heinonen, K. (2011). Consumer activity in social media: Managerial approaches to consumers' social media behavior. *Journal of Consumer Behaviour*, *10*(6), 356–364. doi:10.1002/cb.376

Heitz-Spahn, S. (2013). Cross-channel free-riding consumer behavior in a multichannel environment: An investigation of shopping motives, sociodemographics and product categories. *Journal of Retailing and Consumer Services*, *20*(6), 570–578. doi:10.1016/j.jretconser.2013.07.006

Helal, G., & Ozuem, W. (2018). Social Identity Matters: Social Media and Brand Perceptions in the Fashion Apparel and Accessories Industries. In Digital Marketing Strategies for Fashion and Luxury Brands (pp. 326-361). IGI Global.

Helal, G., & Ozuem, W. (2017). Social Identity Matters: Social Media and Brand Perceptions in the Fashion Apparel and Accessories Industries. In W. Ozuem & Y. Azemi (Eds.), *Digital Marketing Strategies for Fashion and Luxury Brands* (pp. 326–361). Hershey, PA: IGI Global.

Heller Baird, C., & Parasnis, G. (2011). From social media to social customer relationship management. *Strategy and Leadership*, *39*(5), 30–37. doi:10.1108/10878571111161507

Helm, A. E., Moulard, J. G., & Richins, M. (2015). Consumer cynicism: Developing a scale to measure underlying attitudes influencing marketplace shaping and withdrawal behaviours. *International Journal of Consumer Studies*, *39*(5), 515–524. doi:10.1111/ijcs.12191

Hennig-Thurau, T., Gwinner, K., Walsh, G., & Gremler, D. (2004). Electronic word-of-mouth via consumer-opinion platforms: What motivates consumers to articulate themselves on the Internet? *Journal of Interactive Marketing*, *18*(1), 38–52. doi:10.1002/dir.10073

Hennig-Thurau, T., Malthouse, E. C., Friege, C., Gensler, S., Lobschat, L., Rangaswamy, A., & Skiera, B. (2010). The Impact of New Media on Customer Relationships. *Journal of Service Research*, *13*(3), 311–330. doi:10.1177/1094670510375460

Hennig-Thurau, T., Walsh, G., & Walsh, G. (2003). Electronic word-of-mouth: Motives for and consequences of reading customer articulations on the Internet. *International Journal of Electronic Commerce*, *8*(2), 51–74. doi:10.1080/10864415.2003.11044293

Herget, J., & Mader, I. (2009). Social software in external corporate communications – a conceptional approach towards measuring, assessment and optimization of Web 2.0 activity [Social Software in der externen Unternehmenskommunikation – ein Gestaltungsansatz zur Messung, Bewertung und Optimierung von Web 2.0-aktivita¨ten]. *Information-Wissenschaft und Praxis*, *60*(4), 233–240.

Herrero, Ã., Martín, H. S., & Hernández, J. M. (2015). How online search behavior is influenced by user-generated content on review websites and hotel interactive websites: 1. *International Journal of Contemporary Hospitality Management*, *27*(7), 1573–1597. doi:10.1108/IJCHM-05-2014-0255

Herrmann, A., Xia, L., Monroe, K. B., & Huber, F. (2007). The influence of price fairness on customer satisfaction: An empirical test in the context of automobile purchases. *Journal of Product and Brand Management*, *16*(1), 49–58. doi:10.1108/10610420710731151

Herr, P., Kardes, F., & Kim, J. (1991). Effects of Word-of-Mouth and Product-Attribute Information on Persuasion: An Accessibility-Diagnosticity Perspective. *The Journal of Consumer Research*, *17*(4), 454–462. doi:10.1086/208570

Hershatter, A., & Epstein, M. (2010). Millennials and the World of Work: An Organization and Management Perspective. *Journal of Business and Psychology*, *25*(2), 211–223. doi:10.100710869-010-9160-y

He, S., & Wen, N. (2015). A Cautious Pursuit of Risk in Online Word-Of-Mouth: The Effect of Truncated Distribution on Consumer Decisions. *Advances in Consumer Research. Association for Consumer Research (U. S.)*, *43*, 736.

Hess, R. L. Jr, Ganesan, S., & Klein, N. M. (2003). Service failure and recovery: The impact of relationship factors on customer satisfaction. *Journal of the Academy of Marketing Science*, *31*(2), 127–145. doi:10.1177/0092070302250898

He, W., Zha, S., & Li, L. (2013). Social media competitive analysis and text mining: A case study in the pizza industry. *International Journal of Information Management*, *33*(3), 464–472. doi:10.1016/j.ijinfomgt.2013.01.001

Hew, K. F., & Cheung, W. S. (2012). *Use of Web 2.0 technologies in K-12 and higher education: The search for evidence-based practice. In Education Research Review 9.* Singapore: National Institute of Education, Nanyang Technological University.

Hewlet, S., Sherbin, L., & Sumberg, K. (2009, July). How Gen Y & Boomers Will Reshape Your Agenda. *Harvard Business Review*.

Hill, T. P. (1977). On Goods and Services. *Review of Income and Wealth*, *23*(4), 315–318. doi:10.1111/j.1475-4991.1977.tb00021.x

Hinz, O., Schulze, C., & Takac, C. (2014). New product adoption in social networks: Why direction matters. *Journal of Business Research*, *67*(1), 2836–2844. doi:10.1016/j.jbusres.2012.07.005

Hinz, O., Skiera, B., Barrot, C., & Becker, J. (2011). Seeding Strategies for Viral Marketing: An Empirical Comparison. *Journal of Marketing*, *75*(6), 55–71. doi:10.1509/jm.10.0088

Hirschman, E. C., & Holbrook, M. B. (1982). Hedonic consumption: Emerging Concepts, Methods and Propositions. *Journal of Marketing*, *46*(3), 92–101. doi:10.1177/002224298204600314

Hlebec, V., Manfreda, K. L., & Vehovar, V. (2015). The social support networks of internet users. *New Media & Society*, *8*(1), 9–32. doi:10.1177/1461444806058166

Ho, H. Y., & Chang, C. P. H. (2010). Influence of message trust in online word-of-mouth on consumer behaviour - By the example of food blog. In *International conference on electronics and information engineering*. Los Alamitos, CA: IEEE.

Hocutt, M. A., Bowers, M. R., & Donavan, T. (2007). The art of service recovery: Fact or fiction? *Journal of Services Marketing*, *20*(3), 199–207. doi:10.1108/08876040610665652

Hoeffler, S., & Keller, K. (2002). Building Brand Equity Through Corporate Societal Marketing. *Journal of Public Policy & Marketing*, *21*(1), 78–89. doi:10.1509/jppm.21.1.78.17600

Hoerner, J. (1999). Scaling The Web: A Parasocial Interaction Scale for World Wide Web Sites. In D. Schumann & E. Thorson (Eds.), *Advertising and the World Wide Web* (1st ed.; pp. 135–147). Mahwah, NJ: Lawrence Erlbaum Associates.

Hoffman, D.L., & Novak, T. (2013). *Online Experience in Social Media: Two Paths to Feeling Close and Connected.* Academic Press.

Hoffman, K. D., & Bateson, J. E. (2010). *Services Marketing: Concepts, Strategies, & Cases.* Mason, OH: Cengage Learning.

Hoffman, D. L., & Fodor, M. (2010). Can You Measure the ROI of Your Social Media Marketing? *Sloan Management Review*, *52*, 1.

Hoffman, D., & Fodor, M. (2016). Can you measure the ROI of your social media marketing? *Sloan Management Review*, *52*(1), 41–49.

Hoffman, D., & Novak, T. (1996). Marketing in Hypermedia Computer-Mediated Environments: Conceptual Foundations. *Journal of Marketing*, *60*(3), 50–68. doi:10.2307/1251841

Hoffman, K. D., Kelley, S. W., & Rotalsky, H. M. (2016). Retrospective: Tracking service failures and employee recovery efforts. *Journal of Services Marketing*, *30*(1), 7–10. doi:10.1108/JSM-10-2015-0316

Hogan, E. J., & Armstrong, G. (2001). Toward a Resource Based Theory of Business Exchange Relationships: The Role of Relational Asset Value. *Journal of Business-To-Business Marketing*, *8*(4), 3–28. doi:10.1300/J033v08n04_02

Hogg, M. (2001). A Social Identity Theory of Leadership. *Personality and Social Psychology Review*, *5*(3), 184–200. doi:10.1207/S15327957PSPR0503_1

Hogg, M., & Abrams, D. (1988). *Social identifications.* London: Routledge.

Hogg, M., Banister, E., & Stephenson, C. (2009). Mapping symbolic (anti-) consumption. *Journal of Business Research*, *62*(2), 148–159. doi:10.1016/j.jbusres.2008.01.022

Hogg, M., & Reid, S. (2006). Social Identity, Self-Categorization, and the Communication of Group Norms. *Communication Theory*, *16*(1), 7–30. doi:10.1111/j.1468-2885.2006.00003.x

Hogg, M., Sherman, D., Dierselhuis, J., Maitner, A., & Moffitt, G. (2006). Uncertainty, entitativity, and group identification. *Journal of Experimental Social Psychology*, *43*(1), 135–142. doi:10.1016/j.jesp.2005.12.008

Hogg, M., & Terry, D. (2000). Social Identity and Self-Categorization Processes in Organizational Contexts. *Academy of Management Review*, *25*(1), 121–140. doi:10.5465/amr.2000.2791606

Hogg, M., Terry, D., & White, K. (1995). A Tale of Two Theories: A Critical Comparison of Identity Theory with Social Identity Theory. *Social Psychology Quarterly*, *58*(4), 255–269. doi:10.2307/2787127

Hogg, M., & Turner, J. (1987). Intergroup behaviour, self-stereotyping and the salience of social categories. *British Journal of Social Psychology*, *26*(4), 325–340. doi:10.1111/j.2044-8309.1987.tb00795.x

Holbrook, M. B., & Corfman, K. P. (1985). Quality and Value in the Consumption Experience: Phaedrus Rides Again. In C. V. S. How, J. J. Merchandise, & J. C. Olson (Eds.), *Perceived Quality*. Lanham, MD: Lexington Books.

Holbrook, M. B., & Gardner, M. P. (2000). Illustrating a dynamic model of the mood-updating process in consumer behavior. *Psychology and Marketing*, *17*(3), 165–194. doi:10.1002/(SICI)1520-6793(200003)17:3<165::AID-MAR1>3.0.CO;2-5

Hollande, F. (2014). France Tries to Tempt In More Foreign Investment. *International Business*, p. B1. Retrieved from https://www.nytimes.com/2014/02/18/business/international/hollande-throws-open-frances-doors-to-business.html

Holland, J., & Baker, S. (2001). Customer participation in creating site brand loyalty. *Journal of Interactive Marketing*, *15*(4), 34–45. doi:10.1002/dir.1021

Hollebeek, L. D. (2011). Demystifying customer brand engagement: Exploring the loyalty nexus. *Journal of Marketing Management*, *27*(7-8), 785–807. doi:10.1080/0267257X.2010.500132

Hollebeek, L. D., Glynn, M., & Brodie, R. J. (2014). Consumer Brand Engagement in Social Media: Conceptualization, Scale Development and Validation. *Journal of Interactive Marketing*, *28*(2), 149–165. doi:10.1016/j.intmar.2013.12.002

Holloway, B. B., & Beatty, S. E. (2003). Service failure in online retailing: A recovery opportunity. *Journal of Service Research*, *6*(1), 92–105. doi:10.1177/1094670503254288

Holloway, B. B., & Beatty, S. E. (2005). Customer Retention Online: The Influence of Switching Barriers. *Asia Pacific Advances in Consumer Research*, *6*, 104.

Holmes, J. (2015). *Instagram black book*. Lexington, KY: Academic Press.

Holsapple, C. W., Hsiao, S.-H., & Pakath, R. (2018). Business social media analytics: Characterization and conceptual framework. *Decision Support Systems*, *110*, 32–45. doi:10.1016/j.dss.2018.03.004

Homburg, C., Ehm, L., & Artz, M. (2015). Measuring and managing consumer sentiment in an online community environment. *JMR, Journal of Marketing Research*, *52*(5), 629–641. doi:10.1509/jmr.11.0448

Homburg, C., Wieseke, J., & Hoyer, W. D. (2009). Social Identity and the Social Profit chain. *Journal of Marketing*, *73*(2), 38–54. doi:10.1509/jmkg.73.2.38

Hong, H., Xu, D., Xu, D., Wang, G. A., & Fan, W. (2017). An empirical study on the impact of online word-of-mouth sources on retail sales. *Information Discovery and Delivery*, *45*(1), 30–35. doi:10.1108/IDD-11-2016-0039

Horgan, B., & Quan Haase, A. (2010). Persistence and Change in Social Media. *Bulletin of Science, Technology & Society*, *30*(5), 309–315. doi:10.1177/0270467610380012

Hornik, J., Satchi, R. S., Cesareo, L., & Pastore, A. (2015). Information dissemination via electronic word-of-mouth: Good news travels fast, bad news travels faster! *Computers in Human Behavior*, *45*, 273–280. doi:10.1016/j.chb.2014.11.008

Horton, D., & Wohl, R. (1956). Mass Communication and Parasocial Interaction: Observations on Intimacy at a Distance. *Psychiatry*, *19*(3), 215–229. doi:10.1080/00332747.1956.11023049 PMID:13359569

Hosein, N. Z. (2012). Measuring the purchase intention of visitors to the auto show. *Journal of Management and Marketing Research*, *9*, 1–18.

Ho, T. (2016). Private Entrepreneurs in China: Social Entrepreneurs or Social Menaces? *Chinese Public Administration Review*, *3*(1/2), 14. doi:10.22140/cpar.v3i1/2.52

Howell, K. (2012). *An Introduction to the Philosophy of Methodology* (1st ed.). London: Sage Publications Ltd.

Howe, N., & Strauss, W. (2000). *Millennials Rising: The Next Great Generation*. New York: Vintage Books.

Hoyer, W. D., & Ridgway, N. M. (1984). Variety seeking as an explanation for exploratory behaviour: A theoretical model. In T. C. Kinnear (Ed.), *Advances in Consumer Research* (Vol. 11, pp. 114–119). Provo, UT: Association for Consumer Research.

Hoyer, W., & Brown, S. (1990). Effects of Brand Awareness on Choice for a Common, Repeat-Purchase Product. *The Journal of Consumer Research*, *17*(2), 141–148. doi:10.1086/208544

Hsiao, C.-C., Yen, H. J. R., & Li, E. Y. (2012). Exploring consumer value of multi-channel shopping: A perspective of means-end theory. *Internet Research*, *22*(3), 318–339. doi:10.1108/10662241211235671

Hsieh, J., & Tseng, C. (2018). Exploring social influence on hedonic buying of digital goods- online games' virtual items. *Journal of Electronic Commerce Research*, *19*(2), 164–185.

Hsu, C., Chuan-Chuan Lin, J., & Chiang, H. (2013). The effects of blogger recommendations on customers' online shopping intentions. *Internet Research*, *23*(1), 69–88. doi:10.1108/10662241311295782

Hsu, C., & Lin, J. (2008). Acceptance of blog usage: The roles of technology acceptance, social influence and knowledge sharing motivation. *Information & Management*, *45*(1), 65–74. doi:10.1016/j.im.2007.11.001

Hsu, L. C., & Liou, D. K. (2017). Maintaining Customer-Brand Relationships in the Mobile Industry: The Mediation Effects of Brand Relationship Benefits and Quality. *International Journal of Mobile Communications*, *15*(4), 388. doi:10.1504/IJMC.2017.084861

Hu, M., Kumar, R., & Sumit, C. (2014, March). Best practices in strategic multichannel fulfillment. *Ivey Business Journal,* 1-6.

Huang, C., Shen, Y., Lin, H., & Chang, S. (2007). Bloggers' Motivations and Behaviors: A Model. *Journal of Advertising Research*, *47*(4), 472–484. doi:10.2501/S0021849907070493

Huang, J., Baptista, J., & Galliers, R. (2013). Reconceptualizing rhetorical practices in organizations: The impact of social media on internal communications. *Information & Management*, *50*(2-3), 112–124. doi:10.1016/j.im.2012.11.003

Huang, M., Zhou, Y., Tsang, A. S., & Zhou, N. (2013). Recovery strategy for group service failures The interaction effects between recovery modes and recovery dimensions. *European Journal of Marketing*, *47*(8), 1133–1156. doi:10.1108/03090561311324255

Huang, M., Zhou, Y., Tsang, A. S., & Zhou, N. (2014). Group service recovery strategies effectiveness: The moderating effects of group size and relational distance. *Journal of Business Research*, *67*(11), 2480–2485. doi:10.1016/j.jbusres.2014.03.008

Huang, R., & Sarigöllü, E. (2012). How brand awareness relates to market outcome, brand equity, and the marketing mix. *Journal of Business Research*, *65*(1), 92–99. doi:10.1016/j.jbusres.2011.02.003

Huang, W., Schrank, H., & Dubinsky, A. (2004). Effect of brand name on consumers' risk perceptions of online shopping. *Journal of Consumer Behaviour*, *4*(1), 40–50. doi:10.1002/cb.156

Huang, Y., Chen, C. H., & Khoo, L. P. (2012). Products classification in emotional design using a basic-emotion based semantic differential method. *International Journal of Industrial Ergonomics*, *42*(6), 569–580. doi:10.1016/j.ergon.2012.09.002

Huang, Z., & Benyoucef, M. (2013). From e-commerce to social commerce: A close look at design features. *Electronic Commerce Research and Applications*, *12*(4), 246–259. doi:10.1016/j.elerap.2012.12.003

Hudson, S., Huang, L., Roth, M. S., & Madden, T. J. (2016). The influence of social media interactions on consumer–brand relationships: A three-country study of brand perceptions and marketing behaviors. *International Journal of Research in Marketing*, *33*(1), 27–41. doi:10.1016/j.ijresmar.2015.06.004

Hudson, S., Roth, M. S., Madden, T. J., & Hudson, R. (2015). The effects of social media on emotions, brand relationship quality, and word of mouth: An empirical study of music festival attendees. *Tourism Management*, *47*, 68–76. doi:10.1016/j.tourman.2014.09.001

Hughes, D. E., & Ahearne, M. (2010). Energizing the Reseller's Sales Force: The Power of Brand Identification. *Journal of Marketing*, *74*(4), 81–96. doi:10.1509/jmkg.74.4.81

Hu, H. H., Lin, J., Qian, Y., & Sun, J. (2018). Strategies for new product diffusion: Whom and how to target? *Journal of Business Research*, *83*, 111–119. doi:10.1016/j.jbusres.2017.10.010

Hui, M. K., Ho, C. K., & Wan, L. C. (2011). Prior relationships and consumer responses to service failures: A cross-cultural study. *Journal of International Marketing*, *19*(1), 59–81. doi:10.1509/jimk.19.1.59

Hung, K., & Li, S. (2007). The Influence of eWOM on Virtual Consumer Communities: Social Capital, Consumer Learning, and Behavioral Outcomes. *Journal of Advertising Research*, *47*(4), 485–495. doi:10.2501/S002184990707050X

Hunt, S., & Madhavaram, S. (2015). The Service-Dominant Logic of Marketing: Theoretical Foundations, Pedagogy, and Resource-Advantage Theory. In R. Lusch & S. Vargo (Eds.), *The Service-dominant Logic of Marketing: Dialog, Debate, and Directions* (2nd ed.; pp. 67–84). New York: Routledge.

Hur, J., & Jang, S. (2016). Toward service recovery strategies: The role of consumer-organization relationship norms. *Journal of Services Marketing*, *30*(7), 724–735. doi:10.1108/JSM-08-2015-0263

Hutter, K., Hautz, J., Dennhardt, S., & Fuller, J. (2013). The impact of user interactions in social media on brand awareness and purchase intention: The case of MINI on Facebook. *Journal of Product and Brand Management*, *22*(5/6), 342–351. doi:10.1108/JPBM-05-2013-0299

Hutton, G., & Fosdick, M. (2011). The globalisation of SM, consumer relationships with brand evolve in the digital age. *Journal of Advertising Research*, *3*(4), 564–570. doi:10.2501/JAR-51-4-564-570

Huy, Q., & Shipilov, A. (2012). The key to social media success within organisations. *Sloan Management Review*, *54*(1), 73–81.

Hwang, J., & Kandampully, J. (2012). The role of emotional aspects in younger consumer-brand relationships. *Journal of Product and Brand Management*, *21*(2), 98–108. doi:10.1108/10610421211215517

Iacobucci, D. (1994). Analysis of Experimental Data. In R. P. Bagozzi (Ed.), *Principles of Marketing Research*. Cambridge, MA: Blackwell Publishing.

Inditex. (2017). *Inditex's net sales climb 10% to €17. 96 billion in the first nine months of fiscal 2017*. Retrieved from https://www.inditex.com/article?articleId=541893&title=Inditex's+net+sales+climb+10%25+to+€17.96+billion

Insider, B. (2018). These Are The 35 Biggest Advertisers On Facebook. *Business Insider*. Retrieved 1 May 2018, from http://www.businessinsider.com/top-advertisers-on-facebook-2013-11

Ioniţă, I. M. (2017). Digitalization influence on shopping centers strategic management. *Proceedings of the International Conference on Business Excellence, 11*(1), 750-758.

Iosifidis, P., & Wheeler, M. (2016). *Public spheres and mediated social networks in the western context and beyond*. Retrieved from https://ebookcentral.proquest.com

Irani, N., & Hanzaee, K. H. (2011). The mediating role of hedonic value in apparel shopping satisfaction. *World Applied Sciences Journal*, *12*(3), 1715–1729.

Islam, A., Agarwal, N. K., & Ikeda, M. (2015). Conceptualizing value co-creation for service innovation in academic libraries. *Business Information Review*, *32*(1), 45–52. doi:10.1177/0266382115573155

Israeli, A. A., Lee, S. A., & Karpinski, A. C. (2017). Investigating the dynamics and the content of customers' social media reporting after a restaurant service failure. *Journal of Hospitality Marketing & Management*, *26*(6), 606–626. doi:10.1080/19368623.2017.1281193

Istanbulluoglu, D. (2017). Complaint handling on social media: The impact of multiple response times on consumer satisfaction. *Computers in Human Behavior*, *74*, 72–82. doi:10.1016/j.chb.2017.04.016

Itami, H., & Roehl, W. T. (1987). Mobilizing Invisible Assets. Harvard University Press.

Jaakkola, E., Helkkula, A., & Stenroos, L. A. (2012). Service experience co-creation: Conceptualization, implications, and future research directions. *Journal of Service Management*, *26*(2), 182–205. doi:10.1108/JOSM-12-2014-0323

Jackson, T., & Shaw, D. (2006). *The fashion handbook*. Oxon, UK: Routledge.

Jaffe, E. D., & Nebenzahl, I. D. (2001). *National Image & Competitive Advantage: The Theory and Practice of Country-of-Origin Effect*. Copenhagen Business School Press.

Jagongo, A., & Kinyua, C. (2013). The Social Media and Entrepreneurship Growth (A New Business Communication Paradigm among SMEs in Nairobi). *International Journal of Humanities and Social Science*, *3*(10), 213–227.

Jan, A., & Khan, M. F. (2014). Social Media Is Nothing but a Public Relation Tool. *International Journal of Business and Management*, *2*(12), 272–277.

Jang, H., Olfman, L., Ko, I., Koh, J., & Kim, K. (2008). The Influence of On-Line Brand Community Characteristics on Community Commitment and Brand Loyalty. *International Journal of Electronic Commerce*, *12*(3), 57–80. doi:10.2753/JEC1086-4415120304

Jansen, B. J., Zhang, M., Sobel, K., & Chowdury, A. (2009). Twitter power: Tweets as electronic word of mouth. *Journal of the American Society for Information Science and Technology*, *60*(11), 2169–2188. doi:10.1002/asi.21149

Järvinen, J., Tollinen, A., Karjaluoto, H., & Jayawardhena, C. (2012). Digital and social media marketing usage in B2B industrial section. *Marketing Management Journal, 22*(2).

Jayachandran, S., Gimeno, J., & Varadarajan, P. (1999). The Theory of Multimarket Competition: A Synthesis and Implications for Marketing Strategy. *Journal of Marketing*, *63*(3), 49–66. doi:10.2307/1251775

Jenkins, R. (2008). *Social identity (Key Ideas)* (3rd ed.). London: Routledge.

Jeong, S. H., Kim, H. J., Yum, J. Y., & Hwang, Y. R. (2016). What Type of Content are Smartphone Users Addicted to? SNS vs Games. *Journal of Computers in Human Behavior*, *54*, 10–17. doi:10.1016/j.chb.2015.07.035

Jia, A. L., Shen, S., Li, D., & Chen, S. (2018). Predicting the implicit and the explicit video popularity in a User-generated Content site with enhanced social features. *Computer Networks*, *140*, 112–125. doi:10.1016/j.comnet.2018.05.004

Jiang, Z., Chan, J., Tan, B. C. Y., & Chua, W. S. (2009). Effects of interactivity on website involvement and purchase intention. *Journal of the Association for Information Systems*, *11*(1), 34–59. doi:10.17705/1jais.00218

Jiao, Y., Ertz, M., Jo, M., & Sarigollu, E. (2018). Social value, content value, and brand equity in social media brand communities: A comparison of Chinese and US consumers. *International Marketing Review*, *35*(1), 18–41. doi:10.1108/IMR-07-2016-0132

Jiao, Y., Gao, J., & Yang, J. (2014). Social value and content value in social media: Two ways to flow. *Journalof Advanced Management Science*, *3*(4), 299–306.

Jin, S. A. A. (2012). The potential of social media for luxury brand management. *Marketing Intelligence & Planning*, *30*(7), 687–699. doi:10.1108/02634501211273805

Jin, S. V., & Phua, J. (2016). Making Reservations Online: The Impact of Consumer-Written and System-Aggregated User-Generated Content (UGC) in Travel Booking Websites on Consumers' Behavioral Intentions. *Journal of Travel & Tourism Marketing*, *33*(1), 101–117. doi:10.1080/10548408.2015.1038419

Jin, S., & Phua, J. (2014). Following Celebrities' Tweets About Brands: The Impact of Twitter-Based Electronic Word-of-Mouth on Consumers' Source Credibility Perception, Buying Intention, and Social Identification With Celebrities. *Journal of Advertising*, *43*(2), 181–195. doi:10.1080/00913367.2013.827606

John, D., Loken, B., Kim, K., & Monga, A. (2006). Brand Concept Maps: A Methodology for Identifying Brand Association Networks. *JMR, Journal of Marketing Research*, *43*(4), 549–563. doi:10.1509/jmkr.43.4.549

Johnson, M. D., & Gustafsson, A. (2003). *Competing in a Service Economy: How to Create a Competitive Advantage Through Service Development and Innovation*. San Francisco, CA: John Wiley & Sons.

Jones, S. (2002). *3G Launch Strategies, Early Adopters, Why & How to make them yours*. Tarifica report.

Jones, S. (2015). *How should luxury brands navigate advertising controversies?* Retrieved August 19, 2016, from https://www.luxurydaily.com/how-should-luxury-brands-navigate-advertising-controversies/

Jones, H., & Farquhar, J. D. (2007). Putting it right: Service failure and customer loyalty in UK banks. *International Journal of Bank Marketing*, *25*(3), 161–172. doi:10.1108/02652320710739869

Jones, M. A., Weun, S., & Beatty, S. E. (2004). The impact of service failure severity on service recovery evaluations andpost-recovery relationships. *Journal of Services Marketing*, *18*(2), 133–146. doi:10.1108/08876040410528737

Jones, S. (1998). Information, Internet and community: Notes toward an understanding of community in the information age. In S. Jones (Ed.), *Cybersocierty 2.0: Revisiting computer-mediated communication and community* (2nd ed.; pp. 1–34). London: Sage Publications. doi:10.4135/9781452243689.n1

Jung, J., Hun, H., & Oh, M. (2017). Travellers Switching Behaviour in the Airline Industry from the Perspective of the Push-Pull-Mooring Framework. *Journal of Torurism Management.*, *59*, 139–153. doi:10.1016/j.tourman.2016.07.018

Jung, N. Y., & Seock, Y. K. (2017). Effect of service recovery on customers' perceived justice, satisfaction, and word-of-mouth intentions on online shopping websites. *Journal of Retailing and Consumer Services*, *37*, 23–30. doi:10.1016/j.jretconser.2017.01.012

Jung, Y. (2014). What a smartphone is to me: Understanding user values in using smartphones. *Information Systems Journal*, *24*(4), 299–321. doi:10.1111/isj.12031

Jung, Y., Pawlowski, S. D., & Kim, H.-W. (2017). Exploring associations between young adults' Facebook use and psychological well-being: A goal hierarchy approach. *International Journal of Information Management*, *37*(1), 1391–1404. doi:10.1016/j.ijinfomgt.2016.10.005

Jun, S.-Y., Cha, T., & Aggarwal, P. (2011). How Much Better? The Effect Of Tensile Information On Word-Of-Mouth Effectiveness. *Journal of Marketing Theory and Practice, 19*(3), 263–276. doi:10.2753/MTP1069-6679190301

Kadam, A., & Ayarekar, S. (2014). Impact of Social Media on Entrepreneurship and Entrepreneurial Performance: Special Reference to Small and Medium Scale Enterprises. *SIES Journal of Management, 10*(1).

Kahn, B. E., & Louie, T. A. (1990). Effects of Retraction of Price Promotions on Brand Choice Behaviour for Variety-Seeking and Last-purchase Loyal Consumers. *JMR, Journal of Marketing Research, 27*(3), 279–289. doi:10.2307/3172586

Kaikati, A., & Kaikati, J. (2004). Stealth Marketing: How to Reach Consumers Surreptitiously. *California Management Review, 46*(4), 6–22. doi:10.2307/41166272

Kalamas, M., Laroche, M., & Makdessian, L. (2008). Reaching the Boiling Point: Consumers' Negative Affective Reactions to Firm-Attributed Service Failures. *Journal of Business Research, 61*(8), 813–824. doi:10.1016/j.jbusres.2007.09.008

Kalyanam, K., McIntyre, S., & Masonis, J. T. (2007). Adaptive experimentation in interactive marketing: The case of viral marketing at Plaxo. *Journal of Interactive Marketing, 21*(3), 72–85. doi:10.1002/dir.20086

Kamboj, S., & Sarmah, B. (2018). Construction and validation of the customer social participation in brand communities scale. *Internet Research, 28*(1), 46–73. doi:10.1108/IntR-01-2017-0011

Kamboj, S., Sarmah, B., Gupta, S., & Dwivedi, Y. (2018). Examining branding co-creation in brand communities on social media: Applying the paradigm of Stimulus-Organism-Response. *International Journal of Information Management, 39*, 169–185. doi:10.1016/j.ijinfomgt.2017.12.001

Kandampully, J., Zhang, T., & Bilgihan, A. (2015). Customer loyalty: A review and future directions with a special focus on the hospitality industry. *International Journal of Contemporary Hospitality Management, 27*(3), 379–414. doi:10.1108/IJCHM-03-2014-0151

Kane, G. C., Alavi, M., Labianca, G., & Borgatti, S. P. (2014). What's different about social networks? A framework and research agenda. *Management Information Systems Quarterly, 38*(1), 274–304. doi:10.25300/MISQ/2014/38.1.13

Kang, I. (2016). Web 2.0 UGC, and citizen journalism: Revisiting South Korea's Oh my News model in the age of social media. *Telematics and Informatics, 33*(2), 546–556. doi:10.1016/j.tele.2015.07.007

Kang, J.-Y. M., Johnson, K. K. P., & Wu, J. (2014). Consumer style inventory and intent to social shop online for apparel using social networking sites. *Journal of Fashion Marketing and Management, 18*(3), 301–320. doi:10.1108/JFMM-09-2012-0057

Kang, Y. M., Cho, C., & Lee, S. (2011). Analysis of factors affecting the adoption of smartphones. In *International Technology Management Conference (ITMC)* (pp. 919–925). IEEE.

Kang, Y. M., Lee, M., & Lee, S. (2014). Service-oriented factors affecting the adoption of smartphones. *Journal of Technology Management & Innovation, 9*(2), 98–117. doi:10.4067/S0718-27242014000200008

Kanning, L. (2008). *Evolvement and Prospect of Study on Word-of-Mouth Communication.* Working paper.

Kao, T. Y., Yang, M. H., Wu, J.-T. B., & Cheng, Y.-Y. (2016). Co-creating value with consumers through social media. *Journal of Services Marketing, 30*(2), 141–151. doi:10.1108/JSM-03-2014-0112

Kapferer, J. N. (1997). *Strategic Brand Management: Creating and Sustaining Brand Equity Long Term.* London: Kogan Page Ltd.

Kapferer, J. N. (2008). *The New Strategic Brand Management, Creating and Sustaining Brand Equity Long Term.* London: Kogan Page.

Kaplan, A. M., & Haenlein, M. (2010). Users of the world, unite! The challenges and opportunities of Social Media. *Business Horizons*, *53*(1), 59–68. doi:10.1016/j.bushor.2009.09.003

Kaplan, A. M., & Haenlein, M. (2011). The early bird catches the news: Nine things you should know about micro-blogging. *Business Horizons*, *54*(2), 105–113. doi:10.1016/j.bushor.2010.09.004

Kaplan, A. M., & Haenlein, M. (2011). Two hearts in three-quarter time: How to waltz the social media/viral marketing dance. *Business Horizons*, *54*(3), 253–263. doi:10.1016/j.bushor.2011.01.006

Kapoor, K. K., & Dwivedi, Y. K. (2015). Metamorphosis of Indian electoral campaigns: Modi's social media experiment. *International Journal of Indian Culture &Business Management*, *11*(4), 496–516. doi:10.1504/IJICBM.2015.072430

Karahanna, E., Straub, D. W., & Chervany, N. L. (1999). Information technology adoption across time: A cross-sectional comparison of pre-adoption and post-adoption beliefs. *Management Information Systems Quarterly*, *23*(2), 183–213. doi:10.2307/249751

Karikari, S., Osei-Frimpong, K., & Owusu-Frimpong, N. (2017). Evaluating individual level antecedents and consequences of social media use in Ghana. *Technological Forecasting and Social Change*, *123*, 68–79. doi:10.1016/j.techfore.2017.06.023

Karimi, S. (2013). *A purchase decision-making process model of online consumers and its influential factor a cross sector analysis*. University of Manchester.

Karjaluoto, H., & Ulkuniemi, P. (2015). Digital communications in industrial marketing. *Journal of Business and Industrial Marketing*, *30*(6). doi:10.1108/JBIM-04-2013-0092

Karpinski, R. (2005). The next phase: Bottom-up marketing. *BtoB Magazine*, *90*(5), 38.

Katawetawaraks, C., & Wang, C. L. (2011). Online shopper behavior: Influences of online shopping decision. *Asian Journal of Business Research*, *1*(2), 66–74. doi:10.14707/ajbr.110012

Katz, E., & Lazarsfeld, P. (1955). *Personal influence*. Glencoe, IL: Free Press.

Kau, A., & Loh, E. W. (2006). The effects of service recovery on consumer satisfaction: A comparison between complainants and non-complainants. *Journal of Services Marketing*, *20*(2), 101–111. doi:10.1108/08876040610657039

Kaur, P., Dhir, A., Rajala, R., & Dwivedi, Y. (2018). Why people use online social media brand communities: A consumption value theory perspective. *Online Information Review*, *42*(2), 205–221. doi:10.1108/OIR-12-2015-0383

Kayastha, S. (2011). Defining Service and Non-Service Exchanges. *Service Science*, *3*(4), 313–324. doi:10.1287erv.3.4.313

Kaynama, S., Black, C., & Keesling, G. (2000). Impact of the internet on internal service quality factors: The travel industry case. *Journal of Applied Business Research*, *19*, 135–146.

Kazakeviciute, A., & Banyte, J. (2012). The relationship of consumers' perceived hedonic value and behavior. *Inzinerine Ekonomika-Engineering Economic*, *23*(5), 532–540.

Keaveney, S. M. (1995). Customer switching behaviour in service industries: An exploratory study. *Journal of Marketing*, *59*(2), 71–82. doi:10.2307/1252074

Kedmenec, I., Rebernik, M., & Perić, J. (2015). The Impact of Individual Characteristics on Intentions to Pursue Social Entrepreneurship. *Ekonomski Pregled*, *66*(2), 119–137.

Keller, K. (2001). Building Customer-Based Brand Equity: A Blueprint for Creating Strong Brands. Marketing Science Institute, 3-23.

Keller, K. (1993). Conceptualizing, Measuring, and Managing Customer-Based Brand Equity. *Journal of Marketing*, *57*(1), 8. doi:10.1177/002224299305700101

Keller, K. (2001). *Building a Customer-Based Brand Equity: A Blueprint for Creating Strong Brands*. Marketing Science Institute.

Keller, K. (2009). Building strong brands in a modern marketing communications environment. *Journal of Marketing Communications*, *15*(2-3), 139–155. doi:10.1080/13527260902757530

Keller, K. (2012). *Strategic brand management* (4th ed.). Upper Saddle River, N.J.: Prentice Hall.

Keller, K. L., & Lehmann, D. R. (2006). Brands and Branding: Research Findings and Future Priorities. *Journal of Marine Science*, *25*(6), 740–759. doi:10.1287/mksc.1050.0153

Kelley, H. (1952). Two functions of reference groups. In G. Swanson, T. Newcomb, & E. Hartley (Eds.), *Society for the psychological study of social issues, readings in social psychology* (1st ed.; pp. 410–414). New York: Holt.

Kelley, S. W., & Davis, M. A. (1994). Antecedents to customer expectations for service recovery. *Journal of the Academy of Marketing Science*, *22*(1), 52–61. doi:10.1177/0092070394221005

Kelley, S. W., Hoffman, K. D., & Davis, M. A. (1993). A typology of retail failures and recoveries. *Journal of Retailing*, *69*(4), 429–452. doi:10.1016/0022-4359(93)90016-C

Kelly, L., Kerr, G., & Drennan, J. (2010). Avoidance of Advertising in Social Networking Sites. *Journal of Interactive Advertising*, *10*(2), 16–27. doi:10.1080/15252019.2010.10722167

Kelman, H. C. (1958). Compliance, Identification, and Internalization: Three Processes of Attitude Change. *The Journal of Conflict Resolution*, *2*(1), 51–60. doi:10.1177/002200275800200106

Kent, M. L., Taylor, M., & White, W. J. (2003). The relationship between Web site design and organizational responsiveness to stakeholders. *Public Relations Review*, *29*(1), 63–77. doi:10.1016/S0363-8111(02)00194-7

Kerr, G., Mortimer, K., Dickinson, S., & Waller, D. S. (2012). Buy, boycott or blog: Exploring online consumer power to share, discuss and distribute controversial advertising messages. *European Journal of Marketing*, *46*(3/4), 387–405. doi:10.1108/03090561211202521

Kiecker, P., & Cowles, D. (2002). Interpersonal Communication and Personel Influence on the Internet. *Journal of Euromarketing*, *11*(2), 310–321. doi:10.1300/J037v11n02_04

Kietzmann, J. H., Hermkens, K., McCarthy, I. P., & Silvestre, B. S. (2011). Social media? Get serious! Understanding the functional building blocks of social media. *Business Horizons*, *54*(3), 241–251. doi:10.1016/j.bushor.2011.01.005

Kilgour, M., Sasser, S. L., & Larke, R. (2015). The social media transformation process: Curating content into strategy. *Corporate Communications*, *20*(3), 326–343. doi:10.1108/CCIJ-07-2014-0046

Kilian, T., Hennigs, N., & Langner, S. (2012). Do Millennials read books or blogs? Introducing a media usage typology of the Internet generation. *Journal of Consumer Marketing*, *29*(2), 114–124. doi:10.1108/07363761211206366

Kim, A. J., & Johnson, K. K. (2016). Power of consumers using social media: Examining the influences of brand-related user-generated content on Facebook. *Computers in Human Behavior*, *58*, 98–108. doi:10.1016/j.chb.2015.12.047

Kim, A. J., & Ko, E. (2012). Do social media marketing activities enhance customer equity? An empirical study of luxury fashion brand. *Journal of Business Research*, *65*(10), 1480–1486. doi:10.1016/j.jbusres.2011.10.014

Kim, C. K., Han, D. C., & Park, S. B. (2001). The Effect of Brand Personality and Brand Identification on Brand Loyalty: Applying the Theory of Social Identification. *The Japanese Psychological Research*, *43*(4), 195–206. doi:10.1111/1468-5884.00177

Kim, D. (2016). Value ecosystem models for social media services. *Technological Forecasting and Social Change*, *107*, 13–27. doi:10.1016/j.techfore.2016.03.010

Kim, D., Chun, H., & Lee, H. (2014). Determining the factors that influence college students' adoption of smartphones. *Journal of the Association for Information Science and Technology*, *65*(3), 578–588. doi:10.1002/asi.22987

Kim, D., & Lim, U. (2017). Social Enterprise as a Catalyst for Sustainable Local and Regional Development. *Sustainability*, *9*(8), 1427. doi:10.3390u9081427

Kim, D., Nam, J. K., Oh, J. S., & Kang, M. C. (2016). A Latent Profile Analysis of the Interplay between PC and Smartphone in Problematic Internet Use. *Journal of Computers in Human Behavior*, *56*, 360–368. doi:10.1016/j.chb.2015.11.009

Kim, E. E. K., & Lee, C. H. (2015). How do consumers process online hotel reviews? The effects of eWOM consensus and sequence. *Journal of Hospitality and Tourism Technology*, *6*(2), 113–126. doi:10.1108/JHTT-09-2014-0045

Kim, H. D., Lee, I., & Lee, C. K. (2013). Building Web 2.0 enterprises: A study of small and medium enterprises in the United States. *International Small Business Journal*, *31*(2), 156–174. doi:10.1177/0266242611409785

Kim, H. W., Chan, H. C., & Gupta, S. (2007). Value-based adoption of mobile internet: An empirical investigation. *Decision Support Systems*, *43*(1), 111–126. doi:10.1016/j.dss.2005.05.009

Kim, J. (2012). The institutionalisation of YouTube: From user-generated content to professionally generated content. *Media Culture & Society*, *34*(1), 53–67. doi:10.1177/0163443711427199

Kim, J. E., Lloyd, S., & Cervellon, M. C. (2016). Narrative-transportation storylines in luxury brand advertising: Motivating consumer engagement. *Journal of Business Research*, *69*(1), 304–313. doi:10.1016/j.jbusres.2015.08.002

Kim, J., Choi, J., Qualls, W., & Han, K. (2008). It takes a marketplace community to raise brand commitment: The role of online communities. *Journal of Marketing Management*, *24*(3-4), 409–431. doi:10.1362/026725708X306167

Kim, M., Chung, N., & Lee, C. (2011). The effect of perceived trust on electronic commerce: Shopping online for tourism products and services in South Korea. *Tourism Management*, *32*(2), 256–265. doi:10.1016/j.tourman.2010.01.011

Kim, M.-K., Chang, Y., Wong, S. F., & Park, M.-C. (2013). The effect of perceived risks and switching barriers on the intention to use smartphones among non-adopters in Korea. *Information Development*, 1–12.

Kim, M., & Lee, M. (2017). Brand-related user-generated content on social media: The roles of source and sponsorship. *Internet Research*, *27*(5), 1085–1103. doi:10.1108/IntR-07-2016-0206

Kim, N., & Ulgado, F. M. (2012). The effect of on-the-spot versus delayed compensation: The moderating role of failure severity. *Journal of Services Marketing*, *26*(3), 158–167. doi:10.1108/08876041211223960

Kim, S. H., Park, N., & Park, S. H. (2013). Exploring the Effects of Online Word of Mouth and Expert Reviews on Theatrical Movies' Box Office Success. *Journal of Media Economics*, *26*(2), 98–114. doi:10.1080/08997764.2013.785551

Kim, S., & Stoel, L. (2004). Apparel retailers: Website quality dimensions and satisfaction. *Journal of Retailing and Consumer Services*, *11*(2), 109–117. doi:10.1016/S0969-6989(03)00010-9

Kim, W., Jeong, O. R., & Lee, S. W. (2010). On social web sites. *Information Systems*, *35*(2), 215–236. doi:10.1016/j.is.2009.08.003

Kim, Y.-K. (2002). Consumer value: An application to mall and internet shopping. *International Journal of Retail & Distribution Management*, *30*(12), 595–602. doi:10.1108/09590550210453075

King, R.A., Racherla, P. & Bush, V.D. (2014). What We Know and Don't Know About Online Word-of-Mouth: A Review and Synthesis of the Literature. *Journal of Interactive Marketing, 28*(3), 167-183.

King, C. W., & Summers, J. O. (1970). Overlap of opinion leadership across consumer product categories. *JMR, Journal of Marketing Research*, *7*(1), 43–50. doi:10.2307/3149505

King, C., So, K. K. F., Sparks, B. A., & Wang, Y. (2016). The Role of Customer Engagement in Building Consumer Loyalty to Tourism Brands. *Journal of Travel Research*, *55*(1), 64–78. doi:10.1177/0047287514541008

Kireyev, P., Kumar, V., & Ofek, E. (2015). *Match your own price? Self-matching as a multichannel retailer's pricing strategy. Harvard Business Review.*

Kirgiz, A. (2014). Hedonism, A consumer disease of the modern age: Gender and hedonic shopping in Turkey. *Global Media Journal*, *4*(8), 200–213.

Kirmani, A., & Zeithaml, V. (1993). Advertising, perceived quality, and brand image. In D. Aaker & A. Biel (Eds.), *Brand Equity & Advertising: Advertising's Role in Building Strong Brands* (1st ed.; pp. 143–162). Hilldale, NJ: Lawrence Erlbaum Associates.

Kiss, C., & Bichler, M. (2008). Identification of influencers—measuring influence in customer networks. *Decision Support Systems*, *46*(1), 233–253. doi:10.1016/j.dss.2008.06.007

Kizgin, H., Jamal, A., Dey, B. L., & Rana, N. P. (2018). The Impact of Social Media on Consumers' Acculturation and Purchase Intentions. *Information Systems Frontiers*, *20*(3), 503–514. doi:10.100710796-017-9817-4

Kleine, R. III, Kleine, S., & Kernan, J. (1993). Mundane Consumption and the Self: A Social-Identity Perspective. *Journal of Consumer Psychology*, *2*(3), 209–235. doi:10.1016/S1057-7408(08)80015-0

Kleine, S. S., Kleine, R. E. III, & Allen, C. T. (1995). How is a Possession 'Me' or 'Not Me'? Characterizing Types and Antecedents of Material Possession Attachment. *The Journal of Consumer Research*, *22*(12), 327–343. doi:10.1086/209454

Knoll, J. (2015). Advertising in social media: A review of empirical evidence. *International Journal of Advertising*, *35*(2), 266–300. doi:10.1080/02650487.2015.1021898

Knox, G., & Van Oest, R. (2014). Customer complaints and recovery effectiveness: A customer base approach. *Journal of Marketing*, *78*(5), 42–57. doi:10.1509/jm.12.0317

Koch, H., Leidner, D., & Gonzalez, E. (2013). Digitally enabling social networks: Resolving IT-culture conflict. *Information Systems Journal*, *23*(6), 501–523. doi:10.1111/isj.12020

Koh, J., & Kim, Y. (2004). Knowledge sharing in virtual communities: An e-business perspective. *Expert Systems with Applications*, *26*(2), 155–166. doi:10.1016/S0957-4174(03)00116-7

Kohli, C., Suri, R., & Kapoor, A. (2015). Will social media kill branding? *Business Horizons*, *58*(1), 35–44. doi:10.1016/j.bushor.2014.08.004

Kotler, P. (2009). *Marketing Management* (1st ed.). Harlow: Pearson Education.

Kotler, P., Armstrong, G., Harris, L., & Piercy, N. F. (2013). *Principles of marketing* (European edition). Pearson Education Limited.

Kotler, P., & Gertner, D. (2002). Country as brand, product, and beyond: A place marketing and brand management perspective. *Journal of Brand Management*, *9*(4/5), 249–261. doi:10.1057/palgrave.bm.2540076

Koufaris, M., & Hampton-Sosa, W. (2004). The development of initial trust in an online company by new customers. *Information & Management*, *41*(3), 377–397. doi:10.1016/j.im.2003.08.004

Kozinets, R. (2002). The Field Behind the Screen: Using Netnography for Marketing Research in Online Communities. *JMR, Journal of Marketing Research*, *39*(1), 61–72. doi:10.1509/jmkr.39.1.61.18935

Kozinets, R. V. (1999). E-Tribalized Marketing? The Strategic Implications of Virtual Communities of Consumption. *European Management Journal*, *17*(3), 252–264. doi:10.1016/S0263-2373(99)00004-3

Kozinets, R. V., De Valck, K., Wojnicki, A. C., & Wilner, S. J. (2010). Networked narratives: Understanding word-of-mouth marketing in online communities. *Journal of Marketing*, *74*(2), 71–89. doi:10.1509/jmkg.74.2.71

Kozub, K. R., O'Neill, M. A., & Palmer, A. A. (2014). Emotional antecedents and outcomes of service recovery: An exploratory study in the luxury hotel industry. *Journal of Services Marketing*, *28*(3), 233–243. doi:10.1108/JSM-08-2012-0147

Kuksov, D., Shachar, R., & Wang, K. (2013). Advertising and Consumers' Communications. *Marketing Science*, *32*(2), 294–309. doi:10.1287/mksc.1120.0753

Kulmala, M., Mesiranta, N., & Tuominen, P. (2013). Organic and amplified eWOM in consumer fashion blogs. *Journal Of Fashion Marketing And Management: An International Journal*, *17*(1), 20–37. doi:10.1108/13612021311305119

Kumar, A., Bezawada, R., Rishika, R., Janakiraman, R., & Kannan, P. K. (2016). From social to sale: The effects of firm-generated content in social media on consumer behaviour. *Journal of Marketing*, *80*(1), 7–25. doi:10.1509/jm.14.0249

Kumar, N., Hibbard, J., & Stern, L. (1994). *The Nature and Consequences of Marketing Channel Intermediary Commitment*. Cambridge, UK: Marketing Science Institute.

Kumar, R., Novak, J., Raghavan, P., & Tomkins, A. (2004). Structure and evolution of blogspace. *Communications of the ACM*, *47*(12), 35–39. doi:10.1145/1035134.1035162

Kumar, V., & George, M. (2007). Measuring and maximizing customer equity: A critical analysis. *Journal of the Academy of Marketing Science*, *35*(2), 157–171. doi:10.100711747-007-0028-2

Kumar, V., & Mirchandani, R. (2012). Increasing the ROI of social media marketing. *Sloan Management Review*, *54*(1), 55–61.

Kunz, G. I. (2005). *Merchandising: Theory, principles, and practice* (3rd ed.). New York: Fairchild Books.

Kuo, Y. F., & Wu, C. M. (2012). Satisfaction and post-purchase intentions with service recovery of online shopping websites: Perspectives on perceived justice and emotions. *International Journal of Information Management*, *32*(2), 127–138. doi:10.1016/j.ijinfomgt.2011.09.001

Kuo, Y. F., Yen, S. T., & Chen, L. H. (2011). Online auction service failures in Taiwan: Typologies and recovery strategies. *Electronic Commerce Research and Applications*, *10*(2), 183–193. doi:10.1016/j.elerap.2009.09.003

Kuo, Y., & Hou, J. (2017). Oppositional Brand Loyalty in Online Brand Communities: Perspectives on Social Identity Theory and Consumer-Brand. *Journal of Electronic Commerce Research*, *18*(3), 254.

Kushwaha, T., & Shankar, V. (2013). Are multichannel customers really more valuable? The moderating role of product category characteristics. *Journal of Marketing*, *77*(4), 67–102. doi:10.1509/jm.11.0297

Kuvykaitė, R., & Tarutė, A. (2015). A Critical Analysis of Consumer Engagement Dimensionality. *Procedia: Social and Behavioral Sciences*, *213*, 654–658. doi:10.1016/j.sbspro.2015.11.468

Labrecque, L. I. (2014). Fostering Consumer–Brand Relationships in Social Media Environments: The Role of Parasocial Interaction. *Journal of Interactive Marketing*, *28*(2), 134–148. doi:10.1016/j.intmar.2013.12.003

Lacka, E., & Chong, A. (2016). Usability perspective on social media sites' adoption in the B2B context. *Industrial Marketing Management*, *54*, 80–91. doi:10.1016/j.indmarman.2016.01.001

Ladhari, R. (2010). Developing e-service quality scales: A literature review. *Journal of Retailing and Consumer Services*, *17*(6), 464–477. doi:10.1016/j.jretconser.2010.06.003

Laestadius, L. I., & Wahl, M. M. (2017). Mobilizing social media users to become advertisers: Corporate hashtag campaigns as a public health concern. *Digital Health*, *3*, 1–12. doi:10.1177/2055207617710802 PMID:29942600

Lamb, R., & Kling, R. (2003). reconceptualizing users as social actors in information systems research. *Management Information Systems Quarterly*, *27*(2), 197–235. doi:10.2307/30036529

Lam, S. K., Ahearne, M., Mullins, R., Hayati, B., & Schillewaert, N. (2013). Exploring the Dynamics of Antecedents to Consumer–Brand Identification with a New Brand. *Journal of the Academy of Marketing Science*, *41*(2), 243–252. doi:10.100711747-012-0301-x

Lam, S., Ahearne, M., Hu, Y., & Schillewaert, N. (2010). Resistance to Brand Switching When a Radically New Brand Is Introduced: A Social Identity Theory Perspective. *Journal of Marketing*, *74*(6), 128–146. doi:10.1509/jmkg.74.6.128

Lane, P., Wafa, S., & Hassan, R. (2014). Perceived Usefulness and Perceived Ease of Use of E-Commerce Adoption among Entrepreneurs in Sabah. *Kuwait Chapter of Arabian Journal of Business and Management Review*, *3*(9), 94–103. doi:10.12816/0018333

Lane, W., & Manner, C. (2011). The impact of personality traits on smartphone ownership and use. *International Journal of Business and Social Science*, *2*(17), 22. Retrieved from http://www.ijbssnet.com/journals/Vol_2_No_17/4.pdf

Lang, G., & Bressolles, G. (2013). Economic performance and customer expectation in e-fulfillment systems: a multi-channel retailer perspective. *Supply Chain Forum, 14*(1), 16-27.

Langner, S., Hennigs, N., & Wiedmann, K. (2013). Social persuasion: Targeting social identities through social influencers. *Journal of Consumer Marketing*, *30*(1), 31–49. doi:10.1108/07363761311290821

LaPointe, P. (2012). Measuring Facebook's Impact on Marketing. *Journal of Advertising Research*, *52*(3), 286–287. doi:10.2501/JAR-52-3-286-287

Laroche, M., Habibi, M. R., Richard, M. O., & Sankaranarayanan, R. (2012). The effects of social media based brand communities on brand community markers, value creation practices, brand trust and brand loyalty. *Computers in Human Behavior*, *28*(5), 1755–1767. doi:10.1016/j.chb.2012.04.016

Lastner, M. M., Folse, J. A. G., Mangus, S. M., & Fennell, P. (2016). The road to recovery: Overcoming service failures through positive emotions. *Journal of Business Research*, *69*(10), 4278–4286. doi:10.1016/j.jbusres.2016.04.002

Laudon, K., & Traver, C. (2015). *E-commerce*. Boston: Addison Wesley.

Laverie, D., Kleine, R. III, & Kleine, S. (2002). Reexamination and Extension of Kleine, Kleine, and Kernan's Social Identity Model of Mundane Consumption: The Mediating Role of the Appraisal Process. *The Journal of Consumer Research*, *28*(4), 659–669. doi:10.1086/338208

Leckie, C., Munyaradzi, W. N., & Johnson, L. W. (2016). Antecedents of Consumer Brand Engagement and Brand Loyalty. *Journal of Marketing Management*, *32*(5-6), 5–6, 558–578. doi:10.1080/0267257X.2015.1131735

Lee, H.-H., Kim, J., & Fiore, A. M. (2010). Affective and cognitive online shopping experience: Effects of image interactivity technology and experimenting with appearance. *Clothing & Textiles Research Journal*, *28*(2), 140–154. doi:10.1177/0887302X09341586

Lee, I. (2017). A study of the effect of social shopping deals on online reviews. *Industrial Management & Data Systems*, *117*(10), 2227–2240. doi:10.1108/IMDS-09-2016-0378

Lee, J., & Hong, I. B. (2016). Predicting positive user responses to social media advertising: The roles of emotional appeal, informativeness, and creativity. *International Journal of Information Management*, *36*(3), 360–373. doi:10.1016/j.ijinfomgt.2016.01.001

Lee, K. T., & Koo, D. M. (2012). Effects of attribute and valence of e-WOM on message adoption: Moderating roles of subjective knowledge and regulatory focus. *Computers in Human Behavior*, *28*(5), 1974–1984. doi:10.1016/j.chb.2012.05.018

Lee, K., & Carter, S. (2011). Global marketing management. *Strategic Direction*, *27*(1). doi:10.1108d.2011.05627aae.001

Lee, M. J., Singh, N., & Chan, E. S. (2011). Service failures and recovery actions in the hotel industry: A text-mining approach. *Journal of Vacation Marketing*, *17*(3), 197–207. doi:10.1177/1356766711409182

Leenders, R. A. J. (2002). Modeling Social Influence Through Network Autocorrelation: Constructing the Weight Matrix. *Social Networks*, *24*(1), 21–48. doi:10.1016/S0378-8733(01)00049-1

Lee, S., & Choeh, J. Y. (2018). The interactive impact of online word-of-mouth and review helpfulness on box office revenue. *Management Decision*, *56*(4), 849–866. doi:10.1108/MD-06-2017-0561

Lee, T. Y., & Bradlow, E. T. (2011). Automatic marketing research using online customer reviews. *JMR, Journal of Marketing Research*, *48*(October), 881–894. doi:10.1509/jmkr.48.5.881

Lee, Y., & Wu, W. (2015). Effects of Medical Disputes on Internet Communications of Negative Emotions and Negative Online Word-of-Mouth. *Psychological Reports*, *117*(1), 251–270. doi:10.2466/21.PR0.117c13z1 PMID:26226491

Leibtag, A. (2014). *2013; The Digital Crown: Winning at Content on the Web*. Morgan Kaufmann Publishers Inc.

Lemon, K., Rust, R., & Zeithaml, V. (2001). What drives customer equity. *Marketing Management*, *10*(1), 20–25.

Leonardi. (2014). Social media, knowledge sharing, and innovation. *Information Systems Research*, *25*(4), 796–816. doi:10.1287/isre.2014.0536

Leskovec, J. (2011). *Social media analytics: tracking, modelling and predicting the flow of information through networks*. Tutorial in ACM SIGKDD Conference, San Diego, CA.

Le, T. D. (2018). Influence of WOM and content type on online engagement in consumption communities: The information flow from discussion forums to Facebook. *Online Information Review*, *42*(2), 161–175. doi:10.1108/OIR-09-2016-0246

Leung, L. (2009). User-generated content on the internet: An examination of gratifications, civic engagement and psychological empowerment. *New Media & Society*, *11*(8), 1327–1347. doi:10.1177/1461444809341264

Levin, A. M., Levin, I. P., & Heath, C. E. (2003). Product category dependent consumer preferences for online and offline shopping features and their influence on multi-channel retail alliances. *Journal of Electronic Commerce Research*, *4*(3), 85–93. Available at http://www.csulb.edu/web/journals/jecr/issues/20033/paper1.pdf

Levy, S. (1959). Symbols for Sale. *Harvard Business Review*, (37), 117–124.

Lewis, S. (2015). Reciprocity as a Key Concept for Social Media and Society. *Social Media + Society*, *1*(1).

Lewis, B. R., & Spyrakopoulos, S. (2001). Service failures and recovery in retail banking: The customers' perspective. *International Journal of Bank Marketing*, *19*(1), 37–48. doi:10.1108/02652320110366481

Li, L. (2010). A critical review of technology acceptance literature. *Southwest Decisino Sciences Institute*, 22. Retrieved from http://www.swdsi.org/swdsi2010/SW2010_Preceedings/papers/PA104.pdf

Liang, C., & Chen, H. (2009). How to lengthen, deepen and broaden customer-firm relationships with online financial services. *Journal of Financial Services Marketing*, *14*(3), 218–231. doi:10.1057/fsm.2009.20

Liang, T., & Huang, J. (1998). An empirical study on consumer acceptance of products in electronic markets: A transaction cost model. *Decision Support Systems*, *24*(1), 29–43. doi:10.1016/S0167-9236(98)00061-X

Liang, W. K., & Corkindale, D. (2016). The Effect of Online Word-of-Mouth on Risk Assessment for an Experience Service as Price Acceptability Changes. *Services Marketing Quarterly*, *37*(3), 156–170. doi:10.1080/15332969.2016.1184540

Liao, H. (2007). Do it right this time: The role of employee service recovery performance in customer-perceived justice and customer loyalty after service failures. *The Journal of Applied Psychology*, *92*(2), 475–489. doi:10.1037/0021-9010.92.2.475 PMID:17371092

Li, C., & Bernoff, J. (2008). *Groundswell: Winning in a world transformed by social technologies*. Boston: Harvard Business Press.

Li, H., Zhang, Z., Meng, F., & Janakiraman, R. (2017). Is peer evaluation of consumer online reviews socially embedded? – An examination combining reviewer's social network and social identity. *International Journal of Hospitality Management*, *67*, 143–153. doi:10.1016/j.ijhm.2017.08.003

Li, J., & Su, C. (2007). How face influences consumption. *International Journal of Market Research*, *49*(2), 237–246. doi:10.1177/147078530704900207

Lim, K. H., Leung, K., Sia, C. L., & Lee, M. K. (2004). Is eCommerce boundary-less? Effects of individualism–collectivism and uncertainty avoidance on Internet shopping. *Journal of International Business Studies*, *35*(6), 545–559. doi:10.1057/palgrave.jibs.8400104

Lim, Y.-S., & Heide, B. V. D. (2015). Evaluating the Wisdom of Strangers: The Perceived Credibility of Online Consumer Reviews on Yelp. *Journal of Computer-Mediated Communication*, *20*(1), 67–82. doi:10.1111/jcc4.12093

Lincoln, S. (2010). *Mastering Web 2.0*. London: Kogan Page.

Lingelbach, D., Patino, A., & Pitta, D. (2012). The emergence of marketing in Millennial new ventures. *Journal of Consumer Marketing*, *29*(2), 136–145. doi:10.1108/07363761211206384

Lin, S., Yang, S., Ma, M., & Huang, J. (2018). Value co-creation on social media: Examining the relationship between brand engagement and display advertising effectiveness for Chinese hotels. *International Journal of Contemporary Hospitality Management*, *30*(4), 2153–2174. doi:10.1108/IJCHM-08-2016-0484

Lin, W. B. (2006). Correlation between personality characteristics, situations of service failure, customer relation strength and remedial recovery strategy. *Services Marketing Quarterly*, *28*(1), 55–88. doi:10.1300/J396v28n01_04

Lipman, V. (2013, July). Are smartphones a hidden drag on the economy? *Forbes*.

Lipsman, A., Mudd, G., Rich, M., & Bruich, S. (2012). The Power of "Like": How Brands Reach (and Influence) Fans through Social-Media Marketing. *Journal of Advertising Research*, *52*(1), 40–52. doi:10.2501/JAR-52-1-040-052

Litvin, S. W., Goldsmith, R. E., & Pan, B. (2008). Electronic Word-of-Mouth in Hospitality and Tourism Management. *Tourism Management*, *29*(3), 458–468. doi:10.1016/j.tourman.2007.05.011

Liu, Q., Karahanna, E., & Watson, R.T. (2011). Unveiling user-generated content: Designing websites to best present customer reviews. Elsevier Inc.

Liu, B. S.-C., Sudharshan, D., & Hamer, L. O. (2000). After-service response in service quality assessment: A real-time updating model approach. *Journal of Services Marketing*, *14*(2), 160–177. doi:10.1108/08876040010321000

Liu, S., Moizer, J., Megicks, P., Kasturiratne, D., & Jayawickrama, U. (2014). A Knowledge Chain Management Framework to Support Integrated Decisions in Global Supply Chains. *Journal of Production Planning and Control*, *25*(8), 639–649. doi:10.1080/09537287.2013.798084

Liu-Thompkins, Y. (2012). Seeding viral content: The role of message and network factors. *Journal of Advertising Research*, *52*(4), 465–478. doi:10.2501/JAR-52-4-465-478

Liu, X., Burns, A. C., & Hou, Y. (2017). An Investigation of Brand-Related User-Generated Content on Twitter. *Journal of Advertising*, *46*(2), 236–247. doi:10.1080/00913367.2017.1297273

Liu, X., & Hu, J. (2012). Adolescent Evaluations of Brand Extensions: The Influence of Reference Group. *Psychology and Marketing*, *29*(2), 98–106. doi:10.1002/mar.20507

Liu, Y. (2006). Word of Mouth for Movies: Its Dynamics and Impact on Box Office Revenue. *Journal of Marketing*, *70*(3), 74–89. doi:10.1509/jmkg.70.3.74

Liu, Y., & Shrum, L. J. (2002). What is interactivity and is it always such a good thing? Implications of definition, person, and situation for the influence of interactivity on advertising effectiveness. *Journal of Advertising*, *31*(4), 53–64. doi:10.1080/00913367.2002.10673685

Li, Y. M., Chen, H. M., Liou, J. H., & Lin, L. F. (2014). Creating social intelligence for product portfolio design. *Decision Support Systems*, *66*, 123–134. doi:10.1016/j.dss.2014.06.013

Li, Y. M., & Shiu, Y. (2012). A diffusion mechanism for social advertising over microblogs. *Decision Support Systems*, *54*(1), 9–22. doi:10.1016/j.dss.2012.02.012

Lockshin, L., & McDougall, G. (1998). Service problems and recovery strategies: An examination of the critical incident technique in a business-to-business market. *International Journal of Retail & Distribution Management*, *26*(11), 429–438. doi:10.1108/09590559810246395

Loiacono, E., Watson, R., & Goodhue, D. (2002). WEBQUAL: A measure of website quality. *Journal of Marketing*, *60*, 432–438.

Loomer, J. (2013). *How to Measure Facebook Advertising Success: Monitor These 5 Metrics*. Academic Press.

Lopez-Lopez, I., Ruiz-de-Mayal, R., & Warlop, L. (2014). When sharing consumption emotions with strangers is more satisfying than sharing them with friends. *Journal of Service Research*, *17*(4), 475–488. doi:10.1177/1094670514538835

López, M., & Sicilia, M. (2014). Determinants of E-WOM influence: The role of consumers' internet experience. *Journal of Theoretical and Applied Electronic Commerce Research*, *9*(1), 28–43. doi:10.4067/S0718-18762014000100004

Lovejoy, K., & Saxton, G. (2012). Information, Community, and Action: How Nonprofit Organizations Use Social Media*. *Journal of Computer-Mediated Communication*, *17*(3), 337–353. doi:10.1111/j.1083-6101.2012.01576.x

Lovelock, C. (1991). *Services Marketing*. Prentice Hall.

Lo, Y. H., & Wu, C.-C. (2012). Customer reactions to encountering consecutive service failures. *Journal of Consumer Behaviour, 11*(3), 217–224. doi:10.1002/cb.1376

Lu, B., Fan, W., & Zhou, M. (2016). Social presence, trust, and social commerce purchase intention: An empirical research. *Computers in Human Behavior, 56*, 225–237. doi:10.1016/j.chb.2015.11.057

Lueg, J. E., Ponder, N., Beatty, S. E., & Capella, M. L. (2006). Teenagers' Use of Alternative Shopping Channels: A Consumer Socialization Perspective. *Journal of Retailing, 82*(2), 137–153. doi:10.1016/j.jretai.2005.08.002

Lu, H.-P., & Su, P. Y.-J. (2009). Factors affecting purchase intention on mobile shopping web sites. *Internet Research, 19*(4), 442–458. doi:10.1108/10662240910981399

Luhtanen, R., & Crocker, J. (1992). A Collective Self-Esteem Scale: Self-Evaluation of One's Social Identity. *Personality and Social Psychology Bulletin, 18*(3), 302–318. doi:10.1177/0146167292183006

Lukyanenko, R., & Parsons, J. (2015). Information quality research challenge: Adapting information quality principles to user-generated content. *ACM Journal of Data and Information Quality, 6*(1), 1–3. doi:10.1145/2723166

Lukyanenko, R., Parsons, J., & Wiersma, Y. F. (2014a). The IQ of the crowd: Understanding and improving information quality in structured user-generated content. *Information Systems Research, 25*(4), 669–689. doi:10.1287/isre.2014.0537

Luo, N., Zhang, M., & Lui, W. (2015). The effects of value co-creation practices on building harmonious brand community and achieving brand loyalty on social media. *Computer in Human Behaviour*, 492-500.

Luo, B., Zhang, Z., Liu, Y., & Gao, W. (2016). What does it say and who said it? The contingent effects of online word of mouth in China. *Nankai Business Review International, 7*(4), 474–490. doi:10.1108/NBRI-12-2015-0035

Luo, X., Zhang, J., & Duan, W. (2013). Social Media and Firm Equity Value. *Information Systems Research, 24*(1), 146–163. doi:10.1287/isre.1120.0462

Lu, Q., Ye, Q., & Law, R. (2014). Moderating Effects of Product Heterogeneity Between Online Word-Of-Mouth and Hotel Sales. *Journal of Electronic Commerce Research, 15*(1), 1.

Lusch, R. (2007). Marketing's Evolving Identity: Defining Our Future. *Journal of Public Policy & Marketing, 26*(2), 261–268. doi:10.1509/jppm.26.2.261

Lu, W., & Stepchenkova, S. (2015). User-Generated Content as a Research Mode in Tourism and Hospitality Applications: Topics, Methods, and Software. *Journal of Hospitality Marketing & Management, 24*(2), 119–154. doi:10.1080/19368623.2014.907758

LVMH. (2016). *Interim Financial Report Six-Month Period Ended June 30, 2016*. Retrieved from https://r.lvmh-static.com/uploads/2016/06/lvmh-2016-first-half-financial-report.pdf

LVMH. (2018). *LVMH 2017 record results*. Retrieved from https://r.lvmh-static.com/uploads/2018/01/lvmhannualresults2017va.pdf

Macarthy, A. (2013). *500 Social Media Marketing Tips: Essential Advice, Hints and Strategy for Business*. Charlotte, NC: CreateSpace Independent Publishing Platform.

Madahi, A., & Sukati, I. (2012). The effect of external factors on purchase intention amongst young generation in Malaysia. *International Business Research, 5*(8), 153–159. doi:10.5539/ibr.v5n8p153

Madu, C. N., & Madu, A. A. (2002). Dimensions of e-quality. *International Journal of Quality & Reliability Management, 19*(3), 246–258. doi:10.1108/02656710210415668

Maehle, N., Otnes, C., & Supphellen, M. (2011). Consumers' perceptions of the dimensions of brand personality. *Journal of Consumer Behaviour, 10*(5), 290–303. doi:10.1002/cb.355

Maglio, P. P., & Spohrer, J. (2008). Fundamentals of service science. *Journal of the Academy of Marketing Science, 36*(1), 18–20. doi:10.100711747-007-0058-9

Mahoney, L. M., & Tang, T. (2016). *Strategic Social Media: From Marketing to Social Change* (1st ed.). Hoboken, NJ: Wiley-Blackwell. doi:10.1002/9781119370680

Mahrdt, N., Lessing, M., Wagner, W., & Geissler, H. (2013). *Herausforderung Multi - Channel - Neue Wege zum Markterfolg*. Bad Homburg: Gemini.

Mair, J., & Marti, I. (2006). Social entrepreneurship research: A source of explanation, prediction, and delight. *Journal of World Business, 41*(1), 36–44. doi:10.1016/j.jwb.2005.09.002

Malär, L., Krohmer, H., Hoyer, W., & Nyffenegger, B. (2011). Emotional Brand Attachment and Brand Personality: The Relative Importance of the Actual and the Ideal Self. *Journal of Marketing, 75*(4), 35–52. doi:10.1509/jmkg.75.4.35

Malthouse, E. C., Calder, B. J., Kim, S. J., & Vandenbosch, M. (2016). Evidence that user-generated content that produces engagement increases purchase behaviours. *Journal of Marketing Management, 32*(5-6), 427–444. doi:10.1080/0267257X.2016.1148066

Malthouse, E., Haenlein, M., Skiera, B., Wege, E., & Zhang, M. (2013). Managing Customer Relationships in the Social Media Era: Introducing the Social CRM House. *Journal of Interactive Marketing, 27*(4), 270–280. doi:10.1016/j.intmar.2013.09.008

Ma, M., & Agarwal, R. (2007). Through a Glass Darkly: Information Technology Design, Identity Verification, and Knowledge Contribution in Online Communities. *Information Systems Research, 18*(1), 42–67. doi:10.1287/isre.1070.0113

Mandle, J. (2009). *Rawls's A Theory of Justice: An Introduction*. New York: Cambridge University Press. doi:10.1017/CBO9780511814099

Mangold, W. G., & Faulds, D. J. (2009). Social media: The new hybrid element of the promotion mix. *Business Horizons, 52*(4), 357–365. doi:10.1016/j.bushor.2009.03.002

Mantrala, M., Levy, M., Kahn, B., Fox, E., Gaidarev, P., Dankworth, B., & Shah, D. (2009). Why is assortment planning so difficult for retailers? A framework and research agenda. *Journal of Retailing, 85*(1), 71–83. doi:10.1016/j.jretai.2008.11.006

Manville, B. (2004). Building Customer Communities of Practice for Business Value: Success Factors Profiled from Saba Software and Other Case Studies. In P. Hildreth & C. Kimble (Eds.), *Knowledge Networks: Innovation through Communities of Practices* (pp. 106–123). Hershey, PA: Idea Group Publishing. doi:10.4018/978-1-59140-200-8.ch010

Marca España. (2017). *Activities in the period of 2012-2016*. Retrieved from http://marcaespana.es/actualidad/marca-espa%C3%B1a/marca-espa%C3%B1a-un-proyecto-hecho-realidad

Marine-Roig, E., & Anton Clavé, S. (2016). A detailed method for destination image analysis using user-generated content. *Information Technology & Tourism, 15*(4), 341–364. doi:10.100740558-015-0040-1

Markus, H. R., & Kitayama, S. (1991). Culture and the self: Implications for cognition, emotion, and motivation. *Psychological Review, 98*(2), 224–253. doi:10.1037/0033-295X.98.2.224

Martin, R. L., & Osberg, S. (2007). Social Entrepreneurship: The Case for Definition. Stanford Social Innovation Review, 29–39.

Martinez, J., & Martinez, L. (2010). Some insights on conceptualizing and measuring service quality. *Journal of Retailing and Consumer Services*, *17*(1), 29–42. doi:10.1016/j.jretconser.2009.09.002

Martínez-Navarro, J., & Bigné, E. (2017). The Value Of Marketer-generated Content On Social Network Sites: Media Antecedents and Behavioral Responses. *Journal of Electronic Commerce Research*, *18*(1), 52.

Martínez, P., & del Bosque, I. R. (2013). CSR and customer loyalty: The roles of trust, customer identification with the company and satisfaction. *International Journal of Hospitality Management*, *35*, 89–99. doi:10.1016/j.ijhm.2013.05.009

Martin, K., & Smith, N. (2008). Commercializing Social Interaction: The Ethics of Stealth Marketing. *Journal of Public Policy & Marketing*, *27*(1), 45–56. doi:10.1509/jppm.27.1.45

Mason, W. A., Conrey, F. R., & Smith, E. R. (2007). Situating Social Influence Processes: Dynamic, Multidirectional Flows of Influence within Social Networks. *Personality and Social Psychology Review*, *11*(3), 279–300. doi:10.1177/1088868307301032 PMID:18453465

Mathieson, R. (2010). *The On-Demand Brand: 10 Rules for Digital Marketing Success in an Anytime, Everywhere World* (1st ed.). Amacom, Saranac Lake.

Matos, C. A., Henrique, J. L., & Rossi, C. A. V. (2007). Service recovery paradox: A meta-analysis. *Journal of Service Research*, *10*(1), 60–77. doi:10.1177/1094670507303012

Mattila, A. S., Cho, W., & Ro, H. C. (2011). The role of self-service technologies in restoring justice. *Journal of Business Research*, *64*(4), 348–355. doi:10.1016/j.jbusres.2010.02.014

Matzat, U. U., & Snijders, C. C. (2012). Rebuilding trust in online shops on consumer review sites: Sellers' responses to user-generated complaints. *Journal of Computer-Mediated Communication*, *18*(1), 62–79. doi:10.1111/j.1083-6101.2012.01594.x

Maxham, J. G. III, & Netemeyer, R. G. (2002). A longitudinal study of complaining customers' evaluations of multiple service failures and recovery efforts. *Journal of Marketing*, *66*(4), 57–71. doi:10.1509/jmkg.66.4.57.18512

Maxham, J. III. (2001). Service recovery's influence on consumer satisfaction, positive word-of-mouth, and purchase intentions. *Journal of Business Research*, *54*(1), 11–24. doi:10.1016/S0148-2963(00)00114-4

Maxwell, J. A. (2013). Qualitative research design: an Interactive approach (3rd ed.). Thousand Oaks, CA: Sage Publications, Inc.

Maxwell, J. A. (2012). *Qualitative Research Design: An Interactive Approach* (3rd ed.). London: SAGE Publications, Inc.

Mayzlin, D. (2006). Promotional Chat on the Internet. *Marketing Science*, *25*(2), 155–163. doi:10.1287/mksc.1050.0137

McAlexander, J., Koenig, H., & Schouten, J. (2006). Building Relationships of Brand Community in Higher Education: A Strategic Framework for University Advancement. *International Journal of Educational Advancement*, *6*(2), 107–118. doi:10.1057/palgrave.ijea.2150015

McAlexander, J., Schouten, J., & Koenig, H. (2002). Building Brand Community. *Journal of Marketing*, *66*(1), 38–54. doi:10.1509/jmkg.66.1.38.18451

McCall, G. J., & Simmons, J. L. (1978). *Identities and Interactions* (Revised edition). New York: Free Press.

McColl-Kennedy, J. R., & Sparks, B. A. (2003). Application of fairness theory to service failures and service recovery. *Journal of Service Research*, *5*(3), 251–266. doi:10.1177/1094670502238918

McCollough, M. A., Berry, L. L., & Yadav, M. S. (2000). An empirical investigation of customer satisfaction after service failure and recovery. *Journal of Services Research*, *3*(2), 121–137. doi:10.1177/109467050032002

McCracken, G. (1986). Culture and Consumption: A Theoretical Account of the Structure: A Theoretical Account of the Structure and Movement of the Cultural Meaning of Consumer Goods. *The Journal of Consumer Research*, *13*(1), 71–84. doi:10.1086/209048

McCracken, G. (1989). Who is the Celebrity Endorser? Cultural Foundations of the Endorsement Process. *The Journal of Consumer Research*, *16*(3), 310–321. doi:10.1086/209217

McDougall, G., & Levesque, T. (1994). A Revised View of Service Quality Dimensions: An Empirical Investigation. *Journal of Professional Services Marketing*, *11*(1), 189–210. doi:10.1080/15332969.1994.9985149

McGrath, R. G. (2011, January). When your Business Model is in Trouble. *Harvard Business Review*, 96–98.

McKenna, L., & Pole, A. (2008). What do bloggers do: An average day on an average political blog. *Public Choice*, *134*(1-2), 97–108. doi:10.100711127-007-9203-8

McKinsey. (2016). *The State of Fashion*. Retrieved from https://www.mckinsey.com/industries/retail/our-insights/the-state-of-fashion

McNally, M. B., Trosow, S. E., Wong, L., Whippey, C., Burkell, J., & McKenzie, P. J. (2012). User-generated online content 2: Policy implications. *First Monday*, *17*(6). doi:10.5210/fm.v17i6.3913

McQuail, D. (2005). *McQuail's Mass Communication Theory* (5th ed.). London Sage publishers.

Meeker, M., & Wu, L. (2013). *Internet Trends D11 Conference*. Retrieved from https://www.slideshare.net/kleinerperkins/kpcb-internet-trends-2013

Mehrtens, J., Cragg, P. B., & Mills, A. M. (2001). A model of Internet Adoption by SMEs. *Information & Management*, *38*(3), 165–176. doi:10.1016/S0378-7206(01)00086-6

Melis, K., Campo, K., Breugelmans, L., & Lamey, L. (2015). The impact of the multuchannel retail mix on online store choice: Does online experience matter? *Journal of Retailing*, *91*(2), 272–288. doi:10.1016/j.jretai.2014.12.004

Melissen, J. (2011). Beyond the New Public Diplomacy. The Hague: Netherlands Institute of International Relations 'Clingendael'.

Melissen, J. (2005). *The New Public Diplomacy: Soft Power in International Relations (Studies in Diplomacy and International Relations)*. London: Palgrave Macmillan UK. doi:10.1057/9780230554931

Merrilees, B. (2016). Interactive brand experience pathways to customer-brand engagement and value co-creation. *Journal of Product and Brand Management*, *25*(5), 402–408. doi:10.1108/JPBM-04-2016-1151

Mersey, R. D., Malthouse, E. C., & Calder, B. J. (2010). Engagement with Online Media. *Journal of Media Business Studies*, *7*(2), 39–56. doi:10.1080/16522354.2010.11073506

Messeghem, K. (2003). Strategic entrepreneurship and managerial activities in SMEs. *Estados Unidos*, *21*(2), 197–212.

Meuter, M. L., Ostrom, A. L., Roundtree, R. I., & Bitner, M. J. (2000). Self-service technologies: Understanding customer satisfaction with technology-based service encounters. *Journal of Marketing*, *64*(3), 50–64. doi:10.1509/jmkg.64.3.50.18024

Meyer, J., Gremler, D. D., & Hogreve, J. (2014). Do service guarantees guarantee greater market value? *Journal of Service Research*, *17*(2), 150–163. doi:10.1177/1094670513505359

Michaelidou, N., Siamagka, N., & Christodoulides, G. (2011). Usage, barriers and measurement of social media marketing: An exploratory investigation of small and medium B2B brands. *Industrial Marketing Management*, *40*(7), 1153–1159. doi:10.1016/j.indmarman.2011.09.009

Michel, S. (2001). Analyzing service failures and recoveries: A process approach. *International Journal of Service Industry Management*, *12*(1), 20–33. doi:10.1108/09564230110382754

Michopoulou, E., & Moisa, D. G. (2018). (in press). Hotel social media metrics: The ROI dilemma. *International Journal of Hospitality Management*.

Migacz, S. J., Zou, S., & Petrick, J. F. (2017). The "Terminal" Effects of Service Failure on Airlines: Examining Service Recovery with Justice Theory. *Journal of Travel Research*, 1–16.

Mikalef, P., Giannakos, M., & Pateli, A. (2013). Shopping and word-of-mouth intentions on social media. *Journal of Theoretical and Applied Electronic Commerce Research*, *8*(1), 17–34. doi:10.4067/S0718-18762013000100003

Miles, J. (2014). *Instagram power*. McGraw Hill.

Miller, D. (1983). The Correlates of Entrepreneurship in Three Types of Firms. *Management Science*, *29*(7), 770–791. doi:10.1287/mnsc.29.7.770

Miller, J. L., Craighead, C. W., & Karwan, K. R. (2000). Service recovery: A framework and empirical investigation. *Journal of Operations Management*, *18*(4), 387–400. doi:10.1016/S0272-6963(00)00032-2

Miller, K., Fabian, F., & Lin, S. (2009). Strategies for online communities. *Strategic Management Journal*, *30*(3), 305–322. doi:10.1002mj.735

Miller, R., & Lammas, N. (2010). Social media and its implications for viral marketing *Asia Pacific*. *The Public Relations Journal*, *11*(1), 1–9.

Mintel Group. (2017). *Smartphone Purchasing Process*. London.

Mintel. (2011). *Multi-channel retailing*. Author.

Mintel. (2013). *Clothing retailing*. Author.

Mintel. (2014a). *E-commerce*. Author.

Mintel. (2014b). *Fashion online*. Author.

Mintel. (2015). *Online Clothing Retailing*. Accessed March 30 2018, from http://oxygen.mintel.com

Mintel. (2018). *UK Womenswear Market Report*. Accessed October 15 2018, from https://store.mintel.com/uk-womenswear-market-report

Mitchell, V.-W. (1999). Consumer Perceived Risk: Conceptualisations and Models. *European Journal of Marketing*, *33*(1/2), 163–195. doi:10.1108/03090569910249229

Moeller, S. (2010). Characteristics of services – a new approach uncovers their value. *Journal of Services Marketing*, *24*(5), 359–368. doi:10.1108/08876041011060468

Moe, W., & Schweidel, D. (2017). Opportunities for innovation in social media analytics. *Journal of Product Innovation Management*, *34*(5), 697–702. doi:10.1111/jpim.12405

Mohr, L. A., Harris, K. E., & Bernhardt, K. L. (2006). Online service failure, consumer attributions and expectations. *Journal of Services Marketing*, *20*(7), 453–458. doi:10.1108/08876040610704883

Moilanen, T., & Rainisto, S. (2009). *How to brand nations, cities and destinations: A planning book for place branding*. New York: Palgrave Macmillan. doi:10.1057/9780230584594

Mollá-Descals, A., Frasquet-Deltoro, M., & Ruiz-Molina, M. E. (2011). Internationalization patterns in fashion retail distribution: Implications for firm results. *Service Industries Journal*, *31*(12), 1979–1993. doi:10.1080/02642069.2011.540754

Money, R. B., Gilly, M. C., & Graham, J. L. (1998). Explorations of national culture and word-of-mouth referral behavior in the purchase of industrial services in the United States and Japan. *Journal of Marketing*, *62*(4), 76–87. doi:10.1177/002224299806200406

Moon, S., Park, Y., & Seog Kim, Y. (2014). The impact of text product reviews on sales. *European Journal of Marketing*, *48*(11/12), 2176–2197. doi:10.1108/EJM-06-2013-0291

Moon, Y. (2002). Personalization and personality: Some effects of customizing message style based on customer personalities. *Journal of Consumer Psychology*, *12*(4), 313–326. doi:10.1207/15327660260382351

Moore, M. (2012). Interactive media usage among millennial consumers. *Journal of Consumer Marketing*, *29*(6), 436–444. doi:10.1108/07363761211259241

Moreau, C. P., & Herd, K. B. (2010). To each his own? How comparisons with others influence consumers' evaluations of their self-designed products. *The Journal of Consumer Research*, *36*(5), 806–819. doi:10.1086/644612

Morgan, R., & Hunt, S. (1994). The Commitment-Trust Theory of Relationship Marketing. *Journal of Marketing*, *58*(3), 20. doi:10.2307/1252308

Mort, G. S., Weerawardena, J., & Carnegie, K. (2003). Social entrepreneurship: Towards conceptualisation. *International Journal of Nonprofit and Voluntary Sector Marketing*, *8*(1), 76–89. doi:10.1002/nvsm.202

Mostafa, R. B., Lages, C. R., Shabbir, H. A., & Thwaites, D. (2015). Corporate image: A service recovery perspective. *Journal of Service Research*, *18*(4), 468–483. doi:10.1177/1094670515584146

Mueller, S. L., & Thomas, A. S. (2000). Culture and entrepreneurial potential: A nine-country study of locus of control and innovativeness. *Journal of Business Venturing*, *16*(1), 51–75. doi:10.1016/S0883-9026(99)00039-7

Mulhern, F. (2013). Integrated marketing communications: From media channels to digital connectivity. In *The Evolution of Integrated Marketing Communications* (pp. 19–36). Routledge.

Muller, E., & Peres, R. (2018). The effect of social networks structure on innovation performance: A review and directions for research. *International Journal of Research in Marketing*. doi:10.1016/j.ijresmar.2018.05.003

Müller, H., Gove, J. L., Webb, J. S., & Cheang, A. (2015). Understanding and comparing smartphone and tablet use. In *Proceedings of the Annual Meeting of the Australian Special Interest Group for Computer Human Interaction on - OzCHI '15* (pp. 427–436). New York: ACM Press. 10.1145/2838739.2838748

Munar, A. M., & Jacobsen, J. K. S. (2013). Trust and Involvement in Tourism Social Media and Web-Based Travel Information Sources. *Scandinavian Journal of Hospitality and Tourism*, *13*(1), 1–19. doi:10.1080/15022250.2013.764511

Muñiz, A. M. Jr, & Schau, H. J. (2007a). Vigilante marketing and consumer-created communications. *Journal of Advertising*, *36*(3), 35–50. doi:10.2753/JOA0091-3367360303

Muniz, A. Jr, & O'Guinn, T. (2001). Brand Community. *The Journal of Consumer Research, 27*(4), 412–432. doi:10.1086/319618

Muntinga, D. G., Moorman, M., & Smit, E. G. (2011). Introducing COBRAs: Exploring motivations for brand-related social media use. *International Journal of Advertising, 30*(1), 13–46. doi:10.2501/IJA-30-1-013-046

Murugesan, S. (2007). Understanding Web 2.0. *IT Professional, 9*(4), 34–41. doi:10.1109/MITP.2007.78

Mytko, G. (2012). The United Kingdom and the Rise of Digital Public Diplomacy. *Exchange: The Journal of Public Diplomacy.*

Nadeem, M. (2012). Returning Customer: Was That A Planned Purchase? *Skyline Business Journal, 7*(1), 11–17.

Nagi, T. (2015). Social media research: Theories, constructs, and conceptual frameworks. *International Journal of Information Management, 35*(1), 33–44. doi:10.1016/j.ijinfomgt.2014.09.004

Nah, F. F.-H., Zhao, F., & Zhu, W. (2003). Factors influencing Users' Adoption of Mobile Computing. In J. Mariga (Ed.), *Managing E-commerce and Mobile Computing Technologies Book.* Hershey, PA: Idea Group Inc.

Nambisan, S., & Baron, R. A. (2009). Virtual customer environments: Testing a model of voluntary participation in value co-creation activities. *Journal of Product Innovation Management, 26*(4), 388–406. doi:10.1111/j.1540-5885.2009.00667.x

Nambisan, S., & Nambisan, P. (2008). How to Profit from a Better Virtual Customer Environment? *MIT Sloan Management Review, 49*(3), 53–61.

Nandan, S. (2005). An exploration of the brand identity–brand image linkage: A communications perspective. *Journal of Brand Management, 12*(4), 264–278. doi:10.1057/palgrave.bm.2540222

Nardi, B., Schiano, D., Gumbrecht, M., & Swartz, L. (2004). Why we blog. *Communications of the ACM, 47*(12), 41–46. doi:10.1145/1035134.1035163

Naylor, R., Lamberton, C., & West, P. (2012). Beyond the "Like" Button: The Impact of Mere Virtual Presence on Brand Evaluations and Purchase Intentions in Social Media Settings. *Journal of Marketing, 76*(6), 105–120. doi:10.1509/jm.11.0105

Nelson-Field, K., Riebe, E., & Sharp, B. (2012). What's not to "like?": Can a Facebook fan base give a brand the advertising reach it needs? *Journal of Advertising Research*, 1–8.

Neslin, S., Grewal, D., Leghorn, R., Shankar, V., Teerlin, M., Thomas, J., & Verhoef, P. (2006). Challenges and opportunities in multichannel customer management. *Journal of Service Research, 9*(2), 95–112. doi:10.1177/1094670506293559

Neslin, S., & Shankar, V. (2009). Key issues in multichannel customer management: Current knowledge and future directions. *Journal of Interactive Marketing, 23*(1), 70–82. doi:10.1016/j.intmar.2008.10.005

Newcomb, T. (1953). An approach to the study of communicative acts. *Psychological Review, 60*(6), 393–404. doi:10.1037/h0063098 PMID:13112341

Newman, M. C. (2018). Evidence in Social Networks. In M. Newman (Ed.), *The Nature and Use of Eco toxicological Evidence Natural Science* (pp. 219–243). Statistics, Psychology, and Sociology.

Newman, R., Chang, V., Walters, R. J., & Wills, G. B. (2016). Web 2.0—the past and the future. *International Journal of Information Management, 36*(4), 591–598. doi:10.1016/j.ijinfomgt.2016.03.010

Ngai, E. W., Moon, K. L. K., Lam, S. S., Chin, E. S., & Tao, S. S. (2015). Social media models, technologies, and applications: An academic review and case study. *Industrial Management & Data Systems*, *115*(5), 769–802. doi:10.1108/IMDS-03-2015-0075

Ng, E., Schweitzer, L., & Lyons, S. (2010). New Generation, Great Expectations: A Field Study of the Millennial Generation. *Journal of Business and Psychology*, *25*(2), 281–292. doi:10.100710869-010-9159-4

Ng, M. (2014). Social media and luxury fashion brands in China: The case of Coach. *Journal of Global Fashion Marketing*, *5*(3), 251–265. doi:10.1080/20932685.2014.907607

Nguyen, B., & Mutum, D. S. (2012). A review of customer relationship management: Successes, advances, pitfalls and futures. *Business Process Management Journal*, *18*(3), 400–419. doi:10.1108/14637151211232614

Nicholson, M., Clarke, I., & Blakemore, M. (2002). 'One brand, three ways to shop': Situational variables and multichannel consumer behaviour. *International Review of Retail, Distribution and Consumer Research*, *12*(2), 131–148. doi:10.1080/09593960210127691

Nikbin, D., Marimuthu, M., & Hyun, S. S. (2016). Influence of perceived service fairness on relationship quality and switching intention: An empirical study of restaurant experiences. *Current Issues in Tourism*, *19*(10), 1005–1026. doi:10.1080/13683500.2013.801407

Noble, S. M., Griffith, D., & Weinberger, M. G. (2005). Consumer derived utilitarian value and channel utilization in a multi-channel retail context. *Journal of Business Research*, *58*(12), 1643–1651. doi:10.1016/j.jbusres.2004.10.005

Norazah, M. S. (2013). Students' dependence on smart phones: The influence of social needs, social influences and convenience. *Campus-Wide Information Systems*, *30*(2), 124–134. doi:10.1108/10650741311306309

Noruzi, M. R., Westover, J. H., & Rahimi, G. R. (2010). An Exploration of Social Entrepreneurship in the Entrepreneurship Era. *Asian Social Science*, *6*(6), 3–10. doi:10.5539/ass.v6n6p3

Nowak, A., Szamrej, J., & Latané, B. (1990). From private attitude to public opinion: A dynamic theory of social impact. *Psychological Review*, *97*(3), 362–376. doi:10.1037/0033-295X.97.3.362

Nowak, L., Thach, L., & Olsen, J. (2006). Wowing the millennials: Creating brand equity in the wine industry. *Journal of Product and Brand Management*, *15*(5), 316–323. doi:10.1108/10610420610685712

Nurmikko, S. (2011). *Implications of hedonic and utilitarian information search and social media browsing on purchase value*. Aalto University.

O'Cass, A., & McEwen, H. (2004). Exploring consumer status and conspicuous consumption. *Journal of Consumer Behaviour*, *4*(1), 25–39. doi:10.1002/cb.155

O'Reilly, T. (2005). Web 2.0: Compact Definition? *O'Reilly Radar*. Retrieved from http://radar.oreilly.com/2005/10/web-20-compact-definition.html

O'Reilly, T. (2005). *Web 2.0: Compact Definition?* Retrieved from http://radar.oreilly.com/2005/10/web-20-compact-definition.html

O'Reilly, T., & Battelle, J. (2009). *Web Squared: Web 2.0 Five Years On*. O'Reilly Media, Inc.

O'Shaughenssy, N. J. (2000). Testing the nation as a brand: Some neglected issues. *Journal of Macromarketing*, *20*(1), 56–64. doi:10.1177/0276146700201006

Obeidat, Z. M. I., Xiao, S. H., Iyer, G. R., & Nicholson, M. (2017). Consumer revenge using the internet and social media: An examination of the role of service failure types and cognitive appraisal processes. *Psychology and Marketing*, *34*(4), 496–515. doi:10.1002/mar.21002

Odden, L. (2012). *Optimise: How to Attract and Engage More Customers by Integrating SEO, Social Media, and Content Marketing*. Somerset: Wiley.

OECD. (2006). *OECD Information Technology Outlook, 2006*. OECD. Available at www.oecd.org/sti/ito

OECD. (2007). *Communication Outlook, 2007*. Paris: OECD.

OECD. (2007). *Participative Web: user-created content - OECD*. Available online: http://www.oecd-ilibrary.org/science-and-technology/participative-web-and-user-created-content_9789264037472-en

Ofcom. (2016). *'Smartphone by default' internet users: A qualitative research report*. Ofcom.

Okazaki, S. (2009). The Tactical Use of Mobile Marketing: How Adolescents' Social Networking Can Best Shape Brand Extensions. *Journal of Advertising Research*, *49*(1), 12–26. doi:10.2501/S0021849909090102

Okonkwo, U. (2009). Sustaining the luxury brand on the Internet. *Journal of Brand Management*, *16*(5/6), 302–310. doi:10.1057/bm.2009.2

Okonkwo, U. (2010). *Luxury online: styles, systems, strategies*. Basingstoke, UK: Palgrave Macmillan. doi:10.1057/9780230248335

Olins, W. (2002). Branding the nation - the historical context. *Journal of Brand Management*, *9*(4F0020004), 241–248. doi:10.1057/palgrave.bm.2540075

Olins, W. (2005). Making a National Brand. In J. Melissen (Ed.), *The New Public Diplomacy. Studies in Diplomacy and International Relations*. London: Palgrave Macmillan. doi:10.1057/9780230554931_9

Oliver, R. L. (1980). A cognitive model of the antecedents and consequences of satisfaction decisions. *JMR, Journal of Marketing Research*, *17*(4), 460–469. doi:10.2307/3150499

Oliver, R. L. (1981). Measurement and Evaluation of Satisfaction Processes in Retail Settings. *Journal of Retailing*, *57*(3), 25–48.

Oliver, R. L. (1999). Whence Consumer Loyalty? *Journal of Marketing*, *63*(10), 33–44. doi:10.2307/1252099

Olsen, S. O., & Skallerud, K. (2011). Retail attributes' differential effects on utilitarian versus hedonic shopping value. *Journal of Consumer Marketing*, *28*(7), 532–539. doi:10.1108/07363761111181527

Ombudsman Services. (2018). *Consumer action monitor*. Retrieved October 13, 2018 from https://www.ombudsman-services.org/docs/default-source/downloads/cam-2018-report.pdf?sfvrsn=0

Omosigho, O., & Abeysinghe, G. (2012). Evaluating readiness of organizations to adopt social media for competitive advantage. *Information Society (i-Society), 2012 International Conference on*, 16-21.

Ongori, H., & Migiro, S. (2010). Information and communication technologies adoption in SMEs: Literature review. *Journal of Chinese Entrepreneurship*, *2*(1), 93–104. doi:10.1108/17561391011019041

Onorato, R., & Turner, J. (2004). Fluidity in the self-concept: The shift from personal to social identity. *European Journal of Social Psychology*, *34*(3), 257–278. doi:10.1002/ejsp.195

Opitz, L. (2016). *Luxury fashion meets social media: Gucci vs. Prada*. Retrieved September 10, 2016, from https://www.talkwalker.com/blog/luxury-fashion-social-listening

Organization for Economic Cooperation and Development. (2007, April 12). *Participative web: User-created content.* Retrieved from http://www.oecd.org/sti/38393115.pdf

Oswald, L. R. (1999). Culture Swapping: Consumption and the Ethnogenesis of Middle-Class Haitan Immigrants. *The Journal of Consumer Research*, *25*(3), 303–318. doi:10.1086/209541

Ouirdi, M. E., Segers, J., Ouirdi, A. E., & Pais, I. (2015). *Predictors of job seekers self-disclosure on social media.* Computers in Human Behaviour.

Overby, J. W., & Lee, E. J. (2006). The effects of utilitarian and hedonic online shopping value on consumer preference and intentions. *Journal of Business Research*, *59*(10-11), 1160–1166. doi:10.1016/j.jbusres.2006.03.008

Oxford Economies. (2018). *How Fashion Fuels the Economy*. Retrieved October 7, 2018, from http://www.thecreativeindustries.co.uk/industries/fashion/fashion-facts-and-figures/how-fashion-fuels-the-uk-economy

Oyserman, D. (2009). Identity-Based Motivation: Implications for Action-Readiness, procedural Readiness and Consumer Behaviour. *Journal of Consumer Psychology*, *19*(3), 250–260. doi:10.1016/j.jcps.2009.05.008

Öztamur, D., & Karakadilar, I. S. (2014). Exploring the role of social media for SMEs: As a new marketing strategy tool for the firm performance perspective. *Procedia: Social and Behavioral Sciences*, *150*, 511–520. doi:10.1016/j.sbspro.2014.09.067

Ozuem, W., & Azemi, Y. (2017). Online Service Failure and Recovery Strategies in Luxury Brands: A View From Justice Theory. IGI Global.

Ozuem, W., & Azemi, Y. (2018). Online Service Failure and Recovery Strategies in Luxury Brands: A View from Justice Theory. In Digital Marketing Strategies for Fashion and Luxury Brands (pp. 108-125). IGI Global. doi:10.4018/978-1-5225-2697-1.ch005

Ozuem, W., & Lancaster, G. (2013). Recovery strategies in on-line service failure. *Marketing in the Cyber Era: Strategies and Emerging Trends*, 143-159.

Ozuem, W., & Lancaster, G. (2015). Examining the Dynamics of Value Propositions in Digital Books: A Social Constructivist Perspective. In Handbook of Research on Scholarly Publishing and Research Methods (pp. 295-311). IGI Global. doi:10.4018/978-1-4666-7409-7.ch015

Ozuem, W., & O'Keeffe, A. (2015). Towards Leadership Marketing: An Exploratory and Empirical Study. In Marketing and Consumer Behavior: Concepts, Methodologies, Tools, and Applications (pp. 1570-1590). IGI Global.

Ozuem, W., & Tan, K. (2014). Reconciling Social Media with Luxury Fashion Brands: An Exploratory Study. In Digital Arts and Entertainment: Concepts, Methodologies, Tools, and Applications (pp. 1546-1574). IGI Global.

Ozuem, W., & Tan, K. (2014). Reconciling Social Media with Luxury Fashion Brands: An Exploratory Study. In Handbook of Research on Management of Cultural Products: E-Relationship Marketing and Accessibility Perspectives. IGI Global.

Ozuem, W., & Thomas, T. (2015). Inside the Small Island Economies: Loyalty Strategies in the Telecommunications Sector. In Handbook of Research on Global Business Opportunities (pp. 316-349). IGI Global.

Ozuem, W. (2016). User-generated content and perceived customer value. In *Competitive Social Media Marketing Strategies* (pp. 50–63). IGI Global. doi:10.4018/978-1-4666-9776-8.ch003

Ozuem, W. (Ed.). (2016). *Competitive social media marketing strategies*. IGI Global. doi:10.4018/978-1-4666-9776-8

Ozuem, W. (forthcoming). Social media brand perceptions of millennials in the fashion apparel and accessories industries: A social identity perspective. *International Journal of Retail & Distribution Management.*

Ozuem, W. F. (2004). *Conceptualising marketing communication in the new marketing paradigm: A postmodern perspective*. Universal-Publishers.

Ozuem, W., & Azemi, Y. (Eds.). (2017). *Digital Marketing Strategies for Fashion and Luxury Brands*. IGI Global.

Ozuem, W., Borrelli, M., & Lancaster, G. (2017). Leveraging the co-evolution of offline and online video games: An empirical study. *Journal of Strategic Marketing*, *24*(1), 75–97. doi:10.1080/0965254X.2015.1076883

Ozuem, W., Howell, K. E., & Lancaster, G. (2008). Communicating in the new interactive marketspace. *European Journal of Marketing*, *42*(9/10), 1059–1083. doi:10.1108/03090560810891145

Ozuem, W., Howell, K. E., & Lancaster, G. (2018). Developing technologically induced environments: The case of the Nigerian banking sector. *Journal of Financial Services Marketing*, *23*(1), 50–61. doi:10.105741264-018-0043-z

Ozuem, W., Howell, K., & Lancaster, G. (2016a). An exploration of consumers' response to online service recovery initiatives. *International Journal of Market Research*, *59*(1), 97–115.

Ozuem, W., Howell, K., & Lancaster, G. (2016b). Understanding technologically induced customer services in the Nigerian banking sector: The Internet as a post-modern phenomenon. *International Journal of Information Technology and Management*, *15*(3), 272–290. doi:10.1504/IJITM.2016.077349

Ozuem, W., & Lancaster, G. (2012). Technology-induced customer services in the developing countries. In *Service science research, strategy and innovation: Dynamic knowledge management methods* (pp. 185–201). IGI Global. doi:10.4018/978-1-4666-0077-5.ch012

Ozuem, W., & Lancaster, G. (2014). Recovery strategies in on-line service failure. In *Marketing in the cyber era: Strategies and emerging trends* (pp. 143–159). IGI Global. doi:10.4018/978-1-4666-4864-7.ch010

Ozuem, W., & Mulloo, B. N. (2016). Basics of mobile marketing strategy. In *Competitive Social Media Marketing Strategies* (pp. 155–172). IGI Global. doi:10.4018/978-1-4666-9776-8.ch008

Ozuem, W., O'Keeffe, A., & Lancaster, G. (2015). Leadership Marketing: An exploratory study. *Journal of Strategic Marketing*. doi:10.1080/0965254X.2014.1001867

Ozuem, W., Patel, A., Howell, K. E., & Lancaster, G. (2017). An exploration of customers' response to online service recovery initiatives. *International Journal of Market Research*, *59*(1), 97–116.

Ozuem, W., Prasad, J., & Lancaster, G. (2016). Exploiting online social gambling for marketing communications. *Journal of Strategic Marketing*, *26*(3), 258–282. doi:10.1080/0965254X.2016.1211728

Ozuem, W., & Stokinger, E. (2015). Social media and customer retention: Implications for the Luxury Beauty Industry. In K. Wolfe (Ed.), *Computer-Mediated Marketing Strategies*. Hershey, PA: IGI Global.

Ozuem, W., & Tan, K. (2014). Reconciling Social Media with Luxury Fashion Brands: An Exploratory Study. In L. Aiello (Ed.), *Handbook of Research on Management of Cultural Products: E-Relationship Marketing and Accessibility Perspectives* (pp. 257–285). IGI Global. doi:10.4018/978-1-4666-5007-7.ch013

Ozuem, W., & Tan, K. (2014). Reconciling Social Media with Luxury Fashion Brands: An exploratory study. In L. Aiello (Ed.), *Management of Cultural Products: E-Relationship Marketing and Accessibility Perspective*. Hershey, PA: IGI Publications.

Ozuem, W., Thomas, T., & Lancaster, G. (2016). The Influence of customer loyalty on small island economies: An empirical and exploratory study. *Journal of Strategic Marketing*, *24*(6), 447–469. doi:10.1080/0965254X.2015.1011205

Ozuem, W., & Yankova, I. (2015). Social Media and customer experience. In K. Wolfe (Ed.), *Computer- Mediated Marketing Strategies*. Hershey, PA: Business Science Reference.

Pagani, M., & Malacarne, G. (2017). Experiential engagement and active vs. passive behaviour in mobile location-based social networks: The moderating role of privacy. *Journal of Interactive Marketing*, *37*, 133–148. doi:10.1016/j.intmar.2016.10.001

Palmer, A. (2009). *Study: Online Shoppers Trust Customer Reviews More than Friends*. Progressive Grocer.

Palmer, A. (2014). *Principles of services marketing* (7th ed.). Maidenhead, UK: McGraw-Hill Education.

Palmer, R., Cockton, J., Cooper, G., & Sc, M. (2007). *Managing marketing*. London: Butterworth-Heinemann.

Pamment, J. (2014). Articulating influence: Toward a research agenda for interpreting the evaluation of soft power, public diplomacy and nation brands. *Public Relations Review*, *40*(1), 50–59. doi:10.1016/j.pubrev.2013.11.019

Pang, A., Hasan, N. B. B. A., & Chong, A. C. Y. (2014). Negotiating crises in the social media environment. *Corporate Communications*, *19*(1), 96–118. doi:10.1108/CCIJ-09-2012-0064

Pan, Y., & Zhang, J. Q. (2011). Born Unequal: A Study of the Helpfulness of User-Generated Product Reviews. *Journal of Retailing*, *87*(4), 598–612. doi:10.1016/j.jretai.2011.05.002

Papadopoulos, N., & Heslop, L. (2002). Country equity and country branding: problems and prospects. *Journal of Brand Management, 9*(4-5), 294-314.

Papadopoulos, N., Hamzaoui-Essoussi, L., & El Banna, A. (2016). Nation branding for foreign direct investment: An Integrative review and directions for research and strategy. *Journal of Product and Brand Management*, *25*(7), 615–628. doi:10.1108/JPBM-09-2016-1320

Papthanassis Rodgers, S. L., & Thorson, E. (2017). *Digital advertising: theory and research* (3rd ed.). Abingdon, UK: Routledge. doi:10.4324/9781315623252

Paquette, H. 2013. *Social Media as a Marketing Tool: A Literature Review*. Academic Press.

Parameswaran, M., & Whinston, A. (2007). Research Issues in Social Computing. *Journal of the Association for Information Systems*, *8*(6), 336–350. doi:10.17705/1jais.00132

Parameswaran, M., & Whinston, A. B. (2007). social Computing: An Overview. *Communications of the Association for Information Systems*, *19*, 762–780.

Parasuraman, A., Zeithaml, V., & Berry, L. (1988). SERVQUAL: A multiple-item scale for measuring consumer perceptions of service quality. *Journal of Retailing*, *64*(1), 12–40.

Parasuraman, A., Zeithaml, V., & Malhorta, A. (2005). E-S-QUAL: A multiple-item scale for assessing electronic service quality. *Journal of Service Research*, *7*(3), 213–233. doi:10.1177/1094670504271156

Paris, C. M., Lee, W., & Seery, P. (2010). The role of social media in promoting special events: Acceptance of Facebook events. *Information and Communication Technologies in Tourism*, *14*, 531–541.

Park, C. W., Eisingerich, A. B., & Park, J. W. (2013). Attachment–Aversion (AA) Model of Customer–Brand Relationships. *Journal of Consumer Psychology*, *23*(2), 229–248. doi:10.1016/j.jcps.2013.01.002

Park, C., Jaworski, B., & MacInnis, D. (1986). Strategic Brand Concept-Image Management. *Journal of Marketing*, *50*(4), 135–145. doi:10.1177/002224298605000401

Park, C., & Lee, T. M. (2009). Information direction, website reputation and eWOM effect: A moderating role of product type. *Journal of Business Research*, *62*(1), 61–67. doi:10.1016/j.jbusres.2007.11.017

Park, C., & Srinivasan, V. (1994). A Survey-Based Method for Measuring and Understanding Brand Equity and Its Extendibility. *JMR, Journal of Marketing Research*, *31*(2), 271–278. doi:10.2307/3152199

Park, D., Lee, J., & Han, I. (2007). The Effect of On-Line Consumer Reviews on Consumer Purchasing Intention: The Moderating Role of Involvement. *International Journal of Electronic Commerce*, *11*(4), 125–148. doi:10.2753/JEC1086-4415110405

Parker, B. (2009). A comparison of brand personality and brand user-imagery congruence. *Journal of Consumer Marketing*, *26*(3), 175–184. doi:10.1108/07363760910954118

Parker, M. (2011). *Gender differences between hedonic and utilitarian purchase behaviors concerning out-of-stock apparel*. Ashland University.

Park, J. J., & Park, J. W. (2016). Investigating the effects of service recovery quality elements on passengers' behavioural intention. *Journal of Air Transport Management*, *53*, 235–241. doi:10.1016/j.jairtraman.2016.03.003

Park, J. K., & Yang, S. (2006). The Moderating Role of Consumer Trust and Experiences: Value Driven Usage of Mobile Technology. *International Journal of Mobile Marketing*, *1*(2), 24–32.

Park, J., & Han, S. H. (2013). Defining user value: A case study of a smartphone. *International Journal of Industrial Ergonomics*, *43*(4), 274–282. doi:10.1016/j.ergon.2013.04.005

Paroutis, S., & Al Saleh, A. (2009). Determinants of knowledge sharing using Web 2.0 technologies. *Journal of Knowledge Management*, *13*(4), 52–63. doi:10.1108/13673270910971824

Patten, E., & Rashid, T. (2015). CRM in a German multichannel retailing company: Investigating and evaluating the sales peoples' role. *International Journal of Sales. Retailing and Marketing*, *4*(2), 22–34.

Paulin, M. J., Ferguson, R., Jost, N., & Fallu, J. (2014). Motivating millennials to engage in charitable causes through social media. *Journal of Service Management*, *25*(3), 334–348. doi:10.1108/JOSM-05-2013-0122

Payne, A., Storbacka, K., & Frow, P. (2008). Managing the co-creation of value. *Journal of the Academy of Marketing Science*, *36*(1), 83–96. doi:10.100711747-007-0070-0

Peng, J., Agarwal, A., Hosanagar, K., & Iyengar, R. (2018). Network Overlap and Content Sharing on Social Media Platforms. *JMR, Journal of Marketing Research*, *55*(4), 571–585. doi:10.1509/jmr.14.0643

Pentina, I., Gammoh, B., Zhang, L., & Mallin, M. (2013). Drivers and Outcomes of Brand Relationship Quality in the Context of Online Social Networks. *International Journal of Electronic Commerce*, *17*(3), 63–86. doi:10.2753/JEC1086-4415170303

Pentina, I., Prybutok, V., & Zhang, X. (2008). The role of virtual communities as shopping reference groups. *Journal of Electronic Commerce Research*, *9*(2), 114–136.

Peredo, A. M., & McLean, M. (2006). Social entrepreneurship: A critical review of the concept. *Journal of World Business*, *41*(1), 56–65. doi:10.1016/j.jwb.2005.10.007

Perks, H., Gruber, T., & Edvardsson, B. (2012). Co-creation in Radical Service Innovation: A Systematic Analysis of Microlevel Processes. *Journal of Product Innovation Management*, *29*(6), 935–951. doi:10.1111/j.1540-5885.2012.00971.x

Peter, J., & Olson, C. (1993). *Consumer Behaviour and Marketing Strategy* (European Edition). London: McGraw Hill.

Peters, T. (1987). *Thriving on Chaos*. New York: Alfred A. Knopf.

Petty, R., & Cacioppo, J. (1986). The Elaboration Likelihood Model of Persuasion. *Communication and Persuasion*, 1-24. doi:10.1007/978-1-4612-4964-1_1

PewResearch. (2014). *Social Media Use by Age Group Over Time*. Retrieved 29 September, from http://www.pewinternet.org/data-trend/social-media/social-media-use-by-age-group/

Pfeffer, J., Zorbach, T., & Carley, K. M. (2015, March). 2014. Understanding online firestorms: Negative word-of-mouth dynamics in social media networks. *Journal of Marketing Communications*, *20*(1-2), 117–128. doi:10.1080/13527266.2013.797778

Phan, M., Thomas, R., & Heine, K. (2011). Social Media and Luxury Brand Management: The Case of Burberry. *Journal Of Global Fashion Marketing*, *2*(4), 213–222. doi:10.1080/20932685.2011.10593099

Phelps, J. E., Lewis, R., Mobilio, L., Perry, D., & Raman, N. (2004). Viral Marketing or Electronic Word of-Mouth Advertising: Examining Consumer Responses to Pass Along Email. *Journal of Advertising Research*, *44*(4), 333–348. doi:10.1017/S0021849904040371

Phillips, D., & Young, P. (2009). *Online Public Relations: A practical guide to developing an online strategy in the world of social media* (2nd ed.). London: Kogan Page Limited.

Piercy, N., & Archer-Brown, C. (2014). Online service failure and propensity to suspend offline consumption. *Service Industries Journal*, *34*(8), 659–676. doi:10.1080/02642069.2014.886192

Piff, P. K., Kraus, M. W., Cote, S., Cheng, B. H., & Keltner, D. (2010). Having less, giving more: The influence of social class on prosocial behavior. *Journal of Personality and Social Psychology*, *99*(5), 771–784. doi:10.1037/a0020092 PMID:20649364

Piha, L. P., & Avlonitis, G. J. (2015). Customer defection in retail banking: Attitudinal and behavioural consequences of failed service quality. *Journal of Service Theory and Practice*, *25*(3), 304–326. doi:10.1108/JSTP-04-2014-0080

Pillania, R. (2007). Organisational issues for knowledge management in SMEs. *International Journal of Business and Systems Research*, *1*(3), 367. doi:10.1504/IJBSR.2007.015835

Pinto, N. 2013. Understanding the barriers to online shopping among Indian consumers. *International Journal of Research in Humanities, Arts and Literature, 1*(3), 35–44. Available at: http://oaji.net/articles/488-1393060393.pdf

Piotrowicz, W., & Cuthbertson, R. (2014). Introduction to the special issue: information technology in retail: toward omnichannel retailing. *International Journal of Electronic Commerce*, *18*(4), 5–16. doi:10.2753/JEC1086-4415180400

Pitta, D., & Fowler, D. (2005). Internet community forums: An untapped resource for consumer marketers. *Journal of Consumer Marketing*, *22*(5), 265–274. doi:10.1108/07363760510611699

Pitta, D., & Katsanis, L. (1995). Understanding brand equity for successful brand extension. *Journal of Consumer Marketing*, *12*(4), 51–64. doi:10.1108/07363769510095306

Plummer, J. (2000). How Personality Makes a Difference. *Journal of Advertising Research*, *40*(6), 79–83. doi:10.2501/JAR-40-6-79-83

Poddar, A., Donthu, N., & Wei, Y. (2009). Web site customer orientations, web site quality, and purchase intentions: The role of web site personality. *Journal of Business Research*, *62*(4), 441–450. doi:10.1016/j.jbusres.2008.01.036

Pongsakornrungsilp, S., & Schroeder, J. (2011). Understanding value co-creation in a co-consuming brand community. *Marketing Theory*, *11*(3), 303–324. doi:10.1177/1470593111408178

Porter, M. (1990). *The competitive advantage of nations*. Free Press. doi:10.1007/978-1-349-11336-1

Powell, G., Groves, S., & Dimos, J. (2011). *ROI of Social Media: How to Improve the Return on Your Social Marketing Investment, 1* (1st ed.). Hoboken, NJ: Wiley.

Pozza, I. D. (2014). Multichannel management gets 'social'. *European Journal of Marketing*, *48*(7/8), 1274–1295. doi:10.1108/EJM-10-2012-0598

Prahalad, C. K., & Ramaswamy, V. (2004a). *The future of competition: Co-creating unique value with customers*. Boston, MA: Harvard Business School Press.

Prahalad, C., & Ramaswamy, V. (2000). Co-opting Customer Competence. *Harvard Business Review*, *78*(1), 79–87.

Prahalad, C., & Ramaswamy, V. (2004). Co-creating unique value with customers. *Strategy and Leadership*, *32*(3), 4–9. doi:10.1108/10878570410699249

Pratap, U., & Srivastava, R. (2013). Transforming business with mobile enterprise apps. *International Journal of Engineering And Computer Science*, *2*(6), 2057–2066. Retrieved from http://ijecs.in/issue/v2-i6/54 ijecs.pdf

Preece, J., Nonnecke, B., & Andrews, D. (2004). The Top 5 Reasons for Lurking: Improving Community Experiences for Everyone. *Computers in Human Behavior*, *20*(2), 201–223. doi:10.1016/j.chb.2003.10.015

Prendergast, G., Ko, D., & Siu Yin, V. Y. (2010). Online word of mouth and consumer purchase intentions. *International Journal of Advertising*, *29*(5), 687–708. doi:10.2501/S0265048710201427

Prensky, M. (2001). Digital Natives, Digital Immigrants Part 1. *On the Horizon*, *9*(5), 1–6. doi:10.1108/10748120110424816

Prentice-Dunn, & Rogers, R.W. (1985). Effects of Public and Private Self Awareness on Deindividuation and Aggression. *Journal of Personality and Social Psychology*, *43*, 503–513.

Pressgrove, G., McKeever, B. W., & Jang, S. M. (2018). What is Contagious? Exploring why content goes viral on Twitter: A case study of the ALS Ice Bucket Challenge. *International Journal of Nonprofit and Voluntary Sector Marketing*, *23*(1), e1586. doi:10.1002/nvsm.1586

Putzer, G. J., & Park, Y. (2010). The effects of innovation factors on smartphone adoption among nurses in community hospitals. *Perspectives in Health Information Management*, *7*. Retrieved from http://www.ncbi.nlm.nih.gov/pubmed/20697467 PMID:20697467

PwC. (2011). *Pick 'n' Mix: Meeting the demands of the new multi-channel shopper*. Author.

Qi, J., Monod, E., Fang, B., & Deng, S. (2018). Theories of Social media Philosophical Foundations. *Engineering*, *4*(1), 94–102. doi:10.1016/j.eng.2018.02.009

Quach, S., & Thaichon, P. (2017). From connoisseur luxury to mass luxury: Value co-creation and co-destruction in the online environment. *Journal of Business Research*, *81*, 163–172. doi:10.1016/j.jbusres.2017.06.015

Qualman, E. (2009). *Socialnomics: How social media transforms the way we live and do business*. Hoboken, NJ: John Wiley & Sons.

Qualman, E. (2013). *Socialnomics*. Hoboken, NJ: John Wiley & Sons.

Quinton, S., & Wilson, D. (2016). Tensions and ties in social media networks: Towards a model of understanding business relationship development and business performance enhancement through the use of LinkedIn. *Industrial Marketing Management*, *54*, 15–24. doi:10.1016/j.indmarman.2015.12.001

Rainer, T., & Rainer, J. (2011). *The Millennials*. Nashville, TN: B & H Publishing Group.

Rainer, T., & Rainer, J. (2011). *The Millennials: Connecting to America's Largest Generation*. Nashville, TN: B & H Pub. Group.

Rainie, L., & Wellman, B. (2012). *Networked: the new social operating system*. MIT Press.

Ramaswamy, V. (2008). Co-creating value through customers' experiences: The Nike case. *Strategy and Leadership*, *36*(5), 9–14. doi:10.1108/10878570810902068

Ramayah, T., & Ignatius, J. (2005). Impact of perceived usefulness, perceived ease of use and perceived enjoyment on intention to shop online. *ICFAI Journal of Systems Management, 3*(3), 1–16. Available at: http://ramayah.com/journalarticlespdf/impactpeu.pdf

Ramlugun, V. G. (2014). The Scope of social media browsing and online shopping for mauritian e-retailers: A study based on utilitarian and hedonic values. *Review of Integrative Business and Economics Research*, *3*(2), 219–241.

Raney, A. A., Arpan, L. M., Pashupati, K., & Brill, D. A. (2003). At the movies, on the web: An investigation of the effects of entertaining and interactive web content on site and brand evaluations. *Journal of Interactive Marketing*, *17*(4), 38–53. doi:10.1002/dir.10064

Rangaswamy, A., Burke, R., & Oliva, T. (1993). Brand equity and the extendibility of brand names. *International Journal of Research in Marketing*, *10*(1), 61–75. doi:10.1016/0167-8116(93)90034-V

Rani, S. H. (2013). Antecedents and Consequences of Entrepreneurial Quality among Graduate Entrepreneurs. *Asian Journal of Business and Management Sciences*, *2*(9), 44–55.

Ransbotham, S., Kane, G. C., & Lurie, N. H. (2012). Network Characteristics and the Value of Collaborative User-Generated Content. *Marketing Science*, *31*(3), 387–405. doi:10.1287/mksc.1110.0684

Rasmussen & Merkelsen. (2012). The new PR of states: How nation branding practices affect the security function of public diplomacy. *Public Relations Review, 38*(5), 810-818.

Rathore, A., Ilavarasan, V., & Dwivedi, Y. K. (2016). Social media content and product co-creation: An emerging paradigm. *Journal of Enterprise Information Management*, *29*(1), 7–18. doi:10.1108/JEIM-06-2015-0047

Rauschnabel, P. A., Kammerlander, N., & Ivens, B. S. (2016). Collaborative brand attacks in social media: Exploring the antecedents, characteristics, and consequences of a new form of brand crises. *Journal of Marketing Theory and Practice*, *24*(4), 381–410. doi:10.1080/10696679.2016.1205452

Reichheld, F. F. (2003). The one number you need to grow. *Harvard Business Review*, *81*(12), 46–55. PMID:14712543

Rejón-Guardia, F., & Martínez-López, F. J. (2014). Online advertising intrusiveness and consumers' avoidance behaviors. In *Handbook of strategic e-business management* (pp. 565–586). Berlin: Springer. doi:10.1007/978-3-642-39747-9_23

Renton, M., & Simmonds, H. (2017). Like is a verb: Exploring tie strength and casual brand use effects on brand attitudes and consumer online goal achievement. *Journal of Product and Brand Management*, *26*(4), 365–374. doi:10.1108/JPBM-03-2016-1125

Ren, Y., Harper, M., Drenner, S., Terveen, L., Kiesler, S., Riedl, J., & Kraut, R. (2012). Building member attachment in online communities: Applying theories of group identity and interpersonal bonds. *Management Information Systems Quarterly*, *36*(3), 841–864. doi:10.2307/41703483

Reputation Institute. RepTrack. (2017). *Digital country index*. Retrieved from https://www.reputationinstitute.com

Rettberg, J. (2008). *Blogging: Digital Media and Society Series*. Cambridge, UK: Polity.

Rheingold, H. (2002). *Smart mobs*. Cambridge, MA: Perseus Books Group.

Richard, M., & Habibi, M. R. (2016). Advanced modeling of online consumer behavior: The moderating roles of hedonism and culture. *Journal of Business Research*, *69*(3), 1103–1119. doi:10.1016/j.jbusres.2015.08.026

Richards, K., & Jones, E. (2008). Customer relationship management: Finding value drivers. *Industrial Marketing Management*, *37*(2), 120–130. doi:10.1016/j.indmarman.2006.08.005

Richards, M. (2015). *Social Media: Dominating Strategies for Social Media Marketing*. CreateSpace Independent Publishing Platform.

Richey, M. (2016). *Exploring social media use in small firms: a cultural toolkit perspective* (PhD thesis). Loughborough University.

Richins, M. L. (1983). Negative word-of-mouth by dissatisfied consumers: A pilot study. *Journal of Marketing*, *47*(1), 68–78. doi:10.1177/002224298304700107

Richins, M. L. (1994). Valuing Things: The Public and Private Meanings of Possessions. *The Journal of Consumer Research*, *21*(10), 504–521. doi:10.1086/209414

Richins, M. L., & Root-Shaffer, T. (1988). The role of evolvement and opinion leadership in consumer word-of-mouth: An implicit model made explicit. *Advances in Consumer Research. Association for Consumer Research (U. S.)*, *15*(1), 32–36. Retrieved from http://www.acrwebsite.org/search/view-conference-proceedings.aspx?Id=6790

Ridgway, J., & Myers, B. (2014). A study on brand personality: Consumers' perceptions of colours used in fashion brand logos. *International Journal of Fashion Design. Technology and Education*, *7*(1), 50–57.

Riedinger, D. (2015). *Likeable Social Media, Revised and Expanded* (2nd ed.). McGraw-Hill.

Riley, F. D., & Lacroix, C. (2003). Luxury branding on the Internet: Lost opportunity or impossibility? *Marketing Intelligence & Planning*, *21*(2), 96–104. doi:10.1108/02634500310465407

Ring, A., Tkaczynski, A., & Dolnicar, S. (2016). 2014; "Word-of-Mouth Segments: Online, Offline, Visual or Verbal? *Journal of Travel Research*, *55*(4), 481–492. doi:10.1177/0047287514563165

Ringberg, T., Odekerken-Schröder, G., & Christensen, G. L. (2007). A cultural models approach to service recovery. *Journal of Marketing*, *71*(3), 194–214. doi:10.1509/jmkg.71.3.194

Rio-Lanza, A. B. D., Vazquez-Casielles, R., & Diaz-Martin, A. M. (2009). Satisfaction with service recovery: Perceived justice and emotional responses. *Journal of Business Research*, *62*(8), 775–781. doi:10.1016/j.jbusres.2008.09.015

Rius Ulldemolins, J., & Zamorano, M. (2014). Spain's nation branding project Marca España and its cultural policy: The economic and political instrumentalization of a homogeneous and simplified cultural image. *International Journal of Cultural Policy*, 1–21.

Robards, B., & Bennett, A. (2011). MyTribe: Post-subcultural Manifestations of Belonging on Social Network Sites. *Sociology*, *45*(2), 303–317. doi:10.1177/0038038510394025

Robert, G., Astrid, S., & Bart, N. (2013). Social Media Affecting Tour Operators' Customer Loyalty. *Journal of Travel & Tourism Marketing*, *30*, 1–2, 41–57. doi:10.1080/10548408.2013.750993

Roberts, K. (2006). *Lovemarks: The future beyond brands* (2nd ed.). New York: PowerHouse Books.

Roberts, M. L., Barker, M. S., Zahay, D. L., Bormann, N. F., & Barker, D. (2016). *Social media marketing: a strategic approach* (2nd ed South-Western.

Robins, G., Pattison, P., & Elliott, P. (2001). Network Models for Social Influence Processes. *Psychometrika*, *66*(2), 161–190. doi:10.1007/BF02294834

Robinson, J. A., & Lo, J. (2005). *Bibliography of Academic Papers on Social Entrepreneurship*. New York: New York University.

Rodgers, S. L. & Thorson, E. (2017). Digital advertising: theory and research (3rd ed.). Routledge.

Rodriguez del Bosque, I., & San Martin, H. (2008). Tourist Satisfaction a Cognitive Affective Model. *Annals of Tourism Research*, *35*(2), 551–573. doi:10.1016/j.annals.2008.02.006

Rodriguez-Ardura, I., Martinez-Lopez, F. J., & Luna, P. (2010). Going with the consumer towards the social web environment: A review of extant knowledge. *International Journal of Electronic Marketing and Retailing*, *3*(4), 415–440. doi:10.1504/IJEMR.2010.036885

Rodriguez, M., Peterson, R. M., & Krishanan, V. (2012). Social media's influence on business-to business sales performance. *Journal of Personal Selling & Sales Management*, *32*(3), 365–378. doi:10.2753/PSS0885-3134320306

Rogers, E. M. (1983). *Diffusion of innovations*. NewYork: Free Press.

Rogers, T. B., Kuiper, N. A., & Kirker, W. S. (1977). Self-Reference and Encoding of Personal Information. *Journal of Personality and Social Psychology*, *35*(9), 677–688. doi:10.1037/0022-3514.35.9.677 PMID:909043

Roggeveen, A. L., Tsiros, M., & Grewal, D. (2012). Understanding the co-creation effect: When does collaborating with customers provide a lift to service recovery? *Journal of the Academy of Marketing Science*, *40*(6), 771–790. doi:10.100711747-011-0274-1

Romero, D., & Molina, A. (2011). Collaborative networked organisations and customer communities: Value co-creation and co-innovation in the networking era. *Production Planning and Control*, *22*(5-6), 447–472. doi:10.1080/09537287.2010.536619

Rosa, M. I. (2012). *Omni-channel retailing: Is its 'order online pick-up in store' service viable in the Portuguese grocery industry?* Universidade Católica Portuguesa.

Roschk, H., & Kaiser, S. (2013). The nature of an apology: An experimental study on how to apologize after a service failure. *Marketing Letters*, *24*(3), 293–309. doi:10.100711002-012-9218-x

Rosenmayer, A., McQuilken, L., Robertson, N., & Ogden, S. (2018). Omni-channel service failures and recoveries: Refined typologies using Facebook complaints. *Journal of Services Marketing*, *32*(3), 269–285. doi:10.1108/JSM-04-2017-0117

Ross, C., Orr, E., Sisic, M., Arseneault, J., Simmering, M., & Orr, R. (2009). Personality and Motivations Associated With Facebook Use. *Computers in Human Behavior*, *25*(2), 578–586. doi:10.1016/j.chb.2008.12.024

Rossiter, J., & Percy, L. (1978). *Advertising and Promotion Management*. New York: McGraw Hill.

Rossmann, A., Ranjan, K. R., & Sugathan, P. (2016). Drivers of user engagement in eWoM communication. *Journal of Services Marketing*, *30*(5), 541–553. doi:10.1108/JSM-01-2015-0013

Roth, M. S. (1995). The effects of culture and socioeconomics on the performance of global brand image strategies. *JMR, Journal of Marketing Research*, *32*(2), 163–175. doi:10.2307/3152045

Rowley, J. (2006). An analysis of the e-service literature: Towards a research agenda. *Internet Research*, *16*(3), 339–359. doi:10.1108/10662240610673736

Roy, A., & Chattopadhyay, S. (2010). Stealth marketing as a strategy. *Business Horizons*, *53*(1), 69–79. doi:10.1016/j.bushor.2009.09.004

Royo-Vela, M., & Casamassima, P. (2011). The influence of belonging to virtual brand communities on consumers' affective commitment, satisfaction and word-of-mouth advertising. *Online Information Review*, *35*(4), 517–542. doi:10.1108/14684521111161918

Rud, M., & Wong, S. K. B. (2011). *Turning a new page: Co-creation in practice through the study of C-G lookbook*. Lund University.

Russo, A., Watkins, J., Kelly, L., & Chan, S. (2008). Participatory communication with social media. *Curator (New York, N.Y.)*, *51*(1), 21–31. doi:10.1111/j.2151-6952.2008.tb00292.x

Rust, R. T., & Lemon, K. N. (2001). E-Service and the Consumer. *International Journal of Electronic Commerce*, *5*(3), 85–101. doi:10.1080/10864415.2001.11044216

Rust, R. T., & Oliver, R. L. (2000). Should We Delight the Customer? *Journal of the Academy of Marketing Science*, *28*(1), 86–94. doi:10.1177/0092070300281008

Rust, R. T., & Zahorik, A. J. (1993). Customer Satisfaction, Customer Retention, and Market Share. *Journal of Retailing*, *69*(2), 193–215. doi:10.1016/0022-4359(93)90003-2

Rust, R., Lemon, K., & Zeithaml, V. (2000). *Driving Customer Equity: How Customer Lifetime Value Is Reshaping Corporate Strategy*. New York: The Free Pree.

Rust, R., Lemon, K., & Zeithaml, V. (2004). Return on Marketing: Using Customer Equity to Focus Marketing Strategy. *Journal of Marketing*, *68*(1), 109–127. doi:10.1509/jmkg.68.1.109.24030

Ryan, D. (2014). *Understanding digital marketing: marketing strategies for engaging the digital generation* (3rd ed.). London: KoganPage.

Ryan, D., & Jones, C. (2009). *Understanding Digital Marketing: Marketing Strategies forEEngaging the Digital Generation*. Glasgow, UK: Marketing Industry Network.

Ryan, D., & Jones, C. (2014). *The Best Digital Marketing Campaigns in the World II, Second* (1st ed.). London: Kogan Page Ltd.

Rzemieniak, M. (2015). Measuring the Effectiveness of Online Advertising Campaigns in the Aspect of e-entrepreneurship. *Procedia Computer Science*, *65*, 980–987. doi:10.1016/j.procs.2015.09.063

Sabate, F., Berbegal-Mirabent, J., Cañabate, A., & Lebherz, P. R. (2014). Factors influencing popularity of branded content in Facebook fan pages. *European Management Journal*, *32*(6), 1001–1011. doi:10.1016/j.emj.2014.05.001

Saboo, A. R., Kumar, V., & Ramani, G. (2016). Evaluating the impact of social media activities on human brand sales. *International Journal of Research in Marketing*, *33*(3), 524–541. doi:10.1016/j.ijresmar.2015.02.007

Sadek, Elwy, & Eldallal. (2018). The impact of social media brand communication on consumer-based brand equity dimensions through Facebook in fast moving consumer goods: The case of Egypt. *Journal of Business and Retail Management Research, 12*(2).

Safari, F., Safari, N., Hasanzadeh, A., & Ghatari, A. (2015). Factors affecting the adoption of cloud computing in small and medium enterprises. *International Journal of Business Information Systems*, *20*(1), 116. doi:10.1504/IJBIS.2015.070894

Safko, L. (2010). John Wiley & Sons. In *The social media bible: tactics, tools, and strategies for business success* (2nd ed.; pp. 4–25). Hoboken, NJ: John Wiley & sons.

Safko, L. (2012). *The social media bible* (3rd ed.). Hoboken, NJ: John Wiley & Sons.

Safko, L. (2012). *The social media bible: Tactics, tools, and strategies for business success*. Hoboken, NJ: John Wiley & Sons.

Safko, L., Brake, D., & David, K. (2009). *The Social Media Bible: Tactics, Tools, and Strategies for Business Success*. Wiley.

Saghiri, S., Wilding, R., Mena, C., & Bourlakis, M. (2017). Toward a three-dimensional framework for omni-channel. *Journal of Business Research*, *77*, 53–67. doi:10.1016/j.jbusres.2017.03.025

Salvador, R. O., Folger, R., & Priesemuth, M. (2012). Article. *Journal of Managerial Issues*, *24*(2), 124–139.

Samadi, M., Nagi, R., Semenov, A., & Nikolaev, A. (2018). Seed activation scheduling for influence maximization in social networks. *Omega: The International Journal of Management Science*, *77*, 96–114. doi:10.1016/j.omega.2017.06.002

Sampson, S. E., & Froehle, C. M. (2006). Foundations and implications of a proposed Unified Services Theory. *Production and Operations Management*, *15*(2), 329–343. doi:10.1111/j.1937-5956.2006.tb00248.x

Samson, A. (2006). Understanding the buzz that matters: Negative vs positive word of mouth. *International Journal of Market Research*, *48*(6), 647–657. doi:10.1177/147078530604800603

Sandars, J., & Walsh, K. (2009). 2008; "The use of online word of mouth opinion in online learning: A questionnaire survey. *Medical Teacher*, *31*(4), 325–327. doi:10.1080/01421590802204403 PMID:18937096

Santos, A. T., Alves, L., & Brambilla, F. R. (2016). *Value co-creation in Retail through the use of social networks*. Retrieved from https://online.unisc.br/seer/index.php/cepe/index

Santos, J. (2003). E-service quality: A model of virtual service quality dimensions. *Managing Service Quality*, *13*(3), 233–246. doi:10.1108/09604520310476490

Sapena, J., & Paniagua, J. (2014). Business performance and social media: Love or hate? *Business Horizons*, *57*(6), 719–728. doi:10.1016/j.bushor.2014.07.005

Saravanakumar, M., & Sugantha Lakshmi, T. (2012). Social media marketing. *Life Science Journal*, *9*(4), 2012.

Sarkar, A. (2011). Impact of utilitarian and hedonic shopping values on individual's perceived benefits and risks in online shopping. *International Management Review*, *7*(1), 58–65. Available at http://uxscientist.com/public/docs/uxsci_50.pdf

Sarwar, M., & Rahim Soomro, T. (2013). Impact of smartphones on society. *European Journal of Scientific Research*, *98*(2), 216–226. Retrieved from http://www.europeanjournalofscientificresearch.com

Sashi, C. M. (2012). Customer engagement, buyer-seller relationships, and social media. *Management Decision*, *50*(2), 253–272. doi:10.1108/00251741211203551

Sashittal, H., DeMar, M., & Jassawalla, A. (2016). Building acquaintance brands via Snapchat for the college student market. *Business Horizons*, *59*(2), 193–204. doi:10.1016/j.bushor.2015.11.004

Sathish, M., Kumar, K. S., Naveen, K. J., & Jeevanantham, V. (2011). A Study on Consumer Switching Behaviour in Cellular Service Provider: A Study with reference to Chennai. *Far East Journal of Psychology and Business*, *2*(2), 72.

Saunders, M., Lewis, P., & Thornhill, A. (2009). *Research methods for business students* (5th ed.). Harlow: Pearson Education Limited.

Sawhney, M., Verona, G., & Prandelli, E. (2005). Collaborating to create: The internet as a platform for customer engagement in product innovation. *Journal of Interactive Marketing*, *19*(4), 4–17. doi:10.1002/dir.20046

Saxton, G. D., Guo, C., & Brown, W. (2007). New dimensions of nonprofit responsiveness: The application and promise of Internet-based technologies. *Public Performance & Management Review*, *31*(2), 144–173. doi:10.2753/PMR1530-9576310201

Scarpi, D. (2006). Fashion stores between fun and usefulness. *Journal of Fashion Marketing and Management*, *10*(1), 7–24. doi:10.1108/13612020610651097

Schaffer, N., Safko, L., Korhan, J., Goodman, G. F., Stratten, S., & Zarrella, D. (2013). *Social Marketing Digital Book Set* (1st ed.). Hoboken, NJ: John Wiley & Sons Inc.

Schamari, J., & Schaefers, T. (2015). Leaving the home turf: How brands can use web care on consumer generated platforms to increase positive consumer engagement. *Journal of Interactive Marketing*, *30*(5), 20–33. doi:10.1016/j.intmar.2014.12.001

Schau, H., Muñiz, A. Jr, & Arnould, E. (2009). How Brand Community Practices Create Value. *Journal of Marketing*, *73*(5), 30–51. doi:10.1509/jmkg.73.5.30

Schembri, S., Merrilees, B., & Kristiansen, S. (2010). Brand consumption and narrative of the self. *Psychology and Marketing*, *27*(6), 623–637. doi:10.1002/mar.20348

Schendel, D., & Hitt, M. A. (2007). Introduction to volume 1. *Strategic Entrepreneurship Journal*, *1*(1–2), 1–6. doi:10.1002ej.16

Schewe, C., & Meredith, G. (2004). Segmenting global markets by generational cohorts: Determining motivations by age. *Journal of Consumer Behaviour*, *4*(1), 51–63. doi:10.1002/cb.157

Schivinski, B., & Dabrowski, D. (2016). The effect of social media communication on consumer perceptions of brands. *Journal of Marketing Communications*, *22*(2), 189–214. doi:10.1080/13527266.2013.871323

Schlesinger, L. A., & Heskett, J. (1991). Breaking the Cycle of Failure in Services. *MIT Sloan Management Review*, *32*(3), 17–28.

Schlosser, A. E. (2005). Posting Vs. Lurking: Communicating in a Multiple Audience Context. *The Journal of Consumer Research*, *32*(2), 260–265. doi:10.1086/432235

Schminke, M., Caldwell, J., Ambrose, M. L., & McMahon, S. R. (2014). Better than ever? Employee reactions to ethical failures in organizations, and the ethical recovery paradox. *Organizational Behavior and Human Decision Processes*, *123*(2), 206–219. doi:10.1016/j.obhdp.2013.10.002

Schneider, B., & Bowen, D. E. (1999). Understanding Customer Delight and Outrage. *Sloan Management Review*, *41*(1), 35–45.

Schoefer, K., & Diamantopoulos, A. (2009). A typology of consumers' emotional response style during service recovery encounters. *British Journal of Management*, *20*(3), 292–308. doi:10.1111/j.1467-8551.2008.00589.x

Schoenbachler, D. D., & Gordon, G. L. (2002). Multi-channel shopping: Understanding what drives channel choice. *Journal of Consumer Marketing*, *19*(1), 42–53. doi:10.1108/07363760210414943

Schouten, J., & McAlexander, J. (1995). Subcultures of Consumption: An Ethnography of the New Bikers. *The Journal of Consumer Research*, *22*(1), 43. doi:10.1086/209434

Schröder, H., & Zaharia, S. (2008). Linking multi-channel customer behavior with shopping motives: An empirical investigation of a German retailer. *Journal of Retailing and Consumer Services*, *15*(6), 452–468. doi:10.1016/j.jretconser.2008.01.001

Schultz, C. D. (2016). Insights from consumer interactions on a social networking site: Findings from six apparel retail brands. *Electronic Markets*, *26*(3), 203–217. doi:10.100712525-015-0209-7

Schultz, C. D. (2017). Proposing to your fans: Which brand post characteristics drive consumer engagement activities on social media brand pages? *Electronic Commerce Research and Applications*, *26*, 23–34. doi:10.1016/j.elerap.2017.09.005

Schultz, R. J., Schwepker, C. H., & Good, D. J. (2012). An exploratory study of social media in business-to-business selling: Salesperson characteristics, activities and performance. *Marketing Management Journal*, *22*(2), 76–89.

Schulz, S., Pauw, G., Clercq, O., Desmet, B., Hoste, V., Daelemans, W., & Macken, L. (2016). Multimodular Text Normalisation of Dutch User-Generated Content. *ACM Transactions on Intelligent Systems and Technology*, *7*(4), 1–22. doi:10.1145/2850422

Schwandt, T. A. (2000). *Three epistemological stances for qualitative inquiry: Interpretivism, hermeneutics and social constructivism* (2nd ed.). London: SAGE Publication Ltd.

Sciglipaglia, D., & Ely, D. (2006). Customer account relationships and e-retail banking usage. *Journal of Financial Services Marketing*, *10*(4), 109–122. doi:10.1057/palgrave.fsm.4760026

Scott, D. M. (2015). *The New Rules of Marketing and PR: How to Use Social Media, Online Video, Mobile Applications, Blogs, News Releases, and Viral Marketing to Reach Buyers Directly* (5th ed.). New York: John Wiley & Sons Inc. doi:10.1002/9781119172499.ch02

Scott, J. (2012). *Social network analysis*. Thousand Oaks, CA: Sage.

Scott, S., & Orlikowski, W. (2014). Entanglements in Practice: Performing Anonymity Through Social Media. *Management Information Systems Quarterly*, *38*(3), 873–893. doi:10.25300/MISQ/2014/38.3.11

Seadle, M. & Greifender, E. (2014). *Structuring the digital domain*. Emerald Group Publishing Ltd.

Seargeant, P., & Tagg, C. (2018). Social media and the future of open debate: A user-oriented approach to Facebook's filter bubble conundrum. *Discourse, Context & Media Journal*.

Seck, A. (2013). The issue of multichannel integration, a key challenge for service firms in a context of multichannel services distribution. *International Business Research*, *6*(2), 160–169.

Seck, A., & Philippe, J. (2013). Service encounter in multi-channel distribution context: Virtual and face-to-face interactions and consumer satisfaction. *Service Industries Journal*, *33*(6), 565–579. doi:10.1080/02642069.2011.622370

Seiders, K., & Tigert, D. J. (1997). Impact of Market Entry and Competitive Structure on Store Switching/Store Loyalty. *International Review of Retail, Distribution and Consumer Research*, *7*(3), 227–247. doi:10.1080/095939697343003

Sender, T. (2014). *Top of the online shops: Online fashion clicks with 70% of Brits*. Retrieved April 4, 2018 from http://www.mintel.com/press-centre/retail-press-centre/top-of-the-online-shops-online-fashion-clicks-with-70-of-brits

Sender, T. (2017). *Brits hung up on online fashion: Online sales of clothing, fashion accessories and footwear grow by 17% in 2017*. Retrieved October 5, 2018 from http://www.mintel.com/press-centre/fashion/uk-online-sales-of-clothing-fashion-accessories-and-footwear-grow-by-17-in-2017

Senecal, S., & Nantel, J. (2004). The influence of online product recommendations on consumers' online choices. *Journal of Retailing*, *80*(2), 159–169. doi:10.1016/j.jretai.2004.04.001

Sengupta, S., Ray, D., Trendel, O., & Vaerenbergh, Y. V. (2018). The effects of apologies for service failures in the global online retail. *International Journal of Electronic Commerce*, *22*(3), 419–445. doi:10.1080/10864415.2018.1462951

Seno, D., & Lukas, B. (2007). Exploring the relationship between celebrity endorser effects and advertising effectiveness. *European Journal of Marketing*, *41*(1/2), 121–134. doi:10.1108/03090560710718148

Shane, S. (2003). *A general theory of entrepreneurship: The individual-opportunity nexus*. Cheltenham, UK: Edward Elgar Publishing Limited.

Shang, R., Chen, Y., & Liao, H. (2006). The value of participation in virtual consumer communities on brand loyalty. *Internet Research*, *16*(4), 398–418. doi:10.1108/10662240610690025

Shankar, V., Inman, J. J., Mantrala, M., Kelley, E., & Rizley, R. (2011). Innovations in shopper marketing: Current insights and future research issues. *Journal of Retailing*, *87*(Suppl. 1), S29–S42. doi:10.1016/j.jretai.2011.04.007

Shankar, V., Smith, A. K., & Rangaswamy, A. (2003). 'Customer Satisfaction and Loyalty in Online and Offline Environments'. *International Journal of Research in Marketing*, *20*(2), 153–175. doi:10.1016/S0167-8116(03)00016-8

Shao, G. (2009). Understanding the appeal of user-generated media: A uses and gratification perspective. *Internet Research*, *19*(1), 7–25. doi:10.1108/10662240910927795

Shapiro, L. M. (2010). *Severe Market Dissruption on 6th May, 2010: Congressional Testimony*. Collingdale, PA: Diane Publishing Co.

Shaw, E., & Carter, S. (2007). Social entrepreneurship: Theoretical antecedents and empirical analysis of entrepreneurial processes and outcomes. *Journal of Small Business and Enterprise Development*, *14*(3), 418–434. doi:10.1108/14626000710773529

Shehu, E., Bijmolt, T. H. A., & Clement, M. (2016). Effects of Likeability Dynamics on Consumers' Intention to Share Online Video Advertisements. *Journal of Interactive Marketing*, *35*, 27–43. doi:10.1016/j.intmar.2016.01.001

Sheldrake, P., & Sheldrake, P. P. I. (2011). *The Business of Influence: Reframing Marketing and PR for the Digital Age*, *1* (1st ed.). New York: Wiley.

Shen, A. X. L., Cheung, C. M. K., Lee, M. K. O., & Chen, H. (2011). How Social Influence Affects We-Intention to Use Instant Messaging: The Moderating Effect of Usage Experience. *Information Systems Frontiers*, *13*(2), 157–169. doi:10.100710796-009-9193-9

Sherif, C. W., & Sherif, M. (1967). *Attitude, Ego-involvement, and Change*. Westport, CT: Green Wood Press.

Sherif, M., & Hovland, C. I. (1961). *Social judgment: assimilation and contrast effects in communication and attitude change*. Yale University Press.

Sheth, J. (2011). Impact of Emerging Markets on Marketing: Rethinking Existing Perspectives and Practices. *Journal of Marketing*, *75*(4), 166–182. doi:10.1509/jmkg.75.4.166

Sheth, J. N., Newman, B. I., & Gross, B. L. (1991). Why We Buy What We Buy: A Theory of Consumption Values. *Journal of Business Research*, *22*(2), 159–170. doi:10.1016/0148-2963(91)90050-8

Sheth, J., & Parvatlyar, A. (1995). Relationship Marketing in Consumer Markets: Antecedents and Consequences. *Journal of the Academy of Marketing Science*, *23*(4), 255–271. doi:10.1177/009207039502300405

Sheth, J., & Sisodia, R. (1999). Revisiting Marketing's Lawlike Generalizations. *Journal of the Academy of Marketing Science*, *27*(1), 71–87. doi:10.1177/0092070399271006

Shibutani, T. (1955). Reference Groups as Perspectives. *American Journal of Sociology*, *60*(6), 562–569. doi:10.1086/221630

Shin, D. (2018). Empathy and embodied experience in virtual environment: To what extent can virtual reality stimulate empathy and embodied experience? *Computers in Human Behavior, 78*, 64–73. doi:10.1016/j.chb.2017.09.012

Shin, H., Ellinger, A. E., Mothersbaugh, D. L., & Reynolds, K. E. (2017). Employing proactive interaction for service failure prevention to improve customer service experiences. *Journal of Service Theory and Practice, 27*(1), 164–186. doi:10.1108/JSTP-07-2015-0161

Shneiderman, B., Preece, J., & Pirolli, P. (2011). Realizing the value of social media requires innovative computing research. *Communications of the ACM, 54*(9), 34–37. doi:10.1145/1995376.1995389

Siamagka, N., Christodoulides, G., Michaelidou, N., & Valvi, A. (2015). Determinants of social media adoption by B2B organisations. *Industrial Marketing Management, 51*, 89–99. doi:10.1016/j.indmarman.2015.05.005

Simmons, G. (2008). Marketing to postmodern consumers: Introducing the internet chameleon. *European Journal of Marketing, 42*(3/4), 299–310. doi:10.1108/03090560810852940

Simon, J.P. (2016). User generated content – users, community of users and firms: toward new sources of co-innovation? *Info, 18*(6), 4-25.

Simon, J.P. (2016). User generated content – users, community of users and firms: Toward new sources of co-innovation? *Info, 18*(6), 4–25.

Sinan, A., Dellarocas, C., & Godes, D. (2013). Introduction to the Special Issue—Social Media and Business Transformation: A Framework for Research. *Information Systems Research, 24*(1), 3–13. doi:10.1287/isre.1120.0470

Singaraju, S. P., Nguyen, Q. A., Niininen, O., & Sullivan-Mort, G. (2016). Social media and value co-creation in multi-stakeholder systems: A resource integration approach. *Industrial Marketing Management, 54*, 44–55. doi:10.1016/j.indmarman.2015.12.009

Singh, S., & Sonnenburg, S. (2012). Brand Performances in Social Media. *Journal of Interactive Marketing, 26*(4), 189–197. doi:10.1016/j.intmar.2012.04.001

Singh, T., Veron-Jackson, L., & Cullinane, J. (2008). Blogging: A new play in your marketing game plan. *Business Horizons, 51*(4), 281–292. doi:10.1016/j.bushor.2008.02.002

Sinha, K. S., Subramanian, S., & Bhattacharya, K. C. (2012). The contemporary framework on social media analytics as an emerging tool for behaviour informatics, HR analytics and business process. *Journal of Contemporary Management Issues, 17*(2), 65–84.

Sirgy, M. J. (1982). Self-Concept in Consumer Behaviour: A Critical Review. *The Journal of Consumer Research, 9*(3), 287–300. doi:10.1086/208924

Sirgy, M. J., Grewal, D., & Mangleburg, T. (2000). Retail Environment, Self-Congruity, and Retail Patronage: An Integrative Model and a Research Agenda. *Journal of Business Research, 49*(2), 127–138. doi:10.1016/S0148-2963(99)00009-0

Sitta, D., Faulkner, M., & Stern, P. (2018). What can the brand manager expect from Facebook? *Australasian Marketing Journal, 26*(1), 17–22. doi:10.1016/j.ausmj.2018.01.001

Siu, N. Y., Zhang, T. J., & Yau, C. J. (2013). The roles of justice and customer satisfaction in customer retention: A lesson from service recovery. *Journal of Business Ethics, 114*(4), 675–686. doi:10.100710551-013-1713-3

Sivakumar, K., Li, M., & Dong, B. (2014). Service quality: The impact of frequency, timing, proximity, and sequence of failure and delights. *Journal of Marketing, 78*(1), 41–58. doi:10.1509/jm.12.0527

Slawsby, A., Leibovitch, A. M., & Giusto, R. (2003). *Worldwide Mobile Phone Forecast and Analysis, 2003-2007.* IDC Report, No. 29586.

Sloot, L. M., Verhoef, P. C., & Franses, P. H. (2005). The Impact of Brand Equity and the Hedonic Level of Products on Consumer Stock-Out Reactions. *Journal of Retailing*, *81*(1), 15–34. doi:10.1016/j.jretai.2005.01.001

Smith, A., & Anderson, M. (2018). *Social Media Use in 2018.* PewResearch Center. Retrieved from http://assets.pewresearch.org/wp-content/uploads/sites/14/2018/03/01105133/PI_2018.03.01_Social-Media_FINAL.pdf

Smith, A. K., & Bolton, R. N. (2002). The effect of customers' emotional responses to service failures on their recovery effort evaluations and satisfaction judgments. *Journal of the Academy of Marketing Science*, *30*(1), 5–23. doi:10.1177/03079450094298

Smith, A. K., Bolton, R. N., & Wagner, J. (1999). A model of customer satisfaction with service encounters involving failure and recovery. *JMR, Journal of Marketing Research*, *36*(3), 356–372. doi:10.2307/3152082

Smith, A. N., Fischer, E., & Yongjian, C. (2012). How Does Brand-related User-generated Content Differ across YouTube, Facebook, and Twitter? *Journal of Interactive Marketing*, *26*(2), 102–113. doi:10.1016/j.intmar.2012.01.002

Smith, A., & Anderson, M. (2018). *Social Media Use in 2018.* Pew Research Center. Retrieved from http://assets.pewresearch.org/wp-content/uploads/sites/14/2018/03/01105133/PI_2018.03.01_Social-Media_FINAL.pdf

Smith, K. (2011). Digital marketing strategies that Millennials find appealing, motivating, or just annoying. *Journal of Strategic Marketing*, *19*(6), 489–499. doi:10.1080/0965254X.2011.581383

Smith, P. R., & Zook, Z. (2011). *Marketing communications: integrating offline and online with social media* (5th ed.). London: Kogan Page.

Smith, P., & Chaffey, D. (2012). *Emarketing excellence*. St. Louis, MO: Taylor and Francis. doi:10.4324/9780080504896

Smith, P., & Zook, Z. (2011). *Marketing Communications* (5th ed.). London: Kogan Page.

Smith, R., Bell, R., & Watts, H. (2014). Personality trait differences between traditional and social entrepreneurs. *Social Enterprise Journal*, *10*(3), 200–221. doi:10.1108/SEJ-08-2013-0033

Smith, T. (2009). The social media revolution. *International Journal of Market Research*, *51*(4), 559–561. doi:10.2501/S1470785309200773

Smock, A., Ellison, N., Lampe, C., & Wohn, D. (2011). Facebook as a toolkit: A uses and gratification approach to unbundling feature use. *Computers in Human Behavior*, *27*(6), 2322–2329. doi:10.1016/j.chb.2011.07.011

Snap Inc. (2018). Retrieved from https://www.snap.com/en-US/

Soft Power 30. (2017). A global ranking of soft power. *Portland Communications*. Retrieved from https://softpower30.com/wp-content/uploads/2017/07/The-Soft-Power-30-Report-2017-Web-1.pdf

So, K. F., King, C., & Sparks, B. (2014). Customer engagement with tourism Brands: Scale development and validation. *Journal of Hospitality & Tourism Research (Washington, D.C.)*, *38*(3), 304–329. doi:10.1177/1096348012451456

Solomon, G., & Schrum, L. (2007). *Web 2.0: New Tools, New Schools.* Eugene, OR: International Society for Technology in Education.

Solomon, M. (2012). *Consumer behavior* (10th ed.). Pearson Education Limited.

Solomon, M. R., & Tuten, T. L. (2015). The Fifth P of Marketing. In *Social media marketing* (p. 1). Thousand Oaks, CA: Sage.

Song, Z. L., Di Benedetto, A. C., & Song, M. (2010). Competitive advantages in the first product of new ventures. *IEEE Transactions on Engineering Management*, *57*(1), 88–115. doi:10.1109/TEM.2009.2013836

Son, M., & Han, K. (2011). Beyond the technology adoption: Technology readiness effects on post-adoption behavior. *Journal of Business Research*, *64*(11), 1178–1182. doi:10.1016/j.jbusres.2011.06.019

Sopadjieva, E., Dholakia, U. M., & Benjamin, B. (2017). A study of 46,000 shoppers shows that omni-channel retailing works. *Harvard Business Review*, 3.

Sorensen, A., Andrews, L., & Drennam, J. (2016). *Using social media posts as resources for engaging in value co-creation. The case for social media- based cause brand communities.* doi:10.1108/JSTP-04-2016-0080

Sorenson, O. (2013). Status and reputation: Synonyms or separate concepts? *Strategic Organization*, *12*(1), 62–69. doi:10.1177/1476127013513219

Sousa, R., & Voss, C. (2006). Service quality in multichannel services employing virtual channels. *Journal of Service Research*, *8*(4), 356–371. doi:10.1177/1094670506286324

Sousa, R., & Voss, C. (2012). The impacts of e-service quality on customer behavior in multi-channel services. *Total Quality Management & Business Excellence*, *23*(7), 769–787.

Sousa, R., & Voss, C. A. (2009). The effects of service failures and recovery on customer loyalty in e-services: An empirical investigation. *International Journal of Operations & Production Management*, *29*(8), 834–864. doi:10.1108/01443570910977715

Sparks, B. A., & Bradley, G. L. (2017). A 'triple A' typology of responding to negative consumer-generated online reviews. *Journal of Hospitality & Tourism Research (Washington, D.C.)*, *41*(6), 719–745. doi:10.1177/1096348014538052

Sparks, B. A., So, K. K. F., & Bradley, G. L. (2016). Responding to negative online reviews: The effects of hotel responses on customer inferences of trust and concern. *Tourism Management*, *53*, 74–85. doi:10.1016/j.tourman.2015.09.011

Sparks, B., & Fredline, L. (2007). Providing an Explanation for Service Failure: Context, Content, and Customer Responses. *Journal of Hospitality & Tourism Research (Washington, D.C.)*, *31*(2), 241–260. doi:10.1177/1096348006297292

Spence, C., & Gallace, A. (2011). Multisensory design: Reaching out to touch the consumer. *Psychology and Marketing*, *28*(3), 267–308. doi:10.1002/mar.20392

Spreng, R., & Mackoy, R. (1996). An empirical examination of a model of perceived service quality and satisfaction. *Journal of Retailing*, *72*(2), 201–214. doi:10.1016/S0022-4359(96)90014-7

Stareva, I. (2014). *Social Media and the Rebirth of PR: The Emergence of Social Media as a Change Driver for PR* (1st ed.). Hamburg: Anchor Academic Publishing.

Statista. (2016a). *Global daily social media usage by age 2016.* Retrieved from https://www.statista.com/statistics/613456/daily-social-media-usage-worldwide-age/

Statista. (2016a). London Fashion Week: Social Buzz 2014. Social Media & User-Generated Content. *Statista - The Statistic Portal.* Retrieved 18 January 2016, from http://www.statista.com/statistics/315224/social-media-mentions-london-fashion-week/

Statista. (2016b). *Fashion brands: social visibility score on social networks 2016 | Statistic.* Retrieved from https://www.statista.com/statistics/729691/fashion-brands-social-visibility-score-social-networks-world/

Statista. (2016b). *Leading luxury brands ranked by number of Instagram followers as of October 2016 (in millions).* Retrieved 29 September 2016, from https://www.statista.com/statistics/483753/leading-luxury-brands-instagram-followers/

Statista. (2016c). *Daily time spent on social networking by internet users worldwide as of 2nd quarter 2016, by age group (in minutes).* Retrieved 5 March 2018, from https://www.statista.com/statistics/613456/daily-social-media-usage-worldwide-age/

Statista. (2016c). *Instagram: global brand adoption rate 2016.* Retrieved from https://www.statista.com/statistics/305292/worldwide-instagram-brand-adoption-rate-category/

Statista. (2016d). *Global apparel market size projections from 2012 to 2025, by region (in billion U.S. dollars).* Retrieved 29 September 2016, from https://www.statista.com/statistics/279757/apparel-market-size-projections-by-region/

Statista. (2016d). *Instagram usage during MFW by action Italy 2016.* Retrieved from https://www.statista.com/statistics/676023/instagram-usage-during-mfw-by-action-italy/

Statista. (2016e). *Brand value of the leading 10 apparel brands worldwide in 2016 (in million U.S. dollars).* Retrieved 29 September 2016, from https://www.statista.com/statistics/267931/brand-value-of-the-leading-10-apparel-brands-worldwide/

Statista. (2016f). *Sales of the H&M Group from 2008 to 2015, by country (in million U.S. dollars).* Retrieved 29 September 2016, from https://www.statista.com/statistics/252187/sales-of-the-hundm-group-by-country/

Statista. (2016g). *Leading luxury brands ranked by number of Instagram followers as of October 2016 (in millions).* Retrieved 29 September 2016, from https://www.statista.com/statistics/483753/leading-luxury-brands-instagram-followers/

Statista. (2016h). *Leading high street fashion labels ranked by Instagram user engagement as of May 2016.* Retrieved 6 March 2018, from https://www.statista.com/statistics/677609/high-street-fashion-labels-instagram-engagement/

Statista. (2017). *Apparel market in the United Kingdom (UK) – Statistics & facts.* Retrieved October 5, 2018 from https://www.statista.com/topics/3348/apparel-market-in-the-uk/

Statista. (2017a). *Daily time spent on social media by social video viewers worldwide as of 2nd quarter 2017, by age group.* Retrieved 5 March 2018, from https://www.statista.com/statistics/267138/social-media-usage-per-day-global-social-video-users-age/

Statista. (2017a). *Luxury brands discovery sources among Millennials worldwide 2017 | Statistic.* Retrieved from https://www.statista.com/statistics/441758/sources-for-hearing-about-new-luxury-brands-worldwide/

Statista. (2017b). *Number of worldwide social network users 2010-2021 | Statistic.* Retrieved from https://www.statista.com/statistics/278414/number-of-worldwide-social-network-users/

Statista. (2017b). *Sources used by Millennials to hear about the latest high-end fashion or luxury item trends worldwide in 2017.* Retrieved 5 March 2018, from https://www.statista.com/statistics/441758/sources-for-hearing-about-new-luxury-brands-worldwide/

Statista. (2017c). *Snapchat brand stories by media type and industry 2017 | Statistic.* Retrieved from https://www.statista.com/statistics/753645/snapchat-brand-stories-media-type-industry/

Statista. (2017c). *Worldwide forecasted sales growth in the fashion industry in 2018, by region.* Retrieved 6 March 2018, from https://www.statista.com/statistics/802943/fashion-industry-sales-growth-worldwide-by-region/

Statista. (2017d). *Social network penetration worldwide 2021.* Retrieved from https://www.statista.com/statistics/260811/social-network-penetration-worldwide/

Statista. (2018). *How do online customer reviews affect your opinion of a local business?* Available at https://www.statista.com/statistics/315751/online-review-customer-opinion/

Statista. (2018). *Social media: worldwide penetration rate 2018.* Retrieved from https://www.statista.com/statistics/269615/social-network-penetration-by-region/

Statista. (2018a). *Most famous social network sites worldwide as of January 2018, ranked by number of active users (in millions).* Retrieved 6 March 2018, from https://www.statista.com/statistics/272014/global-social-networks-ranked-by-number-of-users/

Statista. (2018a). Social Media Advertising - worldwide. *Statista Market Forecast.* Retrieved 1 May 2018, from https://www.statista.com/outlook/220/100/social-media-advertising/worldwide#

Statista. (2018b). Facebook ad revenue 2009-2017. *Statista.* Retrieved 1 May 2018, from https://www.statista.com/outlook/220/100/social-media-advertising/worldwide#

Statista. (2018b). *Number of daily active Snapchat users from 1st quarter 2017 to 4th quarter 2017 (in millions).* Retrieved 27 March 2018, from https://www.statista.com/statistics/545967/snapchat-app-dau/

Stepanova, E. (2011). The role of information communication technologies in the "arab spring.". *Ponars Eurasia*, *15*, 1–6.

Stephen, A., & Galak, J. (2010). The Complementary Roles of Traditional and Social Media in Driving Marketing Performance. *INSEAD Working Papers Collections*, *2010*(97).

Stern, B. (1994). A Revised Communication Model for Advertising: Multiple Dimensions of the Source, the Message, and the Recipient. *Journal of Advertising*, *23*(2), 5–15. doi:10.1080/00913367.1994.10673438

Stern, B. B., Thompson, J. C., & Arnould, E. J. (1998). Narrative Analysis of a Marketing Relationship: The Consumer's Perspective. *Journal of Psychology and Marketing*, *15*(3), 195–214. doi:10.1002/(SICI)1520-6793(199805)15:3<195::AID-MAR1>3.0.CO;2-5

Sterne, J. (2010). *Social media metrics: how to measure and optimise your marketing investment.* Hoboken, NJ: John Wiley & Sons.

Stevenson, H. H., & Jarillo, J. C. (1990). A Paradigm of Entrepreneurship: Entrepreneurial Management. *Strategic Management Journal*, *11*, 17–27.

Stockdale, R., & Standing, C. (2004). Benefits and barriers of electronic marketplace participation: An SME perspective null. *Journal of Enterprise Information Management*, *17*(4), 301–311. doi:10.1108/17410390410548715

Stocker, K. (2012). *A look back: How luxury brands made an impact online.* Retrieved September 7, 2016, from https://www.drapersonline.com/retail/ecommerce/a-look-back-how-luxury-brands-made-an-impact-online/5038955.article

Stockinger, E., & Ozuem, W. (2014). Social Media and Customer Retention: Implications for the Luxury Beauty Industry. In *Computer-Mediated Marketing Strategies: Social Media and Online Brand Communities.* Business Science Reference.

Stockinger, E., & Ozuem, W. (2015). Social media and customer retention: implications for the luxury beauty industry. In G. Bowen & W. Ozuem (Eds.), *Marketing strategies: Social media and online brand communities.* Hershey, PA: IGI Global. doi:10.4018/978-1-4666-6595-8.ch009

Stoel, M. D., & Muhanna, W. A. (2016). Online word of mouth: Implications for the name-your-own-price channel. *Decision Support Systems*, *91*, 37–47. doi:10.1016/j.dss.2016.07.006

Stokburger-Sauer, N. (2010). Brand community: Drivers and outcomes. *Psychology and Marketing*, *27*(4), 347–368. doi:10.1002/mar.20335

Stokburger-Sauer, N., Ratneshwar, S., & Sen, S. (2012). Drivers of Consumer-Brand Identification. *International Journal of Research in Marketing*, *29*(4), 406–418. doi:10.1016/j.ijresmar.2012.06.001

Stokburger-Sauer, N., & Teichmann, K. (2013). Is luxury just a female thing? The role of gender in luxury brand consumption. *Journal of Business Research*, *66*(7), 889–896. doi:10.1016/j.jbusres.2011.12.007

Stokinger, E., & Ozuem, W. (2014). Social media and customer retention: Implication for luxury beauty industry. In Computer-mediated marketing strategies: social media and online brand communities. IGI Global.

Stokinger, E., & Ozuem, W. (2015). Social media and customer retention: Implications for the luxury beauty industry. In Computer-mediated marketing strategies: Social media and online brand communities. Hershey, PA: IGI Global.

Stokinger, E., & Ozuem, W. (2018). The intersection of social media and customer retention in the luxury beauty industry. In Digital Marketing and Consumer Engagement: Concepts, Methodologies, Tools, and Applications (pp. 1305-1328). IGI Global.

Strandvik, T., Holmlund, M., & Edvardsson, B. (2012). Customer needing: A challenge for the seller offering. *Journal of Business and Industrial Marketing*, *27*(2), 132–141. doi:10.1108/08858621211196994

Strauss, A. L. (1988). Qualitative Analysis for Social Scientists. *European Sociological Review*, *4*(3), 276–277.

Strauss, W., & Howe, N. (1991). *Generations: The History of America's Future*. New York: Morrow.

Strizhakova, Y., Tsarenko, Y., & Ruth, J. A. (2012). I'm mad and I can't get that service failure off my mind: Coping and rumination as mediators of anger effects on customer intentions. *Journal of Service Research*, *15*(4), 414–429. doi:10.1177/1094670512443999

Stryker, S. (1968). Identity Salience and Role Performance: The Relevance of Symbolic Interaction Theory for Family Research. *Journal of Marriage and the Family*, *30*(40), 558–564. doi:10.2307/349494

Stryker, S. (1987). *The Interplay of Affect and Identity: Exploring the Relationships of Social Structure, Social Interaction, Self, and Emotion*. Presented at the *annual meetings of the American Sociological Association*, Chicago, IL.

Stryker, S., & Serpe, R. T. (1982). Commitment, Identity Salience, and Role Behavior: A Theory and Research Example. In W. Ickes & E. S. Knowles (Eds.), *Personality, Roles, and Social Behavior* (pp. 199–218). New York: Springer-Verlag. doi:10.1007/978-1-4613-9469-3_7

Sung, Y., & Kim, J. (2010). Effects of brand personality on brand trust and brand affect. *Psychology and Marketing*, *27*(7), 639–661. doi:10.1002/mar.20349

Sun, H. (2013). Moderating Role of Online Word of Mouth on Website Attributes and Consumer Trust in E-commerce Environment. *Journal of Applied Sciences (Faisalabad)*, *13*(12), 2316–2320. doi:10.3923/jas.2013.2316.2320

Sun, T., Youn, S., Wu, G., & Kuntaraporn, M. (2006). Online Word-of-Mouth (or Mouse): An Exploration of Its Antecedents and Consequences. *Journal of Computer-Mediated Communication*, *11*(1), 1104–1127. doi:10.1111/j.1083-6101.2006.00310.x

Susarla, A., Oh, J. H., & Tan, Y. (2012). Social networks and the diffusion of user-generated content: Evidence from YouTube. *Information Systems Research*, *23*(1), 23–41. doi:10.1287/isre.1100.0339

Swaid, S., & Wigand, R. (2012). The effective of perceived site-to-store service quality on perceived value and loyalty intentions in multichannel retailing. *International Journal of Management*, *29*(3), 301–313.

Swait, J., & Erdem, T. (2007). Brand Effects on Choice and Choice Set Formation under Uncertainty. *Journal of Marine Science*, *26*(5), 679–697. doi:10.1287/mksc.1060.0260

Swani, K., Brown, B. P., & Milne, G. R. (2014). Should tweets differ for B2B and B2C? An analysis of fortune 500 companies' Twitter communications. *Industrial Marketing Management*, *43*(5), 873–881. doi:10.1016/j.indmarman.2014.04.012

Swanson, S. R., & Hsu, M. K. (2011). The effect of recovery locus attributions and service failure severity on word-of-mouth and repurchase behaviors in the hospitality industry. *Journal of Hospitality & Tourism Research (Washington, D.C.)*, *35*(4), 511–529. doi:10.1177/1096348010382237

Sweeney, J., Soutar, G., & Mazzarol, T. (2008). Factors influencing word of mouth effectiveness: Receiver perspectives. *European Journal of Marketing*, *42*(3/4), 344–364. doi:10.1108/03090560810852977

Tafesse, W. (2016). An experiential model of consumer engagement in social media. *Journal of Product and Brand Management*, *25*(5), 424–434. doi:10.1108/JPBM-05-2015-0879

Tafesse, W., & Wien, A. (2017). A framework for categorizing social media posts. *Cogent Business and Management*, *4*(1), 1284390. doi:10.1080/23311975.2017.1284390

Tajfel, H., & Turner, J. C. (1979). The Social Identity Theory of Inter-Group Behaviour. In *Psychology of Intergroup Relations*. Chicago: Nelson-Hall.

Tajfel, H. (1959). Quantitative Judgement In Social Perception. *British Journal of Psychology*, *50*(1), 16–29. doi:10.1111/j.2044-8295.1959.tb00677.x PMID:13628966

Tajfel, H. (1969). Cognitive Aspects of Prejudice. *The Journal of Social Issues*, *25*(4), 79–97. doi:10.1111/j.1540-4560.1969.tb00620.x PMID:5373848

Tajfel, H. (1972). Social categorization. English manuscript of 'La catégorisation sociale. In S. Moscovici (Ed.), *Introduction à la Psychologie Sociale* (Vol. 1, pp. 272–302). Paris: Larousse.

Tajfel, H. (1978). The achievement of intergroup differentiation. In H. Tajfel (Ed.), *Differentiation between social groups* (pp. 77–100). London: Academic Press.

Tajfel, H. (1982). Social Psychology of Intergroup Relations. *Annual Review of Psychology*, *33*(1), 1–39. doi:10.1146/annurev.ps.33.020182.000245

Tajfel, H., & Turner, J. (1985). The Social Identity Theory of Intergroup Behaviour. In S. Worchel & W. Austen (Eds.), *Psychology of intergroup relations* (2nd ed.; pp. 7–24). Chicago: Nelson-Hall.

Taken Smith, K. (2012). Longitudinal study of digital marketing strategies targeting Millennials. *Journal of Consumer Marketing*, *29*(2), 86–92. doi:10.1108/07363761211206339

Tan, C.-W., Bebasat, I., & Cenfetelli, R. T. (2011). Understanding E-Service Failures: Formation, Impact and Recovery. *SIGHCI Proceedings*.

Tang, C., Mehl, M. R., Eastlick, M. A., He, W., & Card, N. A. (2016). A longitudinal exploration of the relations between electronic word-of-mouth indicators and firms' profitability: Findings from the banking industry. *International Journal of Information Management*, *36*(6), 1124–1132. doi:10.1016/j.ijinfomgt.2016.03.015

Tang, L. (2017). Mine Your Customers or Mine Your Business: The Moderating Role of Culture in Online Word-of-Mouth Reviews. *Journal of International Marketing*, *25*(2), 88–110. doi:10.1509/jim.16.0030

Tang, T., Fang, E., & Wang, F. (2014). Is neutral really neutral? The effects of neutral user generated content on product sales. *Journal of Marketing*, *78*(4), 41–58. doi:10.1509/jm.13.0301

Tan, W., Hsiao, Y., Tseng, S., & Chang, C. (2017). Smartphone Application Personality and its Relationship to Personalities of Smartphone Users and Social Capital Accrued through use of Smartphone Social Applications. *Journal of Telematics and Informatics*, *35*(1), 255–26. doi:10.1016/j.tele.2017.11.007

Tapscott, D., & Williams, A. (2006). *Wikinomics: How Mass Communication Changes Everything*. New York: Penguin Group.

Tate, M., & Evermann, J. (2010). The end of SERVQUAL in online services research: Where to from here? *e-Service Journal*, *7*(1), 60–85. doi:10.2979/esj.2010.7.1.60

Tate, M., Nili, A., & Gable, G. G. (2014). A typology of technological enablers of website service failure prevention. *Pacific Asia Conference on Information Systems (PACIS)*.

Tax, S.S., Chandrashekaran, M., & Christiansen, T. (1993). Word of Mouth in consumer decision making: An agenda for research. *Journal of Consumer Satisfaction and Complaining Behaviour*, *6*(10), 74-80.

Tax, S. S., & Brown, S. W. (1998). Recovering and Learning from Service Failure. *Sloan Management Review*, *40*(1), 70.

Tax, S. S., Brown, S. W., & Chandrasherakan, M. (1998). Customer evaluations of service complaint experiences: Implication for relationship marketing. *Journal of Marketing*, *62*(2), 60–76. doi:10.1177/002224299806200205

Taylor, C. R. (2009). The six principles of digital advertising. *International Journal of Advertising*, *28*(3), 411–418. doi:10.2501/S0265048709200679

Taylor, D. G., Lewin, J. E., & Strutton, D. (2011). Friends, fans, and followers: Do ads work on social networks? How gender and age shape receptivity. *Journal of Advertising Research*, *51*(1), 258–275.

Taylor, D. G., Lewin, J. E., & Strutton, D. (2011). Friends, fans, and followers: do ads work on social networks?: how gender and age shape receptivity. *Journal of Advertising Research*, *51*(1), 258–275. doi:10.2501/JAR-51-1-258-275

Taylor, S. A., & Baker, T. L. (1994). An Assessment of the Relationship between Service Quality and Customer Satisfaction in the Formation of Consumers' Purchase Intentions. *Journal of Retailing*, *70*(2), 163–178. doi:10.1016/0022-4359(94)90013-2

Taylor, S., & Todd, P. (1995). Assessing IT usage: The role of prior experience. *Management Information Systems Quarterly*, *19*(4), 561–570. doi:10.2307/249633

Teas, K. (1993). Expectations, performance evaluation, and consumers' perceptions of quality. *Journal of Marketing*, *57*(4), 18–34. doi:10.2307/1252216

Thang, D., & Tan, B. (2003). Linking consumer perception to preference of retail stores: An empirical assessment of the multi-attributes of store image. *Journal of Retailing and Consumer Services*, *10*(4), 193–200. doi:10.1016/S0969-6989(02)00006-1

The Organisation for Economic Co-operation and Development (OECD). (2017). *Selected indicators for Spain*. Retrieved from https://data.oecd.org/spain.htm

The Real Instituto El Cano. (2017). Retrieved from http://www.realinstitutoelcano.org/wps/portal/rielcano_en

Thoits, P. A. (1986). Multiple Identities: Examining Gender and Marital Status differences in Distress. *American Sociological Review*, *51*(2), 259–272. doi:10.2307/2095520

Thompson, C., Rindfleisch, A., & Arsel, Z. (2006). Emotional Branding and the Strategic Value of the Doppelgänger Brand Image. *Journal of Marketing*, *70*(1), 50–64. doi:10.1509/jmkg.2006.70.1.50

Thompson, J., Alvy, G., & Lees, A. (2000). Social entrepreneurship - A new look at the people and the potential. *Management Decision*, *38*(5), 328–338. doi:10.1108/00251740010340517

Thomsett-Scott, B. C. (2014). *Marketing with Social Media: A LITA Guide*. Chicago: ALA TechSource.

Thorson, K., & Rodgers, S. (2006). Relationships Between Blogs as EWOM and Interactivity, Perceived Interactivity, and Parasocial Interaction. *Journal of Interactive Advertising*, *6*(2), 5–44. doi:10.1080/15252019.2006.10722117

Tiago, M., & Veríssimo, J. (2014). Digital marketing and social media: Why bother? *Business Horizons*, *57*(6), 703–708. doi:10.1016/j.bushor.2014.07.002

Tian, K. T., Bearden, W. O., & Hunter G. L. (2001). Consumers Need for Uniqueness: Scale Development and Validation. *Journal of Consumer Research, 28*(1), 50-56.

Tifferet, S., & Herstein, R. (2012). Gender differences in brand commitment, impulse buying, and hedonic consumption. *Journal of Product and Brand Management*, *21*(3), 176–182. doi:10.1108/10610421211228793

Tikkanen, H., Hietanen, J., Henttonen, T., & Rokka, J. (2009). Exploring virtual worlds: Success factors in virtual world marketing. *Management Decision*, *47*(8), 1357–1381. doi:10.1108/00251740910984596

Tikno. (2017). Measuring performance of facebook advertising based on media used: a case study on online shops in indonesia. *Procedia Computer Science, 111*, 105-112. doi:10.1016/j.procs.2017.06.016

Timm, P. R. (2011). Customer Service: Career Success Through Customer Satisfaction (Illustrated ed.). Prentice Hall.

Timothy, D. J. (2005). *Shopping tourism, retailing and leisure*. Channel View Publications. doi:10.21832/9781873150610

Tirunillai, S., & Tellis, G. J. (2012). Does Chatter Really Matter? Dynamics of User-Generated Content and Stock Performance. *Marketing Science*, *31*(2), 198–215. doi:10.1287/mksc.1110.0682

Tolman, E. (1943). Identification and the postwar world. *Journal of Abnormal and Social Psychology*, *38*(2), 141–148. doi:10.1037/h0057497

Tombs, A. G., Russell-Bennett, R., & Ashkanasy, N. M. (2014). Recognising emotional expressions of complaining customers: A cross-cultural study. *European Journal of Marketing*, *48*(7/8), 1354–1374. doi:10.1108/EJM-02-2011-0090

Torres, E. N., Adler, H., & Behnke, C. (2014). Stars, diamonds, and other shiny things: The use of expert and consumer feedback in the hotel industry. *Journal of Hospitality and Tourism Management*, *21*, 34–43. doi:10.1016/j.jhtm.2014.04.001

Tossell, C. C., Kortum, P., Shepard, C., Rahmati, A., & Zhong, L. (2012). An empirical analysis of smartphone personalisation: Measurement and user variability. *Behaviour & Information Technology*, *31*(10), 995–1010. doi:10.1080/0144929X.2012.687773

Trainor, K. J. (2012). Relating social media technologies to performance: A capabilities-based perspective. *Journal of Personal Selling & Sales Management*, *32*(3), 317–331. doi:10.2753/PSS0885-3134320303

Trainor, K. J., Andzulis, J. M., Rapp, A., & Agnihotri, R. (2013). Social media technology usage and customer relationship performance: A capabilities-based examination of social CRM. *Journal of Business Research, 67*(6), 1201–1208. doi:10.1016/j.jbusres.2013.05.002

Tredinnick, L. (2006). Web 2.0 and business. *Business Information Review*, *23*(4), 228–234. doi:10.1177/0266382106072239

Treem, J. W., & Leonardi, P. M. (2012). Social Media Use in Organizations: Exploring the Affordances of Visibility, Editability, Persistence, and Association. *Communication Yearbook*, *3*(6), 143–189.

Tregua, M., D'Auria, A., & Bifulco, F. (2015). Comparing research streams on smart city and sustainable city. *China-USA Business Review*, *14*(4), 203–215.

Trepte, S. (2008). Social Identity Theory. In J. Bryant & P. Vorderer (Eds.), *Psychology of Entertainment* (2nd ed.; pp. 255–271). New York: Routledge.

Tri Do, T. M., Blom, J., & Gatica-Perez, D. (2011). Smartphone usage in the wild: a large-scale analysis of applications and context. In *ICMI '11 Proceedings of the 13th international conference on multimodal interfaces* (pp. 353–360). Alicante, Spain: ACM. Retrieved from https://infoscience.epfl.ch/record/192383/files/Do_ICMI_2011.pdf

Trivedi, C., & Stokols, D. (2011). Social Enterprises and Corporate Enterprises: Fundamental Differences and Defining Features. *The Journal of Entrepreneurship*, *20*(1), 1–32. doi:10.1177/097135571002000101

Trusov, M., Bodapati, A. V., & Bucklin, R. E. (2010). Determining influential users in internet social networks. *JMR, Journal of Marketing Research*, *47*(4), 643–658. doi:10.1509/jmkr.47.4.643

Trusov, M., Bucklin, R., & Pauwels, K. (2009). Effects of Word-of-Mouth Versus Traditional Marketing: Findings from an Internet Social Networking Site. *Journal of Marketing*, *73*(5), 90–102. doi:10.1509/jmkg.73.5.90

Tsai, H-T., & Bagozzi, R.P. (2014). Contribution behavior in virtual communities: cognitive, emotional, and social Influences. *MIS Quarterly*, *38*(1), 143–163.

Tsai, C. T., & Su, C. S. (2009). Service failures and recovery strategies of chain restaurants in Taiwan. *Service Industries Journal*, *29*(12), 1779–1796. doi:10.1080/02642060902793599

Tsai, H.-T., & Bagozzi, R. P. (2014). Contribution Behaviour in Virtual Communities: Cognitive, Emotional, and Social Influences. *Management Information Systems Quarterly*, *38*(1), 143–163. doi:10.25300/MISQ/2014/38.1.07

Tsai, W. S., & Men, L. R. (2013). Motivations and Antecedents of Consumer Engagement with Brand Pages on Social Networking Sites. *Journal of Interactive Advertising*, *13*(2), 2. doi:10.1080/15252019.2013.826549

Tsai, W., & Ghoshal, S. (1998). Social capital and value creation: The role of intrafirm networks. *Academy of Management Journal*, *41*(4), 464–476.

Tsimonis, G., & Dimitriadis, S. (2014). Brand strategies in social media. *Marketing Intelligence & Planning*, *32*(3), 328–344. doi:10.1108/MIP-04-2013-0056

Turner, H. J. (2007). *Handbook of Sociological Theory*. New York: Springer.

Turner, J. (1982). Towards a cognitive redefinition of the social group. In H. Tajfel (Ed.), *Social Identity and Intergroup Relations* (pp. 15–40). Cambridge, UK: Cambridge University Press.

Turner, J. (1985). Social Categorization and Self-Concept: A Social Cognitive Theory of Group Behavior. In E. Lawler (Ed.), *Advances in Group Process: Theory and Research* (pp. 77–121). Greenwich, CT: JAI Press.

Turner, J., Oakes, P., Haslam, S., & McGarty, C. (1994). Self and Collective: Cognition and Social Context. *Personality and Social Psychology Bulletin*, *20*(5), 454–463. doi:10.1177/0146167294205002

Tussyadiah, I. P. (2015). The Influence of Innovativeness on On-Site Smartphone Use among American. *Journal of Travel & Tourism Marketing*. doi:10.1080/10548408.2015.1068263

Tuten, T., & Solomon, M. (2014). *Social Media Marketing* (2nd ed.). Boston: Pearson.

Twenge, J. (2006). *Generation Me: Why today's young Americans are more confident, assertive, entitled--and more miserable than ever before*. New York: Free Press.

Twenge, J., Campbell, W., & Freeman, E. (2012). Generational differences in young adults' life goals, concern for others, and civic orientation, 1966–2009. *Journal of Personality and Social Psychology*, *102*(5), 1045–1062. doi:10.1037/a0027408 PMID:22390226

United Nations Trade and Development (UNCTAD). (2017). *Amount of Foreign direct investment*. Retrieved from http://unctad.org/en/pages/PublicationWebflyer.aspx?publicationid=1555

Unkwu, Obiajulu, & Ozuem. (2016) Understanding Social Entrepreneurship: An Exploration of Theory and Practice. *World Journal of Social Sciences, 6*(3), 86-99.

Üstüner, T., & Godes, D. (2006). Better sales networks. *Harvard Business Review*, *84*(8), 102–112. PMID:16846193

Uyar, A., & Boyar, E. (2015). An Investigation Into Social Media Usage of Publicly Traded Companies. *Journal of Corporate Accounting & Finance*, *27*(1), 71–78. doi:10.1002/jcaf.22113

Vakeel, K. A., Sivakumar, K., Jayasimha, K. R., & Dey, S. (2018). Service failures after online flash sales: Role of deal proneness, attribution, and emotion. *Journal of Service Management*, *29*(2), 253–276. doi:10.1108/JOSM-08-2017-0203

Valentine, D., & Powers, T. (2013). Generation Y values and lifestyle segments. *Journal of Consumer Marketing*, *30*(7), 597–606. doi:10.1108/JCM-07-2013-0650

Valette-Florence, P., Guizani, H., & Merunka, D. (2011). The impact of brand personality and sales promotions on brand equity. *Journal of Business Research*, *64*(1), 24–28. doi:10.1016/j.jbusres.2009.09.015

Van Birgelen, M., De Jong, A., & Ruyter, K. (2006). Multi-channel service retailing: The effects of channel performance satisfaction on behavioral intentions. *Journal of Retailing*, *82*(4), 367–377. doi:10.1016/j.jretai.2006.08.010

Van den Broeck, E., Poels, K., & Walrave, M. (2018). An experimental study on the effect of ad placement, product involvement and motives on Facebook ad avoidance. *Telematics and Informatics*, *35*(2), 470–479. doi:10.1016/j.tele.2018.01.006

Van Dijck, J. (2013). *The culture of connectivity*. Oxford, UK: Oxford University Press. doi:10.1093/acprof:oso/9780199970773.001.0001

Van Dijck, J., & Poell, T. (2013). Understanding Social Media Logic. *Media And Communication*, *1*(1), 2–14. doi:10.17645/mac.v1i1.70

van Dijk, G., Laing, A., & Minocha, S. (2005). Consumer behaviour in multi-channel retail environments: Consumer movement between online and offline channels. *5th American Marketing Association/Academy of Marketing Joint Biennial Conference 'Marketing: Building Business, Shaping Society'*.

Van Doorn, J., Lemon, K. N., Mittal, V., Nass, S., Pick, D., Pirner, P., & Verhoef, P. C. (2010). Customer engagement behavior: Theoretical foundations and research directions. *Journal of Service Research*, *13*(3), 253–266. doi:10.1177/1094670510375599

van Knippenberg, D., van Knippenberg, B., De Cremer, D., & Hogg, M. (2004). Leadership, self, and identity: A review and research agenda. *The Leadership Quarterly*, *15*(6), 825–856. doi:10.1016/j.leaqua.2004.09.002

Van Trijp, H. C. M., Hoyer, W. D., & Inman, J. J. (1996). Why Switch? Product Category-Level Explanations for True Variety-Seeking Behaviour. *JMR, Journal of Marketing Research*, *33*(3), 281–292. doi:10.2307/3152125

Vandenbosch, L., & Eggermont, S. (2016). The Interrelated Roles of Mass Media and Social Media in Adolescents' Development of an Objectified Self-Concept. *Communication Research*, *43*(8), 1116–1140. doi:10.1177/0093650215600488

Vanmeter, R. A., Grisaffe, D. B., & Chonko, L. B. (2015). Of "Likes" and "Pins": The Effects of Consumers' Attachment to Social Media. *Journal of Interactive Marketing*, 70–78.

Vargo, S. L., & Lusch, R. F. (2006). Service Dominant Logic: Reactions, reflections and refinements. *Marketing Theory*, *6*(3), 281–288. doi:10.1177/1470593106066781

Vargo, S. L., & Lusch, R. F. (2008a). Service Dominant Logic: Continuing the Evolution'. *Journal of the Academy of Marketing Science*, *36*(1), 1–10. doi:10.100711747-007-0069-6

Vargo, S. L., & Lusch, R. F. (2011). It's all B2B . . . and beyond: Toward a systems perspective of the market. *Industrial Marketing Management*, *40*(2), 181–187. doi:10.1016/j.indmarman.2010.06.026

Vargo, S. L., & Lusch, R. L. (2004b, May). The Four Services Marketing Myths: Remnants from a Manufacturing Model. *Journal of Service Research*, 324–335. doi:10.1177/1094670503262946

Vargo, S., & Lusch, R. (2004). Evolving to a New Dominant Logic for Marketing. *Journal of Marketing*, *68*(1), 1–17. doi:10.1509/jmkg.68.1.1.24036

Vargo, S., Lusch, R., & Morgan, F. (2015). Historical Perspectives on Service-Dominant Logic. In R. Lusch & S. Vargo (Eds.), *The Service-dominant Logic of Marketing: Dialog, Debate, and Directions* (2nd ed.; pp. 29–42). New York: Routledge.

Veletsianos, G. (2013). Open practices and identity: Evidence from researchers and educators' social media participation. *British Journal of Educational Technology*, *44*(4), 639–651. doi:10.1111/bjet.12052

Veloutsou, C., & Moutinho, L. (2009). Brand relationships through brand reputation and brand tribalism. *Journal of Business Research*, *62*(3), 314–322. doi:10.1016/j.jbusres.2008.05.010

Vemuri, A. (2010). Getting social: Bridging the gap between banking and social media. *Global Finance*, *24*(5), 20–21.

Venkatesan, M. (1966). Experimental Study of Consumer Behavior, Conformity and Independence. *JMR, Journal of Marketing Research*, *3*(4), 384–387. doi:10.2307/3149855

Venkatesh, V. (2000). Determinants of perceived ease of use: Integrating control, intrinsic motivation, and emotion into the technology acceptance model. *Information Systems Research*, *11*(4), 342–365. doi:10.1287/isre.11.4.342.11872

Venkatesh, V., Morris, M., Davis, G., & Davis, F. (2003). User acceptance of information technology: Toward a unified view. *Management Information Systems Quarterly*, *27*(3), 425–478. doi:10.2307/30036540

Venkatraman, S., & Fahd, K. (2016). Challenges and Success Factors of ERP Systems in Australian SMEs. *Systems*, *4*(2), 20. doi:10.3390ystems4020020

Verhagen, T., Nauta, A., & Feldberg, F. (2013). Negative online word-of-mouth: Behavioural indicator or emotional release? *Computers in Human Behavior*, *29*(4), 1430–1440. doi:10.1016/j.chb.2013.01.043

Verhoef, P. C., Neslin, S., & Vroomen, B. (2007). Multichannel customer management: Understanding the research-shopper phenomenon. *International Journal of Research in Marketing*, *24*(2), 129–148. doi:10.1016/j.ijresmar.2006.11.002

Verhoef, P., Kannan, P. K., & Inman, J. J. (2015). From multi-channel retailing to omni-channel retailing: Introduction to the special issue on multi-channel retailing. *Journal of Retailing*, *91*(2), 174–181. doi:10.1016/j.jretai.2015.02.005

Verkasalo, H., López-Nicolás, C., Molina-Castillo, F. J., & Bouwman, H. (2010). Analysis of users and non-users of smartphone applications. *Telematics and Informatics*, *27*(3), 242–255. doi:10.1016/j.tele.2009.11.001

Vermeulen, I., & Seegers, D. (2009). Tried and tested: The impact of online hotel reviews on consumer consideration. *Tourism Management*, *30*(1), 123–127. doi:10.1016/j.tourman.2008.04.008

Vilnai-Yavetz, I., & Levina, O. (2018). Motivating social sharing of e-business content: Intrinsic motivation, extrinsic motivation, or crowding-out effect? *Computers in Human Behavior*, *79*, 181–191. doi:10.1016/j.chb.2017.10.034

Viswanathan, V., Malthouse, E. C., Maslowska, E., Hoornaert, S., & Van den Poel, D. (2018). Dynamics between social media engagement, firm-generated content, and live and time-shifted TV viewing. *Journal of Service Management*, *29*(3), 378–398. doi:10.1108/JOSM-09-2016-0241

Vivek, S. D., Beatty, S. E., & Morgan, R. M. (2012). Customer engagement: Exploring customer relationships beyond purchase. *Journal of Marketing Theory and Practice*, *20*(2), 127–145. doi:10.2753/MTP1069-6679200201

Vodanovich, S., Sundaram, D., & Myers, M. (2010). Digital Natives and Ubiquitous Information Systems. *Information Systems Research*, *21*(4), 711–723. doi:10.1287/isre.1100.0324

Vogel, J., & Paul, M. (2015). One firm, one product, two prices: Channel-based price differentiation and customer retention. *Journal of Retailing and Consumer Services*, *27*, 126–139. doi:10.1016/j.jretconser.2015.07.007

Vogel, V., Evanschitzky, H., & Ramaseshan, B. (2008). Customer Equity Drivers and Future Sales. *Journal of Marketing*, *72*(6), 98–108. doi:10.1509/jmkg.72.6.98

Voyer, P. A. (1999). *Word-of-mouth processes within a services purchase decision context* (Dissertation thesis). The University of New Brunswick.

v. Wangenheim, F., & Bayón, T. (2004). The effect of word of mouth on services switching. *European Journal of Marketing*, *38*(9/10), 1173–1185. doi:10.1108/03090560410548924

Walden, E. (2000). Some Value Propositions of Online Communities. *Electronic Markets*, *10*(4), 244–249. doi:10.1080/101967800750050362

Wallace, E., Buil, I., de Chernatony, L., & Hogan, M. (2014). Who "Likes" You … and Why? A Typology of Facebook Fans. *Journal of Advertising Research*, *54*(1), 92–109. doi:10.2501/JAR-54-1-092-109

Walsh, S., Gilmore, A., & Carson, D. (2004). Managing and implementing simultaneous transaction and relationship marketing. *International Journal of Bank Marketing*, *22*(7), 468–483. doi:10.1108/02652320410567908

Walther, J. B., Liang, Y. J., Ganster, T., Wohn, D. Y., & Emington, J. (2012). Online reviews, helpfulness ratings, and consumer attitudes: An extension of congruity theory to multiple sources in Web 2.0. *Journal of Computer-Mediated Communication*, *18*(1), 97–112. doi:10.1111/j.1083-6101.2012.01595.x

Wan, F., & Ren, F. (2017). The Effect Of Firm Marketing Content On Product Sales: Evidence From a Mobile Social Media Platform. *Journal of Electronic Commerce Research*, *18*(4), 288–302.

Wang, P., Hongxiu, L., & Suomi. (2016). Value co-creation in Business via social media: A technology Affordance approach. *PACIS Proceedings*, 355.

Wang, D., Xiang, Z., & Fesenmaier, D. R. (2014). Adapting to the Mobile World: A Model of Smartphone Use. *Journal of Tourism Research*, *48*, 11–26.

Wang, P., Sun, L., & Peng, L. (2013). Modeling product attitude formation process in online word-of-mouth. *Nankai Business Review International*, *4*(3), 212–229. doi:10.1108/NBRI-07-2013-0025

Wang, X., & Li, Y. (2016). How Trust and Need Satisfaction Motivate Producing User-Generated Content. *Journal of Computer Information Systems*, *57*(1), 49–57. doi:10.1080/08874417.2016.1181493

Wang, X., Yu, C., & Wei, Y. (2012). Social Media Peer Communication and Impacts on Purchase Intentions: A Consumer Socialization Framework. *Journal of Interactive Marketing*, *26*(4), 198–208. doi:10.1016/j.intmar.2011.11.004

Wang, Y., Wu, Sh., Lin, H., & Wang, Y. (2011). The relationship of service failure severity, service recovery justice and perceived switching costs with customer loyalty in the context of e-tailing. *International Journal of Information Management*, *31*(4), 350–359. doi:10.1016/j.ijinfomgt.2010.09.001

Wang, Z., & Kim, H. G. (2017). Can Social Media Marketing Improve Customer Relationship Capabilities and Firm Performance? Dynamic Capability Perspective. *Journal of Interactive Marketing*, *39*, 15–26. doi:10.1016/j.intmar.2017.02.004

Ward, J. C., & Ostrom, A. L. (2006). Complaining to the masses: The role of protest framing in customer- created complaint web sites. *The Journal of Consumer Research*, *33*(2), 220–230. doi:10.1086/506303

Wattanasuwan, K. (2005). The self and symbolic consumption. *The Journal of American Academy of Business, Cambridge*, *6*(1), 179–184.

Weathers, D., Sharma, S., & Wood, S. L. (2007). Effects of online communication practices on consumer perceptions of performance uncertainty for search and experience goods. *Journal of Retailing*, *83*(4), 393–401. doi:10.1016/j.jretai.2007.03.009

Weber, T. (2010). *Why companies watch your every Facebook, YouTube, Twitter move*. Retrieved January 5, 2018 from http://www.bbc.co.uk/news/business-11450923

Weber, L., & Henderson, L. L. (2014). *The Digital Marketer: Ten New Skills You Must Learn to Stay Relevant and Customer-Centric*. John Wiley & Sons Inc.

Weber, M. (1978). *Economy and Society: An Outline of Interpretive Sociology* (2nd ed.). University of California Press.

Webster, F. (1992). The Changing Role of Marketing in the Corporation. *Journal of Marketing*, *56*(4), 1–17. doi:10.2307/1251983

Webster, J. G. (2014). *Marketplace of Attention: How Audiences Take Shape in a Digital Age*. MIT Press.

Wee, T. (2004). Extending human personality to brands: The stability factor. *Journal of Brand Management*, *11*(4), 317–330. doi:10.1057/palgrave.bm.2540176

Weiger, W. H., Wetzel, H. A., & Hammerschmidt, M. (2017). Leveraging marketer-generated appeals in online brand communities: An individual user-level analysis. *Journal of Service Management*, *28*(1), 133–156. doi:10.1108/JOSM-11-2015-0378

Weinberg, T. (2009). The New Community Rules: Marketing on the Social Web. O'Reilly.

Weinberg, B., & Pehlivan, E. (2011). Social spending: Managing the social media mix. *Business Horizons*, *54*(3), 275–282. doi:10.1016/j.bushor.2011.01.008

Weinberg, T. (2009). *The New Community Rules: Marketing on the Social Web*. Sebastopol, CA: O'Reilly Media, Inc.

Weingart, L. R., Bennett, R. J., & Brett, J. M. (1993). The impact of consideration of issues and motivational orientation on group negotiation process and outcome. *The Journal of Applied Psychology*, *78*(3), 504–517. doi:10.1037/0021-9010.78.3.504

Weitzl, W., & Hutzinger, C. (2017). The effects of marketer-and-advocate-initiated online service recovery responses on silent bystanders. *Journal of Business Research*, *80*, 164–175. doi:10.1016/j.jbusres.2017.04.020

Wen, I. (2009). Factors affecting the online travel buying decision: A review. *International Journal of Contemporary Hospitality Management*, *21*(6), 752–765. doi:10.1108/09596110910975990

Whan Park, C., MacInnis, D., Priester, J., Eisingerich, A., & Iacobucci, D. (2010). Brand Attachment and Brand Attitude Strength: Conceptual and Empirical Differentiation of Two Critical Brand Equity Drivers. *Journal of Marketing*, *74*(6), 1–17. doi:10.1509/jmkg.74.6.1

Whiting, A., & Williams, D. (2013). Why people use social media: A uses and gratifications approach. *Qualitative Market Research*, *16*(4), 362–369. doi:10.1108/QMR-06-2013-0041

Whitlark, D. B., Geurts, M. D., & Swenson, M. J. (1993). New product forecasting with a purchase intention survey. *The Journal of Business Forecasting Methods & Systems*, *12*(3), 18. Available at https://www.questia.com/library/journal/1P3-574939/new-product-forecasting-with-a-purchase-intention

Wiertz, C., & de Ruyter, K. (2007). Beyond the Call of Duty: Why Customers Contribute to Firm-hosted Commercial Online Communities. *Organization Studies*, *28*(3), 347–376. doi:10.1177/0170840607076003

Williams, D., Crittenden, V., Keo, T., & McCarty, P. (2012). The use of social media: An exploratory study of usage among digital natives. *Journal of Public Affairs*, *12*(2), 127–136. doi:10.1002/pa.1414

Williams, R., van der Wiele, T., van Iwaarden, J., & Eldridge, S. (2010). The importance of user-generated content: The case of hotels. *The TQM Journal*, *22*(2), 117–128. doi:10.1108/17542731011024246

Williams, T., & Williams, R. (2008). Adopting social media: Are we leaders, managers or followers? *Communication World*, *25*(4), 34–37.

Willis, E., & Wang, Y. (2016). Blogging the brand: Meaning transfer and the case of Weight Watchers' online community. *Journal of Brand Management*, *23*(4), 457–471. doi:10.1057/bm.2016.16

Wirtz, J., den Ambtman, A., Bloemer, J., Horváth, C., Ramaseshan, B., van de Klundert, J., ... Kandampully, J. (2013). Managing brands and customer engagement in online brand communities. *Journal of Service Management*, *24*(3), 223–224. doi:10.1108/09564231311326978

Wirtz, J., & Mattila, A. S. (2004). Consumer responses to compensation, speed of recovery and apology after a service failure. *International Journal of Service Industry Management*, *15*(2), 150–166. doi:10.1108/09564230410532484

Woisetschläger, D., Hartleb, V., & Blut, M. (2008). How to Make Brand Communities Work: Antecedents and Consequences of Consumer Participation. *Journal of Relationship Marketing*, *7*(3), 237–256. doi:10.1080/15332660802409605

Wolfinbarger, M., & Gilly, M. (2003). eTailQ: Dimensionalizing, measuring and predicting etail quality. *Journal of Retailing*, *79*(3), 183–198. doi:10.1016/S0022-4359(03)00034-4

Wolk, A., & Ebling, C. (2010). Multichannel price differentiation: An empirical investigation of existence and causes. *International Journal of Research in Marketing*, *27*(2), 142–150. doi:10.1016/j.ijresmar.2010.01.004

Wolny, J., & Charoensuksai, N. (2014). Mapping customer journeys in multichannel decision-making. *Journal of Direct, Data and Digital Marketing Practice*, *15*(4), 317–326. Available at: http://www.palgrave-journals.com/doifinder/10.1057/dddmp.2014.24

Wolny, J., & Mueller, C. (2013). Analysis of fashion consumers' motives to engage in electronic word-of-mouth communication through social media platforms. *Journal of Marketing Management*, *29*(5-6), 562–583. doi:10.1080/0267257X.2013.778324

Wood, N. T., & Burkhalter, J. N. (2014). Tweet this, not that: A comparison between brand promotions in microblogging environments using celebrity and company-generated tweets. *Journal of Marketing Communications*, *20*(1-2), 129–146. doi:10.1080/13527266.2013.797784

World Bank. (2017). Retrieved from https://data.worldbank.org/country/spain

World Travel and Tourism Council. (2017). *Travel and Tourism Economic impact – Spain*. Retrieved from https://www.wttc.org/-/media/files/reports/economic-impact-research/countries-2017/spain2017.pdf

WRAP. (2017). *Valuing our clothes: The cost of UK fashion report*. Retrieved October 8, 2018 from http://www.wrap.org.uk/sustainable-textiles/valuing-our-clothes

Wright, E., Khanfar, N. M., Harrington, C., & Kizer, L. E. (2010). The lasting effects of social media trends on advertising. *Journal of Business & Economics Research*, *8*(11), 73–80. doi:10.19030/jber.v8i11.50

WSJ. (2016). *H&M Hennes & Mauritz AB Series B*. Retrieved from http://quotes.wsj.com/SE/XSTO/HMB/financials

Wu, J. J., & Chang, Y. S. (2005). Towards understanding members' interactivity, trust, and flow in online travel community. *Industrial Management & Data Systems*, *105*(7), 937–954. doi:10.1108/02635570510616120

Wu, J., Huang, L., Zhao, J., & Hua, Z. (2015). The deeper, the better? Effect of online brand community activity on customer purchase frequency. *Information & Management*, *52*(7), 813–823. doi:10.1016/j.im.2015.06.001

Xia, L. (2013). Effects of companies' responses to consumer criticism in social media. *International Journal of Electronic Commerce*, *17*(4), 73–99. doi:10.2753/JEC1086-4415170403

Xiang, Z., Du, Q., Ma, Y., & Fan, W. (2017). A comparative analysis of major online review platforms: Implications for social media analytics in hospitality and tourism. *Tourism Management*, *58*, 51–65. doi:10.1016/j.tourman.2016.10.001

Xiang, Z., & Gretzel, U. (2010). Role of social media in online travel information search. *Tourism Management*, *31*(2), 179–188. doi:10.1016/j.tourman.2009.02.016

Xiang, Z., Gretzel, U., & Fesenmaier, D. (2009). Semantic Representation of Tourism on the Internet. *Journal of Travel Research*, *47*(4), 440–453. doi:10.1177/0047287508326650

Xiao, S., & Dong, M. (2015). Hidden semi-Markov model-based reputation management system for online to offline (O2O) e-commerce markets. *Decision Support Systems*, *77*, 87–99. doi:10.1016/j.dss.2015.05.013

Xie, Ch., Bagozzi, R., & Troye, S. (2008). Trying to prosume: Toward a theory of consumers as co-creators of value. *Journal of the Academy of Marketing Science*, *36*(1), 109–122. doi:10.100711747-007-0060-2

Xie, I., & Stevenson, J. (2014). Social media application in digital libraries. *Online Information Review*, *38*(4), 502–523. doi:10.1108/OIR-11-2013-0261

Xie, K. L., Zhang, Z., Zhang, Z., Singh, A., & Lee, S. K. (2016). Effects of managerial response on consumer eWOM and hotel performance: Evidence from TripAdvisor. *International Journal of Contemporary Hospitality Management*, *28*(9), 2013–2034. doi:10.1108/IJCHM-06-2015-0290

Xie, K., & Lee, Y. (2015). Social Media and Brand Purchase: Quantifying the Effects of Exposures to Earned and Owned Social Media Activities in a Two-Stage Decision Making Model. *Journal of Management Information Systems*, *32*(2), 204–238. doi:10.1080/07421222.2015.1063297

Xing, Y., & Grant, D. (2006). Developing a framework for measuring physical distribution service quality of multichannel and 'pure player' Internet retailers. *International Journal of Retail & Distribution Management, 34*(4), 278–289. doi:10.1108/09590550610660233

Xing, Y., Grant, D., McKinnon, A., & Fernie, J. (2010). Physical distribution service quality in online retailing. *International Journal of Physical Distribution & Logistics Management, 40*(5), 415–432. doi:10.1108/09600031011052859

Xiuqing, S., & Haiqing, G. (2007). *Online WOM Marketing and the Application of Its Strategy*. Academic Press.

Xue, F., & Zhou, P. (2010). 2011; "The Effects of Product Involvement and Prior Experience on Chinese Consumers' Responses to Online Word of Mouth. *Journal of International Consumer Marketing, 23*(1), 45–58. doi:10.1080/08961530.2011.524576

Yadav, M., Kamboj, S., & Rahman, Z. (2016). Customer co-creation through social media: The case of 'Crash the Pepsi IPL 2015'. *Journal of Direct, Data and Digital Marketing Practice, 17*(4), 259–271. doi:10.1057/dddmp.2016.4

Yan, Y. & Du, S. (2016). Empirical Study for the Influence Factors of Customer Satisfaction Based on B2C Online Shopping. *Revista Ibérica de Sistemas e Tecnologias de Informação, E14*, 300.

Yanamandram, V., & White, L. (2006). Switching barriers in business-to-business services: A qualitative study. *International Journal of Service Industry Management, 17*(2), 158–192. doi:10.1108/09564230610656980

Yang, H., Lee, J., Park, C., & Lee, K. (2014). The Adoption of Mobile Self-Service Technologies: Effects of Availability in Alternative Media and Trust on the Relative Importance of Perceived Usefulness and Ease of Use. *International Journal of Smart Home, 8*(4), 165–178. doi:10.14257/ijsh.2014.8.4.15

Yang, J., Zheng, R., Zhao, L., & Gupta, S. (2017). Enhancing customer brand experience and loyalty through enterprise microblogs: Empirical evidence from a communication framework perspective. *Information Technology & People, 30*(3), 580–601. doi:10.1108/ITP-09-2015-0219

Yang, K., & Kim, H.-Y. (2012). Mobile shopping motivation: An application of multiple discriminant analysis. *International Journal of Retail & Distribution Management, I*(10), 778–789. doi:10.1108/09590551211263182

Yang, K., & Young, A. P. (2009). The effects of customized site features on internet apparel shopping. *Journal of Fashion Marketing and Management: An International Journal, 13*(1), 128–139. doi:10.1108/13612020910939923

Yang, S., Lin, S., Carlson, J. R. A. N. D., & Ross, W. T. Jr. (2016). Brand engagement on social media on social media: Will firms' social media efforts influence search engine advertising effectiveness? *Journal of Marketing Management, 32*(5&6), 47–63.

Yang, W., & Mattila, A. S. (2012). The role of tie strength on consumer dissatisfaction responses. *International Journal of Hospitality Management, 31*(2), 399–404. doi:10.1016/j.ijhm.2011.06.015

Yang, Z., & Peterson, R. T. (2004). Customer perceived value, satisfaction, and loyalty: The role of switching costs. *Psychology and Marketing, 21*(10), 799–822. doi:10.1002/mar.20030

Yankova, I., & Ozuem, W. (2014). Social Media and its Implications for Marketing Communications. In Computer-mediated marketing strategies: social media and online brand communities. IGI Global.

Yao, P. (2011). Research on WOM Marketing of Forest Products Based on Web 2.0. *Journal of Chinese Marketing, 4*(2), 61–66.

Yates, D., & Paquette, S. (2011). Emergency knowledge management and social media technologies: A case study of the 2010 Haitian earthquake. *International Journal of Information Management, 31*(1), 6–13. doi:10.1016/j.ijinfomgt.2010.10.001

Yeh, C., Wang, Y., & Yieh, K. (2016). Predicting smartphone brand loyalty: Consumer value and consumer-brand identification perspectives. *International Journal of Information Management, 36*(3), 245–257. .2015.11.013 doi:10.1016/j.ijinfomgt

Yeh, C. (2015). Online word-of-mouth as a predictor of television rating. *Online Information Review, 39*(6), 831–847. doi:10.1108/OIR-01-2015-0033

Ying, L., Korneliussen, T., & Grønhaug, K. (2009). The effect of ad value, ad placement and ad execution on the perceived intrusiveness of web advertisements. *International Journal of Advertising, 28*(4), 623–638. doi:10.2501/S0265048709200795

Yoo, B., Donthu, N., & Lee, S. (2000). An examination of selected marketing mix elements and brand equity. *Journal of the Academy of Marketing Science, 28*(2), 195–211. doi:10.1177/0092070300282002

Yoo, J., & Park, M. (2016). The effects of e-mass customization on consumer perceived value, satisfaction, and loyalty toward luxury brands. *Journal of Business Research, 69*(12), 5775–5784. doi:10.1016/j.jbusres.2016.04.174

Yoon, S., & Han, H. (2012). Experiential approach to the determinants of online word-of-mouth behavior. *Journal of Global Scholars of Marketing Science, 22*(3), 218–234. doi:10.1080/21639159.2012.699219

Yoshioka, M. (2016). *How entrepreneurial was the UK in 2015?* Retrieved from https://centreforentrepreneurs.org/how-entrepreneurial-was-the-uk-in-2015/

You, Y., Vadakkepatt, G., & Joshi, A. (2015). A Meta-Analysis of Electronic Word-of-Mouth Elasticity. *Journal of Marketing, 79*(2), 1–39. doi:10.1509/jm.14.0169

Yuki, T. (2015). What Makes Brands' Social Content Shareable on Facebook? *Journal of Advertising Research, 55*(4), 458–470. doi:10.2501/JAR-2015-026

Zafarani, R., & Liu, H. (2014). Behavior Analysis in Social Media. *IEEE Intelligent Systems, 29*(4), 1–4.

Zaglia, M. (2013). Brand Communities Embedded in Social Networks. *Journal of Business Research, 66*(2), 216–223. doi:10.1016/j.jbusres.2012.07.015 PMID:23564989

Zaharna & Uysal. (2016). Going for the jugular in public diplomacy: How adversarial publics using social media are challenging state legitimacy. *Public Relations Review, 42*(1), 109-119.

Zahay, D. (2015). *The impact of digital shopping channels on multi-channel marketing and attribution in the changing retail landscape*. Emerald Group Publishing Ltd.

Zaichkowsky, J. (1985). Measuring the Involvement Construct. *The Journal of Consumer Research, 12*(3), 341. doi:10.1086/208520

Zarrella, D. (2009). *The Social Media Marketing Book*. Sebastopol, CA: O'Reilly Media, Inc.

Zeithaml, V. (1988). Consumer perceptions of price, quality, and value: A means-end model and synthesis of evidence. *Journal of Marketing, 52*(3), 2–22. doi:10.1177/002224298805200302

Zeithaml, V. (2000). Service quality, profitability, and the economic worth of customers: What we know and what we need to learn. *Journal of the Academy of Marketing Science, 28*(1), 67–85. doi:10.1177/0092070300281007

Zeithaml, V., & Berry, L. (1990). *Delivering Quality Service*. New York: The Free Press.

Zemke, R., & Schaaf, R. (1989). *The service edge: 101 companies that profit from customer care*. New York: NAL Books.

Zhang, J., Farris, P., Irvin, J., Kushwaha, T., Steenburgh, T., & Weitz, B. (2010). Crafting integrated multichannel retailing strategies. *Journal of Interactive Marketing*, *24*(2), 168–180. doi:10.1016/j.intmar.2010.02.002

Zhang, K., Benyoucef, M., & Zhao, S. (2016). Building Brand Loyalty in Social Commerce: The case of brand microblogs. *Electronic Commerce Research and Applications*, *15*, 14–25. doi:10.1016/j.elerap.2015.12.001

Zhang, L., Tam, V. C., Wan, W. W., Wu, P., & Luk, C. L. (2015). An exploratory study on school children's intent attributions for parental structuring behaviours. *Psychological Reports*, *116*(1), 249–273. doi:10.2466/21.PR0.116k17w3 PMID:25668329

Zhang, T. T., Omran, B. A., & Cobanoglu, C. (2017). Generation Y's positive and negative eWOM: Use of social media and mobile technology. *International Journal of Contemporary Hospitality Management*, *29*(2), 732–761. doi:10.1108/IJCHM-10-2015-0611

Zhang, X., Yu, Y., Li, H., & Lin, Z. (2016). Sentimental interplay between structured and unstructured user-generated contents. *Online Information Review*, *40*(1), 119–145. doi:10.1108/OIR-04-2015-0101

Zhang, Z., Ye, Q., Song, H., & Liu, T. (2015). The structure of customer satisfaction with cruise-line services: An empirical investigation based on online word of mouth. *Current Issues in Tourism*, *18*(5), 450–464. doi:10.1080/13683500.2013.776020

Zhan, Y., Liu, R., Li, Q., Leischow, S. J., & Zeng, D. D. (2017). Identifying Topics for E-Cigarette User-Generated Contents: A Case Study From Multiple Social Media Platforms. *Journal of Medical Internet Research*, *19*(1), e24. doi:10.2196/jmir.5780 PMID:28108428

Zheng, T., Youn, H., & Kincaid, C. S. (2009). An analysis of customers' e-complaints for luxury resort properties. *Journal of Hospitality Marketing & Management*, *18*(7), 718–729. doi:10.1080/19368620903170240

Zheng, X., Cheung, C., Lee, M., & Liang, L. (2015). Building brand loyalty through user engagement in online brand communities in social networking sites. *Information Technology & People*, *28*(1), 90–106. doi:10.1108/ITP-08-2013-0144

Zhenquan, S., & Xueyin, X. (2009). The Processes of Online Word-of-Mouth on the Purchase Decision. *Proceedings of the 7th International Conference on Innovation & Management*, 2033-2036.

Zhou, L. X., Wu, W. P., & Luo, X. M. (2007). Internationalization and the performance of born-global SMEs: The mediating role of social networks. *Journal of International Business Studies*, *38*(4), 673–690. doi:10.1057/palgrave.jibs.8400282

Zhou, T. (2011). Understanding online community user participation: A social influence perspective. *Internet Research*, *21*(1), 67–81. doi:10.1108/10662241111104884

Zhou, W., & Duan, W. (2015). An empirical study of how third-party websites influence the feedback mechanism between online Word-of-Mouth and retail sales. *Decision Support Systems*, *76*, 14–23. doi:10.1016/j.dss.2015.03.010

Zhou, Z., Wu, J., Zhang, Q., & Xu, S. (2013). Transforming visitors into members in online brand communities: Evidence from China. *Journal of Business Research*, *66*(12), 2438–2443. doi:10.1016/j.jbusres.2013.05.032

Zhu, F. X., Wymer, W. J., & Chen, I. (2002). IT-based services and sevice quality in consumer banking. *International Journal of Service Industry Management*, *13*(1), 69–90. doi:10.1108/09564230210421164

Zhu, Y., & Chen, H. (2015). Social media and human need satisfaction: Implications for social media marketing. *Business Horizons*, *58*(3), 335–345. doi:10.1016/j.bushor.2015.01.006

Zhu, Z., Nakata, C., Sivakumar, K., & Grewal, D. (2013). Fix it or leave it? Customer recovery from self-service technology failures. *Journal of Retailing*, *89*(1), 15–29. doi:10.1016/j.jretai.2012.10.004

Zhu, Z., Wang, J., Wang, X., & Wan, X. (2016). Exploring factors of user's peer-influence behaviour in social media on purchase intention: Evidence from QQ. *Computers in Human Behavior*, *63*, 980–987. doi:10.1016/j.chb.2016.05.037

Zinkhan, G., & Hirschheim, R. (1992). Truth in Marketing Theory and Research: An Alternative Perspective. *Journal of Marketing*, *56*(2), 80–88. doi:10.2307/1252044

About the Contributors

Wilson Ozuem teaches and researches communications issues in computer-mediated marketing environments (CMMEs). The results of his research have been published in scholarly journals and conference papers, including the European Journal of Marketing, Journal of Business Research, International Journal of Market Research. Dr Ozuem was a Senior Research Fellow at the University of Gloucestershire (UK), and a Visiting Professor at the University of Tirana (Albania). He currently teaches MSc and MBA courses in marketing communications, Internet marketing, research methodology, and marketing management. He is Fellow of the Chartered Institute of Marketing (FCIM), Senior Fellow Higher Education Academy (SFHEA), and has worked as a marketing consultant for several companies and organizations. He received his BA in Business from the University of Portsmouth, MA Marketing Communications from University of West London, MBA from London Metropolitan University, MEd (Educational Leadership and Management) from Open University (UK), Doctorate from Anglia Ruskin University and Postgraduate Degree in Educational Research from University of Cambridge.

***

Dominic Appiah is currently a business lecturer at Arden University (UK). He has a PhD from Plymouth University, an MBA from the University of Wales and a Bachelor of Arts (Politics and Philosophy), from the University of Ghana. His research investigates the dynamics of consumer purchase intentions and building resistance to brand switching. Prior to joining academia, he worked at State Insurance Company, Ghana; GIA Insurance and Ghana International Bank, UK. Dominic is a fellow of the Higher Education Academy (HEA) and member of the Chartered Institute of Marketing (CIM), Chartered Institute of Insurance (CII) and the British Academy of Management (BAM).

Kenneth Appiah is a Lecturer in Marketing/international Business Modules with extensive experience teaching undergraduate and postgraduate courses. Adept at creating learning solutions that catalyse student success and boost overall levels of achievement; possess a proactive approach to assessment design, curriculum development, and student feedback. Demonstrate outstanding research skills as evidenced by a broad range of publications. Self-motivated and focused, able to nurture collaborative relationships with fellow committee members. PhD in International Marketing/Business, University of Bedfordshire, 2016 Thesis: Competitiveness of SMEs in International Markets Master of Science in Marketing Management, University of Wales, Cardiff, 2009 Postgraduate Diploma (PgD) in Management Studies, Edexcel (Pearson), 2008 Postgraduate Diploma (PgD) in Strategic Business Information Technology, University of Portsmouth, 2007.

Mario Ciutad has completed a Postgraduate Taught Programme at Northumbria University London Campus.

Esra Güven is a lecturer at the University of Manisa Celal Bayar in Turkey. She holds a PhD on the impact of social media on consumer decision-makings. Her current interests include marketing communications, consumer behaviours and consumer communications in social media. Ph. Dr. Esra Guven is the author of several national and international papers and the marketing advisor of the Association of Strategic Researches in Turkey. The author still gives lectures on marketing, marketing researches, modern business, human resources at Manisa Celal Bayar University.

Guida Helal holds a Bachelor degree in Business Administration from American University of Beirut and a masters degree in Fashion Retailing and Luxury Management (with Distinction). Her dissertation primarily focused on social media and social identity among the millennial generation. She also worked as a marketing consultant in Dubai. Prior to this, she was on the staff of a London-based luxury corporation handling fashion and media accounts in the U.K. and MENA region. She is currently working in a digital marketing firm in Australia. Her research has been published in international conferences, books, and journals. Her research interests include digital marketing, luxury and fashion management, consumer behavior, as well as innovative marketing advancements among modern generations.

Laden Husamaldin is a Senior Lecturer in Information Systems and Project Management at the university of West London. She has over 10 years of research and academic experience which she has balanced with industrial practice gained from consultancy work projects for both private and public sectors. She is a Fellow of the Higher Education Academy (FHEA) and holds a PhD in Information Systems from Brunel University, where her research interest in Information Systems Development (ISD) focused on business and software modelling, model driven information systems development and the Semantic Web. Her current research focuses on business data visualization, business analytics, business modelling, project management and research methods.

Özlem Işık is an Assistant Professor at the University of Manisa Celal Bayar in Turkey. Her current interests include marketing communications, brand management, innovation and strategic innovation management. Asst. Prof. Özlem Işık is at the author of several national and international papers. The author still gives lectures on marketing, marketing researches, marketing communications, brand management, retail management.

Hamid Jahankhani gained his PhD from the Queen Mary College, University of London. In 1999 he moved to the University of East London (UEL) to become the first Professor of Information Security and Cyber Criminology at the university in 2010. Over the last 15 years Hamid have also been involved in developing new and innovative programmes and introducing "block mode" delivery approach at UEL, including MSc Information Security and Computer Forensics, Professional Doctorate Information Security. Hamid's principal research area for a number of years has been in the field of cyber security, information security and digital forensics. In partnership with the key industrial sectors, he has examined and established several innovative research projects that are of direct relevance to the needs of UK and European information security, digital forensics industries, Critical National Infrastructure and law enforcement agencies. Hamid have planned, proposed and managed several collaborative projects, and secured a substantial research income of up to £6m. Professor Jahankhani is the Editor-in-Chief of the International Journal of Electronic Security and Digital Forensics, www.inderscience.com/ijesdf, International Journal of Electronic democracy, www.inderscience.com/ijed, both published by Inderscience and general chair of the annual International Conference on Global Security, Safety and Sustainability (ICGS3). Hamid has edited and contributed to over 15 books and has over 150 conference and journal publications together with Various BBC radio interviews. I have supervised to completion 13 PhD and professional doctorate degree students and overseen 67 PhD students progressing. In summer 2017 Hamid was trained as the GCHQ "cyberist" to train the next generation of cyber security experts through GCHQ CyberFirst initiative.

Charanya Nopnukulvised has a strong academic background in Entrepreneur and Online marketing. She earned her Master degree from both Kingston University and University of Cumbria in England. She is currently a PhD candidate in Cardiff Metropolitan University, UK.

Jim O'Brien has been involved in numerous project within the middle east and MENA regions involving national and regional governments as an external consultant for UNDP in the middle east, specifically in the facilitation of value management techniques as applied to environmental remediation and protection. As a Chartered Engineer Jim O'Brien has been a cost engineer for many years before developing into the environmental arena. As an academic he has been involved in creating and supporting educational provision within developing countries.

Sebastian Okafor is a business and management lecture at University of Cumbria as well as an external MSc Project Supervisor at Warwick University, and a member of Assessment and Moderation team at Institute for Professional & Executive Development (IPED) the UK. He is also an Associate Lecturer at the University of West London and Northampton University. Sebastian is a fellow of Higher Education Academy and Chartered Institute of Educational Assessors and holds a doctorate in Business Administration from Newport University and is also Open University scholar and holds its Master in Education. His research interest includes cooperative learning in a multi-cultural environment, transfer of ownership in the family business and Strategic Management of SMEs.

Dipen Rai has completed Master's degree in Information Technology from the Cardiff Metropolitan University and International Business from Anglia Ruskin University. Currently, Dipen Rai is a doctorate research student in the university of the West of Scotland carrying out research on online service failures and recovery strategies in the banking sector.

Kamna Sahni is a doctoral candidate at the University of the West of the Scotland. Her research interests involve the application of emerging technologies in the hospitality sector, and the interface between social media and consumer value co-creation in the emerging countries. Kamna has a wide range of cognate experience in multinational companies, where she worked as an operation manager and trainer. She completed her BSc in Applied Accountancy from Oxford Brookes University (UK) and MSc Finance, Heriot Watt University (UK).

Tereza Semerádová is a research assistant at the Faculty of Economics, Technical University of Liberec. She received her Ph.D. in Economic Informatics. Her research expertise mainly covers online advertising and website optimization.

Ali Usman is a doctoral student at University of the West of Scotland UK.

Petr Weinlich is a research assistant at the Department of Informatics, Technical University of Liberec. His research interests include graphic design, sound production and implementation of multimedia content in advertising.

Michelle Willis completed BA/Bsc Business Studies with Study Abroad at the University of Hertfordshire and obtained Msc International Business degree.

Index

I

J

L

M

O

P

R

S

T

U

V

W

www.ingramcontent.com/pod-product-compliance
Lightning Source LLC
LaVergne TN
LVHW062106300926
849161LV00010B/2384
* 9 7 8 1 5 2 2 5 7 3 4 4 9 *